Preparing Reading Professionals

A Collection
From the
International
Reading
Association

INTERNATIONAL
Reading Association
800 BARKSDALE ROAD, PO BOX 8139
NEWARK, DE 19714-8139, USA
www.reading.org

The International Reading Association attempts, through its publications, to provide a forum for a wide spectrum of opinions on reading. This policy permits divergent viewpoints without implying the endorsement of the Association.

Editorial Director, Books and Special Projects   Matthew W. Baker
Managing Editor   Shannon T. Fortner
Permissions Editor   Janet S. Parrack
Acquisitions and Communications Coordinator   Corinne M. Mooney
Associate Editor, Books   Charlene M. Nichols
Administrative Assistant   Michele Jester
Assistant Permissions Editor   Tyanna L. Collins
Production Department Manager   Iona Muscella
Supervisor, Electronic Publishing   Anette Schütz
Electronic Publishing Specialist   R. Lynn Harrison
Proofreader   Elizabeth C. Hunt

Collection compiled by Cathy M. Roller and Erin Cushing

Project Editor   Matthew W. Baker

Cover Design   Linda Steere

Library of Congress Cataloging-in-Publication Data
Preparing reading professionals : a collection from the International Reading Association.
    p. cm.
 Includes bibliographical references.
 ISBN 0-87207-564-8
 1. Reading teachers--Training of--Standards--United States. I. International Reading Association. II. Standards for reading professionals.
 LB2844.1.R4P75 2004
 428.4'071--dc22
                                                                                                2004015979

Contents

Introduction

*P*reparing Reading Professionals: A Collection From the International Reading Association is a compilation of previously published pieces from International Reading Association (IRA) books and journals. The collection complements *Standards for Reading Professionals, Revised 2003* (*Standards 2003*), which describes what reading professionals—paraprofessionals, classroom teachers, reading specialists/literacy coaches, teacher educators, and administrators—should know and be able to do when they leave their preparation programs. Community college, college, and university faculties use *Standards 2003* for program planning and evaluation. Accrediting bodies such as the National Council for Accreditation of Teacher Education (NCATE), Teacher Education Accreditation Council (TEAC), and state departments of education certification personnel also use *Standards 2003* to make decisions about accrediting preparation programs.

IRA developed this collection in response to the tension between utility and specificity that surfaced repeatedly during the preparation of *Standards 2003*. Utility requires that standards present a usable number of elements against which programs can be compared and evaluated and also requires succinct statements of those elements. In addition, standards must be explicit enough so that users are clear about the performances the standards describe. Mindful of the need for utility, the Professional Standards and Ethics Committee of the International Reading Association—author of *Standards 2003* and previous editions—reduced the number of standards elements from the 87 in the previous edition to 19 in the new edition.

To address the need for explicitness, the committee introduced a format including performance descriptions or criteria for each of the standard elements. Each of the five standards in *Standards 2003* begins with a statement of the standard; for example, Standard 2 is "Candidates use a wide range of instructional practices, approaches, methods, and curriculum materials to support reading and writing instruction." This statement is followed by, "As a result, candidates:". A chart that lists the standard elements in the left column and the professional categories across the top follows the standard statement. (The table on the next page shows a sample chart for element 2.1 of Standard 2.) Each cell of the chart then describes the specific performance a professional must demonstrate to meet the standards. For example, consider element 2.1: "Use instructional grouping options (individual, small-group, whole-class, and computer based) as appropriate for accomplishing given purposes." The cell under Paraprofessional Candidates provides a specific description of the performance paraprofessionals must exhibit to demonstrate that they meet the standard as described in this element, in this case, "Use a variety of instructional grouping options selected by and supervised by a classroom teacher or reading specialist."

Although this format meets the need for utility and is more specific than previous editions of the *Standards for Reading Professionals*, the writing of the performance criteria, which are necessarily brief, often left the author team feeling that the standards were not specific enough to give an adequate picture of the performances described. IRA book and journal content that can capture much more depth and detail than was possible in *Standards 2003* is very helpful in addressing this specificity. The purpose of *Preparing Reading Professionals* is to provide a more complete picture of the performance criteria by gathering pieces that exemplify the standards in action.

STANDARD 2: INSTRUCTIONAL STRATEGIES AND CURRICULUM MATERIALS

Candidates use a wide range of instructional practices, approaches, methods, and curriculum materials to support reading and writing instruction. As a result, candidates:

Element	Paraprofessional Candidates	Classroom Teacher Candidates (plus previous level)	Reading Specialist/ Literacy Coach Candidates (plus previous 2 levels)	Teacher Educator Candidates (plus previous 3 levels)	Administrator Candidates
2.1 Use instructional grouping options (individual, small-group, whole-class, and computer based) as appropriate for accomplishing given purposes.	Use a variety of instructional grouping options selected by and supervised by a classroom teacher or reading specialist.	Match instructional grouping options to specific instructional purposes that take into account developmental, cultural, and linguistic differences among students. They model and scaffold procedures so that students learn to work effectively. They provide an evidence-based rationale for their selections.	Support classroom teachers and paraprofessionals in their use of instructional grouping options. They help teachers select appropriate options. They demonstrate the options and explain the evidence-based rationale for changing configurations to best meet the needs of all students.	Prepare and coach preservice candidates and inservice teachers to use instructional grouping options. They provide the candidates with opportunities to select, use, and practice the options.	Evaluate, support, and coach teachers' use of instructional grouping options for specific purposes based on their appropriateness for those purposes and for accommodating cultural and linguistic differences among their students.

Each of the pieces selected addresses one or more standard elements. Although these pieces can provide readers a much more detailed picture of what is meant by a particular standard element, these examples are not definitive. In most cases the piece represents one among many possible representations of the element. The examples are intended to help readers visualize the standard element and see how it might be instantiated within their own programs.

The collection is organized in five parts that correspond to the five standards:

1. **Foundational Knowledge:** Candidates have knowledge of the foundations of reading and writing processes and instruction.
2. **Instructional Strategies and Curriculum Materials:** Candidates use a wide range of instructional practices, approaches, methods, and curriculum materials to support reading and writing instruction.
3. **Assessment, Diagnosis, and Evaluation:** Candidates use a variety of assessment tools and practices to plan and evaluate effective reading instruction.
4. **Creating a Literate Environment:** Candidates create a literate environment that fosters reading and writing by integrating foundational knowledge, use of instructional practices, approaches and methods, curriculum materials, and the appropriate use of assessments.
5. **Professional Development:** Candidates view professional development as a career-long effort and responsibility.

This collection is valuable to an audience beyond those who have used *Standards 2003* and earlier editions because the topics of the five standards are critical for all reading professionals. *Preparing Reading Professionals* can stand on its own as a treatment of these important topics.

PART 1

Foundational Knowledge

Research about reading processes and instruction began as early as the late 1700s and reading instruction began much earlier (Huey, 1908/1968). In the course of time there has been accumulation of knowledge related to reading processes and reading instruction. This knowledge is the foundation of present-day research and best practices, and the first standard requires entry-level reading professionals to be familiar with foundational knowledge that guides research and grounds practice. Standard 1 is as follows:

> **Candidates have knowledge of the foundations of reading and writing processes and instruction.**

The standard includes four elements.

- **Element 1.1 Demonstrate knowledge of psychological, sociological, and linguistic foundations of reading and writing processes and instruction.**

This element addresses what Pearson (2002) refers to as "Reading as the province of other scholarly traditions." The element focuses on the contributions of other fields to the knowledge base that reading professionals should command. Pearson's piece, which appears in the 2002 edition of Nila Banton Smith's *American Reading Instruction*, provides an overview of the recent history and practice of reading instruction since 1967. The entire book is useful and relevant to reading professionals; however, the piece presented here deals specifically with the influences of linguistics, psycholinguistics, cognitive psychology, sociolinguistics, and literary theory on reading research and instruction.

The Gee (2001) article is included in the collection to provide an example of the ways other scholarly traditions influence our understandings of reading and reading instruction. The author explains that the comprehension of written language is as much about experience with the worlds of home, school, and work as it is about words.

• **Element 1.2 Demonstrate knowledge of reading research and histories of reading.**
This element focuses more directly on reading as a field in its own right. Pearson (2002) characterized the period from 1935 to 1964 as a fine-tuning and elaboration of the instructional models developed in the first third of the 20th century. Pages 11–30 of the Pearson piece provide a survey of reading instructional practices as they evolved from the 1960s to the present. Much of the history delineated in these pages has had a direct influence on the present debates surrounding current best practices. Knowledge of this history, both of the research and of instructional practice, should be shared by reading professionals. The piece also indicates topics and research that more advanced reading professionals should be familiar with.

The body of research literature that surrounds reading and reading instruction is quite vast. The National Reading Panel (National Institute of Child Health and Human Development, 2000) screened more than 100,000 articles about reading and reading instruction in preparation for their report. The Shanahan and Neuman (1997) article, originally published in *Reading Research Quarterly*, lists and describes 10 studies that the authors felt had a major impact on the teaching of reading. Given the extensive research literature on reading, this piece serves merely as an introduction to important research. Advanced reading professional candidates also should be familiar with the work reported in the three editions of *What Research Has to Say About Reading Instruction* (International Reading Association) and in the five editions of *Theoretical Models and Processes of Reading* (International Reading Association). The three editions of the *Handbook of Reading Research* (Longman [volumes one and two] and Erlbaum [volume three]) are also invaluable compilations of research reviews.

Donald Leu's (2002) article addresses the influence of the Internet and technology on literacy. The piece is included as foundational knowledge because technologies are changing the face of literacy, specifically by changing the way people search for, obtain, analyze, and use literacy skills. Leu points out that many professionals do not have the time for the use of the Internet and technology. However, he argues that in order to prepare children for their future, educators must take time to become skilled Internet and technology users. The article provides a framework for integrating technology and Internet use with existing curricula.

• **Element 1.3 Demonstrate knowledge of language development and reading acquisition and the variations related to cultural and linguistic diversity.**
Building a Knowledge Base in Reading (1997) provides an excellent summary of the knowledge base in reading. The chapter presented here provides a succinct summary of language acquisition processes that are the focus of this element. Authors Braunger and Lewis begin with the development of oral language and follow it through the period of emergent literacy. While this explanation is brief, it is well grounded in the research literature, and the list of citations is a good source for further reading.

The Au (2003) chapter from *What Research Has to Say About Reading Instruction*, Third Edition, is a must for all candidates because of dramatically shifting demographics. While the teaching force remains primarily white and female, the student population is increasingly diverse. Some predictions indicate that by 2050 as many as 40% of children entering public schools in the United States will speak a language other than English (Lindholm-Leary, 2000). Au enumerates five challenges that teachers must meet if they are to be successful at teaching all the children in their classrooms. The article and its citations are a good entry point to the issues surrounding the juncture of literacy and multiculturalism.

It is important for reading professionals to be knowledgeable given the rapidly increasing numbers of children from Spanish-speaking backgrounds. Helman's (2004) piece provides crucial knowledge for understanding the literacy learning of Spanish–English bilingual children. Her analysis suggests that the sound system of Spanish may influence the beginning writing behaviors of English-language learners who come from Spanish-speaking backgrounds. The article is also useful to sensitize reading professionals to the more general issues involved in second-language literacy learning.

• **Element 1.4 Demonstrate knowledge of the major components of reading (phonemic awareness, word identification and phonics, vocabulary and background knowledge, fluency, comprehension strategies, and motivation) and how they are integrated in fluent reading.**

The introductions from each section of *Evidence-Based Reading Instruction: Putting the National Reading Panel Report Into Practice* (2003)—Phonemic Awareness, Phonics, Reading Fluency, Vocabulary Development, Comprehension Strategies, and Putting It All Together—are included here. Each introduction provides a definition, summary of findings from the National Reading Panel report, and a brief explanation of the importance of the element and its role in fluent reading. The articles in the book can provide further information about how each element is enacted in the classroom.

Together the articles in Part 1 provide both a broad overview and more specific examples of relevant foundational knowledge for reading professionals. The pieces suggest what knowledge is essential and how that knowledge plays out in specific examples. It is important to realize that the works presented are not intended to be exhaustive but rather to serve as examples that allow reading professionals to examine the role of foundational knowledge in their practice.

REFERENCES

Huey, E.B. (1968). *The psychology and pedagogy of reading.* Cambridge, MA: MIT Press. (Original work published 1908)

Lindholm-Leary, K. (2000). *Biliteracy for a global society: An idea book for dual language education.* Washington, DC: National Clearinghouse for Bilingual Education.

National Institute of Child Health and Human Development. (2000). *Report of the National Reading Panel. Teaching children to read: An evidence-based assessment of the scientific research literature on reading and its implications for reading instruction* (NIH Publication No. 00-4769). Washington, DC: U.S. Government Printing Office.

AMERICAN READING INSTRUCTION SINCE 1967

P. David Pearson

This chapter is an account of reading instruction in the last third of the 20th century, from roughly the late 1960s onward.[1] In fact, I take the publication of Jeanne Chall's (1967) *Learning to Read: The Great Debate* as my starting point. It will end, as do most essays written at a century's turn, with predictions about the future. My hope is to provide an account of the past and present of reading instruction that will render predictions about the future transparent. I will end this piece with my speculations about pedagogical journeys that lie ahead in a new century and a new millennium.

Beginning at Mid-Century Setting the Scene: Reading in the 1960s

The period that spans roughly 1935 to 1965 is best viewed as a time in which we engaged in fine-tuning and elaboration of instructional models that were born in the first third of the century. Most important, the look-say approach (start off with a corpus of high-frequency sight words practiced often in highly controlled stories and then teach phonics on the basis of already taught words), which had started its ascendancy at the turn of the century, gained increasing momentum throughout the middle third of the century until, as has been documented in survey research conducted in the 1960s, over 90% of the students in the country were taught to read using one commercial variation of this approach or another.[2] So common was this approach that Jeanne Chall (1967) felt comfortable describing the then prevailing approach as a set of principles, which can be roughly paraphrased as follows:[3]

- The goals of reading from the beginning of grade 1 should include comprehension, interpretation, and application, as well as word recognition.
- Instruction should begin with meaningful silent reading of stories that are grounded in children's experiences and interests.
- After a corpus of sight words is learned (between 50 and 100), analytic phonics instruction should begin. Phonics should be regarded as one of many cueing systems, including context and picture cues, available to children to unlock new words.
- Phonics instruction should be spread over several years rather than concentrated in the early grades.
- Phonics instruction should be contextualized rather than isolated from real words and texts.
- The words in the early texts (grades 1–3) should be carefully controlled for frequency of use and repeated often to ensure mastery.
- Children should get off to a slow and easy start, probably through a readiness program; those judged as not ready for formal reading instruction should experience an even longer readiness period.
- Children should be instructed in small groups.

Reprinted from Smith, N.B. (2002). *American reading instruction* (Spec. ed., pp. 419–486). Newark, DE: International Reading Association.

Although a few elements in her list are new, such as the early emphasis on comprehension and interpretation and the contextualization of phonics instruction, virtually all the elements introduced in the early part of the century were included in her description of the conventional wisdom of the 1960s. A few things are missing when one compares Chall's list of principles underlying the conventional wisdom with our earlier account of the key developments through 1935. One is the role of skills in commercial reading programs. Although skills did not make it onto Chall's (1967) list of principles, it is clear from several chapters (specifically, chapters 7 and 8) that she was mindful of their importance and curricular ubiquity. By the 1960s, skills lessons in the teachers' manual, accompanied by workbooks allowing students to practice the skills, were much more elaborate than in the 1930s, 40s, or 50s. The other missing piece is the elaborate development of the teachers' manual. Earlier, I implied that the manuals got larger with each succeeding edition of a series. By the middle 1960s, the small teachers' guide section in the back of the children's book of the 1920s and 30s had expanded to the point where the number of pages devoted to the teachers' guide equaled the number of student text pages in the upper grades, and exceeded it in the primary grades.[4]

The materials of the 1960s continued traditions begun early in the century and documented in great detail in Nila Banton Smith's editions of *American Reading Instruction.*[5] Students read stories and practiced skills. Text difficulty was carefully controlled in the basal reading materials published between the 1930s and the 1960s. In the earliest readers (preprimer through first reader, at least), vocabulary was sequenced in order of decreasing frequency of word usage in everyday written and oral language. Because many of the most frequent words are not regularly spelled (*the, of, what, where,* etc.), this frequency principle provided a good fit with the whole-word or look-say emphasis characteristic of the words-to-reading approach so dominant during this period.

Students were still the recipients and teachers still the mediators of the received curriculum. Meaning and silent reading were more important in the 1960s version of reading curriculum than in 1900 or 1935, as evidenced by a steady increase in the amount of time and teachers' manual space devoted to comprehension activities; but it was still not at the core of the look-say approach. When all is said and done, the underlying model of reading in the 1960s was still a pretty straightforward perceptual process; the simple view—that comprehension is the product of decoding and listening comprehension ($RC = Dec^* LC$)— still prevailed. Readers still accomplished the reading task by translating graphic symbols (letters) on a printed page into an oral code (sounds corresponding to those letters), which was then treated by the brain as oral language. In both the look-say approach to learning sight vocabulary and its analytic approach to phonics, whether the unit of focus is a word or a letter, the basic task for the student is to translate from the written to the oral code. This view of reading was quite consistent with the prevailing instructional emphasis on skills. If sight words and phonics knowledge was what children needed to learn in order to perform the translation process, then decomposing phonics into separable bits of knowledge (letter-to-sound, or in the case of spelling, sound-to-letter, correspondences), each of which could be presented, practiced, and tested independently, was the route to helping them acquire that knowledge.

The Legacy of the Scholarship of the 1960s

In beginning reading, the decade of the 1960s was a period of fervent activity. In the early 1960s, in an effort to settle the debate about the best way to teach beginning reading once and for all (this time with the tools of empirical scholarship rather than rhetoric), the Cooperative Research Branch of the United States Office of Education funded an elaborate collection of "First-Grade Studies," loosely coupled forays into the highly charged arena of preferred approaches to beginning reading instruction.[6] Although each of the studies differed from one another in the particular emphasis, most of them involved a comparison of different methods of teaching beginning reading. They were published in a brand new journal, *Reading Research Quarterly*, in 1966. Jeanne Chall completed her magnum opus, *Learning to Read: The Great Debate*, in 1967. It, too, had been funded in order to put the debate behind, but Chall would use different scholarly tools to accomplish her goals. She would employ critical review procedures to examine our empirical research base, the content of our basal readers, and exemplary classroom practices. In 1965, Lyndon Johnson's Elementary and Secondary Education Act, one key plank in his Great Society platform, brought new resources for compensatory education to schools through a program dubbed Title I. And, Commissioner of Education James Allen would, at decade's end, establish the national Right to Read program as a way of guaranteeing that right to each child in the United States. The country was clearly focused on early reading, and many were optimistic that we would find answers to the questions about teaching reading that had vexed us for decades, even centuries.

Chall's book and the First-Grade Studies had an enormous impact on beginning reading instruction and indirectly on reading pedagogy more generally. One message of the First-Grade Studies was that just about any alternative, when compared to the business-as-usual basals (which served as a common control in each of 20+ separate quasi-experimental studies), elicited equal or greater performance on the part of first graders (and, as it turned out, second graders).[7] It did not seem to matter much what the alternative was—language experience, a highly synthetic phonics approach, a linguistic approach (control the text so that young readers are exposed early on only to easily decodable words grouped together in word families, such as the -*an* family, the -*at* family, the -*ig* family, etc.), a special alphabet (i.e., the Initial Teaching Alphabet), or even basals infused with a heavier-than-usual dose of phonics right up front—they were all the equal or the better of the ubiquitous basal. A second message, one that was both sent and received, was that the racehorse mentality of studies that pits one method against another to see which would win had probably run its course. By accepting this message, the reading research community was free to turn its efforts to other, allegedly more fruitful, issues and questions—the importance of the teacher, quite irrespective of method, the significance of site, and the press of other aspects of the curriculum such as comprehension and writing.[8] With the notable exception of the Follow-Through Studies in the 1970s, which are only marginally related to reading, it would take another 25 years for large-scale experiments to return to center stage in reading.[9]

In spite of a host of other important recommendations, most of which had some short-term effect, the ultimate legacy of Chall's book reduces to just one—that early attention to the code in some way, shape, or form must be reinfused into early reading instruction. For the record, Chall recommended five broad changes, each of which will be discussed later:

(1) make a necessary change in method (to an early emphasis on phonics of some sort),

(2) reexamine current ideas about content (focus on the enduring themes in folktales),

(3) reevaluate grade levels (increase the challenge at every grade level),

(4) develop new tests (both single-component tests and absolute measures with scores that are independent of the population taking the test), and

(5) improve reading research (including its accessibility).

The look-say basals that had experienced virtually uninterrupted progress from 1930 to 1965 never quite recovered from the one-two punch delivered by Chall's book and the First-Grade Studies in 1967. Given the critical sacking they took from Chall and the empirical thrashing they took from the First-Grade Studies, one might have expected one of the pretenders to the early reading throne, documented so carefully in the First-Grade Studies, to assume the mantle of the new conventional wisdom in the years that followed. Ironically, it was the basals themselves, albeit in a radically altered form, that captured the marketplace of the 1970s and 1980s. This feat was accomplished by overhauling basals to adapt to a changing market shaped by these two important scholarly efforts. Basal programs that debuted in the five years after Chall's book appeared were radically different from their predecessors. Most notably, phonics, which had been relegated to a skill to be taught contextually after a hefty bank of sight words had been committed to memory, was back—from day one of grade 1—in the series that hit the market in the late 1960s and early 1970s. Surprisingly, it was not the highly synthetic alphabetic approach of the previous century or the remedial clinics of the 1930s (which one might have expected from reading Chall's book). It is better described as an intensification and repositioning (to grade 1) of the analytic phonics that had been taught in the latter part of grade 1, and in grades 2 to 4 in the look-say basals of the 1960s.[10] Equally significant, there was a change in content, at least in grade 1. Dick and Jane and all their assorted pairs of competing cousins—Tom and Susan, Alice and Jerry, Jack and Janet—were retired from the first-grade curriculum and replaced by a wider array of stories and characters; by the early 1970s, more of the selections were adaptations of children's literature rather than stories written to conform to a vocabulary restriction or a readability formula.

It is difficult to determine how seriously educators and publishers took Chall's other three recommendations. For example, in the basals that came out after Chall, the grade 1 books (the preprimers, primers, and readers) were considerably more challenging than their immediate predecessors, mainly by virtue of a much more challenging grade 1 vocabulary—more words introduced much earlier in the grade 1 program.[11] One series even divided its new vocabulary words into words that ought to be introduced explicitly as sight words, and those words, which they dubbed decodable, which should be recognized by the students by applying the phonics skills they had been taught up to that point in the program.[12] Beyond grade 1, however, changes in difficulty were much less visible, and no appreciable increase in the readability scores of these later levels occurred.

In testing, a major change toward single-component tests did occur, although it is difficult to attribute this change solely to Chall's recommendation. Beginning in the early 1970s and continuing through at least the late 1980s, each successive edition of basal programs brought an increase in the number of single-component tests—tests for each phonics skill (all the beginning, middle, and final consonant sounds; vowel patterns; and syllabication), tests for each comprehension skill (main idea, finding details, drawing conclusions, and determining cause-effect relations) at every grade level, tests for alphabetical order and using the encyclopedia, and just about any other skill that comes to mind.

But, other events and movements of the period also pointed toward single-component tests. For one, owing to the intellectual contributions of Benjamin Bloom and John Carroll, the mastery learning movement[13] was gathering its own momentum during the late 1960s. According to proponents of mastery learning, if a complex domain could be decomposed into manageable subcomponents, each of which could be taught and learned to some predetermined level of mastery, then most, if not all, students should be able to master the knowledge and skills in the domain. Second, criterion-referenced tests were spawned during this same period.[14] The logic of criterion-referenced assessment was that some predetermined level of mastery (say 80% correct), not the average for a group of students in a given grade level, ought to be the reference point for determining how well a student was doing on a test. A third construct from this period, curriculum-embedded assessment,[15] held that students should be held accountable for precisely what was needed for them to march successfully through a particular curriculum—no less, no more. If one could specify the scope and sequence of knowledge and skills in the curriculum and develop assessments for each, then it should be possible to guide all students through the curriculum, even if some needed more practice and support than others. One can imagine a high degree of compatibility among all three of these powerful constructs—mastery learning, criterion-referenced assessment, and curriculum-embedded assessment. All three provide comfortable homes for single-component assessments of the sort Chall was advocating.

With powerful evidence from mastery learning's application to college students,[16] publishers of basal programs and some niche publishers began to create and implement what came to be called skills management systems.[17] In their most meticulous application, these systems became the reading program. Students took a battery of mastery tests, practiced those skills they had not mastered (usually by completing worksheets that looked remarkably like the tests), took tests again, and continued this cycle until they had mastered all the skills assigned to the grade level (or until the year ended). Unsurprisingly, the inclusion of these highly specific skill tests had the effect of increasing the salience of workbooks, worksheets, and other skill materials that students could practice on in anticipation of (and as a consequence of) mastery tests. Thus, the basals of this period were comprised of two parallel systems: (1) the graded series of anthologies filled with stories and short nonfiction pieces for oral and silent reading and discussion, and (2) an embedded skills management system to guide the development of phonics, comprehension, vocabulary, and study skills.

Chall's last recommendation was to improve reading research. Research had been too inaccessible (to the very audience of practitioners who most needed it), too narrow in scope, and too dismissive of its past. All that needed to change, she argued. As I will detail in the next section, reading research changed dramatically, but not necessarily in a direction Chall envisioned.

One other change in basal reading programs in this period worth noting was the technology that placed reduced facsimiles of student text pages onto pages surrounded by teaching suggestions and questions for guided reading. This was hailed as a major advance in the utility of manuals, because teachers did not have to turn back and forth from student text to the teachers' section in order to guide the reading of a story.

This was the scene, then, in the early 1970s, just as the reading field was about to embark on a new curricular trek that continues even today. If the middle third of the century was characterized by a steady, unwavering march toward the ever-increasing prominence of a particular philosophy and set of curricular practices encapsulated in ubiquitous basals that championed a look-say approach,[18] the early 1970s brought major challenges in philosophy and pedagogy—harder texts, more phonics, and a skill development program unlike anything seen before.[19]

But even with some alterations in the materials available and some new pedagogical twists, the pedagogy of the early 1970s revealed little fundamental change in the underlying assumptions about the role of the teacher and learner or the nature of reading and writing. Teachers, armed with their basal manuals, controlled the learning situation as never before, and students continued to play the role of passive recipient of the knowledge and skills mediated by the teacher. Most important, reading was still a fundamentally perceptual process of translating letters into sounds. If anything, the perceptual nature of reading was made more salient in the 1950s and 1960s by the return of phonics to center stage.

Developments in the Last Third of the Century

Reading as the Province of Other Scholarly Traditions[20]

Somewhere during this period (the exact point of departure is hard to fix), we began a journey that would take us through many new twists and turns on the way to different landscapes than we had visited before. Along the way, we confronted fundamental shifts in our views of reading and writing and began to create a variety of serious curricular alternatives to the conventional wisdom of the 1970s. Just beyond the horizon lay even more unfamiliar and rockier territory—the conceptual revolutions in cognition, sociolinguistics, and philosophy—which would have such far-reaching consequences for reading curriculum and pedagogy of the 1980s and 1990s.

Reading became an ecumenical scholarly commodity; it was embraced by scholars from many different fields of inquiry. The first to take reading under their wing were the linguists, who wanted to convince us that reading was a language process closely allied to the language processes of writing, speaking, and listening. Then came the psycholinguists and the cognitive psychologists, followed soon by the sociolinguists, the philosophers, the literary critics, and the critical theorists. It is not altogether clear why reading has attracted such interest from scholars in so many other fields. One explanation is that reading is considered by so many to be a key to success in other endeavors in and out of school; this is often revealed in comments such as, "Well if you don't learn to read, you can't learn other things for yourself." Another is that scholars in these other disciplines thought that the educationists had it all wrong, and it was time for another group to have their say. Whatever the reasons, the influence of these other scholarly traditions on reading pedagogy is significant; in fact, the pedagogy of the 1980s and 1990s cannot be understood without a firm grounding in the changes in world view that these perspectives spawned.

Linguistics. In 1962, Charles Fries wrote a book entitled *Linguistics and Reading*. In it, he outlined what he thought the teaching of reading would look like if it were viewed from the perspective of linguistics. In the same decade, several other important books and articles appeared, each carrying essentially the same message: The perspective of the modern science of linguistics, we were told, would privilege different models and methods of teaching reading. It would tell us, for example, that some things do not need to be taught explicitly because the oral language takes care of them more or less automatically. For example, the three different pronunciations of -ed, (as in *nabbed, capped,* and *jaded*), need not be taught as a reading skill because our oral language conventions determine the pronunciation almost perfectly. English in its oral form demands the voiced alternative /d/ after a voiced consonant such as /b/. It demands the unvoiced alternative /t/ after an unvoiced consonant, such as /p/, and it requires the syllabic version /ǝd/ after either /d/ or /t/. To teach these rules, which are very complex, would likely make things more confusing than simply allowing the oral language to do its work without fanfare.

Another linguistic insight came to us from the transformational generative grammars that replaced conventional structural linguistics as the dominant paradigm within the field during the 1960s and 70s. Noam Chomsky published two revolutionary treatises during this period: *Syntactic Structures* in 1957 and *Aspects of a Theory of Syntax* in 1965. With these books, Chomsky revolutionized the field of linguistics and paved the way, theoretically, for equally dramatic changes in the way that psychologists thought about and studied the processes of language comprehension and language acquisition.

Chomsky also provided the basis for a nativist view about language acquisition—a view that holds that humans come to the world "wired" to acquire the language of the community into which they are born. He and others drew this inference from two basic and contrasting facts about language: (a) language is incredibly complex, and (b) language is acquired quite easily and naturally by children living in an environment in which they are simply exposed to (rather than taught!) the language of their community well before they experience school. Only a view that children are equipped with some special cognitive apparatus for inferring complex rules could explain this remarkable feat.

Because our prevailing views of both reading comprehension and reading acquisition were derived from the same behavioristic assumptions that Chomsky and his peers had attacked, reading scholars began to wonder whether those assumptions would hold up when we applied similar perspectives and criticisms to analyses of written language comprehension and acquisition.[21]

Psycholinguistics. During the decade after the publication of *Syntactic Structures*, a new field of inquiry, psycholinguistics, evolved. In its first several years of existence, the field devoted itself to determining whether the views of linguistic competence and language acquisition that had been set forth by Chomsky and his colleagues could serve as psychological models of language performance. Although the effort to develop a simple mapping from Chomsky to models of language performance waned after a few unsatisfactory attempts, the field of psycholinguistics and the disposition of psychologists to study language with complex theoretical tools had been firmly established.

Particularly influential on our thinking about reading were scholars of language acquisition,[22] who established the rule-governed basis of language learning. In contrast to earlier views, these psycholinguists found that children did not imitate written language; rather, as members of a language community, they were participants in language and invented for themselves rules about how oral language worked. This insight allowed researchers to explain such constructions as "I eated my dinner" and "I gots two foots." Roger Brown and his colleagues showed conclusively that children were active learners who inferred rules and tested them out. Much as Kenneth Goodman would later show with written language, "mistakes," especially overgeneralizations, in oral language could be used to understand the rule systems that children were inventing for themselves.

The analogy with oral language development was too tempting for reading educators to resist. Several adopted something like a nativist framework in studying the acquisition of reading, asking what the teaching of reading and writing would look like if we assumed that children can learn to read and write in much the same way as they learn to talk, that is, naturally. What would happen if we assumed that children were members of a community in which reading and writing are valued activities that serve important communication functions? What if we assumed that the most important factors in learning to read and write were having genuine reasons for communicating in these media and having access to a database in which there was so much print and talk about print that students could discover the patterns and regularities on their own, much as they do when they discover the patterns and regularities of oral language? Although the seminal work involved in putting these assumptions to empirical tests would wait for a couple of decades, the seeds of doubt about our perceptually based views of reading acquisition were firmly planted by the middle 1960s.

Two influential individuals, Kenneth Goodman and Frank Smith, led the reading field in addressing these kinds of questions. In 1965, Goodman demonstrated that the errors children made while reading orally were better viewed as windows into the inner workings of their comprehension processes than as mistakes to be corrected. He found that the mistakes that children made while reading in context revealed that they were trying to make sense of what they read. In another seminal piece, "Reading: A Psycholinguistic Guessing Game," Goodman (1967) laid out the elements of language that he thought readers employed as they constructed meaning for the texts they encountered. In reading, he conjectured, readers use three cue systems to make sense of text: syntactic cues, semantic cues, and graphophonemic cues. By attending to all these cue sources, Goodman contended, readers could reduce their uncertainty about unknown words or meanings, thus rendering both the word identification and comprehension processes more manageable.[23]

Smith's revolutionary ideas were first presented in 1971 in a book entitled *Understanding Reading*.[24] In this seminal text, Smith argued that reading was not something one was taught, but rather something one learned to do. Smith believed that there were no special prerequisites to learning to read, indeed, that reading was simply making sense of one particular type of information in our environment. As such, reading was what one learned to do as a consequence of belonging to a literate society. One learned to read from reading. The implication, which Smith made explicit, was that the "function of teachers is not so much to teach reading as to help children read" (p. 3). This certainly challenged the notion of the teacher as the individual who meted out knowledge and skills to passively waiting students. For Smith, all knowing and all learning were constructive processes; individuals made sense of what they encountered based on what they already knew.[25] Even perception, he contended, was a decision-making, predictive process based on prior knowledge.

Smith also argued that reading was only incidentally visual. By that, Smith meant that being able to see was necessary but not sufficient to achieve understanding. He identified four sources of information: orthographic, syntactic, semantic, and visual, all of which he claimed were somewhat redundant. He argued that skilled readers made use of the three sources that were part of their prior knowledge (the orthographic, syntactic, and semantic) in order to minimize their reliance on visual information. In fact, the danger in relying too heavily on visual information is that readers might lose sight of meaning.

The psycholinguistic perspective had a number of influences on reading pedagogy. First, it valued literacy experiences that focused on making meaning. This meant that many classroom activities, particularly worksheets and games, which focused on enabling skills such as specific letter-sound correspondences, syllabication activities, structural analysis skills, specific comprehension activities, or study skills, were devalued. Second, it helped us to value texts for beginning readers (see Table 1, example 1) in which authors relied on natural language patterns, thus making it possible for emerging readers to use their knowledge of language to predict words and meanings. This meant that texts that relied on high-frequency words in short, choppy sentences (what we have come to call "basalese"; see Table 1, example 2) or those based on the systematic application of some phonics element (i.e., a decodable text; see Table 1, example 3) were correspondingly devalued.

Third, the psycholinguistic perspective helped us to understand the reading process and to appreciate children's efforts as readers. Errors were no longer things to be corrected; instead,

TABLE 1
Sample Texts for Beginning Reading

1. Red Fox, Red Fox, what do you see?
   I see a blue bird looking at me.
   Blue Bird, Blue Bird, what do you see?
   I see a green frog looking at me.
   Anon, anon.

2. Run, John, run.
   Run to Dad.
   Dad will run.
   Run, Dad.
   Run, John.
   See them run.

3. Nat can bat.
   Nat can bat with the fat bat.
   The cat has the fat bat.
   The rat has the fat bat.
   Nat has the fat bat.
   Bat the bat, Nat.

they were windows into the workings of the child's mind, allowing both the teacher and the child to understand more about the reading process and reading strategies. Understanding miscues also helped educators focus on comprehension and appreciate risk-taking.

Fourth, psycholinguists gave us a means (miscue analysis) and a theory (reading as a constructive process) that was remarkably distinct from previous ideas about reading. The perspective made explicit links between oral and written language acquisition and helped us view reading as language rather than simply perception or behavior. In a sense, psycholinguistics continued the changes and traditions begun by the linguistic perspective; however, within the reading field, its influence was deeper and broader than its academic predecessor.

Most important, psycholinguistics affected our views of teaching and learning in a fundamental way. Reading scholars began to rethink ideas about what needed to be taught, as well as the relation between teaching and learning. So, instead of asking, "What can I teach this child so that she will eventually become a reader?" we began to ask, "What can I do to help this child as a reader so she will make the progress she deserves to make?" Some teachers began to welcome all children into what Smith referred to as "The Literacy Club" as an alternative to teaching children so-called prerequisite skills.[26]

Cognitive Psychology. If psycholinguistics enabled psychologists to reexamine their assumptions about language learning and understanding by placing greater emphasis on the active, intentional role of language users, cognitive psychology allowed psychologists to extend constructs such as human purpose, intention, and motivation to a greater range of psychological phenomena, including perception, attention, comprehension, learning, memory, and executive control of all cognitive process. All of these would have important consequences in reading pedagogy.

This was not tinkering around the edges; it was a genuine paradigm shift that occurred within those branches of psychology concerned with human intellectual processes. The previous half-century, from roughly the teens through the fifties, had been dominated by a behaviorist perspective in psychology that shunned speculation about the inner workings of the mind: Show the surface-level outcomes of the processes, as indexed by overt, observable behaviors and leave the speculation to the philosophers. That was the contextual background against which both psycholinguistics and cognitive psychology served as dialectical antagonists when they appeared on the scene in the late 1960s and early 1970s.

The most notable change within psychology was that it became fashionable for psychologists, perhaps for the first time since the early part of the century, to study reading.[27] And, in the decade of the 1970s, works by psychologists flooded the literature on basic processes in reading. One group focused on text comprehension by trying to figure out how it is that readers come to understand the underlying structure of texts. We were offered story grammars—structural accounts of the nature of narratives, complete with predictions about how those structures impede and enhance human story comprehension. Others chose to focus on the expository tradition in text.[28] Like their colleagues interested in story comprehension, they believed that structural accounts of the nature of expository (informational) texts would provide valid and useful models for human text comprehension. And, in a sense, both of these efforts worked. Story grammars did account for story comprehension. Analyses of the structural relations among ideas in an informational piece did account for text comprehension. But, what neither text-analysis tradition really tackled was the relationship between the knowledge of the world that readers bring to text and the comprehension of those texts. In other words, by focusing on structural rather than the ideational, or content, characteristics of texts, they failed to get to the heart of comprehension. That task, as it turned out, fell to one of the most popular and influential movements of the 1970s, schema theory.

Schema theory[29] is a theory about the structure of human knowledge as it is represented in memory. In our memory, schemata are like little containers into which we deposit particular experiences that we have. So, if we see a chair, we store that visual experience in our chair schema. If we go to a restaurant, we store that experience in our restaurant schema, if we attend a party, our party schema, and so on. Clearly schema theory is linked to Piaget's theories of development and his two types of learning: assimilation and accommodation. When we assimilate new information, we store it in an existing schema; when we accommodate new information, we modify the structure of our schemata to fit the new data. The modern iteration of schema theory also owes a debt to Frederic Bartlett, who, in the 1930s, used the construct of schema to explain culturally driven interpretations of stories. For Bartlett, cultural schemata for stories were so strong that they prevented listeners, whether European or native Alaskan in background, from adopting the story schema of the other culture to understand its stories. Bartlett's account predates the current constructivist models of cognition and learning by 60 years; and his view is as inherently constructive as those who have succeeded him. In essence, Bartlett was saying exactly what modern constructivists say, that readers and listeners actively construct meanings for texts they encounter rather than simply "receiving" meaning from the texts.[30]

Schema theory also provides a credible account of reading comprehension, which probably, more than any of its other features, accounted for its popularity within the reading field in the 1970s and 80s.[31] It is not difficult to see why schema theory was so appealing to theoreticians, researchers, and practitioners when it arrived on the scene in the 1970s. First, schema theory provides a rich and detailed theoretical account of the everyday intuition that we understand and learn what is new in terms of what we already know. Second, schema theory accounts for another everyday intuition about why we as humans so often disagree about our interpretation of an event, a story, an article, a movie, or a TV show: We disagree with one another because we approach the phenomenon with very different background experiences and knowledge. Third, schema theory accounts for an everyday intuition that might be called an "it's-all-Greek-to-me" experience: Sometimes we just don't have enough background knowledge to understand a new experience or text.

Although these insights may not sound earthshaking after the fact, for the field of reading, and for education more generally, they were daunting challenges to our conventional wisdom. Examined in light of existing practices in the 1970s, they continued the revolutionary spirit of the linguistic and psycholinguistic perspectives. Schema theory encouraged us to ask:

> What is it that my children already know? And, how can I use that to help them deal with these new ideas that I would like them to know? rather than,
>
> What is it that they do not know? And how can I get that into their heads?

More specifically, with respect to reading comprehension, schema theory encouraged us to examine texts from the perspective of the knowledge and cultural backgrounds of our students in order to evaluate the likely connections that they would be able to make between ideas that are in the text and the schema that they would bring to the reading task. Schema theory, like the psycholinguistic perspective, also promoted a constructivist view of comprehension; all readers must, at every moment in the reading process, construct a coherent model of reading for the texts they read. The most important consequence of this constructivist perspective is that there is inherent ambiguity about where meaning resides. Does it reside in the text? In the author's mind as she sets pen to paper? In the mind of each reader as he or she builds a model of meaning unique to his or her experience and reading? In the interaction between reader and text?

Sociolinguistics. Sociolinguistics as a discipline developed in parallel with psycholinguistics. Beginning with the work of William Labov, and Joan Baratz and Roger Shuy, sociolinguists had important lessons for reading scholars.[32] Mainly, these lessons focused on issues of dialect and reading. Sociolinguists were finding that dialects were not ill- or half-formed variations of standard English. Instead, each dialect constituted a well-developed linguistic system in its own right, complete with rules for variations from standard English and a path of language development for its speakers. Speakers of dialects expressed linguistic differences, not linguistic deficits. The goal of schooling was not, and should not be, to eradicate the dialect in the process of making each individual a speaker of standard English. Instead, sociolinguists stressed the need to find ways to accommodate children's use of their dialect while they are learning to read and write. Several proposals for achieving this accommodation were tried and evaluated. The first was to write special readers for dialect speakers. In the early 1960s, several examples of black-dialect readers appeared and, almost as rapidly, disappeared from major urban districts. They failed primarily because African American parents did not want their children learning with "special" materials; they wanted their children to be exposed to mainstream materials used by other children.[33] The second equally unsuccessful strategy was to delay instruction in reading and writing until oral language became more standardized. Teachers who tried this technique soon found out just how resistant and persistent early language learning can be. The third and most successful approach to dialect accommodation involved nothing more than recognizing that a child who translates a standard English text into a dialect is performing a remarkable feat of translation rather than making reading errors. So, an African American child who says /pos/ when he sees *post* is simply applying a rule of black English, which requires a consonant cluster in ending position to be reduced to the sound of the first consonant. Unfortunately for children who speak a dialect, we, as a field, did not take the early lessons of the sociolinguists to heart. We continue to find schools in which children are scolded for using the oral language that they have spent their whole lives learning. We also continue to find children whose dialect translations are treated as if they were oral reading errors.

Prior to the advent of the sociolinguistic perspective, when educators talked about "context" in reading, they typically meant the print that surrounded particular words on a page. In the 1980s, and primarily because of the work of sociolinguists, the meaning of the word *context* expanded to include not only what was on the page, but what Bloome and Green referred to as the instructional, noninstructional, and home and community contexts of literacy.[34] From a sociolinguistic perspective, reading always occurred in a context, one that was shaped by the literacy event at the same time it shaped the event. The sociolinguistic versions of knowledge and language as socially and culturally constructed processes moved the constructivist metaphor to another plane, incorporating not only readers' prior knowledge in the form of schemata, but also the meanings constructed by peers and by one's cultural ancestors.

The most significant legacy of the sociolinguistic perspective was our heightened consciousness about language as a social and, therefore, cultural construction. Suddenly, reading was a part of a bigger and more complex world. Sociolinguists examined the role of language in school settings. For example, they pointed out that often success in reading was not so much an indication of reading "ability" per se, but of the success the individual experienced in learning how to use language appropriately in educational settings. Thus success, according to a sociolinguistic analysis, was more an index of how well children learned to "do school" than how well they could read. They contrasted the functions that language serves in school with the functions it serves outside of school and helped us rethink the role of language within the classroom. By studying the community outside of school, sociolinguists made us conscious of social, political, and cultural differences; as a result, we began to rethink our judgments of language and behavior. We saw that any judgment call we made, rather than reflecting the "right" way, simply reflected "our" way—the way we as teachers thought, talked, and behaved because of the cultural situation in which we lived, outside as well as inside school. By focusing on the role of community in learning, sociolinguists caused many educators to rethink the competitive atmosphere of classrooms and of school labels and recommended changes within schools so that children could learn from and with each other. With these contributions from sociolinguists, it was becoming more and more apparent that reading was not only not context-free, but that it was embedded in multiple contexts.

Literary Theory Perspective. One cannot understand the pedagogical changes in practice that occurred in the elementary reading curriculum in the 1980s without understanding the impact of literary theory, particularly reader-response theory. In our secondary schools, the various traditions of literary criticism have always had a voice in the curriculum, especially in guiding discussions of classic literary works. Until the middle 1980s, the "new criticism" that had emerged during the post–World War II era had dominated for several decades, and it had sent teachers and students on a search for the one "true" meaning in each text they encountered. With the emergence (some would argue the reemergence) of reader-response theories, all of which gave as much (if not more) authority to the reader than to either the text or the author, the picture, along with our practices, changed dramatically. Although there are many modern versions of reader response available, the work of Louise Rosenblatt has been most influential among elementary teachers and reading educators. In the 1980s, many educators reread (or more likely read for the first time) Rosenblatt's (1938) 1976 edition of *Literature as Exploration*, and *The Reader, the Text, the Poem*, which appeared in 1978. Rosenblatt argues that meaning is something that resides neither in the head of the reader (as some had previously argued) nor on the printed page (as others had argued).[35] Instead, Rosenblatt contends, meaning is created in the transaction between reader and document. This meaning, which she refers to as "the poem," resides above the reader-text interaction. Meaning is, therefore, neither subject nor object nor the interaction of the two. Instead, it is transaction, something new and different from any of its inputs and influences.[36]

The Pedagogical Correlates of New Perspectives

Although the post-Chall basal tradition continued well into the decade of the 1980s, new perspectives and practices began to appear in classrooms, journal articles, and basal lessons in the early 1980s.

Comprehension on Center Stage. Comprehension, especially as a workbook activity and a follow-up to story reading, was not a stranger to the reading classrooms of the 1930s through 1970s. As indicated earlier, it entered the curriculum as a story discussion tool and as a way of assessing reading competence in the first third of the 20th century.[37] Developments during mid-century were highlighted in an earlier National Study of School Evaluation yearbook devoted to reading;[38] by mid-century, the infrastructure of comprehension had been elaborated extensively and infused into the guided reading and workbook task. It was a staple of basal programs when Chall conducted her study of early reading, and had she emphasized reading instruction in the intermediate grades rather than grade 1, it undoubtedly would have been more prominent in her account.

During the late 1970s and through the decade of the 1980s, comprehension found its way to center stage in reading pedagogy. Just as a nationally sponsored set of research activities (i.e., the First-Grade Studies and Chall's book) focused energy on reforms in beginning reading in the late 1960s, it was the federally funded Center for the Study of Reading, initiated in 1976, which focused national attention on comprehension. Although the Center's legacy is undoubtedly bringing schema theory and the knowledge-comprehension relationship into our national conversation, it also supported much research on comprehension instruction,[39] including research that attempted to help students develop a repertoire of strategies for improving their comprehension.[40] This research was not limited to the Center; indeed many other scholars were equally involved in developing instructional strategies and routines during this period, including emphases on monitoring comprehension,[41] transactional strategies instruction,[42] K-W-L graphic organizers,[43] and, more recently, questioning the author.[44] Many of these new strategies found their way into the basals of the 1980s, which demonstrated substantially more emphasis on comprehension at all levels, including grade 1.[45]

Literature-Based Reading. Even though selections from both classical and contemporary children's literature have always been a staple of basal selections dating back to the 19th century (especially after grade 2 when the need for strict vocabulary control diminished), literature virtually exploded into the curriculum in the late 1980s. A short burst in literary content occurred after Chall's critical account of the type of selections and the challenge of basal content; more excerpts from authentic literature appeared, even in the grade 1 readers. But these selections had two characteristics that had always offended those who champion the use of genuine literature: excerpting and adaptation. Rarely were whole books included; instead, whole chapters or important slices were excerpted for inclusion. And, even when a whole chapter was included, it was usually adapted to (a) reduce vocabulary difficulty, (b) reduce the grammatical complexity of sentences, or (c) excise words (e.g., mild profanity) or themes that might offend important segments of the market.

Beyond basals, children's literature played an important supplementary role in the classrooms of teachers who believed that they must engage their students in a strong, parallel independent reading program. Often this took the form of each child selecting books to be read individually and later discussed with the teacher in a weekly one-on-one conference. And, even as far back as the 1960s, there were a few programs that turned this individualized reading component into the main reading program.[46]

But in the late 1980s, literature was dramatically repositioned. Several factors converged to pave the way for a groundswell in the role of literature in elementary reading. Surely, the resurgence of reader response theory as presented by Rosenblatt was important, as was the compatibility of the reader-response theory and its emphasis on interpretation, with the constructivism that characterized both cognitive and sociolinguistic perspectives. Research also played a role; in 1985, for example, in the watershed publication of the Center for the Study of Reading, *Becoming a Nation of Readers*, Richard Anderson and his colleagues documented the importance of "just plain reading" as a critical component of any and all elementary reading programs.[47] This period also witnessed an unprecedented expansion in the number of new children's books published annually. Finally, a few pieces of scholarship exerted enormous influence on teachers and teacher educators. Perhaps most influential was Nancie Atwell's (1987) *In the Middle: Writing, Reading, and Learning With Adolescents*, in which she told her story of how, as a middle school teacher, she invited readers, some of whom were quite reluctant, into a world of books and reading. The credibility of her experience and the power of her prose were persuasive in convincing thousands of classroom teachers that they could use existing literature and "reading workshops" to accomplish anything that a basal program could accomplish in skill development while gaining remarkable advantages in students' literary experience.[48]

In terms of policy and curriculum, the most significant event in promoting literature-based reading was the 1988 California Reading Framework. The framework called for reading materials that contained much more challenging texts at all levels. More important, it mandated the use of genuine literature, not the oversimplified adaptations and excerpts from children's literature that had been the staple of basal programs for decades. Publishers responded to the call of California's framework and produced a remarkably different product in the late 1980s and early 1990s than ever had appeared before on the basal market.[49] Gone were excerpts and adaptations and, with them, almost any traces of vocabulary control. Skills that had been front and center in the basals of the 1970s and 80s were relegated to appendix-like status. Comprehension questions were replaced by more interpretive, impressionistic response to literature activities. All this was done in the name of providing children with authentic literature and authentic activities to accompany it. The logic was that if we could provide students with real literature and real motivations for reading it, much of what is arduous about skill teaching and learning would take care of itself.

Book Clubs and literature circles are the most visible instantiations of the literature-based reading movement.[50] The underlying logic of Book Clubs is the need to engage children in the reading of literature in the same way as adults engage one another in voluntary reading circles. Such voluntary structures are likely to elicit greater participation, motivation, appreciation, and understanding on the part of students. Teachers are encouraged to establish a set of "cultural practices" (ways of interacting and supporting one another) in their classrooms to support students as they make their way into the world of children's literature. These cultural practices offer students both the opportunity to engage in literature and the skills to ensure that they can negotiate and avail themselves of that opportunity.

Process Writing. In the middle 1980s, writing achieved a stronghold in the elementary language arts curriculum that it had never before held. Exactly why and how it achieved that position of prominence is not altogether clear, but certain explanations are plausible. Key understandings from the scholarship of the 1970s and 80s paved the way. Functionality associated with the sociolinguistic perspective, process-writing approaches encouraged teachers to ask students to write for genuine audiences and purposes. The psycholinguistic notion of "error" as a window into children's thinking allowed us to worry less about perfect spelling and grammar and more about the quality of the thinking and problem solving children were producing. The general acceptance of constructivist epistemologies disposed us to embrace writing as the most transparently constructive of all pedagogical activities. All these constructs allowed us as a profession to take a different developmental view on writing, one consistent with the emergent literacy perspective that was gaining strength in early childhood literacy. We came to view all attempts to make sense by setting pen to paper, however deviant from adult models, as legitimate and revealing in their own right if examined through the eyes of the child writer. Led by Donald Graves and Lucy Calkins, we revolutionized our views of early writing development.[51] Finally, we began to see reading and writing as inherently intertwined, each supporting the other.

Integrated Instruction. It is impossible to document the history of reading instruction in the 20th century without mentioning the ways in which we have attempted to integrate reading with other curricular phenomena. Two stances have dominated our thinking about how to integrate reading into other curricula: integration of reading with the other language arts (writing, speaking, and listening) and integration across subject matter boundaries (with mathematics, science, social studies, art, and music). Like literature-based reading, both senses of integration have long been a part of the thinking about elementary reading curriculum.[52] In fact, a look back to the progressivism of Dewey and other scholars in the first part of the century reveals substantial rhetoric about teaching and learning across curricular boundaries.[53] From that early spurt of energy until the late 1980s, however, integrations assumed a minor role in American reading instruction. In basal manuals, for example, integration was portrayed almost as an afterthought until the late 1980s; it appeared in the part of the lesson that follows the guided reading and skills instruction sections, signaling that these are things that a teacher can do "if time permits." Things changed in the late 1980s. For one, integrated curriculum fit the sociolinguistic emphasis on language in use: the idea that language, including reading, is best taught and learned when it is put to work in the service of other purposes, activities, and learning efforts. Similarly, with the increase in importance of writing, especially early writing of the sort discussed by Graves and his colleagues,[54] it was tempting to champion the idea of integrated language arts instruction. In fact, the constructivist metaphor is nowhere played out as vividly and transparently as in writing, leading many scholars to use writing as a model for the sort of constructive approach they wanted to promote in readers. The notion was that we needed to help students learn to "read like a writer."[55] Also influential in supporting the move toward integrated instruction was the work of Donald Holdaway, who, in concert with many teacher colleagues, had been implementing an integrated language arts approach in Australia for a few decades.[56]

Whole Language. Important as they are, comprehension, literature-based reading, process writing, and integrated instruction pale in comparison to the impact of whole language, which is regarded as the most significant movement in reading curriculum in the last 30 years.[57] In fact, one might plausibly argue that whole language co-opted all four of these allied phenomena—comprehension, literature-based reading, integrated instruction, and process writing—by incorporating them, problems along with strengths, into its fundamental set of principles and practices. Whole language is grounded in child-centered pedagogy reminiscent of the progressive education movement (the individual child is the most important curriculum informant).[58] Philosophically, it is biased toward radical constructivist epistemology (all readers must construct their own meanings for the texts they encounter). Curricularly, it is committed to authentic activity (real, not specially constructed, texts and tasks) and integration (both within the language arts and between the language arts and other subject matters). Politically, it is suspicious of all attempts to mandate and control curricular decisions beyond the classroom level; as such, it places great faith and hope in the wisdom of teachers to exercise professional prerogative in making decisions about the children in their care. Whole language owes its essential character and key principles to the insights of linguistics, psycholinguistics, cognitive psychology, sociolinguistics, and literary theory detailed earlier. It owes its remarkable, if brief, appearance in the national limelight of reading instruction to its committed leaders and a veritable army of committed teachers who instantiated it in their classrooms, each with his or her own unique signature.[59]

When whole language emerged as a movement in the 1980s, it challenged the conventional wisdom of basals and questioned the unqualified support for early code emphases that had grown between 1967 and the early 1980s.[60] One of the great ironies of whole language is that its ascendancy into curricular prominence is best documented by its influence on the one curricular tool it has most consistently and most vehemently opposed, the basal reader.[61] As suggested earlier, basals changed dramatically in the early 1990s, largely, I conjecture, in response to the groundswell of support within the teaching profession for whole language and its close curricular allies, literature-based reading and process writing.

Vocabulary control, already weakened during the 1970s in response to Chall's admonitions, was virtually abandoned in the early 1990s in deference to attempts to incorporate more literature, this time in unexpurgated form (i.e., without the practices of adaptation and excerpting that had characterized the basals of the 1970s and 80s) into the grade 1 program.[62] Phonics, along with other skills, was backgrounded, and literature moved to center stage.

Basal programs appropriated or, as some whole language advocates have argued, "basalized" the activities and tools of whole language. Thus, in the basals of the early 1990s, each unit might have a writing process component in which the rhetoric, if not the reality of some version of process writing, was presented to teachers and students. In the 1980s, comprehension questions, probably following a story line, might have sufficed for the guided reading section of the manual (the part that advises teachers on how to read and discuss the story), but in the 1990s, questions and tasks that supported deep probes into students' response to literature became more prevalent. Another concession to literature-based reading was the creation and marketing of classroom libraries—boxed sets of books, usually thematically related to each unit—that teachers could use to extend their lessons and units "horizontally" and enrich children's literary opportunities.

Basals also repositioned their "integrated language arts" and "integrated curriculum" strands. Dating back even to the 1920s and 1930s, basals had provided at least a "token" section in which teachers were encouraged to extend the themes or skills of the basal story into related writing (e.g., rewriting stories), oral language (e.g., transforming a story into a play and dramatizing it), or cross-curricular activities (e.g., conducting community surveys, tallying the results, and reporting them), but these forays were regarded as peripheral rather than core. In the basals of the early 1990s, as skills moved into the background,[63] these integrated language arts activities were featured more prominently as core lesson components.[64]

These changes can, I believe, be traced to the prominent position of whole language as a curricular force during this period.[65] Publishers of basals accomplished this feat of appropriation not by ridding their programs of the skills of previous eras, but by subtle repositioning—foregrounding one component while backgrounding another—and creating optional components or modules (e.g., an intensive phonics kit or a set of literature books) that could be added to give the program one or another spin. Unsurprisingly, this created bulkier teacher's manuals and more complex programs.

Acceptance of whole language was not universal. To the contrary, there was considerable resistance to whole language and literature-based reading throughout the country.[66] In many places, whole language never really gained a foothold. In others, what was implemented in the name of whole language was not consistent with the philosophical and curricular principles of the movement; California, whole language advocates would argue, is a case in point. Whole language got conflated with whole-class instruction and was interpreted to mean that all kids should get the same literature, even if teachers had to read it to them.[67]

Nor was there a single voice within the whole language movement. Whole language scholars and practitioners differed on a host of issues such as the role of skills, conventions, and strategies within a language arts program. Some said, if we can just be patient, skills will emerge from meaningful communication activities; others spurred things on by taking advantage of spontaneous opportunities for minilessons; still others were willing to spur spontaneity a bit.

Even so, it is fair to conclude that by the early 1990s, whole language had become the conventional wisdom, the standard against which all else was referenced. The rhetoric of professional articles belies this change. As late as the mid-1980s, articles were written with the presumption of a different conventional wisdom—a world filled with skills, contrived readers, and workbooks. By 1991–1992, they were written with the presumption that whole language reforms, while not fully ensconced in U.S. schools, were well on their way to implementation. The arguments in the 1990s were less about first principles of whole language and more about fine-tuning teaching repertoires. The meetings of the Whole Language Umbrella grew to be larger than most large state conventions and regional conferences of the International Reading Association. By 1995, whole language was no longer a series of assaults on skills and basals that characterized it through the mid-1980s. It had become the conventional wisdom in rhetoric, if not in reality.

Returning to the lenses outlined at the beginning of this chapter (range of materials and practices, role of teacher, role of learner, and the processes of reading and learning to read), in whole language, we finally encountered major shifts in emphasis in comparison to what we found at the beginning of the century. In whole language, teachers were facilitators not tellers. Teachers observed what children did, decided what they needed, and arranged conditions to allow students to discover those very insights about reading, writing, and learning for themselves. Because this was truly child-centered pedagogy, learners occupied center stage. As Jerome Harste puts it, the child was the primary curriculum informant. Students were decision makers involved in choices about the books they read and the stories they wrote. The materials of reading instruction were the materials of life and living—the books, magazines, newspapers, and other forms of print that children can encounter in everyday life are the materials they should encounter in the classroom—no less, no more. There was no need for the sort of contrived texts and tasks of the sort found in basal reading programs. Instructional practices focused not on presenting a diet of skills carefully sequenced to achieve mastery, but on creating activities and tasks that supported the learning students needed at a particular point in time. If skills and strategies were taught, they were taught in minilessons, highly focused forays into the infrastructure of a skill or strategy followed up by immediately recontextualizing the skill in a genuine reading or writing situation. In contrast to previous periods, reading was now regarded as a meaning-making, not a perceptual, process. The reader was an active participant in creating, not a passive recipient of, the message in a text. The process of acquiring reading was also markedly different from the "readiness" perspective so dominant in the first 80 years of the century. Emergent literacy, the alternative to traditional reading readiness views, did not specify a "prereading" period in which children are prepared for the task of reading. All readers, at all stages, were meaning makers, even those who can only scribble a message or "pretend" to read.[68] Thus, at century's end, reading pedagogy finally developed some viable alternatives to the conventional views of teacher, learner, and process that had dominated pedagogical practice for the entire century. As it turned out, the new directions were short-lived, or at least they appear to be so from the perspective of developments in the first few years of the 21st century.

The Demise of Whole Language

At century's end, just when it appeared as if whole language, supported by its intellectual cousins (process writing, literature-based reading, and integrated curriculum), was about to assume the position of conventional wisdom for the field, the movement was challenged seriously, and the pendulum of the pedagogical debate began to swing back toward the skills end of the curriculum and instruction continuum. Several factors converged to make the challenge credible, among them (a) unintended curricular casualties of whole language; (b) questionable applications of whole language; (c) growing dissatisfaction with doctrinaire views of any sort; (d) a paradigm swing in the ideology of reading research; (e) increasing politicization of the reading research and policy agenda, and (f) increasing pressure for educators of all types, especially reading educators, to produce measurable results; and (g) a dramatic shift in the prevailing model of professional development.

Unintended Curricular Consequences. In its ascendancy, whole language changed the face of reading instruction and, in the process, left behind some curricular casualties, few of which were intended by those who supported whole language. Those, myself included,[69] who supported practices that were discarded during the rise of whole language had difficulty supporting the whole language movement even though we might have been philosophically and curricularly sympathetic to many of its principles and practices. This lack of enthusiasm from curricular moderates meant that whole language failed to build a base of support that was broad enough to survive even modest curricular opposition, let alone the political onslaught that it would experience at century's turn.

There were four casualties: skills instruction, strategy instruction, emphasis on text structure, and reading in the content areas. Earlier, I suggested that one of the consequences of whole language was the relegation of skills to the "appendices" of instructional programs. In accepting whole language, we tacitly accepted the premise that skills are better "caught" in the act of reading and writing genuine texts for authentic purposes than "taught" directly and explicitly by teachers. The argument is the same for phonics, grammar, text conventions, and structural elements. These entities may be worthy of learning, but they are unworthy of teaching. This position presents us with a serious conundrum as a profession. Admit, for the sake of argument, that the skills instruction of the 1970s and earlier, with decontextualized lessons and practice on "textoids" in workbook pages, deserved the criticism accorded to it by whole language advocates (and scholars from other traditions). But, a retreat from most skills instruction into a world of "authentic opportunity" did not provide a satisfactory answer for teachers and scholars who understood the positive impact that instruction can have. Many young readers do not "catch" the alphabetic principle by sheer immersion in print or by listening to others read aloud. For some it seems to require careful planning and hard work by dedicated teachers who are willing to balance systematic skills instruction with authentic texts and activities.[70]

Strategy instruction was another casualty. This loss has been particularly difficult for scholars who spent the better part of the early 1980s convincing basal publishers and textbook authors that the thoughtful teaching of flexible strategies for making and monitoring meaning was a viable alternative to mindless skills instruction, where skills were taught as though they were only ever to be applied to workbook pages and end-of-unit tests. But the strategy lessons that filled our basals in the middle to late 1980s—direct advice from teachers about how to summarize what one has read, how to use text structure to infer relations among ideas, how to distinguish fact from opinion, how to determine the central thread of a story, how to use context to infer word meanings, and how to make and evaluate the accuracy of predictions—were virtually nonexistent in the basals of the early to middle 1990s. Although there is no inherent bias in whole language or literature-based reading against the learning and use of a whole range of cognitive strategies, there is, as with phonics and grammar, a serious question about whether direct, explicit instruction in how to use them will help. The advice is to let them emerge from attempts to solve real reading problems and puzzles, the kind students meet in genuine encounters with authentic text. There may have been reason for concern about the strategy instruction of the 1980s. But revision rather than rejection of these strategies was not a part of the rhetoric of whole language.[71]

Structural emphasis was also suspect within whole language. This suspicion extended to formal grammars, story grammars, rhetorical structures, and genre features of texts. As with skills and strategies, whole language reformers do not claim that students should not learn and develop control over these structural tools; they simply claim that, like skills, they are best inferred from reading and writing authentic texts in the process of making meaning. So, the advocates are comfortable in adopting Frank Smith's[72] admonition to encourage kids to read like a writer (meaning to read the text with a kind of critical eye toward understanding the tools and tricks of the trade that the author uses to make her points and achieve her effects on readers), but they would likely reject a systematic set of lessons designed to teach and assess children's control of story grammar elements (such as plot, characterization, style, mood, or theme) or some system for dealing with basic patterns of expository text. As with skills and strategies, many of us see a compromise alternative to both the formulaic approach of the early 1980s and the "discovery" approach of the new reforms—dealing with these structural elements as they emanate from stories that a group is currently reading can provide some guidance and useful tools for students and teachers.

Content area reading also suffered during the ascendancy of whole language and literature-based reading. Content area texts—expository texts in general, but especially textbook-like entries—were not privileged in a world of literature-based reading. This is not an implicit criticism of the literature-based reading movement; rather it is a comment about the reallocation of curricular time and energy that occurs when a movement gains momentum. There is a certain irony in this development, for it is expository reading, not narrative reading, that most concerns middle and high school teachers. The cost here has been very dear. To enter middle school and high school classrooms in order to examine the role of expository text is to conclude that it has none. Occasionally, teachers assign expository texts for homework, but when students come to class the next day, clearly having avoided the assignment, teachers provide them with an oral version of what they would have gotten out of the text if they had bothered to read it. Most high school teachers have quite literally given up on the textbook for the communication of any important content. Although understandable, this approach is, of course, ultimately counterproductive. There comes a time in the lives of students—when they either go to college or enter the work world—when others expect them to read and understand informational texts on their own and in printed form rather than through oral or video transformation.[73]

Because whole language did not go out of its way to accommodate any of these curricular practices, those who were sympathetic with whole language but also champions of one or another approach were not available to help whole language respond to the criticism leveled at it in the late 1990s.

Questionable Applications of Whole Language. One dilemma faced by any curricular challenge is sustaining the integrity of the movement without imposing the very sorts of controls it is trying to eliminate. Whole language did not find and still has not found a satisfying way of managing this dilemma, and it has suffered as a consequence. Many schools, teachers, and institutions appropriated the whole language label without honoring its fundamental principles of authenticity, integration, and empowerment. Basal reader publishers made the most obvious and widespread appropriation, some even positioning their basal series as "whole language" programs. Earlier, I noted another misapplication in which whole language was confounded with whole-class instruction. Nowhere was this conflation more extreme than in the implementation of the California literature framework. The logic that prevailed in many classrooms was that it was better to keep the entire class together at all costs. Implicit in this practice are two interesting assumptions: (1) that getting the content of the stories is the most important goal for reading instruction, and (2) that the skills and processes needed to read independently will emerge somehow from this environment in which many students are pulled through texts that far exceed the grasp of their current skills repertoire. Needless to say, whole language had enough on its hands dealing with its own assumptions and practices; these philosophical and curricular misapplications exposed the movement to a whole set of criticisms that derived from practices not of its own making.

One of the primary reasons for misapplication of whole language was, in my estimate, the lack of an explicit plan for professional development. Whole language gives teachers a wide berth for making curricular and instructional decisions, for whole classes and for individual children. It assumes that teachers who are empowered, sincere, and serious about their personal professional development will be able to tailor programs and activities to the needs and interests of individual children. Such an approach makes sense only when we can assume that teacher knowledge is widely and richly distributed in our profession. To offer these prerogatives in the face of narrow and shallow knowledge is to guarantee that misguided practices, perversions of the very intent of the movement, will be widespread. The puzzle, of course, is where to begin the reform: by ensuring that the knowledge precedes the pre-rogative, or by ceding the prerogative to teachers as a way of leveraging their motivation for greater knowledge.[74]

Growing Dissatisfaction With Extreme Positions. Although it has reached its peak in the last five years, concern about extreme positions, be they extremely child-centered (such as the more radical of whole language approaches) or extremely curriculum-centered (such as high-ly structured, unswerving phonics programs) is not new. Voices from the middle, extolling balanced approaches or rationalizing the eclectic practices of teachers, began to be heard even in the earliest days of whole language's ascendancy.[75] Scholars and teachers raised a number of concerns about the assumptions and practices of the whole language movement. Most importantly, they expressed concern about the consequences of whole language out-lined earlier in this chapter. They questioned the assumption that skills are best "caught" dur-ing the pursuit of authentic reading activity rather than "taught" directly and explicitly. They also questioned the insistence on authentic texts and the corollary ban on instructional texts written to permit the application of skills within the curriculum. They questioned the zeal and commitment of the movement *qua* movement, with its strong sense of insularity and exclusivity. Finally, they worried that the press toward the use of authentic literature and literature-based reading would eradicate, albeit unintentionally, what little progress had been made toward the use of informational texts and teaching reading in the content areas.[76]

Ironically, in the past few years, these voices from the middle have found themselves re-sponding not to those who hold a radical whole language position, but to those who hold steadfastly to the phonics first position. Even so, the fact that those with centrist positions were not inclined to defend whole language when the political campaign against it began in the middle 1990s, they undoubtedly hastened the demise of whole language as the pre-tender to the title of conventional wisdom.

Changing Research Ideology. Prior to the 1980s, qualitative research in any form had little visibility within the reading research community. Among the array of qualitative efforts, only miscue analysis[77] and some early forays into sociolinguistic and anthropological accounts of literacy had achieved much in the way of archival status.[78] But all that changed in the 1980s and early 1990s. Qualitative research more generally, along with more specific lines of in-quiry taking a critical perspective on literacy as a social and pedagogical phenomenon, be-came more widely accepted as part of the mainstream archival literature.[79] Treatises pointing out the shortcomings of traditional forms of quantitative inquiry, especially experimental re-search, appeared frequently in educational research journals.[80] In terms of curriculum and pedagogy, it is important to remind ourselves that much of the research that undergirds whole language comes from this more qualitative, more interpretive, more critical tradition. Thus the credibility of this type of research increased in concert with the influence of whole language as a curricular movement.

Somewhere in the mid-1990s, the discourse of literacy research began to take a new turn. Stimulated by research supported by the National Institute for Child Health and Human Development, a new brand of experimental work began to appear in the middle 1980s and gathered momentum that has reached a peak in the past year or two.[81] This is experimentalism reborn from the 1950s and 60s, with great emphasis placed on "reliable, replicable research," large samples, random assignment of treatments to teachers and/or schools, and tried and true outcome measures.[82] This work does not build on the qualitative tradition of the 1980s and early 1990s; instead it finds its aegis in the experimental rhetoric of science and medicine and in the laboratory research that has examined reading as a perceptual process.[83] Although not broadly accepted by the reading education community at the turn of the century, this work has found a very sympathetic ear in the public policy arena.[84]

The political positioning of this research is important, but so is its substance. Two themes from this work have been particularly important in shaping a new set of instructional practices: phonemic awareness and phonics instruction.

The absolutely critical role played by phonemic awareness (the ability to segment the speech stream of a spoken word, e.g., /cat/ into component phonemes /cuh + ah + tuh/ and/or to blend separately heard sounds, e.g., /cuh + ah + tuh/ into a normally spoken word /cat/) in the development of the ability to decode and to read for meaning was well documented in research studies spanning the last 25 years of the 20th century.[85] Irrespective of mode of instruction, the overwhelming evidence suggests that phonemic awareness is a necessary but not a sufficient condition for the development of decoding and reading. First, children who possess high degrees of phonemic awareness in kindergarten or early in first grade are very likely to be good readers throughout their elementary school careers.[86] Second, almost no children who are successful readers at the end of grade 1 exhibit a low level of mastery of phonemic awareness. On the other hand, a substantial proportion of unsuccessful end-of-grade-1 readers possess better than average phonemic awareness; this evidence is the critical piece in establishing that phonemic awareness is a necessary but not a sufficient condition for reading success. Although we can be confident of its critical role in learning to read, we are less sure about the optimal way to enhance its development. Many scholars have documented the efficacy of teaching it directly, but they also admit that it is highly likely to develop as a consequence of learning phonics, learning to read, or especially learning to write, especially when teachers encourage students to use invented spellings.[87] Research in whole language classrooms suggests that writing is the medium through which both phonemic awareness and phonics knowledge develop, the former because students have to segment the speech stream of spoken words in order to focus on a phoneme, and the latter because there is substantial transfer value from the focus on sound-symbol information in spelling to symbol-sound knowledge in reading.[88]

The second consistent thread in the new experimentalism of the 1990s is the simple but undeniable emphasis on the code in the early stages of learning to read.[89] Reminiscent of Chall's earlier conclusions, scholars in this tradition tend to advocate phonics—first, fast, and simple.[90] Less well documented, and surely less well agreed upon, is the optimal course of instruction to facilitate phonics development. Even Gough, a classic bottom-up theorist, while arguing that what distinguishes the good reader from the poor reader is swift and accurate word identification, suggests that an early insistence on reading for meaning may be the best way to develop such decoding proficiency. Both Philip Gough and Connie Juel are convinced that students can learn how to read when they have "cryptoanalytic intent" (a disposition to decipher the specific letter-to-sound codes), phonemic awareness, an appreciation of the alphabetic principle (i.e., regardless of the numerous exceptions, letters do stand for sounds), and data (some texts to read and someone to assist when the going gets tough).[91]

After reviewing available instructional evidence, two of the most respected scholars in this tradition, Marilyn Adams and Connie Juel, independently concluded that children can and should learn the "cipher" through a combination of explicit instruction in phonemic awareness and letter-sound correspondences, a steady insistence on invented spellings as the route to conventional spellings in writing activities, and many opportunities to read connected text (especially when the texts contain enough decodable words to allow students to apply the phonics information they are learning through explicit instruction). Both of these reviewers, known for their sympathies toward instruction in the code, are quick to add that rich experiences with language, environmental print, patterned stories, and Big Books should also be a staple of effective early reading instruction.[92]

Politicization of the Reading Research and Policy Agenda. From its beginnings, one of the great hopes of educational research (and those who conduct it) is that policymakers will take research seriously when they establish policy initiatives at a local, state, or national level. After all, the improvement of educational practice is the ultimate goal of educational research, and policy is our society's most transparent tool for educational improvement. Historically, however, research has been regarded as one among many information sources consulted in policy formation, including expert testimony from practitioners, information about school organization and finance, and evaluations of compelling cases. In the past half decade, research, at least selective bits of research, has never been taken more seriously. Several laws in California make direct references to research. For example, Assembly Bill 1086 (1998) prohibited the use of Goals 2000 money for professional developers who advocated the use of context clues over phonics or who supported the use of invented spellings in children's writing. The federally sponsored Reading Excellence Act of 1999, which allocated US$240,000,000 for staff development in reading, requires that both state and local applications for funding base their programs on research that meets scientifically rigorous standards. The "scientifically rigorous" phrase was a late entry; in all but the penultimate version of the bill, the phrase was "reliable, replicable research," which had been interpreted as a code word for experimental research. As of early 1999, "phonics bills" (bills mandating either the use of phonics materials or some sort of teacher training to acquaint teachers with knowledge of the English sound-symbol system and its use in teaching) had been passed or were pending in 36 states.[93] In the early days of the current Bush administration, the goal of "evidence-based practice" was made even more explicit, with the phrase "scientifically based reading research" appearing more than 110 times in the Reading First portion of the No Child Left Behind Act of 2001 reauthorizing Title I.[94]

Policymakers like to shroud mandates and initiatives in the rhetoric of science, and sometimes that practice results in very strained, if not indefensible, extrapolations from research. This has happened consistently in the current reading policy arena. Two examples make the point vividly. First, California Assembly Bill 1086, with its prohibition on context clues and invented spelling, represents an ironic application of research to policy. The irony stems from the fact that many of the advocates of a return to code emphasis, such as Marilyn Adams, read the research as supporting the use of invented spellings in the development of phonemic awareness and phonics.[95] Second, the mandate in several states calling for the use of decodable text (usually defined as text consisting of words that can be sounded out using a combination of the phonics rules taught up to that point in the program plus some instant recognition of a few highly frequent sight words) is based on the thinnest of research bases. The idea is that children will learn to use their phonics better, faster, and more efficiently if the texts they read permit facile application of the principles they are learning.

Although it all sounds very logical, there is precious little research evidence to support the systematic and exclusive use of decodable text.[96] This lack of evidence, however, does not seem to have deterred advocates who, on the phonics issues, championed scientific evidence as the gold standard for policy implementation.

Professional groups have entered the policy fray in recent years. For example, the American Federation of Teachers (AFT) has endorsed a particular set of programs as scientifically validated to produce excellent results. Interestingly, each of the programs on their endorsed list is committed to early, systematic, explicit phonics instruction in a highly structured framework. The AFT influence is evident in some other professional movements, such as the Learning First Alliance.[97]

When research moves into the policy arena, one of two outcomes are most likely. If the research is widely accepted by members of the profession from which it comes, widespread acceptance and implementation usually follows. This often occurs in medical, pharmaceutical, or agricultural research. If widespread consensus on what the research says about practice is not reached, then research-based policy initiatives are likely to sharpen and deepen the schisms that already exist, and the entire enterprise is likely to be regarded as a war among factions within the field. The latter scenario appears to characterize the reading field.[98]

Interestingly, the debate, accompanied by its warlike metaphors, appears to have more life in the public and professional press than it does in our schools. Reporters and scholars revel in keeping the debate alive and well, portraying clearly divided sides and detailing a host of differences of a philosophical, political, and pedagogical nature.[99] Teachers, by contrast, often talk about, and more importantly enact, more balanced approaches. For example, several scholars, in documenting the practices of highly effective, highly regarded teachers, found that these exemplary teachers employed a wide array of practices, some of which appear decidedly whole language in character (e.g., process writing, literature groups, and contextualized skills practice) and some of which appear remarkably skills-oriented (explicit phonics lessons, sight-word practice, and comprehension strategy instruction).[100]

Producing Measurable Results. Evaluation has always posed a conundrum for whole language supporters. First, some oppose the use of any sort of externally mandated or administered assessments as a matter of principle, holding that assessment is ultimately the responsibility of a teacher in collaboration with a student and his or her parents. Second, even those supporters who are open to external forms of accountability, or at least reporting outside the boundaries of the classroom or school, often claim that standardized tests, state assessments, and other external measures of student accomplishment do not provide sensitive indicators of the goals of curricula based on whole language principles. Most appealing would be assessments that are classroom-based and individualized in nature, with the option of aggregating these sorts of data at the classroom and school levels when accountability is required. During the 1990s, many felt that the increased emphasis on performance assessment and portfolios would fill this need.[101] In an age of high expectations, explicit standards, and school- and classroom-level accountability, none of these options is a good fit with the views and desires of policymakers and the public. Both of these constituents seem quite uneasy about the quality of our schools and our educational system, so uneasy that leaving assessment in the hands of our teachers seems an unlikely outcome. It is not at all clear to me that the proponents of at least strong versions of whole language can, or will be willing to, hold themselves accountable to the sorts of measures that the public and policymakers find credible.

A Shift in the Prevailing Model of Professional Development. Fast on the heels of the entry of scientifically based reading research into the professional discourse came a new vision of professional development. The models of teacher reflection and prerogative dominant in the early 1990s were replaced by training models that championed the development of the knowledge and skills required to implement scientifically based reading research. This led to implementation models that put a premium on monitoring for quality control and fidelity to programs touted as "scientific."[102] Earlier models emphasizing reflection and teacher inquiry shared a commitment to research as the basis for practice, but any similarity ends there. In the teacher inquiry models, research is used to inform practice, and practice is expected to vary from teacher to teacher and situation to situation. In the models emerging at the turn of the century, research is used to determine practice, and the expectation is that practice should vary minimally from teacher to teacher and situation to situation.

Who Holds the High Ground? One other factor, both subtle and speculative (on my part) seems to be an undercurrent in the rhetoric of the field in the first years of the 21st century. Whole language has always privileged the role of the teacher as the primary curriculum decision maker. Teachers, the argument goes, are in the best position to serve this important role because of their vast knowledge of language and literacy development, their skills as diagnosticians (they are expert "kidwatchers"), and the materials and teaching strategies they have at their disposal. And, in the arguments against more structured approaches, this is exactly the approach whole language advocates have taken: "Don't make these decisions at the state, district, or even the school level. Arm teachers with the professional prerogative (and corollary levels of professional knowledge) they need in order to craft unique decisions for individual children." Although this may seem a reasonable, even admirable position, it has recently been turned into an apology for self-serving teacher ideology.[103] The counter argument suggests that the broad base of privilege accorded to teachers may come at the expense of students and their parents. Thus, those who advocate a strong phonics-first position often take the moral high ground: "We are doing this for America's children (and for YOUR child!), so that they have the right to read for themselves." Even if one opposes this rhetorical move, it is not difficult to appreciate the clever repositioning on the part of those who want to return to more phonics and skills.

Taken together, these factors created a policy environment in which whole language was unlikely to flourish as the mainstream approach to teaching reading and writing. In the final analysis, however, I believe that the reluctance to own up to the "measurable results" standards was the Achilles heel of whole language. If whole language advocates had been willing to play by the rules of external accountability, to assert that students who experience good instruction based on solid principles of progressive pedagogy will perform well on standardized tests and other standards of performance, they would have stood a better chance of gaining a sympathetic ear with the public and with policymakers. And, as long as the criteria for what counts as evidence for growth and accomplishment are vague or left to individual teachers, the public could question the movement and wonder whose interests were being served by an unwillingness to commit to common standards.

Looking Ahead:
Will We Benefit From the Lessons of History?

So where has this journey taken us? And, where will it take us next? We are, as Regie Routman has suggested, at a crossroads.[104] Many recent developments suggest that we are retreating to a more familiar, more comfortable paradigm of basic skills, in which phonics, skills, and controlled text dominate our practices. Other developments suggest that we are on the verge of a new paradigm, a hybrid that weds some of the principles of whole language (integrated instruction and authentic texts and tasks) with some of the traditions of earlier eras (explicit attention to skills and strategies, some vocabulary control of early readers, and lots of early emphasis on the code) in an "ecologically balanced" approach to reading instruction.[105] The most cynical among us might even argue that we are just riding the natural swing of a pendulum that will, if we have the patience, take us back to whole language, or whatever its child-centered descendant turns out to be, in a decade or so. Before making a prediction about the direction the field will take, let me play out the first two scenarios, phonics first and balanced reading instruction.

One Alternative for the Future

If those who have advocated most strongly for a return to phonics and a heavy skills orientation have their way—if they are able to influence federal, state, and local policy as well as the educational publishing industry—we will experience moderate to substantial shifts on most, but not all, the criteria I have used to measure changes in reading pedagogy over the last 40 years (range of materials, range of pedagogical practices, role of teacher, role of student, and underlying theory of reading and reading acquisition). As I read their views about policy and practice, the greatest changes will occur at the very earliest stages of learning to read: kindergarten and grade 1. They suggest explicit instruction on phonemic awareness and phonics, with a strong preference for decodable texts in the early grades. When it comes to writing, literature, response, and comprehension, they seem quite content to cede curricular authority to the practices that emerged during the 1980s and early 1990s, those associated with whole language, literature-based reading, and process writing.[106] Thus, looking broadly at the entire elementary reading curriculum (the range of materials and the range of pedagogical practices), things might, on the surface, look similar to the early 1990s, with some retreat to the 1980s, especially in terms of skill and strategy instruction.

But, beneath that curricular surface, major changes would have occurred. For example, the role of the teacher and the learner would have reverted to what they have been throughout most of the 20th century. The role of the teacher would be to transmit the received knowledge of the field, as reflected in research-based curricular mandates, to students. Students would eventually be regarded as active meaning makers, but only after they had received the tools of decoding from their teachers. The greatest changes of all would have taken place in the underlying model of reading and reading acquisition. The simple view of reading (RC = Dec * LC) would have returned in full force, and the job of young readers would be to acquire the decoding knowledge they lack when they begin to learn to read.

A Second Alternative

If those who are pushing for ecological balance prevail, the field will experience less dramatic shifts. A balanced approach will privilege authentic texts and tasks, with a heavy emphasis on writing, literature, response, and comprehension, but it will also call for an ambitious program of explicit instruction for phonics, word identification, comprehension, spelling, and writing. A balanced approach is likely to look like some instantiations of whole language from the early 1990s, but recalibrated to redress the unintended curricular consequences outlined earlier in this chapter. Major differences between a balanced approach and the new phonics are likely to manifest themselves most vividly in kindergarten and grade

1, where a rich set of language and literacy experiences would provide the context from which teachers would carve out scaffolded instructional activities to spotlight necessary skills and strategies, for example, phonemic awareness, letter-sound knowledge, concepts of print, and conceptual development. Thus, instruction, while focused and explicit, would also be highly contextualized.

Beneath the curricular surface, balanced approaches seem to share slightly more in common, at least on a philosophical plane, with whole language than with new phonics approaches. The teacher is both facilitator and instructor. The teacher facilitates learning by establishing authentic activities, intervening where necessary to provide the scaffolding and explicit instruction required to help students take the next step toward independence. The student is, as in whole language, an active meaning maker from day one of preschool. Reading is a process of constructing meaning in response to texts encountered in a specific context, and the emergent literacy metaphor, not the readiness metaphor, characterizes the acquisition process.

An Ecologically Balanced Approach

If my personal bias has not emerged, let me declare it unequivocally: I favor the conceptual map of the ecologically balanced approach. There are several reasons for favoring this stance. First, my reading of the research points to the balanced curricular position, not to the new phonics position, both at a theoretical and a pedagogical level. I do not see much support for the simple view of reading underlying the new phonics; readers do construct meaning, they do not find it simply lying there in the text. Regarding pedagogical research, my reading requires me to side with Chall's view that while some sort of early, focused, and systematic emphasis on the code is called for, no particular approach can be singled out. Even the recent report of the National Reading Panel took exactly that position. And, while I readily accept the findings of the phonemic awareness research, I do not read them as supporting drill and practice approaches to this important linguistic understanding; to the contrary, highly embedded approaches, such as invented spelling, are equally as strongly implicated in the research.[107]

Second, an ecologically balanced approach is more respectful of the entire range of research in our field. It does not have to exclude major research paradigms or methodological approaches to sustain its integrity.

Third, an ecologically balanced approach also respects the wisdom of practice. It is no accident that studies of exemplary teachers, those who are respected by their peers and nurture high student achievement, consistently find that they exhibit a balanced repertoire of instructional strategies. Teachers who are faced with the variations in achievement, experience, and aptitude found in today's classrooms apparently need and deserve a full tool box of pedagogical practices.

Finally, an ecologically balanced approach respects our professional history. It retains the practices that have proved useful from each era but transforms and extends them, rendering them more effective, more useful, and more supportive of teachers and students. And, it may represent our only alternative to the pendulum-swing view of our pedagogical history that seems to have plagued the field of reading for most of the 20th century. A transformative rather than a cyclical view of progress would be a nice start for a new century. It will be interesting to evaluate in another twenty years, with the lens of history at our disposal, which path we have followed.

ENDNOTES

1. The work reported herein was supported in part under the Education Research and Development Centers Program PR/Award Number R305R70004, as administered by the Office of Educational Research and Improvement, U.S. Department of Education. However, the contents do not necessarily represent the positions or policies of the National Institute on Student Achievement, Curriculum, and Assessment or the National Institute on Early Childhood Development, or the U.S. Department of Education, and endorsement by the federal government should not be assumed. An earlier and more complete version of this essay, titled "Reading in the Twentieth Century," appeared in Good, Thomas (Ed.). (2000). *American education: Yesterday, today, and tomorrow* (Ninety-ninth yearbook of the National Society for the Study of Education, pp. 152–208). Chicago: University of Chicago Press. Adapted with permission.

2. Austin, Mary C., & Morrison, Coleman. (1963). *The first R*. New York: Macmillan.

3. This account is from Chall, J. (1967). *Learning to read: The great debate* (pp. 13–15). New York: McGraw Hill.

4. Smith, N.B. (1986). *American reading instruction* (p. 276). Newark, DE: International Reading Association.

5. Smith, N.B. (1986). *American reading instruction*.

6. Bond, G.L., & Dykstra, R. (1997). The cooperative research program in first-grade reading instruction, *Reading Research Quarterly, 32*(4). Entire issue.

7. The reporting of data for students through grade 2 did not receive the fanfare that the first-grade report did, an outcome which I find unfortunate because it was, in many ways, even more interesting. It showed stronger effects overall for code-based approaches, and it revealed the most provocative of all the findings in this entire enterprise—the project effect. The project effect was this: Using analysis of covariance to control incoming performance, students were better off being in the poorest performing approach in Project A than they were being in the best performing approach in Project B. This raises the whole issue of impact of contextual factors on reading achievement. See Dykstra, R. (1968). Summary of the second-grade phase of the cooperative research program in primary reading instruction. *Reading Research Quarterly, 4*, 49–70.

8. If focus were on the impact of these studies on research rather than the practice, these issues would occupy more of our attention. In a sense, the First-Grade Studies created an opening for other research endeavors; indeed, the directions that reading research took in the mid-1970s—the nature of comprehension and the role of the teacher—suggest that there were groups of scholars ready to seize the opportunity.

9. When large-scale experiments returned in the early 1990s, it was not the Department of Education, but the National Institute of Child Health and Human Development (NICHD), that led the renaissance. For accounts of the development of the NICHD effort, see Lyon, G.R. (1995). Research initiatives in learning disabilities: Contributions from scientists supported by the National Institute of Child Health and Human Development. *Journal of Child Neurology, 10*, 120–127; or Lyon, G.R., & Chhaba,V. (1996). The current state of science and the future of specific reading disability. *Mental Retardation and Developmental Disabilities Research Reviews, 2*, 2–9. It is also worth noting that one of the likely reasons for the demise of Method A vs. Method B experiments is that scholars in the 1960s were looking for main effects rather than interaction effects. Had they set out to find in this work that methods are uniquely suited to particular populations, they might not have rejected them so completely.

10. The impact of Chall's book, particularly the phonics recommendation, was documented by Helen Popp (1975). Current practices in the teaching of beginning reading. In John B. Carroll and Jeanne S. Chall (Eds.), *Toward a literate society: The report of the Committee on Reading of the National Academy of Education*. New York: McGraw Hill.

11. In an unpublished research study, researchers found two- and three-fold increases in the number of words introduced in the first-grade books for the popular series published by Scott Foresman and Ginn. Hansen, J., & Pearson, P.D. (1978). *Learning to read: A decade after Chall*. Unpublished manuscript, University of Minnesota.

12. The teacher's manuals of the Ginn 360 program provide the most notable example of this new trend. See Clymer, T., et al. (1968). *Ginn 360*. Lexington, MA: Ginn.

13. Mastery learning can trace its intellectual roots to the works of Benjamin Bloom and John Carroll: Bloom, B. (1968). Learning for mastery. *Evaluation Comment, 1*; Carroll, J. (1963). A model of school learning. *Teachers College Record, 64*, 723–732.

14. For an account of criterion-referenced assessment as it emerged during this period, see Popham, J. (1978). *Criterion-referenced measurement*. Englewood Cliffs, NJ: Prentice-Hall.

15. Deno, S.L. (1985). Curriculum-based measurement: The emerging alternative. *Exceptional Children, 52*, 219–232.

16. Bloom, B. (1968). Learning for mastery.

17. During the 1970s, the most popular of these systems was the Wisconsin Design for Reading Skill Development, followed closely by Fountain Valley. Systems like these remained a staple in basal programs in the 1980s and 1990s and were still available as options in most commercial programs as late as 2002. For an account of the rationale behind these systems, see Otto, Wayne (1977). The Wisconsin Design, A reading program for individually guided education. In H.J. Klausmeier, R.A. Rossmiller, & M. Saily (Eds.), *Individually guided elementary education: Concepts and practices.* New York: Academic Press. For a critique of these programs during their ascendancy, see Johnson & Pearson, "Skills Management Systems."

18. This is not to say that there were no challengers to the conventional wisdom that emerged in the middle of the century. To the contrary, the alphabetic approach, now dubbed "synthetic phonics," survived as a force throughout the period, as did the language experience approach and a few assorted alternatives. See Chall, *Learning to Read*, and Mathews, *Teaching to Read*, for accounts of these programs.

19. It should be noted that a major child-centered reform movement, the open classroom, was creating quite a wave in educational circles and elementary schools throughout the United States in the early 1970s. It is hard, however, to find any direct impact of the open-classroom movement on reading instruction. However, one could make the argument that the open-classroom philosophy had a delayed impact in its influence on the whole language movement in the late 1980s.

20. Some portions of the text in this section were adapted in Pearson, P.D., & Stephens, D. (1993). Learning about literacy: A 30-year journey. In C.J. Gordon, G.D. Labercane, & W.R. McEachern (Eds.), *Elementary reading: Process and practice* (pp. 4–18). Boston: Ginn. (Sections adapted with the knowledge and permission of the coauthor and publisher.)

21. To assert that Chomsky laid the groundwork for an essential critique of behaviorism as an explanatory model for language processes is not to assert that he drove behaviorism out of psychology or education.

22. For an account of this view of language development, see Brown, R. (1970). *Psycholinguistics.* New York: Macmillan.

23. Goodman, K.G. (1965). A linguistic study of cues and miscues in reading. *Elementary English, 42,* 639–643; and Goodman, K.G. (1967). A psycholinguistic guessing game. *Journal of the Reading Specialist, 4,* 126–135.

24. Smith, F. (1971). *Understanding reading: A Psycholinguistic analysis of reading and learning to read.* New York: Holt, Rinehart, & Winston.

25. In all fairness, it must be admitted that this contribution was not exclusively Smith's. As we shall point out in later sections, many other scholars, most notably David Rumelhart and Richard Anderson, championed constructivist views of reading. It is fair, however, to say that Smith was the first scholar to bring this insight into the reading field. Rumelhart, D. (1980). Schemata: The building blocks of cognition. In R.J. Spiro, B.C. Bruce, & W.F. Brewer (Eds.), *Theoretical issues in reading comprehension.* Hillsdale, NJ: Erlbaum. Anderson, R.C. & Pearson, P.D. (1984). A schema-theoretic view of basic processes in reading comprehension. In P.D. Pearson, R. Barr, M.L. Kamil, & P. Mosenthal (Eds.), *Handbook of reading research.* New York: Longman.

26. Smith, F. (1983). Reading like a writer. *Language Arts, 60,* 558–567.

27. During this period, great homage was paid to intellectual ancestors such as Edmund Burke Huey, who as early as 1908 recognized the cognitive complexity of reading. Voices such as Huey's, unfortunately, were not heard during the period 1915 to 1965 when behaviorism dominated psychology and education.

28. Walter Kintsch and Bonnie Meyer wrote compelling accounts of the structure of exposition that were translated by others (e.g., Barbara Taylor and Richard Beach) into instructional strategies. See Kintsch, W. (1974). *The representation of meaning in memory.* Hillsdale, NJ: Erlbaum; Meyer, B.J.F. (1975). *The organization of prose and its effects on memory.* Amsterdam: North Holland Publishing; and Taylor, B.M., & Beach, R. (1984). The effects of text structure instruction on middle-grade students' comprehension and production of expository text. *Reading Research Quarterly, 19,* 134–146.

29. The most complete accounts of schema theory are provided by Rumelhart, D., (1980) "Schemata: The Building Blocks of Cognition," and Anderson & Pearson, (1984) "A Schema-Theoretic View of Basic Processes in Reading Comprehension."

30. Bartlett, F.C. (1932). *Remembering.* Cambridge, UK: Cambridge University Press.

31. It is not altogether clear that schema theory is dead, especially in contexts of practice. Its role in psychological theory is undoubtedly diminished due to attacks on its efficacy as a model of memory and cognition. See McNamara, T.P., Miller, D.L., & Bransford, J.D. (1991). Mental models and reading comprehension. In R. Barr, M.L. Kamil, P. Mosenthal, & P.D. Pearson (Eds.), *Handbook of reading research* (Vol. 2, pp. 490–511). New York: Longman.

32. For early accounts of this perspective, see Baratz, J., & Shuy, R. (1969). *Teaching black children to read.* Washington, DC: Center for Applied Linguistics; and Labov, W. (1972). *Language of the inner city.* Philadelphia: University of Pennsylvania Press.

33. Baratz & Shuy (1969). *Teaching black children to read.*

34. See Bloome, D., & Greene, J. (1969). Directions in the sociolinguistic study of reading. *Handbook of reading research* (Vol. 2, pp. 395–421).

35. Rosenblatt, L. (1936/1978). *Literature as exploration.* New York: Appleton Century Croft. Rosenblatt, L. (1978). *Reader, text, and poem.* Carbondale, IL: Southern Illinois University Press.

36. Rosenblatt (1938) credits the idea of transaction to John Dewey, who discussed it in many texts, including *Experience and Education.* New York: Kappa Delta Pi.

37. A very interesting, even provocative attempt to understand comprehension processes appears in Thorndike, Edward L. (1917). Reading as reasoning: A study of mistakes in paragraph reading. *Journal of Educational Psychology, 8,* 323–332. The classic reference for using tests to reveal the psychological infrastructure of comprehension is the first published factor analysis of reading comprehension by Davis, F. (1944). Fundamental factors of reading comprehension. *Psychometrika, 9,* 185–197.

38. Robinson, H.M. (Ed). (1968). *Innovation and change in reading instruction* (Sixty-seventh yearbook of the National Society for Study in Education, Part II). Chicago: University of Chicago Press.

39. Dolores Durkin published a revealing study in 1978 documenting that what went on in the name of comprehension was essentially completing worksheets and answering questions during story discussions. She saw almost no instruction about how to engage in any sort of comprehension task—no modeling, no demonstration, no scaffolding. Durkin, D. (1978). What classroom observations reveal about reading instruction. *Reading Research Quarterly, 14* 481–533.

40. Among the most notable efforts at the Center were the classic works on reciprocal teaching: Palincsar, A., & Brown, A.L. (1984). Reciprocal teaching of comprehension fostering and monitoring activities. *Cognition and Instruction, 1,* 117–175; Raphael, T.E., & Pearson, P.D. (1985). Increasing students' awareness of sources of information for answering questions. *American Educational Research Journal, 22,* 217–236; and explicit comprehension instruction as a general approach in Pearson, P.D., & Dole, J. (1988). Explicit comprehension instruction: A review of research and a new conceptualization of instruction. *Elementary School Journal, 88,* 151–165; Pearson, P.D. (1985). Changing the face of reading comprehension instruction. *The Reading Teacher, 38,* 724–738. This focus on comprehension and reasoning while reading continues today at the Center with the work of Anderson and his colleagues.

41. The work of Scott Paris and his colleagues is exemplary in the area of metacognitive training and comprehension monitoring. Paris, S.G., Cross, D.R., & Lipson, M.Y. (1984). Informed strategies for learning: A program to improve children's reading awareness and comprehension. *Journal of Educational Psychology, 76,* 1239–1252.

42. Michael Pressley, working in conjunction with a group of professionals in Montgomery County, Maryland, developed a set of powerful comprehension routines that, among other things, extended the four strategies of reciprocal teaching (questioning, summarizing, clarifying, and predicting) to include more aspects of literary response (e.g., personal response and author's craft). The best resource on this line of pedagogical research is a 1993 volume of *Elementary School Journal,* edited by Pressley, along with the following articles, one of which is from that volume: M. Pressley et al. Transactional instruction of comprehension strategies: The Montgomery County, Maryland, SAIL Program. *Reading and Writing Quarterly, 10,* 5–19; M. Pressley et al. Beyond direct explanation: Transactional instruction of reading comprehension strategies. *Elementary School Journal, 92,* 513–555.

43. K-W-L, an acronym for a graphic organizer technique in which students chart before and after reading what they know, what they want to know, and what they learned, is an interesting phenomenon, because while it has attracted a great deal of curricular attention in basals, articles for practioners, and staff development materials, it is hard to find much research on its instructional efficacy. See Ogle, D. (1986). The K-W-L: A teaching model that develops active reading of expository text. *The Reading Teacher, 39,* 564–570.

44. Isabel Beck and Margaret McKeown have spent several years in collaboration with a network of teachers perfecting this engaging practice, which focuses on how and why authors put text together the way they do. The net result of this routine is that students learn a great deal about how to read critically (What is the author trying to do to me as a reader?) and about author's craft (How do authors structure their ideas to achieve particular effects?). See Beck, I., McKeown, M., Hamilton, R.L., & Kucan, L. (1997). *Questioning the author: An approach for enhancing student engagement with text.* Newark, DE: International Reading Association.

45. Chall, in the 1991 edition of *Learning to Read,* documented this important increase in basal comprehension activities.

46. Chall devotes a section to individualized reading in her 1967 description of alternatives to the basal (pp. 41–42), but has little to say about it as a serious alternative to basal, phonics, or linguistic approaches. In that same period, it is, undoubtedly, Jeanette Veatch who served as the most vocal spokesperson for individualized reading. She published professional textbooks describing how to implement the program in the classroom, for example, *Individualizing your reading program* (1959). New York: G.P. Putnam. In the middle 1960s, Random House published a "series" of literature books that were accompanied (in a pocket on the inside cover) by a set of vocabulary and comprehension activities that look remarkably like basal workbook pages. The Random House materials remind one of the currently popular computer program, Accelerated Reader, which is similarly designed to manage some assessment and skill activity to accompany trade books that children read on their own.

47. Anderson and his colleagues reported several studies documenting the impact of book reading on children's achievement gains: Anderson, R.C., Hiebert, E., Scott, J., & Wilkinson, I. (1984). *Becoming a nation of readers*. Champaign, IL: Center for the Study of Reading.

48. Atwell, N. (1987). *In the middle: Writing, reading, and learning with adolescents*. Portsmouth, NH: Heinemann. While it is difficult to locate data to document these claims about Atwell's particular influence, the rise of literature in the middle school has been documented by changes in the teacher survey portion of the National Assessment of Educational Progress of Reading.

49. James Hoffman and his colleagues painstakingly documented these sorts of changes in the basals of the early 1990s. Hoffman, J.V., McCarthey, S.J., Abbott, J., Christian, C., Corman, L., Elliot, M.B., Matheme, D., & Stahle, D. (1994). So what's new in the "new" basals. *Journal of Reading Behavior, 26,* 47–73.

50. For a complete account of the Book Club movement, see McMahon, S.I., & Raphael, T. E., with Goatley, V., & Pardo, L. (1997). *The book club connection.* New York: Teachers College Press.

51. Two classic books by Donald Graves were influential in leading the process writing movement at the elementary level, as was Lucy Calkins' (1986) classic, *The Art of Teaching Writing*. Portsmouth, NH: Heinemann; Graves, D. (1983). *Writing: Teachers and students at work.* Portsmouth, NH: Heinemann; and Graves, D. (1984). *A researcher learns to write.* Portsmouth, NH: Heinemann.

52. Perhaps the most complete current reference on integrated curriculum is a new chapter in the third volume of the *Handbook of Reading Research*. Gavelek, J.R., Raphael, T.E., Biondo, S.M., and Wang, D. (in press). Integrated literacy instruction. In M.L. Kamil, P. Mosenthal, P.D. Pearson, & R. Barr (Eds.), *Handbook of Reading Research* (Vol. 3). Hillsdale, NJ: Erlbaum.

53. In Chapter 10 of Huey's 1908 book on reading, two such programs, one at Columbia and one at the University of Chicago, were described in rich detail. It is Dewey's insistence that pedagogy be grounded in the individual and collective experiences of learners that is typically cited when scholars invoke his name to support integrated curriculum. Huey, E.B. (1908). *The psychology and pedagogy of reading*. New York: Macmillan. (Revised 1912, 1915)

54. See Graves (1983) for an explication of his views on writing, and, for an account of how reading and writing support one another in an integrated language arts approach, see Hansen, J. (1987). *When readers write.* Portsmouth, NH: Heinemann.

55. Frank Smith and Robert Tierney and P. David Pearson carried this metaphor to the extreme. All three used the reading "like a writer" metaphor in titles to papers during this period: Smith, F. (1983). Reading like a writer. *Language Arts, 60,* 558–567; Tierney, R.J., & Pearson, P.D. (1983). Toward a composing model of reading. *Language Arts, 60,* 568–580; and Pearson, P.D., & Tierney, R.J. (1984). On becoming a thoughtful reader: Learning to read like a writer. In A. Purves & O. Niles (Eds.) *Reading in the secondary school* (Eighty-third yearbook of the National Society for the Study of Education, pp. 144–173). Chicago: National Society for the Study of Education.

56. Donald Holdaway's (1979) *The Foundations of Literacy*, summarizes this perspective and work.

57. The notion of significance here is intended to capture its impact, not its validity. Even those who question its validity would have difficulty discounting its influence on practice.

58. A rich account of the curricular antecedents of whole language and other progressive and critical pedagogies is found in Shannon, P. (1990). *The struggle to continue.* Portsmouth, NH: Heinemann. See also Goodman, Y. (1989). Roots of the whole language movement. *Elementary School Journal, 90,* 113–127. The phrase, "the child as curriculum informant," comes from Harste, J., Burke, C., & Woodward, V. (1984). *Language stories and literacy lessons.* Portsmouth, NH: Heinemann.

59. One cannot possibly name all the important leaders of the whole language movement in the United States, but surely the list will be headed by Ken Goodman, Yetta Goodman, and Jerry Harste, all of whom wrote important works explicating whole language as a philosophical and curricular initiative.

60. In the third edition of *Learning to Read*, Chall makes the case that phonics instruction increased during the 1970s and began its decline in the middle 1980s, at the time comprehension became a dominant research and curricular issue. She also notes a further decline in phonics instruction in basals, based on the work of James Hoffman et al. (1994). So what's 'new' in the new basals. On this issue, one should also consult Goodman, K.G., Shannon, P., Freeman, Y., & Murphy, S. (1988). *Report card on basal readers*. Katonah, NY: Richard C. Owen.

61. My understanding of the primary focus of the opposition to basals is that whole language advocates regarded basals as a pernicious form of external control on teacher prerogative, one that would lead inevitably to the "deskilling" of teachers. In 1988, several whole language advocates and supporters wrote a monograph documenting what they took to be these pernicious effects (Goodman, Freeman, Shannon, & Murphy, 1988).

62. See Hoffman et al. (1994). So what's 'new' in the new basals?"

63. Perhaps the most compelling sign of the backgrounding of skills was their systematic removal from the pupil books. In the middle and even late 1980s, basal publishers featured skills lessons in the pupil books on the grounds that even teachers who chose not to use the workbooks would have to deal with skills that were right there in the student materials. By the early 1990s, as I noted earlier, they were removed from the student books.

64. One must keep in mind that I am discussing changes in published materials, not necessarily changes in classroom practice. Whether teachers changed their actual classroom practices in a matter consistent with, or at least proportional to, the basal practices is difficult to determine given our lack of broad-based data on classroom practices. One suspects that the pendulum swings of actual classroom practice are never quite as wide as the swings in the rhetoric of policy or even the suggestions in published materials.

65. Pearson, P.D. (1992). *RT* remembrance: The second 20 years. *The Reading Teacher, 45*, 378–385. This analysis documents the increasingly dominant force of whole language, literature-based reading, and process writing in the discourse of elementary reading and language arts instruction.

66. Perhaps the best documentation for the resistance to, or at least a more critical acceptance of, whole language practices comes from studies of exemplary teachers who, it appears, never bought into whole language lock, stock, and barrel, but instead chose judiciously those practices that helped them to develop rich, flexible, and balanced instructional portfolios. See Wharton-MacDonald, R., Pressley, M., & Hampton, J.M. (1998). Literacy instruction in nine first-grade classrooms: Teacher characteristics and student achievement. *The Elementary School Journal, 99*, 101–128.

67. A recent analysis of the basals adopted in the early 1990s in California suggests that the vocabulary load of many of these basals was so great that most first graders could gain access to them only if they were read to them by a teacher: Martin, L.A., & Hiebert, E.H. (in press). *Little books and phonics texts: An analysis of the new alternatives to basals*. Ann Arbor, MI: Center for the Improvement of Early Reading Achievement, University of Michigan.

68. In the late 1970s, Marie M. Clay coined the term *emergent literacy* to signal a break with traditional views of readiness in favor of a more gradual view of the shift from novice to expert reader. See Clay, M.M. (1966). *Emergent reading behavior*. Unpublished doctoral dissertation, University of Auckland, New Zealand.

69. In my own case, it was the disdain that whole language seemed to spawn regarding the explicit teaching of skills and strategies, especially those that promoted the meaning-making goals of the movement: comprehension and metacognitive strategies.

70. Hiebert, E.H., & Taylor, B.M. (Eds.). (1994). *Getting reading right from the start: Effective early literacy interventions*. Boston: Allyn & Bacon. The researchers describe several research-based interventions that balance skills instruction with authentic reading.

71. Interestingly, a recent piece in *The Reading Teacher* makes exactly this point about the comprehension strategy instruction of the 1980s. See Dowhower, S.L. (1999). Supporting a strategic stance in the classroom: Comprehension framework for helping teachers help students to be strategic. *The Reading Teacher, 52*, 672–688.

72. Smith, "Learning to Read like a Writer," makes just this point.

73. For a compelling account of this "no text" phenomenon, see Schoenbach, R., Greenleaf, C., Cziko, C., & Hurwitz, L. (in press). *Reading for understanding in the middle and high school*. San Francisco: Jossey Bass. In this account, the staff developers and teachers of a middle school academic literacy course document the role of text in middle school as well as attempts to turn the tide.

74. Similar arguments have been made for the reform movements in mathematics; for instance, that the reforms got ahead of the professional knowledge base. The results of the reform movement in mathematics have also been similar to the fate of the whole language movement. See Good, T., & Braden, J. (no date). *Reform in American education: A focus on vouchers and charters*. Hillsdale, NJ: Erlbaum.

75. In 1989, a Special Interest Group with the apocryphal label, Balanced Reading Instruction, was organized at the International Reading Association. The group was started to counteract the unchecked acceptance of whole lan-

guage as the approach to use with any and all students and to send the alternate message that there is no necessary conflict between authentic activity (usually considered the province of whole language) and explicit instruction of skills and strategies (usually considered the province of curriculum-centered approaches). For elaborate accounts of balanced literacy instruction, see McIntyre, E., & Pressley, M. (1996). *Balanced instruction: Strategies and skills in whole language*. Boston, MA: Christopher-Gordon; Gambrell, L.B., Morrow, L.M., Neuman, S.B., & Pressley, M. (1999). *Best practices in literacy instruction*. New York: Guilford; Pearson, P.D. (1996). Reclaiming the center. In M. Graves, P. van den Broek, & B.M. Taylor (Eds.), *The first R: Every child's right to read*. New York: Teachers College Press.

76. Pearson details many of these concerns and arguments in "Reclaiming the Center."

77. As early as 1965, Kenneth Goodman had popularized the use of miscues to gain insights into cognitive processes. The elaborate version of miscue analysis first appeared in Goodman, Y., & Burke, C. (1969). *Reading miscue inventory*. New York: Macmillan.

78. For an index of the rising momentum of qualitative research in the early 1980s, see Guthrie, L.F., & Hall, W.S. (1984). Ethnographic approaches to reading research; and Bloome, D., & Greene, J. (1984). Directions in the sociolinguistic study of reading, in *Handbook of Reading Research*.

79. As a way of documenting this change, examine *Handbook of Reading Research*, Vols. 1 (1984) and Vol. 2 (1991). Volume 1 contains only two chapters that could be construed as relying on some sort of interpretive inquiry. Volume 2 has at least eight such chapters. For an account of the historical patterns in nonquantitative inquiry, see Siegel, M., & Fernandez, S.L. (2000). Critical approaches. *Handbook of Reading Research* (Vol. 3).

80. Beginning in the mid-1980s and continuing today, the pages of *Educational Researcher* began to publish accounts of the qualitative-quantitative divide. It is the best source to consult in understanding the terms of the debate.

81. For an account of the evolution of this line of inquiry, consult Lyon, R. (1995). Research initiatives in learning disabilities: Contributions from scientists supported by the National Institute of Child Health and Human Development. *Journal of Child Neurology, 10*, 120–126; and Lyon, R., & Chhaba, V. (1996). The current state of science and the future of specific reading disability. *Mental Retardation and Developmental Disabilities Research Reviews, 2*, 2–9.

82. The most highly touted pedagogical experiment supported by NICHD was published in 1998: Foorman, B.R., Francis, D.J., Fletcher, J.M., Schatschneider, C., & Mehta, P. (1998). The role of instruction in learning to read: Preventing reading failure in at-risk children. *Journal of Educational Psychology, 90*, 37–55. The NICHD work, in general, and the Foorman et al piece, in particular, have been cited as exemplary in method and as supportive of a much more direct code emphasis, even in the popular press (e.g., *Dallas Morning News*, May 12, 1998; *Houston Chronicle*, May 17, 1998; *Minneapolis Star Tribune*, August 5, 1998)

83. Much, for example, is made in this new work of the inappropriateness of encouraging young readers to use context clues as a way of figuring out the pronunciations of unknown words. The data cited are eye-movement studies showing that adult readers appear to process each and every letter in the visual display on a page and, most likely, to then recode those visual symbols into a speech code prior to understanding.

84. Allington, R., & Woodside-Jiron, H. (1998). Thirty years of research in reading: When is a research summary not a research summary? In K.S. Goodman (Ed.), *In defense of good teaching*. York, ME: Stenhouse. These writers document the manner in which Bonnie Grossen's manuscript, which is an alleged summary of the research sponsored by NICHD, was used in several states as the basis for reading policy initiatives: Grossen, B. (1997). *30 years of research: What we now know about how children learn to read*. Santa Cruz, CA: The Center for the Future of Teaching and Learning. Web document: http://www.cftl.org/30years/30years

85. Classic references attesting to the importance of phonemic awareness are Juel, C. (1991). Beginning reading. In R. Barr, M. Kamil, P. Mosenthal, & P. David Pearson (Eds.), *Handbook of Reading Research* (Vol. 2, pp. 759–788). New York: Longman; and Adams, M. (1990). *Beginning to Read*. More recently, it has been documented in Snow, C., Burns, S.M., & Griffith, P. (1998). *Preventing reading difficulties in young children*. Washington, DC: National Academy Press.

86. See Juel, C. (1991). "Beginning Reading."

87. See Juel, C. (1991). "Beginning Reading"; and Adams, M., *Beginning to Read*.

88. The work of Linda K. Clarke (1988), "Invented versus traditional spelling in first graders' writings: Effects on learning to spell and read," *Research in the teaching of English, 22*(3), 281–309; and Pamela Winsor and P. David Pearson (1992). *Children at-risk: Their phonemic awareness development in holistic instruction* (Tech. Rep. No. 556). Urbana, IL: Center for the Study of Reading, University of Illinois, are most relevant on the issue of the various curricular routes to phonemic awareness development.

89. Nowhere is the rationale for the mandate of early, systematic phonics more clearly laid out than in the report of the National Reading Panel that appeared in April of 2000.

90. In Summer 1995, one entire issue of *American Educator*, *19*(2), was devoted to the phonics revival. Authors of various pieces included those who would generally be regarded as leaders in moving phonics back to center stage—Marilyn Adams, Isabel Beck, Connie Juel, and Louisa Moats, among others. One piece by Marilyn J. Adams and Maggie Bruck (1995, Summer), "Resolving the Great Debate," *American Educator*, *19*, 7, 10–20, is one of the clearest expositions of the modern phonics first position I can find. A second issue was also devoted entirely to reading (Spring/Summer, 1998, Vol. 22, No. 1 and 2).

91. See Connie Juel, "Beginning Reading"; and Gough & Hillinger (1980).

92. One of the reasons for the continuation of the debate is that few people seek common ground. Researchers who come from the whole language tradition, were they to read Adams and Juel openly, would find much to agree with about in the common privileging of Big Books, writing, invented spelling, and the like. They would not even disagree with them about the critical role that phonemic awareness or knowledge of the cipher plays in early reading success. They would, however, disagree adamantly about the most appropriate instructional route to achieving early success; phonics knowledge and phonemic awareness are better viewed, they would argue, as the consequence of, rather than the cause of, success in authentic reading experiences.

93. These and other reading policy matters have been well documented in a series of pieces in *Education Week* by Kathleen Manzo Kennedy (1997, 1998, 1999). See No. 99.

94. 107th United States Congress (2002). Public Law 107-110. No Child Left Behind. Washington DC: Government Printing Office.

95. Marilyn Adams (see *Beginning to Read*, and Adams & Bruck, "Resolving the Great Debate") has consistently championed invented spelling.

96. Allington, R., & Woodside-Jiron, H. (1998, Spring). Decodable text in beginning reading: Are mandates and policy based on research? *ERS Spectrum*, 3–11. These researchers have conducted a thorough analysis of the genesis of this "research-based" policy and concluded that it all goes back to an incidental finding from a study by Juel and Roper-Schneider in 1983. They could find no direct experimental tests of the efficacy of decodable text.

97. Learning First Alliance (1998). Every child reading. Washington, DC: Author.

98. The war metaphor comes up time and again when the debate is portrayed in the public press. See, for example, Levine, A. (1994, December). The great debate revisited. *Atlantic Monthly*.

99. Manzo, Kathleen K. (1997, March 12). Study stresses role of early phonics instruction. *Education Week, 16*, pp. 1, 24–25; Manzo, Kathleen K. (1998, February 18). New national panel faulted before it's formed. *Education Week, 17*(23), p. 7; and Manzo, Kathleen K. (1998, March 25). NRC panel urges end to reading wars. *Education Week, 17*(28), pp. 1, 18.

100. Several studies are relevant here: First is the work of Wharton-McDonald and Pressley, cited earlier. Also important is the work of Pressley, M., & Allington, R. (1998); and Taylor, B.M., Pearson, P.D., Clark, K., & Walpole, S. (2000). Effective schools and accomplished teachers: Lessons about primary-grade reading instruction in low-income schools. *Elementary School Journal*, *101*(2), 121–165.

101. See Pearson, DeStefano, & García (1998), for an account of the decrease in reliance on portfolio and performance assessment.

102. The clearest instantiation of this approach occurred in California where professional development-based on scientifically based reading research was transformed into law (AB 466). AB 466 required professional development funds from the state of California to be spent only on the state adopted materials, which were defined, prima facie, as based on scientific reading research. California State Legislature. (2001). Assembly Bill 466. The Mathematics and Reading Professional Development. Sacramento, CA: Author.

103. An interesting aside in all the political rhetoric has been the question, Who is de-skilling teachers? As early as the 1970s, whole language advocates were arguing that canned programs and basal reader manuals were de-skilling teachers by providing them with preprogrammed routines for teaching. Recently, whole language has been accused of de-skilling by denying teachers access to the technical knowledge needed to teach reading effectively; see McPike, E. (1995). Learning to read: The school's first mission. *American Educator*, *19*, 4.

104. Written from a somewhat centrist whole language position, Regie Routman provides a compelling account of the political and pedagogical issues we confront in the current debates. Routman, R. (1996). *Literacy at the crossroads* Portsmouth, NH: Heinemann.

105. The *balance* label comes with excess baggage. I use it only because it has gained currency in the field. Balance works for me as long as the metaphor of ecological balance, as in the balance of nature, is emphasized, and the

metaphor of the fulcrum balance beam, as in the scales of justice, is suppressed. The fulcrum, which achieves balance by equalizing the mass on each side of the scale, suggests a stand-off between skills and whole language—one for skills, one for whole language. By contrast, ecological balance suggests a symbiotic relationship among elements within a coordinated system. It is precisely this symbiotic potential of authentic activity and explicit instruction that I want to promote by using the term *balance*.

106. Adams and Bruck, "Resolving the Great Debate"; Adams, M. (1990). *Beginning to read: Thinking and learning about print*. Cambridge, MA: MIT Press; Fletcher, J., & Lyon, G.R. (1998). Reading: A research based approach. In W. Evers (Ed.), *What's gone wrong in America's classrooms?* Stanford, CA: Hoover Institution Press.

107. See the earlier cited studies by Clarke and Winsor and Pearson, as well as the review of phonemic awareness in Adams, M., *Beginning to Read*. See also the report of the National Reading Panel.

James Paul Gee

Reading as situated language: A sociocognitive perspective

Comprehension of written and verbal language is as much about experience with the worlds of home, school, and work as it is about words.

My main goal here is to situate reading within a broad perspective that integrates work on cognition, language, social interaction, society, and culture. In light of recent reports on reading (National Reading Panel, 2000; Snow, Burns, & Griffin, 1998) that have tended to treat reading quite narrowly in terms of psycholinguistic processing skills, I argue that such a broad perspective on reading is essential if we are to speak to issues of access and equity in schools and workplaces. I also argue that reading and writing cannot be separated from speaking, listening, and interacting, on the one hand, or using language to think about and act on the world, on the other. Thus, it is necessary to start with a viewpoint on language (oral and written) itself, a viewpoint that ties language to embodied action in the material and social world.

I have organized this article into four parts. First, I develop a viewpoint on language that stresses the connections among language, embodied experience, and situated action and interaction in the world. In the second part, I argue that what is relevant to learning literacy is not English in general, but specific varieties of English that I call "social languages." I then go on to discuss notions related to the idea of social languages, specifically Discourses (with a capital *D*) and their connections to socially situated identities and cultural models. In the third part, I show the relevance of the earlier sections to the development of literacy in early childhood through a specific example. Finally, I close

Reprinted from *Journal of Adolescent & Adult Literacy* (2001), 44, 714–725.

the article with a discussion of the importance of language abilities (construed in a specific way) to learning to read.

A viewpoint on language

It is often claimed that the primary function of human language is to convey information, but I believe this is not true. Human languages are used for a wide array of functions, including but by no means limited to conveying information (Halliday, 1994). I will argue here that human language has two primary functions through which it is best studied and analyzed. I would state these functions as follows: to scaffold the performance of action in the world, including social activities and interactions; to scaffold human affiliation in cultures and social groups and institutions through creating and enticing others to take certain perspectives on experience. *Action* is the most important word in the first statement; *perspectives* is the most important word in the second. I will discuss each of these two functions in turn.

Situated action. Traditional approaches to language have tended to look at it as a closed system (for discussion, see Clancey, 1997). Any piece of language is treated as representation (re-presenting) of some information. On the traditional view, what it means to comprehend a piece of language is to be able to translate it into some equivalent representational system, either other language (one's own words) or some mental language or language of thought that mimics the structure of natural languages (e.g., is couched in terms of logical propositions).

However, there are a variety of perspectives today on language that tie its comprehension much more closely to experience of and action in the world. For example, consider these two remarks from work in cognitive psychology: "comprehension is grounded in perceptual simulations that prepare agents for situated action" (Barsalou, 1999a, p. 77); "to a particular person, the meaning of an object, event, or sentence is what that person can do with the object, event, or sentence" (Glenberg, 1997, p. 3).

These two quotes are from work that is part of a family of related viewpoints. For want of a better name, we might call the family "situated cognition studies" (e.g., Barsalou, 1999a, 1999b; Brown,

Collins, & Dugid, 1989; Clancey, 1997; Clark, 1997; Engestrom, Miettinen, raij Punamaki, 1999; Gee, 1992; Glenberg, 1997; Glenberg & Robertson, 1999; Hutchins, 1995; Latour, 1999; Lave, 1996; Lave & Wenger, 1991; Wenger, 1998). While there are differences among the members of the family (alternative theories about situated cognition), they share the viewpoint that meaning in language is not some abstract propositional representation that resembles a verbal language. Rather, meaning in language is tied to people's experiences of situated action in the material and social world. Furthermore, these experiences (perceptions, feelings, actions, and interactions) are stored in the mind or brain, not in terms of propositions or language but in something like dynamic images tied to perception both of the world and of our own bodies, internal states, and feelings: "Increasing evidence suggests that perceptual simulation is indeed central to comprehension" (Barsalou, 1999a, p. 74).

It is almost as if we videotape our experiences as we are having them, create a library of such videotapes, edit them to make some prototypical tapes (or set of typical instances), but stand ever ready to add new tapes to our library. We re-edit the tapes based on new experiences or draw out of the library less typical tapes when the need arises. As we face new situations or new texts we run our tapes—perhaps a prototypical one, or a set of typical ones, or a set of contrasting ones, or a less typical one, whatever the case may be. We do this to apply our old experiences to our new experience and to aid us in making, editing, and storing the videotape that will capture this new experience, integrate it into our library, and allow us to make sense of it (both while we are having it and afterwards).

These videotapes are what we think with and through. They are what we use to give meaning to our experiences in the world. They are what we use to give meaning to words and sentences. But they are not language or *in* language (not even in propositions). Furthermore, since they are representations of experience (including feelings, attitudes, embodied positions, and various sorts of foregrounds and backgrounds of attention), they are not just information or facts. Rather, they are value-laden, perspective-taking movies in the mind. Of course, talking about videotapes in the mind is a metaphor that, like all metaphors, is incorrect if pushed too far (see Barsalou, 1999b for how the metaphor can be cashed out and corrected by a consideration of a more neurally realistic framework for "perception in the mind").

On this account, the meanings of words, phrases, and sentences are always situated, that is, customized to our actual contexts (Gee, 1999a). Here context means not just the words, deeds, and things that surround our words or deeds, but also our purposes, values, and intended courses of action and interaction. We bring out of our store of videotapes those that are most relevant to understanding our current context or those that allow us to create and construe that context in a certain way. We can see this in even so trivial an example as the following: If you hear "The coffee spilled, go get the mop" you run a quite different set of images (that is, assemble a quite different situated meaning) than when you hear "The coffee spilled, go get a broom."

On this account, too, the meaning of a word (the way in which we give it meaning in a particular context) is not different than the meaning of an experience, object, or tool in the world (i.e., in terms of the way in which we give the experience, object, or tool meaning):

> The meaning of the glass to you, at that particular moment, is in terms of the actions available. The meaning of the glass changes when different constraints on action are combined. For example, in a noisy room, the glass may become a mechanism for capturing attention (by tapping it with a spoon), rather than a mechanism for quenching thirst. (Glenberg, 1997, p. 41)

While Glenberg here is talking about the meaning of the glass as an object in one's specific experience of the world at a given time and place, he could just as well be talking about the meaning of the word *glass* in one's specific experience of a piece of talk or written text at a given time and place. The meaning of the word *glass* in a given piece of talk or text would be given by running a simulation (a videotape) of how the glass fits into courses of action being built up in the theater of our minds. These courses of action are based on how we understand all the other words and goings on in the world that surrounds the word *glass* as we read it: "[T]he embodied models constructed to understand language are the same as those that un-

derlie comprehension of the natural environment" (Glenberg, 1997, p. 17).

If embodied action and social activity are crucially connected to the situated meanings oral or written language convey, then reading instruction must move well beyond relations internal to texts. Reading instruction must be rooted in the connections of texts to engagement in and simulations of actions, activities, and interactions—to real and imagined material and social worlds.

Perspective-taking. Let me now turn to the second function of language already mentioned. Consider, in this regard, the following quote from Tomasello (1999):

> [T]he perspectivial nature of linguistic symbols, and the use of linguistic symbols in discourse interaction in which different perspectives are explicitly contrasted and shared, provide the raw material out of which the children of all cultures construct the flexible and multi-perspectival—perhaps even dialogical—cognitive representations that give human cognition much of its awesome and unique power. (p. 163)

Let's briefly unpack what this means. From the point of view of the model Tomasello was developing, the words and grammar of a human language exist to allow people to take and communicate alternative perspectives on experience (see also Hanks, 1996). That is, words and grammar exist to give people alternative ways to view one and the same state of affairs. Language is not about conveying neutral or objective information; rather, it is about communicating perspectives on experience and action in the world, often in contrast to alternative and competing perspectives: "We may then say that linguistic symbols are social conventions for inducing others to construe, or take a perspective on, some experiential situation" (Tomasello, 1999, p. 118).

Let me give some examples of what it means to say that words and grammar are not primarily about giving and getting information but are, rather, about giving and getting different perspectives on experience. I open Microsoft's Web site: Is it selling its products, marketing them, or underpricing them against the competition? Are products I can download from the site without paying for them free, or are they being exchanged for having bought other Microsoft products (e.g., Windows), or are there strings attached? Note also how metaphors (like "strings attached") add greatly to, and are a central part of, the perspective-taking we can do. If I use the grammatical construction "Microsoft's new operating system is loaded with bugs" I take a perspective in which Microsoft is less agentive and responsible than if I use the grammatical construction "Microsoft has loaded its new operating system with bugs."

Here is another example: Do I say that a child who is using multiple cues to give meaning to a written text (i.e., using some decoding along with picture and context cues) is reading, or do I say (as some of the pro-phonics people do) that she is not really reading, but engaged in emergent literacy? (For those latter people, the child is only really reading when she is decoding all the words in the text and not using nondecoding cues for word recognition). In this case, contending camps actually fight over what perspective on experience the term *reading* or *really reading* ought to name. In the end, the point is that no wording is ever neutral or just "the facts." All wordings—given the very nature of language—are perspectives on experience that comport with competing perspectives in the grammar of the language and in actual social interactions.

How do children learn how words and grammar line up to express particular perspectives on experience? Here, interactive, intersubjective dialogue with more advanced peers and adults appears to be crucial. In such dialogue, children come to see, from time to time, that others have taken a different perspective on what is being talked about than they themselves have. At a certain developmental level, children have the capacity to distance themselves from their own perspectives and (internally) simulate the perspectives the other person is taking, thereby coming to see how words and grammar come to express those perspectives (in contrast to the way in which different words and grammatical constructions express competing perspectives). Later, in other interactions, or when thinking, the child can re-run such simulations and imitate the perspective-taking the more advanced peer or adult has done by using certain sorts of words and grammar. Through such simulations and imitative learning, children learn to use the symbolic means that other persons have used to share attention with them: "In imitatively learning a linguistic symbol from other persons in this way, I internalize not

only their communicative intention (their intention to get me to share their attention) but also the specific perspective they have taken" (Tomasello, 1999, p. 128).

Tomasello (1999) also pointed out—in line with my previous discussion that the world and texts are assigned meanings in the same way—that children come to use objects in the world as symbols at the same time (or with just a bit of a time lag) as they come to use linguistic symbols as perspective-taking devices on the world. Furthermore, they learn to use objects as symbols (to assign them different meanings encoding specific perspectives in different contexts) in the same way they learn to use linguistic symbols. In both cases, the child simulates in his head and later imitates in his words and deeds the perspectives his interlocutor must be taking on a given situation by using certain words and certain forms of grammar or by treating certain objects in certain ways. Thus, meaning for words, grammar, and objects comes out of intersubjective dialogue and interaction: "[H]uman symbols [are] inherently social, intersubjective, and perspectival" (Tomasello, 1999, p. 131).

If value-laden perspectives on experience are connected to the situated meanings oral or written language convey, then, once again, we have an argument that reading instruction must move well beyond relations internal to texts. Reading instruction must be rooted in the taking and imagining of diverse perspectives on real and imagined material and social worlds. The moral of both the functions of language that we have discussed is this: Our ways with words (oral or written) are of the same nature as our ways with ways of understanding and acting on the material and social world. In a quite empirical sense, the moral is one Freire (1995) taught us long ago: Reading the word and reading the world are, at a deep level, integrally connected—indeed, at a deep level, they are one and the same process.

Social languages

The perspective taken thus far on language is misleading in one respect. It misses the core fact that any human language is not one general thing (like English), but composed of a great variety of different styles, registers, or social languages. Different patterns of vocabulary, syntax (sentence structure), and discourse connectors (devices that connect sentences together to make a whole integrated text) constitute different social languages, each of which is connected to specific sorts of social activities and to a specific socially situated identity (Gee, 1999a). We recognize different social languages by recognizing these patterns (in much the way we recognize a face through recognizing a certain characteristic patterning of facial features).

As an example, consider the following, taken from a school science textbook: "1. The destruction of a land surface by the combined effects of abrasion and removal of weathered material by transporting agents is called erosion.... The production of rock waste by mechanical processes and chemical changes is called weathering" (Martin, 1990, p. 93).

A whole bevy of grammatical design features mark these sentences as part of a distinctive social language. Some of these features are heavy subjects (e.g., "The production of rock waste by mechanical processes and chemical changes"); processes and actions named by nouns or nominalizations, rather than verbs (e.g., "production"); passive main verbs ("is called") and passives inside nominalizations (e.g., "production…by mechanical processes"); modifiers that are more "contentful" than the nouns they modify (e.g., "transporting agents"); and complex embedding (e.g., "weathered material by transporting agents" is a nominalization embedded inside "the combined effects of…," and this more complex nominalization is embedded inside a yet larger nominalization, "the destruction of…").

This style of language also incorporates a great many distinctive discourse markers, that is, linguistic features that characterize larger stretches of text and give them unity and coherence as a certain type of text or genre. For example, the genre here is explanatory definition, and it is characterized by classificatory language of a certain sort. Such language leads adept readers to form a classificatory scheme in their heads something like this: There are two kinds of change (erosion and weathering) and two kinds of weathering (mechanical and chemical).

This mapping from elements of vocabulary, syntax, and discourse to a specific style of language used in characteristic social activities is just as much a part of reading and writing as is the phonics (sound-to-letter) mapping. In fact, more people fail to become successful school-based, academic, or work-related readers or writers because of failing to master this sort of mapping than the phonics one.

There are a great many different social languages—for example, the language of medicine, literature, street gangs, sociology, law, rap, or informal dinner-time talk among friends (who belong to distinctive cultures or social groups). To know any specific social language is to know how its characteristic design features are combined to carry out one or more specific social activities. It is to know, as well, how its characteristic lexical and grammatical design features are used to enact a particular socially situated identity, that is, being, at a given time and place, a lawyer, a gang member, a politician, a literary humanist, a "bench chemist," a radical feminist, an everyday person, or whatever. To know a particular social language is either to be able to "do" a particular identity, using that social language, or to be able to recognize such an identity, when we do not want to or cannot actively participate.

Let me give two further examples of social languages at work. First, I'll use an example I've used in this journal before. It's about a young woman telling the same story to her parents and to her boyfriend (*JAAL*, February 2000; Gee, 1996). To her parents at dinner she says, "Well, when I thought about it, I don't know, it seemed to me that Gregory should be considered the most offensive character." But to her boyfriend later she says, "What an ass that guy was, you know, her boyfriend." In the first case, the young woman is taking on the identity of an educated and dutiful daughter engaged in the social activity of reporting to her parents her viewpoints on what she has learned in school. In the second case, she is taking on the identity of a girlfriend engaged in the social activity of bonding with her boyfriend.

Here is a second example from Myers (1990, p. 150): A biologist wrote in a professional science journal, "Experiments show that *Heliconius* butterflies are less likely to oviposit on host plants that possess eggs or egg-like structures." Writing about the same thing in a popular science magazine, the same biologist wrote, "*Heliconius* butterflies lay their eggs on *Passiflora* vines. In defense the vines seem to have evolved fake eggs that make it look to the butterflies as if eggs have already been laid on them." In the first case, the biologist is taking on the identity of professional scientist engaged in the social activity of making experimental and theoretical claims (note, for instance, the subject "Experiments") to professional peers. In the second case, the biologist is taking on the identity of a popularizer or scientific journalist engaged in the social activity of telling the educated public a factual story about plants and animals (note, for instance, the subjects "butterflies" and "vines").

Now here is the bite of social languages and genres: When we talk about social languages and genres, oral and written language are inextricably mixed. Some social languages are written; some are spoken. Some have both spoken and written versions; written and spoken versions are often mixed and integrated within specific social practices. Furthermore, social languages are always integrally connected to the characteristic social activities (embodied action and interaction in the world), value-laden perspectives, and socially situated identities of particular groups of people or communities of practice. If discussions about reading are not about social languages (and thus, too, about embodied action and interaction in the world, value-laden perspectives, and socially situated identities), then they are not, in reality, about reading as a semiotic meaning-making process (and it is hard to know what reading is if it is not this).

Here is another part of the bite of talk about social languages and genres. Both inside and outside school, most social languages and genres are clearly not acquired by direct instruction. While some forms of (appropriately timed) scaffolding, modeling, and instructional guidance by mentors appear to be important, immersion in meaningful practice is essential. Social languages and genres are acquired by processes of socialization, an issue to which I will turn below.

It is inevitable, I would think, that someone at this point is going to object that social languages are really about the later stages of the acquisition of literacy. It will be pointed out that the current reading debates are almost always about small children and the earlier stages of reading. What, it will be asked, has all this talk of social languages got to do with early literacy? My answer is, everything. Social languages (and their connections to action, perspectives, and identities) are no less relevant to the first stages of learning to read than they are to the later ones (and there are not so much stages here as the same things going on over time at ever deeper and more complex levels). However, before

I turn to the relevance of social languages to early childhood at the end of this article, I need to develop briefly a few more theoretical notions related to social languages.

Discourses

I said earlier that social languages are acquired by socialization. But now we must ask, socialization into what? When people learn new social languages and genres—at the level of being able to produce them and not just consume them—they are being socialized into what I will call Discourses with a big "D" (I use discourse with a little "d" to mean just language in use, Gee, 1996, 1999a; see also Clark, 1996). Even when people learn a new social language or genre only to consume (interpret), but not produce it, they are learning to recognize a new Discourse. Related but somewhat different terms others have used to capture some of what I am trying to capture with the term *Discourses* are communities of practice (Wenger, 1998), actor-actant networks (Latour, 1987, 1991), and activity systems (Engestrom, Miettinen, raij Punamaki, 1999; Leont'ev, 1978).

Discourses always involve language (i.e., they recruit specific social languages), but they always involve more than language as well. Social languages are embedded within Discourses and only have relevance and meaning within them. A Discourse integrates ways of talking, listening, writing, reading, acting, interacting, believing, valuing, and feeling (and using various objects, symbols, images, tools, and technologies) in the service of enacting meaningful socially situated identities and activities. Being-doing a certain sort of physicist, gang member, feminist, first-grade child in Ms. Smith's room, special ed (SPED) student, regular at the local bar, or gifted upper-middle-class child engaged in emergent literacy are all Discourses.

We can think of Discourses as identity kits. It's almost as if you get a tool kit full of specific devices (i.e., ways with words, deeds, thoughts, values, actions, interactions, objects, tools, and technologies) in terms of which you can enact a specific identity and engage in specific activities associated with that identity. For example, think of what devices (e.g., in words, deeds, clothes, objects, attitudes) you would get in a Sherlock Holmes identity kit (e.g., you do not get a "Say No to Drugs" bumper sticker in this kit; you do get both a pipe and lots of logic). The Doctor Watson identity kit is different. And we can think of the Sherlock Holmes identity kit (Discourse) and the Doctor Watson identity kit (Discourse) as themselves parts of a yet larger Discourse, the Holmes-Watson Discourse, because Watson is part of Holmes's identity kit and Holmes is part of Watson's. Discourse can be embedded one inside another.

One Discourse can mix or blend two others. For example, Gallas (1994) created a sharing-time Discourse (a way of being a recognizable sharer in her classroom) that mixed Anglo and African American styles. Discourses can be related to each other in relationships of alignment or tension. For example, Scollon and Scollon (1981) have pointed out that school-based Discourses that incorporate essayist practices and values conflict with the values, attitudes, and ways with words embedded in some Native American home and community-based Discourses (i.e., ways of being a Native American of a certain sort). These latter Discourses value communicating only when the sender knows the receiver of the communication and his or her context and do not value the sorts of fictionalizing (generalizing) of sender and receiver that essayist practices involve.

Cultural models

Within their socialization into Discourses (and we are all socialized into a great many across our lifetimes), people acquire cultural models (D'Andrade & Strauss, 1992; Gee, 1999a; Holland & Quinn, 1987; Shore, 1996; Strauss & Quinn, 1997). Cultural models are everyday theories (i.e., storylines, images, schemas, metaphors, and models) about the world that people socialized into a given Discourse share. Cultural models tell people what is typical or normal from the perspective of a particular Discourse (or a related or aligned set of them).

For example, certain types of middle-class people in the United States hold a cultural model of child development that goes something like this (Harkness, Super, & Keefer, 1992): A child is born dependent on her parents and grows up by going through (often disruptive) stages toward greater and greater independence (and independence is a high value for this group of people). This cultural model plays a central role in this group's Discourse of par-

ent-child relations (i.e., enacting and recognizing identities as parents and children).

On the other hand, certain sorts of working-class families (Philipsen, 1975) hold a cultural model of child development that goes something like this: A child is born unsocialized and with tendencies to be selfish. The child needs discipline from the home to learn to be a cooperative social member of the family (a high value of this group of people). This cultural model plays a central role in this group's Discourse of parent-child relations.

These different cultural models, connected to different (partially) class-based Discourses of parenting, are not true or false. Rather, they focus on different aspects of childhood and development. Cultural models define for people in a Discourse what counts as normal and natural and what counts as inappropriate and deviant. They are, of course, thereby thoroughly value laden.

Cultural models come out of and, in turn, inform the social practices in which people in a Discourse engage. Cultural models are stored in people's minds (by no means always consciously), though they are supplemented and instantiated in the objects, texts, and practices that are part and parcel of the Discourse. For example, many guidebooks supplement and instantiate the above middle-class cultural model of childhood and stages. On the other hand, many religious materials supplement and instantiate the above working-class model of childhood.

Figure 1 summarizes the discussion so far, defining all the theoretical tools and showing how they are all related to one another.

Early literacy as socioculturally situated practice

I turn now to a specific example involving early literacy from my own research. I do this both to give a more extended example of the perspective I have developed so far and to show the relevance of this perspective to early childhood and the earliest stages of the acquisition of literacy. The event is this: An upper-middle-class, highly educated father approaches his 3-year-old (3:10) son who is sitting at the kitchen table. The child is using an activity book in which each page contains a picture with a missing piece. A question is printed under the picture. The child uses a "magic pen" to rub the missing piece and "magically" uncovers the rest of the picture. The part of the picture that is uncovered is an image that constitutes the answer to the question at the bottom of the page, though, of course, the child must put this answer into words.

In the specific case I want to discuss here, the overt part of the picture was the top half of the bodies of Donald and Daisy Duck. The question printed at the bottom of the page was "In what are Donald and Daisy riding?" (Note the social language in which this question is written. It is not the more vernacular form: "What are Donald and Daisy riding in?") The child used his pen to uncover an old fashioned Model T sort of car with an open top. Donald and Daisy turn out to be sitting in the car.

The father, seeing the child engaged in this activity, asks him, after he has uncovered the car, to read the question printed below the picture. Notice that the father has not asked the child to give the answer to the question, which is a different activity. The father is confident the child can answer the question and has a different purpose here. It is to engage in an indirect reading lesson, though one of a special and specific sort.

The father is aware that the child, while he knows the names of the letters of the alphabet and can recognize many of them in words, cannot decode print. He is also aware that the child has on several previous occasions, in the midst of various literacy-related activities, said that he is "learning to read." However, in yet other activities, at other times, the child has said that he "cannot read" and thereafter seemed more reluctant to engage in his otherwise proactive stance toward texts. This has concerned the father, who values the child's active engagement with texts and the child's belief, expressed in some contexts and not others, that he is not just learning to read, but is in fact "a reader."

We might say that the father is operating with a however tacit theory (cultural model) that a child's assuming a certain identity ("I am a reader") facilitates the acquisition of that identity and its concomitant skills. I believe this sort of model is fairly common in certain sorts of families. Parents co-construct an identity with a child (attribute, and get the child to believe in, a certain competence) before the child can actually fully carry out all the skills associated with this identity (competence before performance).

So, the father has asked the child to read the printed question below the picture of Donald and

Daisy Duck sitting in the newly uncovered car. Below, I give the printed version of the question and what the child offered as his "reading" of the question:

Printed version: In what are Donald and Daisy riding?
Child's reading: What is Donald and Daisy riding on?

After the child uttered the above sentence, he said, "See, I told you I was learning to read." He seems to be well aware of the father's purposes. The child, the father, the words, and the book are all here in sync to pull off a specific practice, and this is a form of instruction, but it's a form that is typical of what goes on inside socialization processes.

The father and son have taken an activity that is for the child now a virtual genre—namely, uncovering a piece of a picture and on the basis of it answering a question—and incorporated it into a different *metalevel activity*. That is, the father and

FIGURE 2
Partial analysis of a literacy event

Text	=	Written:	In what are Donald and Daisy riding?
		Read:	What is Donald and Daisy riding on?
		Remark:	See, I told you I was learning to read.
Social language	=	Classificatory question	
Genre	=	Uncover the piece of the picture, form a classificatory question to which the picture is an answer, and give the answer	
Cultural model	=	Reading is the proactive production of appropriate styles of language (e.g., here a classificatory question) and their concomitant meanings in conjunction with print	
Discourse (identity)	=	Emergent reader of a certain type (filtering school-aligned practice into primary Discourse)	

son use the original activity not in and for itself but as a platform with which to discuss reading or, perhaps better put, to co-construct a cultural model of what reading is. The father's question and the son's final response ("See, I told you I was learning to read") clearly indicate that they are seeking to demonstrate to and for each other that the child can read.

Figure 2, which will inform my discussion that follows, (partially) analyzes this event in terms of the theoretical notions we have developed above.

From a developmental point of view, then, what is going on here? Nothing so general as acquiring literacy. Rather, something much more specific is going on. First, the child is acquiring, amidst immersion and adult guidance, a piece of a particular type of *social language*. The question he has to form—and he very well knows this—has to be a *classificatory question*. It cannot be, for instance, a narrative-based question (e.g., something like "What are Donald and Daisy doing?" or "Where are Donald and Daisy going?"). Classificatory questions (and related syntactic and discourse resources) are a common part of many school-based (and academic) social languages, especially those associated with nonliterary content areas (e.g., the sciences).

The acquisition of this piece of a social language is, in this case, scaffolded by a genre the child has acquired, namely to uncover the piece of the picture, form a classificatory question to which the picture is an answer (when the parent isn't there to

read the question for the child), and give the answer. This genre bears a good deal of similarity to a number of different non-narrative language and action genres (routines) used in the early years of school.

Finally, in regard to social languages, note that the child's question is uttered in a more vernacular style than the printed question. So syntactically it is, in one sense, in the wrong style. However, from a discourse perspective (in terms of the function its syntax carries out), it is in just the right style (i.e., it is a classificatory question). It is a mainstay of child language development that the acquisition of a function often precedes acquisition of a fully correct form (in the sense of contextually appropriate, not necessarily in the sense of grammatically correct).

In addition to acquiring a specific piece of certain sorts of social languages, the child is also, as part and parcel of the activity, acquiring different cultural models. One of these is a cultural model about what reading is. The model is something like this: Reading is not primarily letter-by-letter decoding but the proactive production of appropriate styles of language (e.g., here a classificatory question) and their concomitant meanings in conjunction with print. This is a model that the father (at some level quite consciously) wants the child to adopt, both to sustain the child's interest in becoming a reader and to counteract the child's claims, in other contexts, that he can't read. Of course, the child's claim that he can't read in those other contexts reflects that, in other activities, he is acquiring a different cultural model of reading, namely one something like this: Reading is primarily the ability to decode letters and words, and one is not a reader if meaning is not primarily driven from decoding print. As his socialization proceeds, the child will acquire yet other cultural models of reading (or extend and deepen ones already acquired).

The genres, social languages, and cultural models present in this interaction between father and son existed, of course, in conjunction with ways of thinking, valuing, feeling, acting, interacting and in conjunction with various mediating objects (e.g., the book and the "magic pen"), images (the pictures of Donald, Daisy, and the car), sites (kitchen table), and times (morning as father was about to go to work). In and through the social practices that recruit these genres, social language, and cultural models, the 3-year-old is acquiring a Discourse. The father and the child are co-constructing the child as a reader (and, indeed, a person) of a particular type, that is, one who takes reading to be the proactive production of appropriate styles of language and meanings in conjunction with print. This socially situated identity involves a self-orientation as active producer (not just consumer) of appropriate meanings in conjunction with print; meanings that, in this case, turn out to be school and academically related.

However, this Discourse is not unrelated to other Discourses the child is or will be acquiring. I have repeatedly pointed out how the social language, genre, and cultural models involved in this social practice are in full alignment with some of the social languages, genres, cultural models, and social practices the child will confront in the early years of school (here construing schooling in fairly traditional terms).

At the same time, this engagement between father and child, beyond being a moment in the production of the Discourse of a certain type of reader, is also a moment in the child's acquisition of what I call his primary Discourse. The child's primary Discourse is the ways with words, objects, and deeds that are associated with his primary sense of self formed in and through his (most certainly class-based) primary socialization within the family (or other culturally relevant primary socializing group) as a "person like us." In this case, the child is learning that "people like us" are "readers like this."

Now consider what it means that the child's acquisition of the reader Discourse (being-doing a certain type of reader) is simultaneously aligned with (traditional) school-based Discourses and part of his acquisition of his primary Discourse. This ties school-related values, attitudes, and ways with words, at a specific and not some general level, to his primary sense of self and belonging. This will almost certainly affect how the child reacts to, and resonates with, school-based ways with words and things.

Reading and early language abilities

Many of the recent reading reports (e.g., see Gee, 1999b; National Reading Panel, 2000; Snow, Burns, & Griffin, 1998) have stressed that there is significant correlation between early phonological awareness and later success in learning to read and, thus, called for early phonemic awareness training in schools and early sustained and overt instruction on phonics. However, some of these reports are aware that a good many other things, besides early phonological awareness, correlate with successfully learning to read in the early years of school. It turns out, for instance, that the correlation between early language abilities and later success in reading is just as large as, if not larger than, the correlation between early phonological awareness and success in reading. Indeed, as one might suspect, early language abilities and early phonological awareness are themselves correlated (Snow, Burns, & Griffin, 1998):

[P]erformance on phonological awareness tasks by preschoolers was highly correlated with general language ability. Moreover it was measures of semantic and syntactic skills, rather than speech discrimination and articulation, that predicted phonological awareness differences. (p. 53)

…

What is most striking about the results of the preceding studies is the power of early preschool language to predict reading three to five years later. (pp. 107–108)

…

On average, phonological awareness (r. = .46) has been about as strong a predictor of future reading as memory for sentences and stories, confrontation naming, and general language measures. (p. 112)

So what are these early language abilities that seem so important for later success in school? According to the National Research Council's report (Snow, Burns, & Griffin, 1998), they are things like vocabulary—receptive vocabulary, but more especially expressive vocabulary—the ability to recall and comprehend sentences and stories, and the ability to engage in verbal interactions. Furthermore, I think that research has made it fairly clear what causes such verbal abilities. What appears to cause enhanced school-based verbal abilities are family, community, and school language environments in which children interact intensively with adults and more advanced peers and experience cognitively challenging talk and texts on sustained topics and in different genres of oral and written language.

However, the correlation between language abilities and success in learning to read (and in school generally) hides an important reality. Almost all children—including poor children—have impressive language abilities. The vast majority of children enter school with large vocabularies, complex grammar, and deep understandings of experiences and stories. It has been decades since anyone believed that poor and minority children entered school with "no language" (Gee, 1996; Labov, 1972).

The verbal abilities that children who fail in school lack are not just some general set of such abilities, but rather specific verbal abilities tied to specific school-based practices and school-based genres of oral and written language of just the sort I looked at in the earlier example of the 3-year-old making up a classificatory question. This 3-year-old will have been exposed to a great number of such specific, but quite diverse, practices, each offering protoforms of later school-based and academic social languages and genres. These protoforms, always embedded in specific social practices connected to specific socially situated identities (and useless when not so embedded), are the stuff from which success in school-based and academic reading flows. These are the sorts of protoforms that must be delivered to all children—amidst ample practice within socialization in specific Discourses—if we are to have true access and equity for all children.

REFERENCES

Barsalou, L.W. (1999a). Language comprehension: Archival memory or preparation for situated action. *Discourse Processes, 28*, 61–80.

Barsalou, L.W. (1999b). Perceptual symbol systems. *Behavioral and Brain Sciences, 22*, 577–660.

Brown, A.L., Collins, A., & Dugid, P. (1989). Situated cognition and the culture of learning. *Educational Researcher, 18*, 32–42.

Clancey, W.J. (1997). *Situated cognition: On human knowledge and computer representations.* Cambridge, England: Cambridge University Press.

Clark, A. (1997). *Being there: Putting brain, body, and world together again.* Cambridge, MA: MIT Press.

Clark, H.H. (1996). *Using language.* Cambridge, England: Cambridge University Press.

D'Andrade, R., & Strauss, C. (Eds.). (1992). *Human motives and cultural models.* Cambridge, England: Cambridge University Press.

Engestrom, Y., Miettinen, M., & raij Punamaki (Eds.). (1999). *Perspectives on activity theory.* Cambridge, England: Cambridge University Press.

Freire, P. (1995). *The pedagogy of the oppressed.* New York: Continuum.

Gallas, K. (1994). *The languages of learning: How children talk, write, dance, draw, and sing their understanding of the world.* New York: Teachers College Press.

Gee, J.P. (1992). *The social mind: Language, ideology, and social practice.* New York: Bergin & Garvey.

Gee, J.P. (1996). *Social linguistics and literacies: Ideology in Discourses* (2nd ed.). London: Taylor & Francis.

Gee, J.P. (1999a). *An introduction to discourse analysis: Theory and method.* London: Routledge.

Gee, J.P. (1999b). Reading and the New Literacy Studies: Reframing the National Academy of Sciences report on reading. *Journal of Literacy Research, 31*, 355–374.

Glenberg, A.M. (1997). What is memory for? *Behavioral and Brain Sciences, 20*, 1–55.

Glenberg, A.M., & Robertson, D.A. (1999). Indexical understanding of instructions. *Discourse Processes, 28*, 1–26.

Halliday, M.A.K. (1994). *Functional grammar* (2nd. ed.). London: Edward Arnold.

Hanks, W.F. (1996). *Language and communicative practices.* Boulder, CO: Westview Press.

Harkness, S., Super, C., & Keefer, C.H. (1992). *Learning to be an American parent: How cultural models gain directive force.* In R. D'Andrade & C. Strauss (Eds.), *Human motives and cultural models* (pp. 163–178). Cambridge, England: Cambridge University Press.

Holland, D., & Quinn, N. (Eds.). (1987). *Cultural models in language and thought.* Cambridge, England: Cambridge University Press.

Hutchins, E. (1995). *Cognition in the wild.* Cambridge, MA: MIT Press.

Labov, W. (1972). *Language in the inner city.* Philadelphia, PA: University of Pennsylvania Press.

Latour, B. (1987). *Science in action.* Cambridge, MA: Harvard University Press.

Latour, B. (1991). *We have never been modern.* Cambridge, MA: Harvard University Press.

Latour, B. (1999). *Pandora's hope: Essays on the reality of science studies.* Cambridge, MA: Harvard University Press.

Lave, J. (1996). Teaching, as learning, in practice *Mind, Culture, and Activity, 3,* 149–164.

Lave, J., & Wenger, E. (1991). *Situated learning: Legitimate peripheral participation.* New York: Cambridge University Press.

Leont'ev, A.N. (1978). *Activity, consciousness, and personality.* Englewood Cliffs, NJ: Prentice-Hall.

Martin, J.R. (1990). Literacy in science: Learning to handle text as technology. In F. Christe (Ed.), *Literacy for a changing world* (pp. 79–117). Melbourne, NSW, Australia: Australian Council for Educational Research.

Myers, G. (1990). *Writing biology: Texts in the social construction of scientific knowledge.* Madison, WI: University of Wisconsin Press.

National Reading Panel. (2000). *Report of the National Reading Panel: Teaching children to read.* Washington DC: Author. Available online: www.nationalreadingpanel.org.

Philipsen, G. (1975). Speaking "like a man" in Teamsterville: Culture patterns of role enactment in an urban neighborhood. *Quarterly Journal of Speech, 61,* 26–39.

Scollon, R., & Scollon, S.W. (1981). *Narrative, literacy, and face in interethnic communication.* Norwood, NJ: Ablex.

Shore, B. (1996). *Culture in mind: Cognition, culture, and the problem of meaning.* New York: Oxford University Press.

Snow, C.E., Burns, M.S., & Griffin, P. (Eds.). (1998). *Preventing reading difficulties in young children.* Washington, DC: National Academy Press.

Strauss, C., & Quinn, N. (1997). *A cognitive theory of cultural meaning.* Cambridge, England: Cambridge University Press.

Tomasello, M. (1999). *The cultural origins of human cognition.* Cambridge, MA: Harvard University Press.

Wenger, E. (1998). *Communities of practice: Learning, meaning, and identity.* Cambridge, England: Cambridge University Press.

Timothy Shanahan

Susan B. Neuman

Literacy research that makes a difference

In 1961, David H. Russell published an article entitled, "Reading Research that Makes a Difference." In it, he chronicled 10 studies that he claimed had significantly influenced the "curriculum in reading and related areas" (p. 74). He also explained why these studies had been significant. Later, Harry Singer (1970, 1976) published two rejoinders to this article. He neither challenged Russell's original premise—that research could or should influence teaching—nor argued with the specific choices of studies. Instead, he challenged Russell's explanation of why some studies mattered. He presented two lists in support of his position: influential studies that misdirected practice, and positive studies that, though they met Russell's criteria, failed to have any discernible sway.

As we write this article, 35 years after Russell's, more than 50,000 new studies on literacy have appeared. Which studies have changed how we teach literacy? What are the fundamental characteristics of studies that make a difference? At the invitation of the Editors of *Reading Research Quarterly*, we have carried on a stimulating, and at times contentious, conversation exploring these issues. Here, we will propose a list of studies that have influenced instructional practice and consider the role of research in instruction.

How we worked

We have never written together before, though we have served together on professional committees and have become friends during the past few years. We share a deep and abiding interest in family literacy and in the literacy learning of poor children. Susan is interested, also, in preschool development, how children's play supports learning, and the role of media—particularly television—in literacy learning. Tim's other research interests include beginning reading development, the connections between learning to read and write, and the use of classroom assessment to inform teachers' decisions.

We live and work in different regions of the U.S. so we carried on our conversation over electronic mail. Sometimes we exchanged several notes in a single day, a brief sustained conversation of a specific point. Often a single note would be sent one day with a response the next, while at other times there were long delays. In all, we exchanged more than 80 e-mail notes, some several pages long. We often disagreed about which studies mattered or even as to what should count as a study.

The discussion of the practical influence of research has been too rare in the public discourse of our field, such topics usually being relegated to the safety of graduate seminars. This is unfortunate as such discussion, we found, requires nothing less than a construction of the state of the field: power and authority, the current state of practice, the nature and source of knowledge, and even whether education is improving or declining. These issues are entailed in the imaginative narrative history of the changing classroom that each of us conjures. We believe that open discussion of these issues can expose and correct bias and illogic in our perceptions of the status of our field.

Lest readers think this to be overstated, consider one recent example from public discussions of reading achievement. Such discussions have often been based on the premise that reading instruction has changed, and that, consequently, reading achievement has declined. As a result, more than a dozen U.S. states are exploring legislation to better regulate reading instruction, despite the fact that national achievement data do not support an achievement decline.

Although we often disagreed, the quality of discussion was high, and mutual respect was always evident. No matter how formidable the disagreement, we always assumed the possibility of persuasion through information and logic. We sometimes found to our consternation that our conversational partner wasn't the one who lacked sufficient knowledge on a particular point. We strove to agree on a single list of studies rather than to argue for two separate, personal lists, as we hoped that this approach would make it easier for others to join the conversation.

Our first task was actually the most difficult: how to define *influence*. Citation rates, we agreed, were an inadequate measure. Although they give us some idea of *impact*, they tend to reflect interest rather than importance. Tim noted the example of cloze—among the hottest research topics during the 1950s through the 1970s. Yet neither Russell nor Singer even mention cloze. Why not? "Might have been that it was a well-researched topic, but not particularly important," Tim said.

Further, rather than one study, "isn't it a body of work, like schema theory, that really makes an influence on practice?" Susan wondered. "The body of work idea is one that we need to think about," Tim said. "We could highlight two or three studies in a section." Returning again to Russell and Singer's efforts, however, we decided to "bite the bullet." Tim suggested, "Let's point to the important work done by various people in an area, but select and highlight one that stands out and explain why. If we don't point to single studies no one can argue with us, and that goes against the real idea of the article."

Likewise, we chose to consider empirical studies only; that is, investigations in which the researcher collected or analyzed data. There are many integrative literature reviews, theoretical treatises, and practical recommendations available concerning literacy education. As valuable as these are, they are not primary research and, thus, were not considered. This approach required the omission of influential literature reviews such as Chall's (1967) and Adams's (1990) analyses of phonics, Hiebert's (1983) review on ability grouping, Stanovich's (1986) on phonological awareness, Hillocks's (1986) on composition instruction, and some reviews in the *Handbook of Reading Research* (Barr, Kamil, Mosenthal, & Pearson, 1991; Pearson, 1984). These syntheses used research to suggest valuable directions for instruction. However, Russell's original purpose was to show how particular

empirical studies altered practice, and we stayed true to this despite our own misgivings. Moreover, we see it as a sign of the growing sophistication of the field that accumulations of studies have become so influential.

We limited ourselves to those works published since Russell's article appeared. And, of course, there was the recency effect. "Doesn't it take time to have influence?" Susan asked. "No question about it," Tim said. "Work done in the 1960s has a greater chance of having a stronger impact than something done in the 1990s." But given our contrary nature and reluctance to neglect newer work, we agreed to "not hesitate to make a mistake."

Finally, we broadened Russell's criteria to reflect the important conceptual changes that have taken place within the field. We have considered *literacy* research as opposed to reading research. Thus, work on writing and spelling, for instance, could be considered. We also did not limit ourselves to elementary and secondary school considerations. Russell noted with great satisfaction that reading research had expanded the scope of reading instruction into high school. The broader enfranchisement for literacy teaching has continued since then and now includes preschoolers and adults. These changes are reflected in our selections.

Our first approach was straightforward. We proposed studies, traded lists, and added more studies. We were not yet attempting to make our cases, so these proposals were made without explanation or challenge. As we discussed the relative merits of these, however, it became apparent that we were on the wrong track. For example, studies like Heath's (1983) *Ways with Words* or Scribner and Cole's (1981) *The Psychology of Literacy* powerfully influenced cultural theory and methodology. Susan argued that Heath popularized ethnography as a research strategy. "If you look at the *NRC (National Reading Conference) Yearbook*, it is amazing how many ethnographic or qualitative studies there are in comparison to good ol' quantitative studies. These methodological changes essentially led to a broadened definition of what literate behavior might be." Tim responded, "You raise some interesting issues, but I think you are ranging too wide. The issue that we are revisiting is research that has made a difference to practice. Many of the studies that we have been discussing have been important in changing our research conceptions, but have they had any practical significance? We've got to stick to what made a difference in classroom practice: who is taught, what is taught, and how it is taught."

Practical influence had to be the hallmark for inclusion. We did not consider quality, value, citation rate, or any other way of appraising research. We agreed that our list should not reveal much about changes we hope will take place or about current practices that we abhor.

Our task would have been easier if we could have focused on our favorite studies, model research, or those that have influenced our own thinking. Russell established this standard, but he failed to honor it entirely. Curiously, some of the studies that he proposed had not influenced practice, even in his own opinion. In his article, Russell included Nila Banton Smith's chronicle of U.S. reading instruction "as an example of the historical method of research" (1956, p. 75), and a study by William S. Gray "not because its impact has yet been great, but because it points the way to important future developments" (1934, p. 77). We tried to avoid such inconsistency. However, by thinking "from studies to practice," we were neglecting many important changes that had taken place in literacy instruction.

We began to think more about how literacy instruction has changed. Fortunately, Austin and Morrison's survey, *The First R* (1963), provides a useful baseline description of classroom practices at that time. Our perceptions of current practices, however, were still often in disagreement. Each of us is a prisoner of experience, and instructional practices can differ by grade level, socioeconomic status, recency of teacher education, district policies, and even regional concerns. The status of reading achievement has been monitored for decades, but instruction has not. The most recent national examinations of classroom instructional practice are Applebee's (1993) analysis of secondary literature instruction, and the National Assessment of Educational Progress's (NAEP) descriptions of classroom practice (Mullis, Campbell, & Farstrup, 1993). Unfortunately, the NAEP information is sketchy, and Applebee's considers only one area of instruction. Thus, there is little normative empirical data about classroom practices against which to test our own perceptions.

How has literacy instruction changed?

We, nevertheless, constructed our own shared personal portrait of the changes that have taken place in literacy instruction since the early 1960s. This rather impressionistic sketch became the basis for additional brainstorming of potential studies, and it guided our final selection. The major features of that sketch are as follows:

Literacy is taught both earlier (kindergarten and preschool) and later (adult literacy) than before. Readiness activities once so ubiquitous in kindergartens and the first half of first grade have generally disappeared and have been replaced with reading instruction. Ability grouping has probably declined, especially in the primary grades where it had been so popular. Remedial reading in the U.S. grew dramatically through Chapter/Title I programs since the mid 1960s, but these have begun to be supplanted or supplemented with early interventions such as Reading Recovery.

Elementary instruction became increasingly eclectic, but the past decade witnessed the rise of a new factionalism with regard to instructional methods. Phonemic awareness, fluency instruction, and the use of invented spelling have all become part of the literacy curriculum. Self-selected reading in elementary classrooms is more likely to take place now. Worksheets became popular, though we discern some recent decline in their use. Management systems, in which collections of discrete skills are tested and taught, appeared, gained wide use, and have largely disappeared again. The minilesson and the literacy club have emerged as popular instructional activities.

The books used to teach elementary literacy have changed rather dramatically in content and style. Such books, whether referred to as basals or literary anthologies, are probably used less now than even a decade ago. Initially, basal stories were written specifically to be used for teaching reading. Later, these were replaced with adaptations of more widely known trade books. More recently, the mainstay of textbooks has been nonadapted original trade book selections, though publishers continue to alter the graphic aspects of these. Reading textbooks no longer use careful vocabulary controls; these have been replaced by a predictable or patterned style of writing in the beginning levels. These changes have elevated the quality of what children read but might be making it more difficult to teach and learn reading. Textbooks and trade books have become more reflective of diversity in the U.S., so minority children in 1996 read stories more reflective of their racial and ethnic heritages. Textbook use may be down, but the growth of trade book availability, both in and out of schools, has been remarkable, and this growth is reflected in the expansion of children's book clubs and bookstores. Readability controls are used less often than before in reading textbooks. This shift is particularly intriguing as such controls became commonplace around the time of Russell's article, and he praised them as an important advance.

Elementary writing instruction, after decades of neglect, has become the norm in U.S. schools. Children, even those in kindergarten, now usually receive some writing instruction. Preservice and inservice teachers learn more about the teaching of writing than in 1961, and the writing achievement of their elementary and secondary students will probably be tested now. Textbooks of all kinds now stress the value of writing activities and instruction.

There is more instruction devoted to reading comprehension than before, and certainly such instruction is more varied than when its scope was governed mainly by the questions to be asked. Ideas like strategic comprehension and metacognition have become widespread since the mid 1970s—though still probably not the norm—and related instructional practices like ReQuest, DRTA (Directed Reading-Thinking Activity), mapping, story structure summaries, and other related techniques have greatly expanded the instructional repertoires of many teachers.

Teachers are more likely to use informal assessments such as portfolios, and student achievement now is widely and publicly evaluated with large-scale assessment tests. Parents in the 1990s receive more encouragement to help their children with academic work. Different kinds of literacy are now recognized—at least beyond the K–12 curricula—through family literacy and workplace literacy programs. The canon certainly remains, but it has broadened a bit to include more recently published pieces, especially those by women or racial/ethnic minorities. Inclusion of such authors is evident in elementary materials as well. Media and technology, still limited in most schools, are far beyond what was available in 1961. The focus of technology in literacy instruction seems to have changed, too, from machines that teach reading to teaching children to use literacy with various technological tools (word processors, CD-ROM reference materials, hypercards, Internet). Teachers are better educated with regard to reading, literature, and writing, and teacher research has grown.

This brief sketch became the basis for considering a wider range of studies in our conversation. For some changes, it was easy to select an appropriate influential investigation, while others did not seem to develop directly from research findings.

The role of research in instructional change

In fact, many changes that have occurred in literacy instruction have been due less to research than other factors. Worksheet use in reading is a case in point. We could find no research antecedent to this. It occurred more because of the development of the photocopier and decline of bulk paper prices than because of research. Similarly, many of the changes noted in large-scale assessment or textbook design have been due to economic, political, and social factors. This is not to say that research has not been used to develop such measures or that these tests have not been used to generate worthwhile data. The point is simply that large-scale assessments are not used *because* some influential research study found this to be helpful. Accountability is a political issue, not an educational one, and this has driven the expanded use of large-scale assessments. Similarly, the growth in availability of children's trade books has been fueled more by demographic and economic changes outside of school than by school actions instigated by research.

Research does play a role in educational change, but it might be more like the view of history implied by Singer than by Russell. Russell apparently subscribed to so-called "Great Man" theories of history (or, in this case, a "great study" theory). According to such views, history is determined by the actions of a particularly forceful individual. For Russell, simply designed, well-written, utilitarian studies are influential by dint of their quality, utility, and simplicity. Singer made it clear that more is going on here than just well-executed research. The features of research highlighted by Russell are more important than the methodology used, but possibly no study will have much impact if it does not match the Zeitgeist. Certainly, it is rare that research sets or reverses major practical trends in education. The idea is not that studies are just material objects in space with no force, but that this force is necessarily mediated by other, possibly more fundamental, forces.

In both Russell and Singer, there is a strong sense that research can and should influence instructional practice. Certainly, such views are held by many researchers and policymakers. Our view is more conflicted. We hope our studies will influence practice, but we recognize the real limits on the applicability of most findings. Research is complicated, and the results of a single study can be woefully wrong and misleading. Attempts to apply research too quickly can do harm. Also, as valuable as research can be, there are important epistemological, social, and economic forces at work in determining the nature of instruction in schools and how research is used.

Our previous examples of economic and social forces should suffice, though the value of teacher autonomy and professionalism deserves note. How research findings are applied must be determined, in part, by the professional who has to apply them. Views of research as *the* determining factor in educational history supposes a hierarchical field in which researchers, at the top of the pyramid, make decisions about how teachers, lower in status, will conduct their work. Teaching is difficult, and research is only one source of information used along with teacher lore, community values, and experience (Shanahan, 1994).

Research findings should be viewed as a powerful, but partial, form of rhetoric. The idea that any study can provide sufficient perspective on which to determine practice is naive. Research is one of our most useful

A chronological list of the 13 most influential literacy studies since 1961

Goodman, K.S. (1965). A linguistic study of cues and miscues in reading. *Elementary English, 42*, 639–643.

Durkin, D. (1966). *Children who read early.* New York: Teachers College Press.

Bond, G.L., & Dykstra, R. (1967). The cooperative research program in first-grade reading instruction. *Reading Research Quarterly, 2*, 5–142.

Children's Television Workshop. (1969). *Sesame Street.* New York: Public Broadcasting System.

Freire, P. (1970). *Pedagogy of the oppressed* (Trans. M.B. Ramos). New York: Herder & Herder.

Read, C. (1971). Preschool children's knowledge of English phonology. *Harvard Educational Review, 41*, 1–34.

Sticht, T.G., Caylor, J.S., Kern, R.P., & Fox, L.C. (1972). Project REALISTIC: Determination of adult functional literacy skill levels. *Reading Research Quarterly, 7*, 424–465.

Pichert, J.W., & Anderson, R.C. (1977). Taking different perspectives on a story. *Journal of Educational Psychology, 69*, 309–315.

Stein, N.L., & Glenn, C.G. (1977). An analysis of story comprehension in elementary school children. In R. Freedle (Ed.), *New directions in discourse processing: Vol. 2. Advances in discourse processing* (pp. 53–120). Norwood, NJ: Ablex.

Durkin, D. (1978–79). What classroom observations reveal about reading-comprehension instruction. *Reading Research Quarterly, 14*, 481–533.

Clay, M.M. (1979, 1985). *The early detection of reading difficulties.* Auckland, New Zealand: Heinemann.

Graves, D.H. (1981). *A case study observing the development of primary children's composing, spelling, and motor behaviors during the writing process.* Final report. NIE Grant No. G-78-0174. Durham, NH: University of New Hampshire. (ERIC Document Reproduction Service No. 218 653)

Atwell, N. (1987). *In the middle.* Portsmouth, NH: Boynton/Cook, Heinemann.

tools for constructing knowledge. However, a basic part of the research process is to conduct multiple studies of the same phenomenon using different conceptualizations of the problem, samples of participants, measures of success, and so on. Practitioners and policymakers are frustrated by the messiness of this process, as it often leads to conflicting results. However, research discourse through which such differences are analyzed, argued over, and, eventually, understood is a major part of what research brings to practice. To us, the determinants should not be individual studies, but the accumulation of knowledge across lines of research.

Educational research can be thought of as a process that develops transportable technologies that can be applied easily and homogeneously. Alternatively, it can be seen as a reasoning process in which empirical data are used to help formulate more useful conceptualizations of the world. Though we have disagreed about the premises underlying these fundamental notions, we both are aware that individual studies influence practice, and we both hope for an application process that would be considered, deliberate, and reliant on larger collections of studies.

The studies that have influenced practice

By these different approaches we actively considered about 40 studies. We narrowed the field, from there, by logical discussion. In a number of cases, the process was easy, and one interchange sufficed. Other

times we argued. Which studies have influenced practice the most? Russell proposed a top 10, but our conversations led us to what we hope is a "thoughtful 13." Although a top 10 list would have been more consistent with Russell's original plan, we allowed the list to grow a bit longer as we were reviewing a larger and more varied corpus of studies that had been produced over a shorter period of time. Descriptions of the 13 most influential studies since 1961 follow and appear chronologically in the accompanying list.

Most research usually ends up as a paper or book, but in the case of our first selection the research culminated in an ongoing television program for children. Now more than a quarter of a century old, *Sesame Street* (Children's Television Workshop, 1969), the educational and entertainment program for preschoolers, is an exemplar of a successful research experiment: the collaboration of educational advisors and professional researchers with TV production. Susan had to argue strenuously for this one. "But is it research?" Tim had challenged. Her response, and, indeed, the history of the project, proved persuasive. "Research usually ends up as a paper or book, but here the 'treatment' and the 'effect' is actually a TV show for children." From its inception—under the brilliant leadership of Joan Ganz Cooney along with her colleagues, Director of Research Ed Palmer and Chairperson of the Board of Advisors Gerry Lesser—the show was designed as an experimental research project. Together, this team refined child watching to an art form. Prior to broadcasting, researchers estimated what children knew about a topic; program materials were created and tested on target audiences for appeal, comprehensibility, and educational value; researchers then reported back to producers who modified or discarded materials based on these continuous reports from the field. This approach proved highly beneficial for the beginning literacy development of Sesame Street viewers as revealed in summative analysis (Ball & Bogatz, 1970) and led to the creation of a new model for **educational television production.** This innovative experiment proved beyond doubt, the potential of television as an educational asset in the lives of young children. As a result of Sesame Street, beginning reading curricula in schools began to assume greater literacy knowledge among young children.

No study has so successfully influenced remedial reading instruction as Marie Clay's *Reading Recovery* program, described in her book, *The Early Detection of Reading Difficulties* (1979, 1985). In a series of studies conducted over a 5-year period, Clay examined the effects of her innovative **one-on-one tutorial program to intervene early in reading failure.** Up to then, remediation was usually delayed until students were in the fourth grade, as it was assumed that they might catch up on their own. Clay intervened, often successfully, after only 1 year of instruction. Unlike traditional remedial programs, Clay emphasized instruction in the context of real reading, observation as a key assessment technique, high-quality teacher education as a fundamental part of the intervention, and individualized instruction that would raise student achievement to the average level of class performance. The program began in New Zealand but rapidly spread to Australia, England, Canada, and the United States.

Another influential study of early literacy learning was conducted by Charles Read (1971). Read studied how young children understood the phonemic aspects of English as related to the spelling system. His analysis of the attempted spellings of preschool children showed that they were able to use their tacit knowledge of phonological relations and could make sense of highly abstract principles of spelling even without formal instruction. Initially, this work exerted little impact on instruction as it was assumed that Read's subjects were particularly gifted. However, work by Carol Chomsky (1971) and Ed Henderson and his students at the University of Virginia (Henderson & Beers, 1980) showed the relevance of Read's findings to more typical school settings. As a result, we no longer assume that children enter school with little knowledge of the phonological-orthographic features of language, and **invented spelling** has become a popular instructional activity that allows earlier writing and provides children a venue to explore the orthography of their language.

Paulo Freire's (1970) concept of literacy for liberation, beautifully articulated in *Pedagogy of the Oppressed*, is another highly influential study. Working with Brazilian peasants, Freire recognized that literacy was not merely a technical skill, but one that was rooted in the histories, cultures, and day-to-day experiences of learners. His notion of **emancipatory literacy** argued against a *banking* concept of education in which teachers simply deposited information into learners. In its place, he successfully tried a *problem-posing education* in which ideas take shape and change as the learners critically think about their lives and the conditions of state and society. For Freire, literacy was essentially a political act in which individuals assert their rights and responsibilities not only to read, but also to restructure their relationship with society. His work has had a transforming influence in adult literacy education. Today, programs using a Freirian approach focus on collaborative relationships among learners and teachers and involve participants in curriculum development that is centered on their own characteristics, aspirations, backgrounds, and needs.

Another influential study in adult literacy is Tom Sticht's work on literacy in work training and job performance (Sticht, Caylor, Kern, & Fox, 1972). Working with military personnel, he developed an innovative approach that continues to influence **workplace literacy**. He reasoned that effective reading strategies could be taught using job-related materials so that students would learn both skills and the technical content of the job. He based his approach on a functional-context principle—that new knowledge must build on old knowledge, and that literacy instruction could be made more meaningful by using *real life* situations, tasks, and materials. Intertwining transferable processing skills and situation-specific job and career knowledge, his research on functional contexts for literacy and technical training evolved into the concept of workplace literacy used in industry training programs across the U.S. This approach has been extended conceptually into other functional approaches such as family literacy and health literacy.

One of the most ambitious ventures in reading research, the U.S. Cooperative First-Grade Studies, remains a classic in research collaboration as well as literacy education. Written by Guy Bond and Robert Dykstra (1967), the study represented a compilation of data from 27 individual studies examining the effects of instructional approaches on beginning reading and spelling achievement. The study was set up by Donald Durrell, and the list of project directors reads like a Who's Who of Reading Research (Jeanne Chall, Donald L. Cleland, Edward B. Fry, Albert J. Harris, Arthur W. Heilman, Thomas D. Horn, John C. Manning, Helen Murphy, Olive

S. Niles, Robert B. Ruddell, William D. Sheldon, George D. Spache, Russell G. Stauffer, and others). Programs studied included phonics, linguistic readers, basals, initial teaching alphabet, individualized reading, the language experience approach, and various grouping schemes and combinations of instruction. These studies found that no instructional method was superior to the others for students at either high or low levels of readiness. Susan was troubled by this choice, as she felt that much of its influence was based upon false warrants—it had not actually found that teachers made a difference, only that instructional method had not. Tim was able to win the argument by noting that this study did more than highlight "teacher effects"; it also demonstrated that although no single method proved best, combinations of methods were associated with the highest achievement. In other words, it encouraged greater **methodological eclecticism** in elementary instruction than had previously existed. Although no study has successfully challenged these basic findings, eclecticism has been under renewed attack recently. Increasingly rancorous arguments about the superiority of various instructional approaches are evident, and some members of the research community have again become involved in the search for best method. An enduring legacy of this study has been a greater focus on teacher and learning situation characteristics rather than on methods and materials.

The next two classic studies, both conducted by Dolores Durkin, have powerfully influenced reading instruction. Recognizing the incongruity between what early precocious readers knew and what first-grade programs offered, Durkin's studies of *Children Who Read Early* (1966) raised questions about reading readiness. Both of us thought this belonged on the list, but we were concerned that the findings of the study did not line up with the outcome we have attributed to it. Durkin conducted longitudinal studies of precocious readers in California and New York and reported findings that challenged the prevailing view that early readers would suffer problems in school. She found quite the opposite. Early readers maintained their achievement lead. Children who read early typically showed early interest in reading, were read to regularly by parents or siblings, and their parents believed themselves to be their young children's teachers. Although in this study Durkin did not show benefits of earlier school instruction—she hadn't even studied that—she did show that children could learn to read successfully without delay, and this was a critical reason for the eventual **demise of reading readiness programs**. More than any other study, this highlighted the role of parents in literacy learning and set the stage for later emergent literacy views.

Durkin (1978–79) also helped to focus needed attention on reading comprehension. Relatively little work on reading comprehension was done until the 1970s. Durkin, on the basis of a carefully conducted observational study that examined classrooms under nearly ideal conditions, concluded that virtually no reading comprehension instruction was taking place in U.S. classrooms. Her findings indicated that most comprehension instruction took the form of questioning students about what they had read. Durkin's unflattering portrait of instructional neglect set off a series of efforts in research, material development, and teacher training. After Durkin's stark portrait of **reading comprehension instruction** appeared, it became increasingly difficult to ignore this critical area of concern.

This was not the only major influence on reading comprehension instruction, however. Pichert and Anderson (1977) demonstrated convincingly that a reader's perspective influences comprehension and recall. Although they worked from a framework first proposed by Bartlett in 1932, and other notable researchers were conducting similar studies (such as John Bransford's fine work), this study was particularly persuasive because of its ingenious design. They asked participants to read a complete story from one of two perspectives, that of a home buyer or a thief, and found that these pretend perspectives affected what was remembered. This study became a cornerstone in the literature on schema theory and led to a **greater emphasis on instructional techniques that activate prior knowledge** as part of the comprehension process.

Cognitive psychologists wondered what makes a story a story, and how people remember and create narratives; the idea of **story grammar** emerged from this work. A story grammar is a set of tacit rules that determines the essential parts or structures of a story and how these parts relate. Researchers such as Mandler and Johnson (1977) and Stein and Glenn (1977) developed story construction rules, on the basis of analyses of children's recall of story elements and experiments that showed what readers do when particular elements are omitted or disorganized. This was a difficult choice. Susan pointed out that Mandler and Johnson seemed to be cited most often by researchers, but Tim suggested that "if you look at teacher journals, basals, or magazines, they propose activities that are more like the Stein and Glenn's categories." Thus, though both grammars have been widely used by the research community, we think Stein and Glenn's work has been more directly influential on instructional practice. Their grammar, probably as a result of its simpler categories and more parsimonious description of relationships, has become the basis of a number of story mapping and summarizing techniques that are now a mainstay of narrative instruction in U.S. schools.

Before Donald Graves's research (1981), elementary writing, if taught at all, was dominated by grammar, spelling, and usage. Influenced by Donald Murray, Graves, along with his students Lucy Calkins, Mary Ellen Giaccobe, and Susan Sowers, carefully observed what children did within the writing process. Graves's thoughtful instructional recommendations and keen observations of elementary school writers showed that children could successfully engage in writing activities similar to those used by professional writers. His **writing conference method** of instruction emphasized revision processes especially, in which students would write and rewrite drafts with teacher and peer feedback. At a time when many teachers were wondering what to do with this long neglected aspect of the curriculum, Graves's research dramatically created an attractive approach to elementary writing instruction. Although Graves's research has been criticized in terms of methodological adequacy, the effects of his work are seen widely in classrooms throughout the U.S., as well as in many other countries.

Graves helped to bring about another trend, best exemplified by the influential work of Nancie Atwell (1987). Atwell's *In the Middle* describes how the writing workshop in Boothbay, Maine, developed into a complete, and very progressive, approach to the teaching of middle school literacy. Using yearlong case studies, logs of observations, and portfolios, this classic of teacher research demonstrated how a responsive classroom literacy context could be created. Together, she and her students tried out and tested their beliefs about written language, creating solutions grounded in their particular experiences and not in a prescribed curriculum. Her **full-immersion approach to reading and writing**, including minilessons and status reports, has been used in classrooms across the U.S. Most enduring, perhaps, will be the possibilities that her work suggests to future teacher researchers. Written from the inside, Atwell's compelling research details the principles, complexities, and practicalities that define literacy teaching.

Kenneth Goodman's (1965) study of oral reading miscues has been central to what eventually became known as the **whole language** movement. At the time of his study, instructional practices in reading often emphasized word recognition in isolation from meaningful contexts. Goodman argued, from a psycholinguistic perspective, that reading involves the use of multiple cue systems rather than only the cues within printed words. Investigating the role of decoding skill in isolation and context, he examined primary students' ability to read words in lists and texts. He found that children could recognize words in context that they could not in isolation, and that this ability increased with age. Children had used syntactic and semantic cues to better anticipate and recognize unfamiliar words. From this, Goodman and his colleagues challenged oral reading, phonics drills, word lists, and other skills-based approaches that take words out of context. The findings of this study have been severely challenged and certainly much of what has been inferred from it exceeds the actual limits of the study. Nevertheless, there is little doubt that it has been influential on instructional practice.

A summing up

What are the common bonds of these studies? First, they tend to address what could be characterized as *important* issues—all of them set out to answer genuine questions rather than simply to add items to somebody's vita. They often reflected efforts to reconsider current practices or views of learning in new, refreshing, and unique ways. Second, these studies were strongly driven by theory. In some, the authors proposed new theoretical principles, while in others there were clear attempts to extend theory into issues of practice; in each case, it meant that the fruits of the studies could be brought to bear on a set of issues that exceeded those directly addressed by the single investigation alone. Third, each was rhetorically powerful, and simply—perhaps even elegantly—executed. Finally, the researchers were not timid; they boldly speculated on broad issues of learning, teaching, and instruction, drawing fully on the implications of their findings.

Nevertheless, though we were able to arrive at a single list, we could not entirely agree on the true source of power that these studies exerted. Research is influential, according to Susan, when it is creative, tied to important ideas, and sensible to practitioners. Consequently, the researcher is in the saddle and can choose, to some extent, whether or not to be influential. Contrarily, Tim noted that each of these studies somehow matched the social, political, and economic tenor of its times. In other words, studies that demonstrate something that the field or society apparently wanted to believe at a given moment are the ones that matter. According to this view, research will be most influential not necessarily when it provides the right answers, but the answers that we most hope to hear. This disagreement has not been resolved. Let the conversation continue....

REFERENCES
ADAMS, M.J. (1990). *Beginning to read: Thinking and learning about print.* Cambridge, MA: MIT Press.

APPLEBEE, A.N. (1993). *Literature in the secondary school: Studies of curriculum and instruction in the U.S.* (ERIC Document Reproduction Service No. 357 370)

AUSTIN, M.C., & MORRISON, C. (1963). *The first R.* New York: Macmillan.

BALL, S., & BOGATZ, G.A. (1970). *A summary of the major findings in the first year of Sesame Street: An evaluation.* (ERIC Document Reproduction Service No. 122 799)

BARR, R., KAMIL, M.L., MOSENTHAL, P., & PEARSON, P.D. (Eds.). (1991). *Handbook of reading research, Volume II.* New York: Longman.

BARTLETT, F.C. (1932). *Remembering.* Cambridge, England: Cambridge University Press.

CHALL, J.S. (1967). *Learning to read: The great debate.* New York: McGraw-Hill.

CHOMSKY, C. (1971). Approaching reading through invented spelling. In L. Resnick & P. Weaver (Eds.), *Theory and practice of early reading* (Vol. 2, pp. 43–65). Hillsdale, NJ: Erlbaum.

GRAY, W.S. (1956). *The teaching of reading and writing.* Glenview, IL: UNESCO and Scott, Foresman.

HEATH, S.B. (1983). *Ways with words.* New York: Cambridge University Press.

HENDERSON, E.H., & BEERS, J.W. (Eds.). (1980). *Developmental and cognitive aspects of learning to spell.* Newark, DE: International Reading Association.

HIEBERT, E.H. (1983). An examination of ability grouping for reading instruction. *Reading Research Quarterly, 18,* 231–255.

HILLOCKS, G., JR. (1986). *Research on written composition.* Urbana, IL: National Conference on Research in English.

MANDLER, J.M., & JOHNSON, N.S. (1977). Rememberance of things parsed: Story structure and recall. *Cognitive Psychology, 9,* 111–151.

MULLIS, I.V.S., CAMPBELL, J.R., & FARSTRUP, A.E. (1993). *NAEP 1992 reading report card for the nation and the states.* Princeton, NJ: Educational Testing Service.

PEARSON, P.D. (Ed.). (1984). *Handbook of reading research.* New York: Longman.

RUSSELL, D.H. (1961). Reading research that makes a difference. *Elementary English, 38,* 64–68.

SCRIBNER, S., & COLE, M. (1981). *The psychology of literacy.* Cambridge, MA: Harvard University Press.

SHANAHAN, T. (1994). (Ed.). *Teachers thinking, teachers knowing.* Urbana, IL: National Conference on Research in English & National Council of Teachers of English.

SINGER, H. (1970). Research in reading that should have made a difference. *Elementary English, 47,* 27–34.

SINGER, H. (1976). Research in reading that should make a difference in classroom instruction. In S.J. Samuels (Ed.), *What research has to say about reading instruction,* (pp. 57–71). Newark, DE: International Reading Association.

SMITH, N.B. (1934). *American reading instruction.* New York: Silver Burdett.

STANOVICH, K.E. (1986). Matthew effects in reading: Some consequences of individual differences in the acquisition of literacy. *Reading Research Quarterly, 21,* 360–407.

Exploring Literacy on the Internet

Internet Workshop: Making time for literacy

Donald J. Leu, Jr.

"I just don't have the time." Whenever literacy educators tell me they have not integrated the Internet with their literacy curriculum, this is almost always the explanation they provide. When I ask what they mean, I hear two different explanations. Some teachers say they don't have time in their schedule; other teachers say they don't have time to learn new instructional strategies for using a complex tool like the Internet.

I understand. The demands on us today, especially in the world of reading and writing, are enormous. Where do you find the time to fit another period into an already crowded schedule? You can't. How do you find the time to learn complicated new instructional strategies? Impossible! There is never enough time in any day to do all that needs to be done. Extras have to rest on the back burner while priorities are met first.

And yet, I *don't* understand. To me, preparing children for their future is not an extra, it is central to our role as literacy educators. Clearly we require an instructional framework that takes little time to learn and does not require us to sacrifice another element of the curriculum. It should also be consistent with what we know about the new literacies of the Internet.

In search of a theoretical framework

For several years, a number of us in the literacy community (Karchmer,

2001; Kinzer & Leander, in press; Labbo & Reinking, 1999; Leu, 2000; Reinking, McKenna, Labbo, & Kieffer, 1998; and many others) have been exploring the changing nature of reading and writing. We believe that the Internet and other information and communication technologies (ICT) are changing the nature of literacy and literacy learning as they become an increasingly important part of our lives. This work is leading toward a theoretical framework in which to understand the changes to literacy that are taking place today.

We have argued that global economic changes have generated new information technologies that generate new literacies. In this new world, what becomes critical to our students' literacy future is the ability to identify important problems, gather and critically evaluate relevant information from information networks, use this information to resolve central issues, and then clearly communicate the solution to others. In short, a global economy and the changes to ICT that accompany it change the nature of work (Mikulecky & Kirkley, 1998) and change the nature of literacy (Leu, 2000; Luke, 2000; Warschauer, 2000).

At least three themes emerge from this exploration, each of which is essential to understanding the new literacies of our future. First, literacy is deictic; new literacies emerge from new technologies, regularly changing what it means to read and write (Leu, 2000).

Second, literacy learning becomes increasingly social as multiple literacies emerge from rapidly changing technologies (Leu & Kinzer, 1999). No individual can be expected to be literate in all of the new technologies for reading and writing. Instead, what becomes important is knowing how to acquire a new literacy from others when we need it as we share and exchange strategies useful in the new literacies of reading and writing. Finally, learning how to learn continuously new literacies becomes just as important as becoming proficient in a current definition of literacy (Leu, in press); learning to learn is at the core of the new literacies. It is not just that we want students to know how to read and write; we want them to know how to continuously learn new skills and strategies required by the new technologies of literacy that will regularly emerge.

There is much to add and to revise as we build this theoretical framework. As we do, we must also seek instructional practices consistent with what we know about the changes taking place in literacy as the Internet and other ICT become increasingly important to our literacy lives.

Internet Workshop

This column describes a new instructional framework, Internet Workshop, one designed around the three themes identified in this emerging framework

Reprinted from *The Reading Teacher* (2002), 55, 466–472.

of how literacy is changing. Because Internet Workshop fits easily into the instructional schedule of any classroom, it can be used without sacrificing another element of the curriculum. In the time it takes to read this article you could learn how to use Internet Workshop in your classroom, preparing students for the literacy future they deserve. Give me 10 minutes of your time, and I'll show you how to integrate the Internet with your literacy program.

Internet Workshop (Leu & Leu, 2000) consists of an independent reading of information on the Internet around a topic and a location initially designated by the teacher; it concludes with a short workshop session where students can share and exchange the ideas and strategies they discovered during their work on the Internet. Internet Workshop permits students to learn from one another about content information, critical literacy skills, and the new literacies of Internet technologies. It is one of the easiest approaches to use with the Internet, being familiar to anyone who is already using a workshop approach for reading or writing instruction.

Internet Workshop has many variations. It may be used as a directed learning experience, a simulation, a center activity, or with many other instructional practices you already use. Generally, though, it contains these procedures:

1. Locate a site on the Internet with content related to a classroom unit of instruction and set a bookmark for the location.

2. Design an activity, inviting students to use the site as they accomplish content, critical literacy, or strategic knowledge goals in your curriculum. (As children progress, you may also invite them to develop independent inquiry projects.)

3. Complete the research activity.

4. Have students share their work, questions, and new insights at the end of the week during a workshop session. You may also use this time to prepare students for the upcoming workshop experience.

Locate a site. Prepare for the Internet Workshop by locating an Internet site containing information at an appropriate level for your students and related to your classroom unit. Once you have found the site, set a bookmark for your students. This limits random surfing and

Table 1
Central sites for major content areas

Content area	Website	
Science	Eisenhower National Clearinghouse	http://www.enc.org:80/
	Science Learning Network	http://www.sln.org/index.html
Math	Eisenhower National Clearinghouse	http://www.enc.org:80
	The Math Forum	http://mathforum.com./
Social studies	History/Social Studies for K–12 Teachers	http://www.execpc.com~dboals/boals.html
Reading/literature	SCORE Cyberguides to Literature	http://www.sdcoe.k12.ca.us/SCORE/cyberguide.html
	The Children's Literature Web Guide	http://www.ucalgary.ca/~dkbrown/index.html
	The Literacy Web	http://www.literacy.uconn.edu

exploration of sites unrelated to your unit, an important child safety issue, especially in the younger grade levels.

How do you quickly find a site on the Internet containing useful information related to your classroom unit and at an appropriate grade level? One strategy is to simply use a search engine or a directory organized for teachers and children, one that also screens out inappropriate sites for children. You might begin with one of these locations:

- Yahooligans (http://www.yahooligans.com/) is a directory and a Web guide designed for children. Sites are appropriate for ages 7 to 12.

- Ask Jeeves for Kids (http://www.ajkids.com/) is a directory and a search engine based on natural language. You simply type in a question, and it finds the best site with the answer. Sites are appropriate for use by children.

- Searchopolis (http://www.searchopolis.com/) is a directory and search engine organized for students in the elementary grades, middle grades, and high school.

- KidsClick! (http://sunsite.berkely.edu/KidsClick!/) is a directory and search engine

developed for kids by the Ramapo Catskill Library System.

A second strategy is to select one of several central sites for each subject area and explore the resources for use during Internet Workshop. A central site is one that contains an extensive and well-organized set of links to resources in a content area. In a sense, it is like a directory for a content area: reading, math, science, social studies, or another topic. Most are located at stable sites that will not quickly change. As you explore the Internet, you will discover these well-organized treasure troves of information. They will become homes to which you will often return, and you will develop your own favorites. (Table 1 lists some of the better central sites within content areas common to schools.)

Design an activity. The second step is to design an activity related to the learning goals of your unit, using the site you have bookmarked. The activity may be designed for several purposes:

Exploring Japan

Internet researcher: _____   Date: _____

Objectives

This Internet Workshop will introduce you to our unit on Japan. You will have an opportunity to explore an important resource on the Internet for our unit. You will also learn about recent news events from Japan and learn to think more critically about what you read on the Internet. Take notes in your internet journal and share them at our workshop session.

News about Japan

1. Go to the bookmark I have set for Kids Web Japan (http://jinjapan.org/kidsweb/) and scroll down to the bottom of this page. Now click on the button Monthly News (http://jinjapan.org/kidsweb/news.html) and read several recent news stories from Japan. Choose ones of interest to you. Find out what is happening in Japan, take notes, and be ready to share them during Internet Workshop.

_____

_____

_____

Critical thinking

2. Be a detective. What clues can you find at Kids Web Japan (http://jinjapan.org/kidsweb/) to indicate that the information at this site comes from the government of Japan? Write them down and bring these clues to Internet Workshop. How did you find them? Write down the strategies you used.

_____

_____

_____

3. If the information at this location comes from the government of Japan, how might this shape the news stories presented in Monthly News (http://www.jinjapan.org/kidsweb/news.html)? Write down your ideas and bring them to Internet Workshop.

_____

_____

_____

Your choice

4. Visit at least one of the many other locations at Kids Web Japan. You decide where to go! Write down notes of what you discovered and share your special discoveries with all of us during Internet Workshop.

_____

_____

_____

Evaluation rubric

  8 points—You recorded important information for each item (4 × 2 = 8 points).
  2 points—You effectively shared important information with us during our workshop session, helping each of us to learn about Japan.
  _____
  10 points—Total

Table 2
A weekly computer schedule posted for Internet Workshop

Time	Monday	Tuesday	Wednesday	Thursday	Friday
8:30–9:00 a.m.	Michelle	Michelle/Becky	Chris/Emily	Shannon/Cara	Cynthia/Alana
9:00–9:30 a.m.	Chris	Julio/Miguel	Jeremy/Tyna	Kati	Patti
9:30–10:00 a.m.	**Internet Workshop**	Ben	Aaron	Lisa	Julia
10:00–10:30 a.m.	Shannon	**Physical education**	Paul	**Physical education**	Andy
10:30–11:00 a.m.	**Library**	Mike	Scott	Faith	Melissa
11:00–11:30 a.m.	Cynthia	Eric	James	Linda	Sara
11:30 a.m.–12:30 p.m.	**Lunch**	**Lunch**	**Lunch**	**Lunch**	**Lunch**
12:30–1:00 p.m.	Alana	Tyna	Miguel	Cara	Emily
1:00–1:30 p.m.	Becky	Jeremy	Ben/Sara	Mike/Linda	Julio
1:30–2:00 p.m.	Eric/James	Aaron/Melissa	**Music**	Paul/Scott	**Class meeting**
2:00–2:30 p.m.	Kati/Lisa		Faith/Andy	Patti/Julia	

- to introduce students to a site that you will use in your instructional unit;
- to develop important background knowledge for an upcoming unit;
- to develop navigation strategies; or
- to develop the critical literacies so important to effective Internet use.

It is important during this step to provide an open-ended activity for students, one where they have some choice about the information they will bring back to the workshop session. If everyone brings back identical information, there will be little to share and discuss during the workshop session. You may wish to prepare an activity page for students to complete and bring to the Internet Workshop session, or you may simply write the assignment in a visible location in your classroom. An example of an activity page appears in Figure 1.

The activity page in Figure 1 was created by two sixth-grade teachers to develop background knowledge about Japan and to help students think more critically about information they find on the Internet. The teachers located Kids Web Japan (http://www.jinjapan.org/kidsweb/), a site developed by the Japanese Information Ministry for students in other countries who want to learn more about Japan. They set a

bookmark to this central site on the classroom computers.

Notice how the tasks on the activity page are open ended, inviting students to make their own discoveries at this location and bring these to Internet Workshop to share at the beginning of the unit. For example, each student is invited to read different news articles about events in Japan. This is an essential aspect of any assignment prepared for Internet activity. Open-ended questions invite students to bring many different types of information to Internet Workshop for discussion. Little discussion will take place if you have students search only for facts like "How high is Mt. Fuji?" Discussion is at the heart of Internet Workshop.

Notice also how critical thinking is supported by asking students to think about who created the website and how the stance of the authors might shape the information they place there. Critical literacy skills are essential to develop as you use the Internet.

Complete the research activity. The third step is to complete the research activity during the week. If you have access to a computer lab at your school you may wish to schedule a period to complete the activity in that facility. This is essential if you have a departmentalized program in the upper grades

and see your students for only one or two periods each day.

In self-contained classrooms with one or two Internet computers, you may wish to assign students to a schedule such as the one in Table 2. This provides each student with 1 hour of Internet access each week—30 minutes by themselves and 30 minutes with a partner. This is usually sufficient time to complete the research activity for Internet Workshop.

A schedule, such as the one in Table 2, is possible only when you control your time. It will also require one or two students to be working on their Internet Workshop research activity while other lessons take place in your classroom. Students quickly catch up on these experiences, but you should regularly change your schedule so that no student misses the same lesson each week. In addition, you should never schedule your weakest student in any subject area to miss that subject during the day. Having 30 minutes with a partner every week can effectively help students learn from each other and lets them try out new skills independently.

Have students share their work. The concluding experience each week is a short workshop session where students share and compare the information they discovered, discuss their developing skills in critical analysis, and raise new

Figure 2
An activity on the Internet designed to help students practice letter-name knowledge

ABC Gulp (http://www.brainconnection.com/teasers/?main=bc/gulp)

ABC Gulp

This game is powered by Macromedia's Shockwave. If you see a broken icon instead of a game, download Shockwave now.

Instructions

The friendly frog is very hungry. Help her catch a tasty fly by demonstrating your knowledge of the alphabet.

1. Adjust the volume on your computer to a comfortable level.
2. When you are ready, click once on the frog. You will

Used with permission of Brainconnection.com and Scientific Learning Corporation

questions to be explored in upcoming weeks. In the example on Japan, students brought notes from the news articles they read to the workshop session. The discussion of current events proved useful in introducing the unit on Japan because it developed background knowledge for future reading experiences. At the same time, the unit introduced the resources at this Internet site, one the class would use many more times in upcoming Internet Workshop activities.

The most exciting parts of this workshop session, however, were the second and third activities. Students reported finding many different clues that led them to believe that the site was developed by the Japanese government. This prompted a discussion of how important it is to look for a link that explains who developed any website you discover. These links are often labeled "About this site." Students learned that infor-

mation at this location helps them to understand who created the information on a website. It also helps them to think carefully about how this determines the author's stance toward the information presented. The students also learned how an author's stance shapes the information provided to readers. Each weekly workshop session will provide many opportunities to learn critical literacy skills and strategies like this as you work with your students.

Internet Workshop can be concluded with ideas to explore in the next research activity, and the Internet Workshop cycle continues. Over time, as students become familiar with the purpose and practices of Internet Workshop, they may begin inquiry projects as groups or individuals and bring the information they discover back to the next workshop session.

Internet Workshop: Variations on a theme

Internet Workshop may take a variety of forms. As I worked to develop this instructional framework, I invited teachers from around the world to share their instructional needs with me and allow me to design lessons based on this model. The process has helped me better understand the potentials of Internet Workshop and expand my thinking about its use.

A simulation. A particularly challenging assignment came from a reading and language arts teacher in Wisconsin, USA. Her class was reading about the sinking of the *Titanic*, and she wanted to conduct a simulation of the U.S. Senate hearings on that disaster. She also wanted four students to take the roles of U.S. senators and listen to testimony from survivors, ask questions, and write a final report with recommendations to steamship lines. The other students were to each take the role of a survivor or newspaper reporter and research the story of a survivor, then compose a written presentation with testimony about that passenger's experience aboard the fateful ship. The teacher planned to use the simulation experience to conclude her unit on this topic in an engaging fashion as she helped students develop research and writing skills.

In half an hour of searching, I found all of the resources needed for the simulation and quickly put up a Web page for her class to use. You may view the Internet Workshop we developed at Ms. Fields' Internet Workshop on the Titanic (http://sp.uconn.edu/~djleu/titanic.html). An especially important central site for this activity was The Encyclopedia Titanica (http://www.encyclopediatitanica.org/index.html), an extensive collection of links to resources about the disaster, including a database of the passengers, with links to information on the Internet about many of them.

Letter names in kindergarten. Internet Workshop is not limited to the upper elementary grades; it may be used at every grade level, even as low as kindergarten. Another teacher who was interested in trying Internet Workshop with his students had been told that they were too young to use the Internet. We developed an Internet Workshop activity for his writing center to help students develop letter-name knowledge and the ability to form letters.

First, we found a multimedia resource to help children learn letter names, ABC Gulp (http://www.brainconnection. com/teasers/?main=bc/gulp), and quickly developed an age-appropriate Internet Workshop activity. At ABC Gulp (see Figure 2) you click on the frog's belly to hear the name of one of the letters displayed on the right side of the screen. Then you select the letter to match the name you hear and click on it. If you select the correct letter, the frog's tongue whips out and eats it. If you select the incorrect letter, a fly appears in one of the boxes at the top. At the end of a session you can see how many letters you correctly identified. Young children enjoy watching the frog eat the various letters.

I suggested that we place ABC Gulp on this teacher's Internet computer before students arrived in the morning and provide them with a simple assignment when it was their turn to visit the reading and writing center. Each child was to play the game with the frog, attempting to identify each letter correctly. When he or she completed the experience, each child was to write his or her favorite letter on a large piece of paper with a crayon and bring it to the Internet Workshop session. At the end of the week, each did so and shared the letter name with everyone else. The children engaged in several quick activities around the names of all the letters they had selected. One was to name as many letters as they could. Another was to stand up with other students and use their letters to spell a child's name.

It was a great workshop session and showed how the Internet can be used effectively with children at the kindergarten level. In addition to learning letter names, the children developed several new literacies of the Internet as they showed one another various strategies. These included how to use the Reload button on the browser software to call up the site again when it didn't completely download to their computer. Some students also learned how to use the mouse to navigate on the screen and how to use the clicker to select an item. These new literacy skills were important for many

children and were used by them frequently during the rest of the year.

Children's literature. Another variation, suitable for any grade, is to develop independent Internet Workshop activities around the works of exceptional literature children read in class. In this model, students read a work of literature and then complete an activity from the Internet related to the work they have read. Afterwards, they share their experience with the rest of the class during the weekly Internet Workshop session. An exceptional central site for Internet Workshop literature experiences is Cyberguides (http://www.sdcoe.k12.ca. us/SCORE/cyberguide.html), organized around standards developed in California, USA. Linda Taggart-Fregoso and her colleagues in San Diego have done an exceptional job of developing Internet activities around major works of children's and adolescents' literature for Grades K–12. Each cyberguide has four different activities for each book, with links to resources on the Internet needed to complete each activity. Students choose at least one of these activities to complete each week and then share their work and the book they read, prompting others to consider the book for their next reading experience.

Author studies. Is your class reading the works of an important author (or illustrator) in the world of children's literature? You can easily have an Internet Workshop session on that person. Locate the author's home page on the Internet and invite students to search for two or three important ideas about the person's life to share at the workshop session. I like to use the extensive collection located at Authors and Illustrators on the Web (http://www. acs.ucalgary.ca/~dkbrown/authors.html).

Mathematics. Internet Workshop may also be used in a content area such as mathematics. Here, you might assign students a challenging math problem of the week. You can use locations such as the following, which provide a different weekly math challenge for students to solve.

- Math Forum Problems (http://mathforum.com/library/problems/)

- Brain Teasers (http://www.eduplace.com/math/brain/)

- Problem of the Week Homepage (http://www.sits.ac.za/ssproule/pow.html)

When Internet Workshop is used in math, students can bring back to the workshop session the strategies they used to solve a problem, as well as the answer to it. In this way Internet Workshop may be used to develop new insights and problem-solving strategies in mathematics while introducing important new resources to your math program.

Internet Workshop can have as many variations as a creative teacher can have good ideas. We have seen how it may be used to introduce a unit in a content area, conduct a simulation, teach letter-name knowledge, develop critical literacy skills, integrate the Internet with a literature program, conduct author studies, and develop problem-solving skills in math. Internet Workshop is a very flexible tool, designed to assist you in your important work.

Developing the new literacies with Internet Workshop

Another important aspect of Internet Workshop is that it permits you to discover the new literacies emerging from Internet technologies with your students. These new literacies emerge as rapidly as new technologies and new websites develop. It is hard to keep up, but Internet Workshop will provide a vehicle for you to do so.

Some of the new literacies you can uncover during Internet Workshop might include skills and strategies such as how to do the following:

- use all of the features effectively on a new search engine,

- find out who developed a Web page and how this developer might shape the information presented,

- determine when a Web page was last updated,

- find an online expert to assist with an important classroom project and how to do this safely,

- discover more information about an author you have read,

- use the URL for a site to uncover clues about who created it and why, and

- find out what other classrooms around the world are doing in your area of study.

All of these tasks reveal new literacies important for our students to develop. Many of them will be discoveries your students will make and then teach you. Discovering the new literacies and learning together with your students is one of the important aspects of Internet Workshop; it models for students how they will need to learn from others the continuously emerging new literacies of Internet technologies.

Using Internet Workshop as an action forum for discovering and exchanging the new skills, strategies, and insights demanded by the new literacies of the Internet will help you to prepare students in important ways for their future. In addition, Internet Workshop is consistent with what we are discovering about the new literacies of Internet technologies including these observations: Literacy is increasingly deictic, literacy learning is increasingly social, and the new literacies require you to learn how to learn continuously emerging new literacies from new technologies. Used in this way, Internet Workshop may become an important new tool for you to begin using in your classroom. And because it's so similar to other workshop approaches that may already be familiar to you, it requires little additional time to integrate the Internet with your reading and writing curriculum.

Today we all face many new challenges and responsibilities in our work. We can begin using the Internet in our reading and writing classrooms quickly with Internet Workshop; we can learn new lessons together as we begin our Internet journeys. The Internet can become a regular part of our classroom literacy program, allowing us to prepare students for the futures they deserve.

Now, be honest. Did that take much more than 10 minutes of your time?

References

Karchmer, R.A. (2001). Teachers on a journey: Thirteen teachers report how the Internet influences literacy and literacy instruction in their K–12 classrooms. *Reading Research Quarterly, 36,* 442–466.

Kinzer, C. K., & Leander, K.M. (in press). Reconsidering the technology/language arts divide In J. Flood, D. Lapp, J.M. Jensen, & J.R. Squire (Eds.), *Handbook of research on teaching the English language arts* (2nd ed.). Mahwah, NJ: Erlbaum.

Labbo, L.D., & Reinking, D. (1999). Negotiating the multiple realities of technology in literacy research and instruction. *Reading Research Quarterly, 34,* 478–492.

Leu, D.J., Jr. (2000). Literacy and technology: Deictic consequences for literacy education in an information age. In M.L. Kamil, P. Mosenthal, P.D. Pearson, & R. Barr (Eds.), *Handbook of reading research: Volume III* (pp. 743–770). Mahwah, NJ: Erlbaum.

Leu, D.J., Jr. (in press). The new literacies: Research on reading instruction with the Internet and other digital technologies. In S.J. Samuels & A. Farstrup (Eds.), *What research has to say about reading instruction.* Newark, DE: International Reading Association.

Leu, D.J., Jr., & Kinzer, C.K. (1999). *Effective literacy instruction* (4th ed.). Upper Saddle River, NJ: Prentice Hall.

Leu, D.J., Jr., & Leu, D.D. (2000). *Teaching with the Internet: Lessons from the classroom* (3rd ed.). Norwood, MA: Christopher-Gordon.

Luke, C. (2000). Cyber-schooling and technological change: Multiliteracies for new times. In B. Cope & M. Kalantzis (Eds.), *Multiliteracies: Literacy learning and the design of social futures* (pp. 69–91). London: Routledge.

Mikulecky, L., & Kirkley, J.R. (1998). Changing workplaces, changing classes: The new role of technology in workplace literacy. In D. Reinking, M. McKenna, L.D. Labbo, & R. Kieffer (Eds.), *Handbook of literacy and technology: Transformations in a post-typographic world* (pp. 303–320). Mahwah, NJ: Erlbaum.

Reinking, D., McKenna, M., Labbo, L., & Kieffer, R. (Eds.). (1998). *Handbook of literacy and technology: Transformations in a post-typographic world.* Mahwah, NJ: Erlbaum.

Warschauer, M. (2000). The changing global economy and the future of English teaching. *TESOL Quarterly, 34,* 511–535.

Acquiring Language: Basic Understandings

Jane Braunger and Jan Patricia Lewis

How Do We Learn?

Young children are, to say the least, sponges. Current research in the early development of the brain assigns more and more emphasis to the experiences and interactions that occur. Interaction is the key: How those around the child—parents, siblings, caregivers—talk and engage in experiences with the child seems to hold critical importance. Ability is not fixed within each individual, but rather a process where experience and environment are key factors in development of potential. Such research has powerful implications for work with beginning readers.

A study synthesizing research on brain development within the first three years points to five key findings (Carnegie Task Force on Meeting the Needs of Young Children, 1994):

1. Brain development that takes place before age one is more rapid and extensive than we previously realized.

2. Brain development is much more vulnerable to environmental influence than we ever expected (Hart & Risley, 1995).

3. The influence of early environment on brain development is long lasting.

4. The environment affects not only the number of brain cells and number of connections among them, but also the way these connections are "wired."

5. We have new scientific evidence for the negative impact of early stress on brain function (pp. 7-9).

Work in the cognitive sciences and the neurosciences as well as advances in other fields builds upon these notions. It shows effective learning occurs when these factors are in place: direct engagement of the learner; social process; the learner's purposes and intentions driving the learning; hypothesis testing; and a search for meaning (Caine & Caine, 1991, 1997).

Patterning (maps and categories, both acquired and innate) is emphasized as a critical learning strategy, including emotions as an important aspect. Caine & Caine's research has also found that the brain simultaneously perceives and creates parts and wholes; that is, the brain reduces information into parts and perceives wholistically at the same time. Learning involves both focused attention and peripheral perception; it always involves conscious and unconscious processes. In sum, learning is a complex process, embedded within our social interactions. This is compatible with meaning-centered literacy instruction, that is, instruction that focuses on the construction of meaning (1991, p. 80).

How children learn, be it language or any other knowledge, has long been at the heart of research in psychology, the sciences, and education. Brain research extends and supports this tradition. Currently, most models of how children acquire language knowledge have a foundation based in Piagetian (1969) constructs; that is, children learn via interactions and experiences within their environment. The work of Russian psychologist Vygotsky (1978) adds another critical dimension to children's learning with an emphasis on the importance of *social* interaction. Vygotsky's theories put a focus on the construction of mean-

Reprinted from Braunger, J., & Lewis, J.P. (1997). *Building a knowledge base in reading* (pp. 11–18, 68–73). Portland, OR: Northwest Regional Educational Laboratory; Urbana, IL: National Council of Teachers of English; Newark, DE: International Reading Association.

ing as central: Both personal and social meanings are socially constructed. In contracts to Piaget's theories, language is central to this process rather than reflecting but not determining thought (Pace, 1993).

Vygotsky's work also describes a "zone of proximal development" in children's learning. This is the range of social interaction between a novice and more knowledgeable other in which the child can perform with degrees of assistance from an adult that which s/he cannot yet perform independently. The zone of proximal development ends at the level at which the child can operate independently. These social interactions involve scaffolding—the support needed by the learner—to progress in understanding and ability. Cognitive development is promoted since thought and language processes that begin interpersonally later become intrapersonal (Pace, 1993).

Critical to this evolving view of early language learning is the increasing number of researchers focusing on the child's perspective on learning, rather than focusing on an adult's perspective of what learning ought to be (Dahl & Freppon, 1995; Ferreiro & Teberosky, 1982; Teale, 1982). Research methodologies have emerged that allow a closer view of what children do as they learn, particularly as they learn to speak, listen, write, and read; of their developing understandings of reading; and of how they learn to make sense of the meaning they create. Dahl & Freppon (1995) believe these developments to be particularly important in the context of current debates about differing instructional approaches, particularly for low-income children who are most at risk for failure. It is important to better understand how children view reading and writing behaviors from different perspectives in order to provide instruction and experience that best meet their needs.

In the same way, the teachers in the Webster Grove (Missouri) Action Research Project learned to look closely at interactions between themselves and their students to see ways in which they could better support students in becoming effective writers. Teachers took the learners' perspective to see how to help them capitalize on their strengths as writers (informal voice and personal engagement with their subject). Basically, their study began with a goal of "fixing" the students' writing, and, through their case study research, that goal shifted to "fixing the teaching methods" and finally, "fixing the relationships between teachers and students" (Webster Groves Action Research Project, 1994).

Clearly, the need for rich language experiences based in everyday experiences is critical to the cognitive and language development of young children. Educators must be aware of this important element and continue to provide rich experiences for children as they begin formal education.

Language Learning: Acquisition and Development

> …anything that can be said of human language and language learning has some vital bearing upon the processes of literacy. (Holdaway, 1979, p. 13)

Investigation into how children acquire language has grown immensely during the past 40 years. Chomsky's (1959, 1967) notion that all humans actively construct meaning led to questions beyond the long-held behaviorist view of response theory. Chomsky's new perspective and alternative questions have led to a series of investigations that have given increasing insight into how children learn oral language, which, in turn, invites consideration of how children then acquire written language. Because of the relative newness of this area of investigation, consensus remains elusive on many points. Disciplines and subdisciplines interested in such investigations—e.g., cognitive and developmental psychology, psycholinguistics/sociolinguistics/linguistics, anthropology, education—consider questions from such a wide variety of perspectives that difference is found more often than is similarity. These investigations have, however, helped us to gain insight into the processes of acquisition and development of children's language. In general, this research helps us to understand that oral language development is:

- *A process of reconstructing the child's home language through interactions with more sophisticated language users.* Language learning is much more than simple imitation; rather, it is a complex process of trial and error through approximations. Learning language is an intellectual, cognitive process (R. Brown, 1973; R. Brown, Cazden, & Bellugi-Klima, 1968; Halliday, 1975; Piaget & Inhelder, 1969).

- *Meaning based.* Language has a purpose: to communicate needs, wants, feelings. Halliday (1975) suggests learning language is "learning how to mean" in one's culture. Children will take on a language form because of its function—initially understanding the function, and through use, becoming clear about the form itself.

- *Social.* Language is for communication among people, and it is acquired through purposeful and meaningful interactions (Bruner, 1975; Harste, Woodward, & Burke, 1984; Neuman & Roskos, 1993; Vygotsky, 1978; Wells, 1986).

- *Interactive.* Children learn language via scaffolds provided by sophisticated language users; that is, they offer opportunities for children to try out approximations and through constructive and positive feedback, assist children toward gaining conventions of the language (Applebee & Langer, 1983; Bruner, 1975; Cambourne, 1988; Vygotsky, 1978; Wells, 1986).

- *Developmental.* Children's language acquisition occurs in stages that are documentable. Often, children's processes of hypothesis generation (i.e., figuring out how language works) are demonstrated through their language "errors" (R. Brown, 1973; Wells, 1986).

- *In a dynamic relationship with listening, reading, and writing: Each influences the other in the course of development.* Brown and Cambourne (1990), elaborating on a visual metaphor designed by Harste, Burke, and Woodward (1983), describe this relationship in terms of a "linguistic data pool"; this means that all language learners have an ever-increasing pool of knowledge about language, and are continually adding to it whether reading, writing, listening, or speaking (p. 24).

Language as function. It is important to consider Halliday's (1975, pp. 19-21; cf. Pinnell, 1985) notion that language is functional. According to his theory of developmental language, what a child can do during interactions with others has meaning and meaning can be turned into speech: What can be said reflects what can be done. In his work, he describes the following functions of language:

Instrumental:　language to satisfy a personal need and to get things done

Regulatory:　language to control the behavior of others

Interactional:　language to get along with others

Personal:　language to tell about oneself

Imaginative: language to pretend, to make believe

Heuristic: language to find out about things, to learn things

Informative: language to communicate something for the information of others

Children's acquisition of oral language does seem to follow a pattern: Children seem to be more interested in the functions of literacy first, then the form, and later the conventions (Halliday, 1973, 1975; cf. Morrow, 1996, p. 141).

A model of acquisition. Based on a synthesis of Halliday's (and others') work and his own investigations, Cambourne (1988, pp. 28-75) provides a useful model of conditions that support successful oral language learning:

- *Immersion.* From birth we are immersed in the language of our culture. Learners need to be immersed in all kinds of language.

- *Demonstration.* Learners need to receive many demonstrations of how language is constructed and used.

- *Engagement.* Deep engagement with demonstrations is maximized when learners are convinced that (a) they are potential doers of whatever is being demonstrated; (b) engaging with what is being demonstrated will further the purposes of the potential learner's lives; (c) engagement with whatever is being demonstrated will not lead to pain, humiliation, denigration—it is safe to have a go at it. In addition, learners are more likely to engage with the demonstrations provided by those who are significant to them.

- *Expectation.* Expectations of those to whom learners are bonded send clear messages to children as to what they are expected to learn AND what they are capable of learning. Learners respond positively and confidently to supportive expectations.

- *Responsibility.* Learners need to participate in making decisions about when, how, and what bits to learn in any learning task.

- *Approximation.* Learners must be free to approximate the desired model—mistakes are essential for learning to occur.

- *Use.* Learners need time and opportunity to use, employ, and practice their developing control in functional, realistic, nonartificial ways.

- *Response.* Learners must receive feedback from exchanges with more knowledgeable others. Response must be relevant, appropriate, timely, readily available, nonthreatening, with no strings attached.

Connections between oral language and the "language of print." Cambourne (1988) believes these conditions also support the learning of written language. While there is much debate over the parallels between the learning of oral language and the learning of print (reading and writing), it is important to note both the similarities and the differences, and how these apply to acquisition and development.

Similarities. Reading, writing, speaking, and listening, at the deep levels of production and comprehension, are parallel manifestations of the same vital human function—the mind's effort to create meaning (Cambourne, 1988, p. 29). Cognitively, the same processes seem to be in effect with all language processes. Children go through developmental stages in ways similar to oral language development.

Differences. The two modes of language differ in many complex and interesting ways. These differences are due to such pragmatic factors as psychological and physical distance from audience, function, amount of time people have to produce language, and degree of permanence (Chafe & Danielewicz, 1987; Olson, 1977; Rubin, 1978; Tannen, 1982). Most obviously, the two require different kinds of knowledge which learners must acquire in order to operate with and on them. And, of course, there are certain aspects of the use of the written mode that require specific knowledge which can't be carried over from the oral mode and vice versa. Cambourne (1988) discusses these differences in detail.

- Written language is not merely oral language which has been written down. For example, it is used for quite different purposes, in quite different contexts, under quite different conditions.

- The same privileges for learning the written mode are not as available as those for the oral. That is, while oral language is constantly surrounding us in a variety of means (personal, recorded, and so on), print language must be created and made accessible. Someone must construct a text—a newspaper, a letter, a list, a sign, a billboard—and make it available for others to read. Classrooms must provide a wide variety of opportunities to access print—through books, charts, lists, labels—so that children have opportunities to interact with them in real and meaningful ways parallel to oral language (cf. Cambourne, pp. 29, 43-45).

Moustafa (1997) suggests that children need to learn the language of print, that is, based upon their knowledge of oral language, they need to learn how the language of print works. Just as with oral language, children are figuring out how print works concurrently with learning to read (reminiscent of Halliday's learning through language and about language while learning language). Clay (1972) similarly speaks of children's "concepts about print"; that is, they understand the concepts of a book, of how to turn the pages, read from left to right, that meaning comes from print and pictures, and so on. Most importantly, children understand the concept that reading is for enjoyment and for information—it is purposeful and functional in their lives. These must be learned through scaffolded experiences specifically with print. Wells (1986) points out that reading to children also helps them acquire the language of print. The work of Mason (1992), Sulzby (1985), and Purcell-Gates (1988) also supports the importance of reading aloud to children. These experiences give children a sense of the language of print, putting them in an even better position to figure out print on their own (Moustafa, 1997).

Cambourne's (1988) work suggests this learning must be supported by the same conditions as oral language. In fact, Cambourne goes further, saying that his model of language learning reflects how humans go about learning in general. His conditions for learning language reflect basic principles that can guide effective teaching and learning of language. Thus, experiences in and out of schools must be provided by teachers and parents to assist children in their development (pp. 40-42).

Emergent Literacy

Traditionally, adults viewed a discrete set of skills deemed necessary for children to begin to read as "readiness." Typically, this included knowledge of colors, shapes, and the alphabet. The notion of emergent literacy—coined by Marie Clay (1966)—turned the focus from this adult idea of readiness to what children acquired from their surrounding environments that provides a foundation for beginning literacy. Research across cultures has provided substance to the idea of emergent literacy. These researchers have focused explicitly upon how children go about their learning, rather than upon a set of tasks configured by adults to represent the learning. In a very general sense, emergent literacy describes those behaviors show by very young children as they begin to respond to and approximate reading and writing acts. By the time children enter first grade, they are often ready to move into more sophisticated behaviors. However, development varies. Ferreiro and Teberosky (1982); Harste, Woodward, and Burke (1984); Heath (1983); Morrow (1978, 1997); Sulzby (1985); Taylor (1983); Teale (1982, 1986); and Wells (1986) provide insight into how young children use the same type of learning strategies seen in oral language to begin to make sense of the print they find in their world. Generally, children:

- *Have gained oral language structures*: syntax (structure) and meaning, in particular. In oral language, they have begun to experiment with the sounds language makes. This understanding and knowledge is an important foundation transferred to learning the language of print.

- *Find meaning in symbols around them.* Early on, signs and symbols (e.g., McDonald's golden arches, labels from familiar products) take on important meaning: The environmental print in children's lives has a real function. These signs and symbols reflect what is available and meaningful within the lives of those around the child, from letters to symbols found in everyday life (Goodman, 1984; Harste, Woodward, & Burke, 1984; Mason, 1980; Smith, 1971).

- *Begin to write, using symbols, signs, and letters in their attempts to reconstruct the symbolic language around them* (Bissex, 1980; Harste, Woodward, & Burke, 1984; Sulzby, 1986).

- *Begin to approximate print behaviors modeled to them*: storybook reading, use of storybook language and behaviors, approximation of writing tasks modeled (lists, stories, etc.). Often, these approximations occur within the child's play (Heath, 1983; Sulzby, 1985; Wells, 1986).

- *Follow a developmental pattern in reading and writing* (Morrow, 1997, p. 141). These patterns reinforce the use and emergence of language cues for the knowledge systems of sound-symbol relationships, meaning, structure, and purpose. The patterns suggest process, and as these processes are repeated they are refined. Language acquisition is not additive; rather, children are repeating the whole process, refining, getting clearer and clearer with time and experience.

- *Begin to categorize speech sounds to print patters* (Read, 1975). They create their own spelling patterns, based upon their perception of how language works, and how they can fit it together.

Importance of family in emergent literacy. Literacy is deeply embedded in the social process of family life (Taylor, 1983). Families influence literacy development in three ways (Leichter, 1984): through interpersonal interaction (literacy experiences shared by family members), the physical environment (literacy materials found in the home), and the emotional and motivational climate (the relationships and their attitudes toward literacy). In general, parent involvement in education is directly related to significant increases in overall student achievement (Bloom, 1985; Clark, 1983).

Home and school connections are critical to learning to read. Children who have had a wide variety of language experiences—in both oral and written modes—fare better as they begin to learn to read within the school setting. These experiences include:

- *Many opportunities to talk*: descriptions and conversations with positive interactions and feedback from those around the child (Bruner, 1975; Cazden, 1988; Hart & Risley, 1995; Ninio & Bruner, 1978).

- *Experiences with stories, both oral (storytelling) and written (storybook reading)* (Holdaway, 1979; Sulzby, 1985; Teale, 1978, 1982; Wells, 1986). Storybook reading experiences are considered by many to be the most important aspect of emergent literacy experiences (Purcell-Gates, McIntyre, & Freppon, 1995), giving children the structure and syntax of written language as well as demonstrating purpose and function of reading (Heath, 1982; Morrow, O'Connor, & Smith, 1990; Sulzby, 1985; Taylor & Strickland, 1986). If children do not have this background framework upon which to hang the more explicit literacy experiences received in schools, lack of success can occur.

- *Appropriate verbal interaction between adult and child during story readings* (Cochran-Smith, 1984; Ninio, 1980). Edwards (1989, 1991) found that nonmainstream parents can successfully be taught how to interact with books in ways that support successful literacy development.

- *Opportunity to draw and write* (Clay, 1979). Drawing and writing support children's interest in and growing awareness of print in their environment.

References

Applebee, A.N., & Langer, J.A. (1983). Instructional scaffolding: Reading and writing as natural activities. *Language Arts*, 60(2), 168–175.

Bissex, G.L. (1980). *GNYS AT WRK: A child learns to write and read.* Cambridge, MA: Harvard University Press.

Bloom, B.S. (1985). *Developing talent in young people.* New York, NY: Ballantine.

Brown, R. (1973). *A first language: The early stages.* Cambridge, MA: Harvard University Press.

Brown, H., & Cambourne, B. (1990). *Read and retell: A strategy for the whole language/natural learning classroom.* Portsmouth, NH: Heinemann.

Brown, R., Cazden, C.B., & Bellugi-Klima, U. (1968). The child's grammar from one to three. In J.P. Hill (Ed.), *Minnesota symposium on child development.* Minneapolis, MN: University of Minnesota Press.

Bruner, J.S. (1975). The ontogenesis of speech acts. *Journal of Child Language*, 2(1), 1–19.

Caine, R.N., & Caine, G. (1991). *Making connections: Teaching and the human brain.* Alexandria, VA: Association for Supervision and Curriculum Development.

Caine, R.N., & Caine, G. (1997). *Education on the edge of possibility.* Alexandria, VA: Association for Supervision and Curriculum Development.

Cambourne, B. (1988). *The whole story: Natural learning and the acquisition of literacy in the classroom.* Auckland, NZ: Ashton Scholastic.

Carnegie Task Force on Meeting the Needs of Young Children. (April, 1994). *Starting points: Meeting the needs of our youngest children. The report of the Carnegie Task Force on Meeting the Needs of Young Children.* New York, NY: Carnegie Corporation of New York.

Cazden, C.B. (1988). *Classroom discourse: The language of teaching and learning.* Portsmouth, NH: Heinemann.

Chafe, W., & Danielwicz, J. (1987). Properties of spoken and written language. In R. Horowitz & S.J. Samuels (Eds.), *Comprehending oral and written language.* New York, NY: Academic Press.

Chomsky, N. (1959). A review of B.F. Skinner's *Verbal Behavior. Language*, 35(1), 26–58.

Chomsky, N. (1965). *Aspects of the theory of syntax.* Cambridge, MA: MIT Press.

Clark, R. (1983). *Family life and school achievement: Why poor black children succeed or fail.* Chicago, IL: University of Chicago Press.

Clay, M.M. (1966). *Emergent reading behavior.* Doctoral dissertation, University of Auckland, NZ.

Clay, M.M. (1972). *The early detection of reading difficulties: A diagnostic survey with recovery procedures.* Exeter, NH: Heinemann.

Clay, M.M. (1979). *What did I write?* Exeter, NH: Heinemann.

Cochran-Smith, M. (1984). *The making of a reader.* Norwood, NJ: Ablex.

Dahl, K.L., & Freppon, P.A. (1995). A comparison of innercity children's interpretations of reading and writing instruction in the early grades in skills-based and whole language classrooms. *Reading Research Quarterly, 30*(1), 50–74.

Edwards, P. (1989). Supporting lower SES mothers' attempts to provide scaffolding for bookreading. In J. Allen & J.M. Mason (Eds.), *Risk makers, risk takers, risk breakers: Reducing the risks for young literacy learners.* Portsmouth, NH: Heinemann.

Edwards, P. (1991). Fostering early literacy through parent coaching. In E.H. Hiebert (Ed.), *Literacy for a diverse society: Perspectives, practices, and policies.* New York, NY: Teachers College Press.

Ferreiro, E., & Teberosky, A. (1982). *Literacy before schooling.* Exeter, NH: Heinemann.

Goodman, Y.M. (1984). The development of initial literacy. In H. Goelman, A.A. Oberg, & F. Smith (Eds.), *Awakening to literacy.* Exeter, NH: Heinemann.

Halliday, M.A.K. (1973). *Explorations in the functions of language.* London, UK: Edward Arnold.

Halliday, M.A.K. (1975). *Learning how to mean: Exploration in the development of language.* London, UK: Edward Arnold.

Harste, J.C., Burke, C.L., & Woodward, V.A. (1983). Children's initial encounters with print, N.I.E. Grant proposal, cited in V.H. Hardt (Ed.), *Teaching reading with the other language arts* (p. 44). Newark, DE: International Reading Association.

Harste, J.C., Woodward, V.A., & Burke, C.L. (1984). *Language stories and literacy lessons.* Portsmouth, NH: Heinemann.

Hart, B., & Risley, T.R. (1995). *Meaningful differences in the everyday experience of young American children.* Baltimore, MD: P.H. Brookes.

Heath, S.B. (1982). What no bedtime story means: Narrative skills at home and school. *Language in Society, 11*(2), 49–76.

Heath, S.B. (1983). *Ways with words: Language, life, and work in communities and classrooms.* Cambridge, UK: Cambridge University Press.

Holdaway, D. (1979). *The foundations of literacy.* Portsmouth, NH: Heinemann.

Leichter, H. (1984). Families as environments for literacy. In H. Goelman, A.A. Oberg, & F. Smith (Eds.), *Awakening to literacy.* Exeter, NH: Heinemann.

Mason, J.M. (1980). When do children begin to read? An exploration of four-year-old children's letter and word reading competencies. *Reading Research Quarterly, 15*(2), 203–227.

Mason, J. (1992). Reading stories to preliterate children: A proposed connection to reading. In P.B. Gough, L.C. Ehri, & R. Treiman (Eds.), *Reading Acquisition.* Hillsdale, NJ: L. Erlbaum Associates.

Morrow, L.M. (1978). Analysis of syntax in the language of six-, seven-, and eight-year-old children. *Research in the Teaching of English, 12*(2), 143–148.

Morrow, L.M. (1996). *Motivating reading and writing in diverse classrooms: Social and physical contexts in a literature-based program* (NCTE Research Report No. 28). Urbana, IL: National Council of Teachers of English.

Morrow, L.M. (1997). *Literacy development in the early years: Helping children read and write* (3rd ed.). Boston, MA: Allyn & Bacon.

Morrow, L.M., O'Connor, E., & Smith, J. (1990). Effects of a story reading program on the literacy development of at-risk kindergarten children. *Journal of Reading Behavior, 22*(3), 255–275.

Moustafa, M. (1997). *Beyond traditional phonics: Research discoveries and reading instruction.* Portsmouth, NH: Heinemann.

Neuman, S., & Roskos, K. (1992). Literacy objects as cultural tools: Effects on children's literacy behaviors in play. *Reading Research Quarterly, 27*(3), 202–225.

Ninio, A. (1980). Picture-book reading in mother-infant dyads belonging to two subgroups in Israel. *Child Development, 51*(2), 587–590.

Ninio, A., & Bruner, J. (1978). The achievement and antecedents of labelling. *Journal of Child Language, 5*(1), 1–15.

Olson, D.R. (1977). From utterance to text: The bias of language in speech and writing. *Harvard Educational Review, 47*(3), 257–281.

Pace, G. (1993). *Making decisions about grouping in language arts.* Portland, OR: Northwest Regional Educational Laboratory.

Piaget, J., & Inhelder, B. (1969). *The psychology of the child.* New York, NY: BasicBooks.

Pinnell, G.S. (1985). Ways to look at the functions of children's language. In A. Jaggar & M.T. Smith-Burke (Eds.), *Observing the language learner.* Newark, DE: International Reading Association.

Purcell-Gates, V. (1998). Lexical and syntactic knowledge of written narrative held by well-read-to kindergartners and second graders. *Research in the Teaching of English, 22*(2), 128–160.

Purcell-Gates, V., McIntyre, E., & Freppon, P. (1995). Learning written storybook language in school: A comparison of low-SES children in skills-based and whole language classrooms. *American Educational Research Journal, 32*(3), 659–685.

Read, C. (1975). *Children's categorization of speech sounds in English* (NCTE Committee on Research Report No. 17). Urbana, IL: National Council of Teachers of English.

Rubin, A.D. (1978). *A theoretical taxonomy of the differences between oral and written language* (Technical Report No. 35). Urbana, IL: University of Illinois, Center for the Study of Reading.

Smith, F. (1971). *Understanding reading.* New York, NY: CBS College.

Sulzby, E. (1985). Children's emergent reading of favorite storybooks: A developmental study. *Reading Research Quarterly, 20*(4), 458–481.

Sulzby, E. (1986). Writing and reading: Signs of oral and written language organization in the young child. In W.H. Teale & E. Sulzby (Eds.), *Emergent literacy: Writing and reading.* Norwood, NJ: Ablex.

Tannen, D. (Ed.). (1982). *Spoken and written language: Exploring orality and literacy. Vol. IX: Advances in discourse processes.* Norwood, NJ: Ablex.

Taylor, D. (1983). *Family literacy: Young children learning to read and write.* Exeter, NH: Heinemann.

Taylor, D., & Strickland, D.S. (1986). *Family storybook reading.* Portsmouth, NH: Heinemann.

Teale, W.H. (1978). Positive environments for learning to read: What studies of early readers tell us. *Language Arts, 55*(8), 922–932.

Teale, W.H. (1982). Toward a theory of how children learn to read and write naturally. *Language Arts, 59*(6), 555–570.

Teale, W.H. (1986). The beginning of reading and writing: Written language development during the preschool and kindergarten years. In M.R. Sampson (Ed.), *The pursuit of literacy: Early reading and writing.* Dubuque, IA: Kendall-Hunt.

Webster Groves Action Research Project. (1994). *Mirror images: Teaching writing in black and white.* Portsmouth, NH: Heinemann.

Vygotsky, L.S. (1978). *Mind in society: The development of higher psychological processes.* Cambridge, MA: Harvard University Press.

Wells, C.G. (1986). *The meaning makers: Children learning language and using language to learn.* Portsmouth, NH: Heinemann.

Multicultural Factors and the Effective Instruction of Students of Diverse Backgrounds

Kathryn H. Au

What does research have to say about multicultural factors in the teaching of reading? This question has practical importance, because many teachers will find themselves teaching students of diverse backgrounds. In this chapter, I will use the phrase *students of diverse backgrounds* to refer to students who differ from the mainstream in terms of ethnicity, primary language, and social class. In the United States, these students often are African American, Asian American, Latino/a, or Native American in ethnicity; speak home languages other than standard American English; and come from poor or working class families. In discussing multicultural factors in the teaching of reading, I will focus on students of diverse backgrounds and what teachers and other educators might do to improve their reading achievement. I have chosen this approach, with its emphasis on learning, because of the pressure on students and teachers alike to achieve high standards.

The National Assessment of Educational Progress (NAEP), popularly known as the Nation's Report Card, has documented for many years the lower reading achievement of students of diverse backgrounds in the United States. The results of the 1998 reading assessment (Donohue, Voelkl, Campbell, & Mazzeo, 1999) show several important findings. At all three grades tested (grades 4, 8, and 12), white students had higher average reading scores than African American, Hispanic, and Native American students. This difference is notable, because the average reading scores of African American and Hispanic students at grade 12 were at roughly the same level as white students at grade 8. The NAEP evaluates reading performance in terms of three levels: basic, proficient, and advanced. Across all grade levels, 39–47% of white students were at or above the proficient level, compared with 10–18% of African American students and 13–26% of Hispanic students. Results of the 2000 reading assessment, in which only fourth-grade students were tested, indicate that African American, Hispanic, and Native American students continued to perform below their peers (Donahue, Finnegan, Lutkus, Allen, & Campbell, 2001).

The gap between the reading achievement of students of diverse backgrounds and mainstream students has been a concern for many years. However, it is becoming an even greater cause of concern because of the changing demographics of the United States. In the 1990s, students of diverse backgrounds constituted 35% of the enrollment in public schools in grades 1 through 12 (National Center for Education Statistics, 1997a), and approximately 13% of all students spoke a language other than English at home. In 2025, the population of students of diverse backgrounds will be even larger, and an equal or even greater proportion of children will be growing up in poverty. Poverty appears to be the factor most highly associated with low reading achievement. The scores of all students are depressed when half or more of the students in a school are from poor families, and the effect is even stronger when 75% of the students are from poor families (Puma et al., 1997).

As noted, there is a trend toward greater diversity in the student population. However, this same trend is not evident when we look at the population of teachers. Only approximately 13% of the teachers in the United States are of diverse ethnic backgrounds (National Center for Education Statistics, 1997b), and this situation is not likely to change in the near future. What this means is that at some time in their careers most teachers, who are generally of mainstream backgrounds, will find themselves working with students whose backgrounds are quite unlike their own. It is important, then, for teachers to understand how they can successfully teach

Reprinted from Farstrup, A.E., & Samuels, S.J. (Eds.). (2002). *What research has to say about reading instruction* (3rd ed., pp. 392–413). Newark, DE: International Reading Association.

reading to students of diverse backgrounds, especially when they may be starting out with little knowledge of the communities their students come from.

The theoretical perspective taken in this chapter is that of constructivism. In this perspective, people are seen as social actors who understand the world in terms of their lived experience (Schwandt, 1994). Learning takes place as people construct their own understandings of the world, based on what they have experienced. Our perceptions are shaped by our interactions with those around us, often the members of our cultural group. People may see the world differently, in part because of their interactions within one cultural group rather than another.

Extending the constructivist perspective, we can say that both language and literacy are human constructions or social artifacts. Children learn to read through social interactions with those around them, which permits them to construct their own understandings of what reading is and how it works. On a larger scale, we can see that learning to read and failure in learning to read are human constructions or the products of social systems (Cole & Griffin, 1983). To help students of diverse backgrounds, we must understand these social systems and how they can be changed to promote success, rather than failure, in learning to read in school (for a detailed discussion, see Au, 1998).

A growing body of studies points to the effectiveness of constructivist approaches in promoting the literacy achievement of students of diverse backgrounds (Au & Carroll, 1997; Dahl & Freppon, 1995; Guthrie et al., 1995; Morrow, 1992; Morrow, Pressley, Smith, & Smith, 1997). The approaches studied all involved the use of literature-based instruction. In this case, the term *literature* refers to good books, as contrasted with contrived texts, for example, those written to give students practice reading words with the *-at* pattern. Instruction is defined as the process of getting students interested and involved in an activity, then providing them with the support needed to complete the activity successfully (Au & Raphael, 1998). My own research has centered on the use of readers' workshops that include both teacher-directed activities, such as minilessons and guided discussions of literature, and student-directed activities, such as paired and independent reading. Literature-based instruction involves a continuum of strategies to be applied as children move up through the grades in elementary school: shared reading, guided reading, guided discussion, and literature discussion groups (also known as literature circles or book clubs). In addition, two strategies are considered important across the grade levels: teacher read-alouds and sustained silent reading (for a detailed description, see Au, Carroll, & Scheu, 2001).

This chapter discusses implications for improving the reading performance of students of diverse backgrounds, within the framework provided by constructivist approaches and literature-based instruction. I have chosen this focus because available studies conducted in actual classrooms suggest to me that these approaches provide students of diverse backgrounds with the best opportunities for overall growth in all aspects of literacy, including ownership and comprehension. Building from this constructivist perspective, five steps that can be taken based on research are recommended. First, teachers can attend to issues of motivation by establishing positive relationships with students and showing them that literacy is powerful and rewarding. Second, if students struggle as readers, teachers can provide them with rich instruction in the context of a readers' workshop, including instructional strategies such as guided reading, repeated reading, and reciprocal teaching. Third, teachers will want to understand how to conduct a readers' workshop with second language learners, focusing not on surface features of language but on the different life experiences and world views students may bring to class. Fourth, teachers can learn to teach in a culturally responsive manner, using a repertoire of instructional strategies and interactional patterns so that all students can be included in literacy learning activities. Finally, teachers can implement forms of assessment, such as portfolios, that provide multiple indicators of students' progress in reading and lead to implications for improving instruction. I discuss research related to each of these challenges, along with implications for practice.

First Challenge: How Can I Motivate My Students?

When I work with teachers in schools with students of diverse backgrounds, one of the teachers will always ask, "How can I motivate my students to read? If I could just get them to care about reading, I know I could teach them all the skills they need to know." Teachers often observe the following behaviors: Students get up from their seats several times during sustained silent reading to get another book and do not seem willing to read a book from start to finish. When the class visits the library, students wander around and often end up choosing books they do not really want to read. Students do not appear to be reading at home, although independent reading is a regular homework assignment. Often, students' indifference to reading appears to be part of a larger pattern of indifference to school.

Although students' lack of motivation to read may seem on the surface to be a rather simple problem, it is actually an extremely complex one. Students of diverse backgrounds may show not just indifference but resistance to school. Ogbu (1981) suggests that this resistance develops because students do not believe that cooperating with teachers and staying in school will do them any good in the long run. Realizing that students may have such a belief system often comes as a shock to teachers of mainstream backgrounds, who have been raised to view education as the route to a better life. Ogbu points out that students of diverse backgrounds may not place a high value on education because the connection between education and job opportunities has not been illustrated in the history of their own families. In his research in an African American community, Ogbu discovered the existence of a job ceiling. The job ceiling meant that, regardless of how far African Americans had advanced in education, they were always consigned to menial, low-paying jobs (see also Bartoli, 1995). The correlation of education with job prestige and income was much weaker for African Americans from this community than it was for middle class whites. The indifference and oppositional behavior students of diverse backgrounds show in school may result from their families' experience that education does not necessarily lead to a better life.

D'Amato (1988) extends Ogbu's views by analyzing the differences between classrooms of mainstream students and classrooms with many students of diverse backgrounds. In the former, D'Amato suggests, teachers hold control. Students are willing to comply and follow the teacher's directives, even when they are bored and see little personal value in the activities. The mainstream students comply because they understand the importance of remaining in the teacher's good graces, getting good grades, graduating from high school, and continuing on to college. Their family histories usually illustrate a strong connection between schooling and employment and other life opportunities, so mainstream students understand how important it is to remain in school and do well.

In classrooms with many students of diverse backgrounds, students, not the teacher, hold control. Teachers new to these classrooms often experience difficulties with classroom management and feel that students are working against the order they are trying to establish. According to D'Amato, these perceptions are accurate. For example, in classrooms with Hawaiian children, D'Amato observed a phenomenon he termed "acting." Acting, which begins as a playful form of misbehavior, is the students' way of testing the teacher. If the teacher fails to strike the proper balance between being strict and being kind and fair to students, acting will escalate into increasingly disruptive behavior. The standoff between students and teacher can continue for the entire school year. During this time, when the teacher has been unable to establish a positive relationship with the students, little instruction and academic learning can occur, because the teacher's and students' time in the classroom is consumed with management issues.

This broad view of schooling and its significance (or lack of significance) to students of diverse backgrounds provides a context for better understanding students' apparent lack of interest in reading and learning to read. Several steps may be helpful in this regard. First, the teacher will want to establish positive relationships with students. It may be helpful for the teacher to have an understanding of the students' cultural backgrounds and the values they bring to school. Once positive relationships and open communication have been established, students will accept the teacher as a role model and as a model of literate behavior.

Second, to serve as a good model of literate behavior, teachers must demonstrate the kind of literacy they want students to show. As Graves (1990) and others have argued, teachers must see themselves as readers and writers if they want students to read and write. Only then can they provide the sincere demonstrations of literate behavior that will convince students of the value of reading and writing (for classroom examples, see Carroll, Wilson, & Au, 1996). If teachers want students to read books of their own choosing during sustained silent reading, teachers must read books they have chosen for their own enjoyment. If teachers want students to share their chosen books with the class, teachers must participate by sharing the books they have enjoyed. If teachers want students to participate in literature circles, they must participate by presenting their own responses to literature.

The teacher cannot stop with demonstrations of literate behavior. If students respect the teacher, they are likely to follow his or her lead and read. However, the problem remains of helping students to gain a deep appreciation for literacy in their own lives. The teacher must somehow win the students over to schooling and to reading. How might this goal be accomplished? D'Amato (1988) suggests that teachers must show students, on a daily basis, how reading can be rewarding. Teachers can read a chapter a day aloud from high-interest, page-turning novels such as *Roll of Thunder, Hear My Cry*. They can have students read and discuss challenging and thought-provoking novels, such as *Tuck Everlasting* or *The Giver*. They can build on students' interests in working with peers by organizing book clubs or student-led literature discussion circles (McMahon & Raphael, 1997). Teachers can interview students to identify their interests and then connect them to books they will enjoy. Although we might wince at recommending books with titles such as *Extreme Skateboarding*, we should keep in mind the importance of helping students to develop their own tastes and interests as readers.

Ultimately, our goal with students of diverse backgrounds, and with all students, is to promote ownership of literacy (Au, 1997). Ownership has to do with valuing literacy, having a positive attitude toward literacy, and having the habit of using literacy. Students who have ownership make reading a part of their everyday lives outside of school. They read for purposes they set for themselves, perhaps to escape into another world, to follow the progress of a favorite singing group, or to learn the strategy for playing a new video game. Ownership is promoted as teachers develop classrooms as a community of readers. In a community of readers, participants gain a common literary background by reading, listening to, and discussing the same books. They learn to contribute to the community by introducing their classmates to new books and recommending books to their peers. Although all students can benefit from belonging to a classroom community of readers (Cairney & Langbien, 1989), this experience may be especially important to students of diverse backgrounds, by giving them a reason for staying in school.

Second Challenge: What Should I Do About Struggling Readers?

Another question teachers frequently ask me is how they can help the struggling readers in their classrooms. Often, teachers working with students of diverse backgrounds find that many in the class are reading far below grade level. Second-grade teachers tell me that their classes include several students whose reading is still emergent. These students cannot name all the letters of the alphabet and are not tracking print but still attending primarily to pictures when they read. Fourth-grade teachers report experiencing difficulty with students who can decode words accurately but have no understanding of the text. Naturally, these teachers are concerned about providing their students with the powerful instruction that will move them forward as readers.

To understand the kind of instruction likely to be beneficial to struggling readers of diverse backgrounds, it is helpful to look at what research says about the instruction these students usually receive. We begin with the observation that classrooms with students of diverse backgrounds are heterogeneous in many ways, including the range of reading achievement. The same second-grade classroom that includes emergent readers may have other students reading at the fourth- or fifth-grade level. It takes a great deal of expertise on the part of teachers to manage this range and conduct a classroom reading program that meets the needs of the emergent readers, the advanced readers, and all the students in between.

Often, as teachers and schools struggle to address this range of students, they resort to ability grouping and tracking. In elementary schools, students of diverse backgrounds are usually assigned to the lowest reading group in the classroom or sent out to receive remedial reading instruction. In high schools, students of diverse backgrounds are generally placed in the lower tracks. Many studies have documented differences in the nature of the instruction given to elementary students in high versus low reading groups (e.g., Allington, 1983) and to high school students in high versus low tracks (e.g., Oakes, Gamoran, & Page, 1992). In general, students placed in high groups and high tracks do more reading and receive instruction oriented toward comprehension and higher level thinking. Students placed in low groups and low tracks generally do less reading and receive instruction oriented toward word identification and lower level skills. Due to the limited learning opportunities associated with their assignment to low groups and low tracks, students of diverse backgrounds tend to make little progress in reading.

The challenge for teachers is to figure out how to work with struggling readers in a manner that addresses their needs in learning to read, within the context of the rich instruction provided by a readers' workshop, normally available only to stronger readers. The general principle is to use the same continuum of strategies with struggling readers (including teacher read-alouds, sustained silent reading, shared reading, guided reading, guided discussion, and literature discussion groups), but to augment these strategies with intensive instruction on the specific skills students need to succeed. For example, during shared reading, struggling readers will benefit from masking activities in which the teacher isolates particular words and calls children's attention to the initial consonant and other letters (Holdaway, 1979). In guided reading, students can benefit from minilessons that call their attention to spelling patterns, such as -it or -ight. Making words (Cunningham & Cunningham, 1992), an activity in which students spell words using a limited set of letters, may be used to supplement shared and guided reading. For example, if students have read *The Doorbell Rang*, the target word may be *doorbell*. Children will be given small trays with letter cards for *d, o, o, r, b, e, l, l*. The teacher will have them spell shorter words with these letters, such as *or, be, bed, rod, rode*, and so on, and finally *doorbell*. Making words encourages children to study how letters go together to form words, to look beyond the initial consonant, and to notice vowels as well as consonants.

Repeated reading (Samuels, 1979) is an activity effective in building students' fluency. In repeated reading, students tape record their reading of a short passage and keep track of how long each reading takes. Over time, by reading the same passage over and over, students gain the feeling of what it is like to be a proficient reader who experiences a smooth and easy flow through the text. Repeated reading can be used when students are engaged in guided reading, guided discussion, and literature discussion groups. Students can choose the passage they want to learn to read fluently from among the books their group is reading.

Comprehension is usually the biggest problem teachers face with struggling readers from the third grade and higher. Often, students seem to go on "automatic pilot" and decode words without being actively involved in comprehending the text. These students are not monitoring their own comprehension to see if what they are reading is making sense (Wagoner, 1983). Reciprocal teaching is an approach shown to be effective in improving students' comprehension by promoting active engagement with the text (Palincsar & Brown, 1984). Cooper (1997) suggests a simplified strategy for teaching comprehension monitoring based on reciprocal teaching. This strategy can be used as part of guided discussion. After students have silently read a brief section of the text, the teacher stops the group and does a think-aloud. In Cooper's example, the text is *The Bicycle Man.* The teacher says,

> This is a good place for me to stop and ask myself, *Does this make sense?* I understand that the author is telling this story and it takes place in Japan. I'm not sure if I know what a sportsday is. I think I'll reread page 3. (Reread page 3 aloud.) A sportsday must be like our field day where we have different events. (1997, p. 402)

The teacher then directs students to read the next part of the text silently to see if it makes sense to them. After students have finished reading, one of them is chosen to act as the teacher, to do a think-aloud just as the teacher did. The teacher prompts the student-teacher if help is needed, asking about unknown words, parts of the text that were poorly understood, and the section that might need to be reread. This procedure will need to be repeated on many occasions, but if it is implemented consistently, students will gradually learn to monitor their own comprehension.

Many other teaching strategies for assisting struggling readers have been developed. A good reference containing a thorough discussion of instruction and assessment of struggling readers, with numerous instructional strategies, is Lipson and Wixson (1997). Remember that these strategies will be most effective if they occur within the context of reading activities students find motivating and meaningful.

Third Challenge: How Can I Help Second Language Learners?

Frequently, teachers in schools with students of diverse backgrounds find that their classrooms include children who speak a first language other than standard English. Often, the children come from several different language backgrounds. Although some help may be available from a special teacher with training in teaching English as a Second Language (ESL) students, the main responsibility for the children's learning to read usually falls on the classroom teacher. Teachers want to know how they can help English language learners, students who may have varying degrees of proficiency in speaking English, learn to read well in English.

English language learners, like struggling readers, are often subject to instruction oriented toward lower level skills rather than higher level thinking. A review of research by Fitzgerald (1995b) and a recent study by Valdes (1998) suggest that commonly used activities include round robin oral reading, with the emphasis on correct pronunciation, grammar exercises, and copying sentences from the chalkboard. These activities limit students' opportunities in learning to read, hold little interest, foster boredom and disenchantment with school, and lead English language learners to fall even further behind in reading.

Another factor affecting the progress of English language learners is the limited availability of bilingual education. Research summarized by Snow (1990) suggests that the most effective way to build students' English literacy is to begin by teaching them to read and write in their home language. That is the approach recommended here. Yet, even if schools and parents support this view, the demographics and logistics in many schools can make it difficult to implement bilingual education. In some areas, most English language learners come primarily from one or two language backgrounds, making it feasible to have, for example, a Spanish or Cantonese bilingual program. Often, however, students are from many different language backgrounds, and qualified teachers who speak these different languages may be in short supply. It is not uncommon, then, for the classroom teacher to have the responsibility of teaching English language learners to read, perhaps with some assistance from a bilingual aide.

What can teachers do to help English language learners learn to read and write in English? These students will benefit from all the approaches recommended so far in this chapter: literature-based instruction and the readers' workshop, the continuum of strategies, and intensive instruction to develop reading skills and strategies (see also Fitzgerald, 1995a; Freeman & Freeman, 1992). Fitzgerald's (1995b) review of research identifies areas in which focused, intensive instruction appears beneficial for English language learners. These include vocabulary, expository text structure, and metacognition.

While working with English language learners within these approaches, teachers will want to be aware of other factors affecting their learning to read. One of the factors discussed by Valdes (1998) is the difference in the life experiences and world views of the teacher versus the students and their families. Valdes writes about Garden School, representative of many schools witnessing sweeping changes:

> According to one teacher who worked closely with the Latino community, most teachers at Garden School could predict few of the problems their new students would encounter. Most knew little about poverty. They had little notion of why working parents might not be able to make midday appointments with their children's teachers. They suspected disinterest, apathy, and even antagonism, and were baffled and troubled by the failure of these parents to "care" about their children.
>
> The new students, on the other hand, did not quite yet know how to be American middle school students. They knew little about school spirit. They were not sure why being in band or in chorus or in the computer club might be important. They frequently confused teachers' friendly demeanor with permissiveness, and they quickly found themselves in trouble. They understood little of what went on around them and often they became discouraged and disinterested. (p. 5)

As Valdes implies, the issue is not simply one of language but of cultural differences. Sometimes students will need to be taught how to participate appropriately in a reading activity. For example, some students may have learned not to respond until they are sure they know the right answer. These students will need to understand that, in a literature discussion group, there may be questions without right answers, to invite the sharing of best guesses and opinions. If students are not participating or not participating appropriately in a reading activity, teachers may want to discuss the situation with students and model and explain the desired behavior. Teachers may also want to make use of bilingual students who may be able to act as translators or as cultural mediators. Observations by Valdes suggest that one of the difficulties is the tendency for schools to isolate English language learners from English-speaking students. To solve this difficulty, teachers may want to pair English language learners with students who are proficient speakers of English and familiar with classroom routines, so that both language and classroom social skills can be learned from peers.

English language learners differ widely in the literacy abilities they bring to school. Research suggests that children only need to learn to read and write once (Snow, 1990). If a student is already literate in another language, the teacher should seek to build on this ability when teaching the student to read in English. In some cases, for example if the student speaks Spanish, the teacher may encourage the student to use his or her knowledge of cognates (words similar in both languages). In other cases, if the language is not related to English, for example if the student speaks Japanese, the teacher may encourage the student to use existing reading strategies, such as accessing prior knowledge related to the topic of the text.

A factor that handicaps the academic advancement of English language learners is teachers' tendency to be overly concerned about surface features of language, such as correct pronunciation of English, rather than the content of the ideas students are trying to communicate. Minor errors in students' pronunciation may lead teachers to underestimate students' ability to read and comprehend English texts (Moll & Diaz, 1985). Instead of focusing on surface features, teachers should respond to students at the level of ideas. In their responses, teachers should model the use of standard English, so that students will hear and learn the conventional way in which their ideas can be expressed. If students believe that what they have to say is important, they will have the confidence to learn the language needed to express those ideas. Although skills such as grammar and pronunciation are important, in general, corrections in these areas should be made only after teachers are certain that correcting a student will not lead him or her to withdraw from active participation in reading activities.

Fourth Challenge: How Can I Teach Reading in a Culturally Responsive Manner?

Often, teachers find themselves working in classrooms with students from cultural backgrounds unlike their own. The teacher may be of one ethnicity, the students of another. For example, I have worked with many Japanese American teachers in classrooms with Hawaiian students. More commonly, especially in urban areas, the students may be of more than 10 different ethnicities and speak more than six different home languages. The teacher is unlikely to have knowledge of all these cultures and languages. Also, the teacher may reside in a middle-class suburb some distance from the school and so be unfamiliar with the community where the students live. In essence, the teacher is from one world, and the students are from another.

Many teachers are well aware of the distance that separates them from their students, and they want to gain an understanding of how to teach reading effectively, while showing respect for their students' cultures. The phrase *culturally responsive instruction* refers to teaching that reflects the values and standards for behavior of students' home cultures. Over the years, I have given numerous presentations on the concept of culturally responsive instruction, using examples from research that my colleagues and I have conducted in classrooms with Hawaiian children. This research shows that Hawaiian children pay better attention, discuss more text ideas, and make more logical inferences during reading lessons when the teacher structures interaction following the rules for talk story, a common speech event in the Hawaiian community (Au & Mason, 1981). In conventional classroom recitation, the teacher asks a question, calls on one student to answer, and then evaluates the student's response. In talk-story-like reading lessons, the teacher asks a question and then allows the children to respond as they see fit. Usually two or three students will answer at once, using overlapping speech. Gradually, other students join in. In effect, the students collaborate to answer the teacher's question and to interpret the text. Of course, it takes practice for teachers to learn how to manage talk-story-like discussions effectively.

Anthropologists remind us that culture is a whole, and that each aspect of a culture reflects the underlying values of that cultural group (Spindler & Spindler, 1990). In the case of talk story, the underlying value reflected is that of cooperation. In many Hawaiian families, children are raised to value cooperation and the contributions they can make to the well being of the extended family, rather than to value competition and individual achievement. Other research in classrooms with Hawaiian children indicates that the students prefer to work in groups with their peers, rather than completing assignments individually (Jordan, 1985). This preference, too, reflects the value the students attach to cooperation as opposed to competition.

Considerable research has been conducted on culturally responsive instruction. Au and Kawakami (1994) summarized many of these studies in a review. The practical implications that can be drawn from this review are the following: Teachers will want to develop a repertoire of strategies for student participation, having students work as a whole class, in small groups, in pairs, and as individuals. Through experimentation, teachers will discover which types of groupings seem effective for various students. Teachers will want to understand different ways of inviting students' responses to activities, whether through calling on individual students, having each student give a brief response, or reviewing students' written responses to literature. Again, through experimentation, teachers will discover which modes of responding seem most comfortable for various students and draw out their best thinking. However, the idea is not just to persist with the types of groupings and ways of responding that seem most comfortable for students. Teachers need to help students learn to respond in ways that may be unfamiliar and uncomfortable for them, so that they will be prepared to succeed in the variety of classroom situations they are likely to encounter. For example, teachers will want to prepare Hawaiian children, who are comfortable with the talk story style of participation, to behave appropriately in conventional classroom recitation lessons, in which they are required to raise their hands and speak one at a time.

The purpose of culturally responsive instruction is to promote academic achievement, not just to build self-esteem or cultural identity, although these may be added benefits of the approach. Delpit (1991) and Ladson-Billings (1995) have stressed the importance of making sure that African American and other students of diverse backgrounds develop the academic skills to be able to compete in the larger society, because students will be judged on the basis of how well they can speak, read, and write in standard English. The main difference between culturally responsive instruction and other approaches to the education of students of diverse backgrounds, such as basic skills approaches, is that an effort is made to teach students in a manner that does not require them to give up the values of their home cultures.

Ladson-Billings (1995) has used the term *culturally relevant pedagogy* to describe an approach that addresses student achievement and cultural identity while challenging the inequities that exist in school. In her research (1994), she studied eight teachers, some African American and some white, who were able to promote the academic achievement of their African American students. She points out that African American students may see a conflict between negotiating the academic demands of school while at the same time displaying their cultural competence. The teachers in her study were adept at reducing this conflict by bridging the gap or making links between the students' culture and academic learning. For example, one teacher used rap songs as a way of teaching the elements of poetry. Ladson-Billings noted that the teachers were quite different in their styles of teaching, some appearing more structured and traditional, and others more flexible and progressive. What united the teachers was a common set of beliefs. Some of the beliefs the teachers shared were that all students could learn and be successful academically; that they, as teachers, needed to become members of the community surrounding the school; and that they should build positive relationships with students and develop a community of learners in the classroom. Ladson-Billings concludes,

> A common question asked by practitioners is, "Isn't what you described just 'good teaching'?" And, while I do not deny that it is good teaching, I pose a counter question: why does so little of it seem to occur in classrooms populated by African American students? Another question that arises is whether or not this pedagogy is so idiosyncratic that only "certain" teachers can engage in it. I would argue that the diversity of these teachers and the variety of teaching strategies they employed challenge that notion. The common feature they shared was a classroom practice grounded in the educability of the students. (1994, p. 484)

Fifth Challenge: How Can I Assess My Students' Progress in Reading?

Educators' thinking about assessment has changed dramatically over the past decade, making assessment one of the most challenging issues faced by classroom teachers. Teachers usually are most interested in using assessment to improve instruction, which in the view of Valencia (1998) and other experts is the main purpose for assessment. However, in pursuing this view of assessment, teachers in schools with students of diverse backgrounds often find themselves caught in the middle, between meeting the demands of standardized tests and attempting to implement authentic or classroom-based forms of assessment, such as portfolios.

The tension comes about in the following way: Schools in low-income areas that have a large number of students of diverse backgrounds typically have standardized test scores much lower than schools in affluent areas. As mentioned earlier, standardized test scores in schools drop as the percentage of students from low-income families increases. In Hawaii, as well as other states and districts, standardized test scores are the primary means used to ensure accountability. That is, the public looks at standardized test scores as the main indicator of whether the public schools are doing a good job of educating students. When the standardized test scores for individual schools are published in the newspaper, the low scores shown by schools in low-income areas cause the public to assume that these schools are not doing as good a job as schools in affluent areas. Another possibility, not considered by the public, is that standardized tests are actually measures of the cultural capital of middle-class students, rather than measures of students' literacy, broadly defined (Au & Raphael, 2000).

Educators working in schools with low test scores feel pressure to raise test scores. On the surface, this approach seems synonymous with improving reading instruction and helping students to become better readers. In reality, however, efforts to raise standardized test scores rarely have a positive effect on students' learning to read in school and may increase the already detrimental effects of these tests on students' well-being (Paris, Lawton, Turner, & Roth, 1991). One reason is that standardized tests tend to be based on a view of reading that is necessarily limited because of the format of the test. Although this situation is slowly changing, standardized tests have centered on multiple-choice questions with right or wrong answers. Higher level thinking with text, such as interpreting a character's motives or constructing a theme, is difficult to assess with such a restricted format. When teachers are asked to raise test scores, they usually respond by narrowing the curriculum to focus on the lower level skills and content covered in the test. Although this approach is unethical and should be avoided (Haladyna, Nolen, & Haas, 1991), those who work with schools in low-income areas will recognize it to be a common practice. An emphasis on test scores leaves teachers with less time for meaningful, motivating activities emphasizing higher level thinking and involving students in the full process of reading, such as literature discussion groups focused on the interpretation of novels. In this sense, an emphasis on standardized testing can have a detrimental effect on the learning to read of students of diverse backgrounds, because it may move instruction away from higher level thinking about text and because it may make instruction less meaningful and motivating for students.

Many teachers are willing to try new forms of assessment that can reflect the view of reading as a process of constructing meaning, capture students' strengths and weaknesses as readers, and guide instruction. Portfolio assessment has gained popularity because it can meet all of these goals. However, my initial research with portfolios in classrooms with Hawaiian students (Au, 1994) taught me an important lesson: Changing the form of assessment does not automatically change the achievement results. In this instance we had introduced a new language arts curriculum, centered on literature-based instruction, taught during the readers' workshop, and on the process approach to writing, taught during the writers' workshop (for a full description, see Au et al., 1997). The new curriculum incorporated portfolio assessment tied to grade-level benchmarks based on national standards and other reference points, such as the scope and sequence charts of basal reading programs. In the first 2 years of implementing this curriculum, the results obtained for reading comprehension with portfolio assessment were similar to those obtained with standardized tests, indicating that approximately two thirds of the students were performing below grade level. My colleagues and I learned that, important as it was to use an appropriate form of assessment, it was even more important to change instruction. In this case, we found that more time needed to be devoted to reading comprehension through small-group, teacher-led, guided discussion of texts (or experience-text-relationship lessons, see Au et al., 2001), and through lessons with teacher modeling of specific comprehension strategies, such as comprehension monitoring.

Notable improvements in reading comprehension were obtained after these changes in instruction were implemented, as shown by the results of portfolio assessment (Au & Carroll, 1997). Only slight improvements were seen on standardized test scores. We had anticipated this outcome, because we knew that standardized tests were likely to be less sensitive than portfolio assessment to the gains made by low-income students in areas of higher level thinking, such as reading comprehension. One benefit of portfolio assessment in schools with students of diverse backgrounds is that it may offer a means of demonstrating gains in student learning not captured by standardized tests.

One of the possible drawbacks of portfolios used for the purposes of evaluation is that they are directed toward an external standard for achievement. For example, the portfolios described earlier were directed toward grade-level benchmarks. Such an approach may leave little room for students to set their own goals for themselves as readers. For example, a sixth-grade student may want to read all the books by Lawrence Yep. Although worthy, this goal is unlikely to match a particular grade-level benchmark. To promote the ownership so important to the reading development of students of diverse backgrounds, portfolios should be designed not just for their connection to external standards but also to support students' goal setting and reflection on their own learning.

Conclusion

One of the greatest challenges faced by educators is that of bringing students of diverse backgrounds to high levels of reading achievement. This chapter has discussed research related to five issues commonly raised by teachers: how to motivate students, how to help struggling readers, how to work effectively with English language learners, how to teach in a culturally responsive manner, and how to assess students' progress. One of the main themes growing from the research is that traditional approaches to teaching reading to students of diverse backgrounds have not been effective. Instead, these traditional approaches, such as grouping and tracking and a heavy emphasis on skill instruction, have formed systems or patterns that put students of diverse backgrounds at a continued disadvantage in learning to read. The solution to the problem seems to be that we must put new systems or patterns in place. Our overall philosophy of teaching, learning, and literacy must be the same for students of diverse backgrounds as for all other students. We must make sure that students of diverse backgrounds have the opportunity to participate in literature-based instruction and the readers' workshop, following a continuum of teaching strategies that involves them in motivating, meaningful reading experiences. The continuum of strategies is supplemented with intensive instruction, as needed, in areas such as decoding and comprehension. Although the challenge is great, recent research with constructivist approaches appears to offer educators the best chance of narrowing the literacy achievement gap.

Questions for Discussion

1. Create a profile showing the diversity among the students enrolled in a particular school. Go over any statistics available for the school that indicate the ethnicity of the students, their language backgrounds, and how many are eligible for free lunches. Interview several teachers who have been in the school for a while to find out whether the profile of the

student body has changed in recent years or remained the same over time. Discuss your findings.

2. For the same school, identify the programs or initiatives in place to support the literacy learning of students of diverse backgrounds. Interview the principal, another administrator, a curriculum specialist, or a resource teacher to learn more about these programs. Analyze the possible strengths and weaknesses of these programs and initiatives in light of the ideas presented in this chapter.

3. Make arrangements to observe for a least 1 hour in a classroom with many students of diverse backgrounds. Make notes about the classroom environment and instructional approaches. What factors seem to support the students' academic learning? What factors seem to hinder their learning? Consider your observations in light of the recommendations in this chapter.

4. Find out about the assessment procedures used at the school, district, and state level. Analyze the pros and cons of these assessment procedures in terms of the goal of improving instruction for students of diverse backgrounds.

REFERENCES

Allington, R.L. (1983). The reading instruction provided readers of differing reading abilities. *The Elementary School Journal, 83,* 548–559.

Au, K.H. (1994). Portfolio assessment: Experiences at the Kamehameha Elementary Education Program. In S.W. Valencia, E.H. Hiebert, & P.P. Afflerbach (Eds.), *Authentic reading assessment: Practices and possibilities* (pp. 103–126). Newark, DE: International Reading Association.

Au, K.H. (1997). Ownership, literacy achievement, and students of diverse cultural backgrounds. In J.T. Guthrie & A. Wigfield (Eds.), *Reading engagement: Motivating readers through integrated instruction* (pp. 168–182). Newark, DE: International Reading Association.

Au, K.H. (1998). Social constructivism and the school literacy learning of students of diverse cultural backgrounds. *Journal of Literacy Research, 30,* 297–319.

Au, K.H., & Carroll, J.H. (1997). Improving literacy achievement through a constructivist approach: The KEEP Demonstration Classroom Project. *The Elementary School Journal, 97,* 203–221.

Au, K.H., Carroll, J.H., & Scheu, J.A. (1997). *Balanced literacy instruction: A teacher's resource book.* Norwood, MA: Christopher-Gordon.

Au, K.H., Carroll, J.H., & Scheu, J.A. (2001). *Balanced literacy instruction: A teacher's resource book* (2nd ed.). Norwood, MA: Christopher-Gordon.

Au, K.H., & Kawakami, A.J. (1994). Cultural congruence in instruction. In E.R. Hollins, J.E. King, & W. Hayman (Eds.), *Teaching diverse populations: Formulating a knowledge base* (pp. 5–23). Albany, NY: State University of New York Press.

Au, K.H., & Mason, J.M. (1981). Social organizational factors in learning of read: The balance of rights hypothesis. *Reading Research Quarterly, 17,* 115–152.

Au, K.H., & Raphael, T.E. (1998). Curriculum and teaching in literature-based programs. In T.E. Raphael & K.H. Au (Eds.), *Literature-based instruction: Reshaping the curriculum* (pp. 123–148). Norwood, MA: Christopher-Gordon.

Au, K.H., & Raphael, T.E. (2000). Equity and literacy in the next millennium. *Reading Research Quarterly, 35,* 170–188.

Bartoli, J.S. (1995). *Unequal opportunity: Learning to read in the U.S.A.* New York: Teachers College Press.

Cairney, T., & Langbien, S. (1989). Building communities of readers and writers. *The Reading Teacher, 42,* 560–567.

Carroll, J.H., Wilson, R.A., & Au, K.H. (1996). Explicit instruction in the context of the readers' and writers' workshops. In E. McIntyre & M. Pressley (Eds.), *Balanced instruction: Skills and strategies in whole language* (pp. 39–63). Norwood, MA: Christopher-Gordon.

Cole, M., & Griffin, P. (1983). A socio-historical approach to re-mediation. *The Quarterly Newsletter of the Laboratory of Comparative Human Cognition, 5,* 69–74.

Cooper, J.D. (1997). *Literacy: Helping children construct meaning* (3rd ed.). Boston: Houghton Mifflin.

Cunningham, P.M., & Cunningham, J.W. (1992). Making words: Enhancing the invented spelling-decoding connection. *The Reading Teacher, 46,* 106–115.

Dahl, K., & Freppon, P. (1995). A comparison of innercity children's interpretations of reading and writing instruction in the early grades in skills-based and whole language classrooms. *Reading Research Quarterly, 30,* 50–74.

D'Amato, J. (1988). "Acting": Hawaiian children's resistance to teachers. *The Elementary School Journal, 88*, 529–544.

Delpit, L.D. (1991). A conversation with Lisa Delpit. *Language Arts, 68*, 541–547.

Donahue, P.L., Finnegan, R.J., Lutkus, A.D., Allen, N.L., & Campbell, J.R. (2001). *The nation's report card: Fourth-grade reading 2000* (NCES 2001-499). Washington, DC: National Center for Education Statistics, U.S. Department of Education.

Donohue, P.L., Voelkl, K.E., Campbell, J.R., & Mazzeo, J. (1999). *NAEP 1998 reading report card for the nation and the states*. Washington, DC: National Center for Education Statistics, U.S. Department of Education.

Fitzgerald, J. (1995a). English-as-a-second-language learners' cognitive reading processes: A review of research in the United States. *Review of Educational Research, 65*, 145–190.

Fitzgerald, J. (1995b). English-as-a-second-language reading instruction in the United States: A research review. *Journal of Reading Behavior, 27*, 115–152.

Freeman, Y.S., & Freeman, D.E. (1992). *Whole language for second language learners*. Portsmouth, NH: Heinemann.

Graves, D. (1990). *Discover your own literacy*. Portsmouth, NH: Heinemann.

Guthrie, J.T., Van Meter, P., McCann, A.D., Wigfield, A., Bennett, L., Poundstone, C.C., et al. (1995). Growth of literacy engagement: Changes in motivations and strategies during concept-oriented reading instruction. *Reading Research Quarterly, 31*, 306–332.

Haladyna, T.M., Nolen, S.B., & Haas, N.S. (1991). Raising standardized achievement test scores and the origins of test score pollution. *Educational Researcher, 20*, 2–7.

Holdaway, D. (1979). *The foundations of literacy*. Sydney: Ashton Scholastic.

Jordan, C. (1985). Translating culture: From ethnographic information to educational program. *Anthropology and Education Quarterly, 16*, 104–123.

Ladson-Billings, G. (1994). *The dreamkeepers: Successful teachers of African-American children*. San Francisco: Jossey-Bass.

Ladson-Billings, G. (1995). Toward a theory of culturally relevant pedagogy. *American Educational Research Journal, 32*, 465–491.

Lipson, M.Y., & Wixson, K.K. (1997). *Assessment and instruction of reading and writing disability: An interactive approach*. New York: Longman.

McMahon, S.I., & Raphael, T.E. (Eds.). (1997). *The Book Club connection: Literacy learning and classroom talk*. New York: Teachers College Press; Newark, DE: International Reading Association.

Moll, L.C., & Diaz, S. (1985). Ethnographic pedagogy: Promoting effective bilingual instruction. In E. Garcia & R.V. Padilla (Eds.), *Advances in bilingual education research* (pp. 127–149). Tucson, AZ: University of Arizona Press.

Morrow, L.M. (1992). The impact of a literature-based program on literacy achievement, use of literature, and attitudes of children from minority backgrounds. *Reading Research Quarterly, 27*, 251–275.

Morrow, L.M., Pressley, M., Smith, J.K., & Smith, M. (1997). The effect of a literature-based program integrated into literacy and science instruction with children from diverse backgrounds. *Reading Research Quarterly, 32*, 54–76.

National Center for Education Statistics. (1997a). *The condition of education 1997*. Washington, DC: U.S. Department of Education, Office of Educational Research and Improvement.

National Center for Education Statistics. (1997b). *Mini-digest of education statistics 1997*. Washington, DC: U.S. Department of Education, Office of Educational Research and Improvement.

Oakes, J., Gamoran, A., & Page, R.N. (1992). Curriculum differentiation: Opportunities, outcomes, and meanings. In P. Jackson (Ed.), *Handbook of research on curriculum* (pp. 570–608). New York: Macmillan.

Ogbu, J.U. (1981). School ethnography: A multilevel approach. *Anthropology & Education Quarterly, 12*, 3–29.

Palincsar, A.S., & Brown, A.L. (1984). Reciprocal teaching of comprehension-fostering and comprehension-monitoring activities. *Cognition and Instruction, 2*, 117–75.

Paris, S.G., Lawton, T.A., Turner, J.C., & Roth, J.L. (1991). A developmental perspective on standardized achievement testing. *Educational Researcher, 20*, 12–20.

Puma, M.J., Karweit, N., Price, C., Riciutti, A., Thompson, W., & Vaden-Keirnan, M. (1997). *Prospects: Final report on student outcomes*. Washington, DC: U.S. Department of Education.

Samuels, S.J. (1979). The method of repeated readings. *The Reading Teacher, 32*, 403–408.

Schwandt, T.A. (1994). Constructivist, interpretivist approaches to human inquiry. In N.K. Denzin & Y.S. Lincoln (Eds.), *Handbook of qualitative research* (pp. 118–137). Thousand Oaks, CA: Sage.

Snow, C.E. (1990). Rationales for native language instruction: Evidence from research. In A.M. Padilla, H.H. Fairchild, & C.M. Valadez (Eds.), *Bilingual education: Issues and strategies* (pp. 60–74). Thousand Oaks, CA: Sage.

Spindler, G., & Spindler, L. (1990). *The American cultural dialogue and its transmission*. Lewes, UK: Falmer.

Valdes, G. (1998). The world outside and inside schools: Language and immigrant children. *Educational Researcher, 27*, 4–18.

Valencia, S.W. (1998). *Literacy portfolios in action*. Fort Worth, TX: Harcourt Brace.

Wagoner, S.A. (1983). Comprehension monitoring: What it is and what we know about it. *Reading Research Quarterly*, *18*, 328–346.

LITERATURE CITED

Babbit, N. (1975). *Tuck everlasting.* New York: Farrar, Straus & Giroux.
Hutchins, P. (1986). *The doorbell rang.* New York: Morrow.
Lowry, L. (1994). *The giver.* New York: Bantam Doubleday Dell.
Say, A. (1982). *The bicycle man.* Boston: Houghton Mifflin.
Taylor, M. (1976). *Roll of thunder, hear my cry.* New York: Dial.

LORI A. HELMAN

Building on the sound system of Spanish: Insights from the alphabetic spellings of English-language learners

The sound system of Spanish may influence the beginning writing behaviors of English-language learners who come from Spanish-speaking backgrounds. Teachers who have background knowledge about Spanish, as well as the factors that influence students' language and literacy development in English, have more tools to effectively scaffold instruction for Spanish-speaking students.

In the year 2000, 15% of the population in the United States between the ages of 5 and 17 had difficulty speaking English; of that group, 73% spoke Spanish (United States Census Bureau, 2002). The most recent census also documented that over half of the U.S. foreign-born population in 1999 originated from Latin America, and that, demographically, more and more of the Hispanic population has moved from larger cities into smaller cities and rural areas (Population Reference Bureau, 2002). The Spanish-speaking population in the United States is projected to reach 51 million, or 18% of the total, by the year 2025 (United States Census Bureau, 1995). It is imperative for educators who are concerned with meeting all their students' instructional needs to consider how a Spanish-language background may affect students' progress.

This article examines how the sound system of Spanish may influence the pronunciations and, in turn, the beginning writing behaviors of English-language learners who come from a Spanish-speaking background. Why is it that Spanish-speaking students learning to read in English may write *espoyo* when trying to spell a word like *spoil*? Why might a word like *sub* be written *sav*, or *the*, *da*? As more students enter school with Spanish as their primary language, linguistic information that addresses these issues should prove helpful to understanding the strengths, as well as the areas of support needed, for this sizable linguistic community (Bear, Templeton, Helman, & Baren, 2002; Invernizzi, Abouzeid, & Gill, 1994).

The importance of sounds

Literacy learning has been characterized as the internalization of ever more complex understandings about written language, or orthographic knowledge (Ehri, 1997; Ellis, 1997; Henderson & Beers, 1980; Templeton & Morris, 2000). This development proceeds through a series of phases, or stages, that describe students' understandings about print at a given time. Ehri (1997) outlined development from prealphabetic to partial alphabetic, full alphabetic, and finally the consolidated alphabetic stage. Henderson and Beers (1980) described five stages of spelling: preliterate, letter-name, within-word pattern, syllable juncture, and derivational principles. These models delineate students' progress along a continuum beginning with limited print awareness and moving to an initial understanding of the alphabetic principle. Development then expands to full phonemic awareness and the representation in writing of all salient sounds; continues to grow as spelling patterns that move

Reprinted from *The Reading Teacher* (2004), 57, 452–460.

beyond one-letter, one-sound approaches become understood; and blossoms at the more advanced levels where an understanding of the spelling-meaning connection is necessary to be successful at literacy tasks. Henderson and his students have outlined three layers of ever-deepening orthographic knowledge—the sound, pattern, and meaning layers (Bear, Invernizzi, Templeton, & Johnston, 2000; Henderson, 1981; Henderson & Templeton, 1986; Morris, Nelson, & Perney, 1986; Templeton & Bear, 1992). Students' fundamental understandings about written language continue to be refined as they assimilate their knowledge of the sound, pattern, and meaning layers of written language.

Beginning readers' knowledge about how words are written may be best classified as "spelling by sound." Students at this alphabetic stage of spelling rely on hearing and articulating the sound features of words to support their developmental writing (Bear et al., 2000; Bradley & Bryant, 1983; Ehri, 1998; McBride-Chang, 1998; Read, 1971; Salgado, 1995). Students challenge themselves to hear as many sounds as possible in a word, and to encode these sounds with letters they believe represent them.

Comparing the sounds of Spanish and English helps us to clarify possible difficulties that learners may have in distinguishing specific sounds in English; being aware of these sounds and attaching letters to represent them are key aspects of the alphabetic spelling that beginning readers do (Ehri, 1998). Alphabetic writing builds a foundation for the development of more complex levels of reading and writing, which is a primary mission of schooling (Cronnell, 1985; Labov, 2003).

The sound systems of English and Spanish

In the sections that follow I compare several key areas of the sound systems of English and Spanish. First of all, I examine the similarities and differences in consonant sounds between the two languages. Next, I explore how the more complex system of English vowels may cause confusion for second-language learners. Finally, I look at the positions for the consonant sounds, consonant clusters, and vowels in each language. The permissible combinations and placements vary between the two languages and may also be responsible for difficulties in pronunciation that can be reflected in student writing.

Although many dialects and regional variations of Spanish exist, the current discussion refers to the sounds associated with "General American Spanish" (Dalbor, 1997, p. 23). This is the principal dialect heard on radio and television and spoken by Spanish speakers in the southwest United States and Mexico, and by many urban residents in Central and South America.

Consonant sounds

English and Spanish share many of the same phonemes, yet they each also contain sounds that are not recognized as distinct in the other language. What follows is an outline of consonant commonalities, distinctions, and possible areas of difficulty for Spanish speakers learning English.

Commonalities. English and Spanish share many of the same consonant sounds, although they may be spelled differently. The Figure on the following page shows the sounds that exist in both languages (represented by their English letter symbol). The graphic shows much phonemic commonality between English and Spanish. These shared sounds provide a base for working with an unfamiliar oral language (Cárdenas, 1960; Goldstein, 2001; Nash, 1977). These letters also represent a good starting place for teaching Spanish speakers letter-sound correspondences in English.

Similarities also exist between consonant clusters in Spanish and English. These shared consonant blends include *pl, pr, bl, br, tr, dr, cl, cr, gl, gr, fl,* and *fr* (Goldstein, 2000). Although the /r/ will be pronounced differently in English, the fact that these clusters are used in both languages (e.g., *gris/green*) offers some support to the English-language learner.

Distinctions. Spanish and English each contain several consonant sounds that do not occur in the other language (Cárdenas, 1960; Dalbor, 1997; Goldstein, 2001; Nash, 1977; Zutell & Allen, 1988). Table 1 shows some examples of consonant sounds that occur in English (but not Spanish) and

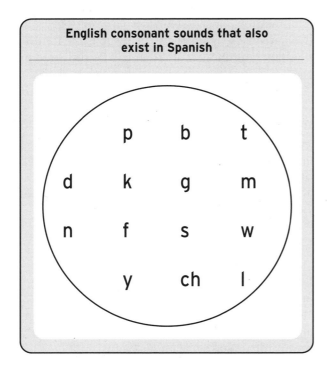

English consonant sounds that also exist in Spanish

p b t

d k g m

n f s w

y ch l

might therefore be tricky for English-language learners to say and, in turn, write.

Possible areas of difficulty for Spanish speakers learning English. A sound that is not present in one's native language will likely be difficult to hear and, in turn, produce (Goldstein, 2000; Kress, 1993). The phonemes and blends that are present in English but not present in Spanish are apt to cause the most problems for Spanish speakers learning English.

By examining Table 1 for features that are present in English but not in Spanish, we can project possible phonemic difficulties for our Spanish-speaking students, as well as sounds that are close and may be used as replacements.

D as in *den*: The /d/ in Spanish has a sound similar to the /th/ of *then* in English. Students are likely to substitute this sound, or simply the /t/ sound. Students who are attempting to spell the English /d/ sound may also be tempted to use the /r/, which has a similar flapped sound in Spanish.

J as in *juice*: Spanish does not have this sound, so it may be substituted with the /ch/ as in *choke* for *joke*.

R as in *rope*: This will be a difficult sound for Spanish speakers, and they may try to compensate

by rolling the *r* as in the Spanish words *rosa* or *carro*. Students may also use a /w/ or /u/ to create a glide, such as in *waipen* for *ripen*.

V, z, th (as in *thick*), sh, zh: These sounds may be difficult for Spanish speakers to recognize, produce, and write. Students are likely to freely substitute /b/ for /v/, producing words orally like *berry* for *very*. In writing, students may not know whether /b/ or /v/ is correct in a given word that they are sounding out. An example spelling of *big* might be *vig*. Z may be said as /s/ (*sue* for *zoo*); *th* as /t/ (*tink* for *think*); *sh* as /ch/ (*chew* for *shoe*); and *zh* as /ch/ (*treachure* for *treasure*).

Table 1 shows some expected pronunciation errors for Spanish speakers learning English. The student spellings noted in the third column show examples of writing confusions that may result from these distinctions.

Consonant blends. In addition to individual consonant sounds, there are also variations between English and Spanish in relation to what consonant clusters can occur in a language. English has many more possibilities for consonant blends than Spanish. Table 2 shows consonant clusters that are permissible in English, but not in Spanish, with some example words. From Table 2 we see that the main category of blends that are distinct in English are blends beginning with the letter *s*. Because Spanish doesn't allow *s*- blends at the beginning of a word, students may try to change these words slightly to make them sound more familiar. In Spanish, *spirit* or *structure* would be *espíritu* or *estructura*. Students may take other words that begin with *s*- blends and add an *e* to the beginning (e.g., *esmile* for *smile*, *esnake* for *snake*). Another possible approach to producing the unfamiliar consonant blends is to reduce them, such as substituting *tars* for *stars* (Goldstein, 2001).

Vowel sounds

The Spanish system of vowel sounds is much simpler than that of English (Foster, Altamiranda, & de Urioste, 1999). The English system, for a second-language learner, may at times seem overwhelming. The following subsections quickly outline common vowel sounds between the two languages, what differences exist, and possible

TABLE 1		
Possible errors caused by distinct English sounds		
Distinct English sound	May be pronounced	Example spelling error
/d/ as in den	*then*	dem (them)
/j/ as in joke	*choke*	gob (job)
/r/ as in rope	(rolled r) *rope, wope*	waipen (ripen)
/v/ as in van	*ban*	surbing (serving)
/z/ as in zipper	*sipper*	sivalais (civilize)
/sh/ as in shell	*chell*	ched (shed)
/th/ as in thick	*tick*	tenk (think)
/zh/ as in treasure	trea*ch*ure	chesher (treasure)

areas of difficulty for Spanish speakers learning the English system.

Commonalities. Both English and Spanish have the vowel sounds listed in Table 3, although they are at times spelled with different letters. Because these vowels do exist orally in both languages, they should generally not cause problems being distinguished or spoken. Where the letters used to represent the sounds differ between languages, however, confusion can arise. Table 3 outlines the differences in how the two languages represent various sounds. Column 3 shows some sample errors that students have made as they use the Spanish code to write in English. For example, a Spanish-speaking student attempting to encode the long /a/ sound may revert to the Spanish /e/, which stands for a similar sound.

Distinctions. Spanish does not contain four of the short-vowel sounds from English (*man, pen, tip, up*), *r*-controlled vowels (e.g., *her*), the schwa sound (e.g., a*way*), or the vowel sounds in *could* or *caught* (Cárdenas, 1960; Dalbor, 1997, Goldstein, 2001; Nash, 1977). With approximately double the number of vowel sounds, the English system is much more complex than that of Spanish.

Possible areas of difficulty for Spanish speakers learning English. Given that Spanish has only one sound per vowel, we can see that the addition of the distinct vowel sounds of English must seem quite complicated to the English-language learner. The schwa sound (e.g., de*ve*l*op*, a*loof*) is the most

common vowel sound in English and does not even occur in Spanish. If the home language does not have the specific English vowel sound, a student may try to use the closest sounding vowel to substitute (Goldstein, 2001). We might therefore find oral, and possibly written, substitutions such as those outlined in Table 4. Students at the alphabetic stage of spelling are likely to spell words as they pronounce them (Stage & Wagner, 1992). An example of spelling substitution that might be predicted from Table 4 is the use of *a* in place of the short *u* (*lamp* for *lump*), or /u/ for *r*-controlled vowels (*sur* for *sir*).

TABLE 2	
English consonant blends not in Spanish	
English consonant blend	Sample word
st	star
sp	spirit
sk/sc	scar
sm	small
sl	sleep
sn	snack
sw	swim
tw	twice
qu (kw)	quick
scr	scrap
spl	splash
spr	spray
str	straight
squ (skw)	square

TABLE 3
Vowel sounds common to English and Spanish

English vowels	Similar vowel sound used in a Spanish word	Example spelling error
a as in cake	e as in *hecho*	shek (shake)
e as in bean	i as in *ido*	spic (speak)
i as in like	ai as in *aire*	nait (night)
o as in hope	o as in *ocho*	flout (float)
o as in top	a as in *ajo*	jab (job)
u as in June	u as in *Usted*	flut (flute)

Positioning of sounds

Each language has its own system of positioning vowels and consonants in words. These "permissible placements" involve not only which sounds can go together but also which sounds may begin or end words and how sounds may change based on their position in a word. Spanish and English share some commonalities and also have distinctive rules about these positions.

Commonalities. Neither Spanish nor English has many limits about what sounds may begin words. All of the consonant phonemes in their respective sound systems, aside from the English /ng/, may begin a word. All of the vowels in their respective sound systems may begin words as well.

Distinctions. Most consonants in English are permitted to end words. The exception to this is the sound of /h/, as heard in the Spanish word *reloj* (Nash, 1977). In contrast, there are only five consonants that may appear in final position in Spanish (*l, r* [flap], *d, n,* and *s*). The vowels take on opposite roles in these two languages. In Spanish, most vowels may end a word. The exception to this is /eu/. In contrast, there are five vowels in English that may not end words (short *a*, short *e*, short *i*, short *u*, and *ou/oo*).

Possible areas of difficulty for Spanish speakers learning English. Two key areas stand out as possibly causing difficulty for Spanish speakers learning English. First, there are many more consonants that may end words in English. Some of these sounds will be difficult for Spanish speakers to get used to and articulate at the end of words. For ex-ample, words that end with sounds that wouldn't be permissible in Spanish such as *crab* (/-b/), *sniff* (/-f/), *beg* (/-g/), or *flop* (/-p/) may cause problems. Consonant clusters that come at the end of words will represent even more of a challenge (e.g., *hard, curl, best*). Spanish speakers may respond to these challenges by deleting sounds at the end of words or substituting sounds with which they are more comfortable. Table 5 gives some examples of possible substitutions a Spanish speaker might make with English words that have unfamiliar endings. Table 5 provides some ideas for how Spanish speakers might try to adapt English to align more closely with their native language. These adaptations help create what is currently described as "Spanish-influenced English" (Goldstein, 2001). Simplifying consonant clusters and substituting permissible consonant and vowel endings in words are logical actions in this process.

Implications for instruction

The preceding discussion has brought out many key points about similarities and differences between the sound systems of Spanish and English, and how these may influence Spanish speakers' pronunciation and developmental spelling in English. The following ideas can guide us as we look toward classroom implications.

Begin with commonalities

There are numerous areas of commonality between Spanish and English sounds on which to base a transfer of skills for English-language learners. It is helpful for second-language learners to build on what is common between their home

TABLE 4
Spanish speakers' possible vowel substitutions

Vowel sound, as in the following:	Closest Spanish vowel sound	May be pronounced
man	A	"mahn" for man
pen	E	"pain" for pen
tip	I	"teep" for tip
up	A	"op" for up
her	U	"who" for her
could	U	"cooed" for could
away	A	"ahway" for away
caught	A	"cot" for caught

language and the new one. For instance, Spanish and English are both alphabetic languages where students match sounds to letter symbols. The Figure illustrates the many common sounds between the two languages. It may be helpful for students to begin learning English phonics with letters in this graphic such as *m, s, l, f,* and *p*.

Use knowledge of Spanish to understand students' developmental reading and writing

Before critiquing students' developmental writing attempts, teachers might try to sound out the words that have been spelled with a Spanish pronunciation. For instance, *da* (sounded out /thah/) becomes more easily understood as *the*. When it is acknowledged that students' developmental spelling attempts make sense, the alphabetic understandings they are trying to represent are validated. At first, it is enough to praise the effort of having written *da*, "Yes! /th/, /ah/—the." As students refine their sound-symbol correspondences, differences between English and Spanish can be explicitly noted—"In English the sound at the beginning of *them* is written with *th*, not the *d* like in Spanish." If teachers do not feel comfortable trying to sound out writing using a Spanish pronunciation, they can ask students to read their writing and listen for matches between pronunciation and spelling.

In the area of reading, teachers can pay attention to sounding-out errors that may have a base in Spanish phonology as well. A student who reads *sit* as *seat* may either be applying the Spanish vowel

sound to the word (very possible if the student has previous literacy experiences in Spanish), or the student may be saying the closest vowel sound that exists in Spanish (a pronunciation issue). In other words, this error is not haphazard, and it gives a teacher clues about what kind of help a student may need.

What should a teacher do with a pronunciation error in reading? It is always important to provide a low-anxiety environment that encourages student participation. Thus, at first, it is wise not to focus on the error as long as meaning is being communicated. The data a teacher gathers in these informal assessments can be noted, and guided practice can be provided in supportive contexts at a later time. Activities that encourage pronunciation practice in a low-stress environment may include choral reading, echo reading, sound sorting of pictures, and using poetry and music.

These examples show us that the more that teachers know about students' home languages, the more the specific errors of the students can tell us. We can then use this information to clarify or provide extra support in our literacy instruction.

Identify areas of distinction and provide explicit support

Variations in consonant and vowel sounds between Spanish and English may create possible confusion for second-language learners in their speech and writing. After a foundation has been built on the commonalities of the two languages, it will be necessary to systematically outline how the two languages differ and provide added support as

TABLE 5 Possible substitutions for difficult words		
Example challenging sound	Sample spelling error	Logic of substitution
Final -rd	har (hard)	Simplifying the consonant cluster
Final -st	tos (toast)	
Final -ng	sirvin (serving)	
Final -sk	as (ask)	
Final -ng	chopen (shopping)	Substituting for a permissible ending
Final -z	praes (prize)	
Final -t	tha (that)	Trying to get a vowel ending
Final -oil	espollo (spoil)	
Final -mp	lanpa (lump)	

needed for the parts that are different. Teachers should plan on doing explicit lessons relating to the sounds listed in Table 1. Venn diagrams can be used to compare sounds or words in English and Spanish. Student-made bilingual dictionaries or bilingual classroom word walls can be visual supports to the differences between the two languages. Teachers often find it helpful to color code the two languages for easy reference.

Use developmental spelling tasks to assess students' learning

Second-language learners are likely to substitute a sound from Spanish for an unfamiliar English consonant or vowel sound. The developmental writing of Spanish speakers is a visual representation of what is confusing to them as they learn English. A developmental spelling assessment (e.g., Bear et al., 2000) that includes words that are likely to cause confusion or a dictation assessment (e.g., Clay, 2002) provides valuable informal data for teachers to use in planning phonics lessons that build on students' understandings of letter-sound correspondences. Particular letter-sound correspondences that are of concern to Spanish-speaking students (e.g., *shell*, *thick*, *joke*) can be inserted into these developmental writing tasks if they are not already present.

Ensure that students understand foundational concepts

Learning to read in a new language while simultaneously learning to speak it is a challenging

process (Garcia, 2000). It is critical that the input students receive makes sense to them, and that it builds on their background knowledge. The complex vowel system of English may seem confusing for Spanish speakers who are trying to get a handle on sound-symbol correspondences. Care should be taken that students are very comfortable with the short-vowel system before beginning with long vowels and other vowel patterns in their literacy instruction.

Include students in think-aloud processes comparing Spanish and English

We have seen that Spanish and English vary in the way that vowels and consonants are used, and in how sounds are positioned in words. Students may attempt to make an English word more "Spanish-like" because that feels more natural. The kinds of substitutions students make have been illustrated throughout this article. What are some ways that students can become more aware of the commonalities and differences between English and Spanish so that they can apply this knowledge in their writing? While instructing small groups and the whole class, teachers can use real examples of Spanish-influenced spelling that come up in students' writing. Teachers may verbalize their thinking in a modeled writing activity as they ponder which sounds they hear in a tricky word. They may even model being confused and self-correcting based on a Spanish sound. Students' writing samples can also be typed on a word processor and then analyzed anonymously with the whole class so that all students can profit from examining the spellings together.

Students should have plenty of opportunities to write for authentic purposes in a low-pressure environment in the classroom. When given these opportunities, students will provide many examples for us to notice, work with, and build upon as we move to more advanced skills in English reading and writing.

Helping students build on similarities

In order to be successful readers and writers in English, students must have a clear understanding of the sound-symbol correspondences of its alphabetic system. The more that teachers know about the similarities and differences between the English and Spanish sound systems, the more they can support their students in overcoming challenges in oral language development, and understanding the phonics of English. Teacher knowledge about how pronunciation influences writing at the alphabetic stage of development is crucial to providing effective literacy instruction. Teachers should not assume that a variant pronunciation reflects an articulation problem. These pronunciations may be artifacts of Spanish-influenced English. As we provide occasions for students to share their growing knowledge of written English, we find out what native-language skills they are bringing to the task. These teacher-student interactions make it possible to clarify students' understandings of English sounds and letter knowledge.

This article has outlined and compared the sound systems of English and Spanish. Where there are distinctions between the two languages, speaking and writing tasks will be more challenging for Spanish speakers learning English. Knowing this, teachers would do well to begin their work with students on letter-sound correspondences that are common to both languages, transferring first-language knowledge to the target language. Once a foundation has been established, it is important that distinct features are brought to students' attention and taught explicitly. Sounds that are different or that are placed in unfamiliar positions in words can be given extra focus and study.

Teachers are likely to see phonemic understandings (or misunderstandings) represented in student writing. For example, a student who is interchanging *b* and *v* in oral language will probably do the same in his or her written language. Correcting the spelling without discussing the misconception will not lead to long-term understanding and growth. Teachers are also likely to hear reading errors that reflect Spanish sounds being transferred to English. A student who reads *bed* as *bade* is applying a Spanish phoneme to the letter *e*. A student who reads *first* as *firs* *cat* as *ca*, or *mutual* as *moo-too-al* is also using Spanish-influenced phonology. Teachers can use assessment to help create instruction that best meets the linguistic needs of their students.

This article has focused on specific information comparing the sound systems of English and Spanish. The general principles outlined here can be extended to work with students from many other language backgrounds as well; only the specific commonalities and distinctions will vary. English-language learners bring many tools with them to the classroom setting, including a home language and knowledge about sounds and words. The more we know about the relationship between sounds in their first language and sounds in English, the more we can help our students build on the similarities and understand the differences as they become proficient speakers, readers, and writers in a new language.

References

Bear, D.R., Invernizzi, M., Templeton, S., & Johnston, F. (2000). *Words their way: Phonics, spelling and vocabulary instruction, K-8* (2nd ed.). Columbus, OH: Merrill/Prentice Hall.

Bear, D.R., Templeton, W.S., Helman, L.A., & Baren, T. (2002). Orthographic development and learning to read in different languages. In G.G. García (Ed.), *English learners: Reaching the highest level of English literacy* (pp. 71-95). Newark, DE: International Reading Association.

Bradley, L., & Bryant, P.E. (1983). Categorizing sounds and learning to read—A causal connection. *Nature, 301,* 419-421.

Cárdenas, D.N. (1960). *Introducción a una comparación fonológica del español y del ingles* [Introduction to a phonological comparison of Spanish and English]. Washington, DC: Center for Applied Linguistics.

Clay, M. (2002). *An observation survey of early literacy achievement.* Portsmouth, NH: Heinemann.

Cronnell, B. (1985). Language influences in the English writing of third- and sixth-grade Mexican-American students. *Journal of Educational Research, 78*, 168-173.

Dalbor, J.B. (1997). *Spanish pronunciation: Theory and practice*. Fort Worth, TX: Harcourt Brace College Publishers.

Ehri, L.C. (1997). Learning to read and learning to spell are one and the same, almost. In C.A. Perfetti, L. Rieben, & M. Fayol (Eds.), *Learning to spell: Research, theory, and practice across languages* (pp. 237-269). Mahwah, NJ: Erlbaum.

Ehri, L.C. (1998). Grapheme-phoneme knowledge is essential for learning to read words in English. In J.L. Metsala & L.C. Ehri (Eds.), *Word recognition in beginning literacy* (pp. 3-40). Mahwah, NJ: Erlbaum.

Ellis, N. (1997). Interactions in the development of reading and spelling: Stages, strategies, and exchange of knowledge. In C.A. Perfetti, L. Rieben, & M. Fayol (Eds.), *Learning to spell: Research, theory, and practice across languages* (pp. 271-294). Mahwah, NJ: Erlbaum.

Foster, D.W., Altamiranda, D., & de Urioste, C. (1999). *The writer's reference guide to Spanish*. Austin, TX: University of Texas Press.

Garcia, G.E. (2000). Bilingual children's reading. In M.L. Kamil, P.B. Mosenthal, P.D. Pearson, & R. Barr (Eds.), *Handbook of reading research* (Vol. 3, pp. 813-834). Mahwah, NJ: Erlbaum.

Goldstein, B. (2000). *Resource guide on cultural and linguistic diversity*. San Diego: Singular Publishing Group.

Goldstein, B. (2001). Transcription of Spanish and Spanish-influenced English. *Communication Disorders Quarterly, 23*(1), 54-60.

Henderson, E.H. (1981). *Learning to read and spell: The child's knowledge of words*. DeKalb, IL: Northern Illinois University Press.

Henderson, E.H., & Beers, J. (Eds.). (1980). *Developmental and cognitive aspects of learning to spell: A reflection of word knowledge*. Newark, DE: International Reading Association.

Henderson, E.H., & Templeton, S. (1986). A developmental perspective of formal spelling instruction through alphabet, pattern and meaning. *Elementary School Journal, 86*, 305-316.

Invernizzi, M., Abouzeid, M., & Gill, J.T. (1994). Using students' invented spellings as a guide for spelling instruction that emphasizes word study. *Elementary School Journal, 95*, 155-167.

Kress, J.E. (1993). *The ESL teacher's book of lists*. West Nyack, NY: The Center for Applied Research in Education.

Labov, W. (2003). When ordinary children fail to read. *Reading Research Quarterly, 38*, 128-131.

McBride-Chang, C. (1998). The development of invented spelling. *Early Education & Development, 9*, 147-160.

Morris, D., Nelson, L., & Perney, J. (1986). Exploring the concept of "spelling instructional level" through the analysis of error-types. *Elementary School Journal, 87*, 181-200.

Nash, R. (1977). *Comparing English and Spanish phonology and orthography*. New York: Regents.

Population Reference Bureau. (2002). *English-speaking ability*. Retrieved April 22, 2003, from http://www.prb.org/Template.cfm?Section=PRB&Template=/ContentDisplay.cfm&ContentID=7905

Read, C. (1971). Preschool children's knowledge of English phonology. *Harvard Educational Review, 41*, 1-34.

Salgado, H. (1995). *De la oralidad a la escritura* [From oracy to writing]. Buenos Aires, Argentina: Editorial Magisterio del Río de la Plata.

Stage, S.A., & Wagner, R.K. (1992). Development of young children's phonological and orthographic knowledge as revealed by their spellings. *Developmental Psychology, 28*(2), 287-296.

Templeton, S., & Bear, D.R. (1992). *Development of orthographic knowledge and the foundations of literacy: A memorial Festschrift for Edmund H. Henderson*. Hillsdale, NJ: Erlbaum.

Templeton, S., & Morris, D. (2000). Spelling. In M.L. Kamil, P.B. Mosenthal, P.D. Pearson, & R. Barr (Eds.), *Handbook of reading research* (Vol. 3, pp. 525-544). Mahwah, NJ: Erlbaum.

United States Census Bureau. (1995). *Statistical abstract of the United States: 1995* (115th ed.). Washington, DC: U.S. Department of Commerce.

United States Census Bureau. (2002). *Census 2000 supplementary survey*. Retrieved April 22, 2003, from http://www.census.gov/c2ss/www/Products/Rank/RankOLO40.htm

Zutell, J., & Allen, J. (1988). The English spelling strategies of Spanish-speaking bilingual children. *TESOL Quarterly, 22*, 333-340.

Readings from *Evidence-Based Reading Instruction: Putting the National Reading Panel Report Into Practice*

Phonemic Awareness

> Phonemic awareness is the ability to hear, identify, and manipulate the individual sounds, or phonemes, in spoken words.

Findings in the National Reading Panel Report

Phonemic awareness can be taught and learned.

Phonemic awareness taught with letters was more effective than phonemic awareness taught without letters.

Teaching one or two phonemic awareness skills was more effective than teaching three or more skills.

Phonemic awareness teaching sessions of about 30 minutes for a total of 5 to 18 hours were most effective.

Computers were effective in teaching phonemic awareness.

Phonemic awareness was most effective with pre-K and K children and children at risk.

Phonemic awareness is an important predictor of early reading achievement. A study by Share, Jorm, Maclean, and Matthews (1984) found that of a variety of measures taken at school entry, phonemic awareness and letter knowledge were the two best predictors of reading achievement at the end of kindergarten and at the end of first grade. Teaching phonemic awareness is important because it helps children understand the alphabetic structure of the English writing system—that is, the basic relationship between letters in written words and sounds in spoken words. It is not easy to distinguish the individual sounds in spoken words because in speech the sounds are not distinct and blend into one another. The point at which one sound ends and another begins is not clear or easy to identify, hence the importance of phonemic awareness training.

Consider the following example: In the word *hat* there are three sounds, /h/, /a/, and /t/, each represented by a single letter. The most common skills

Reprinted from International Reading Association. (2002). *Evidence-based reading instruction: Putting the National Reading Panel report into practice* (pp. 3–4, 35–36, 83–84, 112–113, 137–138, 183–184). Newark, DE: Author.

taught in phonemic awareness are segmenting—taking the sounds of the word *hat* and breaking them into /h/, /a/, and /t/, and then blending them together to say "hat."

In recent volumes of *The Reading Teacher*, there have been many articles related to phonemic awareness, a sign that the profession recognizes phonemic awareness as important in teaching reading. The first article in this section, "Supporting phonemic awareness development in the classroom," by Hallie Kay Yopp and Ruth Helen Yopp, provides an excellent overview of phonemic awareness instruction. The authors give a clear definition and distinguish phonemic awareness from some terms with which it is frequently confused. They then provide a survey of phonemic awareness instruction and conclude with specific activities for teaching phonemic awareness.

The second article, "Developing a kindergarten phonemic awareness program: An action research project," by Kathleen Reiner, is a report of one teacher's implementation of a phonemic awareness program. The article chronicles Reiner's reasons for teaching phonemic awareness, describes the teaching activities she used, summarizes the data collection, and reports how the data

analysis confirmed the value of teaching phonemic awareness and led to changes in her practice.

"Word boxes help children with learning disabilities identify and spell words" by Laurice M. Joseph is included because it gives a detailed description of the use of word boxes, a commonly used activity for teaching phonemic awareness. The author notes that Clay's word boxes are an extension of Elkonin's sound boxes and provides a strong rationale for their use. She then reports the improvement in word identification and spelling of her learning disabled readers after their use of word boxes. She also suggests adaptations for classroom use.

The final article, "Children's books to develop phonemic awareness—for you and parents, too!" by Michael F. Opitz, is included because it provides a list of children's books, specific activities, and a straightforward record-keeping system that teachers can use with parents so that parents' interactions with their children around books can reinforce phonemic awareness skills being taught and learned in the classroom.

Reference

Share, D., Jorm, A., Maclean, R., & Matthews, R. (1984). Sources of individual differences in reading acquisition. *Journal of Educational Psychology, 76,* 1309–1324.

Phonics

Phonics is the understanding that there is a predictable relationship between phonemes, the sounds of spoken language, and graphemes, the letters and spelling that represent those sounds in written language.

Findings in the National Reading Panel Report

Systematic phonics instruction (i.e., synthetic, larger unit, and miscellaneous phonics as defined in the report) made a more significant contribution to children's growth in reading than did alternative programs providing unsystematic or no phonics instruction.

Specific systematic phonics programs (synthetic and larger unit programs) were all more effective than non–phonics programs, and they did not appear to differ significantly from one another in their effectiveness.

Systematic phonics instruction was effective when delivered through tutoring, through small groups, and through teaching classes of students.

Systematic phonics instruction produced the biggest impact on growth in reading when it began in kindergarten or first grade before children had learned to read independently.

Systematic phonics instruction was significantly more effective than unsystematic or no phonics instruction in helping prevent reading difficulties among at-risk students and in helping to remediate reading difficulties in disabled readers. No conclusion was drawn in the case of low achieving readers because it was unclear why systematic phonics produced little growth in their reading and whether the finding is even reliable.

Phonics involves learning letter-sound correspondences and learning how to apply this knowledge in reading. There are many different approaches to teaching phonics, and the National Reading Panel (NRP) focused on systematic—as opposed to unsystematic or no phonics—instruction. Systematic phonics is distinguished from unsystematic or no phonics by delineating a planned, sequential set of phonics elements and teaching them systematically. The phonics elements taught include both consonants and vowels.

There are many different types of systematic phonics approaches. The NRP Report mentions synthetic phonics, analytic phonics, embedded phonics, analogy phonics, onset-rime phonics, phonics through spelling, and phonics in context approaches. The basic finding was that systematic phonics is more effective than unsystematic or no phonics instruction. The panel did not find differences in effectiveness for the different types of systematic phonics. The panel did determine that it is essential for a planned sequence (including consonants and vowels) to be taught explicitly.

In searching past volumes of *The Reading Teacher*, articles that focused explicitly on teaching a sequence of phonic elements could not be found. However, one of the successful systematic phonics approaches from the NRP Report was published in another Association journal, *Reading Research Quarterly*. "An assessment of Early Steps: A program for early intervention of reading problems," by Carol M. Santa and Torleiv Høien, has been included in this volume because the program is well described and exemplifies the way systematic phonics can be integrated into a balanced program.

In addition, Steven A. Stahl's classic article "Saying the 'p' word: Nine guidelines for exemplary phonics instruction" has been included. This article was selected because it gives an excellent overview of phonics instruction, and is consistent with the NRP's findings because it includes a number of the methodologies listed as systematic. One point that is not emphasized is the use of a planned sequence of elements. Stahl addresses this issue by commenting that in many basals the patterns taught in the phonics lessons appear infrequently in the text, leading students to believe that phonics is unrelated to the task of reading. He suggests that teachers using a basal might rearrange the phonics lessons so that a more appropriate element is taught with each story. Although no particular sequence of phonic elements has been demonstrated to be more effective than any other, the use of a planned sequence is more effective than random order.

"Strategies used for phonics instruction in early childhood classrooms," by Lesley Mandel Morrow and Diane H. Tracey, provides a description of actual phonics instruction observed in preschool through grade 2 classrooms. The authors report a change in the type of instruction used between preschool and kindergarten and first and second grades. Direct explicit instruction of phonics increased dramatically in the first and second grades. The descriptions of direct instruction in the article will be helpful for clarifying the range of instruction that is explicit. The focus on a specific sequence is not obvious in the descriptions but is there implicitly as most of the teachers in these grades were using commercial materials that included a specific sequence of phonic elements, one of the key characteristics of systematic phonics instruction.

The article "Building practical knowledge of letter-sound correspondences: A beginner's Word Wall and beyond" by Janiel M. Wagstaff shows how Word Walls can be used to reinforce the teaching of initial phonics lessons. The Word Wall in itself would not qualify as systematic teaching of phonics. It is included here, however, to show how a particular strategy in elementary classrooms can be used as part of systematic phonics instruction if the implementation is guided by the use of a specific sequence of phonic elements. The use of sequence does not mean that all children need to be taught each phonic element. Some children may already know a particular element. Diagnostic information should be used to determine which children know which sounds and which need to have direct instruction in particular elements in the sequence.

Reading Fluency

Fluency is reading with speed, accuracy, and proper expression without conscious attention.

Findings in the National Reading Panel Report

Repeated and monitored oral reading had a significant positive impact on word recognition, fluency, and comprehension.

Fluency instruction was appropriate for children in grades 2 through high school, particularly for struggling readers.

Fluency instruction was equally effective for good and poor readers.

There was no evidence to support the effectiveness of encouraging independent and recreational reading, as for example in sustained silent reading programs.

Fluency has been called the neglected reading skill (Allington, 1983). Until recently, teachers and researchers assumed that fluency would follow accurate word identification, so efforts were focused on word identification. In general it was possible to teach struggling readers to identify words. However, accurate word identification was not necessarily accompanied by fluent word identification. For many struggling readers, word identification remained a slow and laborious process requiring significant conscious attention. In recent years the need to be fluent as well as accurate in word identification has received more attention.

The NRP Report lists several procedures that are included in repeated reading, the first major category of fluency instruction the panel focused on—repeated reading, neurological impress, radio reading, paired reading, and a variety of similar techniques. The panel also investigated formal efforts to increase the amounts of independent or recreational reading that children had, including sustained silent reading programs. There was evidence that fluency instruction in the first category was effective; however, there was insufficient evidence to draw a conclusion about the effectiveness of encouraging independent and recreational reading. Because the one uncontested belief in the field is that children who read more read better, the lack of research is not surprising. It probably has not occurred to researchers to test the hypothesis because it is such a widely held assumption and there is such a broad evidence base in correlational studies (see Anderson, Wilson, & Fielding, 1988).

The first article in this section, "The method of repeated readings," by S. Jay Samuels, is included here because it is the seminal article in this area and one that readers frequently request. It has had a profound impact in the field of reading instruction. The article provides a clear description of the procedures involved in repeated reading and sample data for a mentally retarded student reading five different passages. The effectiveness of repeated reading has been replicated with many different types of students of different abilities and ages. The concluding sentence, "the theoretical and empirical evidence leads us to believe that the method of repeated readings deserves to be more widely used as a technique for building fluency in reading," is strongly supported by the NRP Report.

"Speed does matter in reading," by Timothy V. Rasinski, gives a good explanation of the need for fluency and provides an overview of a number of techniques and procedures that teachers can use with dysfluent readers to improve their fluency. The author ends the article with a caveat, "Do not ignore reading rate."

"'I never thought I could be a star': A Readers Theatre ticket to fluency," by Miriam Martinez, Nancy L. Roser, and Susan Strecker, gives a more in-depth description of one of the techniques recommended by Rasinski—Readers Theatre. It provides an overview of the procedures, describes a weekly routine for implementation, and includes a list of books that are good prospects for Readers Theatre.

The final article in this section is "Be a good detective: Solve the case of oral reading fluency," by Meribethe Richards. The article again provides a sound rationale for fluency instruction and describes another set of activities for fluency instruction. The final section deals with the relationships between fluency and comprehension.

References

Allington, R.L. (1983). Fluency: The neglected goal. *The Reading Teacher*, *36*, 556–561.

Anderson, R.C., Wilson, P.T., & Fielding, L. (1988). Growth in reading and how children spend their time outside of school. *Reading Research Quarterly*, *23*, 285–303.

Vocabulary Development

> Vocabulary is stored information about the meanings and pronunciations of words necessary for communication.

Findings in the National Reading Panel Report

Children learned the meanings of most words indirectly, through everyday experiences with oral and written language.

Some vocabulary, particularly technical and very subject-specific words, was learned through direct instruction.

Quality vocabulary instruction led to gains in reading comprehension.

The following were found to be effective: keyword method, incidental learning, repeated exposure, preteaching of vocabulary, restructuring reading materials, context method.

Vocabulary development has a long history of study in relation to reading. There are five types of vocabulary:

- Listening vocabulary—the words needed to understand what is heard

- Speaking vocabulary—the words used when speaking

- Reading vocabulary—the words needed to understand what is read

- Writing vocabulary—the words used in writing

- Sight vocabulary—those words that can be identified without explicit decoding during reading

The NRP Report notes that the importance of vocabulary in reading achievement has been recognized for more than half a century. Many studies have shown that reading ability and vocabulary size are related. Early descriptions of reading comprehension viewed reading as consisting of two skills, word knowledge, or vocabulary, and reasoning in reading (Davis, 1944).

In early reading the reader translates the relatively unfamiliar words in print into more familiar speech forms of the words. If readers recognize and have meanings stored for the spoken forms (i.e., the word is in their speaking vocabulary), they gradually add such words to their reading vocabulary. Later in reading development, readers are able to add both pronunciations and meanings for words encountered first in print rather than in speech to their reading vocabulary.

Despite the fact that there are strong correlations between vocabulary size and reading achievement, it has been difficult to demonstrate that teaching vocabulary improves reading comprehension. The difficulty is probably related to the fact that vocabulary is learned both directly and indirectly. Estimates of how many words elementary children learn per year vary, but an estimate of over 2,000 words per year is quite reasonable (Nagy & Scott, 2000). Direct teaching of vocabulary cannot possibly account for the learning of so many words; however, research has shown that teaching of particular vocabulary such as technical words and words central to understanding narrative text can improve reading comprehension. It is clear, as the NRP Report specifically states, "vocabulary should be taught both directly and indirectly" (p. 4-27).

The first article in this section, "Vocabulary instruction in a balanced reading program," by William H. Rupley, John W. Logan, and William D. Nichols, provides an explanation of indirect vocabulary learning and presents a number of techniques for direct instruction of vocabulary. The article highlights concept wheel/circle, semantic word map, webbing, concept of definition, and semantic feature analysis.

The remaining four articles in this section are brief descriptions of particular vocabulary instructional strategies. "Word detectives," by Dodie Ainslie, addresses incidental learning of vocabulary and provides a strategy to encourage incidental learning. The strategy immerses children in reading while encouraging them to find out the meaning of unknown words. "Said Webs: Remedy for tired words," by Kathryn L. Laframboise, is an instructional technique specifically directed at developing synonyms for the overused word *said*. "Vocabulary anchors: Building conceptual connections with young readers," by Rod Winters, draws from strategies developed by upper grade content area teachers to help elementary teachers with strategies for dealing with technical vocabulary in informational prose. The final article, "Fun with vocabulary," by Janet Towell, uses a vocabulary acrostic to introduce enjoyable and effective strategies and activities for vocabulary instruction.

References

Davis, F.B. (1944). Fundamental factors in reading comprehension. *Psychometrika, 9*, 185–197.

Nagy, W.E., & Scott, J.A. (2000). Vocabulary processes. In M.L. Kamil, P.B. Mosenthal, P.D. Pearson, & R. Barr (Eds.), *Handbook of reading research* (Vol. 3, pp. 269–284). Mahwah, NJ: Erlbaum.

Comprehension Strategies

> *Reading comprehension is the construction of the meaning of a written text through a reciprocal interchange of ideas between the reader and the message in a particular text.*

Findings in the National Reading Panel Report

When readers were given cognitive strategy instruction, they made significant gains on measures of reading comprehension over students trained with conventional instruction procedures.

The following specific strategies were found to be effective—comprehension monitoring, cooperative learning, graphic organizers, story structure, question answering, question generating, summarization.

Teaching a variety of reading comprehension strategies in natural settings and content areas was most effective.

Comprehension is the essence of reading. Since the 1970s, researchers have developed a substantial body of knowledge about comprehension processes and strategies. The conceptualization of comprehension in this research departed from the previous conceptualizations of comprehension as the automatic byproduct of deciphering words. Rather, comprehension was thought of as intentional thinking during which meaning is constructed through the interactions between text and reader. This conceptualization of reading comprehension as the active construction of information led to the investigation of the strategies readers use in the construction process. As specific strategies were identified, researchers moved to investigating the explicit teaching of those strategies, and the research on single strategies indicated that the strategies could be taught and that they did improve reading comprehension. Next the field investigated whether combinations of strategies could be taught, and once again the answer was affirmative. Reciprocal teaching (Palincsar, David, Winn, & Stevens, 1991), direct explanation (Duffy, 1993), and transactional strategy instruction (Pressley et al., 1992) are examples of the multiple strategy approach. Most recently, researchers have focused on the effective preparation of teachers for teaching students to use effective comprehension strategies, such as summarizing, questioning, and comprehension monitoring.

The first article, "Supporting a strategic stance in the classroom: A comprehension framework for helping teachers help students to be strategic," by Sarah L. Dowhower, provides a framework and routines for incorporating multiple comprehension strategies in classroom instruction. It organizes instruction into three phases—prereading, active reading, and postreading—and provides direction for teachers in planning and implementing multiple comprehension strategies instruction that is consistent with the NRP Report.

The last three articles in this section—"Character Perspective Charting: Helping children to develop a more complete conception of story," by Timothy and Sherrell Shanahan; "Guidelines for implementing a graphic organizer," by Donna M. Merkley and Debra Jefferies;

and "Self-monitoring in beginning reading," by Robert M. Schwartz—are all examples of single-strategy instruction for strategies deemed effective in the NRP Report—story structure, graphic organizers, and self-monitoring. All give good direction for teachers to incorporate the teaching of single strategies in their instruction. These strategies also might be incorporated in multiple strategy comprehension instruction.

References

Duffy, G. (1993). Rethinking strategy instruction: Four teachers development and their low achiever's understandings. *The Elementary School Journal, 93*(3), 231–247.

Palincsar, A.S., David, Y.M., Winn, J.A., & Stevens, D.D. (1991). Examining the context of strategy instruction. *RASE: Remedial and Special Education, 12*(3), 43–53.

Pressley, M., El-Dinary, P.B., Gaskins, I., Schuder, T., Bergman, J., Almasi, J., & Brown, R. (1992). Beyond direct explanation: Transactional instruction of reading comprehension strategies. *The Elementary School Journal, 92*(5), 513–555.

Putting It All Together

The five essential components in the Reading First portion of the No Child Left Behind Act are based on the findings of the *Report of the National Reading Panel*. Each of the previous sections began with a brief summary of the findings related to one of the five essential components—phonemic awareness, phonics, reading fluency, vocabulary development, and comprehension strategies. Indeed, the findings of the panel document the positive effects of instruction in each of these areas on reading development.

The NRP Report provides a list of five specific types of instruction that "work." However, there is much that the report does not and cannot provide. This list is not an exhaustive list and the panel did not intend it to be exhaustive; they had limited time and resources and included in their topics those they believed to be most important. The panel members would be the first to acknowledge that although the report is important and worthy of serious consideration by all reading educators, it is not a prescription for providing good reading instruction.

An analogy may help: The five essential components are the equivalent of a list of ingredients. For some of the ingredients (phonemic awareness and phonics) there is information about the amounts (5–18 total hours for phonemic awareness and 2–3 years for phonics) and timing (pre-K–K for phonemic awareness and K–2 for phonics), but this information is lacking for the other components. The Report, because of its approach and organization, cannot provide the mixing and cooking instructions that will turn the list of ingredients into a successful reading program. A reading program that taught a rotation of lessons on the five essential components would be unsuccessful because instruction in these components must be combined in a coherent instructional design.

The articles included in this section emphasize the ways that skilled professionals incorporate the five essential components in coherent instructional designs. None of the articles refer to all five of the components and all the articles focus on more than one component. The first article, "Effective schools/accomplished teachers," by Barbara M. Taylor, P. David Pearson, Kathleen F. Clark, and Sharon Walpole, summarizes the results of a study designed to uncover the practices of effective teachers. The article highlights several findings. In relation to time, the findings show that in the most effective schools, teachers spent more time working with small groups. The NRP findings addressed small-group issues in some of the areas and found that small groups were effective—in some cases more effective than one-to-one instruction. Taylor et al. also report that the most effective and moderately effective schools spent more time in independent reading, adding to the correlational evidence that supports independent silent reading. The authors also found that in the area of phonics, explicit direct instruction of phonics was present in all the schools and that what distinguished the most effective schools was coaching in how to use phonics knowledge during reading. The observations of comprehension instruction indicated that the effective schools were distinguished by higher level comprehension questions.

"Singing and songwriting support early literacy instruction," by John A. Smith, describes activities organized around songs that teach letter names and sounds, phonemic awareness, print conventions, background knowledge and vocabulary, and word identification. The author describes familiar routines with whimsical songs that can provide opportunities for both direct instruction and practice.

In "Sharing informational text with young children," Ruth Helen Yopp and Hallie Kay Yopp share ways to incorporate informational text into the primary grade literacy program. They note that alphabet books can be used to help children learn letter names and sounds, support development of phonemic awareness, build vocabulary, and are an excellent environment for using comprehension strategies such as graphic organizers. They also provide an annotated bibliography of alphabet books.

In "'Doing' literature: Using drama to build literacy," Jennifer Catney McMaster suggests a number of drama activities that can be used to provide both direct instruction and practice related to the five essential components. For example, she explains how drama can be used for direct vocabulary instruction in ways that help students acquire definitions that go beyond surface verbalizations. She also writes about developing comprehension monitoring and mental imaging through the use of drama.

Linda D. Labbo, in "12 things young children can do with a talking book in a classroom computer center," lists activities that focus on several of the essential components. She explains how repeated reading can be integrated with computer technology; how word searches for similar letter-sound elements such as beginning sounds, vowel patterns, and syllable structures can be used to reinforce phonics; and how telling how one screen fits with other screens can encourage inferencing and the development of higher order thinking skills.

The final article, "Promoting reading comprehension, content learning, and English acquisition through Collaborative Strategic Reading (CSR)," by Janette K. Klingner and Sharon Vaughn, demonstrates another way to combine the essential components in teaching routines.

CSR specifically combines several of the strategies found effective by the panel, including cooperative learning with previewing, click and clunk, getting the gist, and wrapup.

In each of these articles, the authors have used some of the essential components and combined them in a coherent instructional design. The articles describe teaching routines or practices that allow for direct instruction and practice. Each of the articles provide examples of accomplished teachers' abilities to coordinate complex instructional needs and to facilitate systematic and explicit instruction in phonemic awareness, phonics, vocabulary development, reading fluency, and comprehension strategies. The provision of excellent reading instruction extends far beyond the teaching of five discrete components of reading. Teacher expertise is the most important component in excellent reading instruction (Jordan, Mendro, & Weerasinghe, 1997; Sanders & Rivers, 1996; Whitehurst, 2002). Skilled teachers go beyond the bounds of these articles to orchestrate activities and routines that are effective, efficient, and include the five essential components and more, with the goal of meeting the needs of all the children they teach.

References

Jordan, H.R., Mendro, R., & Weerasinghe, D. (1997, July). Teacher effects on longitudinal student achievement: A preliminary report on research on teacher effectiveness. Paper presented at the National Evaluation Institute, Indianapolis, IN.

Sanders, W., & Rivers, J. (1996). Cumulative and residual effects of teachers on future student academic achievement. Knoxville, TN: University of Tennessee Value-Added Research and Assessment Center.

Whitehurst, G.J. (2002, March). *Research on teacher preparation and professional development.* Paper presented at the White House Conference on Preparing Tomorrow's Teachers.

PART 2

Instructional Strategies and Curriculum Materials

Reading professional candidates must have a broad knowledge of instructional strategies and curriculum materials—the basic tools available to teachers for providing instruction. Appropriate selections of strategies and materials are a crucial determinate of a teacher's effectiveness. Teachers who are familiar with a wide range of instructional practices, approaches, methods, and curriculum materials, and who are capable of selecting those most appropriate for specific purposes and for children with specific needs, will be more effective. Standard 2 is as follows:

> **Candidates use a wide range of instructional practices, approaches, methods, and curriculum materials to support reading and writing instruction.**

This standard has three elements.

- **Element 2.1 Use instructional grouping options (individual, small-group, whole-class, and computer based) as appropriate for accomplishing given purposes.**

The Opitz (1998) and Hoeck-Buehler (2001) articles focus on the use of small groups for reading instruction. The first two pieces focus on ways to include children of different ability levels in the same group, and the third piece focuses on how to use and manage ability groups. The types of groups, mixed-ability and homogenous ability, can serve different purposes and provide different learning opportunities. Both types of groups can be used effectively.

The articles do not provide an example of whole-class instruction. Whole-class reading instruction is best used when all the children in the class need to learn the same thing—whether it be class routines or specific information related to a class project. The articles give a good picture of how teachers use different types of grouping to accomplish different purposes and to adjust instruction so that it is appropriate for each child.

Neither of the articles that correspond to Element 2.1 specifically addresses computer-based instruction. However, the Doherty (2003) article that appears later in Part 2 provides a good example of integrating computer-based reading instruction as a type of instructional grouping. The message that various types of grouping can be used to achieve various purposes, and that grouping practices play a crucial role in adapting instruction to particular children's needs, comes through clearly in this article.

- **Element 2.2 Use a wide range of instructional practices, approaches, and methods, including technology-based practices, for learners at differing stages of development and from differing cultural and linguistic backgrounds.**

This set of readings reflects the ambiguity of the term *instructional strategies*. That ambiguity is obvious in the standard that resorts to listing a set of terms that are often used to represent strategies—"practices, approaches, methods, and curriculum materials." The Duffy-Hester (1999) article captures the sense of "methods" or programs. She describes a number of different reading programs that some think of as methods and that actually involve an orchestration of instructional strategies through a set of instructional routines and activities. These programs provide a structure and a set of activities that accommodate children with differing abilities and differing cultural and linguistic backgrounds. At the end of the article, the author offers some general principles that ground these programs and that may be helpful to teachers in creating or adapting a reading program to meet the needs of the children in their classrooms.

The Fischer (1999/2000) article is included to address instructional strategies at the secondary level. The article gives an excellent overview of a master teacher orchestrating instructional strategies that allow her to meet the needs of all students.

The Tatum (2000) article presents an instructional framework specifically directed to providing excellent reading instruction to students he characterizes as disenfranchised African American adolescent readers in low-level tracts. He reports results of a study of 29 below grade level students of whom 25 were promoted to high school under the Chicago Public School's reform initiative requiring eighth-grade students to achieve a minimum grade-level equivalent of 7.0 on the Iowa Test of Basic Skills.

- **Element 2.3 Use a wide range of curriculum materials in effective reading instruction for learners at different stages of reading and writing development and from different cultural and linguistic backgrounds.**

The Doherty (2002) article provides a good example of using technology to meet the needs of diverse students. The piece reports on a project developed and implemented to give students the opportunity to learn critical technological literacy skills and become comfortable in a university setting. The Duffy-Hester article that appears earlier in Part 2 is also useful with respect to curriculum materials because the description of reading programs gives a good sense of the materials used in early reading instruction. The author discusses a wide variety of materials including trade books, commercial published readers, and specialized books including predictable texts (books that have repetitive patterns and strong picture clues) and decodable texts (books that include only the sounds that have been taught) that are important and useful in early reading programs. There are also references to nonfiction and multicultural literature. The Jenkins et al. (2003) article explains in more depth the rationale behind decodable text and how to locate these texts that are truly decodable given the reader's particular knowledge about sound–symbol relationships.

The Hefflin and Barksdale-Ladd (2001) article is an example of using appropriate children's literature in productive ways. Because reading professionals are predominantly white and middle class and the school population in the United States is increasingly diverse, reading professionals must seek out literature to meet the needs of children who are not "like them."

The Ivey (1999) article highlights the importance of access to books for struggling middle school readers. These readers like to read when they have access to materials that span a range of interests and difficulty levels. The piece provides middle schoolers' specific comments about books and the reasons for their appeal. The article also includes a bibliography of appealing books and information about where to find more.

It is important that readers view the articles in Part 2 as exemplars only. Standard 2 is the heart of instruction, and there are infinite examples of practices and materials. Not all topics could be included. However, the part does provide a model for the relationship between topics, practices, and materials and should help reading professionals identify positive examples of practices and materials for topics not addressed in the articles. The book *Evidence-Based Reading Instruction* (International Reading Association, 2002) also provides many more sound examples of practices and materials specific to the areas of phonemic awareness, phonics, reading fluency, vocabulary development, and comprehension.

REFERENCE

International Reading Association. (2002). *Evidence-based reading instruction: Putting the National Reading Panel report into practice*. Newark, DE: Author.

Text sets: One way to flex your grouping—in first grade, too!

Michael F. Opitz

Grouping children to teach reading is one of the most prevalent practices in schools today. It's a good thing because grouping has several advantages. For example, it enables students to learn from one another as they discuss ideas found in various texts. As a result of listening to and discussing with others, students often gain new insights. Grouping also better ensures that all students will participate. Because groups are usually small, students get the opportunity to share their thoughts.

While grouping in general is advantageous, sole use of ability grouping—the grouping of children according to like overall reading achievement levels—is not. In fact, this type of grouping yields several unintended consequences especially for the children viewed as "low" readers (see Opitz, 1997, for a full review of these consequences). For example, students in the "low" group are often asked to perform low-level tasks and have fewer opportunities to read and write. These students' self-concepts are lowered, and they often feel excluded from the class.

Fortunately, there are alternatives, and the purpose of this article is to explain one—text sets. I have deliberately chosen to focus on first grade because this is when most children begin to see themselves as readers. How important it is, then, to have all children experience the reading of real books right from the start. And how fortunate for the children that authors, illustrators, and publishers have made many excellent titles available for them.

Text sets

What are they?

Text sets are collections of books related to a common element or topic. Single copies of books are often used to create them, with each student reading a different book related to the topic. See the Figure for six sample text sets appropriate for use in first grade.

Why use them?

One of the main reasons for using text sets is that they enable all children to be exposed to "real" books right from the start. The result? Children see themselves as readers.

Moreover, using text sets enables children of different achievement levels to be grouped together to learn about a given topic, thereby warding off the stereotyping and other negative consequences of ability grouping.

Not only do text sets allow for heterogeneous groups, but they also permit the limited resources to be spread further. That is, because only one copy of each book is needed, a variety of books can be purchased rather than multiple copies of a single text.

How are they used?

Text sets are used during guided reading instruction. Once students are grouped, the teacher provides each student with one of the books and conducts the reading lesson. As with any effective guided reading lesson, the teacher provides guidance before, during, and after the reading.

Here's a sample framework:

Before reading

1. Activate background knowledge.
"Today we're going to read some books about gardening. What can you tell me about gardening?" As students share their ideas, they are written on the chalkboard or on a chart for future reference.

2. Set the purposes for reading.
"I have a book for each of you to read. When I give you your book, read the title and take a picture walk through the book. Be ready to tell the rest of us what you think your book will be about." Students are given a few minutes to complete this activity.

During reading

1. Explain to students what they will be doing.
"Now that you've had a chance to look through your book, please read it silently to see if you are right about your book. I'll be here to help you if you need it."

2. Have students read silently to see if their predictions were correct. Provide help as needed.
Note: Because some of the books will take longer to read, students could be provided with some additional activities if they finish reading before others in the group. Writing in a journal, drawing about their favorite part of the book, or reading another book are all viable activities.

After reading

1. Plan time for students to tell about their books. Also ask students what their books have in common. A comparison/contrast lesson in which students tell and list how their books are alike is a natural.

2. Complete additional follow-up activities as desired. Students could read a favorite part of their books or show a picture that they liked the best.

Getting ready

Thinking through the logistics of text sets before students arrive will better ensure their success and yours, too. Here are five suggested steps:

1. Identify the topic you want your students to explore. Ask students what they would like to learn more about.

2. Identify your students' general achievement levels. This can be done by using a set of graded passages or specific books that have been identified as "benchmark books."

3. Locate books with varying reading difficulty levels related to the topic. When determining levels, consider interest, levels of predictability (see Peterson, 1991), as well as appropriateness for your specific students and grade level.

4. Determine how many students you want to have in the group. I have found four or five to be ideal. Make sure that you have a "just right" book for each student—books that correspond to their overall achievement levels.

5. Organize your students into groups so that you can read with one group while the rest are completing other activities.

Concluding thoughts

As you attempt using the text sets shown here or those you create, remember that feeling comfortable with

Reprinted from *The Reading Teacher* (1998), 51, 622–624.

this way of teaching may take some time. This is true with almost any teaching strategy that is new to the repertoire. Take time to celebrate successes along the way.

References

Opitz, M. (1997). *Flexible grouping in reading: Practical ways to help all students become better readers.* New York: Scholastic.

Peterson, B. (1991). Selecting books for beginning readers and children's literature suitable for young readers. In D.E. DeFord, C.A. Lyons, & G.S. Pinnell (Eds.), *Bridges to literacy: Learning from Reading Recovery* (pp. 119 – 147). Portsmouth, NH: Heinemann.

Sample text sets

Alphabet

Grover, M. (1997). *The accidental zucchini.* San Diego, CA: Harcourt (Voyager). ISBN 0-15-201545-0.
McDonnell, F. (1997). *Flora McDonnell's A B C.* Cambridge, MA: Candlewick. ISBN 0-7636-0118-7.
Murphy, C. (1997). *Alphabet magic.* New York: Simon & Schuster. ISBN 0-689-81286-8.
Pomeroy, D. (1997). *Wildflower A B C.* San Diego, CA: Harcourt. ISBN 0-15-201-41-6.
Testa, F. (1997). *A long trip to Z.* San Diego, CA: Harcourt. ISBN 0-15-201610-4.

Animals

Duffy, D. (1996). *Forest tracks.* Honesdale, PA: Boyds Mills. ISBN 1-56397-434-7.
MacDonald, S. (1997). *Peck, slither, slide.* San Diego, CA: Harcourt. ISBN 0-15-200079-8.
Sturges, P. (1996). *What's that sound, wooly bear?* Boston: Little, Brown. ISBN 0-316-82021-0.
Threadgall, C. (1996). *Animal families.* New York: Crown. ISBN 0-517-88548-4.

Counting

Bohdal, S. (1997). *1, 2, 3 What do you see?* New York: North-South. ISBN 1-55858-646-6.
Cousins, L. (1997). *Count with Maisy.* Cambridge, MA: Candlewick. ISBN 0-7636-0156-X.
Sierra, J. (1997). *Counting crocodiles.* San Diego, CA: Harcourt. ISBN 0-15-200192-1.
Tucker, S. (1996). *1, 2, 3 Count with me.* New York: Simon & Schuster. ISBN 0-689-80828-3.

Gardening

Cole, H. (1995). *Jack's garden.* New York: Greenwillow. ISBN 0-688-13501-3.
Florian, D. (1991). *Vegetable garden.* San Diego, CA: Harcourt. ISBN 0-15-201018-1.
Ford, M. (1995). *Sunflower.* New York: Greenwillow. ISBN 0-688-13301-0.
Lobel, A. (1990). *Alison's zinnia.* New York: Greenwillow. ISBN 0-688-08865-1.
Peterson, C. (1996). *Harvest year.* Honesdale, PA: Boyds Mills. ISBN 1-56397-571-8.

Relationships

Bogacki, T. (1997). *I hate you! I like you!* New York: Farrar, Straus, Giroux. ISBN 0-374-33544-3.
Fox, M. (1997). *Whoever you are.* San Diego, CA: Harcourt. ISBN 0-15-200787-3.
Kroll, V. (1997). *Hands.* Honesdale, PA: Boyds Mills. ISBN 1-56397-051-1.
Neitzel, S. (1997). *We're making breakfast for mother.* New York: Greenwillow. ISBN 0-688-14575-2.
Yolen, J. (1997). *Nocturne.* San Diego, CA: Harcourt. ISBN 0-15-201458-6.

Shapes

Dodds, D. (1994). *The shape of things.* Cambridge, MA: Candlewick. ISBN 1-56402-224-2.
Falwell, C. (1992). *Shape space.* New York: Clarion. ISBN 0-395-61305.
Grover, M. (1996). *Circles and squares everywhere!* San Diego, CA: Harcourt. ISBN 0-15-200091-7.
MacDonald, S. (1994). *Sea shapes.* San Diego, CA: Harcourt. ISBN 0-15-200027-5.
Merriam, E. (1995). *The hole story.* New York: Simon & Schuster. ISBN 0-671-88353-4.

Let's play tag! A technique for successful mixed-ability group reading

Susan Hoeck-Buehler

I was searching for a way to involve my mixed-level, third-grade readers more effectively in literature or author studies without limiting their choice of texts. I had noticed that weaker readers' interest flagged when book choices were limited to literature within their independent reading level range. I wanted to be able to use the modeling and cooperative work opportunities that mixed-ability grouping offered, but I didn't want the reading assignments to become a chore. I found that many of my weaker readers had a well-developed listening vocabulary to tap into if I could find a way to use it. As I tried out different ideas to improve my lessons I stumbled onto a very simple idea, which I dubbed Tag Reading. It was a hit with students of all reading abilities and met my goals for reading participation.

I found Tag Reading to have the following benefits:

- It is easy to learn.
- It enables the teacher to offer a greater variety of books to the whole group, thereby increasing student motivation and providing more options for instructional resources.
- It increases success and participation in mixed-ability groups.
- It requires the students to stay connected to the reader's voice as well as to the text in order to hold their place in the text and maintain fluency.
- It gives feedback on difficult or new words as the students hear and see the words within a meaningful context.
- It works well with groups from two children up to about six.
- It enables students to participate more effectively and knowledgeably because they have all met reading goals and are prepared to begin whatever follow-up the teacher has prepared.
- It reduces slower readers' frustration.
- It is easily taught to parents and tutors.

- It can be used to help students conquer longer texts or to read high-interest books that are too difficult for them to read without assistance.
- It encourages participation and feelings of success.
- It's fun!

With Tag Reading, no one was singled out as needing reading support; all students were focused on the text and didn't feel embarrassed when they encountered an unknown word—the students simply "tagged off."

Ready!

In literature circles I offered several book options that met my literature teaching goals and of which I had been able to find multiple copies. For example, when studying characterisation I chose books by Roald Dahl. *The Magic Finger* (Puffin, 1987); *The Giraffe, the Pelly and Me* (Puffin, 1985); *The BFG* (Viking Peguin, 1985); *The Twits* (Peguin, 1997); *The Enormous Crocodile* (Puffin, 1978); *James and the Giant Peach* (Puffin, 1988); *Fantastic Mr. Fox* (Knopf, 1970); *Charlie and the Chocolate Factory* (Puffin, 1995); *Charlie and the Great Glass Elevator* (Knopf, 1972); *George's Marvelous Medicine* (Puffin, 1982); *Danny the Champion of the World* (Puffin, 1984); and *Matilda* (Knopf, 1994) were all available in usable quantities. Dahl wrote books at many different levels of sophistication and reading difficulty, with strongly developed characters, so they suit my purpose well. His books are popular, so many students could add additional copies from home to the ones I was able to glean from the school library and from colleagues. They also have not been adapted for a United States audience as many British books have been. Therefore, vocabulary stayed consistent. I teach at an international school in Germany, so students' home libraries are filled with books from a variety of English-speaking countries, and adaptation is an issue.

To get us started, I gave a book talk for each book. The students then chose a book to study based on interest, reading level, or other criteria. Students who chose the same book formed a literature circle. They set a schedule with teacher guidance and received a teacher-made set of discussion starter questions and a menu of possible response activities to choose from, prepare, and present to the class. Students were also encouraged to come up with response ideas of their own to submit for teacher approval.

I borrowed some of the organisation format for my literature groups from the book *Grand Conversations: Literature Groups in Action* (Peterson & Eeds, 1994). Using modifications of forms from *Grand Conversations*, each group recorded its participation in the sessions. Students created a rubric for good participation, supportive behavior, and preparedness to use with the literature circles. They rated their own work as weak, good, or excellent at the end of the session for each criterion. In addition I kept anecdotal notes while circulating, observing, and participating in group work and used the same rubric for feedback to students, evaluation, and record keeping. We finished off the Roald Dahl characterisation unit with a class study of his biography, *Boy*, and found plenty of reflections of the villainous characters from his books in the descriptions of his own experiences. Tag Reading was used as literature circles read all or parts of the text together.

Get set!

To tag read, the group sits in a tight circle, and one student begins to read. The rest of the group follows along, each in his or her own book. Some of my students need to use their fingers to track the text effectively or to help them stay focused. The first reader tags another random student to carry on by tapping him or her on the knee. The trick is to keep the text flowing as if one voice were reading. Students can also choose to tag off in the middle of a word, such as after a syllable or before a suffix, to make the tag off more playful.

While teaching the Tag Reading technique, I joined the circle. Initially, all students tagged off to me, and I controlled who would be tagged next. As the students took over more control I would sometimes tag (tap) the student reading and begin to read before tagging off to another child who had been left out in order to ensure that all children

Reprinted from *The Reading Teacher* (2001), 54, 477–478.

were getting a turn. This is called tagging away, and helped to emphasise taking turns at reading. I found that this was no longer necessary once the children were used to Tag Reading. Tagging away can be useful if a student is reading too long and needs to be encouraged to tag more often or if you want to head off a rough passage for an insecure reader. If there are not enough strong readers in a group the teacher can become part of the circle and have the children tag off to him or her for the rough parts and then can tag them back on passages they can read more successfully.

The children soon caught on and invented elaborations. Weaker readers could tag off as soon as they hit a tricky word and could control the length of the section they read. We kept the atmosphere playful, and the children soon learned to see that everyone was tagged and to keep a steady, natural reading pace. My students began to create their own variations; Tag Reading leaked into partner reading, subject reading, and homework. One pair of boys even worked out a system to tag read on the telephone. Many parents expressed pleasure at seeing their reluctant readers choosing to read at home.

Go!

Tag Reading requires the well-developed listening vocabulary, good sense of story language and sequencing, and prediction skills typical of older, more experienced readers. It is therefore less helpful for younger children who have not yet had enough experience with book language. I recommend Tag Reading as an ideal technique for stress-free reading from Grade 3 on up. Tag Reading gives weaker readers access to more complex literature and enables them to work more effectively with a cooperative, mixed-ability learning group. In my class, students using Tag Reading demonstrated higher motivation; completed their reading tasks without reminders; and participated more actively in discussions, activities, and presentations. They were able to support their opinions by referring to the text more often and had a better grasp of the sequence of story events when preparing their reading response activities. Tag Reading was definitely a success in my third-grade class. It is simple to learn and simple to apply, so give it a try.

Reference

Peterson, R., & Eeds, M. (1994). *Grand conversations: Literature groups in action.* New York: Scholastic.

Ann M. Duffy-Hester

Teaching struggling readers in elementary school classrooms: A review of classroom reading programs and principles for instruction

This article examines model reading programs for struggling readers in which instruction is delivered in the students' regular classrooms. The author also proposes a set of guidelines or principles for developing such programs.

What are the components of elementary school classroom reading programs that promote the reading growth of students with reading difficulties? What are the strengths of these programs, and how can these strengths be used to help educators design or implement other effective reading programs? In this article, I address these questions. The purpose of this article is to discuss six classroom programs that improve the reading growth of elementary school struggling readers and to derive principles for instruction from these programs, other reading research, and my experiences as a reading educator. Through this discussion, I intend to provide information other educators can use to design and implement their own reading instructional programs that work within their particular teaching environments.

Elementary school classroom teachers are increasingly expected to take the crucial and primary role of accelerating the reading growth of elementary school struggling readers (e.g., Walmsley & Allington, 1995), a shift from the

Reprinted from *The Reading Teacher* (1999), 52, 480–495.

previous reliance upon compensatory and special education teachers to teach children with reading difficulties (e.g., McGill-Franzen, 1994). Thus, this review of research-based elementary school classroom reading programs that have been described in the literature as effective in improving the reading growth of struggling readers seems warranted. Although other reviews of such literature have described reading instructional models (e.g., Stahl & Hayes, 1997); combinations of classroom reading programs, tutoring programs, literacy tools and materials, and small-group reading supplements or interventions (Allington & Walmsley, 1995; Hiebert & Taylor, 1994a); elements of effective reading tutoring programs (Juel, 1996; Wasik & Slavin, 1993); components of effective reading programs, program supplements, and interventions for first-grade students struggling in reading (Pikulski, 1994); and characteristics of Reading Recovery that can be used as guidelines for other remedial reading programs (Spiegel, 1995), no one review has looked exclusively at elementary school classroom reading programs that support the reading growth of struggling readers.

Struggling readers in regular classroom reading programs

Why should the reading growth of struggling readers be supported in the context of elementary school regular classroom reading programs? First, many students struggling in reading do not qualify for special or compensatory education support services because of the differing criteria used in various school districts for student entry into these programs or the lack of sufficient funding in some school districts for support programs (Spear-Swerling & Sternberg, 1996; Wang, Reynolds, & Walberg, 1988). Second, even if struggling readers do receive reading support through special or compensatory education programs, the majority of their teacher-directed reading time still occurs in the regular classroom reading program (Allington & McGill-Franzen, 1989; Cunningham & Allington, 1994; Haynes & Jenkins, 1986; O'Sullivan, Ysseldyke, Christenson, & Thurlow, 1990). Third, most remedial and special education support programs have not proven to be effective in accelerating the reading growth of struggling readers (e.g., Johnston & Allington, 1991;

Walmsley & Allington, 1995). Fourth, support programs that are effective in accelerating the reading growth of struggling readers, such as Reading Recovery (e.g., Pinnell, Lyons, DeFord, Bryk, & Selzer, 1994) or small-group interventions (e.g., Hiebert, 1994a), are not available for all children, as they are designed to support limited numbers of students (Baumann & Ivey, 1997), and may not be sufficiently effective to accelerate and maintain the reading growth of struggling readers over time (Center, Wheldall, Freeman, Outhred, & McNaught, 1995; Hiebert, 1994b; Shanahan & Barr, 1995).

In short, struggling readers need more than effective short-term interventions; they also need effective reading instruction in their regular classroom programs (Hiebert & Taylor, 1994b). Exemplary classroom programs cannot always ensure that all children will become proficient readers (Slavin, 1996), but they can dramatically reduce the number of children who are currently classified as reading disabled or remedial readers.

Although the need exists for elementary school classroom teachers to support the growth of struggling readers, a recent national survey of elementary school teachers revealed that many were unsure of how to meet the needs of readers who struggle. Many teachers stated that teaching struggling readers was one of their greatest challenges (Baumann & Duffy, 1996). Many preservice or inservice teacher education programs do not provide teachers adequate training in designing classroom environments that support students with disabilities in reading and related areas (e.g., Fisher, Sax, & Pumpian, 1996). Additionally, few comprehensive and concrete models of classroom programs that support the growth of all students, including struggling readers, have been provided for teachers (e.g., Hiebert, 1991; Loucks-Horsley & Roody, 1990; Schirmer, Casbon, & Twiss, 1995). Thus, additional research on the instruction of struggling readers in classroom reading programs seems necessary.

A review of elementary school classroom reading programs

In this section, I describe six elementary school classroom reading programs: the Book Club Program, Concept-Oriented Reading Instruction, Fluency-Oriented Reading Instruction, the Four Blocks Approach, the Kamehameha Early Education Program Whole Literacy Curriculum, and Success for All. I do not attempt to discuss all programs designed for or implemented with elementary school struggling readers. Rather, the programs I selected were ones that I concluded (a) have been described in recent literature as being effective in promoting the reading growth of elementary school

---

A recent national survey of elementary school teachers revealed that many were unsure of how to meet the needs of readers who struggle.

---

struggling readers; (b) were implemented in diverse, multiple, public school classrooms; (c) provided a complete description of the overall reading program structure; (d) were based on reading research and practice; and (e) included a detailed account of the progress of struggling readers as it was explained by the program developers and researchers through qualitative and/or quantitative measures of student success in these programs.

Book Club Program (BCP)

The BCP is implemented in a variety of ways and modified based on student and teacher needs. Current versions of the BCP (e.g., Goatley, Brock, & Raphael, 1995; McMahon, Raphael, Goatley, & Pardo, 1997) have four common components:

Community Share. Community Share takes place in a whole-class context. In this component, teachers often review reading or discussion strategies, summarize texts they have read out loud to the class, preview new texts, read a new book or selection aloud, allow students to share or discuss their small-group or individual readings, and help students to make connections between their books in discussions. Through this component, students join a community of readers and writers.

Reading. Teachers and students read texts for different purposes and in a variety of ways. Teachers and students sometimes read books or portions of texts out loud to other class members. At other times, students read silently to themselves or with other members of their discussion group the texts they will be using. Students also read self-selected texts to themselves during independent reading times. Teachers meet with small groups or individual children to provide them with explicit instruction in reading based on students' needs (e.g., in comprehension or discussion strategies) or curriculum requirements. Teachers select the books students read in their discussion groups, often giving students some choice about what texts to read. Students select their own texts to read during independent reading periods. For teachers using the BCP as the organizational structure for their entire reading program, trade books are the sole materials used for the reading component.

Writing. During this component, students write for brief (e.g., writing in response or reading logs) and extended (e.g., writing stories or informational texts) periods of time. The writing prepares students for discussions of texts and extends their thinking about these texts. Students write for their own purposes and for purposes set by the teacher.

Book Club. This is the heart of the BCP. In Book Club, diverse groups of students discuss a common text in small groups. These discussions are primarily student led and take place along with extended teacher and student instruction and modeling of discussion techniques and behaviors.

The BCP is used primarily as the organizational structure for the entire reading program (and thus is included in this review), although some teacher-researchers (e.g., Grattan, 1997) use the BCP as one component of their overall reading program. The BCP has been implemented in elementary and secondary classrooms. One of the strengths of the BCP is its broad theoretical base. The program draws on sociocultural perspectives (e.g., Vygotsky, 1978), research on discursive practices (e.g., Cazden, 1988; Gee, 1990), and reader response theories (e.g., Rosenblatt, 1983). In addition, BCP is described clearly and thoroughly, allowing other educators to learn from and build on these descriptions (Wells, 1997). Finally, BCP provides opportunities for students to work both independently and with others on authentic literacy tasks, while at the same time providing explicit instruction in reading strategies, creating a motivating yet supportive literacy environment.

Concept-Oriented Reading Instruction (CORI)

In CORI (e.g., Guthrie, McGough, Bennett, & Rice, 1996; Guthrie, Van Meter, McCann, Anderson, & Alao, 1996), an integrated approach to teaching reading, writing, and science implemented in diverse third- and fifth-grade classrooms, teaching and learning proceed in four phases:

Observe and personalize. In this phase, teachers provide students opportunities to observe occurrences and objects in nature, with students formulating questions from these observations. The student-developed questions are used as the basis for students' future literacy-related activities.

Search and retrieve. Here, students learn how to locate texts and information within texts to answer the questions they previously formulated. Students learn how to use strategies such as goal forming, organizing, locating relevant and important information, and gaining a general understanding of material when using resources to answer their questions.

Comprehend and integrate. Next, students learn various comprehension, notetaking, and analysis strategies in order to help understand and integrate the information they are reading to answer their questions. In addition, students learn various "fix-up" strategies to help them if they encounter difficulties when reading and synthesizing information.

Communicate to others. In this final phase, students present the information they learned to their peers through communications such as written reports, oral presentations, and artistic endeavors. Through these communications, students develop a sense of audience in reading and writing.

CORI occurs in the context of thematic units, which are developed around science instructional goals, objectives, and processes. Trade books are used extensively, with science textbooks used on occasion for reference purposes. The main purpose of the program is to improve students' science and literacy engagement.

CORI is broad based, drawing on theories of conceptual learning, reading strategy instruction, motivation, and integrated instruc-tion. Descriptions of CORI provide a needed, concrete example of how to implement an integrated curriculum and suggest principles that other educators can use to create engaging classroom literacy programs. CORI uses "real-world" events and objects as the basis for instruction, thus creating an authentic purpose for teaching literacy and science strategies.

Fluency-Oriented Reading Instruction (FORI)

The primary objective of the FORI (e.g., Stahl, Heubach, & Cramond, 1997) program is to help children become fluent readers so they can focus on text comprehension. To achieve this objective, the authors developed five goals for their program: (a) to keep the focus of reading lessons on students' comprehension of text, (b) to have students read material on their instructional reading levels, (c) to support students in their reading of instructional level text through repeated readings, (d) to provide opportunities for children to engage in text-based social interactions through partner reading, and (e) to expand the amount of time children spend reading at home and school. To accomplish these goals, the authors designed and helped to implement a reading program through three main components:

Redesigned basal reading lesson. In this component, the teacher reads the selected basal story out loud to the class, and teachers and students discuss the story using such tools as story maps, questioning, or graphic organizers. Depending on the difficulty level of the selected story, the teacher echo reads the story with either a small group of students who need extra assistance or with the whole class if the story is particularly difficult. Then, students read the selection with a partner; usually, students select their own partners for reading. Finally, students respond to the text through journals or dramatizations.

Home reading. In this segment, students read basal selections to themselves or with a family member and also read books of their choice. The intent of this segment is to increase the amount of time children spend reading and to extend their reading beyond the school day.

Free-choice reading period. During free-choice reading, students read self-selected books independently and with partners. This reading takes place in a scheduled 15- to 20-minute independent reading time period, as well as after students complete their assignments during the day.

FORI was implemented in 14 diverse second-grade classrooms in two different elementary schools over the course of 2 years. The program is unique in that it combines several research-based elements of effective reading instruction into a coherent classroom structure that can be readily implemented by elementary classroom teachers; indeed, many teachers who implemented this program with the researchers continue to use this program. Finally, the program has as its focus an often-neglected aspect of reading instructional programs: developing fluent readers (Allington, 1983a).

Four Blocks Approach (FBA)

The FBA (e.g., Cunningham & Hall, 1997; Cunningham, Hall, & Defee, 1998; Hall & Cunningham, 1996; Hall, Prevatte, & Cunningham, 1995) has evolved and expanded over 8 years of development and implementation. It began in first- and second-grade classrooms and now is being implemented in kindergarten and upper elementary classrooms (although only the first- and second-grade program implementations will be included in this review). In recent descriptions of the FBA program, literacy instruction takes place in the context of "four blocks" of time:

Guided reading block. Instruction in this block occurs in a variety of ways. In some classrooms, teachers choose two selections per week from basal readers, trade books, big books, magazines, or other reading materials. One of these selections is written on grade level, and the other selection is written below grade level. Students read the selections several times individually, with a partner, or in small groups. Before and after reading, students are involved in whole-group comprehension instruction, discussions, or response activities.

In other classrooms, students choose from several sets of trade books within a common theme or genre, and then read and discuss these books in small groups. The texts students read are intended to be on or close to their instructional reading levels. After the small-group readings, a whole-class discussion that ties together common elements of the small-group discussions takes place.

In addition, teachers initiate daily, 10-minute "easy reading support groups" in which struggling and nonstruggling readers are included. Different students meet in these groups every day, with struggling readers included more often in these groups than nonstruggling readers. In these groups, students read materials that are written on their instructional levels.

Self-selected reading block. This block begins with the teacher reading a book out loud to the class. Then students choose texts from a variety of genres written on differing difficulty levels and then read these books to themselves. While the students are reading, the teacher is listening to and conferring with several children and taking anecdotal notes. At the end of this block, several students share what they were reading with other class members.

Writing block. In the writing block, the teacher models writing for students, beginning with a minilesson that focuses on various aspects of writing. Then students write independently on topics of their own choosing, moving through the various stages of the writing process (e.g., prewriting, drafting, revising, editing, or publishing). The teacher holds individual conferences with several children daily. At the end of this block, several students share their writing with other members of the class.

Working with words block. In this block, students learn how to read and spell high-frequency words, and to decode and spell other words. These goals are accomplished in several ways. To learn how to spell and read high-frequency words, the teacher displays approximately five new high-frequency words a week on the class Word Wall. Both old and new Word Wall words are reviewed in a variety of ways. The Word Wall is maintained all year, with students using these words in other blocks. Words that include common spelling patterns or that are used frequently are placed on the Word Wall. To help students learn how to decode words, several activities are implemented, including "Rounding up the Rhymes," "Making Words" (Cunningham & Cunningham, 1992; Cunningham & Hall, 1994), and "Guess the Covered Word." (See Cunningham et al., 1998, for a description of these activities.)

The FBA program is unique in two respects. First, the program combines several ways of teaching reading into one program. Realizing that children learn to read in different ways, teachers using this program attempt to teach all children to read by combining several methods of teaching reading into a cohesive yet diverse framework for reading instruction. Second, the program strives to provide instruction that is multilevel; specifically, within each of the instructional blocks, activities are included for readers on varying levels of proficiency.

Perhaps one of the greatest strengths of this program is that it provides a concrete, instructional model for elementary school teachers to use when implementing their reading instructional programs. As Cunningham and Hall (1997) reflected,

> The last eight years have been exciting and satisfying years for us. We have seen the four blocks framework implemented in hundreds of classrooms in diverse settings, with varied populations of children. This framework is based on research but has few revolutionary ideas. It provides teachers a way to implement a balanced program and more nearly meet the needs of children with a range of levels who do not all learn in the same way. (p. 28)

The Kamehameha Early Education Program (KEEP) Whole Literacy Curriculum

Recent characterizations of KEEP (e.g., Au, 1997; Au & Carroll, 1997; Carroll, Wilson, & Au, 1996) use six aspects of literacy as the base for instruction and program design:

- Ownership of reading and writing.
- Reading comprehension.
- The writing process.
- Language and vocabulary knowledge.
- Word-reading strategies and spelling.
- Voluntary reading. (Au & Carroll, 1997, pp. 204–205)

These literacy aspects are used to create a program used with Native Hawaiian students in kindergarten through Grade 6 that includes readers' and writers' workshops, portfolio assessment, and established literacy benchmarks for student success. Grounded in social constructivist thinking and sociocultural perspectives on literacy, this program combines the explicit teaching of reading skills and strategies with literacy experiences meaningful for Native Hawaiian students (e.g., "overlapping talk" structures, in which students' and teachers' conversations overlap, as is the common mode of discourse in many Native Hawaiian students' homes). Teachers participate in ongoing staff development opportunities prior to and during their implementation of this program.

KEEP was designed to help Native Hawaiian children develop higher levels of literacy. As many challenges faced by Native Hawaiian students are similar to challenges faced by other nonmainstream students (Au, 1997), some aspects and design principles of KEEP may be effective with other groups of students as well.

Success For All (SFA)

SFA (e.g., Slavin, Madden, Dolan, & Wasik, 1996) is a comprehensive school restructuring program that includes tutoring; family support services; and, recently, instruction in writing/language arts, mathematics, social studies, and science. For purposes of this review, only the K–5 regular classroom English reading program is described. The program utilizes materials often found in elementary schools (e.g., basal readers and children's literature) as well as commercial materials related to the program (e.g., a detailed SFA teacher's manual that outlines how teachers are to implement all aspects of the program). Although varying somewhat from school to school, there are three basic types of reading programs within SFA: (a) the preschool or early kindergarten program, (b) the Beginning Reading or Reading Roots program, and (c) the Beyond the Basics or Reading Wings program.

The preschool or early kindergarten program is implemented in the preschool program or during the first semester in kindergarten and "uses a thematically based curriculum that is intended to develop oral language, literacy, listening skills, numeracy, creative expression, and positive self-esteem" (Slavin et al., 1996, p. 98). In addition to thematic units and learning center activities, this program contains four reading instruction components:

Story telling and retelling (STaR). In this component, the teacher selects a piece of children's literature that may be related to a thematic unit and reads this story out loud to the class. Intended to develop young children's oral language and comprehension abilities, STaR includes six activities: (a) *story introduction*, in which the teacher tells the students something about the book to be read, discusses some of the challenging vocabulary students will hear, and elicits students' predictions about the text; (b) *interactive story reading*, in which the teacher reads the story out loud to children while questioning them about the story and summarizing key text elements as needed; (c) *story structure review*, in which the teacher reviews the story with the students using summary questions; (d) *group story retelling or individual story conference*, in which students retell the story in groups with props and visual aids or individually retell the story to the teacher or teaching assistant; (e) *story critique*, in which students are encouraged to give their opinions about the story the teacher reads; and (f) *story extension activities*, in which students make personal responses to the story through art, music, cooking, or journals.

Emergent writing. In this component, children are encouraged to write, with the teacher accepting students' various forms of writing and providing opportunities for students to further develop their writing abilities.

Rhyme with reason. The purpose of this component is to develop students' phonemic awareness. Rhyme with reason is based on seven aspects of phonemic awareness, including hearing ending rhymes, producing beginning sounds, and segmenting syllables.

Shared book experience. Teachers and students share in the reading of a common big book. The teacher models various print concepts for children through this experience.

Peabody Language Development kit. With this kit, the teaching assistant works with small groups of children to increase their receptive and expressive language skills. While one group is working with the teaching assistant, the other children are working in center activities that are related to the thematic unit.

Alphabet activities. Teachers present various letters of the alphabet to children throughout the day and review letters through rereading alphabet books. Students use and see the letters on which they are working during morning activities, as part of their center work, and during STaR time.

The Beginning Reading or Reading Roots program usually begins in the second half of the kindergarten year and continues until students reach the primer level of reading. Students are grouped across grade levels based on their reading levels to participate in this reading program. In addition to a listening comprehension component similar to the STaR

activity and a Peabody unit similar to the Peabody Language Development kit activities described above, students in this program engage in 50-minute "shared story" lessons. There are five basic components to the shared story lessons, and activities within these components vary across the school year:

Showtime (reading rehearsal and letter formation review). Students begin by rereading a familiar book or story in order to practice reading and build fluency. Then the teacher directs a review of letter formation and sound-symbol correspondence, giving students oral directions on how to write letters and telling students letter sounds. Later in the year, the teacher reviews words and sentences the students read previously.

Thinking about reading. Students learn how to use metacognitive reading strategies. They learn four basic comprehension strategies: setting purposes for reading, previewing, monitoring, and summarizing. Students apply these strategies in their reading.

Presenting the story. The teacher reads a selected story out loud to the class. She or he provides background information about the story, asks questions, and elicits predictions from the students.

Sound, letter, and word development activities. In this component, students are taught to

> discriminate sounds in language and to know the shapes of the letters and the sounds they represent. The lessons are designed to begin with the isolation of specific sounds within the context of meaningful language; then, to teach sound/letter correspondence using a wide variety of practice techniques; and, finally, to apply those techniques directly to the words to be read in the story. (Slavin, Madden, Dolan, & Wasik, 1996, p. 18)

These goals are accomplished by having students sing the alphabet song, engaging students in games that focus on phonemic awareness and letter formation, and having students identify words beginning with various letter-sound correspondences.

Story activities. Before students read the story selection, they practice decoding and recognizing various high-frequency and other words that they will encounter in their reading. Using a shared story text with the teacher reading part of the story and the students reading mostly phonetically regular words or words with rebus clues, the students read the story with the whole class and then with a partner.

After reading, the students practice spelling words they read in the story. At the conclusion of this component, two students read a portion of the story aloud to the class.

The Beyond the Basics or Reading Wings program begins when students are reading on a first-grade level and continues through the elementary school years. Adapted from the Cooperative Integrated Reading and Composition (CIRC) program (e.g., Stevens, Madden, Slavin, & Farnish, 1987), Beyond the Basics groups students across grade levels based on their reading levels, as they were in the Beginning Reading or Reading Roots program. Students work mainly with cooperative learning groups or with partners in this program, which has four main components:

Story-related activities. After the teacher introduces the story to students, preteaches story vocabulary, reviews decoding skills, sets purposes for student reading, and builds students' background knowledge, students read the selection silently and then with partners. Partners correct each other's reading errors and answer story structure questions. Partners also work with each other to pronounce and define vocabulary words from the reading selection and quiz each other on a weekly spelling list. At the end of this component, students take a comprehension test on the story.

Direct instruction in reading comprehension. Students learn comprehension skills that include finding main ideas, comparing and contrasting, and drawing conclusions. Students complete reading worksheets to use these skills.

Independent reading. Students are encouraged to check out a book from the classroom library to read at home. Students complete book reports based on their reading and share these reports with the class.

Listening comprehension. Teachers read various books or stories aloud to the class during this component. Teachers model comprehension skills and literary analyses in conjunction with the text reading.

The key premise of the SFA program is that students should be prevented from experiencing reading difficulties. Students receive the support they need to become proficient readers; for example, students are assessed every 8 weeks to determine whether they should attend a different reading group or if they need tutorial or family support services to improve their reading abilities. SFA is usually implemented in high-risk elementary schools with large proportions of students living in poverty.

Principles for designing elementary school classroom reading programs that support the reading growth of struggling readers

All of the elementary classroom reading programs I reviewed were successful to varying degrees and in different ways in supporting the reading growth of struggling readers. Drawing on the unique strengths I found in each of the programs, my own experiences as a former elementary school classroom teacher and reading specialist, and selected substantive theories related to elementary school reading instruction, I suggest 10 guiding principles for designing or implementing elementary school classroom reading programs that support the growth of struggling readers:

1. *A reading program should be balanced, drawing on multiple theoretical perspectives.* Many definitions and examples of balanced literacy instructional programs have been described in the literature (e.g., Baumann & Ivey, 1997; Johns & Elish-Piper, 1997; McIntyre & Pressley, 1996). A balanced reading program may include not only a balance of teaching methods, but also a balance of theoretical perspectives. All of the reviewed programs included this balance of perspectives; for example, CORI is based on theories of conceptual learning, comprehension, integrated instruction, and motivation.

Goodman (1992) has criticized eclectic approaches to reading instruction, stating that "eclecticism, taking useful bits and pieces from here and there, is probably the best policy for teachers who have a sense of what they don't like but who don't have a well articulated belief system and knowledge base" (p. 361). Nevertheless, implementing a balanced or eclectic reading program should not imply a lack of theoretical grounding. As Stahl (1997) explained, "principled eclecticism is what good teachers have always done. This eclecticism is not just 'a little of this and a little of that,' nor is it the result of teachers' failure to commit to a particular philosophy" (p. 25).

How can teachers implement reading programs based on a principled mix of theoretical perspectives? Duffy (1997) detailed how excellent teachers accomplish this goal through "conceptual selectivity" in which teachers "never follow a single program, theory, model, or philosophy, nor do they play a single role or employ one set of materials to the exclusion of others. Instead, the best teachers draw thoughtfully from various sources, play many roles and use many techniques and materials" (p. 360). Through implementing balanced reading instruction programs based on theoretical perspectives within and outside the field of reading education, we are more likely to support the reading and overall literacy growth of the children we teach, particularly children who struggle with reading.

2. *There should be a practical and theoretical justification for every component and element in the reading program.* Cunningham (1997) stated that a reading instructional program is not balanced unless every part of it has a unique justification that is supported by teacher experience and research. Building on this view, I suggest that not only should every part or component of the reading instructional program be justified theoretically and practically, but also every activity or element within the component should have instructional and theoretical merit. For example, the FBA manages the reading instructional time to maximum advantage by arranging literacy instruction in four blocks of instruction.

Educators often feel pressed to "make every minute count" in the school day. By engaging children in program elements that have instructional and theoretical merit rather than requiring struggling readers to participate in low-level tasks that do not contribute to their reading growth, as often happens in the reading instruction of struggling readers (e.g., Allington, 1983b), the reading needs of more students could be better supported in regular classroom reading programs.

3. *The explicit teaching of word identification, comprehension, and vocabulary strategies may take place in conjunction with authentic reading and writing tasks.* Debate continues not so much on whether to teach phonics, vocabulary, and comprehension strategies, but rather on how and when to teach them. Some whole language advocates state that reading skills and strategies should be taught only when students show the need to

learn them through the use of minilessons. Some advocates of balanced literacy instruction explain that the explicit teaching of reading skills and strategies should occur, but only within the context of reading and writing. However, these "teachable moments" may simply not arise for all the reading skills and strategies that students need to learn (e.g., Baumann, 1991), or the teacher may not recognize or be able to teach children reading skills or strategies when they show this need (Spiegel, 1992) perhaps due to the complexities of teaching in diverse regular classrooms. Additionally, phonics, comprehension, or vocabulary minilessons that take place only in the context of reading and writing experiences may not be sufficient to teach struggling and nonstruggling readers what they need to know to become more proficient readers.

Often, students need extended, explicit, or direct instruction to learn how to use particular reading skills and strategies in addition to the unplanned, teachable moments that may arise (Durkin, 1990). This extended teaching may be *connected* to what students are reading or writing, but may not necessarily be *integrated* into these authentic experiences. For example, Trachtenburg (1990) detailed how this kind of teaching can be accomplished through teaching phonics via a "whole-part-whole" strategy.

The FBA program utilizes this principle often, particularly in the Working with Words block. Making Words, for example, begins with the teacher choosing a "big word" from a text the students will read, proceeds to students making words from this "big word" and sorting those words, continues with the students reading the text from which the "big word" came, and ends with students using the word patterns employed in the Making Words lesson in their future reading and writing. In SFA much explicit phonics instruction occurs in connection with student and teacher reading.

If reading skills and strategies are sometimes taught explicitly and in conjunction with rather than in the context of authentic reading and writing events, struggling readers could learn more successfully needed reading skills and strategies as well as the connection of these skills and strategies to their own reading and writing.

4. *On a daily basis, teachers should read aloud to students from a variety of genres and*

create opportunities for students to read instructional and independent level texts. Within their framework for early literacy learning, Fountas and Pinnell (1996) described how teachers can create opportunities for students to engage in reading and listening to a variety of texts. Through the elements of reading aloud, guided reading, shared reading, and independent reading, students hear quality literature read to them (reading aloud), read materials written on their instructional level with teacher guidance and minimal support (guided reading), read materials that may be too difficult for them to read independently with the support of other students and the teacher (shared reading), and read easy materials (independent reading). In so doing, students receive a balanced "literacy diet" (e.g., Abouzeid, 1997) that is likely to result in all students, including struggling readers, making progress in their reading and writing growth.

Many of the programs I described afforded students opportunities to read diverse texts in a variety of ways. For example, in the FORI program, students were read to, read texts with partners during the modified basal reader lesson, and read texts independently during the free-choice reading period. There are many ways to design a classroom reading program to enable students to listen to and read a variety of texts, and the programs I reviewed offer several good examples of how to accomplish this goal.

5. *Reading instruction should be informed by and based on meaningful reading assessments.* FORI, KEEP, and the FBA utilized meaningful reading assessments such as informal reading inventories, portfolios, and anecdotal records to inform instruction. For example, KEEP benchmarks provided a way for teachers to document the reading skills or strategies students used well and those skills that needed focused instruction. In many reading programs, instruction is based not on students' needs as revealed through meaningful reading assessments, but rather on a prescribed scope and sequence of reading materials, skills, and strategies as dictated by basal reader teacher editions, curriculum guides, or commercial reading programs (e.g., Duffy, 1997). For struggling readers to make optimal progress, reading instruction must be responsive to their needs rather than based on a fixed scope and sequence.

By using meaningful assessments to inform reading instruction on students' instructional levels, more struggling readers could be supported in regular classroom reading programs. As Gill (1992) concluded, "Lots of reading in materials that can be read with accuracy and fluency, lots of writing, and direct help with those features appropriate for each child when needed—these have been the necessary and sufficient circumstances for children for many generations" (pp. 451–452).

6. *Teachers should be decision makers, using their practical, personal, and theoretical knowledge to inform their reading instruction.* There is no single prescribed or published reading program that meets the needs of all readers, as all teachers and students have unique strengths and needs and are members of distinct and diverse communities of readers and writers that they form with one another. Therefore, although teachers should use published research to inform the design of their reading programs, their implementation of these programs must also be paired with their practical knowledge of and beliefs about the best ways to teach reading to students (Vacca, Vacca, & Gove, 1995). Aspects of reflective teachers' reading programs change over the course of the school year as they decide what students learned and what they still need to learn to become more proficient readers, and whether the teaching and the instructional environment they created was helping students to improve their reading.

In many of the classroom programs I reviewed, teachers adapted the established reading programs to meet their own needs and preferences as well as the reading needs of their students. For example, Grattan (1997) adapted the BCP because the program was not meeting the reading needs of her first- and second-grade students. When teachers are decision makers in their own classrooms, using research-based reading programs, materials, and tools along with their knowledge of what works with the children they are teaching, struggling readers in particular stand to benefit. As Duffy (1997) explained, "the best literacy instruction is provided by independent, enterprising, entrepreneurial teachers who view instructional models as ideas to be adapted rather than as tenets to be followed" (p. 351).

7. *Staff development for preservice and practicing teachers of reading may include providing opportunities for teachers to reflect on their practice.* One of the greatest strengths of the BCP is that it is continually evolving and supports teachers in becoming "reflective practitioners" (e.g., Schon, 1987). Rather than teachers attending a staff development session to learn about how to implement a particular reading program and then being expected to implement the program verbatim, BCP teachers learn how to make the program work for themselves and their students by trying out aspects of the program in their own classrooms, reflecting on how the program works, and modifying the program based on what they learn through their reflections.

Although there is research that addresses how to support practicing and preservice teachers in becoming reflective educators (e.g., Clark, 1988; Clark & Yinger, 1987; Duffy, 1991; McCarthey et al., 1994), this research suggests ways to promote reflective teaching and was not intended to focus on the context of teaching; that is, teachers working with diverse students, including struggling readers, in actual classrooms over time. Perhaps through providing teachers with concrete models or frameworks of theoretically based reading programs in preservice or inservice educational opportunities and then encouraging teachers to undertake teacher research (e.g., Baumann, Bisplinghoff, & Allen, 1997) or engage in formative experiments (e.g., Newman, 1990; Reinking & Pickle, 1993; Reinking & Watkins, 1996) to explore how to modify and expand these programs in ways congruent with their own teaching situations, teacher educators can begin to make the elusive and needed link between research and practice related to teaching struggling readers.

8. *Reading programs may be based on multiple goals for student success.* Several of the programs I reviewed set and achieved, with varying degrees of success, different goals for students, such as improving their reading motivation, discursive practices, reading fluency and automaticity, word identification, comprehension, vocabulary, and reading of increasingly difficult texts. As a recent national survey of elementary school teachers reveals, most teachers do set multiple instructional goals for their reading programs (Baumann & Duffy, 1996).

Programs that focus on a variety of reading goals are more likely to produce engaged readers who are skilled and strategic, motivated, socially interactive, and knowledgeable (e.g., Alvermann & Guthrie, 1993). In FORI, for example, the researchers set five program goals and designed their program to enable the students enrolled to reach these goals. Reading instructional programs that expect struggling and nonstruggling readers to achieve multiple goals for reading instruction are likely to produce students who can and will read. Early and Ericson (1988) stated, "for all students, the ultimate goal must be: 'I can read it myself—and I will'" (p. 42). To achieve this ultimate goal, eclectic goals for elementary school classroom reading programs that support struggling readers must be established and achieved.

9. *Reading programs may provide multiple contexts for student learning.* Hiebert and Fisher (1991) suggest two classroom structures that form the core of classroom literacy programs: *task* structures, or what students are doing, and *talk* structures, or the discourse that occurs among students and between students and teachers. These factors transcend arguments over the "best" approaches to teaching reading (J. Baumann, personal communication, April 29, 1997) and focus instead on the design of optimal talk and task structures that benefit students with diverse literacy needs within the context of classroom reading programs.

In most of the programs I reviewed, students participated in diverse learning tasks and multiple talk structures. As students learn to read in different ways (e.g., Erickson, 1991), students in these programs are provided with varied opportunities to engage in reading in the classroom program. For example, in the KEEP program, students participate in "overlapping talk" as well as more traditional talk structures, and engage in a variety of reading tasks in reading and writing workshops. As Hiebert and Fisher (1991) concluded, "rather than attempting to identify a single best approach to literacy instruction, we argue for attending to the distributions of task and talk structures and for turning these distributions to local pedagogical contexts" (p. 153).

10. *Reading programs should be designed to support the reading growth of all children, both struggling and nonstruggling readers.* In all of the programs I reviewed, both struggling and nonstruggling readers made progress in their reading abilities. Although admittedly not easy to accomplish, our goal as reading educators must be to design and implement reading programs flexible and diverse enough to accelerate the reading growth of all children (e.g., Spear-Swerling & Sternberg, 1996).

Strickland (1994) proposed guidelines for the effective literacy instruction of African American children who are at risk for school failure, and concluded that these guidelines "are learner centered and thus adapt to and support all learners, no matter who they are" (p. 334). I conclude that this same idea holds true in classroom reading instructional programs that support the growth of struggling readers: Quality reading instructional programs for struggling readers may be based on the same principles as programs for nonstruggling readers. It is within these programs and principles that instruction must be individualized to meet the specific reading needs of each child. However, if what Strickland (1994) and I are describing is "just good teaching," then why, as Ladson-Billings (1995) asks, "does so little of it seem to occur in classrooms populated by African-American students?" (p. 484), or, in the case of my review, in so many elementary school regular classrooms where there are struggling readers? This question leads me to some concluding questions and concerns related to teaching struggling readers.

Questions and concerns

I am left with three questions regarding teaching struggling readers in elementary classrooms: (a) Do we as educators have the will to teach all children, including struggling readers, to read? (b) What should count as success for struggling readers in the elementary classroom reading program? and (c) What is the relationship between reading research and practice, particularly as it relates to struggling readers? As is the case with all aspects of this review, these concerns are influenced by my experiences as a former elementary teacher, my values regarding the importance of accelerating the reading growth of struggling readers, and the theoretical perspectives on which my research and teaching interests are based (i.e., balanced literacy instructional programs, reading teacher education, and the literacy environments of struggling readers).

First, I question whether the will truly exists to teach all children to read. Hilliard (1991) explained that the predominant problem we face in education may rest on how we

Removing students from the regular classroom and placing them in resource rooms for special or compensatory education services prevents classroom teachers from realizing that something is wrong with the instruction in their own classroom.

answer the question "Do we truly will to see each and every child in this nation develop to the peak of his or her capacities?" (p. 36). Several studies (e.g., Baker & Zigmond, 1990; Schumm & Vaughn, 1991; Zigmond, Jenkins, Fuchs, Deno, & Fuchs, 1995) suggest that some regular classroom teachers are not willing to make accommodations or modifications for students with disabilities (e.g., learning disabilities) in their classrooms, as they are committed to their established teaching structures and routines and find making adaptations for students with disabilities difficult. Skrtic (1995) explained that this resistance to change the regular classroom program may be due to organizational structures in the educational system:

> Structurally, schools are nonadaptable at the classroom level because professionalization ultimately results in convergent thinking. Given a finite repertoire of skills, students whose needs fall outside a teacher's standard practices must be forced into them, or forced out of general education classrooms and into the special education system (or one of the other special needs programs such as compensatory, bilingual, migrant, or gifted education). (p. 213)

The mere existence of special education, compensatory education, and even early intervention tutoring programs such as Reading Recovery often serves to reduce regular classroom teachers' feelings of responsibility toward supporting the reading growth of struggling readers, instead placing the responsibility of teaching these students on the resource teachers, or even placing the blame for children's lack of reading success on the children themselves or their families (e.g., Allington, 1991a; Dudley-Marling & Murphy, 1997). Skrtic (1995) explained that removing students from the regular classroom and placing them in resource rooms for special or compensatory education services prevents classroom teachers from realizing that something is wrong with the instruction in their own classrooms, hence strengthening "teachers' belief in both the validity of their conventional practices and the notion that school failure is a human pathology" (p. 213).

Do we expect all children to learn to read well? Allington (1991c) argued that it is educators' beliefs or "conventional wisdoms" regarding the potential and instruction of struggling readers that limit these students' successes in reading. Building on a study by Winfield (1986), Allington (1991a) concluded that "teachers who believe in children's potential as learners and who accept responsibility for children's learning are more likely to offer children more and better instruction than teachers who do not share these beliefs" (p. 247).

Morris, Ervin, and Conrad (1996) detailed how a classroom teacher enrolled in a reading education course where she tutored Brett, a struggling middle school reader, changed her thinking about struggling readers after she accelerated the reading growth of this student. As she explained, "In many ways I have changed after working with Brett. Certainly, I have learned things from the tutoring experience, but more important I have come to believe even more strongly that it is never too late to help a child learn to read" (p. 377). We need to instill the confidence, knowledge, and will in preservice and practicing teachers to teach struggling readers. A starting point to achieving this goal may be to create opportunities for teachers to teach one child to read successfully.

Second, I question what should count as success for struggling readers in elementary classroom reading programs. For example, McLeskey and Waldron (1995), in an article describing how success for students with learning disabilities (which are often reading based; see Spear-Swerling & Sternberg, 1996) should be measured in inclusive classrooms,

state that "any objective observer would judge as an unqualified success a program in which two-thirds of the students are gaining ground on their non-learning disabled peers" (p. 302). Allington (1991b) posited that success in reading "must be cast more broadly than group achievement test scores" (p. 25).

In the programs I reviewed, the success of struggling readers was described in various ways. All of the programs I reviewed were described in the literature as being successful in supporting the reading growth of struggling readers, but none, regardless of how it defined success for struggling readers, enabled every child to succeed. I am left with the sobering question of whether "success for all" struggling readers in classroom reading programs is really possible; indeed, perhaps a more realistic goal for elementary school classroom reading programs should be "success for most" children if based on the quality reading instruction they receive in the regular classroom reading program, but "success for all" children if based on exemplary classroom programs combined with outstanding reading support services.

In sum, we need both the *will* and the *skill* to teach all students to read well. As McGill-Franzen and Allington (1991) concluded,

> It is a question of will. We know how to accelerate the literacy development of low achieving children.... We can organize our schools so that all children are entitled to literacy.... It will require changing not only the way we teach, but also our beliefs about the capabilities of low achieving children. It will require both more and better instruction than is available in the regular education program today. (p. 28)

Finally, I question the relationship between reading research and practice. I am convinced that the teacher is more important and has a greater impact that any single, fixed, reading program, method, or approach. It is through reading about and analyzing exemplary reading programs such as the ones I described in this article that educators can induce their own principles of reading instruction, create their own frameworks for teaching reading, and discover for themselves what aspects of extant programs work and do not work in accelerating the reading growth of the struggling readers in their own classrooms.

I believe that good teachers base their instructional decisions, in part, on reading research and theory; likewise, the reading research I value has practical applications and implications.

Alvermann (1990) stated that "reading teacher education lacks status as a topic in the field of reading research" (p. 698). It is time to change this situation, move beyond the political rhetoric that has become almost commonplace in our field, and work toward conducting research that truly moves reading educators along in their thinking about and implementation of reading curricula and instruction that support struggling readers. As Dixon and Carnine (1994) concluded, "when ideological rhetoric is set aside, mainstream educational researchers' (and other educators') best hope for advancing the field might be realized through our commitment to develop and verify the best possible curricular and instructional practices" (p. 364).

Where do we go from here? Erickson (1991) summed up the basic conclusion I draw from my review of exemplary elementary school reading programs that support struggling readers:

> In human literacy learning and teaching there are many differing ladders, many ways to climb, many kinds of powers in climbing, and an amazing capacity in human learners of all ages to climb on more than one ladder at once. How to organize schools genuinely for diversity in literacy, treating its multidimensionality as a resource rather than a liability and providing various ways to climb high, is a challenge we continue to face as educators and citizens. (p. x)

May we as reading educators begin to climb our literacy ladders together. By analyzing and reflecting on existing, research-based classroom reading programs such as the ones included in this review and creating new programs based on meaningful reading research and principles of exemplary reading instructional practices, I hope that more educators can and will design and implement reading instructional environments that better meet the needs of all children.

References

Abouzeid, M. (1997, September). *Teaching and learning strategies for student literacy in elementary schools.* Paper presented at the Northeast Georgia Regional Educational Service Agency Conference, Athens, GA.

Allington, R.L. (1983a). Fluency: The neglected reading goal. *The Reading Teacher, 36,* 556 – 561.

Allington, R.L. (1983b). The reading instruction provided readers of differing reading ability. *Elementary School Journal, 83,* 549 – 559.

Allington, R.L. (1991a). Children who find learning to read difficult: School responses to diversity. In E.H. Hiebert (Ed.), *Literacy for a diverse society: Perspectives, practices, and social policies* (pp. 237 – 252). New York: Teachers College Press.

Allington, R.L. (1991b). Effective literacy instruction for at-risk children. In M. Knapp & P. Shields (Eds.), *Better schooling for the children of poverty: Alternatives to conventional wisdom* (pp. 9 – 30). Berkeley, CA: McCutchan.

Allington, R.L. (1991c). The legacy of "slow it down and make it more concrete." In L. Zutell & S. McCormick (Eds.), *Learner factors/teacher factors: Issues in literacy research and instruction* (pp. 19 – 29). Chicago: National Reading Conference.

Allington, R.L., & McGill-Franzen, A. (1989). School response to reading failure: Instruction for Chapter I and special education students in grades two, four, and eight. *Elementary School Journal, 89,* 529 – 542.

Allington, R.L., & Walmsley, S.A. (Eds.). (1995). *No quick fix: Rethinking literacy programs in America's elementary schools.* New York and Newark, DE: Teachers College Press and International Reading Association.

Alvermann, D.E. (1990). Reading teacher education. In W.R. Houston, M. Haberman, & J. Sikula (Eds.), *Handbook of research on teacher education: A project of the Association of Teacher Educators* (pp. 687 – 704). New York: Macmillan.

Alvermann, D.E. & Guthrie, J.T. (1993). *Themes and directions of the National Reading Research Center* (Perspective No. 1). Athens, GA and College Park, MD: National Reading Research Center.

Au, K.H. (1997). A sociocultural model of reading instruction: The Kamehameha elementary education program. In S.A. Stahl & D.A. Hayes (Eds.), *Instructional models in reading* (pp. 181 – 202). Mahwah, NJ: Erlbaum.

Au, K.H., & Carroll, J.H. (1997). Improving literacy achievement through a constructivist approach: The KEEP demonstration classroom project. *Elementary School Journal, 97,* 203 – 221.

Baker, J.M., & Zigmond, N. (1990). Are regular education classes equipped to accommodate students with learning disabilities? *Exceptional Children, 56,* 515 – 526.

Baumann, J.F. (1991). Of rats and pigeons: Skills and whole language. *Reading Psychology, 12,* iii – xiii.

Baumann, J.F., Bisplinghoff, B.S., & Allen, J. (1997). Methodology in teacher research: Three cases. In J. Flood, S.B. Heath, & D. Lapp (Eds.), *Handbook of research on teaching literacy through the communicative and visual arts* (pp. 121 – 143). New York: Simon & Schuster Macmillan.

Baumann, J.F., & Duffy, A.M. (1996, December). *Elementary teachers' descriptions and evaluations of classroom and school reading programs.* Paper presented at the annual meeting of the National Reading Conference, Charleston, SC.

Baumann, J.F., & Ivey, G. (1997). Delicate balances: Striving for curricular and instructional equilibrium in a second-grade, literature/strategy-based classroom. *Reading Research Quarterly, 32,* 244 – 275.

Carroll, J.H., Wilson, R.A., & Au, K.H. (1996). Explicit instruction in the context of the readers' and writers' workshops. In E. McIntyre & M. Pressley (Eds.), *Balanced instruction: Strategies and skills in whole language* (pp. 39 – 63). Norwood, MA: Christopher-Gordon.

Cazden, C. (1988). *Classroom discourse: The language of teaching and learning.* Portsmouth, NH: Heinemann.

Center, Y., Wheldall, K., Freeman, L., Outhred, L., & McNaught, M. (1995). An evaluation of Reading Recovery. *Reading Research Quarterly, 30,* 240 – 263.

Clark, C.M. (1988). Asking the right questions in teacher preparation: Contributions of research on teacher thinking. *Educational Researcher, 17,* 5 – 12.

Clark, C.M., & Yinger, R.J. (1987). Teacher planning. In J. Calderhead (Ed.), *Exploring teachers' thinking* (pp. 84 – 103). London: Cassell Education Limited.

Cunningham, J.W. (1997). *What balance is and isn't and how to achieve it*. Paper presented at the 42nd annual convention of the International Reading Association, Atlanta, GA.

Cunningham, P.M., & Allington, R.L. (1994). *Classrooms that work: They can all read and write*. New York: HarperCollins.

Cunningham, P.M., & Cunningham, J.W. (1992). Making words: Enhancing the invented spelling-decoding connection. *The Reading Teacher, 46*, 106–115.

Cunningham, P.M., & Hall, D.P. (1994). *Making words*. Carthage, IL: Good Apple.

Cunningham, P.M., & Hall, D.P. (1997, May). *A framework for literacy in primary classrooms that work*. Paper presented at the 42nd annual convention of the International Reading Association, Atlanta, GA.

Cunningham, P.M., Hall, D.P., & Defee, M. (1998). Nonability-grouped, multilevel instruction: Eight years later. *The Reading Teacher, 51*, 652–664.

Dixon, R., & Carnine, D. (1994). Ideologies, practices, and their implications for special education. *Journal of Special Education, 28*, 356–367.

Dudley-Marling, C., & Murphy, S. (1997). A political critique of remedial reading programs: The example of Reading Recovery. *The Reading Teacher, 50*, 460–468.

Duffy, G.G. (1991). What counts in teacher education? Dilemmas in educating empowered teachers. In J. Zutell & S. McCormick (Eds.), *Learner factors/teacher factors: Issues in literacy research and instruction* (pp. 1–17). Chicago: National Reading Conference.

Duffy, G.G. (1997). Powerful models or powerful teachers? An argument for teacher-as-entrepreneur. In S.A. Stahl & D.A. Hayes (Eds.), *Instructional models in reading* (pp. 351–365). Mahwah, NJ: Erlbaum.

Durkin, D. (1990). Dolores Durkin speaks on instruction. *The Reading Teacher, 43*, 472–476.

Early, M., & Ericson, B.O. (1988). The act of reading. In B.F. Nelms (Ed.), *Literature in the classroom: Readers, texts, and contexts* (pp. 31–44). Urbana, IL: National Council of Teachers of English.

Erickson, F. (1991). Foreword. In E.H. Hiebert (Ed.), *Literacy for a diverse society: Perspectives, practices, and social policies* (pp. vii–x). New York: Teachers College Press.

Fisher, D., Sax, C., & Pumpian, I. (1996). From intrusion to inclusion: Myths and realities in our schools. *The Reading Teacher, 49*, 580–584.

Fountas, I.C., & Pinnell, G.S. (1996). *Guided reading: Good first teaching for all children*. Portsmouth, NH: Heinemann.

Gee, J.P. (1990). *Social linguistics and literacies: Ideology in discourses*. London: Falmer.

Gill, J.T. (1992). Development of word knowledge as it relates to reading, spelling, and instruction. *Language Arts, 69*, 444–453.

Goatley, V.J., Brock, C., & Raphael, T.E. (1995). Diverse learners participating in regular education "book clubs." *Reading Research Quarterly, 30*, 352–380.

Goodman, K.S. (1992). Why whole language is today's agenda in education. *Language Arts, 69*, 54–363.

Grattan, K.W. (1997). They can do it too! Book club with first and second graders. In S.I. McMahon, T.E. Raphael, V.J. Goatley, & L.S. Pardo (Eds.), *The book club connection* (pp. 267–283). New York and Newark, DE: Teachers College Press and International Reading Association.

Guthrie, J.T., McGough, K.M., Bennett, L., & Rice, M.E. (1996). Concept-oriented reading instruction: An integrated curriculum to develop motivations and strategies for reading. In L. Baker, P. Afflerbach, & D. Reinking (Eds.), *Developing engaged readers in school and home communities* (pp. 165–190). Mahwah, NJ: Erlbaum.

Guthrie, J.T., Van Meter, P., McCann, A., Anderson E., & Alao, S. (1996). *Does concept-oriented reading instruction increase motivation, strategies, and conceptual learning?* (Research Report No. 66). Athens, GA and College Park, MD: National Reading Research Center.

Hall, D.P., & Cunningham, P.M. (1996). Becoming literate in first and second grades: Six years of multimethod, multilevel instruction. In D.J. Leu, C.K. Kinzer, & K.A. Hinchman (Eds.), *Literacies for the 21st century* (pp. 195–204). Chicago: National Reading Conference.

Hall, D.P., Prevatte, C., & Cunningham, P.M. (1995). Eliminating ability grouping and reducing failure in the primary grades. In R.L. Allington & S. Walmsley (Eds.), *No quick fix: Redefining and reforming instructional support programs for at-risk students* (pp. 137–158). Newark, DE and New York: International Reading Association and Teachers College Press.

Haynes, M.C., & Jenkins, J.R. (1986). Reading instruction in special education resource rooms. *American Educational Research Journal, 23*, 161–190.

Hiebert, E.H. (1991). Literacy contexts and literacy processes. *Language Arts, 68*, 134–139.

Hiebert, E.H. (1994a). A small-group literacy intervention with Chapter I students. In E.H. Hiebert & B.M. Taylor (Eds.), *Getting reading right from the start: Effective early literacy interventions* (pp. 85–106). Boston: Allyn & Bacon.

Hiebert, E.H. (1994b). Reading Recovery in the United States: What difference does it make to an age cohort? *Educational Researcher, 23*, 15–25.

Hiebert, E.H., & Fisher, C.W. (1991). Task and talk structures that foster literacy. In E.H. Hiebert (Ed.), *Literacy for a diverse society: Perspectives, practices, and policies* (pp. 141–156). New York: Teachers College Press.

Hiebert, E.H., & Taylor, B.M. (Eds.). (1994a). *Getting reading right from the start: Effective early literacy interventions*. Boston: Allyn & Bacon.

Hiebert, E.H., & Taylor, B.M. (1994b). Interventions and the restructuring of American literacy instruction. In E.H. Hiebert & B.M. Taylor (Eds.), *Getting reading right from the start: Effective early literacy interventions* (pp. 201–217). Boston: Allyn & Bacon.

Hilliard, A. (1991). Do we have the will to educate all children? *Educational Leadership, 49*, 31–36.

Johns, J.L., & Elish-Piper, L. (1997). (Eds.), *Balanced reading instruction: Teachers' visions and voices*. Dubuque, IA: Kendall/Hunt.

Johnston, P., & Allington, R. (1991). Remediation. In R. Barr, M.L. Kamil, P. Mosenthal, & P.D. Pearson (Eds.), *Handbook of reading research* (Vol. II, pp. 984–1012). New York: Longman.

Juel, C. (1996). What makes literacy tutoring effective? *Reading Research Quarterly, 31*, 268–289.

Ladson-Billings, G. (1995). Toward a theory of culturally relevant pedagogy. *American Educational Research Journal, 32*, 465–491,

Loucks-Horsley, S., & Roody, D.S. (1990). Using what is known about change to inform the regular education initiative. *Remedial and Special Education, 11*, 51–56.

McCarthey, S.J., Hoffman, J.V., Stahle, D., Matherne, D., Elliot, B., Dressman, M., & Abbott, J. (1994). "Very sweet, but very very slow": How teachers' "ways of knowing" are reflected in their assumptions about students. In C.K. Kinzer & D.J. Leu (Eds.), *Multidimensional aspects of literacy, research, theory, and practice* (pp. 507–516). Chicago: National Reading Conference.

McGill-Franzen, A. (1994). Compensatory and special education: Is there accountability for learning and belief in children's potential? In E.H. Hiebert & B.M.

Taylor (Eds.), *Getting reading right from the start: Effective early literacy interventions* (pp. 13 – 35). Boston: Allyn & Bacon.

McGill - Franzen, A., & Allington, R.L. (1991). The grid - lock of low reading achievement: Perspectives on practice and policy. *Remedial and Special Education, 12*, 20 – 30.

McIntyre, E., & Pressley, M. (1996). *Balanced instruction: Strategies and skills in whole language*. Norwood, MA: Christopher - Gordon.

McLeskey, J., & Waldron, N.L. (1995). Inclusive elemen - tary programs: Must they cure students with learning disabilities to be effective? *Phi Delta Kappan, 77*, 300 – 303.

McMahon, S.I., Raphael, T.E., Goatley, V.J., & Pardo, L.S. (Eds.). (1997). *The book club connection: Literacy learning and classroom talk*. New York and Newark, DE: Teachers College Press and International Reading Association.

Morris, D., Ervin, C., & Conrad, K. (1996). A case study of middle school reading disability. *The Reading Teacher, 49*, 368 – 377.

Newman, D. (1990). Opportunities for research on the orga - nizational impact of computers. *Educational Researcher, 19*(3), 8 – 13.

O' Sullivan, P.J., Ysseldyke, J.E., Christenson, S.L., & Thurlow, M.L. (1990). Mildly handicapped elementary students' opportunity to learn during reading instruc - tion in mainstream and special education settings. *Reading Research Quarterly, 25*, 131 – 146.

Pikulski, J.J. (1994). Preventing reading failure: A review of five effective programs. *The Reading Teacher, 48*, 30 – 39.

Pinnell, G.S., Lyons, C.A., DeFord, D.E., Bryk, A.S., & Seltzer, M. (1994). Comparing instructional models for the literacy education of high - risk first graders. *Reading Research Quarterly, 29*, 8 – 39.

Reinking, D., & Pickle, M. (1993). Using a formative ex - periment to study how computers affect reading and writing in classrooms. In D.J. Leu & C.K. Kinzer (Eds.), *Examining central issues in literacy research, theory and practice* (pp. 263 – 270). Chicago: National Reading Conference.

Reinking, D., & Watkins, J. (1996). *A formative experiment investigating the use of multimedia book reviews to increase elementary students' independent reading*. Athens, GA and College Park, MD: National Reading Research Center.

Rosenblatt, L.M. (1983). *Literature as exploration*. New York: Modern Language Association of America.

Schirmer, B.R., Casbon, J., & Twiss, L.L. (1995). Inclusion of children with disabilities in elementary school class - rooms. *The Reading Teacher, 49*, 66 – 68.

Schon, D.A. (1987). *Educating the reflective practitioner*. San Francisco: Jossey - Bass.

Schumm, J.S., & Vaughn, S. (1991). Making adaptations for mainstreamed students: General classroom teach - ers' perspectives. *Remedial and Special Education, 12*, 18 – 27.

Shanahan, T., & Barr, R. (1995). Reading Recovery: An independent evaluation of the effects of an early in - structional intervention for at - risk learners. *Reading Research Quarterly, 30*, 958 – 996.

Skrtic, T.M. (1995). Special education and student dis - ability as organizational pathologies: Toward a metatheory of school organization and change. In T.M. Skrtic (Ed.), *Disability and democracy: Reconstructing (special) education for postmodernity* (pp. 190 – 232). New York: Teachers College Press.

Slavin, R.E. (1996). Neverstreaming: Preventing learning disabilities. *Educational Leadership, 53*, 4 – 7.

Slavin, R.E., Madden, N.A., Dolan, L.J., & Wasik, B.A. (1996). *Every child, every school: Success for all*. Thousand Oaks, CA: Corwin.

Spear - Swerling, L., & Sternberg, R.J. (1996). *Off - track: When poor readers become "learning disabled."* Boulder, CO: Westview Press.

Spiegel, D.L. (1992). Blending whole language and system - atic direct instruction. *The Reading Teacher, 46*, 38 – 44.

Spiegel, D.L. (1995). A comparison of traditional remedi - al programs and Reading Recovery: Guidelines for success for all programs. *The Reading Teacher, 49,* 86 – 96.

Stahl, S.A. (1997). Instructional models in reading: An in - troduction. In S.A. Stahl & D.A. Hayes (Eds.), *Instructional models in reading* (pp. 1 – 29). Mahwah, NJ: Erlbaum.

Stahl, S.A., & Hayes, D.A. (Eds.). (1997). *Instructional models in reading*. Mahwah, NJ: Erlbaum.

Stahl, S.A., Heubach, K., & Cramond, B. (1997). *Fluency - oriented reading instruction* (Research Report No. 79). Athens, GA and College Park, MD: National Reading Research Center.

Stevens, R.J., Madden, N.A., Slavin, R.E., & Farnish, A.M. (1987). Cooperative integrated reading and com - position: Two field experiments. *Reading Research Quarterly, 21*, 433 – 454.

Strickland, D.S. (1994). Educating African - American learners at risk: Finding a better way. *Language Arts, 71*, 328 – 336.

Trachtenburg, P. (1990). Using children's literature to en - hance phonics instruction. *The Reading Teacher, 43*, 648 – 654.

Vacca, J.A.L., Vacca, R.T., & Gove, M.K. (1995). *Reading and learning to read* (3rd ed.). New York: HarperCollins.

Vygotsky, L.S. (1978). *Mind in society: The development of higher mental psychological processes*. Cambridge, MA: Harvard University Press.

Walmsley, S.A., & Allington, R.L. (1995). Redefining and reforming instructional support programs for at - risk students. In R.L. Allington & S.A. Walmsley (Eds.), *No quick fix: Rethinking literacy programs in America's el - ementary schools* (pp. 19 – 44). New York and Newark, DE: Teachers College Press and International Reading Association.

Wang, M.C., Reynolds, M.C., & Walberg, H.J. (1988). Integrating the children of the second system. *Phi Delta Kappan, 70*, 248 – 251.

Wasik, B., & Slavin, R.E. (1993). Preventing early read - ing failure with one - to - one tutoring: A review of five programs. *Reading Research Quarterly, 28*, 178 – 200.

Wells, G. (1997). Learning to be literate: Reconciling con - vention and invention. In S.I. McMahon, T.E. Raphael, V.J. Goatley, & L.S. Pardo (Eds.), *The book club con - nection: Literacy learning and classroom talk* (pp. 107 – 116). New York and Newark, DE: Teachers College Press and International Reading Association.

Winfield, L.F. (1986). Do Chapter I programs promote ed - ucational equity? A review and some comments. *Journal of Educational Equity and Leadership, 6*, 61 – 71.

Zigmond, N., Jenkins, J., Fuchs, D., Deno, S., & Fuchs, L.S. (1995). When students fail to achieve satisfactori - ly: A reply to McLeskey and Waldron. *Phi Delta Kappan, 77*, 303 – 306.

Cynthia Fischer

An effective (and affordable) intervention model for at-risk high school readers

This research-based model includes tailor-made assignments for each student, the use of community volunteer and peer tutors, and regular opportunities for the students to read to elementary school children.

In an article entitled "Catch Them Before They Fall," Torgesen (1998) made the case for early identification of and intervention with young children who have reading problems. This emphasis is logical given that in the United States "38% of our 4th graders are struggling to learn" basic reading skills (Riley, 1999). Nevertheless, many children are not caught early and continue into high school reading at low levels. Increasingly, these students are in danger of completing their education without the skills necessary to function in a technological society or of not completing their education at all. According to Vacca and Alvermann (1998), our complex society requires not just basic literacy, but "an unprecedented level of...literacy" (p. 6).

By the time students who are not reading well reach high school, the implications for those attempting intervention are grave. "The consequences of a slow start in reading become monumental as they accumulate exponentially over time" (Torgesen, 1998, p. 32). These consequences "do not diminish over time and continue to adulthood without appropriate intervention" (Grossen, 1997, p. 6).

There is an urgent need, then, for thoughtful and persistent interventions for those students who reach high school without necessary reading skills. But there are problems. Most high school teachers, including English teachers, are not trained to teach reading. Even those content area teachers who have taken preservice or inservice reading courses generally avoid incorporating literacy prac-

136

tices into their lessons (O'Brien & Stewart, 1992; Vacca & Vacca, 1996). Content area teachers who do try to use literary strategies are most often not able to provide help for a student who is reading on a very low level. Start-up time and running costs of programs for these students can be exorbitant (Office of Educational Research and Improvement, 1991).

This article describes an affordable program to catch those high school students who must raise their literacy levels if they are to become independent learners, successfully complete a secondary education, and function in today's society. The program is implemented in a public high school (Grades 9 through 12) with an enrollment of approximately 975 students. However, the model can work in any setting by simply increasing the number of teachers facilitating it. Although the school has a rural setting in the foothills of the Blue Ridge Mountains in the eastern U.S., it is located in a county (population 72,000) surrounding the city that is home to the University of Virginia and thus the area must be described as suburban. Approximately 80% of the graduates go on to higher education; 12.9% of the students are classified as gifted, 10% receive free or reduced-price lunch, and 13.4% require special education. The population is predominately white and English speaking. Not many students in the school have low reading scores, but all those who do are given an opportunity to improve their literacy competencies through this program.

Components of the model

Three years ago I was asked to develop an intervention model for these students, most of whom are from working class families. I was to be the only teacher facilitating the program. The budget for the year was US$500. Additional outlays were my salary and the cost of reproducing materials ranging from a newsletter to fliers that advertise the program in the community. (I already had some of the assessment and teaching materials.)

At that time as now, I found in the literature very little about establishing and implementing this type of program on the high school level. Of 18 exemplary reading programs listed in the Office of Educational Research and Improvement's publication *Educational Programs That Work: A*

Collection of Proven Exemplary Educational Programs and Practices (1991), only 7 were secondary programs, and only 3 of the 7 specifically addressed the needs of remedial students. Journal articles and books described particular strategies that worked well with these students, but few gave concrete prescriptions for comprehensive programs. After reviewing the literature, I decided that such a program has to incorporate the following components if it is to succeed in raising reading levels and in providing other benefits to at-risk students:

• Students must be at least minimally motivated to improve their reading.
• Students should receive daily reading practice.
• Assignments should be tailor made for each student with an emphasis on direct, explicit instruction.
• Adult volunteers, peer tutors, and the teacher should provide as much one-to-one tutoring as possible.
• There should be opportunities for verbal sharing as well as writing and publishing.
• Students should read to younger children regularly.
• Materials should be at an appropriate level and hold students' interest.

Why these components?

The research of Brophy (1988) and Leinhardt and Bickel (1987) underscored the interdependence of motivation and success in academic tasks. I require that the students express a desire, however minimal, to improve their literacy skills because I can serve only a limited number and want to benefit these students. Having been an English, reading, and special education teacher for over 20 years, I know that if students are able to meet me one or two steps of the way, their successful experiences can provide the momentum to increase motivation. Often one must acknowledge a problem before being able to solve it. By expressing interest in the course, the students are admitting that they need help with their literacy skills.

Allington (1977) cited an informal study that found that students in a remedial reading course did little reading. Because daily reading is vital, I built into the program consistent opportunities for the students to read to me, to volunteers, to each other, to elementary school children, and to themselves. The importance of daily reading practice was underscored by student responses to an exit evaluation at the end of the first year. One activity many of the students would have liked to do more of was Sustained Silent Reading (SSR).

I chose tailor-made programs and one-to-one tutoring because "instruction that fits the needs of the problem reader improves reading performance and promotes fluent reading with comprehension" (Walker, 1992, p. 1). The diversity of their problems means that these students cannot all be required to progress through the same materials at the same pace. Both tailor-made instruction and one-to-one tutoring are components of successful elementary programs (Clay, 1979/1985) and also work well in adult literacy programs such as that of the Literacy Volunteers of America. Slavin and Madden (1989, p. 4) wrote that "given a skilled one-to-one tutor...every student without severe dyslexia or retardation...[can] attain an adequate level of basic skills." In addition, case studies of the use of tailor-made programs and one-to-one tutoring with a middle school student (Lee & Neal, 1992/1993) and a high school student (Ballash, 1994) indicated positive results.

Moreover, because high school students with reading problems are at high risk, these two components address this population's needs for direct, explicit instruction and customized reading material particularly well. When the tutors see problems, they or I can break down the processes and teach personalized strategies using concrete, hands-on types of instruction, as well as provide follow-up practice. Tutors can also help find materials related specifically to the interests of the student with whom they are working. They know quickly which content area course is giving the student problems, and they provide specific help in that area. Aside from the relevant, customized content and hands-on instruction available with a tutorial program, the interpersonal aspects also fulfill many emotional needs of at-risk learners, such as the need for individual rapport with a "teacher," personal connection with the school ("Can't be absent tomorrow—my tutor's coming"), a structured but not rigid environment, and immediate feedback and recognition (Hodge, 1991).

Because recognition is important for every student but especially for this population, several components of the program provide it. In addition to writing daily about their readings and being given opportunities to share these ideas verbally, students have a forum for publishing their writings so that they gain recognition from a larger group of people.

Requiring the students to read to elementary children regularly (Maheady, Mallette, Harper, Sacca, & Pomerantz, 1994) addresses their need for increased self-esteem, again provides recognition, and offers practice in fluency.

The last component, access to level- and interest-appropriate materials, is the dream of every literacy teacher. If the materials are interesting, the students usually have the motivation to continue and often also have at least some of the experiential background necessary to aid comprehension. Although students must be taught to understand content area textbooks, starting or enriching with self-selected materials of high interest can only increase the amount of time spent reading. Students in the program are aided in their selection of high-interest materials with an annotated bibliography of some of the books available in the reading classroom and school library. The reading levels of the books listed allow for success. We borrow the books the students read to the younger children.

I spend the major part of the budget for the program on high-interest trade books and magazines. Often books are purchased specifically to meet the interests of a particular student. The tutors sometimes contribute newspapers, books, and magazines they purchase to match the interests of their students, or they donate ones their own children have outgrown. In addition to materials purchased for the program, the students' own textbooks are used, when possible, to implement vocabulary development and teach comprehension and study strategies.

I also make many of the materials. For example, vocabulary (other than the specific vocabulary needed for content area subjects) is developed mainly through the study of Latin and Greek roots, prefixes, and suffixes. I write exercise sheets that explain and give practice in the use of homophones. Students make the pieces for their matching games from index cards. Sometimes I rewrite the information in a content area text so that it is on a student's level.

Recruitment and assessment of potential students

Regular and special education teachers recommend most of the candidates for the program. Low standardized test scores and failure of state minimum competency tests also trigger scrutiny, and guidance counselor, administrator, and parental requests contribute to the pool. Ninth and tenth graders constitute the majority of students; however, the program is open to all. In the spring, recommendations are solicited from eighth-grade teachers regarding incoming students.

After recommendation, I interview each candidate. These interviews, which take approximately 40 minutes each, help me formulate diagnostic hypotheses. A combination of formal and informal measures is used. The reading subtest of the Kaufman Test of Educational Achievement (KTEA), Brief Form, gives a broad picture of decoding, fluency, and comprehension skills. After the formal testing is completed, I return to some of the test's tasks to assess miscues (Cohn & D'Alessandro, 1978) and vocabulary knowledge. In addition, silent reading passages are sometimes included in the session using the think-aloud format and diagnostic questions suggested by Walker (1992). Throughout, I observe the strategies and cues the student uses to extract meaning. I also discuss with the students their concerns about and assessments of their reading performances.

At this point, if a student needs literacy intervention and seems to be a good candidate, I explain the procedural aspects of the program (i.e., the classes meet for one block per day as all other classes do, successful completion earns one credit toward graduation, the course is taken in addition to English, each student has a tailor-made program, students can expect at least 15 minutes of homework each night, a student may have a tutor). Next, I ask a most important question: "Do you think a program like this could help you, and [if so] would you like to be in it?" I accept students only if they express at least a minimal desire to participate.

Students may enter the program at any time during the school year, as space permits. Space depends on the number of tutors and the needs of the students as a group. At present, the program is able to serve up to about 30 students per year.

Tailor-made assignments

The model allows the teacher to use any strategies she or he feels will help the student to be successful. It does not dictate one type of lesson plan for all students. However, it does require (a) that instruction be provided through interaction with authentic, meaningful texts and (b) that students be given direct, explicit instruction in the use of skills and strategies. Such instruction may include prediction through Directed Reading-Thinking Activities, Self-Monitoring Approach to Reading and Thinking, Know–Want to Know–Learned Plus, Guided Reading Procedure, Question-Answer Relationships, story mapping, the use of other types of graphic organizers, Survey-Question-Read-Recite-Review, decoding and word attack, structured notetaking, summary and restate practice, and using text structure frames. These skills are, when possible, taught using content and subject area materials because at-risk students need to feel that what they are learning relates immediately to their lives.

With the two ground rules in mind, I formulate an initial program using instructional techniques chosen on the basis of the diagnostic hypothesis for each student as derived from the interview, school records, and consultations with teachers. This initial program is flexible; I expect it to change as the needs of the student change. Assessment of needs and performance is informal, personal, and ongoing.

A look at the information gathered about a student we will call Sally indicates that she was referred by her middle school guidance counselor. She had been dropped from special education services because recent testing found that the discrepancy between her aptitude and achievement scores was no longer great enough for her to be eligible. Her counselor knew she would need extra help with reading if she were to have a chance of success in high school. He added that she had good relationships with peers and adults, was hard-working, and would seek assistance when she needed it.

The interview session revealed that Sally had excellent verbal fluency and the ability to attend to and recall details. She had low decoding skills and no real decoding system that worked. If she did not know a word, she often just looked at the initial letters and guessed. This behavior was noted with words both in and out of context. This lack of decoding skills severely hampered her fluency. Her literal comprehension was not strong, and summarizing seemed to be very difficult. Further, she often did not demand that her reading make sense. Checking school records added the information that she had poor receptive language skills and could benefit from repetition of new concepts and lots of practice with the skills being learned. Her standardized test scores were below average in all areas, and she had had to take the state minimum competency test in reading three times before she passed it.

Sally's initial program, then, included a phonogram approach to decoding, repeated readings for fluency, and reciprocal teaching using content area texts (if possible because of her low reading level). Figure 1 is a sample week's schedule for Sally.

Tutors

Literacy volunteers are recruited from the community through a media campaign I conduct during the opening weeks of school. Newspapers, TV, and radio stations carry free announcements that the school is looking for volunteers. I post fliers in shops. In addition, during those first weeks, the school distributes to parents interest and availability questionnaires covering many types of volunteer activities. Sometimes older students are tutors. Frequently, tutors from previous years volunteer again. Next year I will have as tutors some "graduates" of the program who volunteered to tutor the new students. (What better way to practice and reinforce the skills they have learned?)

I meet with each volunteer in order to explain the program and get to know with what type of student the tutor would work best. I try to elicit and intuit as much information as I can, including

FIGURE 1
A student's sample schedule

Sally			September	8–12
Monday	Tuesday	Wednesday	Thursday	Friday
1. Large-group homophones	With tutor	1. Work with Kaneesha	With tutor	Read to elementary children
2. Large-group SQ3R Start to use SQ3R with volcanoes article	1. Decoding clusters, review 18 & 19 new 20 & 21 *Follow Through* book, pp. 20 & 21	Review clusters 4 & 5 new 6 *Follow Through* book p. 6	1. Decoding clusters, review 20 & 21 new 22 & 23 *Follow Through* book, pp. 22 & 23	
	2. Fluency readings	2. Finish SQ3R with article if not finished	2. Practice reading two or three children's books with expression and make up questions	
	3. Check SQ3R work she did Monday	3. SSR		
	4. Summary and restate practice with earth science text		3. Continue summary and restate practice with earth science text	

the extent of the person's experience with teenagers, amount and type of education, warmth, patience, ability to take rejection, reliability, and availability. I then try to match the students' literacy and personality needs with the tutors' characteristics. After tutor and student are paired, I discuss the student's tailor-made assignments with the tutor, who has been given a manual I developed containing instructions on how to perform every activity used in the lessons. This not only provides explanations of strategies but also contains information about how to be an effective tutor (Herrmann, 1994) in the sections on getting to know the students and interacting with them. I explain the first specific lesson plans I have written, which include rapport-building activities and interest inventories as well as reading materials and suggested strategies, and I give the volunteer practice in using the techniques if necessary.

The lesson plans are on forms that have much space for a dialogue between the volunteer tutor and the teacher. Through this dialogue, the tutor can signal when a strategy is not working, when an activity worked well, or if the student's needs have changed. I can then offer strategies that fit these situations. This process sounds terribly time-consuming for the teacher, and in the beginning it is. However, soon the tutors become confident and comfortable enough to write their own lesson plans. The rapport they establish helps them find materials that interest the students, such as magazine and newspaper articles.

A few times each year the tutors get together for program-sponsored pizza socials, where they can meet and share experiences. At the end of the year they are honored with a luncheon and given a framed certificate attesting to their selfless help.

Sometimes the students serve as tutors, which is especially helpful if volunteers are scarce. For example, with some older students who have decoding problems, it is beneficial to use a phonogram approach that introduces phonic principles by using sound clusters within whole words (Glass, 1973). Once students have mastered the method and a specific cluster, they can teach the cluster to another student, thus reinforcing their own learning and boosting their self-esteem. This procedure also frees the teacher to work individually with other students on days when the tutors are not present.

Whole-group activities

Because tutors usually volunteer for a period per day, 2 days a week, at times the class must function as a whole, or at least I must work with groups of three or four students at a time. Most of the fun we have in the classes occurs during these times. For example, we play a version of the word game Blurt! in which I substitute their vocabulary words for the words included on the game cards. Or they use flashcards with vocabulary words, homophones, or content area facts to play a matching game; in the process they learn that this technique is a good study method.

Often, some time is spent introducing and practicing various sound clusters. Most of these students have been in the same classes for years and are used to giving one another the correct pronunciation of a word. At the beginning of the year I tell them that I think they are all wonderful for trying to help, but that I would like them to let me help in a special way so that the person will be able to read the word when alone. I tell them that unless they are prepared to marry the person they are helping and always be there when a word is not known, it is better not to help. This leads to much laughter when various pairs of students forget to be quiet. While we are practicing the clusters and reading aloud, I maintain a list, for each student, of personal pronunciation demons. Usually they groan when another word is added to this list. I tell them I could not sleep at night if I thought they would go through life not knowing that word. Recently, I was amazed when Terrell, very seriously, reminded me to put a word on his list because, he said, he knew I would not want him to not know that word for his whole life

These whole-group times offer opportunities for other activities including book shares, opportunities for writing, and explanations of strategies everyone in the class can benefit from, such as Survey-Question-Read-Recite-Review, mnemonic devices, and notetaking. Recently we were doing a Know–Want to Know–Learned Plus (Carr & Ogle, 1986) activity with a lesson in their earth science book about volcanoes. After we had completed the K–W–L part and the graphic organizer, the students proposed that they draw figures on the graphic organizer to help them "see" the list on the organizer better (see Figure 2). Now we

FIGURE 2
K-W-L Plus with additional figures

Know	Want to Know	Learned
Kill them destroy land and people kill wildlife pollution Mt. St. Helens Kilauea	name of other – active volcanoes – where location – how hot they are – how ~~often~~ they ~~erupt~~ – ~~where is lava going~~ – ~~how much do the H islands grow every 15 years~~	Pinatubo—Philippines nearly 900 people killed Unzen—Japan 1991 + 1993 41 people killed Kilauea—world's most active—Hawaii –1990 no one hurt—slow flow of lava Mt. St. Helens—Washington state 1980 –hot enough to melt snow from last peaks and caused flooding 63 people killed

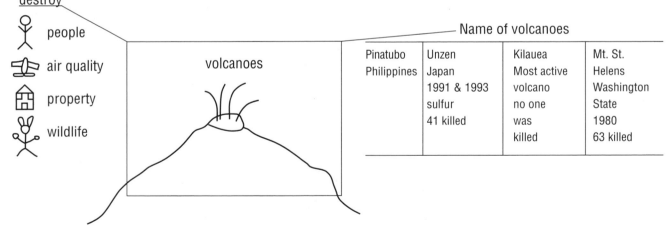

destroy

people
air quality
property
wildlife

volcanoes

Name of volcanoes

Pinatubo Philippines	Unzen Japan 1991 & 1993 sulfur 41 killed	Kilauea Most active volcano no one was killed	Mt. St. Helens Washington State 1980 63 killed

use this suggestion every time it is possible with the graphic organizers we are working on.

A lesson the students have enjoyed is one in which they read "The Sniper" by Liam O'Flaherty. We start by discussing how a civil war is different from other wars, filling in a Venn diagram with civil war on one side and other wars on the other. Luckily, most of the students are somewhat familiar with the U.S. Civil War. I thought they would not know what a sniper is but most of them do. After reading the boldfaced introduction in the textbook to them and discussing it, I write the following question on the chalkboard to establish a purpose for their reading: "How does the writer want us to feel about war and what it does to people?" I then give them copies of the story on which, at various points, I have written a *P* and told them to work in pairs. I pair stronger readers with weaker ones and have them read together. Every time a *P* appears in the story, they stop reading and write a prediction about what will happen next. At the end of reading the next section, they discuss their predictions, place a plus sign if they are accurate or a minus sign if they are not, and make their next predictions.

When they finish reading the story I ask five true-false questions to assess how well they have understood it. Finally, I use the following writing prompt: "The author does not tell us what happens to the sniper after he discovers he has killed his brother. Write what you imagine happened." My knowledge of their interests, their prior knowledge, a visual cue about how civil wars are similar to and different from other wars, prediction questions to facilitate attention and comprehension, and paired reading to ensure that each person can experience the story provide a whole-group reading activity we all thoroughly enjoy.

I also use these periods to present minilessons, such as explaining sets of homophones that are frequently used incorrectly. In addition, when the tutors are not there, students may work independently on implementing the strategies they have been taught, tutor one another, or do SSR.

Another whole-group activity the students enjoy immensely is reading to kindergarten students every Friday at the elementary school that is within walking distance of the high school. To prepare, in the beginning of the year they all receive direct instruction in how to read to children. Pace and expression are modeled. Especially important, they are taught how to question the students to whom they read ("What do you think will happen next?" "How do you think the kitten felt when that happened?") in order to ensure attention and comprehension. Often, at some time during the week they practice (with tutor, teacher, or classmate) the books they will read on Friday.

With the help of a volunteer, the class also publishes newsletters, which contain mostly book reviews and other end-of-the-book activities. Pictures of and interviews with tutors, snapshots

of each student reading to an elementary child, annotated suggestions for summer reading, and ideas for how parents can encourage reading at home have also appeared. These publications—distributed to the volunteers, administrators, and all students in the program and their parents—offer many opportunities for the students to raise their self-esteem and receive positive recognition while sharing with a larger group than just their classmates. The recognition from tutors, administrators, parents, siblings, and classmates is a very positive aspect of the program. As one administrator, who made it a point to compliment the students on their writing, wrote, "It is so good to see these kids, who at times don't make good decisions, being productive and doing well" (E. Browder, personal communication, December 19, 1996).

Homework

All students are required to read from a book of their choice for 10 to 15 minutes every night and to write a few sentences about their reading. After recording the number of pages read, they can summarize what they read or give their reactions or both. ("Bob is looking in Jenny's windows at night, and she doesn't know it. She'd better watch out.") In addition to keeping this action/reaction log, the students record in their notebooks the book's genre, author's name, title, setting, characters, conflict(s), resolution(s), and ending. They fill in the relevant notebook sections as they encounter the information in their readings. For example, characters' names are listed with large spaces after them. The student adds new information about a character piece by piece until a character sketch emerges. I call this procedure "keeping GAT SCCORE"—genre, author, title, setting, characters, conflict(s), order of key events (the action/reaction part), resolution(s), and ending. Using this format immediately provides students with a connection to their English classes in that they are improving their literacy skills at the same time as they are learning and using literary terms. Obviously, this format does not lend itself to nonfiction. With this type of book the students are required to make longer notations about the main ideas and important details in their action/reaction homework.

Grading

Because students receive credit toward graduation when they pass the course, grading must be considered. The major portion of the grade is based on completion of the short homework assignments. Each night's readings and log entry are carefully tracked and recorded. End-of-the-book activities such as book reviews and book talks also are part of the grade. Primarily because of the tailor-made assignments and the fact that students help each other through peer tutoring, there is a noncompetitive atmosphere in the classes. This is another important factor when dealing with at-risk students (Hodge, 1991).

Evaluation of the model

Until early interventions are successfully used everywhere, there will be a need for last-ditch interventions at the high school level. The model illustrates that a program need not be expensive or require much staffing to be effective. During the 3 years of the program's existence, pre- and post-intervention scores on the KTEA Brief Form have shown skills growing at an average rate of 2.2 years (and students gaining an average of 14 national percentage points) over the 9 months of instruction. This measure may not be the most sensitive for detecting specific results of many of the interventions used. However, it does indicate the overall effectiveness of the model, as does the fact that to date only 1.4% of the students who have finished the course have not continued with or completed their schooling. The overall dropout rate for the high school is approximately 5%.

Significant changes in the students also take place in the affective domain. Feedback from teachers includes stories of students volunteering to read aloud and generally participating more in class. Recently a student complained to me, "You know, Nat and Terrell [students in the program] would never read aloud in earth science, and now they won't let anyone else have a chance. You've got to talk to that teacher." Students actively seek books by favorite authors, and they often share opinions of books in their informal conversations. Students become elated when a study strategy enables them to pass a test in another course. Students do not want to be absent on the day

their tutor comes or on Fridays when we read to the younger children. Parents comment on the gains the children have made in reading and self-confidence.

Because there is a lot of camaraderie associated with having a reading problem and overcoming it, these students form close, healthy bonds with one another and with me. They read to "the little ones who need your help because no one at home reads to them," and they become more willing to help others. For example, when school started this year, I had a room to myself for the first time. It badly needed painting, and I was told that I was on the list and it would be done in a few weeks. Two former students, knowing how excited I was to have a room, obtained the paint through the assistant principal and painted the room for me in two of their free periods.

A parent whose son was in the program last year shared this story with me. During their annual beach vacation, 14-year-old A.J. met his first girlfriend. At the end of the vacation they decided to write to each other. When the first letter arrived, the mother, who usually had to help her son with reading, asked whether he wanted her help or, because of the personal nature of the letter, that of his older sister. He informed her that he could now read it by himself. Later in the summer he told her that he would be taking 2 semesters of the program this year instead of the single semester he had originally intended to take. He is one of the boys who volunteered to tutor next year. Last year he entered the program reading at the 1st percentile (grade equivalent 2.8) and ended the year at the 21st percentile (7.3 grade equivalent level).

Future benefit

Parts of the program positively touch each student each day. However, the aspect that I believe has the most promise for the students' future, even if they do not complete their education, is their reading to elementary children. Although many students are initially fearful or resistant, every one of them—from the school "tough" to the painfully withdrawn student reading on a second-grade level—has come to enjoy, to be effective at, and to realize the importance of reading to young children. If this program did nothing more than give them the skills to read to their own children, and a realization of how necessary that activity is, maybe the cycle of functional illiteracy in these students' families would be broken. Until we get to the point where we catch all youngsters before they fall, this type of program is a last opportunity to catch them at all.

REFERENCES

Allington, R.L. (1977). If they don't read much, how can they ever get good? *Journal of Reading, 21*, 57–61.

Ballash, K.M. (1994). Remedial high school readers can recover, too! *Journal of Reading, 37*, 686–687.

Brophy, J. (1988). Research linking teacher behavior to student achievement: Potential implications for instruction of Chapter 1 students. *Educational Psychologist, 23*(3), 235–286.

Carr, E., & Ogle, D. (1987). A strategy for comprehension and summarization. *Journal of Reading, 31*, 626–631.

Clay, M.M. (1979/1985). *The early detection of reading difficulties.* Auckland, New Zealand: Heinemann.

Cohn, M., & D'Alessandro, C. (1978). When is a decoding error not a decoding error? *The Reading Teacher, 32*, 341–344.

Glass, G. (1973). *Teaching decoding as separate from reading.* Garden City, NY: Adelphi University Press.

Grossen, B. (1997). *30 years of research: What we know about how children learn to read.* Santa Cruz, CA: Center for the Future of Teaching and Learning. (ERIC Document Reproduction Service No. 415 492)

Herrmann, B.A. (1994). *The volunteer tutor's toolbox.* Newark, DE: International Reading Association.

Hodge, E.A. (1991). *Intervention for at-risk students at the secondary level.* Montgomery, AL: Alabama State University. (ERIC Document Reproduction Service No. ED 339 764)

Lee, N.G., & Neal, J.C. (1992/1993). Reading rescue: Intervention for a student "at promise." *Journal of Reading, 36*, 276–282.

Leinhardt, G., & Bickel, W. (1987). Instruction's the thing wherein to catch the mind that falls behind. *Educational Psychologist, 22*(2), 177–207.

Maheady, L., Mallette, B., Harper, G.F., Sacca, K.C., & Pomerantz, D. (1994). Peer-mediated instruction for high-risk students. In K.D. Wood & B. Algozzine (Eds.), *Teaching reading to high-risk learners* (pp. 269–290). Needham Heights, MA: Allyn & Bacon.

O'Brien, D., & Stewart, R. (1992). Resistance to content area reading: Dimensions and solutions. In E. Dishner, T. Bean, J. Readence, & D. Moore (Eds.), *Reading in the content areas: Improving classroom instruction* (3rd ed., pp. 30–40). Dubuque, IA: Kendall/Hunt.

Office of Educational Research and Improvement. (1991). *Educational programs that work. A collection of proven exemplary educational programs and practices* (17th ed.). Washington, DC: National Diffusion Network. (ERIC Document Reproduction Service No. ED 338 618)

Riley, R. (1999, February 16). Sixth annual state of American education address, given at California State University at Long Beach.

Slavin, R.E., & Madden, N.A. (1989). What works for students at risk: A research synthesis. *Educational Leadership, 46*, 4–12.

Torgesen, J. (1998). Catch them before they fall. *American Educator, 22*, 32–39.

Vacca, R., & Alvermann, D. (1998). The crisis in adolescent literacy: Is it real or imagined? *NASSP Bulletin, 82*, 4–9.

Vacca, R., & Vacca, J. (1996). *Content area reading* (5th ed.). New York: HarperCollins.

Walker, B.J. (1992). *Diagnostic teaching of reading: Techniques for instruction and assessment.* New York: Macmillan.

Alfred W. Tatum

Breaking down barriers that disenfranchise African American adolescent readers in low-level tracks

A teacher researcher explored ways of helping African American adolescents with poor reading skills read, understand, and respond to literature with word study activities, fluency development exercises, literature, and writing.

A nationwide thrust in the United States to adopt high-stakes testing for promotion in Grades 6, 8, and 11 is forcing many teachers to adopt a test-driven approach to increase the achievement of struggling adolescent readers. District officials assume that high-stakes testing will produce improved learning outcomes. Proponents of high-stakes testing argue that it is students who have done least well in school who will benefit from test-driven instruction. Support for test-driven reform based on standards is not found in analysis of the National Assessment of Educational Progress's 1994 reading assessment (Campbell, Donahue, Reese, & Phillips, 1996). In fact, lower reading achievement is associated with practices that accompany test-driven instruction (Smith, 1991). Evidence suggests that students in states without high-stakes testing perform better than those in states with it (Neill, 1998).

The gap between a comprehensive approach to literacy teaching and the widespread practice of teachers of African American adolescent students with poor reading skills is widening because meeting minimum standards is being emphasized. As an eighth-grade teacher in a low-income African American neighborhood in a large urban area I became concerned about the emphasis being placed on standardized scores as part of a school reform initiative. I wanted to help students nurture their identities so that they would not limit themselves but would seek opportunities not readily available in their community.

Reprinted from *Journal of Adolescent & Adult Literacy* (2000), *44*, 52–64.

Darling-Hammond and Falk (1997) pointed out that

> depending on how standards are shaped and used, either they could support more ambitious teaching and greater levels of success for all students, or they could serve to create higher rates of failure for those who are already least well-served by the education system. (p. 191)

The proliferation of standards and the high rates of retention that result from not meeting these standards indicate that a move toward standards does not always lead to greater levels of success. For example, in Chicago, one of the largest urban school districts in the U.S., alternative high schools have been created to accommodate students who repeatedly fail to meet standards. Parents, educators, and members of local school councils have referred to these schools as warehouses for underachieving students of color.

Standards are minimal and do not begin to adequately address the needs of African Americans struggling with reading if the approach to meeting those standards depends on a basic skills orientation. This "goes against the grain of pushing them toward their maximum competency level" (Hillard, 1995, p. 108). As a result, many students will be remanded to the margins of society, never to experience full political, economic, and social participation.

The problem of how to increase the literacy achievement of African Americans is embedded in social, cultural, economic, and historical dynamics. Educational inequities, cultural alienation, and economic deprivation play out in very subtle and pernicious ways in U.S. classrooms. This situation, along with ill-framed misconceptions about African Americans, by both black and white teachers, have a negative impact on literacy achievement for this group.

A closer look at the "good teaching" (Foster, 1993, 1997; Ladson-Billings, 1995a) of African American students has emerged during the past decade. A distinctive educational philosophy and pedagogy along with the aspects of teacher behavior students considered effective have been pointed out. The "good teachers" of African Americans, whose major attributes were revealed by these studies, may be described as follows:

1. They are concerned individuals who command respect, respect pupils, and are strict, although caring, in requiring all students to meet high academic and behavioral standards.
2. They are concerned not only with the students' cognitive development, but also with their affective, social, and emotional development.
3. They use a culturally relevant approach to literacy teaching.

A culturally relevant approach involves talking to black students about the personal value, the collective power, and the political consequences of choosing academic achievement. In such an approach, activities based on African American community norms are incorporated into the classroom, cooperation is emphasized over competition, and learning is structured as a social activity.

Several other requisites have been offered by Ladson-Billings (1995b) for a culturally relevant approach to literacy teaching:

1. Students must experience academic success, develop and maintain cultural competence, and develop a critical consciousness to challenge the status quo.
2. Teachers should attend to students' academic needs, not merely make them feel good.
3. Students' culture should be made a vehicle for learning.
4. Students need help to develop a broader sociopolitical consciousness that allows them to critique the cultural norms, values, mores, and institutions that produce and maintain social inequities.

Using culturally relevant literature is key to a culturally relevant approach. It has been suggested that African American adolescents in low-level reading tracks (particularly those who live in poverty and in politically and socially defunct communities) need to read, write about, and discuss literature that would help them develop cultural competence (Ladson-Billings, 1995b).

There is a fundamental tension between a basic skills approach to meet standards and a culturally relevant approach. Developing cultural competence with culturally relevant literature does not solve the problems of teachers confronted with students who lack reading skills, and increasing reading scores by focusing on skills in isolation will not strengthen cultural competence or nurture students' identities. Economically disadvantaged African American adolescents in low-level tracks need reading instruction that incorporates a culturally relevant framework with explicit strategy and skill development.

Purpose and description of the study

An 8-month inquiry into classroom dynamics and instructional practices was conducted to gain insights on ways of integrating explicit strategy and skill development with culturally relevant literature. A literacy framework (Figure 1) was devised for addressing four areas of reading development: fluency, word study, comprehension, and writing.

These four areas were integrated in a meaningful way and not addressed as disparate, isolated skills.

Three major strands evolved from the inquiry: barriers that prevented students from reading at their grade level, restructuring the classroom to create a supportive environment, and meshing explicit strategy instruction and culturally relevant literature. In this article I discuss these strands and the instructional approaches used to break down the barriers that prevented students' literate behaviors.

The inquiry was conducted in a class of 29 eighth-grade students (13 boys and 16 girls) who attended a Chicago public school and had reading stanines of 4 or below from the previous year's Iowa Test of Basic Skills. Two students had been retained, and 6 were receiving special education

FIGURE 1
Instructional framework adapted from Timothy Shanahan's (in preparation) Literacy Framework

	Word study	Fluency	Comprehension	Writing
What is included?	• Sight vocabulary • Spelling • Structural analysis • Word meaning	• Reading speed • Oral reading accuracy • Intonation	• Strategies for constructing meaning	• Purposes • Products • Audiences
*How much instructional time?	• 20 minutes daily	• Brief monitoring to as much as 30 minutes daily	• 30 minutes or more daily	• 30 minutes or more daily
How does it change?	• From word recognition to word meaning	• Text difficulty increases • Less repetition to fluency	• Text difficulty increases • Text length increases • Greater individual control	• Text difficulty increases • More distant audiences • Greater individual control
Application	• Individual drill • Provides opportunities to apply knowledge versus teaching rules	• Place emphasis • Silent and oral reading	• Use high interest materials • Make students responsible • Expand range of responses	• Have authentic purposes for writing • Read student writing

* Adjustments were made based on student's needs and time available for instruction.

services. The class met for 50 minutes of reading instruction during the first period of the school day.

Half of the students lived in a neighborhood that was recently dubbed the "Second America," one of the U.S.A's darkest places, in *Life and Death on the South Side of Chicago* (Jones, Newman, & Isay, 1997). Living in this neighborhood gave the students a warped perception of their African American identities. Their identities were closely aligned with the racial dehumanizing of inner city urban youth. They had limited exposure to positive cultural and social experiences.

These students needed literacy instruction to help sustain them for what I have called the 4 critical years—after elementary school and before college—to avoid the negative trappings of their community. Many students from this school go on to surrounding area high schools that send a relatively small percentage of students to college. Going away to college is an escape from the neighborhood and entry to a new realm of possibilities, and it's something that many students hear discussed as happening to others, not them.

Being disengaged from the reading and writing process put these students at a great disadvantage. They were reluctant to read orally, seldom completed assigned readings, and refused to answer questions when called upon. Students in this class rarely ventured into independent reading. They had become accustomed to worksheets and assessment questions from their basal readers as the primary mode of reading instruction. Dictates for these students were more comprehensive than equipping them with basic skills, "remediating" their shortcomings, or increasing scores on a standardized assessment.

Identifying barriers

The inquiry was initiated by interviewing four boys during the third week of the school year to determine what prevented their participation in reading. Aaron, Chad, Leroy, and Rufus (pseudonyms are used for all students) were selected because of an observed unwillingness to participate during reading instruction. When asked why they thought students in this class refused to participate in reading and writing activities, Rufus offered, "Students are scared to say something; they talk after school but not in class." Leroy added, "Not just the boys, the girls too." It was at this point that I asked the boys if we should include the girls in our conversations. They thought it was a good idea, and I included the entire class.

As the interviews continued, students blamed derogatory remarks from previous teachers as powerful deterrents to reading. "People think most black people are going to fail, so we don't do the work," stated Rufus. Another student added, "We are not used to reading and writing. It's like we are starting over in eighth grade." They also felt they had limited vocabularies, deficient decoding skills, and poor comprehension strategies. In addition to these reading difficulties, students were reluctant readers because of a fear of embarrassment. To avoid negative comments from a classroom teacher or peers, one student suggested that many of them would rather say nothing than risk opportunities for potential embarrassment. These students were inadvertently pushed away from reading, and barriers had been constructed that prevented their access to highly literate behaviors such as reading, writing about, and discussing literature.

Fear of embarrassment, deficient word-attack strategies, and limited vocabularies were identified as the major barriers to students' success in reading. These "big three" seemed to prevent them from reading materials at their grade level because of the high level of frustration they experienced. Three goals were developed to get all the students involved: reduce fear of embarrassment; decrease the levels of frustration experienced because of their inability to employ word attack strategies; and have students read, understand, discuss, and write about literature.

Creating a supportive community

Creating a supportive environment was important for reducing the potential for embarrassment. The classroom was reorganized and instruction was restructured. There were three major goals of these changes. The first was building a classroom community. Openly acknowledging that reading problems existed in the classroom and establishing the goal of helping everyone become better readers was important for letting the students know that there was nothing to be embarrassed about. It was also acknowledged that students did not have to accept all the blame for their problems. By year's

FIGURE 2
Students' assessments of their participation, contribution, and reading strengths and weaknesses

Lillie: I contributed my picture (visual representation) pretty good, but I did not talk at all. Next time I will contribute what I learn. Today I think I learned a lot but sometimes when I do not talk that do not mean I am not paying attention.

Tisha: We did good as a group today and I think I should get a 3 because everyone in our group did 100% participation. I make up a ideal for my group and they use it but it did not sound right so we chose another topic.

Pam: I spoke on a subject to the class. It felt good to speak on a subject wear everyone want to learn. Now I am not afraid to speak out loud. I did good because I felt the feeling how we really are in life with pain and fear.

Tamara: My attitude is very positive about reading now, but my real attitude in school is bad. I read fluent now that we decode. Now I can read any types of words just calling them out. At home I read a little not a lot, but in school I keep going over those words on the board. Well I'm still not talking wright, but I correct myself a little, that still has a lot of coming together to take place.

Chuck: My vocabulary is getting better by the day. When I learning something new I don't have to be timid. I can be tranquil. Reading is not boring. It is good, excellent. You can feel the breeze. But now I read much better at home or in school by myself. I read fluency.

---

end the teacher has to accept some of the responsibility, and I acknowledged that I would accept mine. Also, some of the reading instruction took place as I sat among the students in a circle of chairs that were placed in the center of the class. Placing myself alongside the students gave them the sense that I was on their side.

Involving students in the assessment process was the second goal of creating a supportive environment. Student self-evaluations were included as part of the grading, which gave them some control over the process. They were asked to rate their participation in and contribution to the lesson after each reading session on a scale of 1–5.

Students started assessing their own strengths and weaknesses (see Figure 2). They were given the language to communicate their strengths and weaknesses (i.e., "chopped up reading" to assess fluency, "listening to my little critters" to describe comprehension monitoring).

The third goal of creating a supportive environment involved providing space for students to "safely fail" and recover. Before each assessment, students had the opportunity to practice with a cooperating student. If cooperating teachers can assist student teachers and give them feedback to help them become better teachers, I believed that cooperating students could help one another become better readers. Cooperating students would devise ways to remember new vocabulary, monitor one another's reading miscues (omissions, substitutions, or repetitions), time readings to gauge fluency, or work together to identify textual references when responding to comprehension questions. If the cooperating teams had difficulty figuring out something I would model specific reading strategies to help answer their concerns. The students were given time to practice, fail, and recover in a supportive environment.

Reducing embarrassment

The voices of young people must be heard and acknowledged in their own way, or they will excuse themselves early from the table of learning (Livdahl et al., 1995). I wanted to give my students a voice. In Livdahl et al., Herbert suggests ways of inviting reluctant readers to respond. One of her practical ideas was the "one-pager," which allows for multiple ways of responding. A one-pager consists of a visual representation (picture or symbol) of a quote that is significant, and a paragraph of the reader's reflection on the reading. This invitation to respond in a variety of ways enhances student participation successfully. The students' confidence grows, thereby supplanting feelings of learned helplessness. Also, using the one-pager is less intimidating because it is an activity that is not teacher centered and makes possible more than one interpretation. Students have to search for what is meaningful to them and not just what the teacher thinks. This had, then, the potential to propel them into more meaning-oriented activities that could foster appreciation for literature.

The visual or picture/drawing aspect was important to students and elicited the following responses:

Martha: Giving a visual representation helped me with what I wanted to say. And then I could explain it.

Tamera: I liked that part it was fun, we got to draw and have fun and all at the same time.

Chad: Well, it was hard because it's very hard for me to draw with no experience at all. I thought it was good because it showed me where I was coming and how I understood it.

Low-ability readers do not spontaneously employ mental imagery as a strategy; they are thereby deprived of full evocation and participation in the story world (Gambrell & Bales, 1986). Also, less proficient readers are at a loss for strategies for stepping into and sustaining "envisionments" (Purcell-Gates, 1991). Thus, the one-pager "nudged" the students to employ this visualizing. Students who had difficulty finding the words to express themselves were given a passageway into classroom activities. Value was placed upon what they had to say. The classroom environment became less threatening as students were assigned to work both collectively and individually on their one-pagers. To eliminate the fear of embarrassment, a supportive classroom environment was created, and the opportunities for failure were reduced.

Attacking the small puppies to get to the big dogs

The one-pagers led to increased levels of participation, but the students continued to struggle with decoding. Strategies were needed to break down this barrier without reducing reading to isolated skill and drill. Increasing the students' comprehension was a primary goal, and for this group word knowledge skills were integrally related to such an aim.

When the students had difficulty reading words, their attention was diverted from comprehension and they became preoccupied with decoding individual words. They did not comprehend what they were attempting to read when they focused on individual words. The statement "I do not want

to read now" or a deafening silence at my request for a student to read orally became a part of their "refusal to read repertoire."

"Attacking the small puppies to get to the big dogs" was the slogan the class adopted for thinking about decoding. All of the students in the class admitted that they were not afraid of small puppies, and that they would much rather wrestle with a small puppy than a big dog. The small puppies in this analogy were syllables and phonogram patterns. The multisyllable words were the big dogs. This strategy was based on the idea of decoding by analogy where students are taught how to decode words by comparing an unknown word with known "key words" (Gaskins, Gaskins, & Gaskins, 1991).

Students were taught decoding by analogy through direct instruction and by incorporating the strategy into purposeful reading and writing throughout the day. A public display of phonogram patterns was created. Knowledge of phonogram patterns gives students an advantage when determining the pronunciation of words with more than one syllable (May, 1990). Also to assist with decoding, students were taught a shortened version for syllabicating words. They were told that if they could identify the letters *a, e, i, o*, and *u*, and count to 1 and count to 2, that they could decode a large number of multisyllable words. Four rules were given:

1. Split two consonants between vowels (e.g., bal / lad)
2. Move one consonant between vowels to the next syllable (e.g., te / na / cious)
3. Separate neighboring vowels (e.g., jo / vi / al)
4. Do not separate blends or word groupings that needed each other (e.g., ous, qu)

A word-study activity to practice decoding that made a positive impact on the students' self-esteem and supplanted their feelings of learned helplessness while challenging them to perform at a high level of mastery was incorporated. Each morning before the students entered the class five word lists with five words each were placed on the chalkboard. Each student would decode the lists independently in writing. The 25 words were selected from the article, novel, or text the class was required to read. In this manner decoding

FIGURE 3
Syllabication sheet with lowercase letters used during the first month of the inquiry

Instructions: Capitalize the first letter of each syllable.

Hint: Look for blends   bl, cl, gl, cr, dr,.......
       and digraphs   sh, th, ...

Ex # 1 redundant = *Re Dun Dant* (3)
Ex # 2 ludicrous = *Lu Di Crous*

1. resolution _____

2. argument _____

3. unanimity _____

4. incredible _____

5. independence _____

6. anonymous (unknown) _____

7. tyrant _____

8. denunciation _____

9. insistence _____

10. unalterable _____

The class was reading an excerpt from the U.S. Declaration of Independence.

served as a prereading activity that moved the ensuing substantive reading along at a faster pace. Students were expected to successfully make the transfer to the text. In some cases, those who have trouble with reading do not successfully make this transfer. If strategic decoding is effectively used to break down one of the barriers that inhibit many poor readers the connection is made explicit.

Each word was written using lowercase letters unless a proper noun was used; in that case, the first letter was capitalized (see Figure 3). At the beginning of the year, the students were given 5 minutes to syllabicate the words. The written portion of this activity was graded daily to assess which students needed more individual attention. After each student decoded the word lists independently, the work was collected and a whole-group activity began.

A visual and an auditory component were added during the whole-group activity. The students, speaking in unison, called out the syllabicated version. The syllabicated version was written on the board. *Indefatigable* would sound like this: Big *I*, little *n*, big *D*, little *e*, big *F*, little *a*, big *T*, little *i*, big *G*, little *a*, big *B*, little *l*, little *e*, and the rewrite above the word would look like *In De Fa Ti Ga Ble*. They would say each syllable independently of the others before attempting the entire word. This activity was kept at a quick rhythmic pace.

The students stood during the whole-group activity because it removed them from a physical "position of passivity." Seated students use their desks as a barricade to avoid instruction. They slump, fidget, hide behind other students, or pretend to be involved with other tasks not related to the lesson. Students' attention was heightened throughout this activity because they knew their ability to decode one of the word lists individually at a rate of 1 second per word earned them their seat (an idea set forth by the class). Timing the activity was used to emphasize fluency. The lists were assigned in a nonpredictable manner so that the students focused on all the words.

If a student was having difficulty earning a seat, an echo-reading approach was used. Students became eager to demonstrate their ability to perform. "Can I read all 25 words?" was one question that caused a time management constraint as the year progressed. As these students began to decode successfully, there was a shift from the avoidance techniques used to volunteerism. They became more confident in their abilities to decode words. The time allotted for decoding the words decreased. Five months into the study, 2 minutes were allotted to decode the 25 words in writing. In a class with 29 students, each child was seated in less than 3 minutes. The daily syllabication lasted for approximately 7 minutes.

Dictation

A paragraph was dictated to the students after the syllabication activity. They were made aware that the same way they attacked the small puppies to get to the big dogs when decoding words, they were to use those same puppies when spelling words. On occasion, the same words from the syllabication lists were used for the dictated exercises to strengthen the connection between the two.

A dictation, usually two to four sentences, that provoked interest, impregnated thought, or gave information pertinent to understanding the reading was given. The students were instructed to write the paragraph verbatim and underline eight preselected words. Words were selected to emphasize common spelling patterns or to bring attention to the essential vocabulary in the literature that was used during instruction. The syllables of these eight words were clearly articulated so that the students could "tune in." Following each dictation, the students exchanged their papers and spelling was assessed. Common mistakes were discussed. The mistakes were highlighted, spelling patterns were discussed, and more opportunities to practice with these spelling patterns were given in subsequent dictated exercises.

Several questions always followed the dictated exercise and were discussed as a prereading activity. Volunteers were called upon to reread the dictated exercise and respond to the questions before the reading selection (see Figure 4).

Vocabulary development

The students were informed why they were learning to decode and encode words (i.e., to handle the print when reading and writing), yet many of them were failing to construct meaning from the assigned readings because of their small vocabulary base. An ever-growing word wall was created to strengthen their sight and meaning vocabulary. The words selected for study were from the literature assigned to the students. They were told that

FIGURE 4
A sample dictation

People *usually associate* the word *prejudice* with *intolerance* of a *particular* race or *creed*. Prejudice can also exist, however, within a *minority* group that is the victim of *discrimination*.

1. Can you explain why some members of a racial or ethnic group might be given special treatment?

2. What circumstances lead to discrimination?

Dictation was given before reading an article from a local newspaper about cultural diversity.

the words would appear in their readings. Using literature selections to teach students the meaning of words is more effective than assigning vocabulary words at random (Dole, Sloan, & Trathen, 1995).

The word wall was designed to strengthen the relationship between knowing words and reading well. These words were used to address decoding and vocabulary development simultaneously. Students need to see and hear new words repeatedly if they are going to remember them and use them when writing.

The students read the word wall every other day to build their sight vocabulary. Excerpts from songs were associated with the words to enhance their meaning (see Figure 5). Pronouncing the words and singing the excerpts was done every other day during the fourth and fifth month of the study. This approach helped improve new vocabulary retention and gave a sense of music history. It became too time-consuming as the year progressed, so Friday became Word Wall Day. The word wall was also read on occasion when the principal was observing the class and students wanted to show off. The power the students received from this new and highly visible word wall was not anticipated. They became excited about learning words.

One morning during tutoring, Charisse said, "It feels good to read and know what it means, I see a lot of our words and know them right away." The students benefited by their "new weapons," as Xavier's comments suggest:

FIGURE 5
Excerpts from songs selected by the teacher and the students to build meaning vocabulary

retrospect	(excerpt) Looking back on when I was a little nappy-headed boy—Stevie Wonder
deserted	(excerpt) "On My Own"—Patti Labelle
ambitious	(excerpt) And we're moving on up—theme from *The Jeffersons* sitcom
melancholy	(excerpt) All I really want is to be happy—Mary J. Blige
reciprocate	(excerpt) It's the big payback—James Brown
eternal	(excerpt) "Always and Forever"—Heat Wave
cease	(excerpt) "Stop in the Name of Love"—Diana Ross and the Supremes

The words on the wall are easy, but for other students it is hard. The words help me decode better, do fluent reading all the time. I like getting involved in new words because it helps me know them the next time I see them and it helps my comprehension.

They were asked to read these words quickly to facilitate fluency, as Alvin's remarks suggest:

I think when we decode words it help me know the words better when I read in books and the word be in it and I already know it I don't hesitate to say it, and when you snap your hands it don't scare me or make me nervous. I think it helps me say the words better.

Using a challenging vocabulary wall positively affected the attitudes of many of the students. They began to challenge the advanced reading group from the other eighth-grade class. Words gave them power. Many students added words to the wall that they wanted the other students to learn. They could successfully demonstrate their growth and experience immediate success. Vocabulary tests were given every other Friday to assess the students individually. By the sixth month, a majority of the students consistently earned a score of 90% or better. Using words that they came across in their literature significantly improved their sight-word knowledge. By year's

end the word wall had over 450 multisyllabic words that 25 of the 29 students could recognize on sight and consistently spell correctly. They could also attach a meaningful excerpt from a song to approximately 100 of them.

Culturally relevant literature

Culturally relevant literature should be used to help African American students understand changes in history, substantiate their existence, and critically examine the present as a mechanism for political, social, and cultural undertakings that may arise in the future. Culturally relevant literature should extend toward empowering students to honor their presence, "a powerful demanding presence not limiting the space in which the self can roam" (Achebe, 1988, p. 53). Racial dehumanizing should not inhibit this space.

Culturally relevant literature was incorporated into the instructional framework to strengthen cultural competence, nurture students' identities, and increase their reading achievement. Literature, articles, essays, and activities were selected to give students the opportunity to use their explicit skill development in meaningful and relevant ways.

Students who struggle with reading often have limited strategies for comprehending text. Strategies were modeled. Self-questioning strategies, constructing graphic organizers, tuning in to the "little critters" in their minds to monitor comprehension, and acknowledging different question and answer relationships were explicitly modeled via "think-alouds." The culturally relevant literature was selected to help the students use deep processing strategies such as applying the information to other contexts, in this case their lives. This also allows them to use their cultural schema as an additional cueing system.

Materials that challenged the students to think about the social and cultural traditions associated with growing up black in the U.S. were selected. Historical fiction, contemporary fiction, historical nonfiction, and poetry, with emphasis on the ability to survive both physically and psychologically, were used to help the students understand the changes in history and critique their social realities. For example, Booker T. Washington's (1901) *Up From Slavery* was used to examine how tireless perseverance helps to overcome overwhelming odds. Contextualizing Washington's struggle allowed students to examine their lives. Attempts were made to always connect the historical to the contemporary so that the students would not view the information as outdated and irrelevant.

Cooperative repeated readings

Although many students were decoding better, increasing their word knowledge, and using the strategies that were modeled 3 months into the school year, their oral reading was choppy. The transfer from explicit strategy and skill development to the text was not immediate. It was at this point that cooperative repeated readings of literature, appropriate for middle school settings (Dowhower, 1989) were introduced to the class. During the cooperative repeated readings (see Figure 6) each student was given the opportunity to read a selection to a "cooperating student" three times before class discussion. The first reading was used to identify and attack the words that were difficult to decode. This was an extension of the daily syllabication. The second reading was used to eliminate all substitutions, repetitions, and omissions to build fluency. During the second or third readings, student-initiated questions emerged. The focus of reading shifted from decoding to constructing meaning. The students began to focus on the ideas of the text. They began to incorporate the explicit strategies that were modeled as they moved through the text. This allowed them to participate in class discussions that were anchored by four questions: Which part of the essay was the most meaningful? What was most surprising? What did you disagree with? How is the selection relevant today?

Repeated readings, when discussed and evaluated, gave students a chance to examine their progress and shortcomings. The students became more conscientious in their reading habits and were willing to work toward improvement. As Shaungel wrote, "I noticed that my reading has truly improved because I use to always read chop up reading and now I am *cognizant* that my reading skills are grown up and *mediocre*." The italicized words are from the word wall used to build meaning vocabulary. This is just one example of how students claimed ownership of their words and used them when writing.

FIGURE 6
Selections used for cooperative repeated reading

Speeches/letters/documents
* I Have a Dream—Martin Luther King Jr.
  Appeal to the colored citizens of the world but in particular and very expressly to those of the United States of America—David Walker

The Gettysburg Address—Abraham Lincoln

Declaration of Independence—Thomas Jefferson

The Preamble to the United States Constitution

The Preamble to the Illinois Constitution

Poems
* Lift Every Voice and Sing and The Creation—James Weldon Johnson
* If We Must Die—Claude McKay
* Tableau and Incident—Countee Cullen
* For My People and Lineage—Margaret Walker

Short stories/essays
* from Up From Slavery Boyhood Days— Booker T. Washington
* from Narrative of the Life of Frederick Douglass— Frederick Douglass

---

* Reading sources from *African American Literature, Voices in a Tradition*, ©1992 by Holt Rinehart and Winston.

Other students also supported the beneficial effects of repeated readings:

Donella: The changes that I notice in my reading is that I do not become frustrated when I read. I feel that I am picking up speed in my reading.

Kim: I notice that I'm not stumbling over words that I read out of books.

Ashely: I can read some of the words I never knew before and I'm not scared to read in front of the class like I used to be.

Following the classroom discussions the students were asked to address four questions in writing:

• How do you believe you would have reacted in a similar situation and why?

FIGURE 7
A student's written reflection and attempts to use words (boldface) from the word wall

The Man

I am the black man who ashames his race.
I am the darker brother whom they laugh in my face.
I have many disadvantages that bring me down.
I fight for the power when I know it's not allowed.
Feeling the walls close on to my position in
the center of the earth. Hoping to make peace
inside of the man's world feeling the **dehumanization**
coming from the man who awaits my death.
Making me weak on the inside, taking over my soul,
taking my true love from me, left with nothing to hold.
Lost within myself, this can't be real,
can not stand this **antithesis** of life I feel.
Growing darkness taking dawn I thought I was me,
but now I'm gone.
I have awaited my life too long to let the man pull my arm.
Seeking **chaotic** episodes happening everyday
feeling the critters in my head moaning stay away.
Having my manhood stripped away from me everyday.
Having no respect for society, because I know I must
    turn away.
Running away from my fears all alone.
There's no way in the world I can be strong, but I must,
    because it seems
as if my whole race is depending on me. Walking
    around with
unknown **attributes**. Scared to face the world's
    prevaricating
nations. Hiding from the intimidation that awaits me at
    home.
Feeling the products of **lethal** weapons growing strong.
    The
source that kills my brothers an sisters I know its
    wrong.
I know now I must lend my brothers and sisters a
    hand, and hope
they learn the true meaning of overcoming
The Man.

- What impact does the condition/situation have on you presently?
- How will you make an impact to prevent this situation from taking place in the future?
- How is the information relevant for future societies?

The students were challenged to debate about ideas and concepts and use the literature to support their arguments. One such debate revolved around whether African Americans should integrate or separate. The students pitted the words of Elijah Muhammad in the *Message to the Black Man* (1965) and work of David Walker (1993) against the ideas of Martin Luther King in *A Testament of Hope* (Washington, 1986), and the writings of Frederick Douglass, in front of the principal, other students, and a local news reporter.

Do the "write" thing

Word study, vocabulary development, and confidence in reading became stimuli for writing. I created a bulletin board titled Do the Write Thing. All of the students were familiar with this pun. The movie *Do the Right Thing*, written and directed by an African American, was a favorite among the students. Following class discussions, the students were able to retreat into their "writing zones" and write reflective responses about the readings and discussions. Essays, poems, and short stories were posted on the board. Writing became contagious.

Students responded that they loved to write using the "big words" from the word wall to sound intelligent. I made a big deal of this board, making all the writers feel special. I would ask the students to share their writings orally. Initially I think I might have discouraged some students to add their work. They were willing to place writings on the board, but they did not want to publicly share their personal reflections. Later, students were encouraged to use pseudonyms or sign the writings "anonymous" if they did not want me to bring special attention to the author.

Writing opportunities and literature discussions led to increased usage of new vocabulary. For a sample of one student's writing after reading an article written by Willie Lynch (1712), see Figure 7.

A compelling change in attitude

African American students in low-level tracks are often not required to read literature, and they commonly receive limited amounts of reading instruction. Their reading failures are exacerbated by inadequate or poor quality instruction that focuses solely on improving reading scores. Teachers can increase reading achievement by combining explicit skill and strategy development using a framework to address fluency, word study, comprehension, and writing while using culturally relevant literature to nurture identities and develop cultural competence.

It is difficult to find in the literature a study of African American adolescents in low-level reading tracks that adds to our understanding about the combined use of culturally relevant literature and explicit skill development in reading. This study involved a change in class structure that invited low-achieving adolescent students to learn specific skills and strategies and to read literature. Word study activities, fluency development, and writing in a cooperative environment allowed the students to gain confidence in their reading abilities and to improve reading behaviors. The students in this inquiry did not resist the explicit skills in large part because they were thrust upon them in a very challenging forum, and opportunities to exercise their new knowledge were made available through literature activities.

Culturally relevant literature helped the students develop a broader social consciousness that was observed in their discussions and writings. Students' culture was used as a vehicle to learn new vocabulary. Challenging students to read materials at their grade level and giving them the support to experience academic success contributed to their cognitive development. Restructuring the classroom and engaging the students' voices created a cooperative atmosphere. These goals of a culturally relevant approach for African Americans were meshed with explicit word study, fluency, writing, and comprehension instruction to improve reading skills.

This combination of a culturally relevant approach and explicit strategy and skill instruction resulted in 25 of the 29 students earning promotion to high school under the Chicago Public School System's reform initiative requiring eighth-grade students to achieve a minimum grade-level equivalent of 7.0 on the Iowa Test of Basic Skills. Several students scored well beyond this minimum standard. The quantifiable gains are noteworthy given the fact that all the students were several years below grade level in reading at the beginning of the year.

The shift in attitude that many students experienced from their active involvement in the relevant and meaningful literature experiences was compelling. The reluctance the students exhibited at the onset of the inquiry diminished. The students began to challenge the advanced group of readers and other teachers with ideas and words. They also began to realize that they had the power to break down the barriers that prevented their participation in reading and writing.

> The teaching of reading in the public schools has proceeded as if the content of the text makes no difference. Although schools have been successful in teaching students how to read, they have not been nearly as successful engendering an interest in reading or conveying that reading has some utility outside of the classroom. (Sims, 1990, p. 560)

Using culturally relevant literature helped to engage students and offset much of the resistance and student apathy exercised in low-level reading tracks. It also provided the opportunity to develop deeper processing strategies through reading, writing, questioning, and discussing.

We must rethink the test-driven approach and basic skills indoctrination to bring adolescent students in low-level reading tracks up from the bottom. We also must refine the use of culturally relevant literature. There are limitations with both. But when combined, they make a powerful vehicle for increasing the literate behaviors of African American adolescents. An approach to such instruction has been offered that benefited one group of students, and it has the potential to break down the barriers that disenfranchise other adolescent students assigned to low-level reading tracks.

REFERENCES

Achebe, C. (1988). *Hopes and impediments*. New York: Doubleday.

Campbell, J., Donahue, P., Reese, C., & Phillips, G. (1996). *National Assessment of Educational Progress 1994 reading report card for the nation and the states*. Washington, DC: National Center for Education Statistics, U.S. Department of Education.

Darling-Hammond, L., & Falk, B. (1997). Using standards and assessments to support student learning. *Phi Delta Kappan, 79*, 190–199.

Dole, J., Sloan, C., & Trathen, W. (1995). Teaching vocabulary within the context of literature. *Journal of Reading, 38,* 452–460.

Dowhower, Sarah L. (1989). Repeated reading: Research into practice. *The Reading Teacher, 42,* 502–507.

Foster, M. (1993). Educating for competence in community and culture: Exploring the views of exemplary African American teachers. *Urban Education, 27,* 370–394.

Foster, M. (1997). *Black teachers on teaching.* New York: The New York Press.

Gambrell, L., & Bales, R.J. (1986). Mental imagery and the comprehension-monitoring performance of fourth and fifth grade readers. *Reading Research Quarterly, 21,* 454–464.

Gaskins, R.W., Gaskins, J.C., & Gaskins, I.W. (1991). A decoding program for poor readers—and the rest of the class, too! *Language Arts, 68,* 213–225.

Hillard, A. (1995). *The maroon within us.* Baltimore, MD: Black Classic Press.

Jones, L., Newman, L., & Isay, D. (1997). *Our America: Life and death on the South Side of Chicago.* New York: Washington Square Press.

Ladson-Billings, G. (1995a). But that's just good teaching! The case for culturally relevant pedagogy. *Theory Into Practice, 34,* 159–164.

Ladson-Billings, G. (1995b). Toward a theory of culturally relevant pedagogy. *American Educational Research Journal, 32,* 465–491.

Livdahl, B., Smart, K., Wallman, J., Herbert, T.K., Geiger, D.K., Anderson, J.L. (1995). *Stories from response-centered classrooms: Speaking, questioning, and theorizing from the center of the action.* New York, Teachers College Press

Lynch, W. (1712). Speech on slave control delivered in Jamestown, Virginia. Available [online]: www.blackspeak.com/speeches/slavecontrol.htm

May, F. (1990). *Reading as communication—An interactive approach* (3rd ed.). Columbus, OH: Merrill.

Muhammad, E. (1965). *Message to the black man.* Chicago: Muhammad Mosque of Islam No. 2.

Neill, M. (1998). High-stakes tests do not improve student learning. FairTest Executive Report. Available [online]: www.fairtest.org/k12/naeprep.htm

Purcell-Gates, V. (1991). On the outside looking in: A study of remedial readers' meaning-making while reading literature. *Journal of Reading Behavior, 23,* 235–254.

Shanahan, T. (in preparation). *Literacy framework.*

Sims, R. (1990). Walk tall in the world: African American literature for today's children. *The Journal of Negro Education, 59,* 556–565.

Smith, M.L. (1991). Put to the test: The effects of external testing on teachers. *Educational Researcher, 20*(5), 8–11.

Walker, D. (1993). *An appeal to the colored citizens of the world but in particular and very expressly to those of the United States of America.* Baltimore: Black Classic Press.

Washington, B.T. (1901). *Up from slavery.* New York: Doubleday.

Washington, J.M. (Ed.). (1986). *A testament of hope: The essential writings of Martin Luther King, Jr.* San Francisco, CA: Harper & Row.

Extending horizons: Critical technological literacy for urban Aboriginal students

Catherine Doherty

This literacy project was developed and implemented to give students the opportunity to learn critical technological literacy skills and become comfortable in a university setting.

The explosion of texts on the World Wide Web from uncontrolled sources purportedly offering factual information has alerted educators to the need for "critical literacy" skills to challenge, critique, and evaluate textual meaning (Burbules & Callister, 2000). This is an interesting departure from the practices of textbook pedagogy, where textual meaning was paramount to indisputable truth. Previous "functional" or generic notions of literacy assumed textual meaning to be an inert, stable entity. This approach considered texts as one dimensional inactive objects, rather than recognise the power of any text to interact with the reader and ideologically shape the subject matter (Fairclough, 1989). Similarly, it failed to recognise that readers can engage with any text in different ways that render the meaning problematic and disputed. Texts and readers did these things before the Internet existed, but there is now a moral panic associated with the "risks" of the Internet and the collective will in education circles to acknowledge and foster new roles for readers (Luke & Freebody, 1997).

Earlier approaches to literacy focussing on decoding as a generic skill also failed to recognise the diversity of texts, contexts, and purposes that shape reading and writing practices. Australian literacy educators have invested a lot of energy in developing sociological understandings of literacy in terms of linguistic genre, modes, and the role of cultural context in shaping textual practices (e.g., Christie, 1990; Halliday, 1985). E-mail (Moran & Hawisher, 1998), instant messaging (Lewis & Fabos, 2000), and chat rooms—each with their distinct linguistic and pragmatic protocols—are good examples of how new contexts create new shared understandings of how and why texts are "done" in these worlds. So when it comes to developing and defining literacy competency, to talk of one holistic and transportable "literacy" inadequately addresses the diversity of textual practices and the role of socialisation in communities of textual practice (Baynham & Prinsloo, 2001).

To add to the problem, we are inundated with multimedia texts, interactive screens, and the Internet. Print text does not stand alone and inert, but interacts with image, sound, graphics, animations, and design features to create textual meaning. Dedication to print decoding practice will not develop the skills needed to "read" images, graphics, hyperlinks (Burbules & Callister, 2000), and their collocation. C. Luke (2000) highlighted this "hybridity and intertextuality" of electronic texts as a feature of the current textual environment that literacy pedagogy must address.

Reprinted from *Journal of Adolescent & Adult Literacy* (2002), 46, 50–59.

Lemke (1998) described multimedia texts as "meaning objects" created by the intended and unintended synergy of multimodal elements and argued for multimedia and informatic literacies—not as add-on advanced skills, but as new core competencies. Thus literacies are not only multiple across contexts, but also across modes and encoding choices.

In this article I outline the distinctive features of a small-scale literacy program offered to urban Aboriginal school students, which was premised on understandings of critical multiliteracies and explored through technological environments and texts. The project was devised primarily as a service to a local community, not as an experimental "laboratory school" program. However, the success of the program to engage these disadvantaged students in new ways offers other educators ideas that could be adapted to other settings. This article reports the pedagogical decisions and design that distinguish this program, which were distilled from action research over five program cycles. The first section deals with the project brief and the project's participants and context. The second section outlines the program in more detail and describes the rationale behind nine distinctive pedagogical features: avoiding a deficit paradigm, exploring multiple roles for readers, developing multiliteracies across texts and technologies, building a community of expertise, developing a technical vocabulary, being inclusive of the students' worlds, fostering independent learning and problem-solving strategies, experiencing electronic communities, and including role models.

The PLUS Project

Considerations of the nature of current literacy demands and dimensions have informed the design behind the Positive Links Between Universities and Schools (PLUS) Project. Premised on a critical multiliteracies framework (Luke & Freebody, 1997; C. Luke, 2000), the project offers a literacy program for Aboriginal and Torres Strait Islander students from a cluster of primary and secondary state schools in Ipswich, a town near Brisbane, Australia (Community Services and Research Centre and Graduate School of Education, University of Queensland, 1999; Kapitzke et al., 2000; A. Luke, 2000). The program is devoted to electronic texts and technologies and is thus termed a "technological literacy program." The project aims (a) to give the students in upper primary and lower secondary schools the opportunity to develop critical literacy skills in technological environments and (b) to help the students become familiar and comfortable with a university setting. The idea of "extending horizons" in this article's title captures the goals of extending imagined futures, extending the students' world view access to global technology, and extending the way they see things with more critical insight.

The PLUS Project has been developed through collaboration among multiple parties:

- the government primary and secondary schools in Ipswich, Queensland, that selected the students and advised on programming;

- the Aboriginal and Torres Strait Islander parents and students who participated and helped shape the program;

- Education Queensland's Aboriginal and Torres Strait Islander Education Unit, which funded the program and managed aspects of school liaison;

- the Graduate School of Education, University of Queensland (UQ), Brisbane, which designed and delivered the program and conducted the research agenda in consultation with the other parties;

- the Aboriginal and Torres Strait Islander Unit, UQ, which advised on cultural matters; and

- the Community Service and Research Centre, at the UQ Ipswich campus, which brokered the partnerships and managed logistical aspects of the program.

The project is distinct from other computer skills or literacy courses in the ownership felt and asserted by the local Aboriginal community. Regular advisory meetings involve parents and indigenous staff in the program planning. On their advice, the program purposefully has not pursued an explicit Aboriginal studies curriculum to deliver indigenous knowledge—this is seen as the community's responsibility. The parents are eager to see the project invigorate school efforts and deliver competent skills for vocational and further study purposes. They also look forward to the students bringing these skills into the local community. Parents and friends are regularly invited to visit the project in action for a demonstration of what the students can do. The number of parties involved risks confusion or complication, but there is very much a shared sense of purpose and partnership in wanting to make the most of the opportunities available. There is also the sense that the project, though modest in scope by some criteria, can achieve very significant gains for the students and their community. In other words, there are high expectations of the program and the students.

Ipswich, the context for this program, is a regional town of approximately 127,000 people in South East Queensland. It achieved international notoriety in the 1990s with the emergence of the highly contentious One Nation Party with a conservative backlash agenda. This history has overshadowed efforts by the community to redefine itself in the information age as wired and technologically proactive. The recent development of an Ipswich campus of the University of Queensland has contributed to this proactive profile with its emphasis on high-end computing facilities and Web-enhanced programs.

Ipswich also has significant Aboriginal and Torres Strait Islander populations, whose children typically attend mainstream state schools. The urban Aboriginal and Islander communities, as distinct from more remote communities, speak English with perhaps Aboriginal English or an Islander dialect as their home dialect (Eades, 1995). For these students, standard English is the language of instruction in their schools. They live in a western consumer society, and assertions of essential cultural or linguistic difference don't capture the fact that the students also participate in and are part of the greater urban culture. Cultural difference interacts with political, historical, and socioeconomic disadvantage to marginalise these students in the mainstream school.

The current National Indigenous English Literacy and Numeracy Strategy (Commonwealth of Australia, 1999) attempts to address the fact that many Aboriginal children in urban Australian classrooms face intractable disadvantages when it comes to literacy, school completion, and postschool education pathways. Some extra assistance in terms of indigenous school-based support staff, homework centres, indigenous parent advisory groups, and regional advisory staff is provided to support these communities. The PLUS Project is one region's attempt to invigorate schooling, in particular literacy learning, for these students.

When it comes to the spread of technological literacy competence in the community, acquisition has been shown to happen predominantly in the home—particularly in the higher income home (Meredyth, Russell, Blackwood, Thomas, & Wise, 1999). Formal school programs for technological skills will have the greatest impact for those with restricted home access to technology. As might be expected, this group includes children from lower income homes, the geographically isolated and indigenous students. However, the schools these children rely on to give them these crucial experiences are not necessarily the well-equipped ones. From a sample of 38 of the 70 students who have attended the PLUS Project thus far, 55% had access to a computer at home, and 16% had access to the Internet. Their numbers contrast with the Australian averages of 79% and 36% respectively (Meredyth et al., 1999).

As Gilbert (2000) put it, "the equity picture has been shaken and stirred by the advent of technological changes, and we now have a number of new agendas to address" (p. 43). The coexistence of these two sides of the digital divide, the haves and the have-nots, in a town the size of Ipswich has spawned a project whereby Aboriginal students can have regular, supported access to state-of-the-art equipment and, thus, to the emerging culture of electronically mediated communities.

Programming the PLUS Project

In the PLUS Project, students in groups of 15 to 20 attend eight weekly sessions of two hours in a university computer laboratory. Students have their own machines with Internet access, e-mail accounts, and networked drives. These students are chosen by their schools from amongst the Aboriginal and Islander student population as the ones likely to benefit from the program. In some cases this choice is interpreted selectively as low-literacy achievers, while other schools plan to move all their indigenous students through the program eventually. Students can return for a second program if interested.

The project was at first loosely modelled on the "La Clase Magica" model from the University of California, San Diego (http://communication.ucsd.edu/LCM/), in the way disadvantaged children were given access to high-end technology and a supportive learning environment (Kaptizke et al., 2000). Over the five program cycles to the time of writing this article, the following nine pedagogical features have been trialled and refined. I suggest that these features have contributed to the high degree of engagement, effective learning, and performance by students—improvements recognised by the community in its continued demand for this program and by the Department of Education in its decision to continue funding the project. The explanation of each program feature includes a rationale, illus-

trative examples, and details of how this feature was interpreted and enacted.

Avoiding a deficit paradigm

From a generic, functional approach to literacy, low-literacy performance would indicate the need for remedial effort in the form of more decoding practice. In contrast to such a paradigm, the PLUS Project does not frame the program in terms of deficit and need. The PLUS program adopts a sociological view of literacy as sets of social practices based around texts in different social settings (Baynham & Prinsloo, 2001; Luke & Freebody, 1997). It purposefully designs learning as an induction to the cultural practices of electronic communication environments and an exploration of critical dimensions to these literacy practices. This positions the students not as disadvantaged at school, but rather as experts-to-be, with something valuable to contribute to school and local communities. Students rise to this expectation. Some who would be considered poor readers in functional terms are quick, adept learners across applications in the electronic environment. The students negotiate hierarchical menu options, manage files over a choice of drives, read e-mail screens selectively, and negotiate hyperlinks or directories to get what information they want from Web pages.

Exploring multiple roles for readers

Luke and Freebody (1997) outlined four essential sets of practices or roles that a reader draws on. These four are coding practices, text meaning practices, pragmatic practices, and critical practices.

1. *Coding practices* refer to the effort and resources necessary to "crack the code" of the graphophonic and symbolic interface—what does the text say? PLUS students continually engage in this role as they meet text on screen.

They also learn to decode the pictorial icons (e.g., the pointing hand cursor) and the significance of other semiotic codes (e.g., blue underlined text for hyperlinks).

2. *Text meaning practices* refer to the resources that derive understanding of, and participation with, the intended meaning of the text—what does the text mean? PLUS students engage in this role when they make a selection from menu options informed by the knowledge of the relevant technical terms, when they select the correct icon on the desktop to open the desired application, when they complete an on-screen form, when they can find the answer to a question in a Web page, or when they laugh over the contents of an e-mail.

3. *Pragmatic practices* refer to a reader's cultural knowledge of a textual genre and of how the text is structured. Examples of this role are learning not to read the jumble of computer generated text in an e-mail header; knowing to reply to e-mails above the old posting; and overlooking advertising content on a Web page, with an understanding of why those pieces of text are there.

4. *Critical practices* refer to the reader's being alert to how the text selectively constructs its subject and positions its reader ideologically—what is the text doing? PLUS students are asked to evaluate Web pages by reflecting on authorship (e.g., ".com" in the URL), intended readership, what content has been included, and what has been excluded. For example, PLUS students visited a Web page created by the local government to solicit new investment. With a sense of who created the text, the students were able to articulate the positive spin given to their city and contrast this with the mostly negative "newsworthy" accounts the local press would give of Ipswich. Similarly, students identified the U.S. cultural bias of Internet search engines and language usage (Yates, 1996). For example, *football* is American football (without further search terms) and the Australian word *lollies* (*lollipops* or *suckers* in American terms) is not recognised by Microsoft Word's spell check.

The same four roles are encouraged when students compose their own texts—with a sense of audience, purpose, cultural genre, and linguistic conventions all playing a role. These roles or practices apply to visual literacies as well as print literacies. Interestingly, when facing the visual prompt of a trouble-shooting dialogue box, the students have often interacted with the text pragmatically with "What's this for?" as their first response. Unsure of the text purpose, they need a resolution before moving on to decoding, text meaning, or critical roles.

Developing multiliteracies across texts and technologies

In the PLUS program, the students encounter a variety of texts (e.g., Web pages, e-mails, searches, directions, Microsoft PowerPoint files), and they construct texts using a range of technologies, invoking multiple literacies. The students have to read and construct not just print but also images, videos, and sound texts. An effort has been made in the program to provide hands-on experience with different technologies such as scanners, CD-ROMs, digital cameras, and microphones, as well as computers. The texts students read and create are multimodal. They use text, clip art, graphics, colour, and font design as a minimum. The students become adept users of the design tools in Microsoft Word and put considerable effort into refining these aspects. The presentation application PowerPoint in the Microsoft Office suite provided an immediate and manageable experience in making design decisions about animation, sound effects, use of image, layout, and textual appearance. The format process of PowerPoint is useful in scaffolding a coherent expository text. The bullet points' short syntax is enabling for students with limited writing competency, as opposed to the longer paragraph unit of print exposition. Students also download free images from the Internet, use simple graphics packages, a scanner, and a digital camera to create images or short movies to put in their texts. One cohort of students experimented with capturing simple sound and movie files to use in a collaborative Web page.

Discussion with the teaching team explores the students' reasoning behind design choices in their texts and alerts them to design problems. For example, after writing a text of personal introduction, a student inserted a clip art image of a hypodermic needle. Although there was no mention of drugs in the text, this was the immediate connotation I "read" when viewing the screen. It turned out that a sibling of the student was diabetic, thus the significance of the needle in his personal introduction. He quickly realised that this intended meaning was in no way anchored or indicated by the text, and he chose to remove the image to avoid the potential drug connotation. His multimodal text wasn't saying what he intended.

Model

Before creating a text such as a PowerPoint presentation, e-mail, or a personal Web page, students are given models of similar texts and a conceptual vocabulary to talk about the genre's features. Making a Web page or PowerPoint presentation is difficult if a student doesn't know what one is or how it is done. This stage is often followed by joint construction of an example of the text using students' suggestions carefully scaffolded to elicit appropriate genre choices. A data projector facilitates this kind of activity because everyone shares the view of a "live" screen. Text scaffolds are also provided as paper worksheets to help students plan and develop their texts with tutor assistance.

Building a community of expertise

The project resources provide a core of three members of the teaching team and additional assistance where possible. This arrangement has allowed the team to develop as a community of expertise—no member holds all the requisite knowledge or skills. One member has a computing

background and handles the technical trouble shooting that is inevitable in any technology-driven setting. Another member acts as the webmaster and is particularly skilled in the use of ancillary technology such as the digital camera. The third teacher designs the program details, task sheets, and support materials. Other tutors, including preservice teachers, act as guides. Their facilitative questioning can lead students through the steps to resolving problems for themselves. A team of education academics and the advisory group drawn from the community oversee and inform the design of the program. What seems very generous staffing for each session is more accurately an indicator of the intensity and high expectations of the program sessions.

let allow expert

Within this community of expertise, the students play a crucial part. They bring with them expertise in some applications—all have had some exposure to information technologies at school. Students soon explore beyond what is demonstrated by drilling down hierarchies of choice in menus, and they fast become the experts in new areas of technology. They also are respected as experts in the content of their texts. The teaching team consciously takes opportunities to allow students to act as experts and demonstrate their knowledge to others, either as peer tutors or to the whole group, if they are undaunted being singled out. Back in their school communities, PLUS students have acted as peer instructors and tutors, not just for students but for their teachers as well.

Developing a technical vocabulary

Gee (1991) explained his understanding of "discourses" as sets of meanings across texts that can act to include those who are familiar with it and exclude those who are not. We have all been victims of exclusion by the discourse of computing manuals. Gee talked of "powerful" literacy as control of the secondary discourses that organise life outside the primary personal circle. Technical

Community of experts

vocabularies help to delineate such communities of practice. To enter these communities and demystify the power of jargon, the students need some control of the relevant discourse. For these reasons, the PLUS program actively addresses the information technology discourse rather than avoiding or "dumbing down" technical terms. For each session, the relevant target technical vocabulary is made explicit in the planning stage, strategically used by the teaching team in explanations, reinforced in worksheets and reference notes, and consciously elicited from the students in a supported way. For example, students regularly e-mail their principals with a description of what they have been doing at the PLUS Project. Tutors help them deploy technical terms in their descriptions.

Being inclusive of the students' worlds

This project has aimed to create a cluster setting where students' "Aboriginality" produces no risk of their being under a spotlight as it might in a mainstream setting, especially in the context of the conservative backlash politics mentioned earlier. Australia is currently undergoing a process of reconciliation with its past and the treatment suffered by the indigenous people since the invasion of their land. While the Australian government has rejected a formal apology, and the Australian Prime Minister has refused to say "sorry," thousands of Australians joined nationwide reconciliation marches where the Aboriginal flag, a potent symbol of Aboriginal identity, protest, and strength, was displayed. Cathy Freeman, in the wake of her 2000 Olympics win, attracted considerable media attention by carrying both the Aboriginal and Australian flags. It is significant that many of the PLUS students, when exploring a simple graphics package, immediately express the desire to create an image of the flag—yet often ask permission to do so. Their pride in its symbolism is mixed with the recognition of its powerful connotations of protest and confrontation, and the risk of being in a new setting where

the implications of such a statement are not known. This wariness is soon dispelled, and expressions of Aboriginal and Islander identities are encouraged though not forced.

As previously mentioned, the community advisory group expressed the opinion that the project was not to teach "Aboriginal Studies" because Aboriginal knowledge is the premise of family and community. Within the critical multi-literacies focus of the program, the effort shifts instead to investigating (a) how Aboriginal and Torres Strait Islander worlds are represented on the Web and (b) how the Internet privileges some cultures, agendas, and languages while obscuring and disadvantaging others. Students have found in search activities that Aboriginal people are typically presented as the exotic "other" in commercial, museum, or tourism sites, while in their local communities they are often represented in terms of the exotic cultural activities they can add to the local arts festivals. Culture is effectively reduced to the superficial and commercially exploitable tangibles, revealing a permeating bias on the World Wide Web.

The students are also active and avid members of the global consumer culture based on U.S. movie stars and high-profile pop musicians. This culture is core business for the World Wide Web, which has an amazing depth of multimedia material available. With access to high-speed machines, students enjoy downloading lyrics, sounds, movies, and images of their choice. The expression of such subjectivities is a major motivation behind the students' interest in technology, which the PLUS Project exploits unashamedly to develop their skills and critical literacy. Students are asked to work together to identify sites about their favourite artists by using directory or keyword searches. Then they evaluate the range of sites to select the most appropriate to include as links from their collaborative page. Issues of audience, purpose, authority, and functional design are raised in their website evaluations, making them take a critical role.

Fostering independent learning and problem-solving strategies

Given the rate of change in information technologies, a didactic approach to computer competency would result in rapid redundancy. The students' eagerness to jump into the electronic environments would also make it impossible. These students need to cope with constant updates and exposure to new applications. For these reasons, we have purposefully reduced the traditional emphasis on teacher direction of the whole group and actively work against reliance on the teacher for problem solving. To this end, the project uses these "Four Commandments" as a troubleshooting process:

1. Read the screen
2. Read your notes
3. Ask a friend
4. Ask a tutor

Students are given a summary task sheet for each session that explains the essential details. Accompanying the sheet are more detailed notes and instructions on how to perform certain new tasks, with images of relevant computer screens where necessary. These notes are compiled and used as reference resources in future weeks. The notes and the team of tutors allow the group to multitask. The tutors are often allocated different tasks to oversee and work with small groups rotated through the activities. Students are encouraged to sit in friendship groups and to work together to solve problems or perform tasks. If asked for assistance, a tutor will try to avoid using the keyboard but will lead the student through the steps and decisions to solve the problem.

Another feature of the program is the decision at times to encourage students to work out a program for themselves by "mucking around" (i.e., exploring menus and seeing if they can find another way). Smith and Curtin (1998) called this mode of learning "tinkering with intent." This choice reflects the opportunities children would have to learn in unsupervised play on home computers. In the PLUS Project, "tinkering" also aims to empower the students with a sense of efficacy when faced with an unknown application.

Experiencing electronic communities

E-mail is an integral and ongoing part of the program and works to build an electronic community around the project. E-mail accounts are established for students, and weekly e-mails are exchanged between students and the teaching team. These exchanges are much more than an excuse to make the student write something. E-mails are sometimes broadcast to the whole student group with instructions for the day or to demonstrate some feature such as attachments. More important, the e-mails also can be interpersonal exchanges between the tutor and the student, building up a thread of increasingly familiar dialogue. Students can thereby experience the immediacy and intimate nature of e-mail communication. Harslett (1998) emphasised the importance of rapport and positive interpersonal relationships between staff and urban Aboriginal students in education settings. Kickett-Tucker (1998) recommended two-way sharing of personal information when working with these students. The exchange of e-mails contributes to these relationships in a very real way.

E-mail is also used to connect the students with outside communities. An Aboriginal woman who acts in a cultural advisory capacity to the local government has been our "e-pal" for some student cohorts. Other students have been matched with students from the remote Thursday Island High School and are exchanging e-mails from opposite ends of Queensland. Future effort will be made to connect students with overseas communities. These experiences demonstrate not just the capacity of electronic mail, but also the culture and practices surrounding these texts.

Including role models

As an additional layer to the program, a few guest speakers are invited to talk about their use of computer technology and the Internet at home, study, and work. Guests have included an Aboriginal community leader who talked about using the Internet and e-mail in her work and personal life; a young Aboriginal man, recruited to work as a trainee on mapping for the local council, who talked about his use of mapping software; and other Aboriginal community members who shared their favourite websites with the students. These brief conversations also explore how the guests developed their skills. Meredyth et al. (1999) reported a poor understanding amongst school children of the application of such skills beyond school, particularly amongst indigenous and nonurban students. The PLUS strategy is to provide local role models and narratives to which the students can relate these issues.

Project outcomes

In this article I have argued for literacy programs to address critical practices that interrogate texts across multiple texts and modes. I have also presented a model of this critical multiliteracies framework interpreted in a case-study project that has had significant impact on its students and their community. The project worked with indigenous students and by adopting a sociological approach to literacy pedagogy—that is, by theorising literacy as a set of social practices—aimed to introduce them to the textual practices and emerging culture surrounding electronic texts. Students were required to act in a variety of reading roles across a range of texts and technologies. The program refused to construct these students as deficit or remedial learners and facilitated the students' contribution to the community of expertise built in these classes. The program tried to teach the kind of technical vocabulary that can exclude people who don't have it. The teaching staff welcomed expressions of the Aboriginal and Islander identities and invited Aboriginal role models to share their experiences with electronic texts.

Rather than a didactic approach to teaching students how to operate certain applications, the program design and pedagogy encouraged independent learning and problem solving, and it involved students in electronic communities to experience the cultural practices associated with that medium. These students, though considered disadvantaged by their wider school communities, are powerful learners in this environment when given the opportunity, high expectations, resources, and support. Program outcomes include not just the hypertext and multimedia products the students create, but also their experience of contributing to electronic communities, becoming competent with information technology, and taking a more critical role when engaging with texts. Let us hope that this program can create ripples that reach to the horizon for these children, so they can imagine new futures and build on these skills. Their communities in turn will benefit from their expertise.

In this profile, the particular political and historical context was a significant factor shaping aspects of the project. However, other communities experiencing a similarly intransigent digital divide could benefit from the model of interagency collaboration, sociological understandings of literacy, or aspects of the pedagogical design to bring disadvantaged students into the communities of practice that support and exploit digital texts.

REFERENCES

Baynham, M., & Prinsloo, M. (2001). New directions in literacy research. *Language and Education, 15*(2,3), 83–91.

Burbules, N., & Callister, T. (2000). *Watch IT: The risks and promises of information technologies for education.* Boulder, CO: Westview Press.

Christie, F. (Ed.). (1990). *Literacy for a changing world.* Hawthorn, VIC, Australia: Australian Council for Educational Research.

Commonwealth of Australia. (1999). *National indigenous English literacy and numeracy strategy 2000–2004.* Canberra, ACT, Australia: Department of Education, Training and Youth Affairs.

Community Services and Research Centre and Graduate School of Education, University of Queensland. (1999). *Pilot project report on the Positive Links Between Universities and Schools Project.* Unpublished manuscript, University of Queensland, Brisbane, QLD, Australia.

Eades, D. (1995). *Aboriginal English.* Sydney, NSW, Australia: Board of Studies.

Fairclough, N. (1989). *Language and power.* London: Longman.

Gee, J. (1991). What is literacy? In C. Mitchell & K. Weiler (Eds.), *Rewriting literacy: Culture and the discourse of the other* (pp. 3–11). New York: Bergin & Garvey.

Gilbert, P. (2000). "The deepening divide?": Choices for Australian education. *Australian Educational Researcher, 27*(1), 31–45.

Halliday, M.A.K. (1985). *An introduction to functional grammar.* London: Edward Arnold.

Harslett, M.G. (1998, May). *Relationships, relationships, relationships: That's what sells school to Aboriginal students and parents.* Article written for the Western Australian Secondary School Principals Association, Edith Cowan University, Bunbury, WA, Australia. Available online: http://www.wn.com.au/abled/quality/relation.htm

Kapitzke, C., Bogitini, S., Chen, M., MacNeill, G., Mayer, D., Muirhead, B., & Renshaw, P. (2000). Weaving words with the Dreamweaver: Literacy, indigeneity, and technology. *Journal of Adolescent & Adult Literacy, 44,* 336–355.

Kickett-Tucker, C.S. (1998, December). *Research and urban Aboriginal school children: Considerations and implications.* Paper presented at the conference of the Australian Association for Research in Education, Adelaide, SA, Australia. Available online: http://www.aare.edu.au/98pap/kic98374.htm

Lemke, J.L. (1998). Metamedia literacy: Transforming meanings and media. In D. Reinking, M. McKenna, L. Labbo, & R. Kieffer (Eds.), *Handbook of literacy & technology: Transformations in a post-typographic world* (pp. 283–301). Mahwah, NJ: Erlbaum.

Lewis, C., & Fabos, B. (2000). But will it work in the heartland? A response and illustration. *Journal of Adolescent & Adult Literacy, 43,* 462–469.

Luke, A. (2000). A response to Ann Peterson Bishop. *Journal of Adolescent & Adult Literacy, 43,* 482–484.

Luke, A., & Freebody, P. (1997). The social practices of reading. In S. Muspratt, A. Luke, & P. Freebody (Eds.), *Constructing critical literacies: Teaching and learning textual practices* (pp. 185–225). Cresskill, NJ: Hampton Press.

Luke, C. (2000). Cyber-schooling and technological change: Multiliteracies for new times. In B. Cope & M. Kalantzis (Eds.), *Multiliteracies: Literacy learning and the design of social futures* (pp. 69–91). Melbourne, VIC, Australia: Macmillan.

Meredyth, D., Russell, N., Blackwood, L., Thomas, J., & Wise, P. (1999). *Real time: Computers, change and schooling.* Canberra, ACT, Australia: Department of Education, Training and Youth Affairs.

Moran, C., & Hawisher, G.E. (1998). The rhetorics and language of electronic mail. In I. Snyder (Ed.), *Page to screen: Taking literacy into the electronic era* (pp. 80–101). London: Routledge.

Smith, R., & Curtin, P. (1998). Children, computers and life online: Education in a cyber-world. In I. Snyder (Ed.), *Page to screen: Taking literacy into the electronic era* (pp. 211–233). London: Routledge.

Yates, S. (1996). English in cyberspace. In S. Goodman & D. Graddol (Eds.), *Redesigning English: New texts, new identities* (pp. 106–133). London: Routledge.

Decodable text—Where to find it

JOSEPH R. JENKINS, PATRICIA F. VADASY, JULIA A. PEYTON, ELIZABETH A. SANDERS

In designing reading instruction for beginning readers, one of the first decisions teachers face is whether to supplement phonics instruction with practice in decodable texts. That decision is complicated by the challenge of finding texts suitable for individual students. This article describes a tool for finding texts that match children's decoding skills. We begin with an overview of current thinking and research on the use of decodable text in beginning reading instruction.

Teachers and researchers generally concur that explicit phonics instruction is essential to help struggling readers master the code (National Reading Panel, 2000). However, when it comes to decodable text, opinions vary considerably. Foorman, Fletcher, and Francis (1997) have taken one of the stronger positions in favor of decodable text, writing that

> there is a period during beginning reading instruction when all children benefit from practicing letter-sound connections in decodable text. To immerse children in a print environment without instruction in letter-sound correspondences and practice in decodable text is to doom a large percentage of children to reading failure. (p. 16)

Their position resembles that of many prevention-oriented researchers (e.g., Beck, 1997; Kameenui & Simmons, 1997). Other researchers (e.g., Allington & Woodside-Jiron, 1998) caution against overselling decodable texts. The difference of opinion is not so much whether decodable texts are ever useful, but how much and for whom to use such texts (Hiebert, 1999).

The case for decodable text

The case for using decodable text is an extension of the case for phonics. Alphabetic knowledge (i.e., knowledge of graphophonemic regularities) is essential for literacy acquisition (Ehri, 1998). Acquisition of alphabetic knowledge is enhanced when individuals have plenty of opportunities to read words that exemplify the links between graphemes and their pronunciations. Reading practice with decodable text is thought to help struggling readers in three ways.

First, decodable text may facilitate alphabetic insight, reminding beginning readers that all letters in a word are important and that there are no shortcuts to word learning. Second, reading texts that exemplify specific graphophonemic connections may help children anchor those connections in memory. Establishing these connections in memory not only helps beginning readers decode unfamiliar words but also allows them to form complete connections between printed words and pronunciations, leading to the development of a sight-reading vocabulary. Third, practice in decodable texts may enhance motivation and build confidence because the majority of the text yields to a decoding strategy. This may be especially important for students who are teetering on the brink of discouragement.

Research on decodable text

The empirical basis for decodable text derives from clinical reports and the results of multicomponent interventions that included decodable text as one component. Several studies with at-risk first- and second-grade students reported strong effects from interventions that combine explicit instruction in phonological awareness, phonics, word study, and reading in decodable texts (e.g., Blachman, Tangel, Ball, Black, & McGraw, 1999; Vadasy, Jenkins, & Poole, 2000). None of these studies separated the

Reprinted from *The Reading Teacher* (2003), 57, 185–189.

contributions of reading decodable texts from those of other treatment components (e.g., explicit phonics instruction). Nonetheless, it is noteworthy that the researchers took great pains to match texts with phonics lessons.

Only two studies have attempted to isolate the effects of decodable texts. Within each study, comparison groups used the same phonics program, differing only in the kind of texts they read. In a study of first-grade classrooms, Juel and Roper-Schneider (1985) determined that students who read phonetically controlled texts developed stronger decoding skills relative to students who read from traditional basal stories, although the two groups did not differ on a broader reading measure.

A more recent study (Jenkins, Peyton, Vadasy, & Sanders, in press) examined decodable text in a supplemental tutoring program for at-risk first graders. The latter found no differences in first-grade reading scores between a group tutored in highly decodable storybooks and a group tutored in less decodable storybooks. These results suggest that if decodable texts contribute to reading achievement, even substantial differences in text decodability may not always "power through" other tutorial and background (classroom) factors. The fact that both tutored groups received strong doses of phonics and word study may have reduced the importance of differences in storybook decodability. Moreover, both tutored groups read from a variety of texts during *classroom* instruction, and this may have diluted differences in storybook decodability during tutoring.

Finding decodable text

Although the precise contributions of decodable texts have yet to be pinned down, supplementing reading practice with such texts remains a viable instructional strategy, especially when teaching students who struggle with the alphabetic code. However, finding storybooks that complement phonics instruction can be daunting. Even storybooks that are labeled decodable may not be readable by individual students, because a text's decodability depends on the match between the phonic elements featured in it and the phonic elements students have been taught. To complicate matters, most decodable storybooks do not list the specific phonic elements required to read them,

leaving teachers with a time-consuming analysis of phonic elements featured in each book. A few publishers list featured phonic elements in the back of each book—for example, Educators Publishing Service (1996a, 1996b)—allowing teachers to assess (albeit, inconveniently) individual storybooks for their relevance to individual students.

An analysis of decodable storybooks

Here we describe a simple tool to assist teachers in locating decodable storybooks that match individual students' phonic knowledge. Our approach resembles Trachtenburg's (1990) categorization of trade books that repeat specific vowel sounds, but it goes a step further and analyzes *all* letter-sound relations included in a storybook. Our analysis of decodable storybooks identifies the featured phonic elements, along with nondecodable words, in 138 storybooks representing three popular series that employ phonetically controlled text: Bob Books for Young Readers/Set 1 and More Bob Books for Young Readers/Set 2 (Scholastic, 1994a, 1994b); Primary Phonics and More Primary Phonics (Educators Publishing Service, 1996a, 1996b); and The Wright Skills Decodable Books (The Wright Group, 2001). Below we describe the analysis and provide an example from Scholastic's Bob Books.

The analysis lists the phonic elements by category (e.g., consonants, vowels) that are featured in each storybook. We considered an element to be featured if it appeared in more than one word in a storybook. Words were classified as decodable if application of the featured phonic elements produced either a correct pronunciation or a close approximation of a correct pronunciation. For example, we classified *that* as decodable in one book because the elements *a*, *t*, and *th* were featured in it. Even when words in a book included a mix of voiced and unvoiced *th* pronunciations (e.g., *path, that*), we counted *th* words as decodable because most students can produce correct word pronunciations without explicit instruction on these linguistic discriminations.

The analysis also lists any nondecodable word found in a storybook. We considered words nondecodable if they contained any nonfeatured phonic

Sample analysis from the Bob Books* series

Set number	Title	Consonants	Consonant blends	Vowels	Endings	Not decodable
1	Mat	m, n, s, t		Short–a, o		the, end
1	Sam	c, d, m, n, s, t		Short–a, o		the, end, OK
1	Dot	c, d, g, h, n, r, s, t		Short–a, o		the, end, has, a
1	Mac	b, c, d, g, h, m, n, r, t		Short–a, o		the, end, a
1	Dot and Mit	c, d, h, m, n, p, s, t		Short–a, o, i		the, end, a, is, has
1	Dot and the Dog	b, c, d, g, h, m, n, s, t		Short–a, o, i		the, end, a, is
1	Jig and Mag	b, c, d, g, j, m, n, r, t, w		Short–a, i		the, end, a, is
1	Muff and Ruff	c, d, g, h, m, n, p, r, s, t, ff		Short–a, i, o, u		the, end, is, to, for
1	10 Cut-Ups	b, c, d, g, h, j, m, n, p, r, s, t, w, ff		Short–a, i, u		the, end, a, has
1	Peg and Ted	b, d, g, h, m, n, p, r, t, w		Short–a, e, i, o		the, a, is, pink
1	Lad and the Fat Cat	b, c, d, f, g, h, k, l, m, n, p, s, t, x		Short–all		the, a, has, is
1	The Vet	b, c, d, f, g, h, l, m, n, r, s, t, v, x, y, z		Short–all		the, a, to, into, zoo, OK
2	Ten Men	b, d, f, h, j, l, m, n, r, s, t, w, th	Initial–dr, fl Final–nd, nt, st	Short–all		to, the, of, they, a, into, were, has
2	Bump!	b, j, m, n, p, r, s, v, y, th	Initial–sk, sl, fl Final–mp	Short–a, e, i, u Long–o, er	y, ed	the
2	Cat and Mouse	b, c, d, f, h, k, l, m, n, p, r, s, t, w, ck, th,	Initial–sk, sn, fl, sl, st Final–st, lp, nt	Short–a, e, i, o Teams–ou, er	y	is, the, his, a by, of, too, be, she

* (Scholastic, 1994a, 1994b)

elements. Among words classified as nondecodable were high-frequency "sight" or "exception" words (e.g., *the*, *were*, *said*) that contained an inconsistent phonic element (e.g., the *ai* in *said*) as well as phonetically regular words (e.g., *zoo*) that contained a phonic element not featured in the book (i.e., an element that did not occur in more than one word).

The Table shows the results of an analysis of several storybooks in the Scholastic (1994a, 1994b) Bob Books series. Using the analysis, a teacher can identify the storybook number (publisher's number for the book) and title; the featured consonants (and consonant digraphs), consonant blends (initial and final), vowels (and vowel combinations), and endings; and the nondecodable words (i.e., words requiring knowledge of phonic elements not featured in the book).

How to use the analysis

The following five steps show how teachers can use this analysis to locate decodable texts that match and supplement their phonics instruction.

1. Inspect the phonic elements featured in a specific storybook.

2. Compare the featured elements with the phonics knowledge of individual students.

3. For independent reading practice, select storybooks containing phonic elements that students have mastered.

4. For assisted reading practice, select storybooks containing phonic elements that children are currently learning.

5. Before students read a storybook, note the book's nondecodable words and teach any that students do not already know.

Teachers report that the analysis of decodable storybooks has helped them identify suitable storybooks for individual and small-group instruction. In addition, before purchasing a set of storybooks, teachers can use this analysis to determine if the set meets their instructional needs. Those interested in using this resource are welcome to download the complete analysis (138 storybooks) from the Sound Partners Website: www. wri-edu.org/partners.

Decodable texts represent one of several types of early reading texts, all of which are useful in promoting reading acquisition (Hiebert, 1999). Whereas decodable texts emphasize phonetic control, other kinds of texts emphasize literature, language patterns, predictability, or high-frequency words. Like many other aspects of reading instruction, research has yet to settle questions of when, how much, and for whom different text approaches are beneficial. Decodable storybooks may be useful for beginning readers needing persuasion that phonics has utility, for those requiring additional practice applying phonic knowledge, and for those struggling to secure word-specific graphophonemic linkages in memory.

References

Allington, R.L., & Woodside-Jiron, H. (1998). Decodable text in beginning reading: Are mandates and policy based on research? *ERS Spectrum, 16*, 3-11.

Beck, I. (1997, October/November). Response to "overselling phonics." *Reading Today*, p. 17.

Blachman, B.A., Tangel, D.M., Ball, E.W., Black, R., & McGraw, C.K. (1999). Developing phonological awareness and word recognition skills: A two-year intervention with low-income, inner-city children. *Reading and Writing: An Interdisciplinary Journal, 11*, 239-273.

Educators Publishing Service. (1996a). More Primary Phonics. (Series). Cambridge, MA: Author.

Educators Publishing Service. (1996b). Primary Phonics. (Series). Cambridge, MA: Author.

Ehri, L. (1998). Grapheme-phoneme knowledge is essential for learning to read words in English. In J. Metsala & L. Ehri (Eds.), *Word recognition in beginning literacy* (pp. 3-40). Mahwah, NJ: Erlbaum.

Foorman, B.R., Fletcher, J.M., & Francis, D.J. (1997, October/November). "Do children understand what they're reading?" Yes, when they've been taught to read. *Reading Today*, p. 16.

Hiebert, E.H. (1999). Text matters in learning to read. *The Reading Teacher, 52*, 552-566.

Jenkins, J.R., Peyton, J., Vadasy, P.F., & Sanders, L. (in press). Effects of decodable texts in supplemental first-grade tutoring. *Scientific Studies of Reading*.

Juel, C., & Roper-Schneider, D. (1985). The influence of basal readers on first grade reading. *Reading Research Quarterly, 20*, 134-152.

Kame'enui, E., & Simmons, D. (1997, October/November). Decodable texts and the language of dichotomy: A response to Allington. *Reading Today*, p. 18.

National Reading Panel. (2000). *Summary report*. Washington, DC: National Institute of Child Health & Human Development.

Scholastic. (1994a). Bob Books for Young Readers/Set 1. (Series). New York: Author.

Scholastic. (1994b). More Bob Books for Young Readers/Set 2. (Series). New York: Author.

Trachtenburg, P. (1990). Using children's literature to enhance phonics instruction. *The Reading Teacher, 43*, 648-654.

Vadasy, P.F., Jenkins, J.R., & Pool, K. (2000). Effects of a first-grade tutoring program in phonological and early reading skills. *Journal of Learning Disabilities, 33*, 579-590.

The Wright Group. (2001). The Wright Skills Decodable Books (Levels A-C). (Series). Bothell, WA: Author.

Bena R. Hefflin
Mary Alice Barksdale-Ladd

African American children's literature that helps students find themselves: Selection guidelines for Grades K–3

Guidelines and suggested books can help teachers provide literature that reflects African American children's experiences.

Literature is a powerful medium. Through it, children construct messages about their cultures and roles in society. Literature offers them personal stories, a view of their cultural surroundings, and insight on themselves. When children read books that are interesting and meaningful to them, they can find support for the process of defining themselves as individuals and understanding their developing roles within their families and communities.

From the time they enter school, most African American children read literature that seldom offers messages about them, their past, or their future. All too often books used in primary classrooms contain too few African American characters, or they include characters who are African American in appearance only. Many of these stories say little about African American culture, or they present only the history of African Americans as slaves without including any "nonslavery" or modern representations. In short, today's African American children often cannot find themselves in the literature they are given to read.

The purpose of this article is to suggest guidelines for selecting African American children's literature of high literary and artistic quality for Grades K–3. To validate the importance of African Americans in society, the guidelines are for all teachers, whether they have African American children in their classrooms or not. We also provide a list of selected recent books with an African American context that meet the same criteria for quality.

What if you can't find yourself?

To read for years and not encounter stories that connect closely with one's own cultural understandings and life experiences is problematic. One primary motivation for reading fiction involves the pleasure that can be taken in relating to characters, their lives, their problems, and their experiences. When readers frequently encounter texts that feature characters with whom they can connect, they will see how others are like them and how reading can play a role in their lives. A love of reading will result. Alternatively, when readers do not encounter characters who are like them, reading is likely to be frustrating rather than pleasurable. For children, repeated frustration is not likely to lead to personal affirmations and the development of a love of reading. If teachers continually present African American children with texts in which the main characters are predominantly animals and white people, it stands to reason that these children may begin to wonder whether they, their families, and their communities fit into the

Reprinted from *The Reading Teacher* (2001), 54, 810–819.

world of reading. Our interviews with African American adults, remembering their early years in school, speak of this type of reading experience as being one of isolation. (All adult and student names are pseudonyms.)

> For the first 15 years of my life, I didn't find myself in books, and I didn't relate to them. Once I discovered books and characters I could relate to, I gained the love of reading. (Tracey)

> The joy of reading is in stepping into the experience of the characters. When the characters look like, talk like, think like, and act like us, it's easy to share in the experience. I think that after we've had that experience a few times, it becomes easier to understand the experiences of people who are less like us. But in becoming a reader, and learning to love reading, experiencing books that mirror our own lives is extremely important—which for me began when I became an adult. (Robin)

> I didn't feel a strong connection between my world and classroom-related literature experiences. My learning experiences did not speak to me because people who looked like me weren't in the literature. I didn't value my experiences with literature in my early years of learning. (Tyrone)

Similarly, the third-grade African American students we interviewed voiced their preferences, needs, and concerns:

> Well, we're black, and it doesn't mean that I don't like white people in stories, but I like seeing people in the book that are my same color. I like seeing black people in books because mostly they have white people in commercials and shows and stuff. And it's like in a book you can see black people. (Keisha)

> It's not that I don't like white people or nothing, but you're glad because you don't see a lot of books that have black people in them. And it's not to be rude to white people, but you can imagine what they're [black people] thinking of...it might give you a better idea. Again, nothing against white people, but you like to see blacks because [white authors] portray black people like they don't got no manners or nothing. And white people, they know everything and they get a good education. But, that's not always true cause the black people, they get a good education too. But they portray us as not having any manners. When you see [black] people like that, [white] people think that we're stupid. (Marisa)

> I like reading about my heritage and I like stories about black people. There isn't anything wrong with white people...they're just a different color. They're actually people, so they're the same as us, but a different color. But, I would like to see more, you know, black people in stories. (LaVon)

The problem of not finding oneself in books runs deep and wide in the context of schooling in the United States. Historically, the absence of black images in children's literature was birthed from the social structures that slavery imposed. The inaccurate images of African Americans that appeared in literature from 1830–1900 were nurtured by stereotypes, a publishing industry that was not invested in authentic portrayals of African Americans, and lack of understanding (MacCann, 1998). There was very little change in characterizations of African Americans or the number of texts featuring authentic African American characters from 1900 until about 1970 (Harris, 1997). As a result, historically, the vast content of children's literature connoted a clear message: African American children are not valued in society, and books have little to offer them that is personal, relevant, and affirming (Harris, 1993; Sims-Bishop, 1987).

Given the absence and misrepresentation that so many African Americans—young and old—feel about the literature of their youth, we searched for African American children's literature of high literary and artistic quality for Grades K–3. Our plan was to locate literature that establishes African American children as children, authenticates their own world (Clifton, 1981), and—most important—speaks to these children about themselves and their lives (Harris, 1990; Sims-Bishop, 1993).

But how much of this literature is available? Where do you find it? How do you select high-quality African American literature that will lead to affirming reading experiences in which children will be able to relate to stories and characters?

How much African American children's literature is available?

The number of African American children's books steadily increased in the latter part of the 20th century, especially in the 1990s (Harris, 1997; Rand, Parker, & Foster, 1998; Sims-Bishop, 1997). In real terms, however, the increase was very small. For example, in 1998 approximately 4,500 books were published in the United States for children (Horning, Moore-Kruse, & Schliesman, 1999). Only 3% of these books featured African Americans as main characters or focused on African American culture (Rand et al., 1998). Of this 3%, only two thirds of the books were created by African American authors or illustrators (Horning et al., 1999).

Recommended high-quality African American children's literature, K–3 (continued)

April and her sister love to jump Double Dutch. But nobody in the neighborhood wants to jump rope, until Uncle Zambezi arrives with a pair of brightly dyed jump ropes from Africa and claims that they will grant wishes.

Lester, Julius. *Sam and the tigers.* 1996. Ill. Jerry Pinkney. Dial Books for Young Readers. ISBN 0803720289. US$15.99.

This is a retelling of Helen Bannerman's *The Story of Little Black Sambo* (1923, HarperCollins). In this story a little boy named Sam (in fact all of the characters are called Sam) outsmarts a gang of hungry tigers. The tigers turn into a pool of butter, and that night Sam and his family have tiger-striped pancakes for dinner.

McKissack, Patricia C. *The honest-to-goodness truth.* 2000. Ill. Giselle Potter. Atheneum. ISBN 0689826680. US$16.00.

When a young girl is caught in her first lie to her mother, she decides to tell only the truth. Soon, she begins to spread the truth all over town about how Thomas didn't have enough money for lunch and needed to borrow some from the teacher. She learns there's a right and wrong way to tell the truth.

Medearis, Angela Shelf. *Rum-a-tum-tum.* 1997. Ill. James E. Ransome. Holiday House. ISBN 0823411435. US$16.95.

In the late 1800s, a young girl wakes to the festive, celebratory sounds of street vendors busily selling their produce on Market Street in New Orleans, Louisiana. She is mesmerized by Creole women in red bandannas, baskets of richly colored fresh fruits and vegetables, and a jazz parade that lights up the town.

Miller, William. *The piano.* 2000. Ill. Susan Keeter. Lee & Low. ISBN 1880000989. US$15.95.

This story, set in the early 1900s, is about a unique friendship between a little girl named Tia and her employer, an elderly woman named Miss Hartwell. Tia loves music; Miss Hartwell teaches her how to play the piano. In return Miss Hartwell is given a rare and precious gift.

Mollel, Tololwa M. *My rows and piles of coins* (2000 Coretta Scott King Illustrator Honor Award). 1999. Ill. E.B. Lewis. Clarion Books. ISBN 0395751861. US$ 15.00.

A little boy works very hard and saves his money to buy a new bike, only to discover that he doesn't have enough.

Nolen, Jerdine. *Big Jabe.* 2000. Ill. Kadir Nelson. Lothrop, Lee & Shepard. ISBN 0688136621. US$ 15.95.

In this modern tall tale, Addy, a house slave on Simon Plenty's plantation, finds a little boy floating down the river in a basket. Addy is taken by the boy's ability to call fish to jump out of the river and into her wagon. In no time at all, the little boy grows into a giant named Jabe, who has the strength of 50 men and the ability to transport slaves away to freedom.

Orgill, Roxanne. *If I only had a horn: Young Louis Armstrong.* 1997. Ill. Leonard Jenkins. Houghton Mifflin. ISBN 0395759196. US$16.00.

This autobiographical picture book describes how young Louis Armstrong received his first instruments. Before playing the trumpet, he played the bugle and the cornet. His first musical success occurred in the Colored Waifs' Home Band.

Pinkney, Andrea D. *Duke Ellington: The piano prince and his orchestra* (1999 Caldecott Honor Award & 1999 Coretta

(continued)

Scott King Honor Award). 1998. Ill. Brian Pinkney. Hyperion Books for Children. ISBN 0786801786. US$15.95.

This biographical picture book illustrates the life of the legendary jazz composer Duke Ellington.

Pinkney, Andrea D. *Bill Pickett: Rodeo-ridin' cowboy*. 1996. Ill. Brian Pinkney. Gulliver. ISBN 0152021035. US$6.00.

This biography describes how Bill Pickett became the most famous black rodeo performer who ever lived and the first African American to be inducted into the National Cowboy Hall of Fame.

Schroeder, Alan. *Minty: A story of young Harriet Tubman* (1997 Coretta Scott King Illustrator Award). 1996. Ill. Jerry Pinkney. Dial Books for Young Readers. ISBN 0803718888. US$16.00.

This fictionalized account based upon real events profiles the early life of Harriet Tubman and her relationship with her parents. The story describes how she became a conductor on the Underground Railroad.

Siegelson, Kim. *In the time of the drums* (2000 Coretta Scott King Illustrator Award). 1999. Ill. Brian Pinkney. Hyperion Books for Children. ISBN 078680436X. US$15.00.

This story is based on the Gullah legend of a slave rebellion at Ibo's Landing in South Carolina. Mentu's grandmother Twi was born in Africa and remembers her experiences well. Twi teaches her grandson many things, including how to play ancient rhythms on a goatskin drum. One day, slave ships arrive at Mentu and Twi's island. The slaves refuse to get off the ships because they know they are not home. Twi knows she must take her people back to Africa, so together Twi and the slaves walk into the ocean for home. Mentu is left all alone, but he grows up strong, begins a family of his own, and teaches them all that his grandmother taught him.

Sierra, Judy. *Wiley and the hairy man*. 1996. Ill. Brian Pinkney. Lodestar Books Dutton. ISBN 0525674772. US$15.00.

This African American folk tale describes how Wiley and his mother outsmart the Hairy Man by tricking him into doing things for them. But Wiley's mother warns him that he must trick the Hairy Man two more times in order for the beast to go away forever.

Steptoe, John. *Creativity*. 1997. Ill. E. B. Lewis. Clarion. ISBN 0395687063. US$15.95.

An African American child learns to appreciate his similarities and differences with his friend Hector from Puerto Rico. Once Charlie befriends Hector he helps him adjust to the new school and neighborhood. Charlie even tries to help Hector with his English.

Stewart, Dianne. *Gift of the sun: A tale from South Africa*. 1996. Ill. Jude Daly. Farrar Straus & Giroux. ISBN 0374324255. US$15.00.

This South African tale describes how a farmer named Thulani wants to do no more than lie in the sun all day. After a series of lopsided exchanges with others to make his life easier, he finds that his crop is worth something after all. A pocketful of sunflower seeds proves to be very beneficial.

Tarpley, Natasha. *I love my hair*. 1998. Ill. E.B. Lewis. Little, Brown. ISBN 0316522759. US$15.95.

(continued)

Here is the bottom line: Very few books with African American protagonists are published for children. Our bottom line reduces this number even further: How many of these books are high-quality works of literature for African American children?

What are the characteristics of "good" African American children's literature?

The answer to this question is complex. "Goodness," as it turns out, depends on a number of factors: How the literature evolved, readability, marketing, and audience appeal are essential considerations (Temple, Martinez, Yokota, & Naylor, 1998). For our purposes, two interrelated layers mark the characteristics of good African American children's literature: those characteristics general to all children's literature and those specific to African American children's literature.

General characteristics. Characteristics of excellence in children's books are a result of the literary and artistic craft of the author and illustrator. The skills with which authors and illustrators use the tools of their medium to tell the tale are the most essential characteristics that distinguish good children's literature from the rest. "To know what 'good books' are for different children requires some intelligent way of talking about goodness and mediocrity in books—an accepted set of terms for looking at the literary features of children's books" (Temple et al., 1998, p. 7). By drawing upon Temple et al.'s (1998) framework on the qualities of children's literature, and Huck, Hepler, Hickman, and Kiefer's (2000), Cullinan and Galda's (1994), and Lynch-Brown and Tomlinson's (1999) guidelines for evaluating children's picture books, we outlined the characteristics of an author's and illustrator's craft that mark high-quality children's literature.

In seeking well-developed narratives for primary-grade children, readers should look for works that contain the following characteristics.

1. Books should include memorable, well-portrayed characters; in contemporary stories these characters are usually children the same age as the child reader.

2. Books should present a plot that provides interesting events in an understandable sequence.

Plots produce conflict to build excitement and suspense. For primary-grade readers plots should be direct and clear so that children will not have difficulty following the sequence of events, yet plots should be complex enough to capture the attention and lead to predictions, questions, and wonderings. In realistic stories the plot should deal with problems, events, or issues that children will understand and to which they can relate.

3. Books should incorporate well-crafted language that is concrete and vivid—the language should read smoothly and reflect the mood of the story.

4. Books should contain a worthy and truthful theme. Further, the illustrator's work should catch the attention of the reader, move the story forward, and enhance the meanings and tone presented by the author.

Table 1 outlines these characteristics, along with key questions, so they can be readily used to rate (from 1–5) the overall quality of a children's book.

Specific characteristics. In addition to these general considerations for selecting high-quality children's literature, there are specific guidelines to note with regard to the selection of the most appropriate African American children's literature. We have developed a more detailed set of guidelines aimed specifically at African American children's literature, based upon the work of Sims-Bishop (1997), Banks (1991), our own experiences, and those of teachers with whom we have collaborated. There are specific authors and illustrators who have established solid reputations for publishing culturally sensitive literature for children. While we would not recommend that selections of African American literature for children come exclusively from these works, familiarity with these authors, illustrators, and their works is very helpful in becoming accomplished at selecting high-quality texts to share with children.

As general guidelines (in addition to drawing from works by established well-known African American authors and illustrators) we recommend that teachers and parents look for books that have the following characteristics.

1. Books should include characters who are well developed and portrayed in authentic, realistic contexts.

2. Books should use language that is authentic and realistic, particularly dialogue that

---

Recommended high-quality African American children's literature, K–3 (continued)

This picture book celebrates African American identity through hair. Every night before bedtime Keyana sits down with her mother to get her hair combed. It hurts, but her mother gently reminds her of all the different ways that she can wear her hair.

Thomas, Joyce Carol. *I have heard of a land* (1999 Coretta Scott King Illustrator Honor Award). 1998. Ill. Floyd Cooper. HarperCollins. ISBN 0060234776. US$14.95.

Set in the late 1800s, this lyrical tribute describes what it was like for African American pioneers to journey westward to Oklahoma to begin a new life. Newly freed slaves were anxious to receive railroad tickets to travel to a place where all people were promised free land and a new beginning.

Wilkins, Verna Allette. *Dave and the tooth fairy.* (1998). Ill. Paul Hunt. Gareth Stevens. ISBN 0836820894. US$21.00.

Dave's wobbly tooth finally comes out when he sneezes. But he doesn't know where it went. His grandfather and the tooth fairy get a shock when they look under his pillow later that evening.

Woodtor, Dee Parmer. *Big meeting.* Ill. Dolores Johnson. Simon & Schuster. ISBN 0689319339. US$16.00.

During the midsummer heat, families from all over cross the wooden bridge at Pigeon Creek and travel to grandma and grandpa's home for a special reunion. They gather at church for fellowship, to learn about their heritage, and to celebrate the gospel.

---

correctly portrays African American dialect appropriate to the character.

3. Books should incorporate illustrations that portray African American and other characters and settings authentically and realistically.

4. Books should present accurate information.

We have found these guidelines, as outlined in Table 2, to be workable tenets for the selection of high-quality African American children's literature. While all of these story elements may not be found in every good African American children's book, the more elements that are found, the greater the likely appeal for all children. These guidelines also include key questions and a rating scale (from 1–5) to evaluate the quality of African American children's literature.

How do the characteristics apply to a specific piece of literature?

To illustrate how these general and specific characteristics work in practice, we applied them to the African American children's biography *Duke Ellington: The Piano Prince and His*

Table 1
General characteristics of high-quality primary-grade picture books

Feature	Questions	Rating				
Character	• Does the story contain a memorable character who is about the same age as the students?	1 Low	2	3 Medium	4	5 High
Plot	• Is the plot direct, clear, and stimulating? • Will students understand the problems, events, and issues? • Will students be able to easily follow the sequence of events? • Will students enjoy the story?	1 Low	2	3 Medium	4	5 High
Well-crafted language	• Does the story contain natural, vivid language? • Do the words evoke clear, concrete images of characters and actions? • Does the language reflect the mood of the story?	1 Low	2	3 Medium	4	5 High
Worthy, subtle, and truthful theme	• Is the story's theme one that students will find worthy, subtle, and truthful? • Will the theme interest students? • Is the author's intended message understandable without being heavy-handed?	1 Low	2	3 Medium	4	5 High
Quality of illustrations	• Does the illustrator use elements of media, design, and style in original and expressive ways?	1 Low	2	3 Medium	4	5 High
Function of illustrations	• Do the illustrations establish the mood, theme, and setting as the story unfolds? • Do they add or clarify information? • Do they enrich the story?	1 Low	2	3 Medium	4	5 High

Orchestra by Andrea Davis-Pinkney and Brian Pinkney (Hyperion, 1998). Although biography is nonfiction, it can be evaluated similarly to fiction due to its narrative form. However, there is an additional requirement for biography—accuracy.

The story describes the life of legendary Edward Kennedy "Duke" Ellington and provides a glimpse into one of the liveliest eras of American music history. In this tribute to the jazz legend, the music is portrayed through illustrations that represent constant motion with vivid spirals, waves, and colorful swirls. Table 3 illustrates how we applied the general characteristics of children's literature to the story. Our rating for each of the characteristics is noted in Table 3.

Character. The text is realistic and engaging as it introduces a young Duke Ellington who does not enjoy playing the piano because he finds it boring. As the story progresses, Duke becomes a teenager and begins incorporating sounds and rhythms that he finds exciting. Over time, Duke develops a unique style that transforms the music industry.

Plot. The book chronicles Duke Ellington's musical career. The story begins with his childhood—he was born in 1899 in Washington, D.C.—and ends when he became an adult and played at New York City's Carnegie Hall on January 23, 1943. The story is presented chronologically, so it is easy for children to follow; however, it is written so as to keep children

Table 2
Specific characteristics of high-quality African American children's literature

Feature	Questions	Rating				
Character portrayal	• Does the author identify the characters as African American? • Does the author include current and accurate information about African American beliefs, traditions, shared values, and other cultural referents? • Does the author present realistic and positive images of African Americans?	1 Low	2	3 Medium	4	5 High
Language use	• Does the dialogue correctly portray African American dialect? • Is the language authentic and realistic? • Will students understand, identify with, and accurately reflect upon the characters' language?	1 Low	2	3 Medium	4	5 High
Illustration authenticity	• Do the illustrations reflect reality? • Do they reveal variety in settings and African American physical features and coloring, or are characters merely colored brown? • Do the illustrations present positive images of African Americans in aesthetically pleasing ways?	1 Low	2	3 Medium	4	5 High
Information accuracy	• Does the story contain a motif or an authentic aspect of African American history? • Is the information accurate? • Does the story add a distinctive voice or worldview?	1 Low	2	3 Medium	4	5 High

wondering about what will happen and where the story will lead.

Students will enjoy the story because it addresses a problem that is common for many children. Duke Ellington was introduced to a new skill, and, although he understood that practice was essential in developing this skill, he found that practice was very boring. Duke addressed the problem in a unique way that involved setting and accomplishing personal goals (facets of a child's life that parents and teachers alike impress upon young children). Duke Ellington became successful because he was talented and had the resourcefulness and encouragement to build upon his talents.

Well-crafted language. The story contains natural, vivid language used in culturally appropriate, soulful, descriptive ways. For example, one line reads, "Duke's Creole Love Call was spicier than a pot of jambalaya. His Mood Indigo was a musical stream that swelled over the airwaves" (p. 11).

Worthy, subtle, and truthful theme. Students will identify with and remember the theme of the story—growing up and finding yourself—because it is presented in an entirely believable way. In addition, this is an appropriate literary element for young readers to reflect upon as they look at themselves and their own processes of growing up and finding themselves as individuals with unique talents and qualities.

Quality of illustrations. The illustrator uses the elements of shape, color, texture, rhythm, variety, space, paint, expressionism, and representation in divergent, self-expressive, artistic ways.

Function of illustrations. The illustrations are eye catching. The bold, vibrant colors and intricately detailed scenes set the mood and add

Table 3
General characteristics of high-quality primary-grade picture books applied to *Duke Ellington: The Piano Prince and His Orchestra*

Feature	Response	Rating				
Character	• The story begins with a child protagonist (Duke Ellington) and follows him in his adult life through his musical career.	1 Low	2	3 Medium	4	⑤ High
Plot	• A chronological plot follows the challenges and successes of Duke Ellington's life.	1 Low	2	3 Medium	4	⑤ High
Well-crafted language	• The language is used in ways appropriate for understanding jazz.	1 Low	2	3 Medium	4	⑤ High
Worthy, subtle, and truthful theme	• Students will identify with the theme of growing up and finding yourself.	1 Low	2	3 Medium	4	⑤ High
Quality of illustrations	• The illustrator uses the visual elements of line, shape, and color effectively.	1 Low	2	3 Medium	4	⑤ High
Function of illustrations	• The illustrations are integral to the story and extend the text.	1 Low	2	3 Medium	4	⑤ High

luster to the story. The dancers leap off the page while the visual interpretations of the music serve as devices that transport the reader to this era of music history.

Table 4 demonstrates how we applied the specific characteristics of African American children's literature to the story. The ratings for the characteristics are noted in Table 4.

Character portrayal. The author identifies the characters as African American and presents a positive, realistic message about Duke Ellington's musical career. Duke Ellington's desire was to celebrate the history of African American culture through his music. He accomplished this goal through songs about "the glories of dark skin, the pride of African heritage, and the triumphs of black people from the days of slavery to years of civil rights struggle" (p. 26).

Language use. The story is a narrative in which African American dialogue true to the characters is used in several parts of the story. For example, a section reads, "Yo, you got the Duke?" "Slide me some King of the Keys, please!" and "Gonna play me that Piano Prince and his band" (p. 23). This dialogue represents African American dialect that is historically accurate for the period of time in which Duke Ellington lived. Had the entire story been written in this way, it might have been difficult for many students to understand. Instead, the author has chosen to intersperse this type of dialect in the text, providing readers with a perspective on African American language use in the world of Duke Ellington and, thus, helping the reader enter the world of Duke Ellington.

Illustration authenticity. The illustrations in the story reveal variety in African American physical features and coloring. For example, Duke is referred to as having "honey-colored fingertips" while other characters appear to be darker in color—a reflection of reality (p. 21). The illustrations also present positive images of African Americans as in the scenes portraying New York City's Carnegie Hall and the Cotton Club in Harlem.

Information accuracy. The book contains authentic information about Duke Ellington's musical career. The story highlights the African American experience by describing how African Americans supported and enjoyed listening to Duke Ellington's music. At the end, the author includes facts about Duke Ellington's life and provides the sources used to obtain the information.

Valuable book, valued readers

The guidelines presented in this article provide a way for teachers and parents to thoughtfully

Table 4
Specific characteristics of high-quality African American children's literature applied to *Duke Ellington: The Piano Prince and His Orchestra*

Feature	Response	Rating				
Character portrayal	• The author presents accurate and positive images of an African American whose outstanding musical career is portrayed.	1 Low	2	3 Medium	4	⑤ High
Language use	• The dialogue accurately portrays African American dialect of the time. • The language of the text is rich and flows well.	1 Low	2	3 Medium	4	⑤ High
Illustration authenticity	• The illustrations reveal variety in African American physical features and coloring. • The illustrations reveal a variety of settings. • The illustrations present positive images of African Americans.	1 Low	2	3 Medium	4	⑤ High
Information accuracy	• The story contains authentic, accurate information about Duke Ellington's musical career.	1 Low	2	3 Medium	4	⑤ High

and purposefully evaluate the quality of African American children's literature for the primary grades. Determining quality, in this case, lies in the ability to select literature that is affirming and liberating to children. Historically, African American children did not have literature that reflected their experiences. To find the best of this literature, then, is to help these children find themselves in books. To read literature that mirrors themselves and their lives is to feel valued—to have power.

When African American children encounter literature that offers messages about them, their culture, and their roles in society, they have enhanced opportunities to reflect upon themselves as people and their own development. Culturally sensitive stories, views, and insights can allow children to realize that literature has value for them as individuals. To select a balanced collection of stories, we included in our bibliography (see Sidebar) literature that plays and riffs with everyday events of African American life and literature that represents accurate, authentic accounts of slavery. With repeated exposure to engaging literature in which children find themselves establishing personal connections with characters, the likelihood is great that reading will become an appealing activity. Over time, the love of reading may empower students both as readers and as individuals.

For teachers and parents interested in finding African American children's literature, we have carefully crafted an annotated bibliography of books from 1996–2000 that meet our selection guidelines for high-quality African American children's literature. We suggest the bibliography be used as a starting point in selecting literature, and note that the list should be expanded according to individual needs and preferences. The books are recommended for beginning, young, and early intermediate readers (K–3). The title, author, illustrator, year, summary, publisher, ISBN (International Standard Book Number), and price are provided for each book. The books are arranged in alphabetical order beginning with the author's last name.

References

Banks, J.A. (1991). *Teaching strategies for ethnic studies* (5th ed.). Boston: Allyn & Bacon.

Clifton, L. (1981). Writing for black children. *The Advocate, 1,* 32–37.

Cullinan, B.E., & Galda, L. (1994). *Literature and the child* (3rd ed.). New York: Harcourt Brace.

Harris, V.J. (1990). African American children's literature: The first one hundred years. *Journal of Negro Education, 59,* 540–555.

Harris, V.J. (1993). Contemporary griots: African-American writers of children's literature. In V.J. Harris (Ed.), *Teaching multicultural literature in grades K–8* (pp. 57–108). Norwood, MA: Christopher-Gordon.

Harris, V.J. (1997). Children's literature depicting blacks. In V.J. Harris (Ed.), *Using multiethnic literature in the K–8 classroom* (pp. 21–58). Norwood, MA: Christopher-Gordon.

Horning, K., Moore-Kruse, G., & Schliesman, M. (1999). *Cooperative Children's Book Center choices 1998.* Madison, WI: Friends of the Cooperative Children's Book Center.

Huck, C., Hepler, S., Hickman, J., & Kiefer, B. (2000). *Children's literature in the elementary school* (7th ed.). New York: McGraw-Hill.

Lynch-Brown, C., & Tomlinson, C.M. (1999). *Essentials of children's literature* (3rd ed.). Needham Heights, MA: Allyn & Bacon.

MacCann, D. (1998). *White supremacy in children's literature: Characterizations of African Americans, 1830–1900.* New York: Garland.

Rand, D., Parker, T., & Foster, S. (1998). *Black books galore! Guide to great African American children's books.* New York: John Wiley & Sons.

Sims Bishop, R. (1987). Extending multicultural understanding through children's books. In B. Cullinan (Ed.), *Children's literature in the reading program* (pp. 60–67). Newark, DE: International Reading Association.

Sims Bishop, R. (1993). Multicultural literature for children: Making informed choices. In V.J. Harris (Ed.), *Teaching multicultural literature in grades K–8* (pp. 37–53). Norwood, MA: Christopher-Gordon.

Sims Bishop, R. (1997). Selecting literature for a multicultural curriculum. In V.J. Harris (Ed.), *Using multiethnic literature in the K–8 classroom* (pp. 1–19). Norwood, MA: Christopher-Gordon.

Temple, C., Martinez, M., Yokota, J., & Naylor, A. (1998). *Children's books in children's hands: An introduction to their literature.* Needham Heights, MA: Allyn & Bacon.

Gay Ivey

Reflections on teaching struggling middle school readers

Here are four working generalizations about teaching that should be helpful to both experienced middle school teachers and preservice teachers in university classrooms. Each generalization is supported by research, firsthand experience, and suggested strategies and materials.

Clark [all names are pseudonyms] told me he is interested in historical fiction. He said he guessed that *The Highwayman* (Noyes, 1981), which I read to the class today, was set during the American Revolution because Redcoats were mentioned. During free reading time we explored the classroom library for more historical fiction. I suggested that he take a look at *My Brother Sam Is Dead* (Collier & Collier, 1974).

This afternoon I read *The Little Match Girl* (Andersen, 1975) with Katie and Robin. There was a huge difference in the way these two girls read the story. Robin read very fluently, with no problems. Katie, on the other hand, stumbled through the story. Robin helped her out with every few words. I noticed that, in some instances, Katie was not using beginning consonant sounds to help her figure out words.

At the end of class today, Sarah Ann asked me if I planned to be in their classroom tomorrow. I assured her that I would. She said she likes it when I'm there because the students in the class get to do "fun things." Then she said she really doesn't like reading, though. But she pulled out a picture book, *The Wolf's Chicken Stew* (Kasza, 1987), and asked, "Do we get to read tomorrow? I want to read this book." I wonder how she really feels about reading.

These excerpts from my research journal were recorded during the first several weeks of a 5-month naturalistic investigation on sixth-grade readers (Ivey, in press). These three separate incidents exemplify the interesting and complex nature of what I dis-

Reprinted from *Journal of Adolescent & Adult Literacy* (1999), 42, 372–381.

covered about sixth-grade readers. Clark shows that middle school students can have specific reading preferences. Katie and Robin demonstrate the wide range of abilities among middle school readers. Sarah Ann reveals that some middle school students have mixed attitudes toward reading. As demonstrated by these children and their sixth-grade classmates, middle school students exhibit great range and diversity in their reading behaviors.

What my study revealed, that middle school students as readers are complex, was not surprising to me given my previous experiences with young adolescent readers and their teachers. During my training as a reading specialist, I had the opportunity to work with scores of elementary and middle school students in a university reading clinic. I learned some particularly important lessons about literacy development from tutoring for an entire academic year a fourth-grade student who enrolled in the clinic as an emergent reader. As a middle school Title I (then Chapter 1) reading/language arts teacher, I worked primarily with struggling readers, and I discovered some of the obstacles to learning for students who have not learned to read strategically and purposefully by sixth grade. However, I also saw many students learn to love reading. Now, as a university instructor, I am developing a sense of what concerns preservice and inservice teachers about teaching reading to middle school students.

Through all these experiences, along with my recent research, I have reflected on what it takes for middle school students with persistent reading difficulties to become successful, engaged readers. Throughout these reflections are recurring themes that have led me to form some working generalizations about teaching struggling middle school readers.

My purpose here is to share these working generalizations. In the remainder of this article, I will elaborate on these themes, not because I think they are unique, but because I think they will be recognizable to other middle grades educators who have reflected on how to help young adolescents become readers. Although young adolescent readers do represent a wide range of abilities and habits, those of us who work closely with them are beginning to solve the puzzle of who they are as a group by identifying some important com-

monalties across students. The ones I mention in this article are from a variety of U.S. classrooms in three different states, and I have known them at different points in my 10 years as a reading educator, but their experiences and voices reveal what they have in common.

Recurring themes

Struggling middle school readers like to read when they have access to materials that span the gamut of interests and difficulty levels. Numerous studies have reported that by the time students reach the middle grades, they have become uninterested in reading (Ley, Schaer, & Dismukes, 1994; McKenna, Kear, & Ellsworth, 1995). However, I agree with Bintz (1993), who suggested that many secondary students "do not lose interest in reading per se" (p. 613), but instead they lose interest in the kinds of reading they are typically required to do in school, such as reading textbooks and certain teacher-selected texts. Worthy (1996) discussed the importance of making available interesting materials that "hook" reluctant readers, and in my experience, getting the right books into middle school students' hands has made a world of difference in their inclination to read.

One of the first books to convince me that interesting materials can inspire otherwise reluctant readers was Walter Dean Myers's *Scorpions* (1988). During my first year of teaching Title I classes I bought six copies of this book at a local bookstore. Several of the seventh-grade boys were drawn to it because of its interesting cover, which portrayed two African American teenagers at the front steps of an urban apartment building. My students were fascinated by the story, which is about a boy their own age who reluctantly joins a gang. However, they liked the book mostly because it struck a chord of familiarity with them. Students could relate, for example, to the following excerpt in which Jamal, the main character, is being harassed by Dwayne, his nemesis at school:

"Yo, Jamal, what kind of sneakers you wearin'?" ...
"Why don't you shut your mouth?" Jamal said. There were only fifteen minutes of school left, and he didn't want any garbage out of Dwayne.

"All I did was ask a question," Dwayne said, looking in the direction of Billy Ware. "What kind of sneakers you wearing?"

"None of your business," Jamal said.

"They look like Brand X sneakers to me," Dwayne said.

"I think you got a Brand X face," Jamal said.

"Hey, Billy, I think he got them sneakers from the Salvation Army."

Billy giggled and looked down at Jamal's sneakers. (Myers, 1988, p. 21)

The boys continue to taunt Jamal, and at the end of the scene, Myers writes that "Dwayne made Jamal feel small inside" (p. 22). This scenario was not new to my seventh-grade students who, like many other young adolescents, witnessed and experienced many similar real-life situations daily in school. Real-life language and incidents like these kept my students reading *Scorpions*, which was, for some, the first chapter book they had ever read from cover to cover. Humorous books, such as Roald Dahl's *The Twits* (1980) and Jon Scieszka's Time Warp Trio series (e.g., *Knights of the Kitchen Table*, 1991), have also been popular choices for students who have not previously read an entire chapter book.

Often picture books are the key to motivating middle school students to read. Charlie, a sixth-grade struggling reader, proclaimed *Willy the Wimp* (Browne, 1984) the "book of the year," and his sentiments were shared not only by the other students in Title I, but also by some of my homeroom students identified as gifted who chose to read the book during Sustained Silent Reading (SSR). While spending time in a sixth-grade classroom during a recent study (Ivey, in press), I read aloud to the class *Officer Buckle and Gloria* (Rathmann, 1995). After the reading many students elected to read that book during independent free reading time, and others subsequently checked it out from the school library. Other middle school favorites have been *Buz* (Egielski, 1995), *The Great White Man-Eating Shark* (Mahy, 1989), *The Stinky Cheese Man and Other Fairly Stupid Tales* (Scieszka, 1992), *Meanwhile Back at the Ranch* (Noble, 1987), and *Prince Cinders* (Cole, 1987), to name a few.

The matter of interest pertains not only to reluctant readers, but also to avid and successful middle school readers. Casey, a sixth-grade student who is a capable and highly motivated reader, wrote this note to her teacher:

I used to love to read. But this year it's not as enjoyable. I don't know why but I plainly don't like it anymore. I guess it is because I have better things to do. Another reason may be that I can't find a book in the library that interests me. I mean the school library would be the only place I could get books right now. I have already read my books at home.

I can relate to those people who say reading is boring now. I guess after you read so much you just get tired of it.

Reading is kind of like a boy. You like (him) or reading for a long while. Then after so long you just don't like (him) or reading any longer.

I thought you were suppose to enjoy reading as you got older. But it's just the opposite for me. As I get older reading is starting to interest me the least little bit.

A few weeks later, Casey found a new series of books to read, and she reported that she liked reading again. Thus, regardless of ability or general inclination to read, interesting materials are needed to develop and sustain engaged middle school readers.

Instructional-level materials have similar importance. In order for students to get better at reading, they need many opportunities to read materials they can read with 95% accuracy in word recognition (e.g., Betts, 1954). For middle school students who may be 3 to 4 or more years behind their peers in terms of reading ability, this may present a problem given the difficult materials typically found in their classrooms, but this need not be the case. Fielding and Roller's (1992) *making difficult books accessible and easy books acceptable* principle should apply beyond the early grades and into the upper elementary and middle grades in order to give all students what they need.

Lori Ann, a sixth-grade student who scored a first-grade instructional level on an informal reading inventory, had experienced only embarrassment, frustration, and failure with the grade-level texts she was asked to read year after year in school. When she discovered *The Magic Fish* (Littledale, 1986), an easy-to-read, predictable picture book in her sixth-grade classroom, she experienced fluent reading for the first time, and she asked if she could take the book home to read. Lawrence, a seventh grader whose instructional reading level was second grade, moved from frustration to success when he completed all the books in Marshall's easy-to-read Fox series (e.g., *Fox and His Friends*, 1982; *Fox on Wheels*, 1983).

Preservice teachers often ask, "Aren't middle school students embarrassed to read easy books in front of their peers?" My typical response is consistent with what Worthy, Patterson, Turner, Prater, and Salas (1997) reported about struggling readers in their after-school tutoring program. Like the middle school students I have known, these readers "approached the reading of easy texts with pleasure and a sense of relief," and they read easy books "with gusto and not a hint of embarrassment" (p. 5).

Still, some struggling middle school readers want to read texts that are difficult far beyond their comfort levels. Brock, for instance, my former sixth-grade student who read most comfortably in third-grade materials, wanted to read more challenging and sophisticated books such as Carolyn Reeder's (1989) *Shades of Gray*. Because high interest in a book's topic can often help students transcend their reading level (Hunt, 1971), students like Brock can access the things they want to read, especially with some support from a teacher or a peer.

Transitional chapter books are appropriate for middle students who are just slightly below their grade level in reading and for those who are quite capable of reading, but who are inexperienced or reluctant to read. Books such as Patricia Reilly Giff's The Kids of the Polk Street School series (e.g., *The Secret at the Polk Street School*, 1987), Betsy Byars's *Beans on the Roof* (1988), and Clyde R. Bulla's *Shoeshine Girl* (1975) are particularly appealing because they are fairly short and easy to read so that they do not overwhelm inexperienced readers, and they also bridge the gap between picture books and chapter books. Elizabeth, a seventh-grade student in a learning disabilities resource class, read Roald Dahl's *The Magic Finger* (1993) within a 24-hour period, and when she returned the book to me, she reported proudly that it was the first book she had read.

Allington (1994) discussed how limited experience in reading is commonly misperceived as limited ability. It may seem shocking that students who have been in school for 6, 7, or 8 years could be inexperienced with print, but they cannot become experienced until they actually engage in sustained periods of reading. This can be facilitated only when students are provided time to read and access to books they really can read.

Struggling middle school readers want opportunities to share reading experiences with their teachers and their classmates. If you imagined a classroom scene in which the teacher is sitting on a stool or in a rocking chair reading aloud a story or picture book, with students sitting all around on a rug or on big, comfortable pillows or beanbag chairs, you might assume it must be an early elementary classroom. I have come to believe that this is a perfectly appropriate and desirable scene for middle school classrooms.

Successful environments for struggling middle school readers involve interaction among students and interaction between students and teachers during literacy activities. One of these activities, alluded to previously, is the teacher read-aloud. There is no doubt that reading aloud to students is a powerful practice for promoting literacy appreciation and development, but I have found that read-alouds have specific benefits for struggling middle school readers.

Introducing books and reading aloud to the class gives teachers a chance to show students that teachers themselves value the books they bring to the classroom, thus giving students the impression that reading is pleasurable and worthwhile. Far too often, teachers reveal a lack of enthusiasm for school reading materials, as Casey, a sixth-grade student, aptly observed: "I've had teachers before that just, like, hated to read. It's like 'Uhhh, here's the new book we're going to read today, class.' And that made it even boring-er because you can tell that they're not interested, so you're not going to be interested" (Ivey, in press).

When teachers read aloud interesting books and demonstrate their own enthusiasm for reading, however, their zeal may become contagious. The preservice teachers in my literacy development methods course are becoming convinced of this phenomenon, as one student, Jamie, wrote after reading a story aloud to a group of fourth-grade students for the first time: "I began telling the class that this book was one of my favorites, and as soon as I said that some of the girls were like, 'If it's your favorite, then it's my favorite, too.' It was really funny, but I told them to wait and discover if they like the book themselves." Later, she added, "It really made me smile inside when the story was over and students asked to borrow the book."

I have also observed that when middle school teachers share books regularly, students become inspired to do the same. Dora, a sixth-grade teacher, found that soon after she honored one or two students' requests to share books from home and the school library, she had to create a waiting list for students to read aloud to their classmates. The books they shared ranged from childhood favorites, such as *The Giving Tree* (Silverstein, 1994) and *The Jolly Postman* (Ahlberg & Ahlberg, 1986) to all-time middle school favorites, such as *Scary Stories to Tell in the Dark* (Schwartz, 1981). Still some students introduced their classmates to less familiar genres, such as collections of Greek mythology.

Sharing favorite books with peers is especially appealing to less successful and reluctant readers whose prior experiences with public reading consisted mainly of whole-class, round-robin readings of texts that were either too difficult, uninteresting, or both. When students have a chance to choose the books they will share and to rehearse before they read aloud, they can feel like competent, valued members of their classroom literacy communities. For instance, Joshua, a frustrated seventh-grade student in a learning disabilities resource class, had severely limited word knowledge and had never read a book on his own. Needless to say, his oral reading experiences in school had been torturous. What he desperately needed was plenty of supported reading in simple texts, since there was probably no book he could pick up and read on his own.

What worked for Joshua was echo and choral reading. For example, in an echo reading of the predictable pattern book *Hattie and the Fox* (Fox, 1986), the teacher started by reading a short section of the text, and then Joshua read the same lines, and they continued in this manner until the end of the book. After Joshua gained some confidence through echo reading the book in its entirety several times, they tried choral reading, in which Joshua and his teacher read in unison, with the teacher taking the lead until Joshua felt comfortable enough to do so. After a couple of choral readings, Joshua requested to read it aloud to his class, an incident that ignited a pattern book read-aloud frenzy among his classmates who were also extremely inexperienced as readers in the seventh grade.

A sixth-grade student, Ronnie, who I had assumed was uninterested in all the reading and writing activities in his class, asked me to listen to him read *Private I. Guana: The Case of the Missing Chameleon* (Laden, 1995) in the hallway before he read it to the class. I jumped to the conclusion that this often mischievous student was using this opportunity to get out of the classroom, but he proved me wrong when after practicing his reading on several pages he announced that he felt he was ready to share. He went back into the classroom, took a seat on the stool at the front of the class, and read the story to his classmates, cover to cover.

Shared reading times are also good opportunities for students to learn from their teachers and classmates about how to season their oral reading. I have often noticed students trying to mimic the way the teacher reads, using different voices for different characters. A sixth-grade boy once told me as I read aloud *Johnny Appleseed* (Kellogg, 1988), "When you read, it's like a story." After hearing her sixth-grade teacher read aloud *Elbert's Bad Word* (Wood, 1988), Allison decided to read the book on her own, and she announced, "I'm going to try to read this with expression." One of my preservice teachers reflected on how her reading style affected the fifth-grade students who listened to her: "As I read the book, I noticed that the kids really liked to hear different voices and characters throughout the story, which I thought was fun to do and also seemed to help link the characters with a persona."

Equally important to struggling middle school readers are opportunities to read one-on-one with a peer or a teacher. For many students who struggle with reading, individualization has meant going to a remedial reading class and working alone to complete skill sheets, with the teacher rarely intervening with explanations or instructional support (McGill-Franzen & Allington, 1990). There are obvious instructional benefits to one-on-one reading times, such as impromptu lessons on word

Children's books

Ahlberg, J., & Ahlberg, A. (1986). *The jolly postman* (ill. A. Ahlberg). New York: Little, Brown.

Andersen, H.C. (1975). *The little match girl* (ill. B. Lent). Boston: Houghton Mifflin.

Browne, A. (1984). *Willy the wimp*. New York: Knopf.

Bulla, R.C. (1975). *Shoeshine girl*. New York: HarperCollins.

Byars, B. (1979). *Goodbye, Chicken Little*. New York: Harper & Row.

Byars, B. (1988). *Beans on the roof*. New York: Dell.

Cole, B. (1987). *Prince Cinders*. New York: G.P. Putnam's Sons.

Collier, J.L., & Collier, C. (1974). *My brother Sam is dead*. New York: Macmillan.

Dahl, R. (1980). *The Twits* (ill. Q. Blake). New York: Bantam-Skylark.

Dahl, R. (1983). *Revolting rhymes* (ill. Q. Blake). New York: Bantam.

Dahl, R. (1993). *The magic finger* (ill. T. Ross). New York: Puffin.

Egielski, R. (1995). *Buz*. New York: HarperCollins.

Fleischman, P. (1988). *Joyful noise: Poems for two voices*. New York: HarperCollins.

Fox, M. (1986). *Hattie and the fox* (ill. P. Mullins). New York: Simon & Schuster.

Giff, P.R. (1987). *The secrets at the Polk Street School* (ill. B. Sims). New York: Dell.

Kasza, K. (1987). *The wolf's chicken stew*. New York: G.P. Putnam's Sons.

Kellogg, S. (1988). *Johnny Appleseed*. New York: Morrow.

Laden, N. (1995). *Private I. Guana: The case of the missing chameleon*. San Francisco: Chronicle.

Littledale, F. (1986). *The magic fish* (ill. W.P. Pels). New York: Scholastic.

Lobel, A. (1980). *Fables*. New York: Harper & Row.

Mahy, M. (1989). *The great white man-eating shark* (ill. J. Allen). New York: Dial.

Marshall, E. (1982). *Fox and his friends* (ill. J. Marshall). New York: Dial.

Marshall, E. (1983). *Fox on wheels* (ill. J. Marshall). New York: Dial.

Myers, W.D. (1988). *Scorpions*. New York: Harper & Row.

Noble, T.H. (1987). *Meanwhile back at the ranch* (ill. T. Ross). New York: Dial.

(continued)

identification and comprehension strategies, but perhaps their fundamental value is that they are shared literacy experiences that are both personalized and individualized. If students who struggle with reading are to become better and more enthusiastic, they need many opportunities just to enjoy the literate experience with peers and teachers when they are not also being monitored, corrected, or tested.

Struggling middle school readers need real purposes for reading. When surveyed about their most memorable school assignments, one group of middle school students rated hands-on science and independent research projects as their favorites (Wasserstein, 1995). Although reading and writing were scarcely mentioned as favorites, students did not complain about reading and writing when they were used to accomplish some meaningful task. It is not surprising that middle school readers need real purposes for reading, given that motivation is highest when students engage in tasks for their own intrinsic reasons (Deci & Ryan, 1985).

For middle school students who struggle with reading, having authentic purposes is especially crucial. Unfortunately, the remediation programs provided to struggling readers when they were in the elementary grades may have focused on specific skills and other nonacademic activities rather than on reading for meaning (Johnston & Allington, 1991), and students are likely to encounter a similar skill-and-drill approach in the middle grades (Becker, 1990).

Round-robin reading, a practice that persists in schools despite uncertainty about the origin of its popularity (Hoffman & Segel, 1982), is especially problematic for struggling middle school readers. Many students may share the sentiments of Allison, a sixth-grade student who avoids oral reading because of her limited word identification skills: "I think [other students] be staring at me and stuff" (Ivey, in press). Ryan, a fairly fluent sixth-grade reader, senses the frustration of less able readers in his class during round-robin reading, and he explained why he volunteers to read: "I raise my hand 'cause I want to read and get it done with 'cause the slow people read, and it takes them forever to get it done" (Ivey, in press). If struggling readers' agenda is to avoid being called on to read during round-robin readings, and fluent readers' agenda is to "get it done," the ultimate purpose for the reading, to actively construct meaning, must be lost to most of the class.

In my experience, struggling middle school readers enjoy oral reading activities that culminate with a performance. For instance, Allison, the sixth-grade student mentioned previously, vehemently disliked traditional oral reading activities such as round-robin reading. However, after collaborating with a classmate on an original poem patterned after selections from *Joyful Noise: Poems for Two Voices* (Fleischman, 1988), she voluntarily read it aloud to the class. What made the difference for Allison in this situation was the fact that she was able to rehearse the poem at least a dozen times before performing it, or, as she put it, "I got to practice" (Ivey, in press). Moreover, sharing something she had written gave her an authentic purpose for reading. Readers Theatre performances of a wide range of texts, including poetry (e.g., *Revolting Rhymes*, Dahl, 1983), excerpts from novels (e.g., *Goodbye Chicken Little*, Byars, 1979), and short stories (e.g., *Fables*, Lobel, 1980), provide opportunities for students to practice reading toward a goal. In this activity the text is read aloud as a script, with each student assuming the role of a character or some other part.

I have also come to believe that struggling middle school readers do find their own purposes for reading, but not necessarily for in-school, teacher-assigned reading. For example, Allison, who said she "hates to read," read *Jet* magazine regularly at home and often read aloud to her younger brother. Daisy, a sixth-grade struggling reader, checked out books on cooking from the school library and experimented with brownie baking at home. Joey, a sixth-grade sports fanatic, counted on me to bring the morning newspaper to school each day so that he could borrow the sports section during SSR. Ricky and Tim read books on how to draw and make paper airplanes. Given the importance of students' personal preferences, out-of-school reading interests ought to be welcomed into the classroom and integrated into the reading curriculum.

The strong influence of self-selection on motivation to read makes a good case for free-choice reading, especially for struggling middle school readers. Still, for ease of dealing with comprehension instruction, promoting literary discussions, and developing content knowledge, teacher-

Children's books (continued)

Noyes, A. (1981). *The highwayman* (ill. C. Keeping). Oxford, England: Oxford University Press.

Peterson, J. (1991). *Mystery in the night woods* (ill. C. Szekeres). New York: Scholastic.

Rathmann, P. (1995). *Officer Buckle and Gloria.* New York: G.P. Putman's Sons.

Reeder, C. (1989). *Shades of gray.* New York: Avon.

Rylant, C. (1987). *Henry and Mudge in the green time* (ill. S. Stevenson). New York: Macmillan.

Schwartz, A. (1981). *Scary stories to tell in the dark* (ill. S. Gammell). New York: HarperCollins.

Scieszka, J. (1991). *Knights of the kitchen table* (ill. L. Smith). New York: Puffin.

Scieszka, J., & Smith, L. (1992). *The stinky cheese man and other fairly stupid tales.* New York: Viking.

Silverstein, S. (1994). *The giving tree.* New York: HarperCollins.

Wood, A. (1988). *Elbert's bad word* (ill. A. Wood & D. Wood). New York: Harcourt Brace.

selected, whole-class, common texts are sometimes necessary in middle school classrooms, so a balance between teacher-selected and student-selected reading must be maintained. However, many struggling middle school readers may succeed at reading teacher-assigned texts only when teachers help them set purposes for reading and support their reading by showing them ways to become active, strategic readers. I have found that Directed Reading-Thinking Activities (Stauffer, 1969) help less successful readers become engaged in reading texts they would not necessarily choose for themselves because predicting, based on clues from the book and their prior knowledge, along with monitoring their hypotheses, gives them the purpose they need to keep reading. Still, though, materials for guided reading and discussion must be on students' instructional reading levels.

Struggling middle school readers want to be and can become good readers. In general, students' attitudes toward reading may decline during the middle school years, and they may choose to read less than in previous years (Ley, Schaer, & Dismukes, 1994). For struggling middle school readers, increasingly negative attitudes toward reading are even more pronounced than for average and above-average readers (McKenna, Kear, & Ellsworth, 1995). However, their pessimism toward reading may be caused by feelings of helplessness and hopelessness (e.g., Johnston & Winograd, 1985) rather than by a general dislike of reading (Kos, 1991).

Conversely, I have some lasting recollections of sixth-, seventh-, and eighth-grade students who, despite significant odds and low expectations, actually became willing, skilled readers during the middle grades. Antoine, a frustrated, reluctant seventh-grade reader, began the school year reading on the second-grade level, mainly due to his limited word knowledge. A spelling inventory revealed that Antoine was in the within-word-pattern stage of development (Bear, Invernizzi, Templeton, & Johnston, 1996). His instructional program was multifaceted, but it included two main foci: word study and independent reading.

I taught Antoine within a small pull-out group for just 40 minutes each day, so roughly 30 minutes of that time was devoted to a combination of those two activities. Antoine's word study group, which included three or four other students, began the school year by examining long vowel patterns, one vowel at a time (e.g., v*a*se, tr*ai*n, w*ay*), through conceptual word sorting activities and games (see Bear, Invernizzi, Templeton, & Johnston, 1996). The books Antoine chose for independent reading were mainly easy-to-read picture books, such as *Henry and Mudge in the Green Time* (Rylant, 1987). As Antoine's word knowledge developed, he began to read more challenging titles, such as the short novel *Mystery in the Night Woods* (Peterson, 1991). The most convincing evidence of his growth, however, was his mother's happy and tearful report that she came home from work one day to find Antoine reading to his preschool-aged sister.

There were many students who blossomed as readers like Antoine did, but there were also those who did not. But even my failure to find what worked for these children did not destroy their desire to become more literate nor did it diminish the value they placed on what they could do as readers and writers. I remember vividly Darryl, who

was in my Title I class for sixth and seventh grades, but who was placed in a special education program for his eighth-grade year and could not receive both services. Although, despite our efforts, he had not made tremendous progress in reading and writing by eighth grade, he still had the desire to improve and the desire to read and write, which he demonstrated often by skipping lunch to read picture books and to write poems on the computer in my classroom. I am convinced that helping Darryl with his persistent reading problem was my responsibility, and that he was fully capable of becoming a skilled reader if he had been provided with appropriate instruction. I can only hope that now, 7 years later and much more knowledgeable and experienced as a reading educator, I would know how to help Darryl match his motivation to read with good reading skills.

Perhaps the most compelling story I have read with respect to struggling middle school readers chronicled one sixth-grade boy's growth from a second-grade instructional level to a fourth-grade instructional level during 2 years of tutoring (Morris, Ervin, & Conrad, 1996). Instruction for this student included comprehension practice, word study, fluency practice, and writing, but all were balanced within the context of interesting literature he could read and wanted to read. Morris et al. (1996) attributed this success story, in large part, to the fact that the tutor was well trained and knowledgeable about teaching reading. If we placed struggling middle school readers in classrooms where they could experience good teaching, I believe their potential to improve and their motivation to be literate would become increasingly apparent.

In my experiences, struggling middle school students do want to become better at reading, but this happens only when they experience instructional environments that foster optimism for improvement. I believe the most beneficial learning contexts for struggling readers, whether they are regular classrooms, pull-out programs, or one-on-one tutoring sessions, are those that promote both skill and will (Paris, Lipson, & Wixson, 1983) and combine enablement and engagement (Roe, 1997) for reading and writing.

One barrier to providing struggling middle school readers with the instruction they need is the wide range of reading abilities in any one middle school classroom. In order for middle school teachers to see the potential of struggling readers to improve, they must reconceptualize how the reading/language arts class looks, both physically and instructionally. Roller (1996) described how a workshop concept can facilitate reading and writing growth for all students within the regular classroom. The organization of a workshop classroom is particularly appropriate for struggling readers because it is grounded in the notion that individual children within the same classroom can do a variety of literacy activities at once, thus accommodating variability between students. Reading and writing skills can be taught individually, in small groups, or in whole-class minilessons while students are reading and responding to self-selected, personally interesting children's literature on their independent or instructional reading levels. From a teaching perspective, I value the workshop design because it allows me to work in close proximity to small groups of students and, most importantly, to individual students.

A second organizational plan that allows for struggling readers' needs to be met in the regular classroom is the circle-seat-center format (Bear et al., 1996), with students placed in one of three rotating groups based on their instructional needs. During circle time, the teacher meets with a small group of students for instructional-level, guided reading and word study activities. At seat time, students practice what the teacher modeled or taught in a previous circle time. For instance, students might work independently on word study activities (e.g., word sorts, word hunts, writing sorts) dealing with whatever spelling pattern or concept they are studying, or they might read books on their independent reading level. Center time might consist of writing projects students can work on individually or with partners. Although developmental grouping should not be the only way of grouping students during the school day, struggling readers in particular benefit from developmentally appropriate instruction that is difficult to accomplish in a whole-class, heterogeneous format.

Final thoughts

My working generalizations on teaching struggling middle school readers are not intended to over-simplify the very serious and complex problem of children reaching the middle grades lacking the basic skills, confidence, and motivation they need to learn from the increasingly difficult and diverse materials they are expected to read. Morris et al. (1996) called for improved and more intensive training for reading specialists and learning disabilities teachers who work with struggling readers. I would extend that recommendation to include regular classroom teachers in the middle school. I believe middle school language arts teachers ought to be knowledgeable about how literacy develops from the early years on, and only then will they understand struggling readers' histories and what they need to progress toward independence in reading.

Do current teacher education programs prepare new middle school teachers to be good teachers of struggling readers? Probably not. We still have a long way to go in offering adequate reading methods coursework in general for preservice middle school teachers (Romine, McKenna, & Robinson, 1996). What I hope my working generalizations offer to new and experienced middle school teachers is a place to start with students whose situations seem otherwise hopeless or, at best, extremely difficult. The more I learn about middle school readers the more I am convinced that all of them, even those who have struggled with reading since kindergarten, can become successful, engaged readers with the right kind of instruction and with teachers who are attuned to what they need.

REFERENCES

Allington, R.L. (1994). The schools we have. The schools we need. *The Reading Teacher, 48,* 14–29.

Bear, D.R., Invernizzi, M., Templeton, S., & Johnston, F. (1996). *Words their way: Word study for phonics, vocabulary, and spelling instruction.* Englewood Cliffs, NJ: Prentice-Hall.

Becker, H.J. (1990). Curriculum and instruction in middle-grades schools. *Phi Delta Kappan, 71,* 450–457.

Betts, E.A. (1954). *Foundations of reading instruction.* New York: American Books.

Bintz, W.P. (1993). Resistant readers in secondary education: Some insights and implications. *Journal of Reading, 36,* 604–615.

Deci, E.L., & Ryan, R.M. (1985). *Intrinsic motivation and self-determination in human behavior.* New York: Plenum Press.

Fielding, L., & Roller, C. (1992). Making difficult books accessible and easy books acceptable. *The Reading Teacher, 46,* 678–685.

Hoffman, J.V., & Segel, K.W. (1982). *Oral reading instruction: A century of controversy.* (ERIC Document Reproduction Service No. ED 239 277)

Hunt, L.C. (1971). The effect of self-selection, interest, and motivation upon independent, instructional, and frustration levels. *The Reading Teacher, 24,* 146–151.

Ivey, G. (in press). A multicase study of middle school readers. *Reading Research Quarterly.*

Johnston, P., & Allington, R. (1991). Remediation. In R. Barr, M.L. Kamil, P. Mosenthal, & P.D. Pearson (Eds.), *Handbook of reading research, Vol. 2* (pp. 984–1012). New York: Longman.

Johnston, P.H., & Winograd, P.N. (1985). Passive failure in reading. *Journal of Reading Behavior, 17,* 279–299.

Kos, R. (1991). Persistence of reading disabilities: The voices of four middle school students. *American Educational Research Journal, 28,* 875–895.

Ley, T.C., Schaer, B.B., & Dismukes, B.W. (1994). Longitudinal study of the reading attitudes and behaviors of middle school students. *Reading Psychology, 15,* 11–38.

McGill-Franzen, A., & Allington, R.L. (1990). Comprehension and coherence: Neglected elements of literacy instruction in remedial and resource room services. *Journal of Reading, Writing, and Learning Disabilities, 6,* 149–180.

McKenna, M.C., Kear, D.J., & Ellsworth, R.A. (1995). Children's attitudes toward reading: A national survey. *Reading Research Quarterly, 30,* 934–955.

Morris, D., Ervin, C., & Conrad, K. (1996). A case study of middle school reading disability. *The Reading Teacher, 49,* 368–377.

Paris, S.G., Lipson, M.Y., & Wixson, K.K. (1983). Becoming a strategic reader. *Contemporary Educational Psychology, 8,* 296–316.

Roe, M.F. (1997). Combining enablement and engagement to assist students who do not read and write well. *Middle School Journal, 28*(3), 35–41.

Roller, C.M. (1996). *Variability not disability: Struggling readers in a workshop classroom.* Newark, DE: International Reading Association.

Romine, B.G.C., McKenna, M.C., & Robinson, R.D. (1996). Reading coursework requirements for middle and high school content area teachers: A U.S. survey. *Journal of Adolescent & Adult Literacy, 40,* 194–198.

Stauffer, R.G. (1969). *Directing the reading-thinking process.* New York: Harper & Row.

Wasserstein, P. (1995). What middle schoolers say about their schoolwork. *Educational Leadership, 53*(1), 41–43.

Worthy, J. (1996). A matter of interest: Literature that hooks reluctant readers and keeps them reading. *The Reading Teacher, 50,* 204–212.

Worthy, J., Patterson, E., Turner, M., Prater, S., & Salas, R. (1997, December). *Coming to love books: Reading preferences of struggling readers.* Paper presented at the annual meeting of the National Reading Conference, Scottsdale, AZ.

PART 3

Assessment, Diagnosis, and Evaluation

ecause students may learn to read in different ways and at different rates, assessment, diagnosis, and evaluation are critical tools for reading professionals. Good assessment allows reading professionals to determine where children are in their reading development and helps them decide what instructional strategies and curriculum materials will best meet the needs of groups they teach, as well as to determine which students will need variations and which will need alternate approaches and materials. Reading professionals also must be constantly evaluating the effectiveness of instruction and revising their teaching so that each student receives appropriate instruction. Assessment, diagnosis, and evaluation are critical components of an effective instructional cycle. Standard 3 is as follows:

> **Candidates use a variety of assessment tools and practices to plan and evaluate effective reading instruction.**

The standard has four elements.

• **Element 3.1 Use a wide range of assessment tools and practices that range from individual and group standardized tests to individual and group informal classroom assessment strategies, including technology-based assessment tools.**

Farr (1992) presents a brief history of assessment issues that highlights some of the confusion and debate centered around reading assessment. He provides a chart (see page 198) of assessment audiences including the general public (and the press), school administrators/staff, parents, teachers, and students. The chart highlights what each audience uses assessment information for, whether the information needed pertains to groups of students or individual students, and the frequency with which information is needed. He argues that the needs of each audience are legitimate and that assessment systems need to take each audience into account.

Serafini (2000/2001) provides a broader prospective that goes beyond typical analyses of assessment that focus on differences in intended audience, purposes, and procedures. The article is intended to help teachers and other concerned educators by focusing on assessment frameworks or "paradigms" and how these assessments affect classroom practice. This provides a view of assessments that complements the selected articles by providing a classroom-oriented analysis.

McNamara (2003) presents a similar analysis from an Australian perspective and provides examples and a set of useful questions for making assessment decisions. The Parker et al. (1995) piece is included because it provides myriad examples of assessment possibilities.

- **Element 3.2 Place students along a developmental continuum and identify students' proficiencies and difficulties.**

Braunger and Lewis (1997) state, "Monitoring the development of reading processes is vital to student success" (p. 230). The authors provide a brief analysis of the weaknesses of norm-referenced and criterion-referenced tests for providing information about individual students' reading development, and then they make recommendations for assessment and suggest the critical aspects of reading development to monitor. They also provide brief descriptions of possible assessment tools that assess those critical aspects.

Badger and Wilkinson (2003) address assessment with specific reference to cultural diversity. They argue that instruction and assessment are inextricably intertwined and that assessment systems must change along with instructional practices if students from a variety of cultural and linguistic backgrounds are to become competent readers and writers.

- **Element 3.3 Use assessment information to plan, evaluate, and revise effective instruction that meets the needs of all students, including those at different developmental stages and those from different cultural and linguistic backgrounds.**

Valencia and Buly (2004) provide an excellent data-based example of the various types of assessments and how they complement one another. By using a battery of standardized and informal assessments, the authors identified six reading profiles for children scoring below standard on the state test given at the end of fourth grade. This piece was selected because it is a dramatic illustration of the reality that requires educators to base important promotion, graduation, and instructional assessments on multiple assessments.

Jiménez (2004) provides a succinct description of a feasible alternative to typical assessment procedures. He explains first why current procedures provide an inaccurate picture of Latino students' literacy skills. He then outlines a procedure for improving the accuracy of the assessment process in a way that addresses critical equity issues. This article is a must for reading professionals, especially because of the rapidly increasing proportion of Latinos in the school population.

- **Element 3.4 Communicate results of assessments to specific individuals (students, parents, caregivers, colleagues, administrators, policymakers, policy officials, community, etc.).**

Nelson (1999) gives an account of an Australian assessment system that bridges the needs of the variety of stakeholders. The focus of the article is on which stakeholder needs what kind of information. The piece explains how the system that is organized around the Australian National Curriculum and Standards Framework is then used to communicate with the various stakeholders including students, parents, teachers, and district and state officials.

The articles in Part 3 provide good descriptions of a variety of assessment instruments used for a variety of purposes ranging from high-stakes school accountability to informal classroom assessments designed to provide information for teachers' instructional decisions. In addition, readers many want to read *High-Stakes Assessments in Reading: A Position Statement of the International Reading Association* (1999).

REFERENCES

International Reading Association. (1999). *High-stakes assessments in reading: A position statement of the International Reading Association*. Newark, DE: Author.

Putting It All Together: Solving the Reading Assessment Puzzle

Roger Farr

Reading assessment has become a genuine puzzle. Confusion and debate continue about what the goals of school assessment of reading should be and about what types of tests and other assessments are needed to achieve those goals. That debate should focus on the purposes for assessment and whether current tests achieve those purposes. Too often, however, the focus of the debate is on the latest testing panacea. In this article, I first examine the complex components of the assessment puzzle. Next I propose a solution to the puzzle that involves linkages among various assessment audiences and approaches. I conclude with a few remarks about how school districts in the United States might pull together all the pieces and solve the assessment puzzle for themselves.

Examining the Pieces of the Assessment Puzzle

The pieces of the puzzle represent many types of assessments, critical attitudes about them, and attempts to challenge or improve them. One of the truly puzzling aspects of reading assessment to many educators is that the amount of testing appears to increase at the same time that criticism of it intensifies (Farr & Carey, 1986; McClellan, 1988; Salganik, 1985; Valencia & Pearson, 1987).

Criticism of Schools Has Led to More Assessment

Public disappointment with student achievement has led to extensive criticism of U.S. schools. This dis-

approval intensified in the 1950s with a focus on reading. Reading assessment conducted to prove or disprove the criticism has received a great deal of attention ever since. Could Johnny read or not, and how well or how poorly? By the 1960s, and beyond, score declines on tests used to predict how well high schoolers would do in college compounded public concern and criticism (The National Commission on Excellence in Education, 1983).

The conviction that many students were receiving high school diplomas and yet were almost totally illiterate became firmly established in the public's mind (Purves & Niles, 1984). The Peter Doe case in California exemplified that concern (Saretsky, 1973). The case concerned a high school student who sued the school district for graduating him without teaching him to read. As a result of this kind of dissatisfaction with educational outcomes, the use of standardized, norm-referenced assessment intensified, and state minimum competency testing programs proliferated (Madaus, 1985; Salmon-Cox, 1981).

The data to determine whether scores on reading tests were deteriorating over time are sketchy at best and tend not to substantiate dramatic declines in the reading performance of U.S. students over the years (Farr & Fay, 1982; Farr, Fay, Myers, & Ginsberg, 1987; Stedman & Kaestle, 1987). Nonetheless, the public has remained convinced that performance has dropped rather dramatically. Further, the prevalence of minimum competency programs has not significantly altered the conviction of the public and press that student achievement, particularly in reading, continues to deteriorate.

Reprinted from Barrentine, S.J. (Ed.). (1999). *Reading assessment: Principles and practices for elementary teachers* (pp. 44–56). Newark, DE: International Reading Association. Originally published in *The Reading Teacher* (1992), 46, 26–37.

This unabated critical concern was at least partly responsible for the establishment of the National Assessment of Educational Progress (NAEP), an ongoing federally mandated study that now provides some reading performance data over time. Any declines it has depicted are small compared to the public's determined assumptions (Mullis, Owen, & Phillips, 1990). And although careful analyses of the ACT and SAT score declines has cited several reasonable causes other than poor schools, that phenomenon did much to sustain and cement public conviction and the demand for accountability testing (Popham, 1987; Resnick, 1982).

The continuing debate about the quality of U.S. schools has now given rise to a new focus on standards and assessment. At the same time that they reaffirm their conviction that children are not learning in school, critics like Chester Finn (1992) echo the call from the White House "for new American achievement tests" that compare student performance to "world class standards" that would be set as criterion references. President Bush (1991) has called for "voluntary national tests for 4th, 8th, and 12th graders in the five core subjects" to "tell parents and educators, politicians and employers, just how well our schools are doing."

The Search for Alternative Assessments Has Also Led to More Assessment

In addition to dissatisfaction with the schools, there has been a quest for assessments that are closely aligned with more holistic views of language development. Some curriculum theorists concerned with the mismatch between curriculum and assessment have determined that if curriculum is to change, the reading tests must change. This has brought about a proliferation of new assessments—both formal and informal (Brown, 1986; Burstall, 1986; Priestley, 1982; Stiggins, Conklin, & Bridgeford, 1986).

Included in this mix have been modifications of conventional tests with new item formats and the addition of the assessment of behaviors not often included on traditional tests, such as background knowledge, student interests and attitudes, and metacognition. Other assessments in reading have taken an entirely different approach to assessment, relying entirely on student work samples collected in portfolios (Jongsma, 1989; Valencia, 1990; Wolf, 1989). Portfolios have themselves taken many different forms from *show portfolios*, which include only a few carefully selected samples, to *working portfolios*, which include a broad sample of work and which are used to guide and organize daily instruction. In addition, numerous professional publications have published articles calling for the use of a broader range of teacher observations and informal assessment techniques (Cambourne & Turbill, 1990; Goodman, 1991).

Different Audiences Need Different Information

Thus, it seems that the increased amount of testing has resulted from greater accountability demands as well as from attempts to find alternatives to traditional assessments. In order to bring some sense to this proliferation of assessment, we need to understand that tests have only one general purpose: Tests should be considered as nothing more than attempts to systematically gather information. The information is used to help children learn about their own literacy development and to give teachers and others concerned with students' literacy the information they need for curriculum planning. *The bottom line in selecting and using any assessment should be whether it helps students.*

A book that I first authored more than 20 years ago regarding the assessment of reading was entitled *Reading: What Can Be Measured?* (Farr, 1970; Farr & Carey, 1986). I have always felt that the title gave the wrong focus to the review of assessment issues. That book should have been entitled *Reading: Why Should It Be Measured?* We need to consider who needs information about reading, what kind of information is needed, and when it is needed. Only then can we begin to plan for more sensible assessment.

In order to think more clearly about overall assessment plans, we need to know why we want to test. There are, of course, different groups that need information. Without considering these groups and their information needs, the assessment program in any school system will remain as a set of jumbled puzzle pieces. The general distinctions between audiences are covered in Figure 1.

The public. Members of the general public, who make decisions through their elected officials, including school boards, have a vested interest in the

Figure 1
Assessment audiences

Audiences	The information is needed to:	The information is related to:	Type of information	When information is needed:
General public (and the press)	Judge if schools are accountable and effective	Groups of students	Related to broad goals; norm- and criterion-referenced	Annually
School administrators/ staff	Judge effectiveness of curriculum, materials, teachers	Groups of students and individuals	Related to broad goals; criterion- and norm-referenced	Annually or by term/semester
Parents	Monitor progress of child, effectiveness of school	Individual student	Usually related to broader goals; both criterion- and norm-referenced	Periodically; five or six times a year
Teachers	Plan instruction, strategies, activities	Individual student; small groups	Related to specific goals: primarily criterion-referenced	Daily, or as often as possible
Students	Identify strengths, areas to emphasize	Individual (self)	Related to specific goals; criterion-referenced	Daily, or as often as possible

future of children and in their effective and cost efficient instruction. It is recognized as vital to Americans' and their nation's future that schools produce educated students. Indeed, the most recent federally supported efforts to improve education have been on establishing standards that presumably will result in the development of assessments related to those standards. At the present time, those involved with establishing the standards are moving in the direction of holistic kinds of performance assessment.

Administrators. Ideally school administrators would rely most heavily on performance assessments that are criterion referenced. These performance measures should compare student performance against a clearly defined curriculum. Since we live in a complex world where mobility and diversity are the reality, administrators also need norm-referenced comparisons of their students' performance.

Parents. While parents share the public's interests, they have a vested interest in their own individual children. In order to monitor their children's progress and to be active in their education, parents want criterion-referenced reports; additionally parents are also typically interested in how their children perform on normed tests in comparison to children from across the United States.

Teachers. A teacher's primary concern is helping students learn. While teachers are necessarily aware of normed assessment's comparative reports as a kind of bottom-line accountability, they are primarily interested in the kind of information that will support the daily instructional decisions they need to make. This kind of information has been generated by criterion-referenced tests and by other types of assessment that can be utilized more effectively in the classroom as a part of instruction.

Students. Students need to become good self-assessors if they are to improve their literacy skills. They need to select, review, and think about the reading and writing they are doing. They need to be able to revise their own writing and to revise their comprehension as they read. If students understand their own needs, they will improve. Students should, in fact, be the primary assessors of their own literacy development.

The Wall Between Understanding

It is important for each of these audiences to recognize, understand, and respect the needs of the others if we are to pull the assessment puzzle together. Audience needs cluster around those of teachers and students on the one hand and those of other decision makers on the other.

The assessment needs of these two general groups tend to be dramatically different and even contradictory, and if the users of assessment do not recognize one another's needs, it is because these distinctions create a kind of wall depicted in Figure 2. It is essential that we breach that wall if we are to get our assessment act together!

Some Tests Attempt to Do It All

No single assessment can serve all the audiences in need of educational performance information. Yet developments in standardized tests have attempted to do so. The tests have added criterion-referenced interpretations, special interpretations for teachers, special reports for parents, individual score reports, and instructional support materials of various kinds. These developments have made the tests longer, more expensive, more time-consuming, and more confusing. Consequently, teachers are expected to justify these investments by making more instructional use of the test results.

At the same time, the increased investment in assessment time and money has tended to give these tests even more importance in determining school accountability and in making high-stakes educational decisions. Specifically, four potential problems have arisen.

Teaching to the test. As accountability became more and more of a concern, teachers have felt pressured to place emphasis on what the standardized tests covered, regardless of what the school curricu-

---

Figure 2
Opposing views of assessment

A teacher's view of assessment		Other decision makers' view of assessment
Assessment is for:	A lack of undestanding/acceptance	*Assessment is for:*
Nurturing		Gate keeping
Guiding the development of students and schools		Judging the success of students, teachers,
Promoting student self-reflection		Finding relatively singular correct answers
Enabling the teacher to teach flexibly		Exercising control over school behaviors
Comparing student performance to a task to be completed		Comparing student performance to that of other students
Making decisions based on multiple samples, including student-selected activities		Making decisions based on single test scores

lum called for. Over time, reading curricula have begun to reflect the skill breakdown of many tests, and reading textbooks have tended to emphasize the skills tests cover as well.

Contaminating the evidence. Standardized reading tests used to mean something. They were genuine indications that a student who performed adequately on them could read. This was so because they *sampled* reading behavior. But now that indication is contaminated. If teachers are deliberately stressing the sub-behaviors that they know are on the tests, the assessments are no longer sampling reading behavior—they are, in effect, covering a very limited definition of it. A good score on a standardized reading test no longer indicates that the student can read in general. It means only that the student can do those limited things the test covers.

Crunching objectives. Attempts to make reading assessment tests more encompassing have tended to make them much longer. Even so, tests are forced to cover the numerous subskills they contain with only a few items each. "What does it mean," a teacher may legitimately ask, "if a student misses one of three items that report on comprehending cause-and-effect?"

The potential for a mismatch. Teachers have long noted that nationally normed tests do not reflect particular emphases in their classrooms. How can a standardized reading test, they have correctly argued, tell them much about a particular curriculum they are following? What can it tell the public about how well the teacher has done using the curriculum?

The more a teacher adheres to instruction related directly to the needs, interests, and backgrounds of his or her particular students, the less assured is the match of that instruction to standardized test content—and the less likely the test's scores will serve that instruction.

Good Reading Theory Recommends Authentic Performance Assessment

Most published tests have not adequately responded to emerging reading theory, which explains reading comprehension as a meaning-constructing process. Any subskills factored out of the process are not discrete; if they actually exist as behaviors, they appear to operate in such an intricate fashion that it is difficult if not impossible to isolate them.

Authentic assessment. Relatively wide acceptance of a constructivist, context-specific definition of reading has promoted a careful analysis of current reading and language arts test content and format to see how authentic the testing experience is. This analysis has led to the conclusion that the reading required on most tests is not much like the reading behavior that our new understanding describes. How valid is the content of a reading test in terms of reader purpose, interests, and background, which we now believe are primary influences on reading behavior?

Performance assessment. Attention to authenticity has accompanied and helped generate the development and use of performance assessment. A student's language behaviors need to be assessed, it is contended, as they are used in real-life situations. Students do not comprehend something read, for example, as a multiple-choice response, and marking those answers has nothing to do with the way reading is actually used, except in taking tests. Reading performance assessment must look at the reading act in process or judge comprehension of a text as it is applied in some realistic way.

Observation. Observation is one way to do this and can lead teachers to meaningful insights about the progress and needs of individual students. Yet teachers need to be trained in regard to what they can look for and what those signs suggest. They need to develop useful ways to make discrete notes about observations and to synthesize what they find. Observation generates many details in relatively random order, and they seldom become clearly useful until they are gathered into patterns that can direct instruction.

Portfolios. Another highly valuable form of performance assessment is the portfolio. For these collections, students and teachers select numerous samples from drafts and final versions of various kinds of a student's writing. The idea is to demonstrate the student's progress and development in the combined process of reading, thinking, and writing. Thus many of the samples in the portfolio are responses to reading. The portfolio is reviewed and discussed regularly by the teacher and student, who may arrange it for others to examine.

Integrated assessment. Assessments in which thinking, reading, and writing are integrated have been developed in recent years. Such assessments have been developed by classroom teachers, school districts, and publishers in an attempt to integrate reading and writing and to assess reading and writing with more realistic activities. These vary widely, but for most of them the student is given a writing task related to a text that is supplied. The task has been deemed to be authentic because it is typical of something the student might do in real life, including the kinds of activities often used for learning in the classroom. It is designed to emphasize the use of information in the reading selection in a realistic and interesting writing task.

For example, one such test asks students to read a nonfiction article that categorically discusses and describes how insect-eating plants lure, capture, and digest their victims. The task is to write a fictional piece telling what a mother bug might say to her children in cautioning them about these plants. Teachers use what the students write to assess students' understanding of the text. They rate other integrated behaviors as well, such as the students' organization and application of the text's content to the task and factors related to writing.

Such reading/writing assessments encourage students to develop a variety of responses based on their interpretation of the reading selection, their background knowledge, and the direction they choose to take in constructing a realistic response. These kinds of performance assessments provide teachers with valuable insights regarding a student's ability to read, write, and construct a meaningful response to an interesting task. Prewriting notes, first drafts, and teacher observation notes all make the assessment a valuable source of information.

In addition, the final drafts can be scored to serve as information that can help determine accountability. The responses can be scored following a "rubric," a list of criteria that describes several levels of performance in each of the categories to be analyzed. Samples of actual student papers ("anchors") that represent each score level described by the rubrics can also be used in scoring. Thus these tests are criterion-referenced. Yet the guides to scoring are somewhat equivalent to normed scores in the sense that the anchor papers were taken from many gathered in field testing and were judged to be typical of the range of responses described in the rubric.

A Combined Solution to the Assessment Puzzle

None of the preceding types of assessment should be argued to be the single solution to the testing puzzle. Figure 3 depicts how performance as-

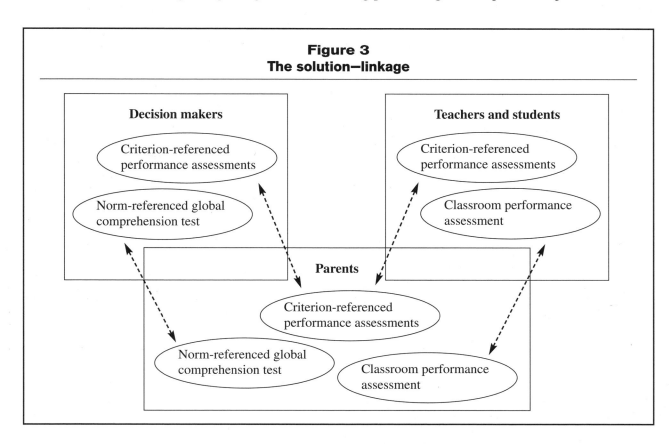

Figure 3
The solution—linkage

Decision makers

Criterion-referenced performance assessments

Norm-referenced global comprehension test

Teachers and students

Criterion-referenced performance assessments

Classroom performance assessment

Parents

Criterion-referenced performance assessments

Norm-referenced global comprehension test

Classroom performance assessment

sessments can provide direct linkage among the main users of assessment and how the three major types of assessment are linked. The chart is a plan for pulling the pieces of the assessment puzzle together into a solution that can inform all the decision makers involved in a student's development into an effective reader and language user.

Solving the Puzzle Will Require Cooperation

Pulling the assessment puzzle together will require tolerance and compromise on the part of many critics of particular types of assessment. The process would be facilitated if:

• Critics of the schools would become aware that assessment must serve more than school accountability. Ideally, critics will inform their concerns with a better understanding of what schools are trying to accomplish.

• Decision makers would understand that assessment is more than numbers on a test paper. They would begin to understand and use the kinds of assessments that are based on real classroom activities and that represent the types of activities in which students who are effective readers and writers should become proficient.

• The most idealistic of the critics of assessment would become more realistic and flexible, tempering their insistence on authentic performance assessment. It seems fruitless, in particular, for some critics to insist that all assessment revolve around observation of activities that are apt not to involve all children and that reveal language use in highly varying degrees.

• Producers of assessments would acknowledge that no one assessment is going to suffice as a school's examination of reading. This would mean that they would no longer promote any of their products as such a test. It would also mean that future revisions of standardized reading tests would undo much of the complexity they now contain.

None of this is to suggest that critical analysis of reading assessment should stop, nor should attempts to improve tests in response to criticism cease. Efforts to develop and institute the new accountability assessments in Illinois (Pearson & Valencia, 1987), where the assessment allows for multiple cor-

rect responses within each multiple-choice item, and in Michigan (Michigan State Board of Education, 1987), where the assessment relies on longer passages followed by more numerous items, have been interesting, if not conclusive, efforts to contribute to a solution to the assessment puzzle. So have attempts to construct items that will reveal students' awareness of how they are processing texts. Although longer reading test passages, different question formats, etc. will not solve the assessment puzzle, they can certainly shape the parts we pull together for a better fit.

Norm-Referenced Tests Need to Change

To solve the assessment puzzle, it will be necessary for teachers and other educators to admit that norm-referenced test results can be of some value to the public and other decision makers, including parents. But these standardized tests should not be of the form that has evolved in response to criticism.

Test authors and publishers should begin to plan assessment *programs* that address multiple audiences. Teachers and schools will need assistance in developing portfolios, planning performance assessments, and integrating assessment information. What are not needed are large single test batteries that promise to meet all of a school's assessment needs from classroom diagnosis to accountability. That attempt, especially linking accountability assessment and instructional assessment, has led to a narrowing of the curriculum.

For the large-scale assessments, this suggests the elimination of the designation of items by subskills and reporting on those sub-behaviors as if they truly are separable and distinct. More publisher efforts should go into the development of a variety of creative and useful curriculum assessments in which students have to actually perform the behaviors the school is attempting to teach.

What large-scale assessment can and should do is to report a global comprehension score, with no special subtests on traditional focuses like word recognition and vocabulary. Without the time-consuming battery of accompanying tests, reading tests can be shorter while using longer passages of a variety of types. These passages must evoke different purposes for reading that reflect the real reasons stu-

Matrix Sampling

dents read in and out of school. Thus, the reading test will be more authentic.

Without the burden of reporting on a host of specific reading and thinking subskills, test makers can write items that truly reflect the balance of a passage, the students' probable purpose for reading such a text, and the aspects of the writing that make the text one of quality and worth the students' time.

It should also be remembered that the long-standing primary purpose of large-scale testing has been to provide a general assessment as to how groups of students are progressing in a school district. Such information, if it does not become the focus of instruction, can be one piece of information used to contribute to a broad base of information for planning, supporting, and evaluating school- and system-wide curricula and instruction.

This approach strongly suggests that *matrix sampling* be used for large-scale assessment, thus eliminating the need to administer to all students the same test items or tasks. Testing time can be considerably shorter if carefully selected samples of students take different parts of a test instead of the whole thing. Good sampling should yield results similar to those obtained when all students take the entire test. Nothing is lost in reporting, since individual scores are of little concern. In addition, matrix sampling provides a general indication of the progress of groups of students, not a blueprint for instruction of individual students.

Performance Assessments Can Provide the Key Linkage

Figure 3 illustrates the linkages across three general audience types that will be essential to solving the assessment puzzle. Norm-referenced information provides a link between parents and decision makers other than teachers. However, the key linkage across all three general audiences is criterion-referenced performance assessments. Various approaches to performance assessment are being developed and tried out in school district assessment programs. Such assessments can be designed by teachers themselves. In fact, this has been done in several local school districts around the United States by teachers cooperating and interacting in order to meet their assessment needs. The same procedures are being tried at the state level in Maryland,

Arizona, California, and Utah, and other states are sure to move in this direction.

The teachers who have been most successful in using this approach have had the support of administrators who could see over the assessment wall. Their support generated public interest and support. In some school systems, published or teacher-created integrated language performance assessment has already become a primary source of information for judging school accountability.

While teachers can create integrated language performance activities on a classroom basis, using them for accountability will require carefully developed or prepared programs that have been made congruent system-wide. This was done in River Forest, Illinois, where teachers developed their own rubrics, anchor papers, and inservice training. This kind of structuring will be necessary if the public, the press, and administrators are to be expected to value these tests as the key indicators of accountability and sources of directions for key decisions, such as curriculum development.

At the same time, of course, these tests can reflect authentic student performance. Not only are they very closely related to instructional activities and thus of high utility to teachers, they are actually instructional activities in and of themselves so the class time they require is doubly well invested.

The Portfolio Is the Flagship of Performance Assessment

Most developers of integrated language assessment programs highly recommend putting the student products into portfolios, a direct acknowledgment that the roots of language performance assessment lie in a portfolio approach to assessment and instruction. Portfolio performance assessment is so integral in good classrooms today that it is vital to note the qualities that make the portfolio approach a successful one.

A successful portfolio approach to assessment must revolve around regular and frequent attention to the portfolio by the student and the teacher. It does minimal good just to store a student's papers in a big folder and let them gather dust for lengthy periods of time. Papers must be added frequently; others can be weeded out in an ongoing rearrangement and selection process; most importantly, the whole process should involve frequent self-analysis by the student and regular conversations between the teacher and the student.

Too many teachers who contend that they are using portfolios do not do these things. Here are a few requirements if portfolios are to provide good assessment:

• The portfolio *belongs* to the student. It is his or her work and property, not some classroom requirement. Students should have choice about what goes in, and they should be encouraged to decorate and personalize their portfolios in unique ways.

• Portfolios are not primarily a display, although students may help arrange them for their parents and administrators to see. They are a shifting, growing repository of developing processes and ideas—a rather personal melting pot that the student uses to reflect on his or her own literacy development and to discuss interesting reading and writing activities with the teacher.

• The teacher's role in portfolio development is that of a consultant who helps convince the student that the work should show a variety of materials reflecting the reading-writing-thinking process as well as examples of responses to common classroom tasks and the student's favorite creations.

• The portfolio should contain numerous and varied pieces written and revised in response to reading. Reading logs reporting ongoing responses to books and articles make valuable contributions to portfolios.

• Portfolios should be reflective collections, revealing genuinely individual and personal responses to classroom activities and to ideas.

• At an absolute minimum, there should be four one-on-one, teacher/student discussions and analyses each semester of a student's developing portfolio. These sessions should not be short and perfunctory. If this requirement is not met, the assessment potential of the portfolio process is forfeited.

• Keeping the portfolio is an ongoing process. Its real value as an assessment tool materializes as the student can analyze his or her progress and development over time.

New Emphases in Assessment Have Common Qualities

Portfolios are part of a group of classroom performance assessments, some of them quite informal, that link the assessment interests of teachers, students, and parents. Portfolios can also be highly revealing to school specialists and administrators who, with the students' permission, take the time to examine them. All of these emerging strategies are both authentic and involve performance assessment. They are:

• Highly individualized, even though they may take place during activities that involve groups of students.

• A part of classroom activities and instruction designed to match an individual student's interests and needs and to use a student's strengths to develop more incisive and creative use of language.

• Activities that integrate several language behaviors.

• Chances to use critical thinking and to express unique and emerging reactions and responses to ideas encountered in text.

• Models that encourage and develop self-assessment by the student, making him or her aware of the language-related strengths that are developing.

How School Districts Can Begin to Solve the Assessment Puzzle

Too often school district testing programs are nothing more than test-and-file procedures. The tests are administered; when the scores are available, they are reported in some way; and teachers are admonished to peruse and use the test results. Yet many educators across the U.S. already embrace the suggestions made here for solving the assessment puzzle. Administrators are aware that testing programs can and do divide educators. Superintendents do not want to abandon their accountability responsibilities, yet they want to support effective ongoing classroom assessment that provides teachers with information that is congruent with current knowledge about reading/writing processes. Teachers want to be more involved in developing an assessment program that serves and matches their instructional needs. They all sense that what is needed is an integrated system that is effective in fostering better teaching and learning.

TRAINING!

Many of these school districts need help with developing an assessment program that links audiences instead of dividing them—one that supplies broad-based accountability information yet is customized to the particular system, its teachers, and its students. One way for school districts to begin is to discuss the pieces of the assessment puzzle in their system. Representatives of all the audiences with assessment needs should take part. As this process develops, the discussions need to be recorded in some way and synthesized. Out of all this can come other brainstorming sessions and ultimately inservice workshops to help all teachers understand how a broad-based assessment program can be pulled together. Equally important, many teachers will welcome inservice training on using different types of informal assessments.

These kinds of workshops can be started within school districts right away. For instance, teachers who are exceptionally good observers or use the portfolio approach with great success are almost always easily identified. They could be enlisted and supported by administrators to run workshops that can be conducted while the discussions about broader reading assessment are helping representative groups define the assessment problems and their district's needs.

The assessment puzzle can be solved. The solution, however, is not as simple as identifying a nonexistent test that will do the whole job nor as arbitrary as eliminating most reading assessment. Rather it takes a vision that focuses on what real literacy means and the awareness that various groups have a stake in helping students to develop as literate citizens. Such a vision must not use assessment to isolate. It must respect the complex nature of literacy, it must serve students and help them to become reflective self-assessors, and it must create links that bring instruction and assessment together.

References

Brown, R. (1986). Evaluation and learning. In A.R. Petrosky & D. Bartholomae (Eds.), *The teaching of writing: Eighty-fifth yearbook of the National Society for the Study of Education* (pp. 114–130). Chicago, IL: University of Chicago Press.

Burstall, C. (1986). Innovative forms of assessment: A United Kingdom perspective. *Educational Measurement: Issues and Practice, 5*, 17–22.

Bush, G. (1991). *America 2000: An education strategy.* Washington, DC: U.S. Department of Education.

Cambourne, B., & Turbill, J. (1990). Assessment in whole language classrooms: Theory into practice. *The Elementary School Journal, 90,* 337–349.

Farr, R. (1970). *Reading: What can be measured?* Newark, DE: International Reading Association.

Farr, R., & Carey, R. (1986). *Reading: What can be measured?* (2nd ed.). Newark, DE: International Reading Association.

Farr, R., & Fay, L. (1982). Reading trend data in the United States: A mandate for caveats and caution. In G. Austin & H. Garber (Eds.), *The rise and fall of national test scores* (pp. 83–141). New York: The Academic Press.

Farr, R., Fay, L., Myers, R., & Ginsberg, M. (1987). *Reading achievement in the United States: 1944–45, 1976, and 1986.* Bloomington, IN: Indiana University.

Finn, C.E., Jr. (1992, January 12). Turn on the lights. *The New York Times,* p. D19.

Goodman, Y. (1991). Evaluating language growth: Informal methods of evaluation. In J. Flood, J. Jensen, D. Lapp, & J. Squire (Eds.), *Handbook of research on teaching the English language arts* (pp. 502–509). New York: Macmillan.

Jongsma, K. (1989). Portfolio assessment. *The Reading Teacher, 43,* 264–265.

Madaus, G.F. (1985). Public policy and the testing profession: You've never had it so good? *Educational Measurement: Issues and Practice, 4,* 5–11.

McClellan, M.C. (1988). Testing and reform. *Phi Delta Kappan, 69,* 766–771.

Michigan State Board of Education. (1987). *Blueprint for the new MEAP reading test.* Lansing, MI: Author.

Mullis, V.S., Owen, E.H., & Phillips, G.W. (1990). *Accelerating academic achievement: A summary of the findings from 20 years of NAEP.* Princeton, NJ: Educational Testing Service.

National Commission on Excellence in Education. (1983). *A nation at risk.* Washington, DC: U.S. Department of Education.

Pearson, P.D., & Valencia, S. (1987). *The Illinois State Board of Education census assessment in reading: An historical reflection.* Springfield, IL: Illinois State Department of Education.

Popham, W.J. (1987). The merits of measurement-driven instruction. *Phi Delta Kappan, 68,* 679–682.

Priestley, M. (1982). *Performance assessment in education and training: Alternate techniques.* Englewood Cliffs, NJ: Educational Technology Publications.

Purves, A., & Niles, O. (1984). The challenge to education to produce literate citizens. In A. Purves & O. Niles (Eds.), *Becoming readers in a complex society: Eighty-third yearbook of the National Society for the*

Study of Education (pp. 1–15). Chicago, IL: University of Chicago Press.

Resnick, D. (1982). History of educational testing. In A.K. Wigdor & W.R. Garner (Eds.), *Ability testing: Uses, consequences, and controversies, Part 2* (pp. 173–194). Washington, DC: National Academy Press.

Salganik, L.H. (1985). Why testing reforms are so popular and how they are changing education. *Phi Delta Kappan, 66,* 628–634.

Salmon-Cox, L. (1981). Teachers and tests: What's really happening? *Phi Delta Kappan, 62,* 631–634.

Saretsky, G. (1973). The strangely significant case of Peter Doe. *Phi Delta Kappan, 54,* 589–592.

Stedman, L.C., & Kaestle, C.F. (1987). Literacy and reading performance in the United States from 1880 to the present. *Reading Research Quarterly, 22,* 8–46.

Stiggins, R.J., Conklin, N.F., & Bridgeford, N.J. (1986). Classroom assessment: A key to effective education. *Educational Measurement: Issues and Practice, 5,* 5–17.

Valencia, S. (1990). A portfolio approach to classroom reading assessment: The whys, whats, and hows. *The Reading Teacher, 43,* 338–339.

Valencia, S., & Pearson, P. (1987). Reading assessment: Time for a change. *The Reading Teacher, 40,* 726–732.

Wolf, D.P. (1989). Portfolio assessment: Sampling student work. *Educational Leadership, 46,* 35–39.

Three paradigms of assessment: Measurement, procedure, and inquiry

When assessment becomes a process of inquiry, teachers can use it to make informed decisions.

Different assessment frameworks have different intended audiences, are used for different purposes and use different procedures to collect information (Farr, 1992). However, these are not the only differences. Each of these assessments may also involve different beliefs about the nature of knowledge, the level of teacher and student involvement, the criteria for evaluating student achievement, and the effects of these assessment frameworks on classroom instruction (Garcia & Pearson, 1994).

The differences between standardized, norm-referenced testing programs and classroom-based assessments have been written about extensively (Neill, 1993). However, as one begins to investigate the various assessment frameworks contained in the professional literature, the distinguishing features of these assessment frameworks, commonly referred to as performance-based, authentic, or classroom-based assessment, tend to overlap and blend.

Various assessment frameworks use similar procedures and data collection methodologies, and many of these "alternative" assessments do not adhere to traditional criteria of standardization, reliability, and objectivity (Linn, Baker, & Dunbar, 1991). This article is intended to help teachers and other concerned educators by providing a broader perspective concerning assessment frameworks or "paradigms" and how these assessments affect classroom practice.

Short and Burke (1994b) described three paradigms of curriculum. They suggested that curriculum could be viewed as Fact, as Activity and as Inquiry. In this description, curriculum as Fact refers to knowledge as a commodity that is "transferrable" and exists separately from the "knower," whereas curriculum as Activity is concerned with the actual activities within the classroom, and curriculum as Inquiry is concerned with the process of creating knowledge in the classroom. As teachers begin to move from a teacher-directed curriculum, based on the transmission of "facts," to a student-centered curriculum, based on inquiry processes, the purposes of assessment and the methods used to collect information may need to be revisited.

In reference to Short and Burke's work, Heald-Taylor subsequently developed three paradigms for literature instruction (1996) and three paradigms for spelling instruction (1998). Heald-Taylor used Short and Burke's curricular paradigms to analyze literature and spelling instruction to help teachers understand their own perspectives, or paradigms, concerning literacy development and classroom practices. This article will look at the distinctions between these three paradigms and use the structure suggested by Short and Burke to shed light on the differences between the various assessment frameworks that operate in schools today.

Short and Burke originally developed these three paradigms to distinguish between the tra-

Reprinted from *The Reading Teacher* (2000/2001), *54*, 384–393.

207

ditional models of curriculum development and an inquiry model. The traditional model, curriculum as Fact, is based on modernist or positivist perspectives of reality and epistemology (Elkind, 1997). From this perspective, knowledge is viewed as an objective commodity that can be transmitted from teacher to student and subsequently measured through standardized forms of assessment (Bertrand, 1991).

In comparison, from a constructivist perspective—curriculum as Inquiry—knowledge is viewed as socially and cognitively constructed by humans as they interact with their environment (Fosnot, 1996). Knowledge is viewed as a construction and not a commodity that exists separately from the "knower." It is this shift from a positivist perspective to a constructivist perspective that underlies the differences in the assessment paradigms to be described in this article.

The curricular paradigms described by Short and Burke are purported to represent different philosophical views of reality, knowledge, and learning (Short & Burke, 1994a). However, in describing the differences between the three paradigms in assessment, one must also look at the level of student and teacher involvement, the methods used to gather information, the purposes or goals of the assessment framework, and the intended audiences for the results. Paralleling the structure used by Short and Burke, the three paradigms of assessment are entitled (a) assessment as measurement, (b) assessment as procedure, and (c) assessment as inquiry.

In this article, I will describe how the three assessment paradigms are similar and how they are different, using various writing assessments —specifically writing portfolios—to help distinguish between the different paradigms. Next, I will present several factors that I believe support teachers making a "paradigm shift" from assessment as measurement to assessment as inquiry. Finally, I will explain several pedagogical suggestions that teachers in transition are using to change their perspectives on assessment.

Assessment as measurement

The first paradigm is assessment as measurement. As mentioned previously, this paradigm is closely associated with a positivist or modernist view of reality and knowledge. The primary instrument of this paradigm is the large-scale, norm-referenced standardized test. These standardized tests are designed to objectively measure the amount of knowledge that a student has acquired over a given time (Wineberg, 1997). A major concern for classroom teachers is whether these assessments provide the necessary information required to make day-to-day instructional and curricular decisions (Johnston, 1992).

In the assessment as measurement paradigm, knowledge is believed to exist separately from the learner, and students work to acquire it, not construct it. The student is seen as an empty vessel, a "blank slate," ready to be filled up with knowledge. Learning is viewed as the transmission of knowledge from teacher to student while meaning is believed to reside within the text, and only one interpretation or judgment is accepted in the standardized tests (Short & Burke, 1994b).

In this paradigm, objectivity, standardization, and reliability take priority over concerns of teacher and student involvement. In these tests, the role of the classroom teacher is scripted, scoring is done by computer, and the tests are kept secured to ensure fairness. The student's primary role in these standardized testing programs is that of test taker. In other words, there is little opportunity for self-evaluation or student reflection. The test is given and a score is tabulated. In this externally mandated form of assessment, classroom teachers have little or no input to the decision-making process and relatively little use for the results of these assessments in directing classroom and curricular decisions (Rothman, 1996).

Primarily, standardized tests are designed to compare large-scale educational programs and to provide accountability to public stakeholders (Murphy, 1997). These tests are used by school districts, state or provincial education departments, and other external stakeholders to rank and compare schools and children (Meier, 1994). Because of the high-stakes agenda associated with these standardized tests, such as funding decisions and school appropriations, they may become highly competitive (Kaufhold, 1995). These tests were not designed to support classroom instruction; rather, they were designed for large-scale educational and program evaluation (Taylor & Walton, 1997).

In the assessment as measurement paradigm, decisions about the information to be collected, and the means of evaluating this information, are usually determined by authorities outside the classroom. For example, writing ability is measured on standardized tests by means of multiple choice questions that focus primarily on issues of grammar, word choice, and spelling. The test items are designed to measure the amount of "writing knowledge" students have accumulated over their school experiences. These tests are also concerned with what a child has not learned or understood. In this way, standardized tests are concerned with deficits of knowledge as well as accumulations.

In this paradigm, portfolios or collections of authentic writing samples are not generally used to evaluate students' writing abilities. In fact, rarely will an actual example of student writing even be evaluated in a standardized testing program.

Assessment as procedure

The assessment as procedure paradigm has elements of the assessment as measurement paradigm as well as the assessment as inquiry paradigm. In this paradigm, the primary focus is on the assessment procedures, not on the underlying purposes of the assessment program or the epistemological stance. Epistemologically, this paradigm is closely related to the assessment as measurement paradigm. Knowledge is still believed to exist independently from the learner; this knowledge can be transmitted to the student and eventually objectively measured.

The main difference between this paradigm and the assessment as measurement paradigm is that the procedures have changed to resemble qualitative data collection methods. However, even though the methods have changed, the underlying beliefs that student achievement can be objectively measured and that knowledge exists independently from the learner have not. In this way this paradigm has elements of the measurement and the inquiry paradigms.

Daly, a social philosopher, referred to a focus on procedures as "methodolatry" (as cited in Noddings, 1992). She described methodolatry as an overemphasis on the correct method of doing things, rather than a focus on the purposes for doing those things. This definition of methodolatry captures the essence of this paradigm very well. The assessment as procedure paradigm is primarily concerned with different methods for collecting data rather than new purposes or audiences for collecting this information.

In this paradigm, like the assessment as measurement paradigm, teachers and students are not directly involved in making decisions concerning the assessment procedures or the purposes for these assessments. The primary concern is with reporting information, albeit information gathered by new methods, to external stakeholders and not with directing classroom instruction (Cizek, 1998).

In Arizona, for example, many portfolio assessment projects were initiated by school district administrations in response to the state-mandated Arizona Student Assessment Program (ASAP). In response to the ASAP, many teachers were directed by their districts to keep portfolios of children's work as part of the state writing assessment. They were required to use a "generic rubric" to score each piece of writing in the student's portfolio and submit a final writing score for each student. This portfolio score would be in lieu of the ASAP performance-based test score. Teachers simply collected the student work, used the rubric to determine a score, and submitted the score to the state department. This was done because an authority outside the classroom directed them to do so.

Because of this situation, these portfolios often become an end in and of themselves. The portfolios were mandated and used to provide scores for the state department. Because of the external mandate, limited teacher input, and little or no staff development, these portfolios became a classroom activity, something teachers were required to administer, rather than a vehicle to promote student or teacher reflection or direct classroom decisions (Smith, 1991).

In this paradigm, the actual procedures for collecting student work, the activities themselves and not the purposes for collecting the student work, have taken priority. As a result of the ASAP, some teachers became more concerned with the type of folders to be used and the procedures for passing these portfolios on to the next grade level than with discussing the various ways these portfolios could be used to promote reflection and self-evaluation.

In the assessment as procedure paradigm, teachers are still being asked to objectively measure students' abilities and report information in numerical form to external audiences. They re-

How new motives become end in themselves

main outside the decision-making process, barely involved in determining the purposes for these assessments.

Many of these "assessment as procedure programs" are destined to fail because they become an end in and of themselves. Classroom teachers have not been involved in the creation of these new methods, which are not intended to provide new insights to a child's learning. Teachers are simply burdened with another set of procedures given to them by their administration in order to provide scores for an external authority.

In effect, the procedure or method of collecting information in and of itself does not determine the assessment paradigm. This paradigm is a blend of two other paradigms. It is the purpose and the audience for these assessments, along with the epistemological stance and methods used to gather information, that helps determine the paradigm.

Assessment as inquiry

In the assessment as inquiry paradigm, assessment is based on constructivist theories of knowledge (Fosnot, 1996), student-centered learning (Altwerger, Edelsky, & Flores, 1987), and the inquiry process (Short, Harste, & Burke, 1995). Here, the teacher uses various qualitative and quantitative assessment techniques to inquire about particular learners and their learning processes. It is a process of inquiry, and a process of interpretation, used to promote reflection concerning students' understandings, attitudes, and literate abilities.

Not only have the procedures changed for collecting information, but so have the levels of teacher and student involvement, the purposes of these assessments, the epistemological perspective, and the audiences for the information created. In the assessment as procedure paradigm, the changes were only at the pedagogical level, concerned with new information-gathering procedures. In comparison, within this paradigm the purpose of the assessments is a deeper understanding of individual learners in their specific learning contexts. The audience has also changed from external authorities to the teachers, parents, and students involved in the classroom.

Assessment, in this paradigm, is viewed as a social, contextually specific, interpretive activity (Crafton & Burke, 1994). Knowledge is believed to be constructed by the individual within the social contexts of the learning event, rather than being acquired solely through transmission or direct instructional techniques. In this paradigm multiple interpretations are encouraged, and each learner transacts with different texts and the world to create meanings (Rosenblatt, 1979).

Using assessment as inquiry, teachers are no longer simply test administrators. Rather, teachers and students are viewed as active creators of knowledge rather than as passive recipients (Wells, 1984). Instead of using tests to measure student abilities and compare children, teachers use these classroom-based assessment procedures to facilitate learning, direct curricular decisions, and communicate more effectively with students and parents (Serafini, 1995).

In this assessment as inquiry paradigm, it is believed there is no simple prescription for each student's ailment or a program that one can administer quickly and relatively effortlessly to eliminate inappropriate behaviors. Assessment is not viewed as an "objective" measurement process, intended for comparisons and prescriptions; rather, it is seen as a human interaction involving the human as the primary assessment instrument (Johnston, 1997). The differences between this paradigm and the assessment as procedure paradigm are in why teachers implement these procedures, not necessarily how these procedures are carried out. What is done with the information and for whom the assessments are conducted has also changed.

Instead of state or provincial education departments mandating a particular portfolio assessment program such as the ASAP example used earlier, teachers implement their own portfolio assessment process to collect samples of student work in order to make appropriate instructional decisions. These portfolios have become vehicles to promote reflection and student self-evaluation (Tierney, 1998). The methods used to collect information may be similar, but the purposes and the goals of the assessment as inquiry paradigm are quite different.

In this paradigm, portfolios are seen as a vehicle for promoting student and teacher reflection, self-evaluation, and goal setting. These portfolios are an ongoing collection of work used to understand a student's interests, abilities, needs, and values. The artifacts in the portfolios are not usually scored or used to compare

children against their same-age cohorts; rather, students reflect upon the contents in order to understand their academic progress and to document their growth. This has been referred to as learner-referenced assessment (Johnston, 1997).

The work included in these portfolios has been created in a more authentic context, rather than in a testing situation (Bergeron, 1996). In this paradigm, classroom instruction does not stop in order to assess learning. Assessment is viewed as part of the learning process, not as separate from it.

Portfolios are noncompetitive and attempt to focus on students' strengths rather than their deficiencies (Murphy, 1997). The portfolios in this paradigm are used to uncover the possibilities for students, to understand each child as a whole, and to attempt to provide a window into a student's conceptual framework and ways of seeing the world.

Educational communities would look radically different if this were the dominant theory of assessment; however, standardized tests will not disappear tomorrow. This shift from assessment as measurement to assessment as inquiry will take time, resources, administrative support, and dialogue among interested educators. Viewing assessment as inquiry would shift the focus of assessment research and practices from the standardized testing programs to the classroom itself, where assessment may be of more service in helping teachers to improve classroom learning experiences (Serafini, 1998).

Supporting teachers in transition

The shift toward an inquiry-based assessment paradigm places different demands not only upon classroom teachers, but also on school administrations, staff development programs, and teacher education models. Making changes in a teacher's practice or educational belief system demands considerable time, research, and the opportunity for teachers to collaborate (Fullan, 1994). In general, teachers need time, support, and the opportunity to have a dialogue with colleagues. Teachers need time to read professional literature concerning assessment, engage in dialogue with other teachers in transition and have the chance to try these new procedures in a supportive, collaborative environment.

Time is already at a premium during the school day for classroom teachers. Paperwork,

school site committees, staff meetings, large classroom enrollments, and shortened preparation periods all contribute to the inadequate amount of time allotted to professional development. Administrators and staff development specialists need to become more creative and supportive in finding time to help classroom teachers understand these new assessment procedures, read about their implementation, try them out in the classroom, and reflect on their progress.

Change can be threatening. Teachers, like other educators, need peer support when working through new ideas. A trusting environment where teachers can enter into open dialogue with one another is of primary importance. However, when teachers are allowed to voice their concerns and ideas, change may become less threatening.

By looking at the existing school structures and developing alternatives to the traditional school day, administrators may find new ways to create time for teachers to collaborate, research new assessment practices, and take the first step toward making a shift in their assessment beliefs and practices. When teachers and administrators come to value the changes necessary to move toward reflective practice and assessment as inquiry, it becomes easier for these groups to justify the time required to support these changes.

In making this shift, teachers will need to reevaluate not only the procedures used to generate information about their students, but also the purposes and audiences for the information collected. In this way it is a "paradigm shift," a new stance toward assessment and knowledge as well as a change in the actual procedures used (Cambourne & Turbill, 1997).

Making the shift

In order to make this paradigm shift from assessment as measurement to assessment as inquiry, teachers need a supportive environment where administration and staff development programs provide time to collaborate with other educators, time to reflect, and the opportunity to work through the new purposes and procedures in the new assessment framework. The general support mechanism needs to be in place to allow teachers the time, dialogue, and collaboration necessary for change to occur.

Along with these general supports, specific changes in a teacher's practice and thinking may support a transition to this new paradigm. Teachers may want to consider the following ideas: (a) teachers as knowledgeable, reflective participants; (b) meaningful student involvement; and (c) negotiating criteria used to assess student performance. Each of these ideas will now be addressed in more detail, including some practical suggestions for teacher consideration.

Teachers as knowledgeable, reflective participants

The teacher as a knowledgeable, reflective participant is the foundation for the assessment as inquiry paradigm. Rather than relying on testing agencies outside the classroom context to evaluate student progress, teachers in this paradigm assume an active role in the assessment process. This new role involves using observational strategies and other classroom-based assessment procedures to gather information about student achievement.

The information collected is then interpreted by teachers on the basis of their existing knowledge and experiences. Teachers reflect on and interpret classroom experiences and student performances to make decisions about curriculum and instruction, rather than relying solely on the interpretations or scores from an externally mandated test. The more extensive the teacher knowledge base, the more effective the interpretations and subsequent instructional decisions (Fenstermacher, 1994). When teachers assume an active role in the assessment process, the audience and purposes for these assessments shift from an external focus on comparison and student ranking to an internal focus on informing classroom practice (Tierney, 1998).

Traditionally, teachers were perceived as "program operators," and the knowledge they needed to be successful was based on how to implement prepackaged curriculum or present the lessons scripted for them in teacher manuals (Bullough & Gitlin, 1985). Subsequent traditional teacher education programs were developed around methods courses that explained how to deliver the curriculum. These notions of teacher as automated program delivery person become problematic in shifting to an assessment as inquiry paradigm.

Many teacher education programs have attempted to restructure their programs to devel-

op teachers who assume an active, reflective role in curriculum and assessment decisions (Ross, 1989). The teacher as a reflective participant is a different stance than the transmission or direct instruction models still taught in some traditional teacher education programs (Zeichner, 1987). If teachers are going to make the transition from assessment as measurement to assessment as inquiry, they need to know more about observing learners, learn how to make curriculum decisions based on these observations, and increase their knowledge base concerning child development and learning processes.

In the assessment as inquiry paradigm, teacher participation means that not only do teachers administer the assessments, but they also have a voice in the decisions as to how, when, and for what purposes these assessments are being used. Teachers are no longer simply the test givers, but become critically involved, deciding which assessments generate the most useful information for their instructional purposes. These new assessments are not blindly accepted, but are judged on the type of information they create, the purposes for these assessments, and the needs of the audiences involved.

As reflective participants, teachers make a commitment to learn from past experiences. It is an intentional, systematic, and deliberate focus on why things occur and what effects these experiences have on student learning (Dewey, 1933). Reflection has been defined as "systematic enquiry into one's own practice to improve that practice and to deepen one's understanding of it" (Lucas, 1991, p. 85).

Reflective thinking is initiated by the perception of a problem (Dewey, 1933). It is this acknowledgement of uncertainty and "unsettledness" that initiates the inquiry process. In other words, in order to be reflective participants, teachers need to be able to discuss their doubts and inquiry questions without being seen as unknowing or incompetent. Being able to make one's practice "problematic" has been observed as a first step in this process (Valli, 1997). When teachers have no doubts about their practice or the programs they are using, reflection remains of minimal importance.

In working toward becoming knowledgeable, reflective participants in the assessment process, teachers have assumed the role of teacher-researcher to better understand the experiences and interactions in their classrooms (Cochran-Smith & Lytle, 1992). In doing so, teachers have become producers of research and knowledge as well as consumers (Richardson, 1994). By video-taping classroom events (Berg & Smith, 1996), observing peers at work in classrooms, and working in team teaching situations, teachers are opening up new avenues for dialogue and collaboration. This has allowed teachers the opportunity to become more reflective about their practice. Teachers also use journal writing as a way to help understand the perspectives and beliefs they bring to their practice and their effect on classroom events (Hubbard & Power, 1993).

Many teachers have used journal writing to create belief statements or platform statements about their philosophy of education in order to understand the expectations and hidden beliefs they bring to the assessment process (Kottkamp, 1990). In writing these statements, teachers have been able to "unpack" their values and biases and to distance themselves from their practice in order to critique it more effectively. The purpose of these procedures is to help teachers see their practice from a different, more critical perspective (Osterman, 1990).

Another way to help teachers make this shift is to support the development of teacher dialogue groups. When teachers come together to discuss educational issues that are relevant to their practice, change and growth become possible (Ohanian, 1994). Teacher-research groups (Queenan, 1988) and assessment-driven teacher dialogue groups (Stephens et al., 1996) help provide a structure for teachers to support one another through the change process. Through these dialogue groups, teacher-research groups, and journal writing, teachers are inquiring into the quality of the learning experiences provided for their students and the effectiveness of the decisions they make in their classroom.

Meaningful student involvement

The assessment as measurement paradigm has historically left students out of the assessment process (Bushweller,1997). Assessment has been something we do "to" students rather than "with" students. Schools administer standardized tests and send them off to be scored by external testing agencies; eventually the results of the tests are reported back. Through this traditional assessment as measurement paradigm,

students and schools have come to rely on external testing agencies to judge their effectiveness and to document their educational progress. This lack of involvement has created passive recipients, not active participants, in the learning as well as the assessment process (Calfee & Perfumo, 1993).

In the assessment as inquiry paradigm, portfolios of student work, student-led conferences, learning response logs, and negotiated reporting procedures include the student in the assessment process (Tierney, Carter, & Desai, 1991). This new level of involvement helps students to accept more responsibility for their learning and to reflect on their own educational progress. Students need to be invited to participate in determining the criteria by which their work will be judged and then play a role in actually judging their work (Kohn, 1993).

Portfolios are used as a vehicle to promote reflection on students' academic progress as well as document their growth in various subject areas (Graves, 1992). Students collect work generated during the school year to evaluate their progress and set goals for their future learning experiences. Many times these portfolios are used in conjunction with student-led conferences where students share their portfolios and reflections with parents and other interested audiences. These portfolios have an authentic purpose and are a primary vehicle for supporting student reflection as well as student involvement in the assessment process.

Another way students are involved in the assessment process is through negotiated reporting configurations (Anthony, Johnson, Mickelson, & Preece, 1991). Students are invited to become intimately involved in the creation of their report cards in a negotiated process with both teachers and parents. This process may begin by allowing students to evaluate their efforts and performances, based on criteria negotiated between the teacher's perspective, the information contained in various standards documents, and the beliefs and values of the community. Opening up the criteria used to evaluate student work and inviting students to participate in the evaluation process helps students begin to feel a part of the assessment process, rather than as passive recipients of someone else's evaluation.

Another way of involving students in assessing their progress is through classroom-designed rubrics (Rickards & Cheek, 1999). Rubrics are negotiated forms of criteria explicitly written for particular classroom work and activities. Again, opening up the conversation to include students in the decisions about what criteria are used to evaluate their progress helps students become involved in the assessment process. When students become an active part of the assessment process, assessment becomes a process of inquiry rather than an external measurement reducing student performance and ability to a numerical score for comparative purposes.

Negotiating the criteria used to assess student performance

The debate over what children should be taught and what they need to know in order to be successful adults has been going on in the United States for centuries (Bracey, 1995). This debate has been rekindled by many of the standards-based restructuring initiatives across the U.S. and other countries (Noddings, 1997). The creation of standards documents by state legislatures and federal education agencies, along with the standardized testing that usually accompanies these documents, has tended to restrict programs to the assessment as measurement paradigm, while at the same time supporting agendas tied to gatekeeping and exclusion (Tierney, 1998). These documents are written as general learning statements by people far removed from actual classrooms and students. The negotiation of educational criteria becomes a highly political issue and hence a highly controversial one (Shannon, 1996).

As educators, we just don't know all that students need to know, nor are we able to teach them everything we do know (Wiggins, 1989). The criteria used for assessing student performance should be open for negotiation and revision to adapt to our changing societal demands. Teachers and students should have a voice in what is taught, how this knowledge is eventually assessed, and what criteria are used for evaluation.

With all of these restructuring efforts, teachers have been bombarded with standards created by federal and state agencies, local school boards, and professional organizations like the National Council of Teachers of English and the International Reading Association. Using these documents as guidelines, teachers may open the

negotiations by writing detailed belief or platform statements concerning their expectations for student learning and behavior (Kottkamp, 1990). These platform statements provide a place to open up a discussion among parents, teachers and school officials about the experiences to be provided for students during the school year. By presenting their criteria to be negotiated, teachers open up a space for different voices to be heard concerning what is of value in education and what place particular content areas and learning processes are to have in the school curriculum.

As mentioned before, classroom rubrics designed with student and teacher input are an excellent vehicle for negotiation and involvement in the assessment process. Students and teachers come together to "unpack" their values and beliefs about education in order to expose these to discussion and negotiation. It is this process of negotiation that is of primary importance, not necessarily the actual documents that are created in the process (Boomer, 1991).

The items included on school district report cards and how amenable these cards are to change should also be open to negotiation. School report cards are a written statement about what the community deems valuable in education. If it is on the report card and it gets a grade, it is probably seen as important by that community. Even the amount of space designated for each subject area is a statement concerning how much value is placed upon that topic. The larger the space, it seems the more value is assigned to that particular subject or topic.

In negotiating the criteria used to assess student performance, educators should consider the "models of excellence" already available in the outside world that classroom teachers and students can use to judge the quality of the work done in schools. Possibly educators can look to various awards, such as the Newbery or Pulitzer prize for writing or the Nobel prize for science, in order to find criteria that are authentic and can be incorporated into the negotiation of student evaluation. What are the authentic models of criteria available for assessing student performance? Instead of school districts and education departments being the sole creators of these criteria of student progress, opening up the discussion to bring in multiple voices may create more authentic, more useful criteria.

No quick fix

When educators begin to acknowledge the complexity and the interpretive nature of the learning and assessment process, traditional assessment as measurement procedures become problematic. All assessments are interpretive; unfortunately teachers and students rarely become involved in large-scale testing programs' interpretations or dissemination of results. The assessment as inquiry paradigm offers teachers another perspective from which to understand the needs and abilities of their students, using different assessment methods for different purposes and audiences.

Making this shift from assessment as measurement to assessment as inquiry takes time, administrative support, collaboration, and the opportunity to engage in dialogue. Simply mandating new procedures for teachers to administer will not help teachers make this shift in assessment paradigms.

It is my hope that classroom teachers will begin to take an active role in the assessments used in their classroom. Teachers need to involve students in the assessment process in meaningful ways, become knowledgeable, reflective participants in the assessment process themselves, and negotiate the criteria used to evaluate academic performances. As educators, we need to acknowledge the complexity of the learning process and stop trying to find the quick-fix solutions to both educational and assessment issues. When assessment becomes a process of inquiry, an interpretive activity rather than simply the "objective" measure of predetermined behaviors, teachers will be able to use assessment to make informed decisions concerning curriculum and instruction in their classrooms.

References

Altwerger, B., Edelsky, C., & Flores, B. (1987). Whole language: What's new? *The Reading Teacher, 41*, 144–154.

Anthony, R., Johnson, T., Mickelson, N., & Preece, A. (1991). *Evaluating literacy: A perspective for change.* Portsmouth, NH: Heinemann.

Berg, M.H., & Smith, J.P. (1996). Using videotapes to improve teaching. *Music Educator's Journal, 22*(5),31–37.

Bergeron, B. (1996). Seeking authenticity: What is "real" about thematic literacy instruction? *The Reading Teacher, 49*, 544–551.

Bertrand, J. (1991). Student assessment and evaluation. In B. Harp (Ed.), *Assessment and evaluation in whole language programs* (pp. 17–33). Norwood, MA: Christopher-Gordon.

Boomer, G. (Ed.). (1991). *Negotiating the curriculum: A teacher-student partnership.* Sydney, Australia: Ashton-Scholastic.

Bracey, G. (1995). *Final exam: A study of the perpetual scrutiny of American education.* Washington, DC: Technos Press.

Bullough, R.V., Jr., & Gitlin, A. (1985). Schooling and change: A view from the lower rungs. *Teachers College Record, 87*, 219–237.

Bushweller, K. (1997). Teach to the test. *The American School Board Journal, 184*, 20–25.

Calfee, R., & Perfumo, P. (1993). Student portfolios: Opportunities for a revolution in assessment. *Journal of Reading, 36*, 532–537.

Cambourne, B., & Turbill, J. (Eds.). (1997). *Responsive evaluation.* Portsmouth, NH: Heinemann.

Cizek, G. (1998). The assessment revolution's unfinished business. *Kappa Delta Pi Record, 34*,144–149.

Cochran-Smith, M., & Lytle, S. (Eds.). (1992). *Inside/outside: Teacher research and knowledge.* New York: Teachers College Press.

Crafton, L., & Burke, C. (1994). Inquiry-based evaluation: Teachers and students reflecting together. *Primary Voices, 2*(2), 2–7.

Dewey, J. (1933). *How we think.* Chicago: Henry Regnery.

Elkind, D. (1997). The death of child nature: Education in the postmodern world. *Phi Delta Kappan, 78*, 241–245.

Farr, R. (1992). Putting it all together: Solving the reading assessment puzzle. *The Reading Teacher, 46*, 26–37.

Fenstermacher, G. (1994). The knower and the known: The nature of knowledge in research on teaching. In L. Darling-Hammond (Ed.), *Review of research in education, 20* (pp. 3–56). Washington, DC: American Educational Resrearch Association.

Fosnot, C.T. (1996). Constructivism: A psychological theory of learning. In C.T. Fosnot (Ed.), *Constructivism: Theory, perspectives and practice* (pp. 8–33). New York: Teachers College Press.

Fullan, M. (1994). Why teachers must become change agents. *Educational Leadership, 50*, 12–17.

Garcia, G.E., & Pearson, P.D. (1994). Assessment and diversity. In L. Darling-Hammond (Ed.), *Review of research in education, 20* (pp. 337–391). Washington, DC: American Educational Research Association.

Graves, D. (1992). Portfolios: Keep a good idea growing. In D. Graves & B. Sunstein (Eds.), *Portfolio portraits* (pp. 1–12). Portsmouth, NH: Heinemann.

Heald-Taylor, B.G. (1996). Three paradigms for literature instruction in grades 3 to 6. *The Reading Teacher, 49*, 456–466.

Heald-Taylor, B.G. (1998). Three paradigms of spelling instruction in grades 3 to 6. *The Reading Teacher, 51*, 404–412.

Hubbard, R.S., & Power, B.M. (1993). *The art of classroom inquiry: A handbook for teacher reseachers.* Portsmouth, NH: Heinemann.

Johnston, P.H. (1992). Nontechnical assessment. *The Reading Teacher, 46*, 60–62.

Johnston, P.H. (1997). *Knowing literacy: Constructive literacy assessment.* York, ME: Stenhouse.

Kaufhold, J.A. (1995). Testing, testing. *The American School Board Journal, 182*, 41–42.

Kohn, A. (1993). Choices for students: Why and how to let students decide. *Phi Delta Kappan, 75*, 8–20.

Kottkamp, R.B. (1990). Means for facilitating reflection. *Education and Urban Society, 22*, 182–203.

Linn, R., Baker, E., & Dunbar, S. (1991). Complex, performance-based assessment: Expectations and validation criteria. *Educational Researcher, 20*(8), 15–21.

Lucas, P. (1991). Reflection, new practices and the need for flexibility in supervising student teachers. *Journal of Higher Education, 15*(2), 84–93.

Meier, T. (1994). Why standardized tests are bad. In *Rethinking our classrooms: Teaching for equity and social justice* (pp. 171–175). Milwaukee, WI: Rethinking Schools Ltd.

Murphy, S. (1997). Literacy assessment and the politics of identity. *Reading and Writing Quarterly, 13,* 261–278.

Neill, M. (1993). A better way to test. *The Executive Educator, 15,* 24–27.

Noddings, N. (1992). *The challenge to care in schools.* New York: Teachers College Press.

Noddings, N. (1997). Thinking about standards. *Phi Delta Kappan, 79,* 184–189.

Ohanian, S. (1994). *Who's in charge? A teacher speaks her mind.* Portsmouth, NH: Heinemann.

Osterman, K. (1990). Reflective practice: A new agenda for education. *Education and Urban Society, 22*(2), 133–152.

Queenan, M. (1988). Impertinent questions about teacher research: A review. *English Journal, 77*(2),41–46.

Richardson, V. (1994). Conducting research on practice. *Educational Researcher, 23*(5), 5–10.

Rickards, D., & Cheek, E., Jr. (1999). *Designing rubrics for K-6 classroom assessment.* Norwood, MA: Christopher-Gordon.

Rosenblatt, L.M. (1979). *The reader, the text, the poem.* Carbondale, IL: Southern Illinois University Press.

Ross, D. (1989). First steps in developing a reflective approach. *Journal of Teacher Education, 40*(2), 22–30.

Rothman, R. (1996). Taking aim at testing. *The American School Board Journal, 183,* 27–30.

Serafini, F. (1995). Reflective assessment. *Talking Points: Conversations in the Whole Language Community, 6*(4), 10–12.

Serafini, F. (1998). Making the shift. *Talking Points: Conversation in the Whole Language Community, 9*(2), 20–21.

Shannon, P. (1996). Mad as hell. *Language Arts, 73,* 14–18.

Short, K., & Burke, C. (1994a). *Creating curriculum.* Portsmouth, NH: Heinemann.

Short, K., & Burke, C. (1994b). *Curriculum as inquiry.* Paper presented at the Fifth Whole Language Umbrella Conference, San Diego, CA.

Short, K., Harste, J., & Burke, C. (1995). *Creating classrooms for authors and inquirers.* Portsmouth, NH: Heinemann.

Smith, M.L. (1991). Put to the test: The effects of external testing on teachers. *Educational Researcher, 20*(5), 8–11.

Stephens, D., Story, J., Aihara, K., Hisatake, S., Ito, B., Kawamoto, C., Kubota, S., Mokulehua, J., Oka-Yamashita, S., Omalza, S., Tsuchiyama, E., Yamate, F., Yoshioka, E., Yoshizaki, L., & Yoshizawa, D. (1996). When assessment is inquiry. *Language Arts, 73,* 105–112.

Taylor, K., & Walton, S. (1997). Co-opting standardized tests in the service of learning. *Phi Delta Kappan, 79,* 66–70.

Tierney, R.J. (1998). Literacy assessment reform: Shifting beliefs, principled possibilities, and emerging practices. *The Reading Teacher, 51,* 374–390.

Tierney, R.J., Carter, M.A., & Desai, L.E. (1991). *Portfolio assessment in the reading-writing classroom.* Norwood, MA: Christopher-Gordon.

Valli, L. (1997). Listening to other voices: A description of teacher reflection in the United States. *Peabody Journal of Education, 72*(1), 67–88.

Wells, G. (1984). *The meaning makers.* Portsmouth, NH: Heinemann.

Wiggins, G. (1989). The futility of trying to teach everything of importance. *Educational Leadership, 47,*14–18.

Wineberg, S. (1997). T.S. Eliot, collaboration and the quandries of assessment in a rapidly changing world. *Phi Delta Kappan, 79,* 59–65.

Zeichner, K. (1987). Preparing reflective teachers: An overview of instructional strategies which have been employed in pre-service education. *International Journal of Education Research, 11,* 565–575.

Reading assessment options for teachers of junior secondary students

Michael McNamara

The purpose of this paper is to consider a range of alternatives for teachers wishing to assess students' reading abilities and behaviours in the junior secondary school and comment on their usefulness. It will be argued that teachers should be aware of the strengths and weaknesses of all options, that those options which seem to offer most stimulating information about students' performance are difficult to implement, and that compromise between what is best and what is possible is a likely component of choosing between means of assessment.

What is the purpose of the assessment?

In a discussion of the purposes of assessment, Broadfoot (1987) specified the difference between assessment for curriculum, assessment for communication, and assessment for accountability. Assessment for curriculum is that which is diagnostic and motivating. It tells the teacher what each pupil has learned, more general information about students' strengths and weaknesses, and how far the teaching has succeeded in its aims. Assessment for communication has a certification function and a selection function. Assessment for accountability is to demonstrate the extent to which the aims of an educational institution have been fulfilled. Broadfoot also reminds us of the distinction between formative and summative assessment, defining the former as a means to encourage learning, and suggesting that the emphasis of the latter is to provide reliable and acceptable information on what has been achieved.

As discussed below, secondary teachers should be clear on the general purposes of assessment and be sure to choose means of assessing students which meet their specific needs.

Assessment for curriculum: Diagnostic and motivating

An assessment mechanism which involves the teacher and student in collaboration, and includes close scrutiny of the process of reading, examination of the text which is read, and consideration of the context of reading, is likely to stimulate detailed diagnosis and motivate teachers and students to take immediate and appropriate action to continue reading development.

There are a number of reasons for choosing a means of assessment with these characteristics. Law (1984) calls for collaboration between teachers and students in the assessment process. He argues that this acknowledges students' responsibility for the way in which they are portrayed. Close scrutiny of the process of reading gives teachers the opportunity to design activities that are appropriate for each student. Examination of the text that is being read involves the teacher in reflection about the demands of the text and the kinds of support that learning readers will need in handling that text and others like it. Consideration of the context of reading gives the teacher the opportunity to reflect on the environmental and other factors that could affect reading behaviour. The influence of this sort of factor is acknowledged in standardised tests. In the *TORCH Manual* (Mossenson et al., 1987, p. 7), teachers are advised to administer the test in the morning and in a suitable room.

Assessment for curriculum using close observation

In the following section, a recording of one Year 8 student reading and discussing a passage required in a Social Education class, is analysed. The act of reading/doing the analysis makes clear the sort of

Reprinted from Fehring, H. (Ed.). (2003). *Literacy assessment: A collection of articles from the Australian Literacy Educators' Association* (pp. 103–117). Newark, DE: International Reading Association. Originally published in *The Australian Journal of Language and Literacy* (November 1992), *15*(4). Reprinted with permission of the Australian Literacy Educators' Association.

support the student requires to make sense of the passage and others like it. The analysis is intended to demonstrate the potential richness of close observation.

The student, S, discusses the passage reproduced below. It should be noted that S read the passage aloud quite fluently and the retelling was done after she had time to re-read the passage silently. The passage itself was part of a longer document used in the fourth term of the previous year in S's Year 7 class.

Ancient Egypt: Pyramids and Herodotus

Almost two and a half thousand years ago Herodotus, an ancient Greek historian, visited the land of the Egyptians. He travelled into the desert to see the great pyramid at Giza. In the history he wrote later, Herodotus described the largest pyramid of the Pharaoh Khufu or Cheops.

> It took twenty years to build and has a square base and its height is equal to the length on each side. It is made of polished stone blocks and all of them at least nine metres long and beautifully fitted together.

> When Herodotus saw the pyramid they were already two thousand years old and the Egyptians themselves had forgotten many of the facts about the construction and how their ancestors had come to build these immense tombs.

S: "This was about...two and a half thousand years ago and it is about an ancient Greek historian named Herodotus and he went to Egypt and he had um built the pyramids and when he came...like he hadn't seen them for about 2000 or something years ago, he didn't see them, and all the Egyptians forgot how to make the pyramids and that and they were very big and they were made out of shiny tomby stones and that is about it."

Table 1 lists the points made in the passage. The points that are marked with an asterisk in the right hand column are those that the student was able to repeat in her first retelling.

Table 1

Herodotus was an ancient Greek historian.	*
2,500 years ago, Herodotus visited Egypt.	*
He traveled to the desert to visit the pyramid at Giza.	
The pyramids were two thousand years old when he saw them.	*
Details of how the pyramids were built were not known by the Egyptians living in Herodotus's time.	
Herodotus wrote the following about the pyramid:	
It took twenty years to build.	
It had a square base.	*
Its height is equal to the length of each side.	
It is made of polished stone blocks.	*
All of the stones are least nine metres long.	
The stones beautifully fitted together.	

In this retelling it appears as if S was able to repeat some significant information but her understanding seems largely confused about time, who had in fact built the pyramids, and Herodotus's role. The text itself is noteworthy in the following ways:

• The passage is from a unit about Ancient Egypt but starts with a description of an Ancient Greek historian.

• The passage includes a quote from Herodotus's writing. It requires that the reader be familiar with the convention of marking a substantial quotation with an indentation.

• While the concept of time is central to the passage, the time segments are not ordered sequentially.

The passage refers to three segments of time, they are:

A   The time of the building of the pyramids;
B   A time in Egypt two thousand years later when a Greek visitor came to Egypt;
C   The time of Herodotus writing the history of the pyramid's construction.

The three segments occur in the passage in the following order: B, C, A, B, A. In the sweep of three paragraphs, four and a half thousand years are covered but they are referred to in two easily confused two thousand year blocks.

The assessor and S discussed the passage further.

A   OK. There is one thing that just when you were telling me about it, I wasn't clear on. You said that he went to visit Egypt and then you said something about the pyramids. Could you just say that again. What was he doing there?

S   I think he was building he was writing on how they were building a pyramid.

A   All right. Were they building them at the time he visited?

S   Yeah.

A   Do you want to check that?

S   While he was visiting there it took twenty years to build so he was there and umm.... No when he saw them they were two thousand years old.

A   All right. So what are....

S   He wasn't actually there. When he came back...when he saw they were two thousand years old, the pyramids.

A   So how do you mean when he came back? Had he been there before?

S   Yeah

A   Just take your time. You are a really terrific reader, S. Don't let me panic you.

S   Yeah, it says here he travelled to see the great pyramid at Giza, right, and in the history he wrote later a book on it and when, yeah...and he described the largest pyramid and now he says how long it took to build the pyramid and it says here when Herodotus saw the pyramid they were two thousand years ago.

In the last attempt at a retelling the student seems surer. She has a much greater sense of the way time is organised in the passage; she is surer that Herodotus's writing has been quoted although there is a sense that she is still not totally at ease with the passage.

What does this brief analysis suggest about assessment? At the beginning of this section it was suggested that "assessment for curriculum" would involve close scrutiny of the process of reading, examination of the text which is read, consideration of the context of reading, and teacher and student acting in collaboration.

Close scrutiny of the process of reading

The analysis shows that S is a very competent decoder of the material she is expected to use in class; that she can struggle to express her understanding when put under pressure; but when encouraged, she can make some sense of quite challenging material.

Examination of the text which is read

The analysis suggests that teachers who use factual material similar to that described above might read it carefully before presenting it in class to see the kinds of difficulty it presents. Teachers could reflect on the background knowledge the students would need to have before they could make best use of the passage. The teachers might note the difficulties presented when moments of history are written about out of sequence.

Consideration of the context of reading

S read and summarised the passage in a one to one conference with a researcher who was not a teacher at the school in a room adjacent to the classroom. One cannot be sure simply from the retelling how her reading was affected by it occurring in these circumstances. Nevertheless, it is clear that when S was given time and encouragement to clarify her summary, she was able to come to a closer understanding of the text by re-reading it and continuing to describe what she understood. Teachers might reflect on the possibility of giving students the opportunity to articulate their understanding to a sympathetic audience (perhaps the student's peers in small group activities). They might also reflect on whether the dynamics of their classrooms are conducive to creating audiences for reading so that understanding can be developed by summariser and listener together.

Teacher and student in collaboration

The process described above brings the teacher and student face to face in a shared experience that can become a stimulus for further growth and a reference point for shared analysis and discussion.

As well, it is clear that the teacher intervenes in the reading assessment process so that half-formed understandings are explored and developed. Other writers have called for this type of intervention. Brozo (1990) advocates what he calls "interactive assessment," the goal of which "is to discover the conditions under which a student will succeed in reading rather than merely describing a student's current status as a reader." Kletzien and Bednar (1990) describe "dynamic assessment" which attempts not only to recognise already mastered abilities but also to identify capabilities that "are in the process of maturing."

The question arises about when and where such detailed attention to the performance of a single student can occur. The student whose reading and discussion are described above participated in a one to one interview lasting fifteen to twenty minutes. To conduct this sort of interview for each of the students in a single class, let alone all the classes a teacher might have, would take a prohibitively long time. An alternative is for teachers to set class time aside in which they observe students at work and then keep an informal record of their observations. This requires a sufficiently orderly class for this sort of observation to be possible and the ability of students in the class to work without disturbing the teacher and student in conference. If these conditions are satisfied, then the assessment process that involves close scrutiny of a student's reading not only provides evidence upon which to base written assessment, it stimulates thought about classroom reading material and ways to assist students to read effectively.

Assessment for curriculum and standardised tests

A criticism levelled at standardised tests is that the use of them denies the teacher the opportunity of observing how a reader makes meaning of a particular text, instead restricting the teacher to being a receiver of a report of reading ability (Johnston, 1989). The teacher, for example, cannot be sure whether students have re-read a piece before committing themselves to paper, or revised their position after an initial attempt. Standardised tests cannot describe the inexact, or half-formed understanding that students can have about a passage, the sort of understanding that is developed and clarified with another's prompts and suggestions. This sort of description is possible when teachers closely observe and interact with students during the assessment process.

A further problem with standardised tests is that there is little opportunity for teachers to consider the demands of the material being read, its similarity to the material that they will require students to use in their subjects, or the way that the purpose of reading (for assessment, for enjoyment, for performance, for information gathering) can affect the way that it is read. A fundamental principle of standardised tests is that we should conceptualise reading as a skill or set of skills which can be articulated in relation to students independent of the particular texts that they are reading. It may be the case, though, that a key item of vocabulary or unfamiliar schematic structure (as in the case described above) could affect the students' understanding or result in relation to a certain skill, while a different result might occur if the tested passage is something different. Standardised test results cannot offer insights into students' performance on reading in content area subjects, because there are not tests which can take into account the breadth of subject areas or the diversity of styles that are possible in content area reading. Understanding of the demands of reading in various situations can best be gauged by observing the reading that occurs in them.

There are standardised tests which do claim to be diagnostic and able to suggest appropriate courses of future action for teachers. The writers of the *Tests of Reading Comprehension (TORCH) Manual* claim that theirs are tests able to be interpreted with reference to particular skills. They give examples of the kind of skills that might become the focus of attention with particular students:

> Susan has a TORCH score of 32 which suggests that she can complete rephrased sentences as well as connect pronouns with previously mentioned nouns. She may not be able to connect ideas separated in text as well as extracting details in the presence of distracting ideas. (Mossenson et al., 1987, p. 17)

The writers suggest that this is one of the features that makes TORCH a useful package. Nevertheless, one fears that emphasis on such skills might prompt teachers to develop them by encouraging students to read and complete activities identical to the activities required in the test. "Teaching to the test" is lamented in a variety of literature (e.g., Cambourne & Turbill, 1991; Johnston, 1989). Mastery of such skills is still no guarantee of mastery of the diversity of reading likely to be encountered at school.

Assessment for communication: Certification and selection

Broadfoot (1987) reminds us of other purposes of assessment, namely certification and selection. When assessment serves the selection function it is necessarily comparative and often competitive. There are a number of possibilities for certification and selection. Assessment can be descriptive, norm-referenced, criterion-referenced, or work-referenced.

Garforth and Macintosh (1986) give examples of descriptive assessment where student performance is recorded in terms of tasks required, goals set, and the skills demonstrated by the student once the task is completed. Descriptive assessment can also document change in students' performance. It can describe typical behaviour before the teaching/learning sequence begins and changes that have occurred during the course. The reference point is the individual child's starting behaviour. There need be no requirement that the tasks be uniform, so direct comparison may be difficult. When this is the case, interpretation is left to the reader who assumes responsibility for attaching weight to various aspects of the description. With regard to reading, interpretation depends on the reader's understanding of the process of reading, the various skills and knowledge required to make reading material meaningful, and his/her familiarity with the material actually read by the student.

Criterion-referenced assessment is a potential way of making the process of interpreting assessment less demanding. In relation to reading, if the criteria for assessment are intended to describe a full range of reading ability, then placing a student in relation to the criteria makes explicit the assessor's opinion about what has been achieved and what has yet to be achieved. Placing a student's reading behaviour by describing it in terms of predetermined criteria relieves the reader of the assessment of the responsibility of deciding the extent of the student's achievement. Similarly, if the criteria are defined hierarchically in a way that does not offend the reader of the assessment, then comparison between students becomes easier and selection simpler. As is indicated above, results of TORCH tests can be given in terms of predetermined and hierarchically defined criteria. Another example in Victoria is the use of criteria by which Victorian Certificate of Education Common Assessment Tasks are graded.

Work-referenced assessment indicates completion of a specified number of work requirements. Certificates record the assessment simply in terms of S or N. The student either has or has not completed the specified minimum number of work requirements. In this form of assessment, performance is not graded.

Norm-referencing is another way of distinguishing between students for selection. Norm-referencing occurs after the test activity and is designed to place a student's performance in relation to others' performance. It does not describe reading behaviour in itself. (As is pointed out by Griffin and Nix [1991, pp. 88–89], informal norm-referencing can take the form of assessment for curriculum. They argue that every time a teacher judges what it is reasonable to expect from a particular student, the implicit standards for assessment are the teacher's own judgements about the capabilities of a wider group of students displaying similar characteristics. This might be limiting or enriching depending on the teacher's expectations and previous experiences.)

Assessment for accountability

Broadfoot suggests that "an educational institution must increasingly be able to demonstrate to both itself and the world outside that it is fulfilling the aims that it has set for itself and the ones expected of it by society in general" (1987, p. 5), and that this has implications for assessment. Some argue that this requirement results in the demand for a readily-defined, comprehensive set of criteria defined publicly before the assessment tasks are completed. This point is made in the introduction to the Victorian Ministry of Education and Training's *English Profiles Handbook.*

> Assessment of a more formal and systematic kind is necessary to ensure that students are making progress in all aspects of a subject. Formal assessments include planned assessment tasks designed to provide information about students' work in relation to specific criteria. (1991, p. 7)

Assessment of reading behaviour for accountability at the system level, it is argued, must be comprehensive, but structured with sufficient simplicity to make comparison over time possible.

One senses, again, that such constraints must inevitably involve compromise. The analysis of the student reading the passage about Herodotus and the pyramids above, gives the beginning of an insight into the complexity of the reading process, how successful reading depends not only on the use of skills that can be brought to every reading situation but on the interaction between reader and text, the student's prior knowledge of the subject of the reading, the vocabulary specific to it, and the attitude the reader brings to the process of reading. Such detail may become too burdensome if the purpose of assessment is for accountability. One (perhaps compromised) solution to this problem that appears to have been implemented up until the present is to describe reading behaviour in terms of *skills and activities without reference to context or material being read.* There is an elaboration of this point in the section below.

How comprehensive is the assessment?

The most detailed methods of assessment are those which enable description of reading behaviour, the texts being read, and the contexts of reading—that is, the environment the reading is done in, the purpose of the reading, the audience for the reading, and the expectations that the audience has of the reader. In this paper, it has been argued that the more detailed the assessment, the greater chance of more useful diagnostic feedback for the teacher. However, detailed assessment is not a guarantee of comprehensive assessment. In the detailed example given above, although there was a lot of useful description of S's reading of the passage about Herodotus, one might be reluctant to generalise on the basis of that reading about S's ability to read other texts.

This is a problem for all kinds of assessment. It has been addressed by distinguishing the concept of "generalisable" reading skills from the concept of particular reading skills-in-use. Practically, there is a risk with individualised assessment of skill-in-use that particular passages which are being read while the student is observed may not give the reader the opportunity to demonstrate all the abilities that he or she has. This problem has been dealt with by predetermining a comprehensive set of skills which become criteria for assessment and which can guide observation of student reading behaviour. Necessarily, these are limited constructs. This can be seen by comparison of two descriptions of sets of desirable skills. They are those used to describe levels of achievement in the *Test of Reading Comprehension (TORCH) Manual* and the *English Profiles Handbook*. It should be noted that the levels of achievement taken from the latter are very brief summaries of behaviours and abilities that are described in much greater detail in various reading bands groupings of descriptors which teachers can match to the performance of their students. Nevertheless the comparison is instructive.

The English Profiles and the Test of Reading Comprehension are designed for different bodies of students, the Profiles being relevant from P–12, while TORCH is intended for use with Years 3 to 10. Nevertheless, there are clear differences between the ways students' potential performances are described. The English Profiles include behaviours ("talks confidently about characters") and attitudes

Table 2

TORCH	ENGLISH PROFILES
Infer emotion from a few scattered clues and the writer's tone	Is skilful in analysing and interpreting wide range of written material.
Reconstruct the writer's general message from specific statements	Has clear ideas about purposes for reading. Reads beyond the literal in search of deeper meaning.
Provide evidence of having understood a motive underlying a series of actions	Reads widely for learning and pleasure and can readily draw together main ideas. Has a critical and analytical outlook towards ideas and writing style.
Provide a detail in the presence of competing answers	Can read different kinds of texts. Interprets and analyses passages and explains personal responses.
Provide a detail in the presence of distracting ideas	Knows how to tackle difficult texts. Experiences with reading reflected in own writing and general knowledge. Talks confidently about characters and settings in literature.
Connect ideas separated in text	Expects what is read to make sense. Talks about what is read and indicates understanding. Absorbs language and ideas.
Connect pronouns with previously mentioned nouns	Seeks meaning from printed text. Wants to read a lot and talk about stories.
Complete rephrased sentences	Is able to recognise many familiar words and tries to read unfamiliar text. Shows signs of becoming an active reader.
Complete very simple rewordings	Knows how a book works, likes to look at books and have stories read.
Complete sentences copied verbatim	
Provide subject of story given multiple references	

("likes to look at books and have stories read") in relation to a range of text types as well as skills of comprehension and analysis. The other describes performance in many instances in terms of behaviour required by the test itself ("connects pronouns with previously mentioned nouns"). The comparison must make one suspicious of the degree of comprehensiveness that scales like those above can claim. Recognising this, the designers of the Reading Profiles add sections for the teacher to note behaviours, attitudes, and skills not accounted for in the descriptors and provide space for teachers to note the type of material being read and the context in which it is read. Such flexibility was not available to the TORCH designers. Indeed, full use of the Profiles requires close observation similar to that described in the section above.

What are the reference points or criteria for the assessment?

The discussion above has already touched on this question. It is worth recapping.

The assessor's reading

When student S was observed reading the passage about Herodotus in Ancient Egypt, the teacher based his assessment of S's performance on his own interpretation of the passage. This involved him in examination of the passage and as a result the prerequisites for reading it successfully became clear.

The student's prior reading behaviour

In future assessment of S's reading behaviour, aspects of her performance detailed above will help determine criteria for growth. Will she be more confident to read over passages that seem immediately inaccessible? Will she acknowledge her doubts about her own understanding—a part of the continuum between self-monitoring and self-correcting? Will she demonstrate behaviour of a reader who is used to being in control of a wide variety of reading material? If she does these things, she will have made significant steps forward. But those criteria will not describe the full range of S's reading ability or behaviour.

Preordinate criteria

Predetermined, or preordinate, criteria offer the security of a reference point from which to make judgements about a broad range of reading abilities. They offer the chance to make comparison between students across schools and over time. However, as has been shown, they are not exhaustive and they might not be sufficiently discriminating to measure significant growth in individual students including their growth shown in particular subjects.

How valid is the assessment?

Much of the discussion of methods of assessment is conducted in terms of their validity, that is the quality of being well-founded and applicable to the students and the circumstances in question. Thus, the writers of the *English Profiles Handbook* argue "entire dependence on informal methods of assessment can mean that coverage of important skills and knowledge may be incomplete for some students, thus limiting their success" (Ministry of Education and Training, Victoria, 1991, p. 7).

On the other hand, there is very vocal condemnation of standardised tests. Kemp (1989) doubts the suitability of tests to monitor the performance of struggling readers. He suggests that the very act of conducting a formal test (in rows, in silence) can be intimidating enough to deny students the chance of displaying their best talents. Tuinman (1986) argues in *Reading is Recognition When Reading is Not Reasoning* that reading comprehension tests assess only formal comprehension which he differentiates from communicative comprehension and private comprehension. Formal comprehension, he argues, is the most complex, involving the ability to utilize a range of skills: the reader has to understand details, relate them to other information presented, make fine distinctions among facts, events, and motives, and recognise and understand abstractions. He suggests that this sort of comprehension involves reasoning, which is not a characteristic of all reading, and adds that, one of the most curious developments in measurements of reading comprehension is that concepts and techniques suitable for the measurement of formal comprehension have come to be used for the measurement of all comprehension! Brown and Cambourne (1989) are quite adamant, "Language is an ever changing medium that always presents new challenges even as we learn to control more. It is qualitative and subjective and therefore must be approached differently when evaluation is considered. Evaluation by testing is not applicable to language."

What view of reading underpins the assessment?

It is impossible to ascribe a view of reading to the designers and users of particular assessment techniques because the measurement devices themselves are not such flexible things that they can be made to reflect every aspect of the designer's understanding. Compromises may have to be made in the design and use of any means of assessment. Assessment of reading ability must be conceptualised in terms of practicality and utility as well as in terms of reading theory.

Nevertheless, close scrutiny of the process of reading over time allows for observation of reading behaviour in relation to a range of texts and in a number of contexts. Such a process is consistent with a view of reading which suggests that reading skill is inseparable from reading material and that skill is only possessed or shown in the act of reading. Use of standardised tests and scales of reading behaviour is consistent with a view that reading can be divided into a hierarchy of isolatable and generalisable skills.

What means of assessment should be used?

As has been suggested, the issue of assessment is a complex one. Choice of means of assessment involves consideration of the needs of the teachers and students involved, the intended audience of the assessment, and the amount of time available for assessment.

You might consider these questions:

Is the assessment for diagnostic purposes?

Will the assessment give you the "opportunity to assess the instructional factors that influence reading performance" (Brozo, 1990)?

Is the assessment going to be the basis for formal reporting?

What skills will the reader or hearer of the assessment be able to bring to the reading or the interview so that description can be interpreted meaningfully?

To what extent is the assessment linked to certification? Is any link with certification appropriate?

Do you have a role in making assessments which show the extent to which the school is fulfilling its aims?

How influenced in the junior level are you by requirements for certification and selection that mark formal assessment at the senior level?

If you imitate practices at the senior level, how flexible are they? Are they useful for the full range of your students?

It will probably be the case that choice of assessment mechanisms will involve compromise. When teachers are aware of the compromises, and why various types of assessment have been developed, they will be in a better position to make what will always be a difficult decision.

REFERENCES

Broadfoot, P. (1987). *Introducing profiling: A practical manual.* London: Macmillan Education.

Brown, H., & Cambourne, B. (1989). Evaluation in the whole language classroom: A collaborative research project. In E. Daly (Ed.), *Monitoring children's language development.* Melbourne: Australian Reading Association.

Brozo, W.G. (1990). Learning how at-risk readers learn best: A case for interactive assessment. *Journal of Reading, 33,* 522–527.

Cambourne, B., & Turbill, J. (1991). Evaluation and the literacy curriculum: Who is in control? *Australian Journal of Reading, 14*(3).

Garforth, D., & Macintosh, H. (1986). *Profiling: A user's manual.* Cheltenham, UK: Stanley Thornes Limited.

Griffin, P., & Nix, P. (1991). *Educational assessment and reporting: A new approach.* Sydney: Harcourt Brace Jovanovich.

Johnston, P. (1989). Constructive evaluation and the improvement of teaching and learning! *Teachers College Record, 90*(4).

Kemp, M. (1989). The holistic classroom: Assessment of children with special needs. In E. Daly (Ed.), *Monitoring children's language development.* Melbourne: Australian Reading Association.

Kletzien, S.B., & Bednar, M.R. (1990). Dynamic assessment for at-risk readers! *Journal of Reading, 33,* 528–533.

Law, B. (1984). *Uses and abuses of profiling.* London: Harper & Row. Quoted in Broadfoot, op. cit.

Mossenson, L., Hill, P., & Masters, G. (1987). *Tests of Reading Comprehension (TORCH) manual.* Melbourne: ACER.

School Programs Division, Ministry of Education and Training, Victoria. (1991). *English profiles handbook: Assessing and reporting students' progress in English.* Melbourne: Education Shop, Ministry of Education and Training, Victoria.

Tuinman, J. Jaap. (1986). Reading is recognition when reading is not reasoning! In S. De Castell, A. Luke, & K. Egan. *Literacy, society and schooling: A reader.* Cambridge: Cambridge University Press.

READING ASSESSMENT

Editor: Peter Afflerbach

Guest authors: Emelie Lowrey Parker, Regla Armengol, Leigh Baxley Brooke, Kelly Redmond Carper, Sharon M. Cronin, Anne Cooper Denman, Patricia Irwin, Jennifer McGunnigle, Tess Pardini, and Nancy P. Kurtz

Teachers' choices in classroom assessment

In this column we will share a variety of assessment practices utilized in our primary classrooms to meet the needs of our diverse student population. Over 80% of our 5- and 6-year-old students are second language learners of English who come from various cultural and economic backgrounds and who have a wide range of literacy experiences for us to build upon.

Our assessment practices are tailored to meet the literacy needs of these children, who range from fluent readers and writers to those with limited or no experience with English. Our goal is to meet students' instructional needs so that we can facilitate their learning. Effective assessment is essential to our instructional program.

We think of assessment as something that permeates every school day. Assessment teaches us not only what our students have learned and are learning, but what they are ready to learn. Information gained through assessment drives our instructional decisions. Long and short range planning is based on this information. Lesson content is determined. Questions are answered, such as "What will we teach tomorrow?" and "Who needs to be engaged in what kind of learning activities?" The assessment practices we describe must be continuously refined and modified to meet the ever-changing needs of our students.

Concepts about print

The beginning of the year presents both a challenge and an opportunity to teachers. One of our first assessments is the child's knowledge of concepts about print, specifically print in books. Our assessment is a modification of the observational survey designed by Marie Clay (1991). This measures the nuts and bolts of print, whether the child knows the front of the book from the back, that print is read rather than illustrations, and that reading is done from left to right and top to bottom. The assessment also measures children's conceptions of word and letter. We work with children individually, using a book selected from our classroom. This 5-minute assessment is invaluable for gauging a beginning point for instruction.

For example, a child who scores low on this assessment needs more exposure to print in various forms. The child probably has not had much experience with print at home, and this alerts the teacher to a potential point of growth for the family. In school the child needs to be surrounded with print, to participate in guided readings and book extensions, and possibly to be paired with another child who has a stronger reading foundation for activities such as buddy reading, listening to books on tape, or writing. On the other hand, a child who already knows print concepts is ready to begin learning other aspects of reading. If the child is able to identify some of the words in the book used for the assessment, similar reading materials could be encouraged. If the child reads the book easily, then more difficult text can be provided, and instruc-

tion can center around different types of writing, story structure, or another topic according to the needs of the student. Overall, the concepts about print observation provides an excellent opportunity to assess how a child deals with print and how much the child has been exposed to print in the past. It provides one snapshot of the child that can be combined with other informal assessment results to establish a point to meet the child's literacy needs.

Running records

Another observational task that we adapted from Marie Clay is the running record. This reading assessment guides our teaching by evaluating students' strengths and needs. We can determine if children are self monitoring their reading, if their reading material is appropriate, and what strategies the children are using to identify unknown words. When analyzing running records, we look for the intelligence in the child's errors. Based on the type of errors made, we can determine what cues they are using and those that they are neglecting.

Using running records with English as a Second Language (ESL) students has given us a great deal of insight into how they learn to read and speak. We often observe an over-reliance on one or two cueing systems. For example, a child may be using picture and letter sounds to decode text but neglect the use of language structure. Our use of running records with ESL students has helped us understand that as their oral language strengthens, ESL children will transfer this knowledge to reading and begin to rely on all cueing systems simultaneously.

Anecdotal notes

Children continually change throughout the school year because they are influenced by their observations and interactions with print, their peers, and their family members. They also learn from formal instruction. Anecdotal notes capture student growth as observed by the teacher. We use the notes to demonstrate growth in all areas of instruction, especially reading, writing, and oral language development. Whatever method is used to make anecdotal notes, the goal is the same: to capture the development of the child as it happens and to create a more complete picture of the whole child. Like other assessment tools, anecdotal notes provide information to further tailor each child's individual instruction.

Anecdotal records are as formal or informal as the teacher wants them to be. They look different in every classroom. For example, when dealing with ESL students, an anecdotal note might relate the day that a child began using complete sentences in class, such as saying "May I go to the bathroom?" as opposed to "Bathroom?" Developments such as this may signal that conventions of oral language are being assimilated and applied by the child.

Writing vocabulary and word dictation

The writing vocabulary assessment is administered at the beginning of the school year to gain baseline data on our students. A small group of children is called together and asked to write all the words that they know. Children begin with their names, then write any other words they think that they can write. Some children write only their names or isolated letters, and others write long lists of words. At the end of 10 minutes each child is asked to read the words that were written. Those words that are spelled correctly and that the child reads back accurately are counted. We use the assessment at the end of each academic quarter to show change over time.

Children's responses provide the teacher with valuable information about how they are building a basic writing vocabulary. The assessment also shows the child's knowledge of spelling, sound-symbol relationships, word families, and usage of capital and lower-case letters. It also provides evidence of the child's recall of high-frequency words used in the classroom. This in turn helps the teacher plan for future instruction.

For children to become proficient writers, it is necessary for them to hear the sounds in words and be able to record them. Teachers need to know what children know about spelling in order to guide their instruction. The word dictation assessment provides this information. The first-grade team generated a list of 20 words that required students to demonstrate their spelling progress. Some were chosen because they were high-frequency words (*my, and*), some were chosen because they included a particular blend (*jump, skip*), vowel sound (*coat, game*), or tense (*played, looking*); and some words were chosen because of their frequent use in our classroom or in the children's writing (*because, then, once*) The writing assessment and the word dictation show the progress our children make in recognizing sounds and linking them to symbols, in noticing word patterns, and in understanding that sounds in words may be represented in different ways.

Self-assessment/goal-setting interviews

We often use self-assessment/goal-setting interviews in our first-grade classrooms for gaining insight into the child's perspective of writing. The following interview questions help us determine our instructional focus, change the physical environment of the classroom to be more conducive to a writer's needs, and determine expectations: What did you do well as an author/writer? What did/will your audience like best? Why? What do you need to work on/learn next to be a better author/writer? How can I or your friends help you?

Students' answers to these interview questions alert us to stumbling blocks:

"I can do the first sound and the last sound. Teach me the middle sounds." The answers are sometimes a humbling assessment of teaching: "You didn't do a good job of teaching us quotation marks. We need to do it again." When we listen to the children, we gather valuable information about guiding and teaching beginning writers. When we use this information to make instructional decisions, the child's writing instruction becomes rich and personalized. Children at all ages can reflect on their learning. Here are questions a kindergarten teacher asks students: How did you learn to read? Which can you do better, read or write? Did writing every day help you to read? How?

The children's responses inform the teacher about their perceptions of literacy. Teachers at our school believe that instruction should lead the children to discover for themselves. Our goal, starting at kindergarten, is to make them a part of the assessment process so that they can take control of their own learning and teachers can facilitate learning.

Nonfiction journals

Nonfiction journals, learning logs, or "learnals" are a form of assessment that some of us have experimented with in our classrooms. We begin slowly with a lot of modeling and encouragement. First we discuss with the students what to include in their nonfiction journals. We differentiate between fiction and nonfiction and model many nonfiction journal entries. At the beginning each entry starts with "I learned about...." I did...," "Today I learned that...." At the end of each day the class brainstorms what they learned that day and makes a list of key words for writing. Next the students choose how to show what they learned: writing, drawings, or diagrams. Finally, the children share and discuss their entries. During this sharing time the first-grade team watches for evidence of higher level thinking, using content-related oral communication, and questioning. Our journal assessment helps us to direct our instruction to the children's needs and interests.

Nonfiction journals are tools for children to express, reflect on, and assess what they have learned. They provide information to the teacher about a child's comprehension of nonfiction reading and of content concepts being studied. The teacher can use this information to further the development and direction of the unit of study, as well as to guide both small and large group lessons.

Scoring rubrics

Our team has begun to experiment with scoring rubrics in order to provide consistency in assessing student progress and to help us clarify instructional goals. The scoring rubric that we developed last year, for example, focused on assessing the children's understanding of the mathematics and science concepts studied in one of our conceptual units. This interdisciplinary unit, entitled "Connections," is organized around the major concept that cycles occur in nature (the cyclical nature of the four seasons, the growth cycle of plants) as well as in mathematics (geometric and numerical patterns). Throughout the unit students are engaged in many activities: comparing versions of the Johnny Appleseed story, summarizing a nonfiction text, conducting scientific experiments, and engaging in real-world experiences such as planting a garden.

We wanted an assessment that would provide our diverse student population a range of options for demonstrating their learning. A scoring rubric with a numerical scale of 1 to 5 was designed. Students who scored a 5 demonstrated an in-depth understanding of the unit's concepts, and those who scored a 1 showed an emergent understanding of the concepts. We developed a scale that described the characteristics of student performance at each level. The students were rated holistically using teacher observation, anecdotal records, and several performance tasks. This form of alternative assessment afforded all of our students, even those who did not have spoken English competency, ways to demonstrate their learning. A child with very limited oral or written English could demonstrate knowledge through art or drama.

Conclusion

These assessments did not evolve quickly or in sequence. Rather, they are still developing as we continue to tailor our instruction to meet the individual needs of our students. Our assessments are designed to be used primarily by the teacher. However, they are often shared with students to show individual growth over the school year, and we use them with parents to pinpoint areas of children's growth and development.

Assessments prove to be most productive when students are assessed as an integral part of the learning process. Assessing the process as well as the product is important to us. We simultaneously assess what has been learned, how it was learned, and the techniques that we used to teach it. Classroom teachers must formulate assessments based on what is meaningful for them and their students. Assessment should be used as teaching tools to benefit the unique individuals within the classroom.

Reference
Clay, M. (1991). *Becoming literate.* Portsmouth, NH: Heinemann.

Monitoring the development of reading processes is vital to student success

Jane Braunger and Jan Patricia Lewis

Monitoring learners' progress calls for a variety of assessment and evaluation strategies. Assessment and instruction are integral processes, each informing the other to meet the individual needs of students. Teachers must constantly use keen observation of student growth and development to inform instruction. Also, students must learn to become critically aware of their own reading processes, that is, to become metacognitive, to facilitate their development as meaningful, fluent readers. Evaluation, on the other hand, takes into account all assessments and observations in order to make a judgment about an individual student for grading and/or placement purposes.

Traditional modes of monitoring development have occurred via standardized/norm-referenced instruments and criterion-referenced tests. While these measures show where an individual falls within a peer group, they do not necessarily show in detail what an individual can do as a reader. Some drawbacks to traditional modes (Allington & Walmsley, 1995) include:

1. They are largely unreliable bases for making any judgments about an individual's reading development.

2. They rarely have much demonstrated validity as they assess only a narrow range of literacy activity.

3. They are given infrequently and at odd times of the year so the results, even if reliable and valid, are not of much use in planning and instruction.

4. They tend to narrow the curriculum as teachers feel the need to "teach the test"; some see this as working to discourage teacher-learner collaborative evaluation of literacy learning.

5. They can play a role in discouraging those children whose performance on the tests suggests that their reading development lags behind that of their peers (pp. 78-79; Darling-Hammond, 1991; Stallman & Pearson, 1990).

Standardized tests will likely remain an important aspect of school literacy programs. However, many standardized tests are being revised to incorporate current definitions of reading. Currently, there are many examples of strategies for monitoring and assessing reading development that incorporate the research developments of the past 25 years, including comprehension monitoring (cognitive development), response to texts beyond a literal level (cognitive development, response theory), errors as ways of indicating knowledge (language acquisition, emergent literacy), strategy use, and attitude. Many reform efforts highlight the need for "performance" assessments: That is, are learners able to actually translate and apply skills and strategies in new, authentic tasks? What do learners do? The impact of research can be seen in both informal, classroom-level assessments and more formal, standardized kinds of assessments.

Reprinted from Braunger, J., & Lewis, J.P. (1997). *Building a knowledge base in reading* (pp. 53–58, 105–106). Portland, OR: Northwest Regional Educational Laboratory; Urbana, IL: National Council of Teachers of English; Newark, DE: International Reading Association.

For example, the most current NAEP reading assessment (Mullis, Campbell, & Farstrup, 1993; Williams, Reese, Campbell, Mazzeo, & Phillips, 1995) reflected this trend toward performance-based assessments grounded in current theories of reading. The construction of this assessment was based upon the general agreement of educators defining literacy learning as occurring through a broad range of oral and written activities including personally meaningful experiences (such as responding to reading), reflection on reading, interacting with others about reading, and choosing to read independently (Ruddell & Ruddell, 1994). Tasks required students to construct, extend, and examine meaning while reading a variety of texts for a variety of purposes (Pinnell, Pikulski, Wixson, Campbell, Gough, & Beatty, 1995, p. 4).

Current understandings of how children learn to read suggest the following assessment recommendations: assess authentic reading and writing in texts that make all cue systems available to students; assess reading in a variety of contexts and situations; assess products as well as processes; use multiple sources of data to find patterns in student growth and development; involve all involved with the student in the assessment process (students, parents, school personnel); and make assessment an ongoing part of everyday reading and writing tasks (Rhodes & Dudley-Marling, 1996). Developmental patterns and behavior in reading and writing are based upon current research (Cochrane, Cochrane, Scalena, & Buchanan, 1984; Holdaway, 1979) as well as on standards for reading as presented by national organizations (IRA/NCTE, 1996), state departments of education (Commission on Student Learning, 1996), and local districts.

Aspects of reading development to monitor.

• *Personal perceptions, attitudes, and interests.* Students' personal perceptions are impacted by their attitudes, beliefs, and interests. Comprehension of texts is always influenced by social and historical values and expectations, both known and unknown. These perceptions help teachers to understand how individuals socially situate the act of reading: How is time spent with reading? Who is involved in conversations about reading? The importance of reading, and the sense of one's ability to read, will affect the choices students make in regard to reading, including types and time of reading.

Ways to document personal perceptions, attitudes, and interests include:

- *interviews* to provide insight into individual perceptions. Teachers can construct their own interviews or use Burke's Reading Interview (Goodman, Watson, & Burke, 1987), which focuses on perceptions of what reading is and what good readers do. Rhodes and Dudley-Marling (1996) also emphasize the particular importance for at-risk readers to gain insight into their own beliefs and perceptions of the reading process, and their interactions with this process.

- *inventories* to help teachers to find out about students' interests and connections to reading in and out of school. This might include inventories of the number of books read and owned at home as well as reading logs of what is read at school.

- *observation* of how students interact in a variety of situations that require reading. How does this individual interact with others in regard to reading and books? What choices do individuals make in regard to reading?

- *anecdotal records* of individual background information that might be helpful in understanding how reading is socially situated.

• *Comprehension.* The meaning made by readers is at the heart of the reading process. How is background knowledge used in constructing meaning? What kind of sense is made of the texts read? What comprehension strategies (e.g. predicting, skimming, rereading) are used in order to construct meaning? Is the appropriate literary knowledge in place to apply to understand this text (e.g., story structure, formats, literary elements, genres, and particular authors)?

Ways to document comprehension include:

- *response*: Responding to texts in a variety of ways helps children to demonstrate a synthesis of what they have gained from interaction with their own lives. How does it apply to their own lives? What sense can they make of the text? How does this compare and contrast to other texts they have read? This may happen through writing in literature logs, through a dramatic presentation, by discussing the book in a literature discussion group with peers, or by book talks as a way to convince others to read the book.

- *retelling*: Brown and Cambourne (1990) and Goodman, Watson, and Burke (1987) encourage teachers to use forms of retelling to get at what students understand about the content of stories read as well as their structure. Retelling is a way of getting to students' comprehension of what has been read. It is an assessment/monitoring strategy as well as a teaching strategy.

- *Informal Reading Inventory (IRI)/Qualitative Reading Inventory (QRI)*: These inventories provide normed assessments that focus on children's comprehension of text. The QRI, in particular, incorporates elements of miscue analysis and retelling in its procedures (Leslie & Caldwell, 1990).

- *interviews*: These can be used to find out what students have gained through their reading of a text.

- *observations*: Teachers can watch as students read, asking questions and keeping anecdotal records.

• *Processing words and other text features.* How students process words and other text features has an integral relationship with their comprehension and understanding of a text. There is probably the most debate about how to view instruction at the word level, and thus of how to best assess and monitor the development of students' ability in this area.

At one level, it is important for students to understand the concepts of letters, of word, and of sentence. Marie Clay's (1972, 1991, 1993) work with children at the emergent stage of literacy development highlights the importance of monitoring the development of concepts about print. Clay highlights the importance of presenting these tasks in ways as authentic and meaningful as possible.

Ways to document the processing of words and text features include:

- *concepts of print*: Children are interviewed, with a book, about directionality (Where is the front of this book? Where do I begin to read? Where do I go from here?), and about their concepts of letters and words (Show me one letter; Show me two letters; Show me a word; Show me a sentence). Clay's (1972) *Sand and Stones* texts provide a structured format from which to assess these concepts.

- *identification of letter names and sounds*: Children point to and tell letter names and sounds they know. At emergent levels, this focuses on single letter names and sounds, but can move to more sophisticated groupings of letters (blends and digraphs) as they are introduced and taught to children.

- *word knowledge*: Children are asked to read familiar words (usually high frequency words with which they have some interaction).

- *writing*: Children are asked to write whatever they would like. Teachers observe how children go about this task: How do they perceive writing? What types of symbols do they choose to use? What does their attempt say about their knowledge of phonemic awareness and phonic knowledge?

- *hearing and recording sounds in words*: Children write a dictated sentence. Teachers analyze their response by counting the representation of sounds by letters.

Some believe it is important to continue to document children's phonemic awareness; that is, how able are they to discriminate and segment letter sounds in speech (e.g., c-a-t). Often, this can be observed in the context of daily classroom experiences by clapping syllables, observing the growth of invented spelling, and work with rhyming words.

At another level, it is important to look at how readers process words and text features within the meaningful context of a text. What kinds of errors (miscues) do readers make? How do these miscues seem to affect comprehension? What do the miscues reveal about the strategies and cues they use to process text? Do students use other text features to comprehend text?

Ways to do this include:

- *error analysis/miscue analysis*: Research in miscue analysis (Goodman, Watson, & Burke, 1987) and running records (Clay, 1972, 1991, 1993) has provided teachers with important insights into how children read, as well as with important tools for documenting reading behaviors of children. All readers make errors; it is through analysis of these errors that intent and strategy can be determined. Oral reading of a text is an important avenue through which teachers can observe reading behaviors (Pinnell, et al., 1995). Clay (1991) highlights the importance of a reader's use of language patterns and text structures in successful reading; error analysis can help teachers to understand the thought processes and problem-solving strategies readers use and do not use. There are many formats to follow for this assessment (Clay, 1993; Goodman, Watson, & Burke, 1987; Rhodes, 1993). In general, students read an unfamiliar text, providing a retelling when they have finished. Teachers record their miscues, analyzing them to discover the strategies used and the ability of the reader to make sense of the text.

- *anecdotal records and observation*: Teachers must carefully watch what readers are doing and continue to record these observations for analysis over time.

- *student self-assessment*: Within a structure and set of expectations provided by the teacher, students reflect upon their abilities (What am I able to do well? What have I learned to do?) and set new personal goals (What is an appropriate next step for me?).

• *Metacognitive strategies.* Students who are able to think and talk about the strategies they use are better able to draw upon their own resources to problem solve as they encounter difficulties in their reading, "thinking about their writing" as they go about a task. Students need to be able to understand when, how, and why they are applying particular reading strategies and skills, and what might be important to help them progress in their development.

Ways to document this include:

- *think-alouds*: Thinking aloud as a text is read gives insight into the strategies readers are using. Teachers can gauge why comprehension is or is not occurring as they listen to what strategy choices the reader is making (Brown & Lytle, 1988).

- *student self-assessment*: Given a set of expectations, students reflect upon their ability to use metacognitive strategies and set new goals as appropriate.

- *interviews*: Teachers interview students as to what they do as they read. This often occurs as students are reading a text.

- *anecdotal records and observations*: Teachers observe and record what they see students doing as they read.

• *Environment and instruction*. Reading is a transaction between the reader, the text, and the environment within which they rest. It is appropriate to move assessment beyond what is perceived to be "in" a student. Home, school, and community environments all contribute to literacy development.

Ways to document this relationship include:

- *teacher self-assessment and reflection*: Teachers must reflect upon the matches necessary among the classroom environment, instructional decisions, and the needs of individual students. When students do not appear to be succeeding, teachers consider why this is so from as many perspectives as possible. What factors might be an obstacle for students? What alternatives might be employed?

- *student self-assessment and reflection*: As students reflect upon their own learning, insights into obstacles and issues can provide new options for instruction.

Recently, the incorporation of student portfolios as a means of gathering and monitoring reading development has gained in favor as performance-based assessments have been developed. Portfolios offer ways to include multiple measures taken over time of an individual's reading as documentation.

References

Allington, R.L., & Walmsley, S.A. (Eds.). (1995). *No quick fix: Rethinking literacy programs in America's elementary schools*. Newark, DE: International Reading Association.

Brown, H., & Cambourne, B. (1990). *Read and retell: A strategy for the whole-language/natural language classroom*. Portsmouth, NH: Heinemann.

Brown, C.S., & Lytle, S.L. (1988). Merging assessment and instruction: Protocols in the classroom. In S.M. Glazer, L.W. Searfoss, & L.M. Gentile (Eds.), *Reexamining reading diagnosis: New trends and procedures*. Newark, DE: International Reading Association.

Clay, M.M. (1972). *The early detection of reading difficulties: A diagnostic survey with recovery procedures*. Exeter, NH: Heinemann.

Clay, M.M. (1991). *Becoming literate: The construction of inner control*. Portsmouth, NH: Heinemann.

Clay, M.M. (1993). *An observation survey of early literacy achievement*. Portsmouth, NH: Heinemann.

Cochrane, O., Cochrane, D., Scalena, S., & Buchanan, E. (1984). *Reading, writing, and caring*. Winnipeg, Manitoba, Canada: Whole Language Consultants (Distributed by R.C. Owen).

Commission on Student Learning. (1996, January). *Essential academic learning requirements: Reading, writing, communication, and mathematics*. Olympia, WA: Author.

Darling-Hammond, L. (1991). The implications of testing policy for quality and equality. *Phi Delta Kappan, 73*(3), 220-225.

Goodman, Y.M., Watson, D.J., & Burke, C.L. (1987). *Reading miscue inventory*. Katonah, NY: R.C. Owen.

Holdaway, D. (1979). *The foundations of literacy*. Portsmouth, NH: Heinemann.

International Reading Association & National Council of Teachers of English. (1996). *Standards for the English language arts.* Newark, DE: International Reading Association & Urbana, IL: National Council of Teachers of English.

Leslie, L., & Caldwell, J. (1990). *Qualitative reading inventory.* Glenview, IL: HarperCollins.

Mullis, I.V.S., Campbell, J.R., & Farstrup, A.E. (1993). *Executive summary of the NAEP 1992 reading report card for the nation and the states: Data from the national and trial state assessments.* Washington, DC: National Center for the Education Statistics.

Pinnell, G.S., Pikulski, J.J., Wixson, K.K., Campbell, J.R., Gough, P.B., & Beatty, A.S. (1995). *Listening to children read aloud: Data from NAEP's integrated reading performance record at grade 4.* Washington, DC: National Center for Education Statistics.

Rhodes, L.K. (1993). *Literacy assessment: A handbook of instruments.* Portsmouth, NH: Heinemann.

Rhodes, L.K., & Dudley-Marling, C. (1996). *Readers and writers with a difference: A holistic approach to teaching struggling readers and writers* (2nd ed.). Portsmouth, NH: Heinemann.

Ruddell, R.B., & Ruddell, M.R. (1994). Language acquisition and literacy processes. In R.B. Ruddell, M.R. Ruddell, & H. Singer (Eds.), *Theoretical models and processes of reading.* Newark, DE: International Reading Association.

Stallman, A.C., & Pearson, P.D. (1990). Formal measures of early literacy. In L.M. Morrow & J.K. Smith (Eds.), *Assessment for instruction in early literacy.* Englewood Cliffs, NJ: Prentice-Hall.

Williams, P.L., Reese, C.M., Campbell, J.R., Mazzeo, J., & Phillips, G.W. (1995, October). *NAEP 1994 reading: A first look. Findings from the National Assessment of Educational Progress* [Revised edition]. Washington, DC: National Center for Education Statistics.

Literacy assessment of students from poor and diverse communities: Changing the programs, changing the outcomes

Lynne Badger and Lyn Wilkinson

This article reports on the concerns and issues about literacy assessment that a small group of selected teachers who work in disadvantaged primary schools are grappling with in the everyday world of their classrooms.

One of the fundamental issues which confronts them is that cohorts of students from poor and disadvantaged communities perform less well on school literacy tasks than do students from more affluent families (Connell, 1992; Freebody & Ludwig, 1995; South Australian Department of Education, 1992; Williams, 1987). A major function of schools, it is often argued, is to sort and classify students, to discriminate among them, and to determine what kinds of socio-economic opportunities will be open to them. Assessment is one way in which schools do this. Because it acts as a gatekeeping mechanism, assessment is therefore heavily implicated in the production and maintenance of socio-cultural privilege (Connell, 1992, p. 20).

This constructs a dilemma for teachers in disadvantaged schools who are mediating between the diverse values and literacy practices of the groups of students they teach and the particular values and literacy practices which are privileged by mainstream curricula and assessment.

About the research project

This project focussed on the questions and concerns that the teachers in the research schools raised about the interrelationship of school literacy programs and assessment outcomes for students from poor and diverse communities. It was felt that these questions and concerns could provide insight for other practitioners in disadvantaged schools. Thus our aim as literacy educators was to explore and document the ways this group of teachers conceptualised their role in promoting students' literacy performance and achieving more equitable literacy outcomes.

The documentation was part of a larger literacy research project conducted in a number of disadvantaged schools across metropolitan Adelaide, South Australia. These schools are designated as disadvantaged because they have large numbers of students whose families are receiving government assistance. The research team had won a grant from the Committee for the Advancement of University Teaching (CAUT) to produce three videos and accompanying written materials which explored the relationship between literacy, poverty, and schooling. It was our belief that the teacher development materials could be used to trigger conversations between other practitioners as they in turn explored this relationship in their own schools and classrooms. Thus we assumed that these materials would generate more genuine dialogue and have greater credibility for teachers and student teachers if they were grounded in the actual practices and concerns of other practitioners.

The research for the video which dealt specifically with literacy assessment was carried out with teachers working in classes from Reception (Kindergarten) to Year 7, the final year of primary schooling in South Australia. Early in the project the teachers simply wanted to know what we wished to see in their classrooms and what we would film. We explained the kinds of ideas we had and some of the issues that concerned us. As we worked with the teachers we observed and heard the interesting and challenging assessment practices that they talked about and that they were putting into practice. But rather than provide exemplars of "good assessment practice" we wanted the materials

Reprinted from Fehring, H. (Ed.). (2003). *Literacy assessment: A collection of articles from the Australian Literacy Educators' Association* (pp. 55–66). Newark, DE: International Reading Association. Originally published in *The Australian Journal of Language and Literacy* (June 1998), *21*(2). Reprinted with permission of the Australian Literacy Educators' Association.

to foreground what was problematic from the viewpoint of teachers and other educators with a commitment to achieving more equitable literacy outcomes for students in disadvantaged schools. We also wanted to situate the classroom footage within a framework which explored the politics of advantage (Eveline, 1994) and structural inequality (Connell, 1992) within our society.

As we discussed this framing with teachers they not only began to respond to the questions we asked about their literacy assessment practices but also to the issues of equity we raised. In doing so they began to see themselves as co-enquirers rather than simply informants. Moreover, as we spent time in classrooms observing and interacting with students and sometimes their parents, as well as getting a "feel" for each classroom community, our discussions with the teachers became increasingly *dialogic* (Shor, 1980, pp. 95–96). That is, we acted as equals engaged in joint research rather than doing research *on* teachers and teaching, and this in turn allowed the teachers to have a significant measure of control. While we, the teacher educators, still formulated the actual framework for the research, in other respects there was genuine participation by our classroom colleagues. In particular, we worked in ways that incorporated their experiences, classroom practice, values, and beliefs, and which encouraged joint decision making about what aspects of their practical and intellectual work should be documented.

The interrelatedness of the classroom literacy program and assessment

Together we explored issues such as how students *at risk* are defined; how each classroom literacy practice privileges some students' knowledge and experiences and marginalises others; the cultural values associated with particular kinds of literacy and certain categories of texts; and how unexamined values and beliefs can unwittingly influence teaching practice in ways that contribute to students' literacy success or failure.

These issues may appear to go beyond the usual discussions of literacy assessment which tend to focus more on changing assessment techniques or developing better, different, or more technically advanced instruments. However, we believed that assessment and assessment techniques cannot be understood outside of what counts in the literacy program, and how this is shaped by what is valued and what counts as mainstream literacy practices and competencies. Such practices and competencies are socially and culturally constructed, which means that assessment of students' literacy competencies is an act of social judgement which has social consequences (Connell, 1993).

Because it is an act of social judgment, assessment of itself never provides a level playing field. No assessment tool is free of bias (Connell, 1992, p. 22). It is a myth that any assessment tool, and this includes standardised tests, teacher-devised assessments, and new approaches such as portfolios, can be objective in the sense that it is unbiassed or value-free. The kinds of tasks and questions that are set, the knowledge that is called on, the processes which students are required to undertake, all privilege some students' knowledge, experience, and practices over others. Teachers in disadvantaged schools have to "consider the extent to which assessment methods distort or reflect the literacy development of students from diverse backgrounds" (Garcia & Pearson, 1991, p. 254).

Thus a recurring feature of the dialogue we had with teachers was their focus on the literacy program. We found it impossible to talk about assessment without constantly coming back to issues of programming. It seemed that the literacy program was the most significant factor in making a difference to students' achievement. The two—the classroom literacy program and assessment of students' achievements—were inextricably linked. In other words, we found that teachers' literacy programs construct the limits and possibilities for students' school literacy performance, which is then the focus for assessment.

The teachers with whom we worked were grappling with the need to radically rethink the literacy programs they had offered to students, and were asking themselves the kinds of questions below.

What does my classroom program make possible?

What competencies are the students able to display?

What competencies are excluded by my program?

Which literacy practices and texts are privileged, and which marginalised by the program I offer?

While part of this rethinking meant reviewing assessment practices, it was clear that making a difference for students in disadvantaged schools is not simply a matter of changing or improving assessment techniques. More equitable outcomes result from literacy programs which reflect, build on, and assess a diversity of literacy practices.

The teachers were also grappling with the way in which assessment permeated their literacy programs. Students' literacy competence was assessed moment by moment throughout every school day, as teachers listened to them speak, heard them read aloud, observed them during writing and silent reading sessions, and interacted with them. From the moment that students entered the classroom, the "production of differences in literate competence begins" (Baker & Freebody, 1993, p. 291). Often subconsciously, teachers begin a mental ledger on each student, entering credits and debits according to how well the student matches up with their expectations about what counts as literate behaviour. This crediting is communicated to students both overtly and covertly, consciously and unconsciously, when teachers respond to their literacy work and behaviour. As Baker and Freebody point out, "[t]eachers do not rely on formal tests to infer how good children are at literacy; they hear this competence minute by minute in exchanges" (1993, p. 287).

The teachers in the project recognised assessment as a pervasive fact of classroom life. One teacher explained her viewpoint as follows.

> I guess assessment goes on in a variety of situations in our classrooms. It is not just contained in language sessions where I go around and collect specific information but most of the assessment is actually found in real life experiences where [students] are writing letters of real importance like last year writing to get donations of food for camps...or class meeting agendas where children fill in the problems and concerns or issues they want to discuss in class meetings. Some children filled in SACON forms [minor works request forms]...and it really shows their power of language and how they can use it to get things done. So language assessment is done all day in a whole range of ways.

If teachers are to make a difference for students from disadvantaged groups, then they need to examine assessment in all its manifestations. Students' success and failure in literacy is not just measured at "transition points" such as the end of the term or the year, or the end of secondary school. It is constructed moment by moment as students engage in the literacy events offered by the teacher's program and as the teacher assesses their competence during these events.

Broadening opportunities for assessing students' literacy competencies

During the project both teachers and researchers have been challenged to take apart what has been naturalised, what is unexamined and assumed, to see how both programs and assessment practices are implicated in the reproduction of disadvantage. In interrogating their programs to achieve more equitable outcomes for students from poor and diverse communities, teachers identified three key interrelated aspects that need to be addressed. These aspects are:

- the diversity of literacy practices which are reflected in the program,
- the constraints and possibilities of classroom literacy practices, and
- student perspectives.

Diversity of literacy practices reflected in the program

Teachers who are concerned about equity place "social justice at the foundation of thinking about curriculum and assessment" (Connell, 1993, p. 83). This leads them to consider the ways in which their programs reflect or fail to reflect the diversity of literacy practice in the wider community. The traditional school literacy curriculum has privileged the practices, texts, content, and forms (Connell, 1992, p. 22) of some groups in the community over others, giving advantage to the children from these groups. If this is to be redressed then researchers and teachers need to:

> look at the different kinds of literacy practices that go on in different subcultures and in different areas and in different workspaces and to look at different kinds of ways in which they are projected back into schooling—to look at the way in which the activities that go on in the classroom reflect or fail to reflect certain sorts of ways in which reading and writing are routinely practised in the everyday lives of people in different sectors of the society, different work sectors, different domestic sectors, different kinds of communities. (Peter Freebody, video transcript in Badger et al., 1997)

The teachers in the project were, to varying extents, trying to broaden the range of literacy practices and texts offered in their classrooms. They realised that the diversity of students' experiences means that they bring to school different strengths and competencies in literacy, many of which are unrecognised and unvalued in the traditional literacy curriculum. For example, in one school, nine- and ten-year-old students were extremely competent in using timetables to travel to a seaside suburb where there is considerable weekend entertainment, adeptly making connections between two buses and a tram. When the teachers recognised the students possessed such skills they were able to credit them and build on them in their classroom literacy programs.

In the same school, teachers saw how other areas of the curriculum offered opportunity for different literacy practices. For example, the students grew vegetables, and as part of that endeavour they read seed packets, brochures, and instructions about planting and caring for the plants as well as for dealing with weeds and pests. They wrote labels for different vegetables, and kept descriptive logs recording the growth (or death!) of their plants. Again, many of the students sang in the school choir, where there were opportunities for them to share their interpretations of lyrics, as well as to discuss the meanings of obscure or unfamiliar words.

In another school, two of the junior primary teachers had a particular interest in understanding the nexus between the practices which counted in their literacy programs, the range of outcomes which their programs made possible and the ways they assessed their students' literacy competencies. These teachers too were involved in an on-going process of modifying the curriculum they offered so as to include opportunities for students to use literacies beyond the usual school literacies. They had a particular focus on using literacy for social action. For instance, the students were involved in writing letters to cereal manufacturing companies to request their support in providing breakfast foods for the school camp because the school community did not have the material resources to meet all the costs required to send students to the camp.

In this same classroom students regularly filled out the forms through which schools request minor works and repairs. When students identified that repairs were needed to school property they obtained and completed the form. To do this successfully they had to make a range of decisions about the location of the problem and the category of repair needed, providing accurate information that could be acted on by the maintenance workers when they came to the site. Those who filled out the form also had responsibility for faxing it to the appropriate authority. The students who had been in the school for some time took this responsibility seriously for themselves, and also inducted new students into the processes.

Additionally, students used the literacy practices involved in democratic decision making. Those with designated executive responsibility regularly ran class meetings where the class responded to items that students placed on the agenda, writing minutes to provide a record of decisions that they could refer to later.

These same teachers worked with students to identify a range of classroom responsibilities (e.g., lunch monitors) and developed position descriptions for them. Individual students then selected a position of interest to them and applied for it in writing, arguing their suitability against the criteria, and providing a reference from a family member or friend. The application was read by a selection committee of peers who made the decision as to which applicant got the position. All the positions were vacated at the end of each term and the process was repeated.

The kinds of literacy events described above are very different from the traditional school literacy tasks which focus on instruction or evaluation. Through these and many other literacy events the teachers provided a variety of opportunities for students to learn and to demonstrate their literacy competencies, usually through tasks that were real and meaningful for them.

Constraints and possibilities of classroom literacy practices

There is more to constructing an inclusive curriculum, however, than simply providing a diversity of literacy events. Literacy events in themselves are not socially or culturally neutral, but may be enacted in a variety of ways depending on the rules for the discourse within particular communities. Therefore literacy events themselves have to provide spaces for students to participate in ways that take cognisance of students' known ways of behaving and which allow them to build on and extend their understandings. Haas Dyson highlights this point when she says, "If a curriculum is to be truly responsive to diversity, truly child-centred, it must be permeable enough to allow for children's ways of participating in school literacy events" (Haas Dyson, 1992, p. 41).

Teachers in the project understood the need to attend to the ways in which different groups of students participated in and were positioned by specific literacy events. This led them to reflect on and try to understand different students' perspectives on and participation in the events.

One teacher explained how this presented her with a major challenge:

> One of the biggest challenges I face in teaching in a disadvantaged school is...constantly questioning what I present to children. So when I'm presenting something to children I examine the impact that it's going to have on them. For example, when I'm presenting a book to children I try to look at it through each individual child's eyes and ask what messages will this give Aboriginal children in my class. What messages will it give the non-English-speaking background children?

The quote demonstrates one of the ways in which the teachers tried to make their teaching more inclusive of a diverse range of students' experiences, serving to render the "socio-educational barriers more permeable" (Connell, Johnston, & White, 1994, p. 211). They sought to understand how students might interpret the classroom literacy events in which they participated (Garcia & Pearson, 1991) and how these events have the potential to both constrain and to enable different groups of students in the class. Two examples from the classroom demonstrate how teachers analysed literacy practices.

One Year 7 teacher came to understand the difficulties and hurdles she had unwittingly constructed when she demanded that during silent reading time students read only novels. She saw that many of the students were selecting familiar formula novel series such as *Sweet Valley High*, *Goosebumps*, *Hair Raisers*, and *Babysitters Club*, or they were only "pretending" to read the book in front of them. She realised that she had been privileging the reading of novels and negating a body of texts which students found interesting and enjoyable, thus limiting the range of texts on which students could develop and demonstrate their reading competencies. She has now changed her practice and permits the reading of magazines and comics during silent reading time.

A junior primary teacher questioned the valorisation of class meetings as a means of allowing students to experience democratic decision making. Her analysis of these meetings helped her to understand that the usual procedures are based on a "white middle class model of operating" which serves to marginalise Aboriginal students in particular.

Sometimes we provide situations in schools where we are actually limiting the information we obtain about students. For example, we have class meetings...which are set up on a white middle class model. We have one person talking at a time, people put their hands up and people vote. This can actually limit the involvement of some of the cultural groups we have in our school. For example Aboriginal children often don't work well on that model, don't work well in that kind of a situation. So even though it is important they are exposed to different situations we really need to incorporate some of the ways that they learn and talk in our class meetings. So we may set up lots of situations where children can come up with ideas in small groups and then have the opportunity to share those back with the class in a class meeting rather than just use the one model.

Rather than assess the students as unable to participate, as inadequate, or as lacking in confidence, this teacher analysed the practice from students' perspectives and modified it to provide a means for all the students to participate. In this way she avoided "reading" the limitations of the practice as limitations of the students. Students cannot receive credit for the literacy understandings and skills they have if the program fails to give them opportunities to show what they know and can do.

Students' perspectives

If a literacy program is to be equitable it needs to reflect the diversity of students' literacy practices, world views, and experiences. In addition, teachers need to find out how students are responding to the program that is being offered to them. It is argued that "[t]o understand...children's perspectives in school is to gain some insight into how they make sense of and interpret instructional experiences" (Dahl, 1995, p. 1). Understanding students' perspectives—what they are taking from the literacy program, their sense of success and failure, their goals and expectations—is important for teachers modifying and adapting the program.

In traditional forms of assessment, the knowledge that "counts" about students' achievement has been predominantly based on the teacher's perceptions. Student knowledge of who they are as literacy users and their literacy achievements has been completely discounted. The teachers in the research project were actively working to redress this, and to include students' perspectives as part of the data which informed their assessment processes and their program evaluation.

The change from student as object of assessment (Edelsky, 1991, p. 87) to student as participant in assessment takes account of the constructed nature of knowledge. If we accept that knowledge is constructed, then the knower is an intimate part of the known (Johnston, 1989), and their perspective should be made to count.

In the same way that classroom programs need to accommodate the multiplicity of literacy experiences, assessment practices have to explore the multiplicity of perceptions (Taylor, 1990) which are reflected in classrooms serving diverse communities.

> To assert privilege for one type of voice among all others in a classroom promotes and maintains a hierarchy based on nationality, gender, race, economic class, and ethnicity. Unless teachers and students are allowed and willing to listen to each other...to use their multiplicity of voices in any classroom, there is little hope for democratic development in our society. (Shannon, 1993, p. 92)

Teachers in the project schools were clear that this sentiment must extend to assessment, given its predominance in shaping the curriculum. Student self-assessment can serve to change the power dimension in classrooms, affirming students as one of the major stakeholders in the assessment process.

While self-assessment is seen to be empowering for students, it is not unproblematic. It cannot be accepted uncritically as a quick route to equity-based assessment. It can be as subject to bias and constraint as other kinds of assessment, with students "locked into seeing things only through the single set of lenses provided for them by their cultural guardians" (O'Loughlin, 1995, p. 107). When students wrote comments such as:

- I can write lots of genres
- I can write neatly with finger spaces between my words
- I'm a good reader because I borrow lots of fiction from the library

project teachers reviewed their programs in the light of the emphases and values on which students were focusing.

Interviews with students revealed that some of the kinds of self-assessment required were difficult. They said that parents and caregivers were likely to ask more questions than previously about their literacy achievement, and that they were expected to be able to give reasons and explanations in a way that they hadn't in the past. They had to take responsibility for their learning, and be able to justify their judgements about their work, and they told us that this was not easy to do.

> I think that the hardest part on the sheet is "How did I go?" because it's really hard to write about yourself because when you show your teacher or your parents at the interview they read it and then you get home and they talk to you about it and it's really hard to talk about yourself and write about yourself. (Kate, Year 7)

When students' perceptions count as a source of information, and teachers understand the complexity of how these perceptions are constructed in the classroom, then they are in a better position to understand the relationship between their programs and students' literacy outcomes.

Conclusion

It can be argued that the whole enterprise of changing literacy outcomes for students from diverse and poor communities is less about finding more technically efficient assessment tools and more about changing classroom literacy programs. As teaching and assessment are inextricably linked, teachers' programs have to provide the spaces and opportunities through which students can demonstrate the diversity of their literacy competencies and build on those to use literacy as a powerful tool for "shaping identity, knowledge and power" (Luke, 1993, p. 48).

REFERENCES

Badger, L., Wilkinson, L., Comber, B., Nixon, H., & Hill, S. (1997). *Literacy assessment in disadvantaged schools*, Video module 6. Melbourne: Eleanor Curtain.

Baker, C., & Freebody, P. (1993). The crediting of literate competence in classroom talk. *The Australian Journal of Language and Literacy, 16*(4), 279–294.

Connell, R. (1992). Measuring up: Assessment, evaluation and educational disadvantage. *ACSA Teaching Resource No. 2*, Belconnen, ACT: Australian Curriculum Studies Association.

Connell, R. (1993). *Schools and social justice*. Toronto: Our Schools/Our Selves Production.

Connell, R., Johnston, K., & White, V. (1994). The issue of poverty and educational measurement. In E. Hatton (Ed.), *Understanding teaching: Curriculum and the social context of schooling*. Sydney: Harcourt Brace.

Dahl, K. (1995). Challenges in understanding the learner's perspective. *Theory Into Practice, 34*(2), 1, 124–130.

Haas Dyson, A. (1992). The case of the singing scientist: A performance perspective on the 'stages' of school literacy. *Written Communication, 9*(1), 3–47.

Edelsky, C. (1991). *With literacy and social justice for all: Rethinking the social in language and education*. London: Falmer Press.

Eveline, J. (1994, Autumn). The politics of advantage. *Australian Feminist Studies, 19*, 129–154.

Freebody, P., & Ludwig, C. (1995). *Everyday literate practices in and out of schools in low socio-economic urban communities: Executive summary*. Canberra: Department of Education, Employment and Training; Melbourne: Curriculum Corporation.

Garcia, G., & Pearson, P. (1991). The role of assessment in a diverse society. In E. Hiebert (Ed.), *Literacy for a diverse society*. New York: Teachers College Press.

Johnston, P. (1989). Constructive evaluation and the improvement of teaching and learning. *Teachers College Record, 90*(4), 509–528.

Luke, A. (1993). The social construction of literacy in the primary school. In L. Unsworth (Ed.), *Literacy learning and teaching: Language as social practice in the primary school*. Melbourne: Macmillan.

O'Loughlin, M. (1995). Daring the imagination: Unlocking voices of dissent and possibility in teaching. *Theory Into Practice, 34*(2), 107–116.

Shannon, P. (1993). Developing democratic voices. *The Reading Teacher, 47*, 86–94.

Shor, I. (1980). *Critical teaching and everyday life*. Boston: South End Press.

South Australian Department of Education. (1992). *Writing reading assessment programme: Final report*. Adelaide: Author.

Taylor, D. (1990). Teaching without testing: Assessing the complexity of children's literacy learning. *English Education, 22*(1), 4–74.

Williams, T. (1987). *Participation in education* (Research Monograph No. 30). Hawthorn, Victoria: Australian Council for Education Research.

SHEILA W. VALENCIA
MARSHA RIDDLE BULY

Behind test scores: What struggling readers *really* need

Why do so many children in the United States fail state and standardized reading tests each year? This analysis is a look behind test scores at the specific reading abilities of students who failed one state reading test.

Every year thousands of U.S. students take standardized tests and state reading tests, and every year thousands fail them. With the implementation of the No Child Left Behind legislation (www.ed.gov/nclb/landing.jhtml), which mandates testing all children from grades 3 to 8 every year, these numbers will grow exponentially, and alarming numbers of schools and students will be targeted for "improvement." Whether you believe this increased focus on testing is good news or bad, if you are an educator, you are undoubtedly concerned about the children who struggle every day with reading and the implications of their test failure.

Although legislators, administrators, parents, and educators have been warned repeatedly not to rely on a single measure to make important instructional decisions (Elmore, 2002; Linn, n.d.; Shepard, 2000), scores from state tests still seem to drive the search for programs and approaches that will help students learn and meet state standards. The popular press, educational publications, teacher workshops, and state and school district policies are filled with attempts to find solutions for poor test performance. For example, some schools have eliminated sustained silent reading in favor of more time for explicit instruction (Edmondson & Shannon, 2002; Riddle Buly & Valencia, 2002), others are buying special programs or mandating specific interventions (Goodnough, 2001; Helfand, 2002), and some states and districts are requiring teachers to have particular instructional emphases (McNeil, 2000; Paterson, 2000; Riddle Buly & Valencia, 2002). Furthermore, it is common to find teachers spending enormous amounts of time preparing students for these high-stakes tests (Olson, 2001), even though a narrow focus on preparing students for specific tests does not translate into real learning (Klein, Hamilton, McCaffrey, & Stecher, 2000; Linn, 2000). But, if we are really going to help students, we need to understand the underlying reasons for their test failure. Simply knowing which children have failed state tests is a bit like knowing that you have a fever when you are feeling ill but having no idea of the cause or cure. A test score, like a fever, is a symptom that demands more specific analysis of the problem. In this case, what is required is a more in-depth analysis of the strengths and needs of students who fail to meet standards and instructional plans that will meet their needs.

In this article, we draw from the results of an empirical study of students who failed a typical fourth-grade state reading assessment (see Riddle Buly & Valencia, 2002, for a full description of the study). Specifically, we describe the patterns of performance that distinguish different groups of students who failed to meet standards. We also provide suggestions for what classroom teachers need to know and how they might help these children succeed.

Study context

Our research was conducted in a typical northwestern U.S. school district of 18,000 students

Reprinted from *The Reading Teacher* (2004), 57, 520–531.

TABLE 1
Diagnostic assessments

Assessment	Word identification	Meaning	Fluency
Woodcock-Johnson-Revised			
Letter-word identification	X		
Word attack	X		
Qualitative Reading Inventory-II			
Reading accuracy	X		
Reading acceptability	X		
Rate			X
Expression			X
Comprehension		X	
Peabody Picture Vocabulary Test-Revised			
Vocabulary meaning		X	
State fourth-grade passages			
Reading accuracy	X		
Reading acceptability	X		
Rate			X
Expression			X

located adjacent to the largest urban district in the state. At the time of our study, 43% were students of color and 47% received free or reduced-price lunch. Over the past several years, approximately 50% of students had failed the state fourth-grade reading test that, like many other standards-based state assessments, consisted of several extended narrative and expository reading selections accompanied by a combination of multiple-choice and open-ended comprehension questions. For the purposes of this study, during September of fifth grade we randomly selected 108 students who had scored below standard on the state test given at the end of fourth grade. These 108 students constituted approximately 10% of failing students in the district. None of them was receiving supplemental special education or English as a Second Language (ESL) services. We wanted to understand the "garden variety" (Stanovich, 1988) test failure—those students typically found in the regular classroom who are experiencing reading difficulty but have not been identified as needing special services or intensive interventions. Classroom teachers, not reading specialists or special education teachers, are solely responsible for the reading instruction of these children and, ultimately, for their achievement.

Data collection and assessment tools

Our approach was to conduct individual reading assessments, working one-on-one with the children for approximately two hours over several days to gather information about their reading abilities. We administered a series of assessments that targeted key components of reading ability identified by experts: word identification, meaning (comprehension and vocabulary), and fluency (rate and expression) (Lipson & Wixson, 2003; National Institute of Child Health and Human Development, 2000; Snow, Burns, & Griffin, 1998). Table 1 presents the measures we used and the areas in which each provided information.

To measure word identification, we used two tests from the 1989 Woodcock-Johnson Psycho-Educational Battery–Revised (WJ–R) that assessed students' reading of single and multisyllabic words, both real and pseudowords. We also scored oral reading errors students made on narrative and expository graded passages from the 1995 Qualitative Reading Inventory–II (QRI–II) and from the state test. We calculated total accuracy (percentage of words read correctly) and acceptability (counting

TABLE 2
Cluster analysis

Cluster	Sample percentage	English Language Learner percentage	Low socioeconomic status percentage	Word identification	Meaning	Fluency
1–Automatic Word Callers	18	63	89	+ +	–	+ +
2–Struggling Word Callers	15	56	81	–	–	+ +
3–Word Stumblers	17	16	42	–	+	–
4–Slow Comprehenders	24	19	54	+	+ +	–
5–Slow Word Callers	17	56	67	+	–	–
6–Disabled Readers	9	20	80	– –	– –	– –

only those errors that changed the meaning of the text). Students also responded orally to comprehension questions that accompanied the QRI–II passages, providing a measure of their comprehension that was not confounded by writing ability. To assess receptive vocabulary, we used the 1981 Peabody Picture Vocabulary Test–Revised (PPVT–R), which requires students to listen and point to a picture that corresponds to a word (scores of 85 or higher are judged to be average or above average). As with the comprehension questions, the vocabulary measure does not confound understanding with students' ability to write responses. Finally, in the area of fluency, we assessed rate of reading and expression (Samuels, 2002). We timed the readings of all passages (i.e., QRI–II and state test selections) to get a reading rate and used a 4-point rubric developed for the Oral Reading Study of the fourth-grade National Assessment of Educational Progress (NAEP) (Pinnell, Pikulski, Wixson, Campbell, Gough, & Beatty, 1995) to assess phrasing and expression (1–2 is judged to be nonfluent; 3–4 is judged to be fluent).

Findings

Scores from all the assessments for each student fell into three statistically distinct and educationally familiar categories: word identification (word reading in isolation and context), meaning (comprehension and vocabulary), and fluency (rate and expression). When we examined the average scores for all 108 students in the sample, students appeared to be substantially below grade level in all three areas. However, when we analyzed the data using a cluster analysis (Aldenderfer & Blashfield, 1984), looking for groups of students who had similar patterns across all three factors, we found six distinct profiles of students who failed the test. Most striking is that the majority of students were not weak in all three areas; they were actually strong in some and weak in others. Table 2 indicates the percentage of students in each group and their relative strength (+) or weakness (–) in word identification, meaning, and fluency.

The profiles

We illuminate each profile by describing a prototypical student from each cluster (see Figure) and specific suggested instructional targets for each (all names are pseudonyms). Although the instructional strategies we recommend have not been implemented with these particular children, we base our recommendations on our review of research-based practices (e.g., Allington, 2001; Allington & Johnston, 2001; Lipson & Wixson, 2003; National Institute of Child Health and Human Development, 2000), our interpretation of the profiles, and our experiences teaching struggling readers. We conclude with several general implications for school and classroom instruction.

Cluster 1–Automatic Word Callers

We call these students Automatic Word Callers because they can decode words quickly and

Prototypical students from each cluster

Cluster 1—Automatic Word Callers (18%)

Word identification	Meaning	Fluency
+ +	-	+ +

Tomas

Word identification = ninth grade (WJ-R)
> fourth grade (QRI-II)
= 98% (state passages)
Comprehension = second/third grade
Vocabulary = 108
Expression = 3
Rate = 155 words per minute
Writing = proficient

Cluster 2—Struggling Word Callers (15%)

Word identification	Meaning	Fluency
-	-	+ +

Makara

Word identification = fourth grade (WJ-R)
< second grade (QRI-II)
= 75% (state passages)
Comprehension = < second grade
Vocabulary = 58
Expression = 2.5
Rate = 117 words per minute
Writing = below proficient

Cluster 3—Word Stumblers (17%)

Word identification	Meaning	Fluency
-	+	-

Sandy

Word identification = second grade (WJ-R)
= second-grade accuracy/third-grade
acceptability (QRI-II)
= 80% accuracy/99% acceptability
(state passages)
Comprehension = fourth grade
Vocabulary = 135
Expression = 1.5
Rate = 77 words per minute
Writing = proficient

Cluster 4—Slow Comprehenders (24%)

Word identification	Meaning	Fluency
+	+ +	–

Martin

Word identification = sixth grade (WJ-R)
> fourth grade (QRI-II)
= 100% (state passages)
Comprehension = > fourth grade
Vocabulary = 103
Expression = 2.5
Rate = 61 words per minute
Writing = proficient

Cluster 5—Slow Word Callers (17%)

Word identification	Meaning	Fluency
+	-	-

Andrew

Word identification = seventh grade (WJ-R)
> fourth grade (QRI-II)
= 98% (state passages)
Comprehension = second grade
Vocabulary = 74
Expression = 1.5
Rate = 62 words per minute
Writing = not proficient

Cluster 6—Disabled Readers (9%)

Word identification	Meaning	Fluency
- -	- -	- -

Jesse

Word identification = first grade (WJ-R)
< first grade (QRI-II)
< 50% (state passages)
Comprehension = < first grade
Vocabulary = 105
Writing = not proficient

accurately, but they fail to read for meaning. The majority of students in this cluster qualify for free or reduced-price lunch, and they are English-language learners who no longer receive special support. Tomas is a typical student in this cluster.

Tomas has excellent word identification skills. He scored at ninth-grade level when reading real words and pseudowords (i.e., phonetically regular nonsense words such as *fot*) on the WJ–R tests, and at the independent level for word identification on the QRI–II and state fourth-grade passages. However, when asked about what he read, Tomas had difficulty, placing his comprehension at the second-grade level. Although Tomas's first language is not English, his score of 108 on the PPVT–R suggests that his comprehension difficulties are more complex than individual word meanings. Tomas's "proficient" score on the state writing assessment also suggests that his difficulty is in understanding rather than in writing answers to comprehension questions. This student's rate of reading, which was quite high compared with rates of fourth-grade students on the Oral Reading Study of NAEP (Pinnell et al., 1995) and other research (Harris & Sipay, 1990), suggests that his decoding is automatic and unlikely to be contributing to his comprehension difficulty. His score in expression is also consistent with students who were rated as "fluent" according to the NAEP rubric, although this seems unusual for a student who is demonstrating difficulty with comprehension.

The evidence suggests that Tomas needs additional instruction in comprehension and most likely would benefit from explicit instruction, teacher modeling, and think-alouds of key reading strategies (e.g., summarizing, self-monitoring, creating visual representations, evaluating), using a variety of types of material at the fourth- or fifth-grade level (Block & Pressley, 2002; Duke & Pearson, 2002). His comprehension performance on the QRI–II suggests that his literal comprehension is quite strong but that he has difficulty with more inferential and critical aspects of understanding. Although Tomas has strong scores in the fluency category, both in expression and rate, he may be reading too fast to attend to meaning, especially deeper meaning of the ideas in the text. Tomas's teacher should help him understand that the purpose for reading is to understand and that rate varies depending on the type of text and the pur-

pose for reading. Then, the teacher should suggest that he slow down to focus on meaning. Self-monitoring strategies would also help Tomas check for understanding and encourage him to think about the ideas while he is reading. These and other such strategies may help him learn to adjust his rate to meet the demands of the text.

Tomas would also likely benefit from additional support in acquiring academic language, which takes many years for English-language learners to develop (Cummins, 1991). Reading activities such as building background; developing understanding of new words, concepts, and figurative language in his "to-be-read" texts; and acquiring familiarity with genre structures found in longer, more complex texts like those found at fourth grade and above would provide important opportunities for his language and conceptual development (Antunez, 2002; Hiebert, Pearson, Taylor, Richardson, & Paris, 1998). Classroom read-alouds and discussions as well as lots of additional independent reading would also help Tomas in building language and attention to understanding.

Cluster 2—Struggling Word Callers

The students in this cluster not only struggle with meaning, like the Automatic Word Callers in Cluster 1, but they also struggle with word identification. Makara, a student from Cambodia, is one of these students. Like Tomas, Makara struggled with comprehension. But unlike Tomas, he had substantial difficulty applying word identification skills when reading connected text (QRI–II and state passages), even though his reading of isolated words on the WJ–R was at a fourth-grade level. Such word identification difficulties would likely contribute to comprehension problems. However, Makara's performance on the PPVT–R, which placed him below the 1st percentile compared with other students his age, and his poor performance on the state writing assessment suggest that language may contribute to his comprehension difficulties as well—not surprising for a student acquiring a second language. These language-related results need to be viewed with caution, however, because the version of the PPVT–R available for use in this study may underestimate the language abilities of students from culturally and linguistically diverse backgrounds, and written language takes longer than oral language to develop. Despite difficulty with meaning, Makara read quickly—117 words per minute. At first glance, this may seem unusual given his difficulty with both decoding and comprehension. Closer investigation of his performance, however, revealed that Makara read words quickly whether he was reading them correctly or incorrectly and didn't stop to monitor or self-correct. In addition, although Makara was fast, his expression and phrasing were uneven and consistent with comprehension difficulties.

Makara likely needs instruction and practice in oral and written language, as well as in constructing meaning in reading and writing, self-monitoring, and decoding while reading connected text. All this needs to be done in rich, meaningful contexts, taking into account his background knowledge and interests. Like Tomas, Makara would benefit from teacher or peer read-alouds, lots of experience with independent reading at his level, small-group instruction, and the kinds of activities aimed at building academic language that we described earlier, as well as a more foundational emphasis on word meanings. Makara also needs instruction in self-monitoring and fix-up strategies to improve his comprehension and awareness of reading for understanding. Decoding instruction is also important for him, although his teacher would need to gather more information using tools such as miscue analysis or tests of decoding to determine his specific decoding needs and how they interact with his knowledge of word meanings. Makara clearly cannot be instructed in fourth-grade material; most likely, his teacher would need to begin with second-grade material that is familiar and interesting to him and a good deal of interactive background building. At the same time, however, Makara needs exposure to the content and vocabulary of grade-level texts through activities such as teacher read-alouds, tapes, and partner reading so that his conceptual understanding continues to grow.

Cluster 3—Word Stumblers

Students in this cluster have substantial difficulty with word identification, but they still have surprisingly strong comprehension. How does that happen? Sandy, a native English speaker from a middle class home, is a good example of this type of student. Sandy stumbled on so many words ini-

tially that it seemed unlikely that she would comprehend what she had read, yet she did. Her word identification scores were at second-grade level, and she read the state fourth-grade passages at frustration level. However, a clue to her strong comprehension is evident from the difference between her immediate word recognition accuracy score and her acceptability score, which takes into account self-corrections or errors that do not change the meaning. In other words, Sandy was so focused on reading for meaning that she spontaneously self-corrected many of her decoding miscues or substituted words that preserved the meaning. She attempted to read every word in the reading selections, working until she could figure out some part of each word and then using context clues to help her get the entire word. She seemed to over-rely on context because her decoding skills were so weak (Stanovich, 1994). Remarkably, she was eventually able to read the words on the state fourth-grade reading passages at an independent level. But, as we might predict, Sandy's rate was very slow, and her initial attempts to read were choppy and lacked flow—she spent an enormous amount of time self-correcting and rereading. After she finally self-corrected or figured out unknown words, however, Sandy reread phrases with good expression and flow to fit with the meaning. Although Sandy's overall fluency score was low, her primary difficulty does not appear in the area of either rate or expression; rather, her low performance in fluency seems to be a result of her difficulty with decoding.

With such a strong quest for meaning, Sandy was able to comprehend fourth-grade material even when her decoding was at frustration level. No doubt her strong language and vocabulary abilities (i.e., 99th percentile) were assets. As we might predict, Sandy was more than proficient at expressing her ideas when writing about her experiences. She understands that reading and writing should make sense, and she has the self-monitoring strategies, perseverance, and language background to make that happen.

Sandy needs systematic instruction in word identification and opportunities to practice when reading connected text at her reading level. She is clearly beyond the early stages of reading and decoding, but her teacher will need to determine through a more in-depth analysis precisely which decoding skills should be the focus of her instruction. At the same time, Sandy needs supported experiences with texts that will continue to feed and challenge her drive for meaning. For students like Sandy, it is critical not to sacrifice intellectual engagement with text while they are receiving decoding instruction and practice in below-grade-level material. Furthermore, Sandy needs to develop automaticity with word identification, and to do that she would benefit from assisted reading (i.e., reading along with others, monitored reading with a tape, or partner reading) as well as unassisted reading practice (i.e., repeated reading, reading to younger students) with materials at her instructional level (Kuhn & Stahl, 2000).

Cluster 4—Slow Comprehenders

Almost one fourth of the students in this sample were Slow Comprehenders. Like other students in this cluster, Martin is a native English speaker and a relatively strong decoder, scoring above fourth-grade level on all measures of decoding. His comprehension was at the instructional level on the fourth-grade QRI–II selections, and his vocabulary and writing ability were average for his age. On the surface, this information is puzzling because Martin failed the fourth-grade state test.

Insight about Martin's reading performance comes from several sources. First, Martin was within two points of passing the state assessment, so he doesn't seem to have a serious reading problem. Second, although his reading rate is quite slow and this often interferes with comprehension (Adams, 1990), results of the QRI–II suggest that Martin's comprehension is quite strong, in spite of his slow rate. This is most likely because Martin has good word knowledge and understands that reading should make sense, and neither the QRI–II nor the state test has time limits. His strong score in expression confirms that Martin did, indeed, attend to meaning while reading. Third, a close examination of his reading behaviors while reading words from the WJ–R tests, QRI–II, and state reading selections revealed that he had some difficulty reading multisyllabic words; although, with time, he was able to read enough words to score at grade level or above. It appears that Martin has the decoding skills to attack multisyllabic words, but they are not yet automatic.

The outstanding characteristic of Martin's profile is his extremely slow rate combined with his relatively strong word identification abilities and comprehension. Our work with him suggests that, even if Martin were to get the additional two points needed to pass the state test, he would still have a significant problem with rate and some difficulty with automatic decoding of multisyllabic words, both of which could hamper his future reading success. Furthermore, with such a lack of automaticity and a slow rate, it is unlikely that Martin enjoys or spends much time reading. As a result, he is likely to fall further and further behind his peers (Stanovich, 1986), especially as he enters middle school where the amount of reading increases dramatically. Martin needs fluency-building activities such as guided repeated oral reading, partner reading, and Readers Theatre (Allington, 2001; Kuhn & Stahl, 2000; Lipson & Wixson, 2003). Given his word identification and comprehension abilities, he most likely could get that practice using fourth-grade material where he will also encounter multisyllabic words. It is important to find reading material that is interesting to Martin and that, initially, can be completed in a relatively short time. Martin needs to develop stamina as well as fluency, and to do that he will need to spend time reading short and extended texts. In addition, Martin might benefit from instruction and practice in strategies for identifying multisyllabic words so that he is more prepared to deal with them automatically while reading.

Cluster 5—Slow Word Callers

The students in this cluster are similar to Tomas, the Automatic Word Caller in Cluster 1. The difference is that Tomas is an automatic, fluent word caller, whereas the students in this cluster are slow. This group is a fairly even mix of English-language learners and native English speakers who have difficulty in comprehension and fluency. Andrew is an example of such a student. He has well-developed decoding skills, scoring at the seventh-grade level when reading words in isolation and at the independent level when reading connected text. Even with such strong decoding abilities, Andrew had difficulty with comprehension. We had to drop down to the second-grade QRI–II passage for Andrew to score at the instructional level for comprehension, and, even at that level, his retelling was minimal. Andrew's score on the PPVT–R, corresponding to first grade (the 4th percentile for his age), adds to the comprehension picture as well. It suggests that Andrew may be experiencing difficulty with both individual word meanings and text-based understanding when reading paragraphs and longer selections. Like Martin, Andrew's reading rate was substantially below rates expected for fourth-grade students (Harris & Sipay, 1990; Pinnell et al., 1995), averaging 62 words per minute when reading narrative and expository selections. In practical terms, this means he read just one word per second. As we might anticipate from his slow rate and his comprehension difficulty, Andrew did not read with expression or meaningful phrasing.

The relationship between meaning and fluency is unclear in Andrew's case. On the one hand, students who realize they don't understand would be wise to slow down and monitor meaning. On the other hand, Andrew's lack of automaticity and slow rate may interfere with comprehension. To disentangle these factors, his teacher would need to experiment with reading materials about which Andrew has a good deal of background knowledge to eliminate difficulty with individual word meanings and overall comprehension. If his reading rate and expression improve under such conditions, a primary focus for instruction would be meaning. That is, his slow rate of reading and lack of prosody would seem to be a response to lack of understanding rather than contributing to it. In contrast, if Andrew's rate and expression are still low when the material and vocabulary are familiar, instruction should focus on both fluency and meaning. In either case, Andrew would certainly benefit from attention to vocabulary building, both indirect building through extensive independent reading and teacher read-alouds as well as more explicit instruction in word learning strategies and new words he will encounter when reading specific texts (Nagy, 1988; Stahl & Kapinus, 2001).

It is interesting that 50% of the students in this cluster scored at Level 1 on the state test, the lowest level possible. State guidelines characterize these students as lacking prerequisite knowledge and skills that are fundamental for meeting the standard. Given such a definition, a logical assumption would be that these students lack basic, early reading skills such as decoding. However, as the evidence here suggests, we cannot assume that students who score at the lowest level on the test need decoding instruction. Andrew, like others in this cluster, needs instruction in meaning and fluency.

Cluster 6—Disabled Readers

We call this group Disabled Readers because they are experiencing severe difficulty in all three areas—word identification, meaning, and fluency. This is the smallest group (9%), yet, ironically, this is the profile that most likely comes to mind when we think of children who fail state reading tests. This group also includes one of the lowest numbers of second-language learners. The most telling characteristic of students in this cluster, like Jesse, is their very limited word identification abilities. Jesse had few decoding skills beyond initial consonants, basic consonant-vowel-consonant patterns (e.g., *hat*, *box*), and high-frequency sight words. However, his knowledge of word meanings was average, like most of the students in this cluster, which suggests that receptive language was not a major problem and that he does not likely have limited learning ability. With decoding ability at the first-grade level and below, it is not surprising that Jesse's comprehension and fluency were also low. He simply could not read enough words at the first-grade level to get any meaning.

As we might anticipate, the majority of students in this cluster were not proficient in writing and scored at the lowest level, Level 1, on the state fourth-grade reading test. It is important to remember, however, that children who were receiving special education intervention were not included in our sample. So, the children in this cluster, like Jesse, are receiving all of their instruction, or the majority of it (some may be getting supplemental help), from their regular classroom teachers.

Jesse clearly needs intensive, systematic word identification instruction targeted at beginning reading along with access to lots of reading material at first-grade level and below. This will be a challenge for Jesse's fifth-grade teacher. Pedagogically, Jesse needs explicit instruction in basic word identification. Yet few intermediate-grade teachers include this as a part of their instruction, and most do not have an adequate supply of easy materials for instruction or fluency building. In addition, the majority of texts in other subject areas such as social studies and science are written at levels that will be inaccessible to students like Jesse, so alternative materials and strategies will be needed. On the social-emotional front, it will be a challenge to keep Jesse engaged in learning and to provide opportunities for him to succeed in the classroom, even if he is referred for additional reading support. Without that engagement and desire to learn, it is unlikely he will be motivated to put forth the effort it will take for him to make progress. Jesse needs a great deal of support from his regular classroom teacher and from a reading specialist, working together to build a comprehensive instructional program in school and support at home that will help him develop the skill and will to progress.

Conclusions and implications

Our brief descriptions of the six prototypical children and the instructional focus each one needs is a testimony to individual differences. As we have heard a thousand times before, and as our data support, one-size instruction will not fit all children. The evidence here clearly demonstrates that students fail state reading tests for a variety of reasons and that, if we are to help these students, we will need to provide appropriate instruction to meet their varying needs. For example, placing all struggling students in a phonics or word identification program would be inappropriate for nearly 58% of the students in this sample who had adequate or strong word identification skills. In a similar manner, an instructional approach that did not address fluency and building reading stamina for longer, more complex text or that did not provide sufficient reading material at a range of levels would miss almost 70% of the students who demonstrated difficulty with fluency. In addition to these important cautions about overgeneralizing students' needs, we believe there are several strategies aimed at assessment, classroom organization and materials, and school structures that could help teachers meet their students' needs.

First and most obvious, teachers need to go beneath the scores on state tests by conducting additional diagnostic assessments that will help them identify students' needs. The data here demonstrate quite clearly that, without more in-depth and indi-

vidual student assessment, distinctive and instructionally important patterns of students' abilities are masked. We believe that informal reading inventories, oral reading records, and other individually tailored assessments provide useful information about all students. At the same time, we realize that many teachers do not have the time to do complete diagnostic evaluations, such as those we did, with every student. At a minimum, we suggest a kind of layered approach to assessment in which teachers first work diagnostically with students who have demonstrated difficulty on broad measures of reading. Then, they can work with other students as the need arises.

However, we caution that simply administering more and more assessments and recording the scores will miss the point. The value of in-depth classroom assessment comes from teachers having a deep understanding of reading processes and instruction, thinking diagnostically, and using the information on an ongoing basis to inform instruction (Black & Wiliam, 1998; Place, 2002; Shepard, 2000). Requiring teachers to administer grade-level classroom assessments to all their students regardless of individual student needs would not yield useful information or help teachers make effective instructional decisions. For example, administering a fourth-grade reading selection to Jesse, who is reading at first-grade level, would not provide useful information. However, using a fourth- or even fifth-grade selection for Tomas would. Similarly, assessing Jesse's word identification abilities should probably include assessments of basic sound/symbol correspondences or even phonemic awareness, but assessing decoding of multisyllabic words would be more appropriate for Martin. This kind of matching of assessment to students' needs is precisely what we hope would happen when teachers have the knowledge, the assessment tools, and the flexibility to assess and teach children according to their ongoing analysis. Both long-term professional development and time are critical if teachers are to implement the kind of sophisticated classroom assessment that struggling readers need.

Second, the evidence points to the need for multilevel, flexible, small-group instruction (Allington & Johnston, 2001; Cunningham & Allington, 1999; Opitz, 1998). Imagine, if you will, teaching just the six students we have described, who could easily be in the same class. These students not only need support in different aspects of reading, but they also need materials that differ in difficulty, topic, and familiarity. For example, Tomas, Makara, and Andrew all need instruction in comprehension. However, Tomas and Andrew likely can receive that instruction using grade-level material, but Makara would need to use easier material. Both Makara and Andrew need work in vocabulary, whereas Tomas is fairly strong in word meanings. As second-language learners, Tomas and Makara likely need more background building and exposure to topics, concepts, and academic vocabulary as well as the structure of English texts than Andrew, who is a native English speaker. Furthermore, the teacher likely needs to experiment with having Tomas and Makara slow down when they read to get them to attend to meaning, whereas Andrew needs to increase his fluency through practice in below-grade-level text.

So, although these three students might be able to participate in whole-class instruction in which the teacher models and explicitly teaches comprehension strategies, they clearly need guided practice to apply the strategies to different types and levels of material, and they each need attention to other aspects of reading as well. This means the teacher must have strong classroom management and organizational skills to provide small-group instruction. Furthermore, he or she must have access to a wide range of books and reading materials that are intellectually challenging yet accessible to students reading substantially below grade level. At the same time, these struggling readers need access to grade-level material through a variety of scaffolded experiences (i.e., partner reading, guided reading, read-alouds) so that they are exposed to grade-level ideas, text structures, and vocabulary (Cunningham & Allington, 1999). Some of these students and their teachers would benefit from collaboration with other professionals in their schools, such as speech and language and second-language specialists, who could suggest classroom-based strategies targeted to the students' specific needs.

The six clusters and the three strands within each one (word identification, meaning, fluency) clearly provide more in-depth analysis of students' reading abilities than general test scores. Nevertheless, we caution that there is still more to be learned about individual students in each cluster,

beyond what we describe here, that would help teachers plan for instruction. Two examples make this point. The first example comes from Cluster 1, Automatic Word Callers. Tomas had substantial difficulty with comprehension, but his scores on the vocabulary measure suggested that word meanings were likely not a problem for him. However, other students in this cluster, such as Maria, *did* have difficulty with word meanings and would need not only comprehension instruction like Tomas but also many more language-building activities and exposure to oral and written English. The second example that highlights the importance of looking beyond the cluster profile is Andrew, our Slow Word Caller from Cluster 5. Although we know that in-depth assessment revealed that Andrew had difficulty with comprehension and fluency, we argue above that the teacher must do more work with Andrew to determine how much fluency is contributing to comprehension and how much it is a result of Andrew's effort to self-monitor. Our point here is that even the clusters do not tell the entire story.

Finally, from a school or district perspective, we are concerned about the disproportionate number of second-language students who failed the test. In our study, 11% of the students in the school district were identified as second-language learners and were receiving additional instructional support. However, in our sample of students who failed the test, 43% were second-language learners who were *not* receiving additional support. Tomas and Makara are typical of many English-language learners in our schools. Their reading abilities are sufficient, according to school guidelines, to allow them to exit supplemental ESL programs, yet they are failing state tests and struggling in the classroom. In this district, as in others across the state, students exit supplemental programs when they score at the 35th percentile or above on a norm-referenced reading test—hardly sufficient to thrive, or even survive, in a mainstream classroom without additional help. States, school districts, and schools need to rethink the support they offer English-language learners both in terms of providing more sustained instructional support over time and of scaffolding their integration into the regular classroom. In addition, there must be a concerted effort to foster academically and intellectually rigorous learning of subject matter for these students (e.g., science, social studies) while they are developing their English-language abilities. Without such a focus, either in their first language or in English, these students will be denied access to important school learning, will fall further behind in other school subjects, and become increasingly disengaged from school and learning (Echevarria, Vogt, & Short, 2000).

Our findings and recommendations may, on one level, seem obvious. Indeed, good teachers have always acknowledged differences among the students in their classes, and they have always tried to meet individual needs. But, in the current environment of high-stakes testing and accountability, it has become more of a challenge to keep an eye on individual children, and more difficult to stay focused on the complex nature of reading performance and reading instruction. This study serves as a reminder of these cornerstones of good teaching. We owe it to our students, their parents, and ourselves to provide struggling readers with the instruction they *really* need.

References

Adams, M.J. (1990). *Beginning to read: Thinking and learning about print.* Cambridge, MA: MIT Press.

Aldenderfer, M., & Blashfield, R. (1984). *Cluster analysis.* Beverly Hills, CA: Sage.

Allington, R.L. (2001). *What really matters for struggling readers.* New York: Longman.

Allington, R.L., & Johnston, P.H. (2001). What do we know about effective fourth-grade teachers and their classrooms? In C.M. Roller (Ed.), *Learning to teach reading: Setting the research agenda* (pp. 150-165). Newark, DE: International Reading Association.

Antunez, B. (2002, Spring). Implementing reading first with English language learners. *Directions in Language and Education, 15.* Retrieved October 15, 2003, from http://www.ncela.gwu.edu/ncbepubs/directions

Black, P., & Wiliam, D. (1998). Assessment and classroom learning. *Assessment in Education, 5*(1), 7-74.

Block, C.C., & Pressley, M. (2002). *Comprehension instruction: Research-based best practices.* New York: Guilford.

Cummins, J. (1991). The development of bilingual proficiency from home to school: A longitudinal study of Portuguese-speaking children. *Journal of Education, 173,* 85-98.

Cunningham, P.M., & Allington, R.L. (1999). *Classrooms that work* (2nd ed.). New York: Longman.

Duke, N.K., & Pearson, P.D. (2002). Effective practices for developing reading comprehension. In A.E. Farstrup & S.J. Samuels (Eds.), *What research has to say about reading instruction* (pp. 9-129). Newark, DE: International Reading Association.

Echevarria, J., Vogt, M.E., & Short, D. (2000). *Making content comprehensible for English language learners: The SIOP model.* Boston: Allyn & Bacon.

Edmondson, J., & Shannon, P. (2002). The will of the people. *The Reading Teacher, 55,* 452-454.

Elmore, R.F. (2002, Spring) Unwarranted intrusion. *Education Next.* Retrieved March 21, 2003, from http://www.educationnext.org

Goodnough, A. (2001, May 23). Teaching by the book, no asides allowed. *The New York Times.* Retrieved March 21, 2003, from http://www.nytimes.com

Harris, A.J., & Sipay, E.R. (1990). *How to increase reading ability* (9th ed.). New York: Longman.

Helfand, D. (2002, July 21). Teens get a second chance at literacy. *Los Angeles Times.* Retrieved March 21, 2003, from http://www.latimes.com

Hiebert, E.H., Pearson, P.D., Taylor, B.M., Richardson, V., & Paris, S.G. (1998). *Every child a reader: Applying reading research to the classroom.* Ann Arbor, MI: Center for the Improvement of Early Reading Achievement, University of Michigan School of Education. Retrieved March 21, 2003, from http://www.ciera.org

Klein, S.P., Hamilton, L.S., McCaffrey, D.F., & Stecher, B.M. (2000). What do test scores in Texas tell us? *Education Policy Analysis Archives, 8*(49). Retrieved March 21, 2003, from http://epaa.asu.edu/epaa/v8n49

Kuhn, M.R., & Stahl, S.A. (2000). *Fluency: A review of developmental and remedial practices* (CIERA Rep. No. 2-008). Ann Arbor, MI: Center for the Improvement of Early Reading Achievement, University of Michigan School of Education. Retrieved March 21, 2003, from http://www.ciera.org

Linn, R.L. (2000). Assessments and accountability. *Educational Researcher, 29*(2), 4-16.

Linn, R.L. (n.d.). *Standards-based accountability: Ten suggestions.* CRESST Policy Brief. 1. Retrieved March 21, 2003, from http://www.cse.ucla.edu

Lipson, M.Y., & Wixson, K.K. (2003). *Assessment and instruction of reading and writing difficulty: An interactive approach* (3rd ed.). Boston: Allyn & Bacon.

McNeil, L.M. (2000). *Contradictions of school reform: Educational costs of standardized testing.* New York: Routledge.

Nagy, W.E. (1988). *Teaching vocabulary to improve reading comprehension.* Urbana, IL: ERIC Clearinghouse on Reading and Communication Skills and the National Council of Teachers of English.

National Institute of Child Health and Human Development. (2000). *Report of the National Reading Panel. Teaching children to read: An evidence-based assessment of the scientific research literature on reading and its implications for reading instruction* (NIH Publication No. 004 769). Washington, DC: U.S. Government Printing Office. Retrieved March 21, 2003, from http://www.nationalreadingpanel.org

Olson, L. (2001). Overboard on testing. *Education Week, 20*(17), 23-30.

Opitz, M.F. (1998). *Flexible grouping in reading*. New York: Scholastic.

Paterson, F.R.A. (2000). The politics of phonics. *Journal of Curriculum and Supervision, 15*, 179-211.

Pinnell, G.S., Pikulski, J.J., Wixson, K.K., Campbell, J.R., Gough, P.B., & Beatty, A.S. (1995). *Listening to children read aloud*. Washington, DC: U.S. Department of Education.

Place, N.A. (2002). Policy in action: The influence of mandated early reading assessment on teachers' thinking and practice. In D.L. Schallert, C.M. Fairbanks, J. Worthy, B. Malock, & J.V. Hoffman (Eds.), *Fiftieth yearbook of the National Reading Conference* (pp. 45-58). Oak Creek, WI: National Reading Conference.

Riddle Buly, M., & Valencia, S.W. (2002). Below the bar: Profiles of students who fail state reading tests. *Educational Evaluation and Policy Analysis, 24*, 219-239.

Samuels, S.J. (2002). Reading fluency: Its development and assessment. In A. Farstrup & S.J. Samuels (Eds.), *What research has to say about reading instruction* (pp. 166-183). Newark, DE: International Reading Association.

Shepard, L.A. (2000). The role of assessment in a learning culture. *Educational Researcher, 29*, 4-14.

Snow, C.E., Burns, M.S., & Griffin, P. (Eds.). (1998). *Preventing reading difficulties in young children*. Washington, DC: National Academy Press.

Stahl, S.A., & Kapinus, B.A. (2001). *Word power: What every educator needs to know about vocabulary*. Washington, DC: National Education Association Professional Library.

Stanovich, K.E. (1986). Matthew effects in reading: Some consequences of individual differences in the acquisition of literacy. *Reading Research Quarterly, 21*, 360-407.

Stanovich, K.E. (1988). Explaining the difference between the dyslexic and garden-variety poor reader: The phonological-core variable-difference model. *Journal of Learning Disabilities, 21*, 590-612.

Stanovich, K.E. (1994). Romance and reality. *The Reading Teacher, 47*, 280-290.

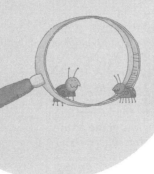

More equitable literacy assessments for Latino students

Robert T. Jiménez

A teacher recently came to me with the end-of-year reading test scores for her Latino students. Her principal wanted to know what she was going to do to improve their scores. The teacher was not provided with any other information useful for interpreting the scores—information that would give her a sense of how well or poorly her students were performing in comparison with other students like hers or mainstream students. One of the problems with assessments like these is that they serve to hierarchically rank children according to their ethnic and social-class backgrounds. Such inequitable assessments often confound students' knowledge of English with literacy. Consider for a moment how literate you might appear if you were given a reading test in the foreign language you studied in high school. Such a test might indicate something about your knowledge of the foreign language but probably not much else. While more in-depth information for assessing the literacy of Latino students is available, my goal is to help you assess your linguistically diverse students more equitably (García, 1994; Pérez & Torres-Guzmán, 1996).

As teachers, we need to assess students within three domains. The first domain involves traditional assessments that indicate how well students are learning the literacy valued in schools. These abilities and forms of knowledge constitute a type of capital necessary for success in the mainstream. Failure to provide students with these forms of literacy constitutes a kind of inequity. The second dimension involves assessing students' knowledge of other literacies. Schools often treat these abilities as a kind of foreign currency, but including them could radically improve perceptions of these stu-

dents as literate persons. Such a change has the potential to provide Latino students with a more equitable learning experience. In the third domain of assessment, information is needed on how students perceive and respond to the process of learning a new language, a new culture, and its associated forms of literacy. Understanding these feelings and beliefs can help us understand how larger inequitable forces adversely affect students' performance and that language and literacy are more than simply what we know and can do—they are a part of who we are.

Traditional literacy assessments

The information derived from traditional assessments can be greatly enhanced with a language profile and an educational history. The profile should include information concerning languages with which the child has had contact and where they were encountered (such as home, school, neighborhood, or church). Some children in countries like Mexico have had the most contact with an indigenous language and encounter Spanish only outside the home. Equitable instruction for these children would include the language necessary to succeed on school literacy tasks. Students might need more contact with native speakers of English, overt instruction on specific linguistic forms, or opportunities to use their native language to clarify misunderstandings. For example, in some schools in Mexico children are not asked to author texts but only to faithfully reproduce them (Smith, Jiménez, & Martinez-León, 2003). Students coming from

Reprinted from *The Reading Teacher* (2004), 57, 576–578.

this background will need extra support to understand different uses of writing.

An educational history also is important for understanding students' learning needs. It is most important to determine whether a student has had gaps in schooling. Students from rural backgrounds are especially vulnerable because schooling may have been unavailable due to a lack of teachers or classroom space, or family poverty may have precluded school attendance because of costs involving school supplies, uniforms, or books. Other students miss portions of their schooling because of frequent mobility.

In addition, students from diverse backgrounds can experience highly fragmented schooling. For example, a child may begin his or her schooling in a mainstream all-English preschool or kindergarten. When the child fails to make adequate or expected progress, he or she might be moved into an English as a Second Language (ESL) or special education classroom. Some children have experienced all of these placements within three to four years of schooling. The changes in placement are seldom planned within a cohesive program but instead reflect educators' confusion. In short, some instruction is repeated and some is omitted. By considering the child's history of schooling, those concerned with equity should identify what components of literacy instruction have been provided and which are still necessary.

Students' test scores should be compared with those of other English-language learners and considered in light of what is expected from native English-speaking children. Factors to consider include the child's age when first exposed to English, the amount of exposure to English, the quality of previous instruction, the child's language learning aptitude, and the quality of current instructional offerings. Research demonstrates that the amount of time necessary to achieve grade-level expectations can vary between two to seven years (Thomas & Collier, 1997). Without making excuses, ask yourself how much time you would need to be as literate as an educated native speaker of another language. As teachers, we can accelerate students' progress by providing excellent instruction (Reyes & Halcón, 2001) and by exposing students to meaningful forms of English. Equity demands that these last two items be considered carefully when assessing English-language learners.

Assessing students' nonschool literacies

It is absolutely essential to assess students' native-language literacy. Students who are literate in their non-English language, particularly Spanish, have an immense advantage in becoming literate in English if we recognize this "treasure trove" and help students link it to English literacy (August & Hakuta, 1997). Too often this knowledge is rejected as "foreign currency." Teachers can get a rough understanding of their students' non-English literacy abilities by conferring with ESL teachers, bilingual teachers, students' parents, and the students themselves. Specific ways to assess students' native-language literacy, like dictations, cloze tests, retellings, and think-alouds, can be found in the work of Pérez and Torres-Guzmán (1996).

Nonschool-based literacies may be more motivating and purposeful to some Latino students, and understanding what students do with these literacies can be informative (Jiménez, 2001). For example, some students have parents who struggle with English. These students often translate for their parents in a process known as language brokering. Research shows that the more young people broker language, the better they perform in school (Orellana, Reynolds, Dorner, & Meza, 2003). A simple and direct way to find out if students serve as language brokers is to ask them about it. Educators can learn more by asking students to keep a journal of their language-brokering activities. Many students see income-tax forms, credit applications, and rental agreements outside of the classroom but seldom see such texts as part of their literacy curriculum. Other alternative literacies include letter writing to distant relatives, the study of popular music lyrics, and the use of handmade texts to communicate commercial interests found in students' communities. By recognizing and valuing these other literacies, we can help students understand the ways that school literacy can support their efforts to be good family and community members.

Assessing students' literate identities

In the United States, it is not unusual for students from linguistically diverse backgrounds to voice feelings of shame, dislike, and alienation toward their non-English language. They may refuse to speak it, or they may make statements to the effect that their language is "stupid," confusing, or not as good as English. While it is almost an irresistible force of nature that children immersed within any given speech community will desire to learn that language, such desire need not be associated with efforts to abandon their native language. Negative feelings toward the non-English language are fueled by messages produced within school. Students who experience debits or bankruptcy in their literate identity accounts will often exhibit related problems with academic learning and may drop out or be attracted by gangs (Flores-Gonzalez, 2002). Although alienation is more prevalent at the secondary school level, researchers recommend that educators establish meaningful relationships with students through extracurricular activities to ameliorate this problem.

Children who do not understand the relationship between their first and second languages often experience more difficulties with English literacy than those students who view their native tongue as a source of strength. For example, Jiménez, García, and Pearson (1996) noted that higher performing bilingual/biliterate Latino students are more likely to see their knowledge of Spanish as a source of information useful for comprehending English text. The students in the 1996 study drew from their prior knowledge of topics learned in Spanish, noted similarities between the meanings of cognate vocabulary items across the two languages, and strategically translated information when they did not understand text in their weaker language. Students who were struggling with English-language literacy reported that Spanish and English were different, that they should not be confused with one another, and that the process of reading was essentially a matter of pronunciation. Equitable instruction needs to include spaces where students can discuss these language relationships. Students are willing to share this information with individuals who want to hear it and with those committed to advocating students' interest, even in the face of inequitable assessment practices.

References

August, D., & Hakuta, K. (1997). *Improving schooling for language-minority children.* Washington DC: National Academy Press.

Flores-Gonzalez, N. (2002). *School kids/street kids: Identity development in Latino students.* New York: Teachers College Press.

García, G.E. (1994). The literacy assessment of second-language learners: A focus on authentic assessment. In K. Spangenberg-Urbschat & R. Pritchard (Eds.), *Kids come in all languages: Reading instruction for second-language learners* (pp. 183–208). Newark, DE: International Reading Association.

Jiménez, R.T. (2001). "It's a difference that changes us": An alternative view of the language and literacy learning needs of Latina/o students. *The Reading Teacher, 54,* 736–742.

Jiménez, R.T., García, G.E., & Pearson, P.D. (1996). The reading strategies of Latina/o students who are successful English readers: Opportunities and obstacles. *Reading Research Quarterly, 31,* 90–112.

Orellana, M.F., Reynolds, J., Dorner, L., & Meza, M. (2003). In other words: Translating or "para-phrasing" as a family literacy practice in immigrant households. *Reading Research Quarterly, 38,* 12–34.

Pérez, B., & Torres-Guzmán, M.E. (1996). *Learning in two worlds.* White Plains, NY: Longman.

Reyes, M., & Halcón, J. (2001). *The best for our children: Critical perspectives on literacy for Latino students.* New York: Teachers College Press.

Smith, P.H., Jiménez, R.T., & Martínez-León, N.C. (2003). Other countries' literacies: What U.S. educators can learn from Mexican schools. *The Reading Teacher, 56,* 777–781.

Thomas, W., & Collier, V. (1997). *School effectiveness for language minority students.* Washington DC: National Clearinghouse for Bilingual Education.

Authentic assessment and system accountability

Anne Nelson

System accountability has assumed prime importance in the last ten years, right across Australia. Most states use some sort of "basic skills" testing as well as curriculum outcome statements against which student progress is measured.

In Victoria, schools are expected to structure their teaching around the Curriculum and Standards Framework (CSF), which was derived from the eight National Profiles.

CSF Levels are tied to particular age-grade expectations: Level 1 is the end of Prep, Level 2 the end of Grade 2, and so on. Each child's progress must be reported as "Beginning," "Consolidating," or "Established" within the relevant Level.

As there are four primary levels, each Victorian child might progress through 12 reporting levels in seven years—from "Beginning Level 1" to "Established Level 4." These reports are made in Mathematics, English, and Science.

Victorian schools are required to list the CSF level and sub-level of all children in their Annual Reports. In the midst of all this grading and levelling it would be easy to surrender authentic practices and just tick the boxes on a report form.

Assessing reading in an authentic way

Anne uses running records several times a term for all children, and more often for those in difficulty or at risk. These are noted on her own running record proforma and kept in a folder.

During guided reading sessions she writes observational notes and sometimes takes informal running records. These observations also record the children's attitudes, engagement, and enjoyment in the task.

Periodically the class has a special performance called "Guest Reader," in which children take turns to read rehearsed text to the others, while Anne takes notes on a guest reader proforma.

Anne's children participate in cross-age tutoring three times a week: "Tutors are trained to note important features of their tutee's reading. They record their comments on a proforma that they helped design."

Anne includes these tutor comments in her own assessment process.

Each child has their own small box of books from which they choose their own book to take home each day.

Teachers at Spensley St. have sorted the home reading books according to broad bands of levelled text, but allow children to borrow outside their supposed level, as their interests dictate. Also in the box is a communication book (an exercise book cut in half). The parent writes the date, title, and a brief comment whenever the child takes a book home to read. Sometimes children write their own evaluative comments in here too.

Anne: "I regularly write comments about the child's reading in here too, because it's part of my reporting process."

Thus Anne has extensive written data to draw on when assessing a child's reading progress, ranging from informal notes to a bank of running records.

Anne's assessment is essentially qualitative, rather than a quantitative measurement:

Reprinted from Fehring, H. (Ed.). (2003). *Literacy assessment: A collection of articles from the Australian Literacy Educators' Association* (pp. 76–80). Newark, DE: International Reading Association. Originally published in "From the Classroom," *Practically Primary* (February 1999), 4(1). Reprinted with permission of the Australian Literacy Educators' Association.

I don't calculate the percentage of errors. I really use them (the running records) for two reasons. One is to check that the child is choosing and reading books at an appropriate level.... I encourage them to balance reading in a comfortable way with taking a challenge. Second I look at the kinds of miscues to see the areas that need work and I note their strengths or gains.

Reporting to parents

This accumulated assessment data helps Anne make "on balance judgments" about each child, which she summarises on the school's Report Form. The reading descriptors for Levels 1, 2, and 3 are shown here (that is, the Victorian expectations for Prep to Grade 4).

The school does not refer to this report as a "profile" but its characteristics are comparable to the National Profile for English, only shorter and more manageable for parents.

Anne explains: "We have developed 'menus' from the CSF, using the Curriculum Focus Statements for each level and incorporating First Steps indicators. We refer to the menus during our planning days when we set the outcomes to focus on for the next term."

Using these menus as a type of school-based profile, Spensley St. teachers show each child's reading development over time.

Key statements from the menu are listed on the Report Form for parents. There are similar statements for Writing, Speaking and Listening, and Mathematics. (Science has not been developed yet.)

"There's a difference between the larger 'menu' and the actual outcome statements we select at any given time. Development over time is shown by keeping some of the outcome statements the same from semester to semester. New statements are added and others dropped according to the topic or genre or focus we've studied."

Key statements from the reading menu as shown on Spensley St.'s Student Progress Report

CSF Level 1
Engages in reading-like behavior, e.g., holds book correctly, turns pages
Invents stories to accompany pictures, using story-like phrases from text
Shows awareness of letter/sound relationships
Recognises a number of works in text

CSF Level 2
Uses strategies for interpreting text, including self-correction
Uses own knowledge and experiences to link to a variety of texts
Reads for meaning, has comprehension strategies
Selects appropriate texts

CSF Level 3
Reflects on text, e.g., plot, characterization, main idea
Clarifies or corrects meaning by pausing, re-reading, and reading on
Can verbalise own reading strategies
Attempts to work out meaning of unknown words

Comprehensive reporting

This article concentrates on "Reading," but Anne's assessment of her children is comprehensive. With "Writing," for example, she uses:

- Work samples to position the child on the writing menu.
- "Research Books" in which each child reports on what she's learnt from the current integrated unit of work. Children put their books together themselves, with teacher consultation. It shows spelling development, finished pieces, reading comprehension, even artwork. (This idea was adapted by Spensley St. teachers from an initiative of Heathcote Primary School, in country Victoria.)
- Projects, displayed around the room, often the result of group work.
- A class presentation for parents and other visitors, called "Ask the Expert" where children show and discuss projects or research (this activity also helps Anne gather data for assessing Listening and Speaking).

Self evaluations

Children at Spensley St. compile a "Self Evaluation Book," which is a student portfolio showing a few pieces of work from each term. Teachers and children jointly select English, Maths, and Integrated Unit samples, without teacher annotation. Many children, however, write evaluative comments for their work samples, for example, "I chose this work because it shows that I know about..."

These samples are discussed at parent teacher interview—children may attend their own interview—and the book is taken home at the end of the year, as a permanent record of work.

Formal self evaluations are included, in the form of learning logs. They are usually directed at the current unit of work. Sometimes children write more general self evaluations ("how I feel about reading/maths," etc.).

Two of Bethany's self evaluations in her end of year Self Evaluation Book

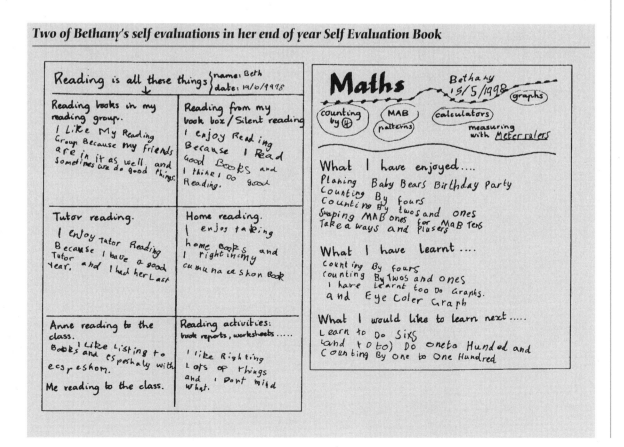

Meeting system requirements

When completed, the Student Progress Report is talked through at the parent—teacher interview. It's typically about eight pages long. The other records mentioned above, the Self-Evaluation Book, and the child's Research Book also inform the interview, and the child shows his or her projects and other work.

But very little of this rich array of data is required by the Victorian Department of Education. The system's requirement is simply that children be put onto a CSF Level, firstly for parent reporting, secondly for annual departmental reporting. Victorian schools are required to list the CSF Level of each and every child in an Annual School Report.

Because the outcome statements on the parent report form are labelled as "CSF Levels," the Victorian departmental requirements are easily met, without affecting the validity or authenticity of the extensive assessment practices.

Essentially, meeting these requirements is irrelevant and superfluous to the real purpose of the assessment—keeping track of kids in order to help them learn better.

PART 4

Creating a Literate Environment

The knowledge and skills detailed in Standards 1 through 3 are not independent of one another, and they all must be integrated to create a literate environment that fosters reading and writing development. Standard 4 emphasizes the use of foundational knowledge along with knowledge and skills related to using a wide range of instructional practices and curriculum materials in conjunction with assessment information at the individual, class, school, and district levels. The integration of these factors is crucial for developing reading instruction that meets the needs of every student. Standard 4 also emphasizes the crucial role that motivation plays in learning to read. The standard is as follows:

> **Candidates create a literate environment that fosters reading and writing by integrating foundational knowledge, use of instructional practices, approaches and methods, curriculum materials, and the appropriate use of assessments.**

The standard has four elements.

- **Element 4.1 Use students' interests, reading abilities, and backgrounds as foundations for the reading and writing program.**
Hunt's (1970) classic article is included in this collection because it reminds us that self-selection, interest, and motivation may have powerful effects on students' ability to read. The piece reminds us that our assessments of student reading ability are usually drawn from a limited set of passages and that as such they are merely estimates. Students' interests and motivation can make a difference, and the article shows us how those interests can be harnessed to motivate students and propel them even when learning to read is difficult.

Blake and Van Sickle (2001) report a case study of two dialect divergent high school students. They provide detailed and clear descriptions of the instruction offered to these students who were at risk of failing a state test that was required to receive a diploma rather than a certificate of attendance. Both students were successful in passing the test and did receive diplomas. The authors explore the implications of their work for teacher education.

Babbitt and Byrne (1999/2000) use three case studies to illustrate the dramatic impact of students' background and language on school achievement. The article is a must for reading professionals because it provides a good example of ways that emotional stresses affect students' lives and learning.

- **Element 4.2 Use a large supply of books, technology-based information, and nonprint materials representing multiple levels, broad interests, and cultural and linguistic backgrounds.**

Book-rich environments are important in fostering the love of reading. Ramos and Krashen (1998) report the effects of increasing children's access to books by a single trip to a public library. They argue that "simply providing interesting books for children is a powerful incentive for reading, perhaps the most powerful incentive possible." The reader may wish to revisit the Duffy-Hester article in Part 2, and all the pieces in Part 2, Element 2.3.

- **Element 4.3 Model reading and writing enthusiastically as valued lifelong activities.**

The Morrow, Barnhart, and Rooyakkers (2002) article focuses on integrating technology in a teacher education environment. It provides detailed descriptions of the strategies and practices used and also shows teacher educators "walking the talk" of technology and literacy. Wickstrom (2003) provides an additional example of a teacher educator modeling the integration of technology with literacy instruction. The author used a Web-based discussion board to promote reflection, encourage engagement, and develop collegiality in preservice teachers.

- **Element 4.4 Motivate learners to be lifelong readers.**

Sweet and Guthrie (1996) provide examples to demonstrate their general finding that children's motivations for literacy are multidimensional and diverse. They speak to internal and external motivation and conclude that

> There are places for both intrinsic and extrinsic motivation in every classroom. At times when skill building and behavior control are necessary, extrinsic incentives are useful. When higher order literacy and self-directed learning are desired, the importance of students' intrinsic motivation should increase. By aligning their motivational support system with their instructional practices, teachers can enhance the development of long-term literacy engagement.

Worthy (2002) reports survey data from intermediate-grade students. She reports that the studies reviewed in the column suggest that "students are savvy in their understanding of reading motivation. If we listen to students and attend to what they say about classroom instruction and reading materials, schools can have profound effects on students' motivation, engagement, and, ultimately, achievement." In a second article by Worthy (1998), the author tells the story of two reluctant middle school readers and makes suggestions for educators who want to improve students' reading motivation. The recommendations drawn from two case studies echo those in the other articles in this part: (1) Let students choose the books they read for class, (2) let students talk to their friends about what they like to read, and (3) get good books and material for students to read in the classroom.

The pieces in this part were chosen to illustrate the ways in which instructional practices and reading materials interact in complex ways that reading professionals must be sensitive to in creating literate environments. Motivation is a key to integrating all the elements of the standards and to creating successful schools, classrooms, and teachers.

Lyman C. Hunt, Jr.

The effect of self-selection, interest, and motivation upon independent, instructional, and frustrational levels

Tears welled up in his eyes. One or two trickled down his cheek. This 7-year-old boy with the round man-in-the-moon appearance was pretty well shook. Moments before he had been eagerly and willingly working away at writing sentences; he had been doing well. Then he encountered the monster word *were*. He could neither recognize it nor write it. For him it was a devastating experience. He quit trying. He couldn't remember a word he was supposed to know. Why so sensitive? Why the tears?

What would diagnosis reveal? What of levels of reading? How could assessment of independent, instructional, and frustration levels contribute to sound reading instruction in this situation? The interplay between interest, motivation, and self-direction on the one hand and the reading levels concept on the other needs careful consideration. In this particular instance, the evidence indicates that adults—both parents and professionals—as well as the child had been confused more than helped in this situation by concern for errors.

More is needed here than an assessment of reading levels. Granted that sound diagnosis is typically centered on a determination of reading levels commonly classified as independent, instructional, and frustration levels, such classification without a fairly sophisticated interpretation of inventory response is insufficient. Any instructional efforts easily go astray unless proper perspective is present. It is perspective about which one must be concerned.

Without question, the reading level concept has contributed greatly to efforts by teachers to teach readers on their own instructional terms. Through application of this concept, teachers have been learning to differentiate instruction. Utilization of the reader levels concept is not only valuable but commonplace. Yet for all its virtues, the conventional use of the reader level concept is not without significant limitations.

Hang up on errors

The concept of reading levels is often based on errors of recognition and comprehen-

Reprinted from *The Reading Teacher* (1996/1997), *50*, 278–282. Originally published in *The Reading Teacher* (1970), *24*, 146–151, 158.

sion. Making mistakes becomes the measure of performance. The more mistakes, the greater the frustration and the lower the corresponding reading level. Concentrating on errors is inherently negative. Unfortunately, efforts to eliminate the negative have resulted in failure to accentuate the positive.

This focus on errors tends to distort perceptions with regard to the primary goal of reading instruction. Mistakes become too important. Teachers tend to overreact to them; young readers become overly sensitive about making them. Once the inventory procedures are learned, teachers often see their role as essentially that of counting mistakes in word recognition. Mispronunciations, substitutions, omissions, repetitions, hesitations, and reversals become the object of teachers' attention if not affection. Counting mistakes can easily become a compulsive activity.

Preoccupation with keeping track of and correcting errors interferes with attending to meaningful reading. It becomes easy for teachers to forget that getting ideas from print is what reading is all about. It makes it easy for teachers to delude themselves that perfect recognition is necessary if acceptable comprehension is to be realized.

At this point teachers must order priorities. The issue concerns perfection of recognition on the one hand and the relativity of comprehension on the other. Conventionally, the premise is that good reading is 100% error-free. This is highly questionable. That all errors are equally bad is also assumed. Again this practice is questionable. Assessment is not necessarily made according to whether or not understandings gained are essential or important. The fact that some ideas are more important than others is overlooked.

It is further assumed that errors are fixed and somehow an integral part of the reader's response. Errors, in fact, are very much a function of the situation. Certainly the question of whether particular errors made in a testing or teaching situation will recur in precisely the same form must be raised.

Transcending the frustrational level

One phenomenon that contradicts the validity of the reading levels theory is readily observed. It is the case of the high-interest book and the low-powered reader. Every observant teacher has seen the highly motivated reader engrossed in a book which for him is obviously of considerable difficulty. But because interest and involvement are high, he persists in the pursuit of ideas and he gets some.

Certainly in such instances the reader does not get all the ideas, not even all important ideas, but he does get enough to sustain his interest. If oral reading renditions were required, his performance would be catastrophic; the material would be classified as well beyond the frustration level. However, when he has chosen the material to read because of personal interest, he can break many of the barriers. Strong interest can frequently cause the reader to transcend not only his independent but also his so-called instructional level. Such is the power of self-motivation.

Given the opportunity, then, the reader who finds a really good book for him, the book that has ideas he truly wants to learn about, frequently will outdo his own instructional level of performance. When the criteria of complete comprehension and perfect oral reading are used, then the power of the interest factor is markedly reduced. By contrast, when the classroom atmosphere encourages self-selection, usual reading level performances become less meaningful. This author has watched many readers spend many rewarding moments with material that by any standard inventory would be classified as too difficult.

The primary consideration centers on the relativity of comprehension. The reader is encouraged to get as many ideas as possible regardless of the number of unknown words. Obtaining a few ideas of importance to the reader is viewed as more vital than getting all the ideas of importance to the teacher. Teacher guidance and assistance can encourage the reader in his search for meaning regardless of the restrictions imposed by standard reading levels.

A variety of reader assists provided by the teacher help the reader transcend his conventional reading levels. The first and most important aid given by the teacher lies in questions asked. The sense of all questions is such that it causes the reader to reflect on his grasp of the ideas. None is more significant than: "Could you get some of the important ideas?" or "Could you follow the ideas as you were reading along?" The teacher, through the ensuing discussion with the reader, helps him focus on the search for meaning. It is amazing how much some readers weak in recognition can get.

The following questions aid in realizing this goal:

1. Did you have a good reading period today? Did you read well? Did you get a lot done?
2. Did you read better today than yesterday?
3. Were you able to concentrate today on your silent reading?
4. Did the ideas in the book hold your attention? Did you have the feeling of moving right along with them?
5. Did you have the feeling of wanting to go ahead faster to find out what happened? Were you constantly moving ahead to get to the next good part?
6. Was it hard for you to keep your mind on what you were reading today?
7. Were you bothered by others or by outside noises?
8. Could you keep the ideas in your book straight in your mind?
9. Did you get mixed up in any place? Did you have to go back and straighten yourself out?
10. Were there words you did not know? How did you figure them out?
11. What did you do when you got to the good parts? Did you read faster or slower?
12. Were you always counting to see how many pages you had to go? Were you wondering how long it would take you to finish?
13. Were you kind of hoping that the book would go on and on—that it would not really end?

By generating a discussion about the nature, quality, and quantity of reading accomplished during silent reading time, the teacher helps to build a concept within each student about the kind of reader he is becoming and of what each needs to do to improve his own reading. Thus the concept of what the good reader does emerges. This concept of the good reader, and what one must do to become one, is the foundation of improved reading performance by each reader.

The theory of relativity

Basically the teacher must realize that much learning at the idea level can occur in spite of a fairly high frequency of mistakes. Whether a relatively acceptable standard of comprehension is gained depends on the teacher's orientation. Teachers can learn to give readers assists that aid understanding in spite of errors made on word recognition. It's a matter of attitude.

To a certain extent teachers must learn how to ignore errors rather than merely count and correct them. The hang-up is on requiring perfection from the outset. This is an impossi-

ble standard for the low-powered reader. A tolerance level for errors can be markedly higher than current standards permit. Much greater success can be realized by working for the perfect standard over a relatively longer period of time (several years in some cases) rather than requiring perfection continuously from the outset. By emphasizing silent reading and tolerating mistakes rather than indulging in endless oral reading and abusing those who make them, ultimately better readers can be developed.

Current convention supports the practice of resorting to greater use of oral reading as the number of mechanical errors increases. The opposite should hold. When oral reading is inadequate, it should be used less. Standards for low-powered readers for oral reading should be lowered.

The reading situation must be turned into a search for ideas. The search should be done silently. Even in group reading each reader can find, by himself, answers to questions. Teacher's commands and questions serve as guides to the reader's silent search for ideas.

USSR but not the Union of Soviet Socialist Republics

USSR should have a special meaning for reading as well as for social studies. The particular meaning of USSR differs for each area, however. For the reading teacher, USSR concerns a fundamental reading skill. Nothing in the area of skill development is of greater consequence. USSR spelled out is Uninterrupted Sustained Silent Reading. USSR is the essence of reading power; the ability to keep going with ideas in print. Without it the reader is crippled; with the power of sustained silent reading the reader is on his own, he can propel himself through print. He is an independent reader and does not depend on outside direction by the teacher.

USSR can be cultivated. The environment in a reading class can be established so that everyone—especially the low-powered readers—can develop greater power of sustained silent reading. To accomplish this the teacher must make silent reading the primary activity of the reading period. Establishing goals so that increasingly greater increments of time are spent in uninterrupted silent reading is fundamental. The skillful and persistent teacher can help the low-powered readers realize real albeit slow progress in this crucial area of skill development. Time charts can be maintained, or daily logs indicating amounts of time spent in pursuit of ideas by oneself can be kept. Even small increases in time spent in silent reading should be rewarded. Basically it is a matter of commitment on the teacher's part.

One teacher's testimony

The testimony of a second-grade teacher perhaps will place one of these ideas in perspective.

In early September I undertook the time-consuming but what I then thought to be the valuable task of assessing the reading performance of all youngsters in my room. More accurately, the process of discerning reading levels by using individual informal inventories could better be called determining reading disabilities; for I was interested not only in obtaining indications of reading levels, but also in recording and categorizing these mistakes. I spent much time going over word lists in basal readers which the youngsters had read and listening to samples of oral reading in order to note both the frequency and types of mistakes. More time was consumed in making comprehension checks, analyzing results and examining the implications of these results.

Based upon these results I proceeded to formulate instructional plans using a basal series that would provide time for the consideration of individual reading problems along with regular group work. Youngsters were grouped in two ways—one grouping for directed reading instruction, another more flexible grouping for needed supplementary work in various skill areas. This program was an effort to give consideration to individual needs.

Progress was slow. The children were struggling but not because of the difficulty of the work. They were appropriately placed according to level. But because the children were concentrating on overcoming previously experienced difficulty, the tasks were unpleasant for them. They wanted to avoid the tasks that were presented and to evade unpleasant associations connected with such activities.

The results of the program proved devastating for children and teacher; for in my effort to assess instructional reading levels and determine problem areas, I had overlooked an important element. I had been stressing a negative rather than a positive measurement. I had been more concerned with what the youngsters could not do than with what they could

do! I had given the youngsters attention for the inabilities and had failed to stress the importance of their abilities.

Of course, this realization involves a philosophical point of view. The effects of stressing either disabilities or abilities can be completely opposite. With youngsters who have achieved well, perhaps the point of view is not of great consequence. With youngsters who have made little academic progress, however, the philosophical and practical point of view becomes a matter of primary importance. Attitudes affect one's approach to the teaching-learning situation. The effect on youngsters can be astounding when one stresses positive rather than the negative.

With the new emphasis on positive performance, the reading program was revised to stress strengths rather than weaknesses. Student creativity and inventiveness regardless of inherent limitations were utilized in the further development of already established abilities. Skills were taught informally when needed, seldom to the entire class, but individually or in small groups. Children were encouraged to pace themselves in their basals with the firm understanding that if they desired or needed help, they are to consult a student helper or the teacher. By capitalizing on their strong points and stressing what they could do, the youngsters were able to make progress in their weak areas. The process of improvement became a natural by-product of positive experiences in the youngster's strong areas. Deficiencies began to diminish without a concentrated effort to specifically overcome these deficiencies. Self-concepts and attitudes toward the reading process improved.

What next?

What about the tears? The happy ending to the story cannot be written yet. Steps to reduce tension have been taken. The fact that he has learned many words is being highlighted. He is being told that if he can learn some words he can learn others, even though it may take him longer. He is being helped to get ideas from print even though he does make mistakes on the monster word *were*. However, the tough task lies ahead; certain adults in his life—both parents and teachers—must be convinced that he is not suffering from a mysterious malady named dyslexia.

Mary E. Blake
Meta Van Sickle

Helping linguistically diverse students share what they know

When students in this case study improved their ability to code-switch from the local dialect to Standard English, they improved their academic achievement — particularly in science and math.

For the past 20 years or more the education of African American children in the United States has been a topic of inquiry (Cartwright, 1993; Hale-Benson, 1986; Hoover, Dabney, & Lewis, 1990; Kozol, 1991), with the policies about the language use of many of these children becoming entangled in controversy (Berdan, 1980; Delpit, 1995). Witness the debate that erupted when the Oakland School Board in California acknowledged Ebonics as the primary language of its students. Further furor followed the Board's advocating the use of Ebonics to facilitate children's acquisition of Standard English—not because it was a pass-through language on the way to acceptable oral fluency but because it was a legitimate system of communication (Perry, 1997). The rationale of the School Board stemmed from the idea that knowing both ways of using language would help Oakland teachers foster their students' acquisition and use of more traditional forms of English (Perry & Delpit, 1997). However, the outcome of the Oakland situation being moot, the roots of this controversy related to African American children, their language learning, and overall academic achievement go back much, much further.

A succinct picture of the background of dialect diversity and education of African American students emerges through both the available literature and our experiences. Although the early, traditional lines of research related to dialect have focused on appropriate language development versus language problems, they have also pointed to the

Reprinted from *Journal of Adolescent & Adult Literacy* (2001), *44*, 468–475.

fact that academic failure of African American children appears to be "the result of political and cultural conflict within the classroom" (Labov, 1972, p. 35). Other approaches have investigated teacher expectations (Good & Brophy, 1987) and teacher and student attitudes (Dandy, 1988; Goodman & Buck, 1973, 1997) as sources of conflict inhibiting academic achievement. While much of the information about academic achievement relates to literacy (Leibowicz, 1984), more recent work focuses on the many indications that African American and Hispanic students lag behind their standard English-speaking peers in the language-rich areas of math and science (National Science Foundation, 1996; Short, 1994), reflecting the close relationship between reading literacy and science literacy (Wellman, 1978).

On a positive note, many teachers believe that students who exhibit language diversity actually know much more than the test scores reflect (Brophy & Good, 1974). Dialect isn't destiny; individuals have the capacity to acquire other modes of speaking and writing (The Linguistic Society of America, 1997). Evidence exists of code-switching between dialects to enhance educational and social functioning (Wolfram, 1998). Combining the ability to code-switch between African American English and Standard English with appropriate hands-on inquiry teaching in science and math may have an impact on the academic achievement of this significant group of students. These beliefs formed the backdrop for our work with African American students on one of the Sea Islands in South Carolina, USA.

Research rationale and study structure

Keeping the prior research in mind, we entered this study knowing that we would have to learn the students' island dialect, and constantly diagnose their understanding of the content being presented at each exchange of information (verbal, nonverbal, and written). The students in our study presented great dialect divergence and resistance to the existing teaching methods and classroom management. These students had the ability to complete the work and subsequently pass the tests. It was our job during the project to learn their dialect and to use it to convey science and mathematics content. Our ultimate goal was to

help the students develop the ability to code-switch between their island dialect and Standard English to communicate their understandings of the science and math concepts and pass mainstream courses and standardized tests.

We chose to use the format of a case study because we wanted to look at specific cases in depth. This research method was used "precisely because the researcher wishes to understand the particular in depth, not to find out what is generally true of many" (Merriam, 1998, p. 208). We specifically kept careful notes about our work with the students and recorded information on a case-by-case basis. We were able to use purposeful sampling in order to keep the research focus at the forefront (McMillan, 1992). The criteria for the purposeful sampling was dialect diversity, failure to pass the exit exam, retention in special education, and lowest level or no course work in math or science as well as limited exposure to English literature classes. Further criteria for selecting these students was the consistent inability to pass various sections of the South Carolina Exit Exam (SCEE) assessing reading, writing, math, and science, a requirement for graduation from high school in South Carolina.

The SCEE exam is based on standards that have been approved by the South Carolina State Board of Education. This is a norm-referenced test in the above-mentioned content areas. The total score for each section is 800, and students must score above 600 to pass. Students who do not pass this basic-skills exam receive a certificate of attendance rather than a high school diploma. The data gathered for each of the students in the case study were in the traditional forms of notes, tapes of conversations, and artifacts concerning progress.

At the request of a resource specialist from the Sea Island high school, we began to work with her students who were having difficulty passing the SCEE. "We" includes a language development person (Blake) and a science education specialist from the College of Charleston (Van Sickle). Because we started with a resource student who exhibited strong characteristics of dialect diversity, we decided to include an English teacher with a background in linguistics as part of our team. Later that year the group expanded to include two other students and another teacher. In the second year, three new students from the class of the resource specialist were added to the program. The third year we worked with nine students.

Our students in this case study were at risk for failing the SCEE and exhibited dialect diversity. The overall demographics of the school population are 84% African American, 13% white, and 3% Hispanic. Because the majority of students at this school are considered dialect divergent, our instructional strategies focused on empowering them with strategies to aid code-switching (Wolfram, 1998) in their own communication (reading and writing) and in understanding math and science concepts. Currently, students on Johns Island typically score 45–48% lower on tests in these areas than more affluent students in neighboring districts, reflecting the national trend of lower scores for economically disadvantaged students.

Our students were relegated to the Resource Room because of failure on a multitude of standardized tests including the SCEE. In addition to being assigned to the least academically challenging courses in the school, each of our students was several years behind peers in completing academic course work. Another outstanding characteristic of the students was their predominant and consistent use of the island dialect, which was represented not only in word usage and grammar but also in pronunciation and tonality. There was a mutual lack of regard between our students and most of their teachers—with the exceptions being a few teachers who believed that the students knew more and were capable of much more than their academic records indicated.

Teaching tactics used

Initially, time was spent talking about the students' interests, using various levels and phases of inquiry. The levels of inquiry were what's the question, what's the procedure, and what's the finding? The iterative phases of inquiry involved exploration, questioning, and testing variables in the areas of science and math. As we helped the students develop new concepts, we made notes and diagnoses about their oral and written responses. Concurrent with our observations, we chose to implement a variety of instructional strategies designed to help the students enhance their language and content learning. The techniques involved were undertaken to accelerate rather than remediate the students and were accompanied by focused discussions, conversations related to differentiating fact and inference, writing workshop and language experience activities, and dialogue journals. Students' reactions to the strategies were noted on a regular basis.

The format for the writing workshop activities was a modification of that developed by Atwell (1987). After each student drafted an initial paper, subsequent sessions most often consisted of the following activities:

1. very brief minilessons addressing mechanics, descriptions, and lead-in paragraphs (Clemmons & Laase, 1995),
2. dialogue about the status of ongoing work,
3. actual writing, and
4. sharing what was written.

The workshop activities consumed most of the time spent with each student and conducting the ongoing dialogue was critical to the progress of each paper. Work was frequently done at the word processor to take advantage of the spontaneity and fluency fostered by the combination of talk and technology (Reinking & Bridwell-Bowes, 1986).

Language experience was the critical part of the writing workshop activities in that everything the students wrote about was based on their personal experiences, which helped them move from the known experiences to the unknown language of communicating about them (Ashton-Warner, 1963). Some of the communication and writing was done as a response to experiences in the classroom; other longer pieces were based on relevant personal experiences that were of great interest to the students. Reflecting Ashton-Warner's work (1958, 1963, 1972) we "used the children's experiences as a basis from which to build learning" (Tierney & Readence, 2000, p. 218). Their own "cultural diversity in the classroom became a strength" (p. 218). By understanding the students' cultural experiences through their own eyes, we were better able to assess their basic knowledge and to enhance their ability to communicate that information to those from other cultures.

Dialogue journals were a direct outgrowth of our use of students' experiences as a basis for promoting writing (Staton, 1980). Our approach to this strategy was to provide an inquiry or writing experience in the classroom and then to follow it with a dialogue journal entry. To facilitate the initial recording of ideas, each entry was started as a dictated experience (Stauffer, 1970). One of the authors would record the date and the salutation on chart paper in the front of the room. Individual students would then offer statements about the recently completed activity that would be recorded. Then the students would complete the entry on their own. Each week the teacher would respond to each student's entry to encourage the students in their work and model the mechanics of appropriate entries. The interaction between the students and their classroom teacher further enhanced their growth as writers.

What we noted

Our initial notes reveal that dialect diversity and community culture are closely related. Observations of the students and consultation with the linguistics specialist involved appear to validate our belief that the Sea Island culture appears to have produced the following modifications to African American English:

1. use of *been* or *had* to replace -*ed* in the past tense,
2. simplification of pronouns to *i (e)*,
3. use of /o/ to indicate possession—John *o*,
4. /um/ to mean it or them, and
5. /okay—all right/ to indicate completion of the dialogue.

In addition to recognizing specific features of the dialect, we realized that speakers were creating visual pictures through their words—pictures easily visible to those who knew the same Johns Island dialect code. However, we can only speak for the students with whom we worked and cannot make any statements about how consistent these observations are with the overall student population. We've included detailed descriptions of our work with two of the students to illustrate how they progressed during our time with them. Students' names are pseudonyms.

Demain

Demain was a 19-year-old senior who was a star football player and captain of the team. He had both an intense interest in and undeniable talent for sports. He was regularly reviewed by college scouts, was part of the Southeast Regional All-Star Team, and consistently received accolades for his prowess in sports. On the other hand, he was ineligible for recruitment because he had failed all three parts of the SCEE three times which kept him from receiving a high school diploma. He was enrolled in classes to help him pass this test; however, the classes, which used traditional linear, sequential methods of teaching, did not meet his needs.

We offer the following example to illustrate Demain's inability to attend to details and analyze sufficiently to accomplish a task related to understanding fractions. He appeared unable to understand the concept of fractions; perhaps because he was not even aware that he could or should number each of the 12 sections that the researcher (R) asked him (D) to create.

R: Fold that paper so you get 12 equal parts.
D: (folds for 45 seconds)
R: How many did you get?
D: 10.
R: You got 10. I didn't get 12; I need 12 equal parts.

For the activity to work each part had to be equal. Demain's sections were not equal, so he had to measure them until he could get the appropriate measurement and all the parts were equal. (To successfully create fractions in this problem, all of the parts had to have equal measurement. This was the great difficulty that Demain was having.)

D: Okay. (refolds) I mean this looks like 45.
R: [It's] 4 point 5. Where does your decimal point go?
D: Point 5.
R: Measure one of your boxes and see if it is 4.5.
D: (measures) Mm hmm.
R. Measure a different box and see if it's 4.5.
D: Mm hmm.
R: Measure another box.
D: Mm hmm.

Demain kept measuring until he got the 12 equal parts. When questioned about the difficulties he was having, he responded that he was looking at the whole piece of paper rather than the 12 sections on which he was supposed to focus. He was looking at the big picture rather than the specific details.

Demain's writing from the beginning of our work with him lacked detail. We include part of the final version of a story about a football game to illustrate how a clearer sequence is evident with more details included. The first version created a picture, but it was not completely sequential or rich enough in specific details for a non-island speaker to understand his position or importance in the North/South game. At the conclusion of our work with Demain, he was able to produce work that was not only sequential but rich in detail. He was able to do this not only in English class but in math and science. The following is an excerpt from his final version of the North/South game.

Demain's story on the North/South game

The game is where I played noseguard position. The game was about 15 minutes in each quarter and included a halftime. As soon as the game was about to start the coaches and the player from each school walked onto the field ands they introduced you to the crowd. The players walked to the side that they play on. Game began with a kickoff to the South. For the first 2 or 3 minutes the South was playing offense and the North team was on defened. The South team made a clear drive down the field and had to punt because we came into fourth down. The North team got the ball and also tried to get a touchdown. That's when I came on the field. Everyone is lined up, and the center snapped the ball to the Quarterback. That's when I made my move. I passed the center; then the Quarterback is ready to hand the ball off to the running back. I hit the running back and caused a fumble. The ball is sitting an the field; the coach from the North team started calling "the ball, the ball" to his team and that's when I jumped on top of it. I gave the ball back, and then South team went back on the field. The first play they threw a interception to the North team. Then the South team lost the ball to the North. Now I came back on the field. The center snapped the ball to the Quarterback, but I did the same thing again. I tackled the running back, but this time he held onto the ball so he kept the ball. But this time, the center got smarter and everytime he snapped the ball, he went for my leg. After that I was popping all around. The two guards started going for my legs and I was "on ice" [couldn't do anything].

Demain's final version included specific details in a sequential way that could be understood easily. Demain subsequently passed all three sections of the SCEE and received his high school diploma. He is now attending a small college because of the numerous gaps in his education.

Josiah

Josiah was a 15-year-old African American high school sophomore, and he was assigned to the resource room. Although the most mathematically minded of the group, he had the greatest gaps in his math education. Other than occasional illness, he consistently attended our sessions.

Josiah could easily tell stories in the traditional island dialect. The following is an example of something he wrote.

Prompt: Tell me a story about matches and starting a fire.

Josiah: i go inne the hou and gette the match. i go uppee [more traditional form would be up nee] the hou. i lightee the match. My grand daddy haul me out and whoop my ass.

This is a story that takes place in the fall. It includes gathering leaves under a house and setting fire to them. These actions created smoke, and the boy's grandfather hauled him from under the house. Our island students understood the first version of the story completely and were laughing hysterically at it. We didn't get it at all until the students translated it for us. Other writing samples illustrated confusion over verb tense as well as lack of description and detail in a more traditional sense.

Josiah's final writing project was a language experience story about rap music. The following excerpts illustrate the attention to detail that Josiah eventually exhibited.

Rap
Rap means rhyming things together.
All the artists write and sing about everyday life.
It's something that you could dance to.
The beat sounds good with what the
person is saying.
It doesn't always have to be fast;

it could be slow too.
Josiah doesn't like Will Smith
because he doesn't
express Josiah's feelings.
Josiah likes R+B better,
but we'll try a rap about Trevor.
Trevor's a rap star
He could start rapping at the bar.
And he could go far.
Josiah feels uncool—
don't want to stay in school.
He wants to go to the pool
Then he'll be cool.

Josiah was also able to describe the essence of tops through an early drawing. Our original challenge to the students was to figure out what made a top work, a classic example of an inquiry task. Josiah created a top, and his words were "top be balance." He was correct, and drew a picture to represent his meaning. The next step to to get Josiah to describe the parts that created the essence or whole meaning of what makes a top work. On the drawing he added the words "must be in the center"—code-switching from his home language to the school language.

What we learned

Both the students benefited from the targeted strategies and made progress in passing the various portions of the SCEE. They passed the reading, writing, and math portions of the test and graduated with diplomas—not certificates of attendance, as they did more than just "their time." Both students gained over 100 points in each of the three testing areas to put their scores in the passing range. Demain is now enrolled in a college program. We hypothesize that through consistent language interactions with us the students became more sensitive to the language of the school and the language of the test. They figured out how to code-switch from the island dialect to Standard English and convey their knowledge in a way that would benefit them in school.

Overall, three main themes emerged from our work: timeframe reference, language development, and code-switching. As we listened to our students' stories, wrote with them, and engaged in inquiry activities, it became apparent that the way they look at the world is different from our way. It also became clear that we would have to do content-specific language development to enable these students to pass tests and communicate with the outside world. Because our goal was not to eradicate their native dialect and culture, we focused on code-switching (Wolfram, 1998) as a means of preserving their heritage while giving them an alternative way to communicate about the same topics.

It is or it isn't—no past, no future. There are certain inconsistencies in time frame reference that showed up as we worked with our students. References to time can consistently be seen only in some of Demain's last sessions with us. A sense of past and future is not a characteristic of the students' world view that can be described in their island dialect; note that most verbs in Demain's writing are used in the present tense.

Josiah's original story is a traditional rendering of the island way of speech. It is told in the present tense. Unless you were an island resident or speaker, you would have no way of knowing what time of the year the story takes place. The story demonstrates the value of inference in the island dialect and culture.

Confusion about verbs and time frame reference shows up in the use of double verbs, such as "is was" or "was play." At times it also resulted in reversion to the singular present tense. To help the students deal with this confusion, we engaged in continuing dialogues about and revisions of multiple drafts of their work. What appeared to aid most in empowering their code-switching and enhancing their writing was specific one-on-one coaching in the writing process.

Language development. For our students, language development was a very complex issue. Often they omitted words or did not know the specific content words. While their island language patterns could create holistic pictures of what we were doing, the dialect did not contain enough words to communicate precise meaning to those unfamiliar with it.

If you look at some of the initial verbal interactions and writings of each of the students, you will notice a paucity of details. A notable example is

Demain's habitual response of "Mm hmm." This finding relates to the observation that the dialect spoken on Johns Island is highly inferential, and most of the details and some of the words are often left out. However, island speakers get the big picture (the whole) from what was said.

Code-switching. All of our students could switch between social and academic languages. In many instances, students were able to understand the science or math concept being presented through the inquiry activity, and they accurately described the learning through the use of island language. For example, when Josiah said "Top be balance," he was indicating that the essence of the object was that it could be balanced. His statement was absolutely correct, but it was looking at the whole of what made a top work. In this case the school science view of how a top works would be to look at the parts or variables: the distribution of mass, the symmetry of distance from the axle, and the center of gravity or how high the top should be on the axle.

For this activity, switching between codes began with an initial drawing where the student wrote his description; recognizing his accurate comprehension of the essence of a top, one of us provided the detailed variable words of *axle, symmetry, mass, height,* and *radius,* as well as *balance.* He immediately began incorporating these words into his next drawing. By the time he was through, he not only had a basic understanding of the whole, he also had the language to communicate about the the parts and pieces (variables of the whole) to others. In addition, he and the other student involved were able to apply all of these understandings (whole and part) to their daily lives in dealing with automobile maintenance and the balancing of tires.

In the writing of stories, initial efforts tended to illustrate the inferential nature of the island language through the absence of details (the parts and pieces that would be variables in science). Through the use of writing workshop activities and continual questioning for details and sequence, a picture emerged that would be comprehensible to both island speakers and those communicating in a standard code.

Teacher education implications

Our experiences with these students have shown how important it is for teacher education programs to acknowledge differences in languages and the ways in which languages make meaning. Schools of education need to promote the types of teaching and learning strategies that don't discount alternative ways of viewing the world and communicating about it.

Because we valued their island dialect, we never tried to get the students to stop using it. What we did try to do was help them acquire some specific terminology, sequencing skills, and alternative grammar structures to use in language, math, and science situations where they had to acquire knowledge through inquiry.

The outcomes of our work indicate that the issues of dialect diversity and its impact on the communication of knowledge need to be recognized and acknowledged by both dialect and nondialect speakers. Teachers of dialect-divergent students need to be aware that there is such a thing as code-switching amongst the various versions of English, and they need to know how to promote such a skill within their classrooms. In that way, the students of the Sea Islands will be able to demonstrate their academic achievements and give testament to the efforts of their teachers. Conversely, the Sea Island students need to appreciate the value of their island heritage and dialect and to be able to implement the same code-switching to communicate with nonisland inhabitants.

In terms of teacher preparation, the project indicates that future teachers need to be exposed to many different cultures and dialects. Initially, students need to recognize both the universals of being human and the unique qualities of their own cultures. Then they need to be able to figure out how different cultures express these human universals. Preservice teachers have to decide how to match the culture with the teaching strategies. As teachers they then need to encourage two things: the use of the child's native dialect or language to communicate within the culture and the use of code-switching to Standard English to communicate with nondialect speakers.

REFERENCES

Ashton-Warner, S. (1958). *Spinster*. New York: Simon & Schuster.

Ashton-Warner, S. (1963). *Teacher*. New York: Simon & Schuster.

Ashton-Warner, S. (1972). *Spearpoint*. New York: Knopf.

Atwell, N. (1987). *In the middle: Writing, reading and learning with adolescents*. Portsmouth, NH: Heinemann.

Berdan, R. (1980). Knowledge into practice: Delivering research to teachers. In M.F. Whiteman (Ed.), *Reactions to Ann Arbor: Vernacular Black English and education* (pp. 77–84). Arlington, VA: Center for Applied Linguistics.

Brophy J., & Good, T. (1974). *Teacher-student relationships: Causes and consequences*. New York: Holt, Rinehart & Winston.

Cartwright, M. (1993). *For the children: Lessons from a visionary principal*. New York: Doubleday.

Clemmons, J., & Laase, L. (1995) *Language arts mini-lessons*. New York: Scholastic.

Dandy, E. (1988, April). *Dialect differences: Do they interfere?* Paper presented at the Fourth Annual Conference of Minority Advising Program and Minority Recruitment Officers, Savannah, GA.

Delpit, L. (1995). *Other people's children: Cultural conflict in the classroom*. New York: New Press.

Good, T., & Brophy, J. (1987). *Looking in classrooms*. New York: Harper & Row.

Goodman, K.S., & Buck, C.L. (1973). *Theoretically based studies of patterns of miscues in oral reading performance*. Tech. Rep. USOE Project 9-0375. Washington, DC: U.S. Department of Education.

Goodman, K.S., & Buck, C.L. (1997). Dialect barriers to reading comprehension revisited. *The Reading Teacher, 50*, 454–459.

Hale-Benson, J.E. (1986). *Black children: Their roots, culture, and learning styles*. Baltimore: Johns Hopkins University Press.

Hoover, M.R., Dabney, N., & Lewis, S. (Eds.). (1990). *Successful black and minority schools*. San Francisco: Julian Richardson.

Kozol, J. (1991). *Savage inequalities: Children in American schools*. New York: Crown.

Labov, W. (1972). *Language in the inner city: Studies in the Black English vernacular*. Philadelphia: University of Pennsylvania Press.

Leibowicz, J. (1984). ERIC/RCS report: Classrooms, teachers, and nonstandard speakers. *Language Arts, 61*(1), 88–91.

Linguistic Society of America. (1997). Resolution on Ebonics. *Rethinking Schools, 12*(1), 27.

Merriam, S. (1998). *Qualitative research and case study applications in education*. San Francisco: Jossey-Bass.

McMillan, J.H., Reed, D., & Bishop, A. (1992). *A qualitative study of resilient at-risk students. Review of Literature.* (ERIC Document Reproduction Service ED 389 779)

National Science Foundation. (1996). *The learning curve: What we are discovering about U.S. science and mathematics education*. (NSF No. 96-53). Arlington, VA: Author.

Perry, T. (1997). I'on know why they be trippin. *Rethinking Schools, 12*(1), 3–5.

Perry, T., & Delpit, L. (1997). An introduction from the guest editors. *Rethinking Schools, 12*(1), 3.

Reinking, D., & Bridwell-Bowles, L. (1986). Computers in reading and writing. In R. Barr, M. Kamil, P. Mosenthal, & P.D. Pearson (Eds.), *Handbook of reading research* (Vol. II, pp. 310–340). New York: Longman.

Short, D. (1994). Expanding middle school horizons: Integrating language culture, and social studies. *TESOL Quarterly, 28*, 581–586.

Staton, J. (1980). Writing and counseling: Using a dialogue journal. *Language Arts, 57*, 514–518.

Stauffer, R.G. (1970). *The language-experience approach to the teaching of reading*. New York: Harper & Row.

Tierney, R., & Readence, J. (2000). *Reading strategies and practices: A compendium* (5th ed.). Boston: Allyn & Bacon.

Wellman, R.T. (1978). Science: A basic for language and reading development. In M.B. Rowe (Ed.), *What research says to the science teacher* (Vol. I, pp. 1–12). Washington, DC: National Science Teachers Association.

Wolfram, W. (1998). Linguistic and sociolinguistic requisites for teaching language. In J.S. Simmons & L. Bains (Eds.), *Language study in middle school, high school, and beyond* (pp. 79-109). Newark, DE: International Reading Association.

Susan Babbitt
Maureen Byrne

Finding the keys to educational progress in urban youth: Three case studies

Three 13-year-olds received individual after-school instruction from a certified reading specialist. The students' level of academic functioning and emotional situation and how their needs were met are described.

Teaching 13-year-olds can be difficult, for they live in a precarious world of transition, straddling childhood and adolescence. When these students have reading or academic problems, teaching becomes even more complicated. Working with urban teenagers who have social or emotional issues caused by life stresses as well as learning problems presents a particularly difficult challenge.

What follows are case studies of three different 13-year-olds, clients of an urban multidisciplinary mental health agency, who participated in the agency's after-school individualized reading program. The students have all been given pseudonyms. For these students, emotional stresses have greatly interfered with their learning and educational progress. What will be shown are the successes and failures that occurred with these students during the course of 9 months of tutoring, as their life stresses continued to affect their educational lives.

Diego: Man of the family

Diego was in a self-contained sixth-grade special education class for severely learning disabled students. He had been in special education since the second grade. He was the oldest boy in a household of five cared for by his mother, a single parent. Charming and sweet, sporting a loopy grin and a diamond stud in his left ear, Diego was earnest and reasonably motivated once engaged. He could generally

Reprinted from *Journal of Adolescent & Adult Literacy* (1999/2000), 43, 368–378.

be counted on to work consistently without interruption for up to 30 minutes. The key was to get him to show up for the sessions.

Marisol: Teenage sophisticate

Marisol was in a regular seventh-grade class, homogeneously grouped to include all seventh graders in her school who read below the 10th percentile as measured by previous citywide testing. She received special education instruction in the form of daily Resource Room teaching. Marisol was very attractive and looked older than her 13 years. She became depressed as a child, and that depression had been made worse by the death of her young mother in the past year. Marisol lived in a household of nine children held together by a strong maternal grandmother who emigrated from Puerto Rico as a young woman and managed to bring a number of family members to the mainland U.S. Marisol came to every session. The key was to get her to do anything.

Lynette: Scholarship student

Lynette was in the eighth grade at an expensive independent school. On scholarship from the school and the agency, she had attended private school since the third grade. Gaps in her knowledge and certain organizational difficulties had become more apparent in the sixth grade, and Lynette had been receiving tutoring at the agency since the seventh grade. Tall for her age and substantially overweight, Lynette stood out at school for her size, for her socioeconomic level, and for being African American. Lynette had carried adult responsibilities in her family for years. She came to every session and was generally motivated. The key was to give her enough foundation so that her potential was not sapped and depleted by family concerns and crises.

Diverse students, common themes

While these students had very different academic and learning needs, there were, nonetheless, some common themes. All three were at that critical developmental stage that occurs during the middle school years, when adolescents' belief in their own competency may decline (Harter, Whitesell, & Kowlaski, 1992). Indeed, researchers suggest the stakes are even higher for students with multiple problems; they are at the greatest risk of dropping out of school during these years (Caldwell & Ginthier, 1996; Dunn & Griggs, 1988; Hobbs, 1990; Tuma, 1989).

Language was a factor for two of the three students. Diego and Marisol, both born in the U.S., grew up in households where Spanish was spoken, although by their own admission they were not fluent in Spanish. More research needs to be done on the impact of this circumstance on literacy acquisition. Despite the growing multiculturalism of the U.S., during the past 10 years only 3% of all literacy research has dealt with cultural or linguistic diversity and less than 1% of the children's literature produced annually features Latino families or communities (Jiménez, Moll, Rodríguez-Brown, & Barrera, 1999).

For each of the three students motivation was an issue, although in different ways. Two of the three students displayed little evidence of what researchers have called "intrinsic" motivation, or motivation internal to the learner (Deci, Vallerand, Pelletier, & Ryan, 1991; Sweet & Guthrie, 1996; Wigfield, 1994). Yet we know from past research that this is necessary in order for children to employ strategies for processing text beyond the literal level (Guthrie, Alao, & Rinehart, 1997).

For Diego and Marisol, motivation was essentially extrinsic, that is, it was imposed on them from someone or for something outside themselves, resulting in compliance motivation (Sweet & Guthrie, 1996). For example, Diego was in serious trouble in school, failing all his subjects. His mother, who had an intense concern for Diego's education and learning, insisted with the support of the family social worker that Diego attend the reading sessions (Baumann & Thomas, 1997). Marisol was not failing in school, but her attendance at the agency was mandated by her grandmother, who recognized Marisol's need for multiple services. While Marisol may eventually rebel from this tight control, at this point in her life she had no choice.

In contrast, intrinsic motivation for educational achievement seemed a possible goal for Lynette. She had been rewarded for her own academic potential by being sent to a school where academic achievement was esteemed. However, living in a family with no previous experience with the intensity and competitiveness of a college-preparatory school made it difficult for her to nurture and sustain inner motivation. As will be shown, nurturing that inner motivation became a major objective of her educational plan.

Educational plan for Diego

At the beginning of the academic year, Diego was assessed as being able to decode and comprehend at the third-grade level, using *Aesop's Stories for Pleasure Reading* (Dolch, Dolch, & Jackson, 1951) as text for an informal reading inventory. On the Surveys of Problem-Solving & Education Skills (SPES, 1986) his decoding score was comparable to that achieved on the informal assessment, but comprehension scores were even lower, presenting the instructor with a student scoring 5 or more years below grade level in reading.

Writing and spelling were also difficult for him. On a written personal questionnaire that he completed in September, Diego wrote "bih clos" for "Buy clothes," "becas she nis" for "because she is nice," and "I get in fithet" for "I get in fights." His invented spelling suggests that despite some knowledge of the alphabetic code, Diego had difficulty retrieving commonly used words.

The educational plan for Diego noted his history of erratic attendance at previous educational activities at the agency. However, it was also observed that he seemed to respond well to incentives. That, coupled with his apparent eagerness to please, were to be the linchpins in motivating him to attend regularly.

A clear statement of attendance standards, and the firm willingness of the teacher to apply them, were critical components of Diego's treatment plan. His family life suffered from a severe lack of order and consistency. Diego had spent several years in foster care as the result of his mother's substance abuse behavior. His father had been incarcerated and subsequently deported to Ecuador. His 21-year-old sister lived in the household but without her four children, all of whom had been placed in foster care. Diego's younger brother was dying of a lung disease. Diego's mother, free of drugs for several years, was struggling to hold the family together.

The tutor determined that Diego would need a structured, skills-based educational approach. He had severe problems at the word level that prevented him from reading connected text and utilizing comprehension strategies. Fast and accurate word recognition is related to proficient reading as well as skillful reading comprehension and was deemed essential for Diego's progress (Adams, 1990; Perfetti, 1985; Stanovich, Cunningham, & Freeman, 1984). Further, despite the fact that 75% of students master the alphabetic code without explicit instruction (Liberman, Shankweiler, & Liberman, 1989), Diego obviously had difficulty automatically applying it to text.

Mastery of specific high-frequency words thus became the criterion for the initial contracts between teacher and student. Diego was to receive prizes for being able to read, write, and spell correctly words in isolation and in sentences. The use of such extrinsic rewards would do little beyond encouraging student compliance, and the instructional methodology was clearly rudimentary, yet the instructor viewed this as a necessary first step in order to motivate Diego to attend the sessions (Sweet & Guthrie, 1996).

The ability to spell the word in a sentence was an important, and more difficult, part of the task. At issue was Diego's ability to process two or more cognitive demands simultaneously. Students with language difficulties present a challenge for the instructor in terms of both the manner and timing in which multiple pieces of verbal information are presented (Bryant, 1980).

As instruction proceeded, certain things became clear. For one thing, the highly structured nature of the task was very appealing to Diego. The predictable nature of the sessions provided a contrast to the unpredictability of his family life, which was dominated by the health problems of the younger brother and the erratic behavior of the oldest sister. Also, he was able to achieve some successes each week, as he made his way through the list of words. For this reason, the goal and the reward seemed reasonable, attainable, and sufficiently challenging (Turner, 1997). Through the end of October, he had missed only one session, and that was an excused absence.

As Diego was making relatively good progress in learning to read and spell the high-frequency words, it was also necessary to ensure that he was reading connected text at his instructional level and given practice applying decoding skills as one of many strategies when encountering difficult material. For a while, he and the teacher read short fables from *Aesop's Stories for Pleasure Reading* (Dolch et al., 1951). Diego was able to comprehend the stories, as measured by his ability to retell them, make accurate predictions, or answer inferential questions. His oral reading, however, remained slow and deliberate, and time limits precluded the application of strategies such as repeated readings (Morris, Ervin, & Conrad, 1996; Samuels, 1979).

During this period, new high-frequency words were being introduced. By the middle of December, Diego seemed less interested in working for specific prizes, but still continued to work diligently at learning his words, a sign that his motivation was becoming more intrinsic. It appeared that this activity managed to advance but not overwhelm Diego's abilities (Turner, 1997). Also, Diego's decreasing need for prizes confirmed our belief that while extrinsic rewards are initially helpful in getting students to do a difficult task, these rewards become less necessary as social interaction and satisfaction with task completion take over (Sweet & Guthrie, 1996).

Unfortunately, Diego's attendance became more problematic at this time. While his absences were usually excused and were occasioned by health problems in the family, they nonetheless interfered with the momentum that had been building. Even worse, Diego received his report card showing he was failing every subject. Ultimately, we agreed upon a system that required Diego to remember his appointments by means of notes he put up in his apartment. The importance of making Diego responsible for getting to sessions and assuming ownership of his own learning was considered integral to a successful outcome (Au, Schen, Kawakami, & Herman, 1990).

For the next several months, Diego's attendance was perfect, and his punctuality, while still somewhat problematic, did improve. During this period, lessons focused less on skills work and more on high-interest, contextual reading (for example, a book about snakes that he chose). The use of such integrated instruction, unifying reading, writing, and science, as well as student-directed material, aided in the gradual development of Diego's intrinsic motivation and his investment in the lessons (Guthrie et al., 1997; Sweet & Guthrie, 1996).

Over the course of the sessions, Diego's tutor noticed that he learned concepts more completely when information was initially presented to him in concrete fashion. Thus, wherever possible, he and the tutor would act out things to understand the content. For example, the notion of comparative sizes of various snakes became more meaningful to Diego when he and the instructor actually paced off together the lengths of a boa, an anaconda, and a python.

By mid-March, Diego was making progress in his tutoring sessions. He was, however, continuing to have difficulties in school, as his brother's medical condition worsened and his sister's problems escalated. In spite of these stressors, for the remaining 2 months of the school term Diego was reasonably on time and missed only a few sessions, always for legitimate reasons. During that time, the family moved into a new apartment away from the oldest daughter, and Diego's mother worked with her social worker to arrange a lung transplant for her youngest son.

At the start of the year, the biggest concern about Diego had been his willingness to attend after-school reading sessions. Establishing a contract between instructor and student and providing external rewards as an incentive both to come to sessions and to work while there proved to be effective in the beginning, but became increasingly less important as time went on. Rather, successful task completion coupled with the need to connect with a stable and caring adult were proving to be strong motivators for Diego once he established a pattern of coming to his sessions. His overall yearly attendance was 80%.

Not all of the educational goals set for Diego at the beginning of the year were realized, and in some cases work was not even begun. Fortunately, though, slowing down does not mean stopping. In June, Diego again took the SPES test. While he continued to be markedly below grade level, his progress exceeded expectations, as he improved one grade level in decoding and three levels in comprehension.

In our view, a major reason for this improvement involved Diego's commitment to the tutoring and his desire to work to see if he could "get" it. What the 9 months of tutoring seemed to have given him were less the specific skills and strategies, although they were certainly important, but more the confidence that he would be able to use those skills and strategies to make some sense out of printed text, which may have represented a shift in self-perception. Diego had, in fact, become "task-involved," assuming greater control over his own learning (Johnson & Winograd, 1985).

Diego's year was deemed a success. He had overcome his attendance problems, demonstrated improvement in his skills, and seemed to have made a commitment to "coming to reading." He graduated from the sixth grade and was accepted at an alternative junior high school with a special education seventh-grade class. He continued with the reading program at the agency for another year.

Educational plan for Marisol

Marisol was reading at the third-grade level, 4 years below her grade placement. On the SPES (1987), she passed all sections at the third-grade level, able to process both isolated words and connected text.

Motivation for Marisol was hindered by two factors. For one thing, she perceived text that she was able to decode as much too childish. Also, her fragile emotional situation often interfered with her willingness to cooperate. Unlike Diego, she was moody and temperamental. She suffered from enuresis as well as depression. Although Diego did not have a father in the household, he did have a mother who cared deeply for him even though life stressors sometimes left her unable to carry out effective parenting. Marisol's much-loved mother had died at 27 years of age, after a lingering illness, when Marisol was 12 years old. In 2 years, Marisol would be the age that her mother had been when Marisol was born.

On the positive side, Marisol demonstrated a flair for fashion and style and expressed interest in pursuing a career as a hair stylist. Like many of her peers, Marisol was beginning to think about her future (Kos, 1991). If anything, her expectations were too low.

Unlike Diego, Marisol was able to write and spell with reasonable accuracy, albeit at a level much lower than her current grade. Her ability to decode unfamiliar words, however, was limited, fitting the profile of many severely disabled readers (Olson, Kliegl, Davidson, & Foltz, 1985; Vellutino, 1979). A psychoeducational evaluation done 4 years earlier indicated the existence of possible cognitive and memory limitations as well as problems with receptive language and verbal fluency. Such difficulties with language proficiency could be expected to have a negative effect on the acquisition of reading skills (Mather, 1992).

Given the severe delay in Marisol's reading skills, it was felt that, like Diego, she could benefit from at least a measure of structured, skills-based instruction. Research findings suggest, in fact, that severely disabled readers need direct instruction; they do not learn "by osmosis" (Haring & Bateman, 1997, p. 148). Glass analysis (Glass & Glass, 1976), an analytic decoding method, was felt to be one appropriate instructional tool. It was decided to use this method because it provides the older student with the opportunity to decode more sophisticated words sooner, rather than later, in the instructional process. For someone like Marisol, sophisticated in so many other ways, this aspect was important.

The Glass analysis words were also used to expand Marisol's limited vocabulary. She often did not know the meaning of the words she was decoding, such as *shabby, establish, brag, scold, brash, ignore,* and *editor.* While this was certainly not formalized vocabulary study, and in fact, is not consistent with the prescribed Glass methodology, it nonetheless served the purpose of providing discussions about language and increasing her knowledge of more complex vocabulary. Although Marisol often appeared depressed and remote during much of her sessions, she nonetheless responded reasonably well to the Glass analysis approach, meaning that she did not refuse to do the task.

Another goal for Marisol, that of reading a minimum amount of connected text each week, proved to be much more difficult. Over a 4-week period several choices were tried from various popular book series, all of which were at her instructional level and would have been theoretically ideal books for teaching both comprehension and word attack skills. However, none were successful, and Marisol continued to essentially disengage herself from any part of the lesson that involved text reading. Possibly Marisol was defending herself from an activity that in the past had been fraught with failure and that she felt might erode her fragile sense of competency (Guthrie et al., 1997; Johnson & Winograd, 1985).

At this juncture the instructor decided to read aloud to Marisol with the goals of exposing her to more language and narrative structure and allowing her to employ many of the comprehension strategies used by good readers (Elley, 1989; Ivey, 1999). For a time, Marisol enjoyed listening to fairy tales from *A Treasury of Stories From H.C. Andersen* (Koralek, 1996). We have found that children referred to our clinic often prefer to work with fairy tales and magical stories. Possibly, these stories are removed from their own stresses yet describe conflict and difficulties that the characters must, and do, overcome (Bettleheim, 1977).

An unexpected benefit of the read-aloud strategy came when Marisol asked to read some of the text herself. Perhaps she was responding to the smaller type and more complex text, which appeared "older" than some of the children's series. Also, Marisol was not being required to read, only to listen. By deciding herself that she wanted to read, she was controlling the situation, rather than having an adult tell her what to do, something very important for young adolescents (Anders & Pritchard, 1993). Present research findings suggest that we can turn over some control to students while maintaining responsibility for flow and content (Pearson, 1996). For children who experience many traumas and uncertainties in life, such as Marisol, being able to control a situation becomes very important. Unfortunately, the success with this genre was short-lived. Marisol's depression made it difficult for her to sustain an interest in almost anything, a situation that had clear implications for her educational progress (Goleman, 1995).

Findings on what makes teachers effective suggest that the failure to adapt or to acknowledge students' feedback is characteristic of poor teaching (Babad, Bernieri, & Rosenthal, 1991; Wubbels, Creton, & Holvast, 1988). As a result of Marisol's resistance, it had become increasingly clear that if there were to be any success, the educational goals must be realistic and decided upon reciprocally. It was hoped that giving Marisol her own choice of reading material would result in increased comprehension and motivation (Andersen, Shirey, Wilson, & Fielding, 1987;

Turner, 1997). However, Marisol's motivation remained fragile and volatile.

Ultimately, her teacher realized that her work with Marisol must somehow connect with those things in Marisol's life that were emotionally sustaining to her at the moment, and to which she would pay attention, if the teacher were going to be even moderately effective with her (King, 1985; Rissler & Steinberg, 1991). Remembering that Marisol had mentioned that she wanted to be a hair stylist, her teacher found several hair style magazines directed toward African American and Latina audiences. These magazines were interesting to Marisol and related to her needs (Farnan, 1996; Ivey, 1999). She was willing to try to read from them, even though the text presented certain problems. The language was relatively complex and occasionally metaphoric; the vocabulary sophisticated. However, this meant that short sections of text were filled with educational opportunities that Marisol did not resist.

The principal structured teaching activity that arose from the shared reading was vocabulary acquisition. Researchers have shown that direct instruction informs reading comprehension when new words can be integrated into already existing schema through a natural print environment (Beck & McKeown, 1991; Harmon, 1998). Contextualized word study has been found to be particularly useful for students with verbal processing difficulties. Because some words recurred in many of the issues, Marisol was able to see them in use and reinforce her learning (Harmon, 1998).

Writing, too, was something Marisol was occasionally interested in. If included intermittently, at appropriate times, it proved to be a powerful instructional vehicle. To be successful, Marisol had to have a story she wanted to tell. During the 9 months, this happened only once, but it enabled her teacher to work with her over five sessions, during which Marisol wrote, rewrote, and edited three drafts before completing her final version. Her motivation to tell this story was high. Because Marisol's expressive language was limited, the effort to produce the story was particularly valuable because she had to search, and re-search, her mind to find appropriate words. With each revision, as she would listen to her teacher read her words back to her, she found new things to say.

Unfortunately, this experience could not be duplicated. However, for a short period after this she became interested in writing poetry. Using *Honey, I Love* by Eloise Greenfield (1986) and *Spin a Soft Black Song* by Nikki Giovanni (1988), she wrote several poems modeled after their work. Provided with the structure and basic key words from individual poems by Greenfield and Giovanni, Marisol was able to create her own poems. Using the computer to write them in attractive fonts and with appropriate illustrations gave her a product that she could be proud of.

Ultimately, Marisol presented a major dilemma for the reading staff at the agency. Clearly in need of academic remediation, she had an attendance rate of well over 90% at her twice-weekly reading sessions. However, her engagement in the learning activities was erratic and often minimal. While she was not confrontational and seemed to have developed a reasonable relationship with the teacher, her depression and general neediness were severe enough to interfere greatly with her learning. With a waiting list of other children who needed remediation, what should be done with a student like Marisol on whom so much effort had been expended, with seemingly little result? The situation seemed to demand a sort of educational triage.

From a teaching perspective, the 9 months of tutoring appeared relatively unproductive. To continue to work with her the next year seemed problematic. However, in Marisol's case, the benefits of an effective multidisciplinary approach became quite clear. What appeared to be problematic for the educational staff was viewed quite differently by the case psychologist. While the inherent difficulties were acknowledged, the bottom line consideration was whether *any* progress had been made during the 9 months and whether Marisol *needed* the educational services. If so, then commitment to the client's well-being demanded ongoing remediation.

As it turned out, there was, indeed, some measure of progress. Marisol did show improvement on the informally administered SPES (1987) assessment, improving one grade level, from the third to the fourth, on one decoding and two comprehension subtests. She remained, however, 4 years below actual grade placement.

As the direct result of close and frank communication between educators and psychologists, a decision was made to continue Marisol in the reading program for 1 more year and to work collaboratively to ensure an appropriate high school placement for Marisol.

In what was a possible indication that the psychologists were right and the educators wrong, when Marisol heard the news that she had to "come to reading" again next year, she seemed pleased. Perhaps she realized that the teacher's educational choices for her throughout the year had been thoughtful and caring attempts to meet her inarticulated needs.

Educational plan for Lynette

Unlike Diego and Marisol, Lynette did not have a reading disability. Instead, she was reading on grade level and attending a respected private school that was associated with a well-regarded graduate school of education. There were multiple goals for this plan: to assist Lynette with organizational skills such that she could successfully meet the high demands of five content areas, to support her unspoken appreciation of learning and knowledge, and to convince her that she had the ability to succeed on her own in a competitive academic environment.

While Lynette's intellectual ability had never been questioned, it had become clear that she needed help using that intellect to produce a consistent body of academic work that reflected it. Her homework was done erratically, usually during free periods at school. Assignments that were completed were often buried in a seemingly bottomless book bag. In general, her approach to the details of producing academic work was disorganized and unsystematic.

Many of these characteristics are familiar to those working with this age group. In some cases, maturation is all that is needed to effect a cure. In other cases, the lack of organization may be a lifelong trait, but not necessarily an impediment to success. In Lynette's case, however, a timely measure of academic success was critical in order to sustain her scholarship.

As a result, the need to teach organizational and study skills and to emphasize the importance of self-monitoring became critical components of Lynette's educational plan. As the year progressed, periodic "book bag checks" were made, and occasionally, half a session might be devoted to filing material in the proper place in Lynette's binder.

As important as this was, an even more important component of her educational plan was the need to show Lynette how to study, to make her aware that when she did study she could do well. The instructor wanted to instill in Lynette the sense that learning was exciting and liberating, and could be an end in itself, so that she could "feel the flow" (Csikzentmihaly & Csikzentmihaly, 1988).

To that end, Lynette and her teacher continued the pattern that had begun the past year; that is, in each session they identified and worked on the most challenging language arts or social studies homework for the week. This year the task was to do more of the same, but with the added goal of weaning Lynette from her teacher's support, because she would no longer have a tutor as a resource when she reached high school. Lynette needed to know that she could do it on her own; the instructor's task was to "get out of her way" (Pearson, 1996).

Sessions with Lynette were much more straightforward and conventional than those with Diego and Marisol. She was motivated to do her work, she realized that this was the best time she had during the week to work on her homework, and she took an intellectual interest in most of the subjects. In contrast to Diego and Marisol, Lynette had an attention span that allowed the instructor to work with her for an hour or more at a time.

Unlike Marisol and Diego, Lynette lived within a nuclear, working-class family. Although Lynette's mother had the strength to escape from what she herself described as a highly dysfunctional home situation, she had nonetheless brought into her own family many of the same behaviors she had run away from. Her marriage to a much older man was troubled. In addition, she had two younger children who were learning disabled, one severely. Her effective and ongoing intervention in the latter's educational life engaged much of her time and effort, often depleting her of the energy needed for other family issues.

To these tensions in Lynette's life were added the burdens occasioned by being a minority scholarship student in an independent school whose population was essentially white, educated, and middle or upper class. Such a situation may create conflict within the student as he or she daily in-

habits two different worlds and has to make adjustments constantly in order to adapt to each world. In addition, there may be conflict within the family because the educational opportunity presented to the child may be perceived as a threat: the more successful the education, the greater the potential distance from the family—socially, economically, and culturally (Ogbu, 1993). Indeed, Lynette's father was at odds with his wife regarding Lynette's schooling and was known to be vocal in his distrust of what Lynette was "becoming."

In addition to these stressors, Lynette's family struggled with how best to support the educational demands being placed on her. While her mother tried to provide quiet places and study times for Lynette, her own inconsistent personality made it difficult for her to be successful. As a result, Lynette had to struggle more than most of her classmates to meet the educational requirements of her school.

The stressors on Lynette affected her academic life somewhat differently than did stressors in the lives of Diego and Marisol. For example, her frequent school lateness kept her from attending important early morning math review sessions or sometimes even first period classes. Occasionally she was not allowed to accompany her class on trips because her harried mother felt that on those days Lynette's time was better spent at home helping in her licensed day care practice. Also, Lynette had to attend weekly church meetings on school nights and all day on Sundays, which sometimes upset the delicate balance between church and school activities.

Fortunately, Lynette's academic performance showed continuing growth during her eighth-grade year. While her school did not give letter grades on their reports, she showed that she was able to handle the intellectual content of her subjects. Although she continued having problems getting work done on time, she was increasingly able to work on major academic tasks at home, an accomplishment that boded well for high school success.

In addition, she acted the part of the Wizard in her eighth-grade play, *The Wizard of Oz*, participated in the class's study of mythology, and ran as her party's candidate for President pro tempore of the class senate during a unit on the U.S. government. After lengthy intervention on the part of the agency, her mother allowed Lynette to accompany her class on the year-end trip to Washington, D.C.

On Lynette's final exams, she achieved solid Bs in both subjects in which she had been tutored. She felt especially proud that she had studied for the exams on her own.

As she enters high school, Lynette and her family will no longer be clients of the agency. While they are still at risk, after many years at the agency, staff felt enough gains had been made for them to attempt to function on their own. Lynette will be attending a small, alternative public high school which is a tier below the city's rigorously selective public high schools but which is nonetheless academically challenging.

At her eighth-grade graduation, Lynette's family repeatedly emphasized that the next milestone for Lynette would be her marriage. Although the agency staff who attended understood their concern, they insisted, with equal emphasis, that they expected to be invited to her college graduation as well.

Finding the key to educational success

In varying degrees, the 9 months of tutoring had been positive for each of these students, an outcome we would not necessarily have predicted when we began our case studies. In each situation, several things conspired to make the year a relative success.

First, and possibly foremost, we have found that progress in meeting educational goals for these children in this clinical setting is more often achieved if a relationship develops between student and teacher, a relationship made more possible by what Tharp and Gallimore (1980) term "responsive teaching." Teacher ingenuity becomes critical to the learning process, as educational goals and strategies may have to be radically adjusted or even abandoned in order to find ways to engage the student. The resulting relationship with a stable, caring adult becomes the connector to achieving longer term, more distant educational goals that otherwise seem very removed from their daily lives. Thus, social exchange between individuals, in this case teacher and student, becomes a source of cognitive growth (Gardner, 1983; Rogoff, 1990; Turner, 1997; Vygotsky, 1978).

In our experience, this is the most critical component to success in working with this at-risk population, as we have seen children and young people, described as trouble-makers at school, often with multiple suspensions, come with reasonable regularity to their reading sessions at the agency because they appear to have made that all important connection with their teachers. Indeed, educators are becoming increasingly aware of the social aspects of instruction and their influence on cognitive outcomes (Pearson, 1996). Clearly, this connection is much more easily made and sustained in a one-to-one setting.

Second, events in these families' lives in this particular year did not spin out of control. In those instances when this might have happened, the agency's therapeutic staff was there to manage and contain any incipient crises. The importance of that support cannot be underestimated as it once again points to the significance of emotional stresses on the learning process and the importance of recognizing and dealing with them.

If there is any lesson to be drawn from this admittedly qualitative research with a very small sample, it is probably one based essentially on common sense. Educational success for urban youth with learning and emotional stressors is certainly achievable when the teacher finds that key, unique to each child, which allows them together to overcome obstacles that might otherwise be insurmountable. The foundations of that success, however, are best supported when the family has available the resources of educational and mental health professionals who are able to work together for the benefit of both child and family. For most of us, but particularly for these children, the world of the mind does not exist apart from the worlds of the heart and the soul.

REFERENCES
Adams, M.J. (1990). *Beginning to read.* Cambridge, MA: The MIT Press.
Anders, P.L., & Pritchard, T.G. (1993). Integrated language curriculum and instruction for the middle grades. *Elementary School Journal, 93,* 611–624.
Anderson, R.C., Shirey, L.L., Wilson, P.T., & Fielding, L.G. (1987). Interestingness of children's reading material. In R.E. Snow & M.J. Farr (Eds.), *Aptitude learning and instruction: Cognitive and affective process analysis.* (pp. 287–299) Hillsdale, NJ: Erlbaum.

Au, K.H., Scheu, J.A., Kawakami, A.J., & Herman, P.A. (1990). Assessment and accountability in a whole literacy curriculum. *The Reading Teacher, 43,* 574–578.

Babad, E., Bernieri, F., & Rosenthal, R. (1991). Students as judges of teachers' verbal and nonverbal behavior. *American Educational Journal, 28*(1), 211–234.

Baumann, J.F., & Thomas, D. (1997). If you can pass Momma's tests, then she knows you're getting your education: A case study of support for literacy learning within an African-American family. *The Reading Teacher, 51,* 108–120.

Beck, I., & McKeown, M.G. (1991). Conditions of vocabulary acquisition. In R. Barr, M. Kamil, P. Rosenthal, & P.D. Pearson (Eds.), *Handbook of reading research: Vol. II.* (pp. 789–814). New York: Macmillan.

Bettleheim, B. (1977). *The uses of enchantment.* New York: Vintage.

Bryant, N.D. (1980). The effects of some instructional variables on the learning of handicapped and nonhandicapped populations: A review. *Integrative Reviews of Research, 1,* 1–70.

Caldwell, G.P., & Ginthier, D.W. (1996). Differences in learning styles of low socio-economic status for low and high achievers. *Education, 117,* 141–147.

Csikzentmihalyi, M., & Csikzentmihalyi, I.S. (1988). *Optimal experience.* Cambridge, England: Cambridge University Press.

Deci, E.L., Vallerand, R.J., Pelletier, L.G., & Ryan, E.M. (1991). Motivation and education: The self-determination perspective. *Educational Psychologist, 26,* 325–346.

Dolch, E.W., Dolch, M.P., & Jackson, B.F. (1951). *Aesop's stories for pleasure reading.* Champaign, IL: Garrard.

Dunn, R., & Griggs, S.A. (1988). High school dropouts: Do they learn differently from those who remain in school? *The Principal, 34,* 1–8.

Elley, W.B. (1989). Vocabulary acquisition from listening to stories. *Reading Research Quarterly, 24,* 174–187.

Farnan, N. (1996). Connecting adolescents and reading: Goals at the middle level. *Journal of Adolescent & Adult Literacy, 39,* 436–445.

Gardner, H. (1983). *Frames of mind: The theory of multiple intelligences.* New York: Basic Books.

Giovanni, N. (1988). *Spin a soft black song.* New York: Farrar, Straus & Giroux.

Glass, G.G., & Glass, E.W. (1976). *Glass analysis for decoding only.* Garden City, NY: Easier-to-Learn.

Goleman, D. (1995). *Emotional intelligence.* New York: Bantam.

Greenfield, E. (1986). *Honey, I love.* New York: Harper Trophy.

Guthrie, J., Alao, S., & Rinehart, J. (1997). Engagement in reading for young adolescents. *Journal of Adolescent & Adult Literacy, 40,* 438–446.

Haring, N.G., & Bateman B. (1997). *Teaching the learning disabled child.* Englewood Cliffs, NJ: Prentice-Hall.

Harmon, J.M. (1998). Vocabulary teaching and learning in a seventh-grade literature-based classroom. *Journal of Adolescent & Adult Literacy, 41,* 518–531.

Harter, S., Whitesell, N., & Kowlaski, P. (1992). Individual differences in the effects of educational transitions on young adolescents' perceptions of competence and motivational orientation. *American Educational Research Journal, 29,* 777–807.

Hobbs, D. (1990). School based community development: Making connections for improved learning. In S. Raferty & D. Mulkey (Eds.), *The role of rural schools in community development* (pp. 57–64). Mississippi State, MS: Southern Rural Development Center.

Ivey, G. (1999). A multicase study in middle-school: Complexities among adolescent readers. *Reading Research Quarterly, 34,* 172–193.

Jiménez, R.T., Moll, L., Rodríquez-Brown, F., & Barrera, R. (1999). Conversations: Latina and Latino researchers interact on issues related to literacy learning. *Reading Research Quarterly, 34,* 217–230.

Johnson, P.H., & Winograd, P.N. (1985). Passive failure in reading. *Journal of Reading Behavior, 17,* 279–301.

King, D.H. (1985). *Writing skills for the adolescent.* Cambridge, MA: Educators Publishing Service.

Koralek, J. (reteller). (1996). *A treasury of stories from H.C. Andersen.* New York: Kingfisher.

Kos, R. (1991). Persistence of reading disabilities: The voices of four middle school students. *American Educational Research Journal, 28,* 875–895.

Liberman, I.Y., Shankweiler, D.P., & Liberman, A.M. (1989). The alphabetic principle and learning to read. In D.P. Shankweiler & A.M. Liberman (Eds.), *Phonology and reading disabilities* (pp. 1–35). Ann Arbor, MI: University of Michigan Press.

Mather, N. (1992). Whole language reading instruction for students with learning disabilities: Caught in the crossfire. *Learning Disabilities Research and Practice, 7,* 87–95.

Morris, D., Ervin, C., & Conrad, K. (1996). A case study of middle school reading disability. *The Reading Teacher, 49,* 368–377.

Ogbu, J.U. (1993). Variability in minority school performance: A problem in search of an explanation. In E. Jacob & C. Jordan (Eds.), *Minority education: Anthropological perspectives* (pp. 83–111). Norwood, NJ: Ablex.

Olson, R., Kliegl, R., Davidson, B., & Foltz, G. (1985). Individual and developmental differences in reading disabilities. In T. Waller (Ed.), *Reading research: Advances in theory and practice* (pp. 1–64). London: Academic Press.

Pearson, P.D. (1996). Reclaiming the center. In M. Graves, P. van den Broek, & B.M. Taylor (Eds.), *The first R: Every child's right to read* (pp. 259–274). New York: Teachers College Press.

Perfetti, C.A. (1985). *Reading ability.* New York: Oxford University Press.

Rissler, J., & Steinburg, C. (1991). In practice. *Training and Development, 45,* 11–12.

Rogoff, B. (1990). *Apprenticeship in thinking: Cognitive development in social context.* New York: Oxford University Press.

Samuels, S.J. (1979). The method of repeated readings. *The Reading Teacher, 32,* 403–408.

Stanovich, K.E., Cunningham, A.E., & Freeman, D.J. (1984). Intelligence, cognitive skills, and early reading progress. *Reading Research Quarterly, 19*, 278–303.

Sweet, A.P., & Guthrie, J.T. (1996). How children's motivations relate to literacy development and instruction. *The Reading Teacher, 49*, 660–662.

Tharp, R.G., & Gallimore, R. (1993). Teaching mind in society: Teaching schooling and literate discourse. In L.C. Moll (Ed.), *Vygotsky and education* (pp. 175–205). Cambridge, England: Press Syndicate of the University of Cambridge.

Tuma, J.M. (1989). Mental health services for children: The state of the art. *American Psychologist, 44*, 188–189.

Turner, J.C. (1997). Starting right: Strategies for engaging young literacy learners. In J.T. Guthrie & A. Wigfield (Eds.), *Reading engagement: Motivating readers through integrated instruction* (pp. 183–204). Newark, DE: International Reading Association.

Vellutino, F.R. (1979). *Dyslexia: Theory and research.* Cambridge, MA: MIT Press.

Vygotsky, L. (1978). *Mind in society: The development of higher psychological processes.* Cambridge, MA: Harvard University Press.

Wigfield, A. (1994). Expectancy-value theory of achievement motivation: A developmental perspective. *Educational Psychology Review, 6*, 49–78.

Wubbels, T., Creton, H., & Holvast, A. (1988). Undesirable classroom situation: A systems communication perspective. *Interchange, 19*, 25–40.

RAPID RESEARCH REPORT

Francisco Ramos
Stephen Krashen

The impact of one trip to the public library: Making books available may be the best incentive for reading

It is well established that children read more when they have more access to books (Krashen, 1993). Children in many schools, however, have little access to books because of the poor condition of some school libraries (Allington, Guice, Baker, Michaelson, & Li, 1995; Krashen, 1996; Pucci, 1994). Here we describe a program, developed by bookless teachers, that attempted to improve students' access to books.

Twenty second-grade and 84 third-grade Hispanic students in an inner city school in Los Angeles, California, USA, served as subjects. All children came from print-poor homes. At school, their access to books was limited to a weekly 30-minute visit to the school library, where they were allowed to check out only one book per visit.

To provide the children with greater access to books, four teachers organized monthly visits to the neighborhood public library during school time, but before it was open to the public in the morning. This allowed the children to explore the library, share books, and not be constrained by the need to remain quiet.

The trips to the library significantly increased access to books: Each student was allowed to check out 10 books, which suddenly produced a substantial classroom library for use during sustained silent reading time. In addition, students were allowed to take the books home. Reading the new books was voluntary, and there were no reading logs or written assignments connected to the reading. Students' parents were, how-

ever, asked to sign a form each day, confirming that they had seen the book the child brought home, in order to avoid losses and subsequent fines from the public library.

Two anonymous surveys were run 3 weeks after the first visit to the public library, one for students and one for their parents (see Table). It was clear that the children enjoyed their visit; most reported reading more, that reading was easier, and that they wanted to return to the library. Parents' responses were consistent with the children's responses and tended to show even more enthusiasm.

During parent-teacher conferences, held 7 weeks after the first visit to the library and 2 weeks after a second visit, parents assured teachers that the level of interest in reading continued.

When asked what they thought contributed to their children's increased interest in books, 22% of the parents felt that the fact that students went as a group, with their friends, was an important factor. But 67% of the students asked their parents to take them back to the library after the first visit, on their own.

There are, of course, other explanations for our encouraging results. Both parents and children could have been attempting to "please the experimenter"; that is, give responses that they thought we were looking for. The results are so strong, however, that we must conclude that at least some of the increased enthusiasm is genuine.

While we plan to continue to bring children to the public library, we do not feel that the implication of our study is that schools should simply take more advantage of the public library to supply a print-rich environment for children. The solution must come from school. We were lucky to have a cooperative, well-supplied public library close to the school. Others are not so lucky.

The clearest implication of our study is that simply providing interesting books for children is a powerful incentive for reading, perhaps the most powerful incentive possible. This conclusion is consistent with research showing that extrinsic incentives for reading have not been successful, while improving access to books has been successful in encouraging reading (Krashen & McQuillan, 1996). Our study not only confirms that providing interesting reading itself is an excellent motivator, it also shows the powerful impact even a single exposure to books can have.

Authors' note

We thank Jose M. Estrada, Dorothy McGuire, and Isela Mendez, the other participants in this project, who enthusiastically took on the task of facilitating students' access to books.

References
Allington, R., Guice, S., Baker, K., Michaelson, N., & Li, S. (1995). Access to books: Variations in schools and classrooms. *The*

Language and Literacy Spectrum, 5,
23 – 24.

Krashen, S. (1993). *The power of reading*.
Englewood, CO: Libraries Unlimited.

Krashen, S. (1996). *Every person a reader*.
Culver City, CA: Language Education
Associates.

Krashen, S., & McQuillan, J. (1996). *The
case for late intervention: Once a good
reader, always a good reader*. Culver City,
CA: Language Education Associates.

Pucci, S. (1994). Supporting Spanish language literacy: Latino children and free
reading resources in schools. *Bilingual
Research Journal, 18*, 67 – 82.

Reactions to library visit

Child survey (*n* = 93)
First time visited the public library: 52%
Returned to the library since the visit: 62%
Returned to the library since the visit; had never been there before: 23%
Would like to return to the library with the school again: 75%
Reading more since the library visit: 75%
Feel reading is easier now: 82%

Parent survey (*n* = 75)
Child more interested in reading since visiting the library: 96%
Notice improvement in child's reading: 94%
Child spends more time with books: 94%
Child reads aloud to family member daily: 96%
Would like the library visiting program to continue: 100%
Child has asked parent to take him/her to the library since the visit: 67%

Lesley Mandel Morrow
Steven Barnhart
Debra Rooyakkers

Integrating technology with the teaching of an early literacy course

The early literacy course described used many kinds of technology to improve teaching and learning.

While studying to become a reading specialist, Debbi Rooyakkers (third author) selected as one of her methods requirements a course called "Literacy Development in the Early Years." Debbi's reflections, which appear in the sidebar on pp. 301–302, illustrate that the technological revolution has doubtless made its mark. It has dramatically changed learning and communication in the process. On a daily basis we check our e-mail, go to automatic teller machines for cash, and coordinate our schedules on handheld computers. With technology an integral part of everyday life, it is our responsibility as educators to teach students how to use relevant equipment.

This article describes a project designed to enhance the technological ability of university students enrolled in an early literacy course. By modeling the use of technology as a tool for literacy instruction for them, we hoped that these teachers and future teachers would become more familiar with technology and use it when teaching their early childhood students to read (Morrow, 2001).

Technology and literacy development

A responsibility of education is to prepare students for the future. We have to teach our students to use technology if we want them to succeed in today's world. Valmont and Wepner (2000) stated,

Functional literacy means that people are able to process print in their environment, whether it be newspapers, train sched-

ules, or official documents. Now included in this array of materials for which people must have functional literacy is information technology. Everywhere we go there is a reference to an online address. Radio and television advertisements send their listeners and viewers to web sites to get additional information about the many items advertised. Retail stores and local services boast about their 24-hour accessibility through their specialized web sites. (p. 5)

In order to prepare our children, we must recognize the impact of technology in today's workplace and train them accordingly. Technology can help to support and enhance the development of reading, writing, and the language arts, which are the foundation for success in school and in life (Reinking, 1999).

We have entered a time when technology is developing rapidly, which has an important effect on literacy development (Leu, 1997; Rickelman & Caplan, 2000). The changing constructions of literacy within new technologies will require us to train teachers to prepare children for these changes (Leu & Kinzer, 2000). The literacy needs and demands of a changing society must be addressed in school when children are very young. The World Wide Web has created the necessity for new literacy abilities such as search and navigation strategies and synthesis and critical thinking (Reinking, 1999). Technology can be used as an instructional tool to support literacy development. Computer technology is effective when it is used to supplement, not to supplant, the teacher (Balajthy, 1989; Labbo, 1996).

Reprinted from *The Reading Teacher* (2002), 56, 218–230.

Using technology in literacy instruction—benefits

Research suggests that there are benefits to using technology as a tool in literacy instruction. Technology appears to motivate children and to increase the time they are willing to spend practicing important academic skills. This is especially helpful to teachers when trying to work with children who have difficulty acquiring reading skills and who may become easily frustrated and disinterested. According to Stanovich (1986), extended involvement in reading is essential for developing reading ability. Daiute (1983) found that students exhibited a higher level of motivational engagement when using technological tools. Studies that compared word processing revision versus handwritten revision commonly found that children were more highly motivated to revise when using the computer, which led to more time spent on the revision process (Kamil, Intrator, & Kim, 2000).

Another benefit of technology use is that computers can provide individual reinforcement of skills. Providing instructional activities designed for individual abilities has always been a challenge for teachers. However, many software programs have adjustable levels of difficulty, and children can be trained to use this software on their own. Children can use it in learning centers when the teacher is working with other children in small groups. The computer provides opportunities for cooperative learning as children work in pairs or small groups. Cooperative learning promotes academic achievement, social interaction, and positive attitudes in the classroom (Baker, 2000).

The computer allows teachers and children to communicate and share ideas with others around the world. At the same time, it offers the opportunity to discuss how to carefully read the information acquired on the Internet and assess its reliability. Computers and Internet use provide teachers and children with access to information all over the globe. Children can direct their own learning as the computer brings them into contact with information not available in print. The computer may provide the most current information and is always being updated. Nevertheless, children must also learn how to evaluate the accuracy of that information. Both verifying and referencing information are important literacy skills whether the information is from the Web or from a book (Baker, 2000).

Using technology in the classroom—challenges

Although there are many benefits, a major challenge with technology is the cost. Many school districts are now equipped with computers, and hardware costs continue to fall; however, the ratio of computers to students is still just 1 to 5 (Symonds, 2000). In addition, keeping up with equipment upgrades, current software, monthly telephone/cable/Internet provider connection charges, printer ink cartridges, paper supply, diskettes for students, and so on is a constant challenge (Leu & Kinzer, 2000).

Training children to use technology is challenging due to time constraints in the school day. The level of technical expertise among the children varies. For example, some students will need instruction in how to use software programs, access the Internet, do searches, and use word processing. Others will already have these skills. Many districts provide a computer class as a special subject, like art or music, where students learn these skills and the burden is not on the classroom teacher. In addition, there are many good software programs that students could use to practice these skills. If teachers incorporate technology into their instruction, this model will heighten their children's awareness about the use of technology.

Technology in preservice and inservice training

Preservice and inservice professional development of teachers is probably the most overlooked yet essential component for integrating technology use with literacy instruction. Teacher training is essential to provide children with quality learning experiences involving technology. As in all educational endeavors, a committed, knowledgeable teacher is the most instrumental factor in effective instruction (Leu & Kinzer, 2000). Because new technologies continuously appear, staff development for practicing teachers must be continuous (Wepner, Valmont, & Thurlow, 2000).

Separate courses in the use of technology are available for inservice and preservice teachers. Although they may be related to educational activities, they are not content specific. Another way of dealing with teacher training and technology is to integrate it with content-area teacher education courses.

Technology in the early literacy course

In the early literacy course discussed here, the instructor (Lesley Morrow, first author) enhanced her instruction with technology use. In this way she modeled how technology could be used in teaching. As the university students learned about instructional approaches to early literacy, they were also learning about the use of technology in teaching. In addition there were explicit activities that required technology use in their assignments.

The purpose of the project. The Graduate School of Education at Rutgers University (New Brunswick, New Jersey) received a grant from the U.S. Department of Education to incorporate technology into different content areas within our education programs. (Steven Barnhart, the second author, was the principal investigator on the grant.) We were to determine the effect that embedding technology in our instruction had on our own students' knowledge of technology and, further, how this affected their use of technology in their own classrooms. The university students in the class were a combination of individuals seeking their initial teacher certification (two thirds) and practicing teachers (one third). Reported here are the results of a course entitled Literacy Development in the Early Years.

Embedding technology in an early literacy course

Procedures. The early literacy course lasted for a 15-week semester and met for 2 hours and 40 minutes a week. The syllabus for the course required university students to use technology in their assignments, and they were given a list of suggestions for doing so. To enhance students' knowledge, the instructor modeled behavior by using the different technologies in every class session. To expose university students to and engage them in technology use, the following activities were required.

1. Chat on the class website at least twice—once to initiate discussion about text read or some class discussion and once to respond to others.
2. Participate in an interactive chat on the class website at least once during the semester.
3. Post some of your projects, your students' projects, or items of interest on the class website.
4. Read and prepare an abstract for an online article from a professional journal about literacy development and describe the experience of getting information this way, as opposed to a paper copy of a journal.
5. Use some type of technology that you haven't used before (i.e., do research on Internet, make a PowerPoint presentation, create a website for your class).
6. Use an educational website to locate practical teaching ideas.
7. Participate in an interactive television (ITV) demonstration.
8. Videotape your class presentation for your own critique of your work.
9. When at your field placement, use technology in three different lessons and in three different ways in your literacy instruction.
10. Preview and critique one piece of software that teaches a literacy skill.

How technology was used during the course

Use of the website. A website was set up for the course (see Figure 1). University students could log on and access it from home. With it, they could check the time and place of the course and view the syllabus. Students could look over the requirements for the course, see the grading system and textbooks required, contact the instructor, participate in online discussions, and post and receive messages from their instructor and classmates. The Web discussions could continue after the course ended because the website remained intact for a year. The website entries were used to discuss reading assignments and class lectures. University students could share thoughts and ideas about these with others and also discuss content that needed clarification. The instructor left a weekly message reminding students about assignments, providing additional explanations for difficult concepts, and adding information she forgot to discuss in class.

Another use of the website was to participate in an online chat. The instructor conducted two chats during the semester. University students logged on from home to participate. After the chat, they discussed their feelings about such

Figure 1
Webpage for early literacy course

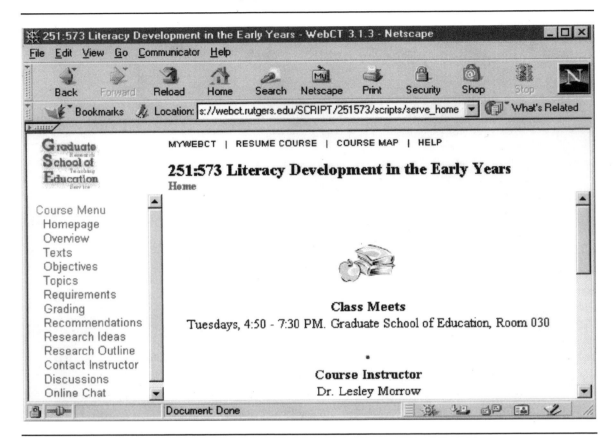

communication and whether it would be useful with young children. Most believed it would be, and their suggestions for using the Web included (a) organize chats with authors of children's literature, (b) organize electronic pen pals (e-pals) and chat with children anywhere in the world, and (c) post children's work on the Web for parents to look at.

The following conversation took place among the university students concerning an assignment. One person started the discussion by posting his thoughts, then others responded to the message. What is important about this chat is how students continue their class discussion on their own time. They are bouncing ideas off one another and entering into a reflective conversation about literacy instruction.

John—As far as the readings go this week, I never imagined how hard it was for young children to retell a story. I read the chapter before I did a retelling with the child I am evaluating and I assumed he would have no problem. I even picked a Franklin story to be sure of the simplicity, but sure enough as soon as I finished reading it he had no idea how to begin to retell the story. I used questions that the text suggested, but it was basically "I don't know," and he was so frustrated...to the point in which he said he didn't like the story even though he clearly enjoyed it while I was reading it. So then I used some more specific prompts and allowed him to use the pictures in the book, and he got started.

Mike—I had a similar problem, and using the pictures in the book as prompts worked for me too. I used the same story as you did and I got my child to retell by starting the story for him. I said "Once upon a time there was a turtle named Franklin," and then I stopped and he began to retell. He didn't do a great job but at least he said something. I did it again another day, and he was much better at it. They do need practice.

What struck me most when reading that chapter 7 in our text was the large number of strategies available to teachers when developing children's comprehension. I remember when I was in elementary school we would read a story and complete a worksheet with questions about the story. It was graded and handed back. Very little discussion took place. In the lower grades I remember being read to, but such strategies as story retelling, KWL, and DLTA/DRTA were never used. The teacher sat at the front of the group and read the story, showing us the pictures as she went. Then she asked us if we liked the story, and maybe we'd draw a picture about it. It certainly is an exciting time to be entering the field of education. So many different modes of teaching and learning are arising as well. Children in this new millennium should be much better prepared as readers at an early age.

Cheryl—I thought that Mike was absolutely correct when saying that children are at a better advantage with their comprehension strategies than we were as kids. I don't remember teachers focusing on thinking skills in order to help us better comprehend the text. You just passed or failed and moved on. Today we teach young children strategies to use graphic organizers such as maps and webs to help them to comprehend.

Currently I am doing my teaching practicum in a third-grade classroom. The teacher that I am observing demonstrates perfect KWL and DRTA teaching methods. She used the KWL approach for *The Hundred Dresses* and the DRTA approach for the basal reading lessons. One day she asked the children to focus on their thinking strategy—whether it is predictions, previewing, or reader response. The children can identify the strategy they are using and will be able to use these strategies for a lifetime of reading.

Each university student was to post comments on the website twice during the semester, and the instructor logged on once a week for a total of 14 entries. In this class of 30 students, there were 142 entries on the Web during the semester. Therefore, on average, the university students logged on to the website four times during the semester when it was only required to do so twice.

Interactive television. The instructor also conducted interactive television demonstrations. ITV is often referred to as videoconferencing. As mentioned earlier, one distance group was always in attendance because it was taking the entire early literacy course. Two other groups participated in three other class sessions, which were selected based on topic. The three groups were made up of teachers and coordinators from three different school districts, and they participated in the course from each school system's ITV room. All involved received course credit or staff development credit. Teachers do not like to travel after school for staff development, and ITV is one way to ensure attendance at such sessions.

ITV allowed the university students to listen to teachers from other parts of the state talk about their ideas and discuss similar problems.

The instructor gave helpful hints about teaching successfully with ITV, based on her experience.

- All sites need a technician in case something goes wrong with the equipment.
- All sites need to have someone in charge such as the main instructor or a teaching assistant.
- Supplies needed for a class must be available at all sites.
- Plan the sessions so that students can interact with one another at their sites, students at other sites, and the instructor.
- Assign names to the groups so that you can address them and they know you are talking to them. The names can be their school districts.
- Students must be aware that whispers are picked up on the microphones from all sites and movements are seen as well.

One class session with ITV involved reviewing story structure for the development of comprehension. University students were to identify the different structural elements within a story such as setting, theme, plot episodes, and resolution. Before viewing a video of a story to identify structural elements, the instructor put a story map on the document camera that pictured the elements of story structure. She assigned a story element to each group to identify in the video. For example, the students in the classroom with the instructor, on TV screen 1, would identify the setting of the story and the characters. The group seen on TV screen 2 would identify the story theme, those on TV screen 3 would identify the

This technologically sophisticated classroom included a large television monitor to project images from the document camera controlled by a remote touch pad in the front of the room. Photo by Lesley Mandel Morrow.

As can be seen on the television screen in the wall, in addition to the students on site in the ITV classroom there was one group of teachers at a different site who were always in attendance for the class sessions. Photo by Lesley Mandel Morrow.

plot episodes, and those on TV screen 4 would identify the resolution of the story.

After watching and listening to the story the instructor called on each of the different sites to fill in their section of the story map. Site 1 started the map by filling in the setting of the story and the story characters, site 2 stated the theme of the story, site 3 listed the plot episodes, and site 4 talked about the resolution of the story. The session was truly interactive with all sites participating and contributing.

From time to time there were technological problems—it was difficult to hear someone at another site, or the picture on the TV wasn't quite clear. Nevertheless, the university students agreed that the ITV experience started them thinking about how to use this technology with the children in their current or future classrooms.

One second-grade teacher, who had never seen this technology in use before taking this course, explored how to use it with her children because her district had an ITV room. She decided to use the ITV to get together with another second-grade class in another state, because they were both studying rain forests. At the end of the unit, both teachers in their districts' ITV rooms, 500 miles away from each other, had their children read stories they had written about the rain forest, share experiences about field trips taken related to the rain forest, and share recipes for snacks made from food that comes from the rain forest. Most important, these second-grade children, who had been pen pals during the school year, got to meet one another on TV.

Literacy software and PowerPoint demonstrations. During the course, the students demonstrated the use of various types of software to develop literacy. One demonstrated a program that provides children with a basic framework for writing a story. One feature, "Story Starters," helps children generate ideas for their story, although they can write original stories as well. The software allows the children to start out with the title page. They type the title of the story, the author (or authors), and a copyright date. They are also able to choose from a selection of colorful thematic borders. Then the children go on to the next page and begin their stories. For the top of the page, the children choose a graphic or background and add objects such as people, cars, or animals. Then on the bottom half of the page they write their text. Spell-check is available to help the children edit their stories.

The university students were each responsible for a presentation. They were to model the teaching of a literacy skill using children's literature and a game or manipulative material they had created. The typical material might be word building using letters on a magnetic board or making little words from big words on a felt board. Several students used PowerPoint presentations and created word-building activities on the computer. In this activity, the child moves an initial consonant in front of phonograms or

Figure 2
Completed technology log

Name: Suzie Student

Date	Technology (program) used	How technology was used
10/00	Microsoft Word	Write a paper
10/00	Web CT	Responded to articles
10/00	Scanner equipment/software	Copied pictures
10/00	Microsoft PowerPoint	Created presentation
10/00	Interactive TV	Participated in class
10/00	Web CT	Class chat
11/00	http://www.alfy.com	Built lesson plans
11/00	ERIC (http://www.libraries.Rutgers.edu)	Searched for articles
11/00	Proquest (http://www.libraries.Rutgers.edu)	Searched for articles
11/00	E-mail (http://www.yahoo.com)	Communicated with teacher/classmates
11/00	http://teachervision.com	Searched for ideas for lesson plans
12/00	http://www.lessonplanet.com	Searched for ideas for lesson plans
12/00	http://www.educationplanet.com	Read articles on guided reading
12/00	Web CT	Class chat
12/00	Jumpstart 2nd Grade	Games/educational lessons w/students
12/00	Where in the World is Carmen Sandiego?	Game with students
12/00	http://www.readingonline.org	Searched for articles
12/00	Bailey's Bookhouse (software)	Game with students
12/00	Jumpstart 3rd Grade	Played educational games

word endings to create new words. As the semester continued, the sophistication of these materials increased. As one university student got up to present she said, "Don't laugh at my PowerPoint presentation. I was determined to do one and I've never done one before. I didn't care how it came out, I just wanted to try." Her presentation turned out to be most effective.

An evaluation of the project

Several measures were used to collect data from the university students concerning the project's success. These measures included the following:

- Students completed a survey designed to determine their knowledge and use of technology at the beginning and end of the semester. The purpose was to determine if technology knowledge was enhanced after completing the course.
- Students filled out logs throughout the semester to record the technology they used for the course. The log required

student to write the date, the type of technology, and how it was used.

- A random selection of 10 university students in the class were interviewed at the end of the semester. They were asked to answer questions about how the course influenced the integration of technology into their present literacy instruction or what they would do in the future.

Analysis of the data collected

Pre- and postsemester survey results. The results of the surveys of the 30 students from the university site, given at the beginning of the semester, show the following:

- 80% rated themselves as capable at word processing
- 57% rated themselves as familiar with and capable with Internet searches for educational information
- 30% rated themselves as capable with chats and online Web discussions
- 87% rated themselves as not familiar with ITV or distance education

Figure 3
Frequency of use of technology

Program	September	October	November	December	Other	Totals
Adobe Premier	1	1				2
Cassette		1	2			3
Digital camera			2	1		3
E-mail	35	39	40	29		143
Flow chart				1		1
Front Page		1				1
ITV		14				14
Individually named webpages	5	10	22	13	7	57
Internet searches	33	40	42	24		139
Microfiche				1		1
Microsoft Paint		1				1
Microsoft Word	1	10	8	12		31
Overhead projector		2				2
Palm Pilot					1	1
PowerPoint		5	2	1		8
Scanner		1	1			2
Software	5	9	9	6		29
Spreadsheet	1	1				2
TV/video		2	1	1		4
WebCT	70	70	68	37		245
Totals	151	207	197	126	8	689

- 60% of the students felt that they were unfamiliar with software programs designed to develop children's literacy skills
- 75% never attempted to develop meaningful literacy learning activities for their students involving technology.

Matched *t*-tests pairs were run to determine if there were significant differences in the post-semester survey as compared to the presemester survey. There were significant differences at the .05 level for the following areas:

- ($p < .03$) for familiarity with and capability with Internet searches for educational information
- ($p < .001$) for capability with chats and online Web discussions
- ($p < .001$) for familiarity with ITV and distance education
- ($p < .001$) for familiarity with software programs designed for children to develop literacy skills
- ($p < .03$) for ability to check spreadsheet for classroom grading
- ($p < .05$) for familiarity with data analysis tools

Although not statistically significant, there were differences in survey responses concerning never attempting to develop meaningful literacy learning activities for the children they teach in their own classrooms or in their practicum experiences.

Technology log results. Completed technology logs (seen in Figure 2) were handed in at the end of the semester. These logs were analyzed to report the number and types of technology used throughout the semester. The results show the peak of use and different types of use during October and November. They demonstrate the university students' use of technology during the middle months of the semester. After students started to learn more, their use of equipment increased. Figure 3 details the frequency and types of technology use reported by the students during the semester.

The technology the students most commonly made use of included the course website (245 times), e-mail (143 times), and Internet searches

Figure 4
Defino Dinosaur Lab, a first-grade website

 # Defino
Dinosaur Lab

Welcome to the Defino Dinosaur Lab! This month the first graders in Ms. Fahey's class and Miss Casola's class will be learning all about dinosaurs. Throughout March we will become scientists in the lab and paleontologists on digs to discover the fascinating world of dinosaurs. Defino Dinosaur Lab would like to invite you to see what we discover this month by coming to see our dinosaur play on April 5, 2001.

Click on *me* to practice our dino song!

Click on *me* to see a list of dinomite dinosaur sites!

Click on *me* to say hi to Ms. Fahey.

Click on *me* to say hi to Miss Casola.

(139 times). The next three most common were not used as extensively: Individually named web-pages (57 times), word-processing programs (31 times), and different types of software (29 times).

Students listed the websites that they used on their technology logs. Those most frequently mentioned were as follows:

Discovery School—http://www.schooldiscovery.com
Scholastic—http://www.scholastic.com
Enchanted Learning—http://www.enchantedlearning.com
White House for Kids—http://www.whitehouse.gov/kids
Reading Online—http://www.readingonline.org
Encyclopedia Britannica—http://www.britannica.com
Lesson Plans—http://www.lessonplans.com
Lesson Plans—http://www.lessonplanspage.com
Yahoo—http://www.yahoo.com
Yahooligans—http://www.yahooligans.com
Ask Jeeves—http://www.ajkids.com
Eduhound—http://www.eduhound.com
International Reading Association—http://www.reading.org

Interview data. The 10 randomly selected university students were interviewed at the end of the semester in person. Their responses were tape-recorded and written. Students who took part in the class answered questions about how the course was influencing their integration of technology with their present or future literacy instruction. The following are a representative selection of quotes from the interviews given by the 10 university students.

After completing this course do you feel any different about using technology in the classroom?

> I feel more comfortable accessing information via the Internet and hopeful of using it frequently as part of my teaching. I will use it to set up a class website, encourage e-mails between myself and students and parents.
>
> I was introduced to different software programs for literacy development such as Storybook Weaver. I will definitely use that software and other.
>
> It improved our class and made it exciting; therefore I feel it is important to use with the children I eventually teach to give them the same exposure.
>
> I was introduced to ITV, which I found we have in my school district, and I will definitely make use of this technology. I learned about a document camera that I would use when available.

How will you use technology in the classroom?

> I will use it to create newsletters, story creations, presentations, science, social studies; the possibilities are endless.

> I can use ITV to share projects with students in other parts of the world and compare data and research.
>
> I will use it to have the children create their own story and illustrations with a program like Storybook Weaver.
>
> The Internet can be used like the library of the future. I will use it for teaching children about research. Children can seek information and learn about things outside of their community or state and anywhere in the world.
>
> I can create a website for my class and use it to post homework, and if anyone is sick they can see what we are doing through pictures. Also, they could get homework and even e-mail questions to the teacher.
>
> I think ITV would be great for staff development.

The instructor received a letter from one university student after the course ended that demonstrated the knowledge she gained from participating in the course and how she was using that information.

> Dear Dr. M.,
> I hope you are well. Enclosed is a copy of the web page I just designed for my first graders about our upcoming dinosaur play. It is under construction right now. I wanted to send these to you to see what you think of them. I'd appreciate any suggestions. I'd also like to thank you for being the catalyst in all of this web exploration. As a result of your course, Literacy Development in the Early Years, technology just stands out in my mind, so I decided to do something about it. Thank you so much for stressing its importance in your course throughout the semester. It really motivated me to try it in my classroom. If you would like to visit the web pages please do so. You can find them at the following address: http://www.hometown.aol.com/krisfahey/dinosaur.html

Another university student described a project she undertook as a result of the exposure to technology in the early literacy course. This first-grade teacher partnered with a sixth-grade teacher in her school. The school was in an inner-city environment, and 90% of the children received free or reduced-cost lunch. The first- and sixth-grade teachers agreed to work on an integrated language arts unit on the theme of agriculture. The children learned about plants and how they grow and survive in different environments.

The children consulted a farmer in Missouri about their planting project. These children in Maryland planted the same seeds as the farmer in Missouri and then communicated through e-mail as to the progress of the plant growth. Sixth-grade children used the Internet to research

Classroom vignette

I never could have anticipated the pedagogical and technological adventure upon which I was about to embark. When I entered the classroom I found a rich literacy environment. In addition, the classroom was equipped with sophisticated technology. The physical layout suggested that this was a true model of an early childhood classroom. I had never seen a classroom quite like this.

The print in the room included a calendar, weather chart, helper chart, and rules for the class. Signs communicated information such as "Take a folder when you arrive," and "Leave your self-addressed stamped envelope on my desk." There was a box called "Messages" that housed the message for the day that class members were to take on their way to their seats. A cork notice board on one wall was for posting news items, conference advertisements, and new book titles for children and teachers. A word wall included high frequency words and phrases that dealt with early literacy such as *emergent reader, invented spelling, phonemic awareness, comprehension, family literacy, fluency,* and *phonics.*

A small table held materials for reading instruction such as an assortment of leveled books, a pocket chart with sentence strips including the words of a poem to welcome the class, and an experience chart that provided directions for binding books. There was a stack of writing slates for working with words and writing. There was a folder for each of us with our name on it that contained materials we needed for class. On a shelf built into the wall were a few sample corrugated cardboard book bins, labeled with names of class members. These would be for storing journals, books being read, homework assignments, and other personal work. In this same area was a sign that read "Literacy Center." On another shelf were books in baskets leveled for difficulty, and books labeled for themes and genres such as fairy tales, good health, animals, plants, and poetry.

There was a rocking chair, some stuffed animals, pillows, and a small area rug. There was a place for headsets with taped stories for listening. There were manipulatives to reinforce word study skills, magnetic boards, sandpaper and felt letters for building words, an alphabet puzzle for sequencing letters, and a bingo game for matching letters and sounds. There were materials for developing comprehension such as a felt board and roll movie for storytelling. The author's spot included markers, pencils, crayons, and various types of paper. There were index cards for "Very Own Vocabulary" word collections, and notebooks for journal writing. Finally, there were materials for writing and mailing letters.

This environment was not only rich in literacy, but also in technology. The technology was woven seamlessly into the class. There was a large TV monitor at the front and six smaller monitors built high into the wall at the back. The rich technology environment also included a long table at the front of the room, which had a touch pad control panel that operated all of the equipment. Built into the table was a document camera, which is a cross between an overhead projector and an old-fashioned opaque projector. The document camera projects images of pictures or objects onto the screens. The book *It Happens to Everyone* (Myers, 1990), about the first day of school, was on the document camera. It could be seen on one of the smaller screens in the back and on one quarter of the large screen at the front. (The large screen was split into four sections.)

The desk in the front of the room was a typical teachers desk at first glance. But there was a computer built into it, and images from the computer could be projected onto the large TV screen in the front as well as on the smaller screens in back. When I entered, the computer displayed the class website that would be used by the instructor and class members between class sessions. The image of the website was on a second quarter of the screen in the front of the room and on one of the screens in the back of the room. Stored in the desk in the front of the room were software programs for early literacy development, a PowerPoint presentation created by the instructor, and a directory for recording student e-mail addresses. There was also a directory of teacher-suggested websites.

Next to the large TV screen in the front of the room was a cabinet with two VCRs, one for playing videotapes and the other for recording. A tape of a first-grade teacher modeling a guided reading lesson was playing on the third quarter of the TV monitor in the front of the room and on one of the televisions in the back of the room. The room also had the capacity for interactive TV (teleconferencing). On the fourth quarter of the large screen was a group of teachers 50 miles away. We could see and hear them as they assembled in their ITV classroom. They were taking this early literacy course with our instructor. Microphones were built into the ceiling so we could hear from the other site and they could hear us. The instructor had a wireless lapel microphone to be sure that her voice carried clearly.

I think the instructor used every piece of equipment during the first night of class. The class began with a PowerPoint presentation, a historical overview of literacy instruction in the United States over the past 100 years. The instructor used the document camera to display original pages from children's materials beginning with the McGuffy Readers. She enlarged the images on the screen that illustrated the many types of reading instruction we have used over the years. The materials included texts that fostered reading development through the use of repeated sight words and controlled vocabularies. There were those that were phonics

(continued)

Classroom vignette (continued)

oriented, with different decoding skills being taught on each page and structural linguistic approaches as well. The instructor enlarged the picture on the document camera to demonstrate a current strategy for building words with manipulative letters in word-study programs. We could see how she built the word *chart* by blending together the *ch* digraph on a letter card with the art phonogram. We watched a few short video clips of more current approaches to literacy instruction. The videos modeled first-grade guided reading instruction, organizing center instruction, and doing a running record.

We were introduced to our class website and we watched how to get online and post messages and how to chat with many students at once. We signed up for dates to discuss readings of the week on the site and to respond to comments made by others in the class. All the time, the professor was using the remote touch pad to work the technology.

After we introduced ourselves, the teachers from the distance site made their introductions. We talked about ITV etiquette, participation, and technical pros and cons of the interactive TV distance learning mode. There would be other groups dropping in during the semester for specific topics of interest to them.

plants and survival in different environments and then shared their information with the first-grade students. Each class participated in activities appropriate for their grade and had opportunities to share what they had learned. There was a website for the two classes to post their work. At the end of the unit the children were interviewed concerning the technology used during the project.

Quotes from students.

What did you know about computers and using the Internet before this unit?

> I didn't really know much about computers. I don't own a computer. Now I know that you can send messages on e-mail and that the Internet is for finding information. The computer also types really good.—girl, age 12

> I thought I knew what computers were used for, but I never had one myself, and I didn't really know how to use them. I can't believe all they can do. We really need to get computers in everyone's house.—girl, age 8

Did the computer help you learn?

> Yes, I learned a lot. I learned you could play games and learned how to type on the computer. You can also write to people and hear back from them really soon on e-mail, even if they're really far away.—boy, age 7

Did you like using the computers and Internet?

> Of course I did! I really didn't know there was so much to know and learn on the Net. It would have taken so much more time to look for the information we needed in the library. We probably wouldn't have found it all.—boy, age 12

Classrooms of the future

According to Symonds (2000), classrooms of the future will be equipped very much like the one used in this project or in even more sophisticated ways. In schools of the future students will carry wireless devices, teachers will collaborate with colleagues across the globe and rely less on textbooks, classrooms will have cooperative learning tables instead of rows of desks, and students will work together to solve problems. Distance learning will provide children with virtual field trips and the ability to meet and talk with people throughout the world, parents will exchange e-mails with teachers and view their child's work online, tests will give way to electronic assessments, homework will be more individualized, and tutors will be available for online help. Some of these predictions are already realized. One cannot accurately speculate about what the future of technology will bring because it changes so rapidly, but most educators would agree that technology will take teachers and children further than most of us could ever imagine. It is an exciting time to be a teacher with so much change. We must embrace these changes with enthusiasm and great expectations.

The purpose of this project was to increase awareness about technologies available and how they can be used with children in literacy development programs. To do this the use of technology was integrated with an early literacy course that required class members to use different technologies in their assignments and in their teaching. The university students were exposed to numerous strategies and techniques to help children develop their abilities in reading, writing, listening, speaking, and viewing. The instructor's use of technology was a model for the students to learn how to use it to support their own instruction of young children. Incorporating technology is no longer a special effect or idea; it is a necessity in preparing teachers for today's and tomorrow's world.

The project was successful in increasing the university students' knowledge of different types of technology and how they are operated. It was also successful in broadening these university students' use of technology in their work for the course and in their own classrooms. Most colleges, universities, and school districts have the types of technology described in this project. Those who try to use the equipment will learn that it isn't as intimidating as it seems, it enriches teaching, and, most important, it enhances children's learning. It is time to turn potential into reality and to use technology in classrooms in every way possible.

References

Baker, E.A. (2000, July). Instructional approaches used to integrate literacy and technology. *Reading Online, 4*(1). Retrieved (June 27, 2002) from http://www.readingonline.org/articles/baker

Daiute, C. (1983). *Writing and computers*. Reading, MA: Addison Wesley.

Kamil, M.L., Intrator, S.M., & Kim, H.S. (2000). The effects of other technologies on literacy and literacy learning. In M.L. Kamil, P.B. Mosenthal, P.D. Pearson, & R. Barr (Eds.), *Handbook of reading research, Vol. III* (pp. 771–788). Mahwah, NJ: Erlbaum.

Labbo, L. (1996) A semiotic analysis of young children's symbol making in a classroom computer center. *Reading Research Quarterly, 51*, 356–385.

Leu, D.J., Jr. (1997). Caity's question: Literacy as deixis on the Internet. *The Reading Teacher, 51*, 62–67.

Leu, D.J., Jr., & Kinzer, C.K. (2000). The convergence of literacy instruction and communication. *Reading Research Quarterly, 35*, 108–127.

Morrow, L.M. (2001). Integrating the language arts with thematic instruction. In L. Morrow (Ed.), *Literacy development in the early years* (pp. 16–17). Needham, MA: Pearson.

Myers, B. (1990) *It happens to everyone*. New York: The Trumpet Club.

Reinking, David. (1999). *Electronic literacy*. (Perspectives in Reading Research No. 4). Athens, GA & College Park, MD: National Reading Research Center, University of Georgia & University of Maryland.

Rickelman, R.J., & Caplan, R.M. (2000). Technological literacy in the intermediate and middle grades. In K.D. Wood & T.S. Dickinson (Eds.), *Promoting literacy in grades 4–9* (pp. 306–316). Boston: Allyn & Bacon.

Stanovich, K.E. (1986). Matthew effects in reading: Some consequences of individual differences in the acquisition of literacy. *Reading Research Quarterly, 21*, 360–407.

Symonds, W.C. (2000, September 25). A technology revolution is about to sweep America's classrooms. *Business Week*, 116–128.

Valmont, W.J., & Wepner, S.B. (2000). Using technology to support literacy learning. In S.B. Wepner, W.J. Valmont, & R. Thurlow (Eds.), *Linking literacy and technology: A guide for K–8 classrooms* (pp. 2–18). Newark, DE: International Reading Association.

Wepner, S.B., Valmont, W.J., & Thurlow, R. (2000). *Linking literacy and technology: A guide for K–8 classrooms*. Newark, DE: International Reading Association.

A "funny" thing happened on the way to the forum

Carol D. Wickstrom

A teacher educator uses a Web-based discussion board to promote reflection, encourage engagement, and develop collegiality in preservice teachers.

For more than half of the 20th century, educational practices supported classroom discourse in which teachers asked questions and students answered them (Hoetker & Ahlbrand, 1969; Mehan, 1979; Thayer, 1928). This discourse pattern was often referred to as "recitation." Discourse is limited in this pattern, and the answers to the questions are often restricted to one word (Mehan, 1979). However, as we moved closer to the 21st century, theorists and researchers (Barnes, 1995; Bruner, 1966; Cazden, 1988; Vygotsky, 1978) supported the view that language is at the heart of teaching and learning. Through various language experiences we acquire knowledge and shape our understandings of the world around us.

Thus, classroom practices began to support different kinds of interaction between students and teachers (Boggs, 1972; Heath, 1983; Tharp & Gallimore, 1991) as well as greater interaction among the students (Barnes, 1990; Johnson & Johnson, 1987/1991; Palincsar & Brown, 1984). These interactions encourage both talk in the classroom and the use of the students' dialect for this talk. Dialogue between students *and* between

the student and the teacher that is not restricted by existing patterns promotes inquiry (Britton cited in Pradl, 1982; Wells & Chiang-Wells, 1992). Using language for inquiry allows the teacher and the students to be problem solvers who generate an idea, reframe the idea through discussion, make connections between experience and knowledge, qualify existing beliefs, as well as judge what might happen next. As a result of this experience, the discourse becomes more reflective rather than being a question-and-answer session.

Simply increasing discourse opportunities does not necessarily change the pattern of discourse. Accordingly, Barnes (1995) suggested using a variety of settings. He claimed that an individual reaches different understandings as a result of the different settings in which the discourse occurs. In other words, learning is shaped not just by the amount of discourse in which we engage but also by the context of these settings.

One strategy used by teachers and teacher educators to vary the manner in which discourse occurs is dialogue journals. A dialogue journal is a log or record of thoughts kept by a writer and responded to by other writers (Staton, Shuy, Peyton, & Reed, 1988). Such journals create a dynamic log of discourse, which is characteristic of reflection because, through writing, reading, and responding in journals, the individuals create mutually constructed knowledge much like the language of inquiry. Through this reflective process teachers

Reprinted from *Journal of Adolescent & Adult Literacy* (2003), 46, 414–423.

and teacher educators have gained a greater under-standing of student thinking.

Dialogue journals, however, still present some limitations on the discourse process as well as on the reflective process (McIntyre & Tlusty, 1995). In general, journals require that students present their discussion in a specific, finalized format. Thus, they are similar to the classroom format because feedback only occurs after the reflective writing is finished. Because there may be a great deal of time between when the entry is written and the response is received, the student may no longer be engaged in that particular "discussion." In addition, the only person to read these journals is the teacher, so that is the only feedback that the students receive. This situation, in itself, can have a limiting effect on the dialogue because of the student's subordinate relationship to the teacher. Today's electronic bulletin boards have the potential to remove some of the obstacles to the discourse process and reflectivity, and since researchers (Guthrie & Richardson, 1995; Leu, 2000) have urged educators to use technology in conjunction with literacy I decided to use it with my students.

The purpose of this study was to investigate the effects that a discussion board (forum) created on a website would have on the discourse and reflection of preservice teachers. Discussion boards are particularly suited to facilitating and improving learning because they provide a place for students to post comments related to the course content and process (Adkins, 1991; Brooks & Kopp, 1989; Chesebro & Bonsall, 1989; Lindsey-North, 2000). Although class time was to be spent in discussion, the bulletin board would provide another opportunity for discourse. In the past, students wrote reflections, but I maintained that the forum had to be a more authentic way to reflect because their peers would be reading their work rather than just the instructor. Thus, it would be viewed as professional dialogue, which facilitates reflection about teaching (Good & Brophy, 2000). I also speculated that the students would be more proactive about their learning. Rather than the topics and ideas coming from the instructor, I anticipated that the students would initiate topics as they "talked" on the forum. Last, because their peers would be reading their ideas and responding, I thought the forum would encourage collegiality and a greater understanding of how important it is to communicate with other teachers once these preservice teachers had their own classrooms. Bakkenes, de Brabander, and Imants (1999) purported that a forum could help teachers overcome professional isolation because it provides an avenue for information exchange between teachers.

Context of the study

There were 45 undergraduate students enrolled in a one-semester reading assessment course at a university in the southwestern United States during the spring of 2001. Of the 45 students, 33 attended class on the main campus, and 12 attended class at a new campus located 56 miles south. All students had taken a foundational reading course as a prerequisite. The course objectives were (a) to develop awareness of maintaining a responsive teacher-pupil relationship, (b) to demonstrate knowledge of strategies to communicate with appropriate teachers and specialists related to the assessment and instructional planning for learners experiencing difficulties in reading and writing, and (c) to develop a reflective mindset about learning and teaching.

In the reading assessment course, the preservice teachers are exposed to informal reading assessments such as miscue analysis, retellings, book handling concepts, think-alouds, writing analysis, writing sprees (opportunities to free-write about anything that comes to mind for about five minutes), and attitude and interest surveys. The preservice teachers are required to use these assessment strategies with a child in order to write a case study, which chronicles their work and develops an instructional plan for the child based on the findings. Preservice teachers develop a portfolio with reflective captioning that allows them to learn about portfolio assessment as well.

Course requirements that semester included reflective responses to readings in their textbook, *Diagnostic Teaching of Reading* (Walker, 2000), and reflective responses to assessment scenarios devised by the instructor. The last two assignments were to be posted on the discussion area.

Reflections and the discussion area

Through a university service, a webpage was created for the course using WebCT. An online discussion area was included. Because I had told the university that this site was just for me, I had to ensure that all of the students entered their identification numbers and password in order to be part of the discussion. I introduced the discussion area during class and, there being no classroom computer access at the time, I walked them through written directions. In retrospect, this was probably the hardest part of the task because of the variance in students' computer skills and computer access.

I set a date for the postings to occur; however, because several students had difficulty, I told the students to ignore the calendar dates and update weekly. The Figure gives the suggested format for the postings, which follow the same format that I give to students for written reflections. I encouraged the students not to let the format restrict their thinking. They were instructed to read the posted topics and other student postings and then add their thoughts to the discussion.

From the beginning, I explained that I did not always want to be the one to start a discussion and emphasized that my objective for the forum was for students to generate their own ideas and dialogue. I did not expect them to take over from the start, but the goal was for my participation to diminish throughout the semester. Students needed to approach the discussion area as a place to talk about what they were learning. What were their questions? What else did they want to know? How were they making sense of their learning? What was the importance of what they were learning? How would they use it in the future? What problems or discoveries were occurring as they were assessing?

Because the forum replaced the written reflections, I included it as a part of the grading. A total of 75 points was delegated to this component of the course, although I was uncertain how those points would be earned. I anticipated that everyone would participate to the same extent, so I did not think that points would be an issue.

Initial student response to the forum

The students' first entry was to let me know that they had successfully reached the site. Once they had reached it, they were to respond to a brief survey. For one of the questions, each student was

---

Reflection format

Part 1: A brief statement is to be written with regard to the topic.
   This may be a description, an opinion, or summary statement.

Part 2: This section makes connections to the individual's experiences or to what she or he learned.

Part 3: This section should illuminate how the individual will use this information or idea. As a result of this reading or experience, what will the individual do next? How will the individual make use of this information?

Student postings	
Number of students	Postings
23	≤13
18	14–24
1	26
1	30
1	31
1	62

Note. Total postings = 639; mean = 14.

could (a) enable them to get help on their coursework, (b) give the "quiet" students a place to speak up; (c) provide a place for students to talk in an open format, and (d) afford one more opportunity to gain experience with technology.

What happened during the semester

Initial analysis of the data occurred through a simple counting of the postings on the discussion board. During the semester there were 639 postings, which sounds like an enormous number. As the instructor, I think that for an initial experience it was significant that there were so many postings. However, a closer look at them presents a clearer idea of student participation over the course of the semester.

Individual students had as few as 2 postings and as many as 62 (see Table). The average number of postings was 14. Twenty-three of the students posted 13 or fewer times. Eighteen students posted 14 to 24 times. Then, there was one student each for 26, 30, 31, and 62 postings. Two of the three students who did not post an opinion about the discussion area also had some of the lowest participation in the forum: 5 postings and 2 postings. When questioned about their lack of participation, they responded that they were having trouble reaching the site because of their computers. The third student had a much higher rate (18 postings); however, these postings only occurred after I sent midterm failing notices.

to indicate her or his attitude about using the discussion area. Of the 45 students (12 of whom I had taught the prior semester) enrolled in two classes, only 6 had ever used a discussion area in any of their courses. All but 3 students had a positive attitude about using the forum. (Those 3 did not respond to the initial prompt, so I am unsure about their attitude.) In general, the students who did respond expressed a variety of ideas that made me believe the forum was going to be extremely valuable. The following are representative of the students' responses (all names are pseudonyms assigned without regard to sex of the student).

Birdie: This [the forum] is a town hall where you can discuss back and forth. I'm glad that you decided to do this.

Libby: It [the forum] will encourage people who don't speak up but want to ask questions.

Carmen: This [the forum] will be important if we have any questions about an upcoming assignment when we are at home.

Roy: I can get assistance, ideas, and feedback. I like the idea of putting a question or idea out there and getting feedback from others.

Edgar: I think it [the forum] is a good way to communicate in and out of the classroom.

These comments and others like them led me to believe that the students were glad that the forum was part of the course. They saw the value of using it in a variety of ways. Using the forum

Beginning the discussions

I continued analysis of the data by looking at the content of the responses to my prompts. At the beginning, prompts were one- or two-word topics generated from readings or class discussions. The prompts were given in either a question or a statement format. Topics were related to the course goals, the assessment texts, and personal classroom experiences as students. I limited the prompts because I did not want to direct the students' postings. I wanted the students to express their ideas rather than strictly answer a question that I had posted.

Student postings ranged from a couple of words to more than a page, single-spaced. Not all students responded to all of the prompts. Generally, the student entries were five to eight sentences. For example, when I posted the subject "Retelling," I wanted to get feedback from the activity that we had done in class. Retellings are used to determine comprehension of a passage that the student has read or that has been read to the student. The following are examples of ways the students responded.

> The class retelling activity was an excellent example of the different ways to approach retellings. It was fun as well. Because I had an increased insight about the possible outcomes, I was much better prepared to work with my assessment student. She impressed me that as a third grader she could recall so many details when she read orally. In the written retelling of a listening passage, she conveyed the main idea succinctly. In working with a class, being aware of possible outcomes and how prior knowledge affects them will be beneficial in both planning and assessment. (Mark)

> The class activity today defiantly [sic] helped clear up any uncertainties I had about retelling. I saw how these retellings could help you learn so much about a student and their comprehension skills and strategies. I think this activity really impressed me. I think you could tell about a person's learning styles and personalities while listening to their retelling of the story. Also, the different types of retellings that people did greatly affected the way they responded. You could use all of these techniques for retelling and see where a student's strengths and weaknesses were. (Carmen)

For another prompt, I simply gave them "Assessment Text." This was done after they had read the first 50 pages of the textbook. In this portion of the text, the author provides definitions for diagnostic teaching, types of readers, and attributes of effective readers. Because I only stated the topic, the students could determine what they wanted to say. These are two typical responses:

> I think the assessment text is a great tool to begin working with. It is laid out quite well and seems easy to use. I think it would be interesting to compare our case study with the student's actual teacher. Judging from what we learned in class and the time I have spent with my student, the assessing will be a skill that we will have to take time to develop. (Edgar)

> I think that the assessment text is an excellent tool for us. It really gives us the tests and strategies to use first-hand. Being able to see the word lists and the miscue analysis material [gives] a much clearer picture of what to do with the student that we are assessing. It also shows us how to manage and take notes on those things in order to record information efficiently. (Phyllis)

Rather than taking the initiative for the postings, the majority of students waited for me to post a prompt. In fact, if I had not kept posting, many of them would have quit. For these students, the teacher maintained control of the discourse.

Final analysis of the data occurred by identifying the students who posted beyond my prompts. Of the 45 students, 14 initiated postings on their own. The entries included (a) reactions to newspaper articles related to educational issues, (b) helpful teacher websites, (c) how to get free books and teaching materials, (d) requests for assistance with assignments, and (e) positive feedback and encouragement to other classmates.

Fortunately, there were three students who were rather prolific. These students initiated topics, wrote the lengthiest entries, and had at least 30 postings on the site. Their postings appeared to demonstrate a greater depth of thought (reflection), whether they were responding to my posting or to a peer's. The students generated ideas, discussed the postings in various ways, made connections with experiences or beliefs, and projected what might happen next. These postings more nearly followed the suggested reflection format. The following is Allen's response to my posting with regard to the retelling demonstration.

> The retelling from class did much in the way of clarifying my understanding. A lot of factors seem to affect the retelling. Prior knowledge definitely plays a role as

evidenced by the substitution of *call* in the place of *write*. I think just background in general and the purpose for reading make a big difference in the comprehension and the retelling. I noticed everyone made a big point of memorizing the details like 12 weeks. The instructor did not give questions on the reading, yet everyone seemed to try to remember the details as if they were to be tested. I think this is probably because in most of our experiences, we were forced to regurgitate details in order to prove our comprehension of a reading. I remember how much I hated comprehension as a young student. I would understand what I read, but sometimes could not remember all of the details and then would not make a very good grade. Also, sometimes, students can learn to answer questions without even understanding the reading. A retelling tells a lot about the student's comprehension and not just her/his memory. I find it interesting that even though all the details remained at least close to the original story, the comprehension failed in many of the cases. I think in the past details have been overemphasized when comprehension is really what is important. Reading does not take place unless comprehension does. Otherwise, it is just sounding out or speaking of words. Plus, I think a retelling would be less formal than a written quiz of questions putting the students more at ease. I also found the difference between the oral and written retelling interesting. One person wanted to write because she thought it would be easier. Maybe some students are more intimidated by having to write while others are more intimidated by having to speak. Maybe as teachers we need to keep that in mind.

This entry clearly shows many more connections between what occurred during the class experience with retellings and the student's personal beliefs and experiences. It goes beyond a simple response as demonstrated in the other examples, which resemble bookish responses. The majority of Allen's postings were similar. The thoughtfulness of his responses added a great deal to the forum.

The following posting is similar to many of the responses that students wrote to one another. Terry had asked for some help with her goals, and Maria wrote this response. Although it sounds like advice, clearly Maria has reflected on what Terry said and then responded using her own educational beliefs and experiences.

Terry, I read your response to your goals and would like to offer a few words of encouragement. First of all, you will be ready when it comes time to teach.... I have faith that all the hours, lectures, information, and materials will come together in the end or should I say the beginning of our careers. I have no doubt I will be looking back at my notes and handouts for ideas and information. What I have done is to try and stay organized now, so it will pay off later. Get a binder folder and file your "Teaching Techniques" from other classes. Go back through your notes and write out any lesson plan ideas. There are many ideas in the book, too. If you do not have this information, let me know and I would be happy to make a copy.... Please respond if you would like and if there is anything I can do, let me know. See you Monday! Maria

What did I notice?

One of my first observations was that some of the students who had given lengthy, thoughtful reflections during the fall semester were not giving me very much on the forum. Although young learners are not intimidated by this technology, Thompson, Nay, and Malone (2000) used a survey to ascertain that forums intimidated their college students *until* the students had opportunities to use this technology for their coursework. I wondered if technology use was the problem with my students.

When I questioned students about their participation, they gave me several responses. For example, Edgar had been in my fall class. He came to me because he was concerned about the brevity of his responses. I, too, had noticed that during the fall his reflections had been much more elaborate. He had made a greater number of connections with the material, and it was obvious that he was formulating his beliefs about literacy practices. When I asked what he thought the problem was, he said that he found it hard to reflect when someone other than the teacher was going to read it.

Several students were embarrassed to have others read what they had written. I thought that was odd because I was reading and "grading" their writing, and that did not seem to bother them. When I questioned several other students about their limited number of postings, they responded that they felt as though others had already said what they wanted to say, so they did not need to say it again.

From the first postings on the forum, I anticipated that this format of discourse would give students who were less likely to speak out in class the opportunity to be "heard." Unfortunately, this was not the case. The students who were silent in class responded in a matter-of-fact way on the forum; there was no increase in their voluntary participation when this new format was a requirement. The forum did give the students who were already very verbal during class discussions one more chance to speak. The more prolific in class were the same students who were more prolific on the forum.

For most students, the length of reflection was limited, especially in response to my prompts. Students were responding as directed (following the reflection format), but they did not seem to go much beyond what was necessary. When I asked a question or posed a topic, they responded. This behavior resembled typical classroom patterns (Cazden, 1988; Mehan, 1979). On the other hand, when the students asked a question or posted an idea, there was conversation, like Maria's response to Terry.

As for the collegiality, the interchanges between students suggest that for some of these preservice teachers there is openness to the idea of sharing once in the classroom. When the students were responding to one another's questions and ideas, there was greater reflection and a more conversational tone. The example of Maria's response to Terry demonstrated that Maria was thinking ahead and that she was willing to share her ideas with a classmate. In addition, while students were conducting the reading assessments and a problem arose, they did seek help on the forum. For example, Kit posed the following problem there.

As you might remember from class discussion, I have an ESL student. He is in the fifth grade, but his independent level is third-grade level. I'm worried because his textbooks are at the sixth-grade level, making it nearly impossible to comprehend what needs to be learned. The only progress I have made with him is allowing him to read text that he is interested in like soccer or baseball. His writing ability is also very low. Does anybody know anything that I can do to help him improve his grade level of reading? I really don't want to just get the information that I need for my case study and leave him high and dry without helping him. I only have one hour a day, twice a week to spend time with him at his school. ANY suggestions are GREATLY appreciated.

Three students offered Kit assistance with her student. Two of the responses provided book titles and authors that might help. Another student offered her some writing ideas that would involve the elementary student in reading his own writing.

Several other students posed questions about their case studies, class goals, and teaching materials. Although not everyone responded to the postings, those who did were positive and helpful. They often expressed similar problems accompanied by suggestions that might help their peers. Generally, the students' responses to one another had a greater sense of thoughtfulness than the ones they gave to my postings. Like the preservice teachers in McIntyre and Tlusty (1995), the students in this study found moral support on the forum. Because the forum was beneficial in this way, participants might use this method to communicate with other teachers once they have their own classrooms.

Several students, Anna, Marlys, and Birdie, did take command of their learning. They posed some conversation-producing topics. Anna posted a newspaper article about a third grader who was suspended from school because he had drawn a picture of a soldier with a gun. Marlys shared information about her daughter's reading disability that required her daughter to use tinted glasses to do her work, which led to another student sharing information about attention deficit disorder. Last, Birdie posted the story of a 16-year-old who committed suicide at school. All of these postings led to extended responses. Edgar, who had been concerned about his shorter, less reflective responses, posted several longer and more reflective postings in response to the article on the suspended child.

What were my problems?

Some "funny" things happened. One of my biggest problems occurred when I decided that the forum would replace the written reflections. Because I still wanted students to be thoughtful and to elaborate on their ideas, my expectations were not being met by responses on the forum. Several weeks after we started, I thought that if I copied postings and responded to them individually then the students might extend their postings. The students were glad to get my responses, but my idea did nothing to change their actions.

With regard to grading, the forum presented more of a problem. Because written reflections were part of my accountability system, I thought that the discussion area needed to be part of it as well. When it came time to give a grade, I found myself counting the number of entries rather than the content of the postings. In an attempt to add a little rigor to the process, I included two other characteristics—responding over the entire semester and responding to the initial prompts. I consider grading in this manner counterproductive to reflectivity.

The forum provided the students with the opportunity to speak more often in a more public place. Although it did cause the quiet ones to speak more often than they did in class, it did not create enough comfort for them to speak there. My belief that the forum would encourage students to participate and create more dialogue because it was less threatening was faulty. Like other classroom practices (Boggs, 1972; Heath, 1983; Tharp & Gallimore, 1991), the forum supported a different type of interaction, but it did not necessarily change the participation level or the manner in which students participated.

I hypothesized that this activity was something in which everyone would take part. Since technology and its use in the classroom have become an important aspect of education and life, I assumed that students would jump at the chance to use this tool. However, as Carboni (1999) determined, it is often the same individuals contributing many of the postings. When I questioned a few who did not participate much, several of the students stated that they did not have time. There were even a few who said that, because they did not know where they were going to teach, they did not even know if their district would have computers, and they would learn about them when the time came. I found these attitudes surprising because I wondered if the students would have made time to do written responses to the initial assignments.

Thinking that the students would be more reflective was also faulty. I believe that I would have gotten more from the majority of them if I had required the written reflections that I had had students do in the past. Perhaps the forum was still too public for students, or this was not the correct way to use it. As pointed out by McIntyre and Tlusty (1995), the frequency of usage and the length of the messages do not create reflective students; the discussion board merely creates another opportunity.

Collegial conversations occurred when the students had real concerns. The authenticity of these concerns is the key to participation. The assignments that instructors create are very important. We can develop assignments that we think are authentic. Unfortunately, if the students do not view them as authentic, then their responses will probably reflect that idea. Spending the time to create authentic assignments is a key factor.

What did I learn?

The most important lesson I learned about using a Web-based discussion board is to incorporate it into the learning environment slowly. Do not try to accomplish too many things at once. Although discussion boards can be created easily, experience, accessibility, and time affect the way that an individual is able to maintain them. I was excited that students were getting one more occasion to talk; however, it meant that it was one more place for me to respond. As a result, I found that my *lack* of experience, accessibility, and time often hindered what I wanted to accomplish. The students often expressed these same hindrances.

What will I do next time?

First, I will not have the forum replace another assignment. If it is important enough to be included, then it needs to be part of the syllabus from the beginning. I will have the students do some kind of introductory entry so that we will know a little bit about people's backgrounds. However, I am going to have them assume pseudonyms and am curious to see if this will help students speak more. Perhaps if no one knows who the other people really are, then the forum will be less threatening.

Next time students will self-assess. We will devise a rubric together, but I think it is important for them to do the grading. Perhaps if they have that knowledge in the beginning, they may be more apt to participate fully.

Last, students will be encouraged to pose questions, provide information related to materials, suggest website addresses, and give any other helpful information. They also will be welcome to bring up topics that they think will be of interest to the group. I will provide some model ideas but will encourage students to take the lead. Encouraging them to identify their major concerns and issues will be one of my focuses for the use of the forum.

Final thoughts

The purpose of this study was to determine the effect that an online discussion board would have on the discourse and reflection of preservice teachers. Like others (Copeland, 1986; Zeichner & Liston, 1996), I believe that discourse is important to the development of reflection that allows the individual to look at the circumstances and then change them, either in process or in future. If we can articulate what we know, then we have the opportunity to reflect on it and make changes (Barnes, 1976). At the same time, I advocated the use of the forum as a means of creating further opportunities for discourse in hopes that it would change some of the existing classroom discourse patterns, promote collegial conversations, and increase the use of technology. For some students, the discourse pattern was different and collegial conversations existed. The volume of messages demonstrates that the forum was well used. Thus, the results of these hypotheses are supported, but refinement is needed. In addition, I now have a clearer understanding of how this technology can work and so I will continue its use in my courses. However, I am going to limit my expectations of what it can do.

REFERENCES

Adkins, M. (1991). *Computer-mediated communication and interpersonal perceptions.* Paper presented at the annual meeting of the Eastern Communication Association, Pittsburgh, PA.

Bakkenes, I., de Brabander, C., & Imants, J. (1999). Teacher isolation and communication network analysis in primary schools. *Educational Administration Quarterly, 35,* 166–202.

Barnes, D. (1976). *From communication to curriculum.* London: Penguin.

Barnes, D. (1990). *Language, the learner, and the school.* Portsmouth, NH: Boynton/Cook.

Barnes, D. (1995). Talking and learning in classrooms: An introduction. *Primary Voices K–6, 3*(1), 2–7.

Boggs, S.T. (1972). *Speaking, relating, and learning: A study of Hawaiian children at home and at school.* Norwood, NJ: Ablex.

Brooks, D., & Kopp, T. (1989). Technology in teacher education. *Journal of Teacher Education, 18,* 2–8.

Bruner, J.S. (1966). *Toward a theory of instruction.* Cambridge, MA: The Belknap Press of Harvard University.

Carboni, L.W. (1999). *How might an online discussion forum support teachers' professional development in mathematics? A first look.* Paper presented at the annual meeting of Mathematics Teacher Educators, Chicago, IL.

Cazden, C. (1988). *Classroom discourse: The language of teaching and learning*. Portsmouth, NH: Heinemann.

Chesebro, J., & Bonsall, D. (1989). *Computer-mediated communication*. Tuscaloosa, AL: The University of Alabama.

Copeland, W.D. (1986). *The RITE framework for teacher education: Preservice applications. Reality and reform in clinical teacher education*. New York: Random House.

Good, T.L., & Brophy, J.E. (2000). *Looking in classrooms*. New York: Longman.

Guthrie, L.F., & Richardson, S. (1995). Turned on to language arts: Computer literacy in the primary grades. *Educational Leadership, 53*(2), 2–7.

Heath, S.B. (1983). *Ways with words*. New York: Cambridge University Press.

Hoetker, W.J., & Ahlbrand, W.P. (1969). The persistence of recitation. *American Educational Research Journal, 6,* 145–167.

Johnson, D.W., & Johnson, R. (1991). *Learning together and alone: Cooperative, competitive, and individualistic learning* (3rd ed.). Englewood Cliffs, NJ: Prentice-Hall. (Original work published 1987)

Leu, D. (2000). Literacy and technology: Deictic consequences for literacy education in an information age. In M.L. Kamil, P. Mosenthal, P.D. Pearson, and R. Barr (Eds.), *Handbook of reading research, Volume 3* (pp. 743–770). Mahwah, NJ: Erlbaum.

Lindsey-North, J.L. (2000). *Incorporating a course website into teaching: A promising practice, especially for teacher education*. (ERIC Document Reproduction Service No. ED447077)

McIntyre, S.R., & Tlusty, R.H. (1995). *Computer-mediated discourse: Electronic dialogue journaling and reflective practice*. Paper presented at the annual meeting of the American Educational Research Association, San Francisco, CA.

Mehan, H. (1979). *Learning lessons*. Cambridge, MA: Harvard University Press.

Palincsar, A.S., & Brown, A.L. (1984). Reciprocal teaching of comprehension fostering and monitoring activities. *Cognition and Instruction, 1,* 117–175.

Pradl, G. (Ed.). (1982). *Prospect and retrospect: Selected essays of James Britton*. Montclair, NJ: Boynton/Cook.

Staton, J., Shuy, R., Peyton, M., & Reed, L. (Eds.). (1988). *Dialogue journal communication: Classroom, linguistic, social and cognitive views*. Norwood, NJ: Ablex.

Tharp, R., & Gallimore, R. (1991). *The instructional conversation: Teaching and learning in social activity*. Santa Cruz, CA: National Center for Research on Cultural Diversity and Second Language Learning.

Thayer, V.T. (1928). *The passing of the recitation*. Boston: Heath.

Thompson, J.C., Jr., Nay, F.W., & Malone, B.G. (2000). *Utilizing the Internet to supplement classroom instruction: An analysis of longitudinal data*. Paper presented at the annual meeting of the Mid-Western Educational Research Association, Chicago, IL.

Vygotsky, L.S. (1978). *Mind in society*. Cambridge, MA: Harvard University Press.

Wells, G., & Chiang-Wells, G.L. (1992). *Constructing knowledge together*. Portsmouth, NH: Heinemann.

Walker, B. (2000). *Diagnostic teaching of reading* (4th ed.). Upper Saddle River, NJ: Merrill.

Zeichner, K.M., & Liston, D.P. (1996). *Reflective teaching: An introduction*. Mahwah, NJ: Erlbaum.

Guest authors: Anne P. Sweet
John T. Guthrie

How children's motivations relate to literacy development and instruction

Helping students become engaged in long-term literacy activity is a challenge for teachers at every grade level. Teachers and researchers agree that motivation is central to literacy development, yet few have asked what we mean by literacy motivation. In this column we look at the spectrum of motivations that children bring into the classroom and discuss how these motivations connect to instruction.

We have asked many children, "Why are you reading this text?" Children's reasons and goals for reading are their literacy motivations. We have used focus groups, clinical interviews, and self-report questionnaires to illuminate the depth and stability of children's motivations for reading and writing. In these different inquiries, children have expressed eight distinct motivations for literacy. A typical child possesses several motivations, but not all are equally powerful. Students in third to fifth grades reported their reasons for reading in the following ways:

• One student noted, "I like reading mysteries because it is fun to get lost in the book," showing *involvement* as a goal for reading.

• Many children report reading about favorite topics. For example, "I like to find out more about cheetahs because they are really amazing," expresses the motivation of *curiosity*. This student's interest in cheetahs propels her to learn about the world around her through reading informational books.

• Some students are attracted by *challenge*. They like figuring out a complex plot or integrating a lot of facts about a topic, such as spiders.

• Children frequently report *social interaction* as motivation for literacy. When students share a book with friends, gain a partner in collaborative writing, become a member of a book club, maintain a friend through sharing books, or exchange interests, they are socially motivated.

• Besides reading for their own interest, children often report reading "because the teacher said to." We characterize this as a *compliance* motivation. These students are interacting with a text in order to meet the teacher's expectation or to conform to a classroom requirement.

• One student reported that she reads or writes "to get as many points as I can." Her motivational goal is *recognition*, the desire to feel publicly acknowledged.

• A frequent goal reported by students is *competition*. These students strive to be the best at literacy tasks, want to demonstrate superiority, and work hard to achieve high grades.

• Last, but not least, students confess *work avoidance* as a goal for some reading and writing. For example one student said, "I am writing this story so I won't have to read my book."

These brief examples illustrate our general finding that children's motivations for literacy are multidimensional and diverse. Children are not merely motivated or unmotivated, but they possess a profile of different types of motivational goals. Just as students bring a diversity of background experiences and knowledge to the classroom, they also bring a variety of motivational orientations. Recognizing the different characteristics of these motivations is the first step toward understanding how to foster the growth of long-term literacy participation.

Intrinsic motivations sustain long-term literacy learning

We distinguish between intrinsic and extrinsic motivations. As described by Deci and his colleagues (Deci, Vallerand, Pelletier, & Ryan, 1991), intrinsic motivations are goals that are internal to the learner. Intrinsic motivations spring from personal interests and private experiences that develop into reasons for reading. These reasons include: involvement, curiosity, social interaction, and challenge. One of our students reported that he reads for involvement:

Last week I was getting into a book I was reading 'cause I was almost done. I

Reprinted from *The Reading Teacher* (1996), 49, 660–662.

carried the book with me in my hand going to meet a friend. I was reading and it was a straight street, so I just went up the street reading the book.

In contrast, extrinsic motivations originate with the teacher or the parent. For example, students who read to receive points or gold stars are motivated by the incentive provided by the teacher. Compliance, recognition, and getting good grades are examples of frequently stated goals that operate as extrinsic motivations for reading and writing.

Intrinsic and extrinsic motivations influence the learner in very different ways. Intrinsic motivations appear to be imperative to lifelong, voluntary reading. Students who read frequently and widely are pursuing personal, internalized goals (Wigfield, in press). Strategies such as finding books, maintaining a place for reading, preserving large amounts of time for reading activities, and coping with distractions are learned and sustained by intrinsic motivations.

Strong internal purposes for reading are needed to persevere in learning complex strategies such as summarizing, self-monitoring, and drawing inferences during reading. Because intrinsic motivations last longer and support sustained thinking, they are vital to higher order strategy development (Pintrich & Schrauben, 1992). Extrinsic motivations lead to shallow processing. If students can finish assignments (fulfill a compliance motivation) by using low-level strategies rather than more difficult ones, they will tend to use the least effort. Extrinsic motivations lead to "least effort" literacy styles, whereas intrinsic motivations are more likely to inspire long-term literacy commitments.

Extrinsic motivation controls behavior temporarily

Extrinsic motivations that students have reported to us include compliance, recognition, competition, and work-avoidance. These goals for reading and writing are powerful because they induce immediate effort and attention, but they are also short-term. For example, telling students that they will win points and/or lose privileges will command attention and effort toward a literacy task such as answering comprehension questions, but only temporarily, because the literacy activity terminates when the goal is attained. If they are reading to complete an assignment, the reading stops when the compliance motivation is fulfilled. Extrinsic motivations do not regenerate themselves. The teacher must provide a new goal to induce new reading activities. One of our students, Kerrin, described to the interviewer how her reading complies with the classroom routine.

I: Did you finish the *Wonderful Flight to the Mushroom Planet* yet?

K: No, we got a few pages yet.

I: Do you think that you will read the whole book?

K: Yeah, she says to finish them.

I: Do you like science fiction books?

K: Uh huh.

I: How do you know when to read?

K: The teacher tells us.

I: Have you finished the book report?

K: The teacher hasn't decided.

Cameron and Pierce (1994) examined more than 150 studies about the effect of extrinsic rewards on intrinsic motivation. They concluded that when students are rewarded for completing tasks, irrespective of success (like winning a prize for finishing a book), intrinsic motivations decrease. Both time engaged in the task and attitude toward the activity (such as reading) decreased. Similarly, McLoyd (1979) found that students who had been rewarded for reading high-interest books subsequently read less in a free time period than children who had also read high-interest books but had not been rewarded. The reward increased the reading time for students with low-interest books. McLoyd (1979) reasoned that children who were not rewarded for reading high-interest books attributed the cause of their reading to positive, internal factors (e.g., interest, curiosity). Their counterparts, who were rewarded, attributed their reading behavior to external factors, so the reading behavior diminished when the external reward was removed.

The distinction between intrinsic motivation and extrinsic motivation, we believe, is pivotal for teachers. Motivations appear to work in different ways. Intrinsic motivations enhance long-term strategy development and time spent in literacy activities. Extrinsic ones have a positive short-term effect on controlling behavior and attention to uninteresting tasks but have a negative long-term effect on building literacy lifestyles.

Intrinsic motivations are needed in integrated instruction

Teachers who want to develop intrinsic motivations may construct integrated instruction that unifies reading, writing, science, and social studies (see Guthrie, McCann, Hynd, & Stahl, in press). Successful integrated instruction is based on learners' curiosities and aesthetic involvements and permits students to connect ideas across many types of texts. Integrated instruction requires self-directed learning. Students identify their own interests, choose appropriate books, and extend their literacy in ways that fulfill their own individual visions. An emphasis on intrinsic motivations leads to collaborative activity, because social motivations are prominent among elementary and middle school learners. Direct instruction in skills and strategies is not neglected, but it is situated in ways that serve content learning.

Teachers who integrate instruction confirm the role of intrinsic motivation (Sweet & Guthrie, in press). They describe highly motivated learners as intrinsically involved, engrossed in learning, and sharply focused on lesson content. They expect these students to use higher order strategies, to interact socially with peers, and to persist in the face of obstacles. In contrast, students who were less intrinsically motivated were expected not to exhibit these behaviors. Integrated instruction cannot easily be built on extrinsic motivational schemes. A system of points and external rewards will not sustain the long-term, self-directed, collaborative learning that is required in highly integrated instruction.

Extrinsic motivations are needed for skill-building

When instruction is organized around skills related to reading, writing, and spelling, ample practice is needed. Because skill-based teachers need to set goals for excellent performance and to cover an important set of objectives, an emphasis on performance incentives is compatible with well-organized, sequential language arts teaching that emphasizes basic skills.

Sequentially organized language arts teaching may not be compatible with an emphasis on intrinsic motivations. Motivations such as curiosity and involvement may lead students to choose topics and books that are inconsistent with the prescribed sequence. The preset instructional organization may be disturbed when intrinsic goals are incorporated into the mainstream of a skill-centered curriculum.

Teachers should align their motivational climate with their instruction

For centuries, teachers have been providing instruction without analyzing children's motivations for reading. Many teachers have inspired lifelong literacy without reflecting on the learners' motivations or on their own beliefs about motivations. However, we cannot afford to ignore the growing knowledge base in literacy motivation. Far too many students fail to acquire basic competencies and choose not to utilize the literacy competence they possess.

There are places for both intrinsic and extrinsic motivations in every classroom. At times when skill building and behavior control are necessary, extrinsic incentives are useful. When higher order literacy and self-directed learning are desired, the importance of students' intrinsic motivation should increase. By aligning their motivational support system with their instructional practices, teachers can enhance the development of long-term literacy engagement.

References

Cameron, J., & Pierce, W.D. (1994). Reinforcement, reward, and intrinsic motivation: A meta-analysis. *Review of Educational Research, 64*, 363 – 423.

Deci, E.L., Vallerand, R.J., Pelletier, L.G., & Ryan, R.M. (1991). Motivation and education: The self-determination perspective. *Educational Psychologist, 26*, 325 – 346.

Guthrie, J.T., McCann, A., Hynd, C., & Stahl, S. (in press). Classroom contexts promoting literacy engagement. In J. Flood, D. Lapp, & S.B. Heath (Eds.), *Handbook for literacy educators: Research on teaching the communications and visual arts.* New York: Macmillan.

McLoyd, V.C. (1979). The effects of extrinsic rewards of differential value on high and low intrinsic interest. *Child Development, 50*, 1010 – 1019.

Pintrich, P.R., & Schrauben, B. (1992). Students' motivational beliefs and their cognitive engagement in classroom academic tasks. In D.H. Schunk & J.L. Meese (Eds.), *Student perceptions in the classroom* (pp. 149 – 184). Hillsdale, NJ: Erlbaum.

Sweet, A.P., & Guthrie, J.T. (in press). *Teacher perceptions and students' motivation to read* (Research Report). Athens, GA: University of Georgia, National Reading Research Center.

Wigfield, A. (in press). *Dimensions of children's motivations for reading: An initial study* (Research Report). Athens, GA: University of Georgia, National Reading Research Center.

The Intermediate Grades

What makes intermediate-grade students want to read?

Jo Worthy

There is wide agreement among literacy researchers that students who read more become more proficient in reading fluency and comprehension, as well as general vocabulary and cognitive development (Anderson, Wilson, & Fielding, 1988; Stanovich, 1986). When students do not read on their own, their general academic progress is in jeopardy. Educational researchers agree that "schools must deliberately and thoughtfully attract children to reading" (Morrow, 1991, p. 682). The question is "how?"

In the past few years, several research studies have gone directly to the source, asking intermediate-grade students to talk about what their language arts teachers can do to make reading more attractive in school. Students who are avid readers, students who say they "hate to read," third graders, sixth graders, and students in between have remarkably similar ideas about which aspects of the classroom environment are the most motivating (Ivey & Broaddus, 2001; Worthy, 1998, 2000; Worthy, Patterson, Salas, Prater, & Turner, in press).

It is important to mention something that, perhaps surprisingly, students did not consider motivating. School programs often use rewards as incentive to read, and many teachers believe they work, but students generally do not consider them to be important (Worthy, 2000). In fact, when points, grades, or other favors are offered for reading tasks, students are given the impression that reading is a chore not worth doing unless it is rewarded (Kohn, 1993). The factors that have been found to be especially relevant to students' reading attitudes and motivation fall into two general categories: engaging instruction and choice and variety in reading materials. In describing the categories, I include student quotes from reading motivation studies.

Engaging instruction

Students offered many suggestions to make reading more appealing in the classroom. In all of the studies reviewed, students asked for more teacher read-alouds and more time to read independently in school. While most students had their own interests and preferences, the majority wanted to hear about good books from teachers, to have teachers introduce books that students would like, and to read segments "to get us interested." They also wanted more time to read in school, "so we get a habit of it," as one student put it. Students commented that teachers' enthusiasm about reading is transparent. "If they show us books they like and they're, like, real excited, we get interested in reading, too." Teachers who treat reading as merely a school subject that "you gotta do," may negatively influence students' feelings toward reading (Worthy, 2000).

Students also requested that they be given some time to read for enjoyment without required assignments such as worksheets or responses. One student asked, "Do we have to have journal entries every time we read?" Creative dramatics such as role-playing, Readers Theatre, and reading poetry aloud were mentioned by many students as motivating (Worthy, 2000).

Choice and variety in reading material

A common characteristic among avid adult readers is that they have had the opportunity to read materials of their own choosing (Carlsen & Sherrill, 1988). Intermediate-grade students also like to choose their own materials and, like adults, their tastes are varied and individual. When students were asked what they would choose to read, the most common choices were magazines, comic books, mysteries or books with scary themes, jokes and humorous stories, materials about sports, series books, and books with relevant characters and themes. Younger students also liked picture books and books that were "easy to read" (Worthy et al., in press).

Students in several classrooms complained about the limited number of books and the lack of new, relevant books in their classroom libraries. One student said, "She could get some new books in the room. Hers are from the 1960s!" (Worthy, 2000).

Many students listed books that their teachers had introduced or read out loud as some of their favorites. Based on this information, it might be tempting to fill a classroom library with the most popular publications along with more conventional school texts. However, it is important to note the wide variety of publications that students mentioned and to consider that each student is an individual with different experiences whose preferences and motivation may change with time and in response to a variety of factors. For example, when asked what he would read if he had unlimited choice, Chris (pseudonym) answered "Nothing. I hate to read." Indeed, he never checked out books from the library and rarely completed reading assignments. Chris had one major interest, wrestling, and he talked of nothing else. Because there were no materials on wrestling available in his school, he simply did not read. When he discovered wrestling magazines and information on the Internet, he began to devour them and, later, to try out other reading materials (Worthy & Sailors, 2001).

Carolina, a recent immigrant from Mexico, quickly learned to communicate in English, but she resisted U.S. culture and English literacy and turned up her nose at the series books other girls her age were reading. When she discovered books written by Mexican American authors, Carolina's world changed. She was enthralled with bilingual picture books and books that included Spanish words embedded in English text, which she would pronounce with a proud flair. She was particularly moved by books about visiting relatives in Mexico (Worthy & Sailors, 2001).

Many educators tend to think they must exert control over the materials that are available for school reading. While it is important for educators to ensure that students have access to high-quality, conceptually challenging literature, it is also essential to address students' preferences in order to capture their attention and engagement and, thus, to foster learning. Fortunately, students seem to know what's good for them. The academic and affective benefits of using materials that students prefer include enhanced fluency, vocabulary, linguistic competence, confidence, and motivation (Carlsen & Sherrill, 1988). Students who can proficiently read a wide variety of materials and formats will be better prepared for the real-world reading tasks they will encounter in their lives. If we want to reach students, it is important to offer them variety in reading formats and to listen to their preferences.

For many students, "young adolescence marks the beginning of a downward trend in academics" (Ryan & Patrick, 2001, p. 438). This situation is especially grievous for reluctant readers, minority students, and students from economically impoverished backgrounds, whose school libraries typically do not provide sufficient types or quantities of books that are necessary for academic growth as well as interesting and relevant to students (Neuman & Celano, 2001). This situation is made worse by the fact that few schools provide reading materials for classroom library collections.

Good news

The studies reviewed in this column suggest that students are savvy in their understanding of reading motivation. If we listen to students and attend to what they say about classroom instruction and reading materials, schools can have profound effects on students' motivation, engagement, and, ultimately, achievement.

References

Anderson, R.C., Wilson, P.T., & Fielding, L.G. (1988). Growth in reading and how children spent their time outside school. *Reading Research Quarterly, 23,* 285–303.

Carlsen, R., & Sherrill, A. (1988). *Voices of readers: How we come to love books.* Urbana, IL: National Council of Teachers of English.

Ivey, G., & Broaddus, K. (2001). "Just plain reading": A survey of what makes students want to read in middle school classrooms. *Reading Research Quarterly, 36,* 350–377.

Kohn, A. (1993). *Punished by rewards: The trouble with gold stars, incentive plans, A's, praise, and other bribes.* Boston: Houghton Mifflin.

Morrow, L. (1991). Promoting voluntary reading. In J. Flood, J. Jensen, D. Lapp, & J. Squire (Eds.), *Handbook of research on teaching the English language arts* (pp. 681–690). New York: Macmillan.

Neuman, S., & Celano, D. (2001). Access to print in low-income and middle-income communities: An ecological study of four neighborhoods. *Reading Research Quarterly, 36,* 8–26.

Ryan, A.M., & Patrick, H. (2001). The classroom environment and changes in adolescents' motivation and engagement during middle school. *American Educational Research Journal, 38,* 437–460.

Stanovich, K. (1986). Matthew effects in reading: Some consequences of individual differences in the acquisition of literacy. *Reading Research Quarterly, 21,* 360–406.

Worthy, J. (1998). "On every page someone gets killed!" Book conversations you don't hear in school. *Journal of Adolescent & Adult Literacy, 41,* 508–517.

Worthy, J. (2000). Teachers' and students' suggestions for motivating middle school students to read. *Yearbook of the National Reading Conference, 49,* 441–451.

Worthy, J., Patterson, E., Salas, R., Prater, S., & Turner, M. (in press). "More than just reading": The human factor in reaching resistant readers. *Reading Research and Instruction.*

Worthy, J., & Sailors M. (2001). "That book isn't on my level": Moving beyond text difficulty in personalizing reading choices. *The New Advocate, 14,* 229–239.

Jo Worthy

"On every page someone gets killed!" Book conversations you don't hear in school

The perspectives of two middle school reluctant readers can inform educators who want to improve students' engagement with reading.

While eating ice cream outside on a warm spring night, my sixth-grade son, Jared, and his friend, Chase, began talking about books they had recently read and books they were planning to read. They weren't talking to me, but I asked them to hold their thoughts while I ran to the car to get my tape recorder. After some self-conscious giggling and posturing, they continued their conversation, with Chase taking the lead.

> Chase: I just read *Cycle of the Werewolf* (King, 1983). It was only 120 pages, and most of Stephen King's books are like 500 pages. And the thing about it is, it's so gripping. On every page someone gets killed.
>
> Jared: Yeah! But I mean it's really, really descriptive, and the pictures are amazing—they look like real photographs. And it's a really good book.
>
> Chase: Yeah! The only thing I don't understand is how he became a werewolf.
>
> Jared: It said that he went to a graveyard and got flowers and the flowers like withered and died and shot some spores at him and made him like a werewolf.
>
> Chase: Oh yeah! Cool!

In my experience as a classroom teacher in middle and elementary school, a reading specialist, and a school-based preservice and inservice teacher educator, I have rarely heard a conversation like this take place in a classroom. Jared and Chase's conversation was spontaneous, informal, self-directed, and similar to a conversation about a book adults might have in the coffee room at work or over the dinner table. Books in which someone gets killed on every page are not the usual school fare, and, to be honest, I am uncomfortable that my son and his friend were so obviously thrilled by this genre. However, after hearing many times from teachers that Jared was not an engaged reader and from him that he hated reading class, I was pleasantly shocked that he would spend his own time voluntarily talking about books.

My sense of the importance of the conversation between Chase and Jared was heightened by my in-

Reprinted from *Journal of Adolescent & Adult Literacy* (1998), *41*, 508–517.

terest in students who are labeled "reluctant readers" and by the fact that the excitement they demonstrated is so rare in school "book talk," particularly beyond the elementary grades. Through my work and interviews with students who say they don't like to read, I have found the reluctant reader label to be ambiguous because what appears to be reluctance may stem from a variety of complex and individual factors (Worthy & McKool, 1996). Jared and Chase were both considered disengaged readers in their language arts classes, but, like other so-called reluctant readers that I've talked to, they were passionate about reading self-selected materials outside of school. Their perspectives, presented here, suggest that we may need to rethink how reading is presented in school if we are to reach preadolescent and older students.

Reluctant readers and school reading

Research about reading attitudes and voluntary reading shows that, in general, both show a steady decline as students progress through school and that negative attitudes become especially prevalent in the middle and high school years (Cline & Kretke, 1980; McKenna, Ellsworth, & Kear, 1995; Shapiro & White, 1991). Despite this grim portrayal, however, researchers have noted that some adolescents read more than educators think they do, even if they do not appear to enjoy reading in school (Alvermann, Young, Green, & Wisenbaker, 1996; Bintz, 1993; Worthy & McKool, 1996). Through interviews with high school students fitting the reluctant reader profile, Bintz concluded that some students "lose interest in school reading as they progress through school but do not lose interest in reading per se" and that one major reason for resistance to school reading is that students "are forced to read materials that they have no voice in selecting" (p. 612).

Perhaps another reason for students' resistance to school reading is their perceived or real lack of control in classroom book talk. Recent research has focused on the desirability of moving from teacher-controlled recitation, in which student participation and interaction are minimal, to discussion or open forum (Alpert, 1987; Alvermann, O'Brien, & Dillon, 1990; Cazden, 1988; Mehan, 1979). Discussion im-

plies active student participation and collaborative construction of meaning, rather than passive answering of teachers' questions. Participating in discussions has potential cognitive, social, and affective benefits (Almasi, 1997). Teacher-led discussions, however, sometimes tend to slip back to the old recitation mode, with the teacher controlling the tone and direction of the conversations, determining turn-taking, and emphasizing specific skills or curricular goals (McMahon, 1997).

Book discussions led by students rather than teachers can allow students to "engage in exploratory thinking, resulting in more extended and more elaborate mental representations and higher level analytical thinking" (Gambrell, 1997, p. 31) as well as to improve communication skills and attitudes toward reading (Almasi, 1997). Researchers and practitioners point out that as long as students are provided instruction and modeling in effective group process (Au, 1993) and have interaction guidelines, topics to discuss, and tasks to complete (Purves, Rogers, & Soter, 1990), student-led discussions can be quite productive.

Jared and Chase's conversation takes student-led discussions a step further. It is student initiated, and there *are* no guidelines, no preset topics to discuss, no tasks to complete, no requirements to cover particular issues or skills, and no teacher or designated leader to make sure the participants stay on task. Because of the informal context and the rather illicit (for school) books they discussed, I have dubbed their conversation a "renegade" book discussion.

In this article, I examine the renegade book conversation of two middle school reluctant readers, provide background information on the participants and on related research, and explore through interviews the participants' perspectives and attitudes toward reading both at the time of the initial conversation and 2 years later. Their perspectives hold implications for educators who are interested in improving students' engagement with reading in school.

Exploring reading with renegade readers

At the time of the book conversation and first interview, Jared and Chase were in sixth grade in a middle school in central Texas, USA, with homogeneously grouped language arts classes. They were in the same basic language arts class in which they kept B averages. Both Chase and Jared had followed a typical course of development in all academic and social areas and had been average to above-average students during their earlier school years. Each had grown up in homes in which literacy was valued and reading materials were abundant, and in which they had rich access to books, magazines, and comics of their choice. Both had enjoyed reading in their preschool and primary years, and both had begun to resist school reading in their upper elementary years and continued to do so. Although they were more likely to spend their free time playing video games, playing sports, or "hanging out" with their friends, they both read regularly from self-selected materials at home. Neither read standard fiction or nonfiction at home except for what was required to complete school assignments. Both Jared and Chase had discovered less conventional materials, such as comics, drawing books, and magazines in elementary school, and had begun before middle school to read horror and suspense books mainly written for adults.

According to Nieto (1994), students' voices are often missing in discussions of educational practice. In consideration of the importance of including students' perspectives, the data examined for this study consist of Jared's and Chase's own words gathered through their renegade book conversation and interviews. In the renegade conversation, I was an observer and participant on the fringe, asking occasional questions to clarify issues that arose but letting the boys do most of the talking. Within a week after the initial conversation, I conducted individual follow-up interviews with both boys in which I inquired about school and home reading and asked them to help me understand better some of the issues brought up in their conversations.

During the 2 years that elapsed between Jared and Chase's renegade conversation and follow-up interviews, I analyzed the transcripts and my notes several times and wrote reflections. Following procedures recommended for constant comparative analysis (Erlandson, Harris, Skipper, & Allen, 1993; Strauss & Corbin, 1990), I first unitized the data into

meaningful segments (phrases, sentences, or paragraphs), wrote summaries and reactions to each unit, and made an exhaustive list of issues and topics that emerged. I shared these with a colleague, who offered advice and new insights. I then grouped the list of issues and topics into broader categories and asked a different peer to comment. I further refined the categories and evaluated my analysis in terms of previous research results, wrote a first draft of the paper, and formulated questions for the follow-up interview (Miles & Huberman, 1994). Two years later, I showed both boys a draft of this article, and we read and discussed it together. They gave feedback on my descriptions and analysis and updated me on their current ideas about reading both in and out of school.

My analysis of Jared and Chase's conversations and interviews is presented in the following sections. I begin with discoveries about their reading habits both in and out of school and follow with their recommendations to teachers for making school reading more engaging for students.

Discoveries about renegade readers

While analyzing the initial renegade book conversation and subsequent interviews, I found three salient themes. Chase and Jared's conversation illustrates that they understood and were engaged in the books they discussed. Their preferences were ardent and discriminating. Chase and Jared expressed general indifference and sometimes distaste toward reading in school.

Demonstrating understanding and engagement through conversation. Following their *Cycle of the Werewolf* discussion, Chase continued the conversation by talking about another book both boys had recently read. They collaboratively summarized and evaluated the book and clarified plot details. As in the first excerpt, their engagement and understanding were readily apparent. They understood the plot at both literal and inferential levels, and when events were unclear, Jared asked a question about a plot point (italicized) and Chase clarified.

> Chase: Oh and I just got done reading *Congo* (Crichton, 1980), too.
> Jared: Oh, yeah!

Chase: Like it's really sick at the beginning. It's like he steps on this, he thought it was like this...

Jared: Berries.

Chase: Yeah, berries. And it was an eyeball. It was like a human eyeball and it was like, squishing.

Jared: They were throwing eyeballs at him, the monkeys.

Chase: And they had, they had like a submarine going underwater searching for the lost city, Congo.... And at the end they find the place Congo but it's like all shredded up and it's really disgusting how they describe it.

Jared: Isn't in *Congo*, isn't it like the monkeys beat people with paddles or something?

Chase: Yeah.

Jared: *How do they stop 'em at the end?*

Chase: They like set this bomb up to stop all the monkeys and it like makes a big explosion....

As the conversation continued, Jared and Chase talked more about *Congo* and *Cycle of the Werewolf*. They had recently seen movie versions of both after having read the books. The movie and book talk included thoughtful evaluations of the similarities, noting differences in plot, character, and detail. Later they both discussed books that they had recently read, giving concise summaries and either recommending or panning the books. Jared discussed and highly recommended John Grisham's books, and Chase had mixed reviews of books by Christopher Pike and Lois Duncan that he had just read. The remainder of the conversation was dedicated to talk about personal preferences and how they chose books.

Even the short segments of the renegade book conversation shown in this article include elements that researchers and teachers find important in book discussion. The boys used and understood vocabulary from the books, and their talk was full of "book language." They compared, synthesized, evaluated, responded personally, and supported their opinions with examples (Rosenblatt, 1983; Zarillo & Cox, 1992). Names of authors were bandied about, and the boys made intertextual and experiential connections (Zarillo & Cox, 1992). They both actively participated, collaboratively constructed meaning (Alpert, 1987; Alvermann, O'Brien, & Dillon, 1990), and clarified and questioned when necessary. Their talk had an authentic "real reader" qual-

ity that teacher-led discussions and even book club meetings usually don't have, because Chase and Jared's talk was unstructured and decidedly informal, and there was no agenda. It seems clear that such talk has led and will continue to lead the boys toward more books.

Book preferences: "What's the big deal About R.L. Stine?" Popular materials don't suit everyone. General preferences for reading materials seem to go in cycles. At any given time there are materials that are wildly popular among most students. However, educators caution that general preferences do not apply to everyone (Monson & Sebesta, 1991). As Howes (1963) pointed out: "Each child is himself no matter what the generalizations about the reading patterns and interests for his age may be" (p. 492). Jared and Chase's conversation underscored these cautions. A major theme of the book discussion and individual interviews was the boys' ardent personal, individualized preferences. They liked many of the same books (especially suspense and horror), but they also had some different personal tastes (Chase liked sports and didn't like fantasy at all, while Jared liked fantasy, science fiction, and suspense novels but only particular authors, such as Piers Anthony and John Grisham).

The boys emphasized that because certain books or genres are generally popular, it doesn't mean that they are universally liked. At the time of the book conversations and interviews, Goosebumps (Stine) were the most popular books among late elementary to middle school students (Worthy & Turner, 1997). Although horror was Jared's and Chase's favorite genre, they didn't like the "childish horror" of Goosebumps or R.L. Stine. Chase spoke with disdain about Stine's popularity among other students in the school by saying "I don't know what's the big deal about R.L. Stine." Jared agreed: "He's a freak! He writes like a book every week." Jared went on to explain that "[R.L. Stine's] books are really childish," they have the "corniest titles," and "they're not really scary." He insisted that he "wouldn't even have liked them in second grade." This disdain for popular books did not seem to be overgeneralized, though. While both boys were quick to reject books that did not immediately grab their attention, they were open to recommendations from peers, parents, and teachers. Jared and his father often read and discussed John Grisham's books, and Chase's father had introduced him to Stephen King's novels. Parent recommendations weren't always successful, though. Chase shared a recent memory of attempting to read a book his mother highly recommended.

> One book I cannot get into. My mom requested it [from the library] and I started to read it: *Gone With the Wind* (Mitchell, 1939). I got 200 pages into it and I fell asleep (laughter). 'Cause all it was was just romance. Like, this guy, at the very beginning he gets home, and they marry, and they start in on the romance. And the next page—romance. Ten pages later—romance. It's like nonstop romance. They could have declared me legally dead, I was so bored.

Chase explained that after that experience he always went to the library and bookstore with his mother "'cause she doesn't really choose good books."

"Chase usually recommends it": *Deciding what to read.* I asked the boys to talk about how they decided what books to read. Consistent with the results of previous studies (Burgess, 1985; Wendelin & Zinck, 1983), Jared and Chase considered the genre, author, title, summary, and physical features of the book, including length, cover illustration, and back cover summary when they chose books. As other researchers have found (Wendelin & Zinck, 1983; Worthy & Turner, 1997), peer recommendations have become increasingly important to Jared and Chase over the years.

Jared: Well, Chase usually recommends it. How do you decide about the books?

Chase: OK, well, I'll tell you. Usually what I do is I go to the bookstore, I go straight to the section I like—suspense—'cause I can get into that. Uh, let's see, drama is dull. Romance—sleep. I don't like Tom Clancy 'cause his books are too much of the cop and CIA type stuff; I don't get into that. Let's see, I'm not into J.R.R. Tolkein; I don't like that fantasy stuff.

Jared: Fantasy's OK. It depends on who the author is.

Chase: Yeah. But, like I said, I go to the bookstore, I pick up the book. If the author I know is recognizable, it grips my attention. The title sometimes gets me and then the cover.

Jo: What kinds of covers and titles do you look for?

Jared: The suspenseful titles, good titles...

Chase: I got *Cujo* (King, 1981). You see the claw and he's like making a big scratch and it's cool...

Jared: A bloody scratch...

Chase: Yeah, and...I always read the back before I buy something, too, and that's basically it.

Jared: You usually recommend them to me.

Chase: Yeah, I usually recommend books to Jared. And I just got done reading *Gone But Not Forgotten*. It's a book by Philip Margolin (1993). It's about this, like this really smart killer who leaves, all he leaves after the killing is just an envelope and a rose on it that says "gone but not forgotten." And at the end they like shoot him. It's so stupid but like they have this rose gun, it's like a gun with a rose on it (laughter). It's so stupid (laughter from both boys).

Jared: I'm gonna read *Gone But Not Forgotten*.

Chase: I have it, do you want to borrow it?

The last segment of conversation above illustrates the power of peer book recommendations for Jared. If not for his talks with Chase, Jared might not have discovered *Gone But Not Forgotten*, a book that he went on to read later. In fact, Jared's reading was often dependent upon a confluence of having the right materials at the right time and "nothing else to do." In the next segment of the renegade conversation, Chase and Jared talked about another book that Chase had recommended.

"There was nothing else I wanted to read right then." After he struggled with reading in his early elementary years, Jared's attitude toward school reading was quite negative by the late elementary years. He had developed intense, personal interests in reading materials that were not typically found in school, and his decision to read or not to read was dependent on the availability of those specific materials. When he had his sights set on a particular book or comic (usually the result of a peer recommendation), a different publication even in the same genre or by the same author wouldn't satisfy him. His self-selected books and comics are still on his shelves, and he revisits them frequently.

Jared and Chase again brought up *Cycle of the Werewolf*, and Jared's sister, who was 7 at the time of the conversation, recalled Jared's exhaustive search for it.

> Jenna: Jared liked that book so much he went to three or four bookstores to get it.

Jared: I went to like five or six bookstores, and they didn't have it anywhere.
Jo: So why didn't you just get another book?
Jared: See, 'cause I really, really wanted to read it, and there was nothing else I wanted to read right then. And [after I got it] I read it in like 2 hours.

In the individual interviews, the boys explored the topic of school reading. Their perspectives on assigned reading were quite different from their voluntary reading and gave me some insight into why they were at best indifferent to reading in school.

School reading. I asked both boys to talk generally about their perspectives and enjoyment of reading in school and probed with additional questions about time for reading and materials available. According to the boys, reading that was done in school was largely teacher selected, teacher directed, and skills focused.

In many classrooms, time allotted for sustained reading is relatively rare, even during instructional periods (Allington, 1994; Morrow, 1991; Ysseldyke & Algozzine, 1982–1983). Jared's and Chase's perspectives of their classrooms were consistent with patterns identified in earlier studies. Jared and Chase said that there was rarely a planned reading time in their classes; that most such times took place serendipitously. Thus, students didn't always have their personal books with them to use during free reading times. In fact, Jared took a personal book to school for a week but found only a few occasional minutes to read it. When the opportunity for free reading finally came, he didn't have his book with him, and he had to read one of his teacher's "booooring" books.

The books they read as assignments, Jared explained, were from a variety of genres ("just not horror"), with a focus on "things like biographical fiction," chosen to follow the school's curriculum. Both boys read the books they were assigned in school, and both had enjoyed some of them but "hated" most. While the teacher's library contained "a couple of good books," according to the boys, "lots of people have already read 'em," and most of the other books are "not very good." According to Chase, a few of the books "look good but you don't have time to read 'em anyway." Thus, their time and opportunities to get involved in books during school were limited.

The boys said that they rarely had time to talk to their peers about books in class, but that they often talked about and recommended books to each other during lunch. Jared said, "Chase really likes horror books and so I usually listen to him and he usually has good books that he recommends." I was encouraged that these boys, who had been labeled reluctant readers by their teachers, were so excited about their own reading that the subject regularly came up at lunch and outside of school.

Eighth-grade update: "I haven't read my own book in like a year." Two years after the initial book conversation, Jared, Chase, and I met to listen to the first tape and to read the first draft of this article together, so they could comment and update me on their current in-school and out-of-school reading attitudes and habits. Even beyond their shrill sixth-grade voices, which had deepened considerably in the 2 years, they insisted that they had changed greatly since the earlier conversation ("I don't know how I could have said that"; "I was an idiot back then"). After the laughter and embarrassment died down, I asked them if they still read a lot outside of school.

Jared: No!
Chase: Absolutely not. I haven't read my own book in like a year. I used to be like a reader in sixth grade. I read all the Stephen King books. I know he has all these new books, but I haven't read them.
Jared: I'm more active. I have more stuff to do now. I actually have friends to play with.

Both added that they were interested in girls now, and that reading time has been displaced by talking on the phone. Despite their protests to the contrary, however, it became clear that they *do* still read outside of school, but that their reading interests have changed. Neither reads books often, but both read parts of the newspaper and subscribe to magazines (Chase to *Sports Illustrated* and Jared to *GamePro* and *Entertainment Weekly*) and read them regularly. In fact, during our meeting, Jared couldn't put down an *Entertainment Weekly* that had just arrived in the mail.

Chase's move in his eighth grade year from basic language arts to advanced had brought some changes in the books read, but he insisted that it was still boring and that "it's still easy but we actually read good books every once in awhile now." He mentioned *The Hobbit* (Tolkein, 1966) and *Alas, Babylon* (Frank, 1959) as examples. Jared reported that in his basic language arts class, the books were mainly "boring and stupid." A case in point was a teacher-chosen book, *Summer of My German Soldier* (Greene, 1973), which both the advanced and basic classes had read. According to Jared, "nobody liked it except a few girls," and Chase labeled it "pointless." Both admitted rather proudly that they had been "getting away" with not doing assigned reading while still receiving adequate grades. Jared's and Chase's apathy about school reading had apparently continued to grow, causing me to wonder: Why can't reading in school engage these boys as much as they obviously have the potential to be engaged? Why is reading in school a turnoff for so many students? Can the enthusiasm found in renegade discussions be transferred to school settings?

Advice for teachers from renegade readers

I asked the boys if there was anything they could suggest to their teachers that would promote reading engagement and enjoyment in school for students who, like they, are not avid school readers. The suggestions that they offered are not new to the literature on voluntary reading. However, according to Jared and Chase, and affirmed by previous research (Worthy, Moorman, & Turner, 1997), this advice is not regularly followed in many language arts classes. Thus, these suggestions warrant repeating and developing.

"Let us choose the books we read for class." Student choice and control in reading material and instruction play an important role in involvement with and enjoyment of reading and in fostering voluntary reading (Bintz, 1993; Turner, 1995). When students are not permitted to exercise choice, they may avoid teacher-selected books as a matter of principle. Thus, when students say they hate the books they read in school, part of this opinion may be due to their perceived lack of voice in the school curriculum. Especially in the upper grades, then, teachers should consider "negotiating the curriculum with their pupils and making their purposes in teaching specific books more explicit" (Thomson, 1987, p. 24). Jared and Chase stated that opportunities for choice were infrequent and that students were given minimal voice in the curriculum or in the selection of instructional materials. Jared's suggestion was modest: "Like she could pick three books and ask the class which they want to read." Chase wanted the choice to be more individualized: "Just have everyone read their own book and like do a project for that book...so they can read the book *they* want to read."

"Let us talk to our friends about what we like to read." Jared and Chase couldn't stop laughing when I asked them if they had opportunities to talk with their friends about books in school: "Talk to our friends? In class?" "Oh yeah, right." As Bintz (1993) contends, "We need to value and legitimate what students do outside of school rather than bemoan what they are not reading in school" (p. 614). Jared and Chase requested the opportunity to spend "just a couple of minutes" in school talking to their friends about books and magazines they read outside of school. While discussions based on teacher-chosen books are an important part of the curriculum, enjoyable, social exchanges and self-initiated interactions with books have been found to be important in the development of reading motivation (Morrow & Weinstein, 1986). In addition, such talk opens the door to peer recommendations that, for adolescents, may be the most important motivator for voluntary reading (Shore, 1968; Wendelin & Zinck, 1983; Worthy & Turner, 1997). Providing a few unstructured minutes for renegade book conversations in class may make an impact on students' attitudes in class as well as on their out-of-school reading habits.

"Get some good books and other stuff to read in the classroom." Thomson (1987) concluded from surveys of the reading habits of British teenagers that "as students progress through secondary school, the gap between what they choose to read and what the school provides and recommends becomes increasingly wider" (pp. 32–33). Jared and Chase also found few materials that they enjoyed in school. Surveys and interviews of U.S. middle school students, librarians, and teachers affirm that most school and classroom libraries have limited numbers of student-preferred materials (Worthy, 1996; Worthy & Turner, 1997). In interviews with middle school librarians and teachers, my colleagues and I found that many are open to the idea of students reading nontraditional materials of interest to them, but that schools don't typically provide money for teachers to buy materials that are not obviously relevant to the school's curriculum. Most teachers who have such materials in their rooms have to solicit donations or use their own money to purchase them (Worthy, 1996; Worthy, Moorman, & Turner, 1997). Until schools offer some support for teachers to buy student-preferred materials, many students will not have access to them.

Discussion

Because student-preferred reading materials often include materials that have been traditionally seen as inappropriate for school, such as light fiction, series books, magazines, comics, horror, and satire, there is ample potential for disapproval of student choice from parents, administrators, and community members. I offer two ideas for educators who have concerns about using students' preferred materials in school.

First, I believe that instruction using high-quality, critically accepted literature is the most essential component of a language arts program and that the major place of student-preferred materials is in free-choice reading, which should supplement rather than replace the instructional curriculum. Even so, educators will find the need to proactively head off complaints that are likely to accompany the addition of such materials. Fortunately, there is ample research evidence of the academic and affective benefits of listening to students' opinions. Encouraging student choice leads to better attitudes toward reading and learning. Many times students' chosen materials are more complex than teacher-chosen materials, and even light materials promote fluent reading and vocabulary development and help to develop the linguistic competence, confidence, and motivation necessary for reading more sophisticated materials (Carlsen &

Sherrill, 1988; Dorrell & Carroll, 1981; Mathabane, 1986; Parrish & Atwood, 1985).

Second, research suggests that students' personal interests need not be static and that teachers can stretch students' topic interests through instructional approaches and materials that are motivating (Schiefele, 1991). Educators can also be encouraged by evidence that personal preferences are not necessarily static and that they can be simultaneously encouraged and broadened. For example, elementary and middle school students value their teachers' recommendations and help in choosing books if the teacher shows genuine interest in the materials (Csikszentmihalyi & McCormack, 1986; Roettger, 1980; Worthy & Turner, 1997). In addition, the transition from light materials to more complex texts can be hastened by providing student-preferred materials for free-choice reading, using more sophisticated works on similar topics for instruction and read-alouds, and encouraging students to adopt a critical stance in comparing the texts.

Coda

Jared and Chase have almost given up on school reading, perhaps due to what they see as limited choice and control in school and the widening gulf between the books they read in school and their personal preferences. According to them, they are "absolutely not" avid readers, yet on closer examination they both admit to reading out of school frequently. Perhaps this incongruity comes from the fact that the materials they read are magazines and not books, and thus perhaps not regarded as "real reading." In many ways, Jared and Chase fit Bintz's (1993) description of adolescents who are reluctant *school* readers but avid *out-of-school* readers.

As did the teenagers in Bintz's study, Jared and Chase think of most school reading as "an imposition, inconvenience, and interference with current reading interests" (p. 612). Fortunately, they are still interested in self-selected reading. Yet there are many students who have similarly negative feelings toward school reading and also do not read outside of school. For these students, Jared's and Chase's suggestions may be vital. Time spent reading is tied to reading and writing competence (Greaney, 1980; Mullis, Campbell, & Farstrup, 1993; Wilson, 1981), and many students who do not read in their free time eventually lose academic ground, even if they are not initially remedial readers (Anderson, Wilson, & Fielding, 1988; Mikulecky, 1990; Stanovich, 1986). Beyond mere time, however, *"involvement* in reading remains the most potent factor in the development of reading processes" (Allington, 1994, p. 21).

References

Allington, R.L. (1994). The schools we have. The schools we need. *The Reading Teacher*, 48, 14–29.

Almasi, J.A. (1997). A new view of discussion. In L.B. Gambrell & J. Almasi (Eds.), *Lively discussions! Fostering engaged reading* (pp. 2–24). Newark, DE: International Reading Association.

Alpert, B.R. (1987). Active, silent, and controlled discussions: Explaining variations in classroom conversation. *Teaching and Teacher Education*, 3(1), 29–40.

Alvermann, D.E., O'Brien, D.G., & Dillon, D.R. (1990). What teachers do when they say they're having discussions of content area reading assignments: A qualitative analysis. *Reading Research Quarterly*, 25, 296–332.

Alvermann, D.E., Young, J.P., Green, C., & Wisenbaker, J. (1996, December). *Adolescents read when they want to and that's more often than we thought.* Paper presented at the National Reading Conference annual meeting, Charleston, SC.

Anderson, R., Wilson, P., & Fielding, L. (1988). Growth in reading and how children spend their time outside of school. *Reading Research Quarterly*, 23, 285–303.

Au, K.H. (1993). *Literacy instruction in multicultural settings.* New York: Harcourt Brace Jovanovich.

Bintz, W.P. (1993). Resistant readers in secondary education: Some insights and implications. *Journal of Reading*, 36, 604–615.

Burgess, S.A. (1985, January). Reading but not literate: The Child Read survey. *School Library Journal*, 31, 27–30.

Carlsen, R., & Sherrill, A. (1988). *Voices of readers: How we come to love books.* Urbana, IL: National Council of Teachers of English.

Cazden, C.B. (1988). *Classroom discourse.* Portsmouth, NH: Heinemann.

Cline, R.K.J., & Kretke, G.L. (1980). An evaluation of long-term SSR in the junior high school. *Journal of Reading*, 23, 502–506.

Crichton, M. (1980). *Congo.* New York: Knopf.

Csikszentmihalyi, M., & McCormack, J. (1986). The influence of teachers. *Phi Delta Kappan*, 67, 415–419.

Dorrell, L., & Carroll, E. (1981). Spider-Man at the library. *School Library Journal*, 27, 17–19.

Erlandson, D.A., Harris, E.L., Skipper, B.L., & Allen, S.D. (1993). *Doing naturalistic inquiry.* Newbury Park, CA: Sage.

Frank, P. (1959). *Alas, Babylon.* Philadelphia: Lippincott.

Gambrell, L.B. (1997). What research reveals about discussion. In L.B. Gambrell & J. Almasi (Eds.), *Lively discussions! Fostering engaged reading* (pp. 25–38). Newark, DE: International Reading Association.

Greaney, V. (1980). Factors related to the amount and type of leisure-time reading. *Reading Research Quarterly*, 15, 337–357.

Greene, B. (1973). *Summer of my German soldier.* New York: Dial.

Howes, V. (1963). Children's interests—a key note for teaching reading. *Education*, 8, 491–496.

King, S. (1981). *Cujo.* New York: Viking.

King, S. (1983). *Cycle of the werewolf.* Westland, MI: Land of Enchantment.

Krashen, S.D. (1992). *The power of reading.* Englewood, CO: Libraries Unlimited.

Margolin, P. (1993). *Gone but not forgotten.* New York: Doubleday.

Mathabane, M. (1986). *Kaffir boy.* New York: Plume.

McKenna, M., Ellsworth, R.A., & Kear, D. (1995). Children's attitudes toward reading: A national survey. *Reading Research Quarterly*, 30, 934–957.

McMahon, S.I. (1997). Guiding student-led discussion groups. In L.B. Gambrell & J. Almasi (Eds.), *Lively discussions! Fostering engaged reading* (pp. 224–247). Newark, DE: International Reading Association.

Mehan, H. (1979). *Learning lessons.* Cambridge, MA: Harvard University Press.

Mikulecky, L.J. (1990). Stopping summer learning loss among at-risk youth. *Journal of Reading*, 33, 516–521.

Miles, M.B., & Huberman, A.M. (1994). *Qualitative data analysis* (2nd ed.). Thousand Oaks, CA: Sage.

Mitchell, M. (1939). *Gone with the wind.* New York: E.B. Greenstone.

Monson, D.L., & Sebesta, S. (1991). Reading preferences. In J. Flood, J. Jensen, D. Lapp, & J. Squire (Eds.), *Handbook of research on teaching the English language arts* (pp. 664–673). New York: Macmillan.

Morrow, L.M. (1991). Promoting voluntary reading. In J. Flood, J. Jensen, D. Lapp, & J. Squire (Eds.), *Handbook of research on teaching the English language arts* (pp. 681–690). New York: Macmillan.

Morrow, L.M., & Weinstein, C.S. (1986). Encouraging voluntary reading. The impact of a literature program on children's use of library centers. *Reading Research Quarterly*, 21, 330–346.

Mullis, I., Campbell, J., & Farstrup, A. (1993). NAEP 1992: *Reading report card for the nation and the states.* Washington, DC: U.S. Department of Education.

Nieto, S. (1994). Lessons from students on creating a chance to dream. *Harvard Educational Review*, 64, 392–426.

Parrish, B., & Atwood, K. (1985). Enticing readers: The teen romance craze. *California Reader*, 18, 22–27.

Purves, A.C., Rogers, T., & Soter, A.O. (1990). *How porcupines make love II: Teaching a response-centered literature curriculum.* White Plains, NY: Longman.

Roettger, D. (1980). Elementary students' attitudes toward reading. *The Reading Teacher*, 33, 451–454.

Rosenblatt, L.M. (1983). *Literature as exploration* (3rd ed.). New York: Noble & Noble.

Schiefele, U. (1991). Interest, learning, and motivation. *Educational Psychologist*, 26, 299–323.

Shapiro, J., & White, W. (1991). Reading attitudes and perceptions in traditional and nontraditional reading programs. *Reading Research and Instruction*, 30, 52–66.

Shore, R.B. (1968). Perceived influence of peers, parents, and teachers on fifth and ninth graders' preferences of reading material. *Dissertation Abstracts International*, 47, 051, No. 86-16, 829.

Stanovich, K. (1986). Matthew effects in reading: Some consequences of individual differences in the acquisition of literacy. *Reading Research Quarterly*, 21, 360–406.

Strauss, A.L., & Corbin, J. (1990). *Basics of qualitative research: Grounded theory procedures and techniques*. Newbury Park, CA: Sage.

Thomson, J.L. (1987). *Understanding teenagers' reading: Reading processes and the teaching of literature*. New York: Nichols.

Tolkein, J.R.R. (1966). *The hobbit*. Cambridge, MA: Houghton Mifflin.

Turner, J.C. (1995). The influence of classroom contexts on young children's motivation for literacy. *Reading Research Quarterly*, 30, 410–441.

Wendelin, K.H., & Zinck, R.A. (1983). How students make book choices. *Reading Horizons*, 23, 84–88.

Wilson, R.M. (1981). Any way you read it, illiteracy is a problem. *Presstime*, 3, 4–8.

Worthy, J. (1996). Removing barriers to voluntary reading: The role of school and classroom libraries. *Language Arts*, 73, 483–492.

Worthy, J., & McKool, S.S. (1996). Students who say they hate to read: The importance of opportunity, choice, and access. In D.J. Leu, C.K. Kinzer, & K.A. Hinchman (Eds.), *Literacies for the 21st century: Research and practice* (pp. 245–256). Chicago: National Reading Conference.

Worthy, J., Moorman, M., & Turner, M. (1997, March). *Can the teacher make a difference in students' attitudes toward reading?* Paper presented at the American Educational Research Association meeting, Chicago.

Worthy, J., & Turner, M. (1997, February). *Motivating students to read: Ideas from 6th grade students and their language arts teachers*. Paper presented at the Southwest Regional conference of the International Reading Association, Fort Worth, TX.

Ysseldyke, J.E., & Algozzine, R. (1982–1983). Where to begin in diagnosing reading problems. *Topics in Learning and Reading Disorders*, 2, 60–68.

Zarillo, J., & Cox, C. (1992). Efferent and aesthetic teaching. In J.E. Many & C. Cox (Eds.), *Reader stance and literary understanding* (pp. 235–249). Norwood, NJ: Ablex.

PART 5

Professional Development

*L*earning plays an important role in a teaching career. The underlying assumption is that quality teaching is not something learned and then repeated as a routine, but rather a constantly evolving activity that requires continuous reflection and revision. One of the important goals of teacher preparation and professional development programs is to convey this expectation and the set of behaviors that will allow teachers to be developing constantly. Standard 5 is as follows:

> **Candidates view professional development as a career-long effort and responsibility.**

The standard has four elements.

- **Element 5.1 Display positive dispositions related to reading and the teaching of reading.**

Wilcox (1996) presents a specific use of portfolios to promote thoughtfulness and the use of strategies to develop thinking. The portfolio process encourages teachers in training to practice strategies that result in thoughtfulness, and it therefore helps them to avoid entrenchment. Responding to reading in writing, sharing ideas with colleagues, and reflecting on one's own ways of knowing are processes that enhance learning and improve thinking. Teachers who learn and adapt the "smart" portfolio treat learning to teach as a lifelong commitment, and thus display a critical positive disposition.

- **Element 5.2 Continue to pursue the development of professional knowledge and dispositions.**

Raphael et al. (2001) describe a good exemplar for teachers continuing development. The piece highlights the importance of peer collaboration to teacher learning and shows how cross-grade interaction can contribute to professional development. The article also reports the life of a community of teachers devoted to improving their practice and demonstrates the tremendous potential of teacher research for solving the problems of practice. The Miller (2002) article is specifically addressed to teachers who wish to become multicultural teachers. The author provides 10 recommendations for reaching that goal.

The Bean, Swan, and Knaub (2003) article is included because it provides a data-based portrait of reading specialists. The piece highlights the diversity of the roles reading specialists enact and the flexibility they demonstrate. The portrait demonstrates the need for a continuous and ongoing commitment to professional development on the part of reading professionals.

The Lefever-Davis et al. (2003) article provides specific and concrete detail for the concept of teacher study groups—one of the more frequently used, popular, and effective ways to provide continuous and ongoing professional development.

Dole (2004) provides an up-to-date picture of the reading specialist and notes the implications of the changing role for professional development initiatives and university preparation programs.

- **Element 5.3 Work with colleagues to observe, evaluate, and provide feedback on each other's practice.**

Jaeger (1996) proposes a model for professional development that involves teachers and a reading specialist as a collaborative consultant. This article is particularly relevant today because of the dramatic increase in the number of teachers who act as literacy coaches. It provides another model for sustained professional development that is more school based and less peer oriented. The model draws from a more experienced other in the form of the reading specialist and is focused at the building level.

- **Element 5.4 Participate in, initiate, implement, and evaluate professional development programs.**

Parish (1995) provides a brief explanation of how to organize a collegial professional development experience. The article gives a good set of directions for organizing and conducting a language arts reading club. In many ways it is similar to the experience described by Raphael et al. earlier in Part 5.

The articles in this part give substance to the concept of professionalism. The pieces are a mixture of some that provide descriptions of the reading professional—particularly the reading specialist/literacy coach—and descriptions of professional development initiatives such as clinical practica and teacher study groups. In these articles we have the embodiment of the term *reading professional*.

Bonita L. Wilcox

Smart portfolios for teachers in training

Portfolios can facilitate and demonstrate professional growth. Smart portfolios contain evidence of thoughtful teaching and learning and make thinking processes visible.

In *Outsmarting IQ: The Emerging Science of Learnable Intelligence*, Perkins writes, "Hardly anything in conventional educational practice promotes, in a direct and straightforward way, thoughtfulness and the use of strategies to guide thinking" (1995, p. 117). I want to argue that a portfolio process that encourages teachers in training to practice strategies that result in thoughtfulness will help them avoid entrenchment. Teachers who understand their own belief structure become less dependent on the existing structure of the school environment. Practicing reflective thinking and new ways of knowing in a direct and focused way ensures that we learn from our own thoughtfulness.

Passive thinking results in passive teaching and learning (Barell, 1995; Fisher, 1995; Kirby & Kuykendall, 1991; Tishman, Perkins, & Jay, 1995). School environments are not always conducive to the professional development of teachers. In fact, schools are often the worst places for teachers to learn. Few schools provide periodicals containing recent research or books on methodology and professional knowledge. Rarely do schools encourage teachers to attend expensive professional conferences. Time to share thoughts and ideas with one another and time to read, write, and reflect are not built into a teacher's schedule. We seem to believe that teachers will be able to mass produce lifelong learners without being lifelong learners themselves.

Given the difficulty teachers may have finding time to consider their own learning, it is imperative that thoughtfulness and a thinking attitude become second nature to student teachers before they ever enter the classroom. Research shows that responding to reading in writing, sharing one's ideas, and reflecting on one's own ways of knowing are processes that enhance learning and improve thinking. Practicing reflective thinking strategies, as easy as "thinking about your thinking processes," enables a good thinker to become a better thinker.

Reprinted from *Journal of Adolescent & Adult Literacy* (1996), 40, 172–179

Figure 1
Integrating five essential elements of a smart portfolio

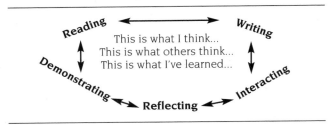

Creating smart portfolios, which requires systematic self-assessment and sharing, allows writers to experience the power of reflective thinking. Thoughtfulness may not come naturally when teaching in a busy classroom, but making a conscious effort to reflect on what we know and can do may cause us to search for new and better ways of teaching.

The portfolio has earned recognition as an assessment tool; however, a portfolio that can generate ideas and teach new ways of thinking offers unlimited possibilities for teaching and learning. Teachers who know about assessment as instruction will never be satisfied with a portfolio *just* for assessment. The smart portfolio is a powerful tool for professional development and lifelong learning.

Getting started

It is easy to organize a smart portfolio. Begin with the five essential elements—reading, interacting, demonstrating, writing, and thinking (see Figure 1). Choose a container for all the contents. A three-ring binder or a pocket portfolio will suffice. Label sections for the essential elements. As you begin to build each section, consider the following.

1. *Reading.* This section of the portfolio is concerned with new knowledge and new perspectives. Whether the texts are compendiums of basic skills and teaching strategies, individual texts on innovative approaches, or handouts from professional journals, new information and new ideas must be introduced. A smart portfolio contains evidence of input.

2. *Interacting.* This section contains artifacts from activities and exercises done in groups to illustrate the importance of thoughtfulness in teaching and learning. Activities focus on group inquiry and problem solving and include analyzing, arguing, and assessing.

3. *Demonstrating.* This is the part of the portfolio where learning is applied. Teachers in training deliver lessons for their peers or present demonstrations that show significant differences between traditional lessons and enhanced lessons that incorporate new teaching and learning strategies.

4. *Writing.* The formal paper is the capstone experience in which reading, thinking, interacting, demonstrating, and viewing come together. Thinking has been extended, presented, defended, and refined. These papers show evidence that prior knowledge has been assessed, new knowledge has been integrated, and current knowledge can be documented.

5. *Thinking.* This section of the portfolio is composed of a journal in which thinking becomes visible. This thinking journal contains three parts: one for book notes and reader responses, one for recording thoughts from class interactions and feedback from lesson demonstrations, and one for reflecting on ideas and strategies under investigation.

When these essential elements are considered holistically, after several months of teacher evaluation, feedback from peers, and personal and professional self-assessment exercises, teachers in training understand how to develop the habits of mind of lifelong learners in themselves and in others.

Building a smart portfolio

The smart portfolio is built in a community of learners where the consensus is that "two heads are better than one." Thoughtfulness and inquiry are built into every activity. When one looks more closely at the artifacts of the smart portfolio, the natural integration of the five essential elements becomes more evident (see Figure 2). As teachers in training record and connect ideas that flow through their experiences—responding, interacting, demonstrating, making meaning, and reflecting—their thinking actually becomes visible.

Responding

Teachers in training respond to current literature on "best practice" using the double-entry journal method. Dividing the pages into two parts, one third on the left and two thirds on the right or half and half, allows room on the left to respond to text notes, which are written on the right. The responses may be questions, comments, reminders to cross-reference, or any thinking related to the reading. Giving the students a page of dialogue from the teacher's journal will demonstrate engagement in a written conversation with the text. Keeping a journal and sharing it with your students is a powerful teaching/learning strategy.

Teachers in training learn to recognize the benefits of journal writing from modeling, but practice is even more important. *Journals in the Classroom: Writing to Learn* (Anson & Beach, 1995) is full of reflective writing prompts for all levels and content areas. Practicing "writing to learn" exercises greatly increases the chance that this strategy will be used again.

After several class meetings, pairs of teachers in training evaluate each other's journals (see Figure 3). This exercise makes them aware of what the instructor thinks is important. After completing the assessment, teachers in training reflect on what they learned from the exercise. Then they write an assessment of their own journals. When they share these final assessments, teachers in training begin to see that learning from assessment can be a valuable experience. Furthermore, they can easily create assessments for journals that extend and support learning.

Interacting

Scaffolding occurs when we interact in small groups responding to activities that require strategic thinking and cooperation. For example, several weeks ago I participated in a seminar on writing across the curriculum. One of the activities we were asked to do required that we read one of five short articles, then move to a new group where each of five participants had read a different one of the five articles. We summarized the article we had read and offered a response. We listened and asked questions as the other four group members talked about their readings.

Figure 2
Contents of a smart portfolio

Reading artifacts
Book list
Book notes
Summaries
Diagrams
Overviews
Outlines

Thinking (journal) artifacts
Thinking about our thinking
Responses to prompts
Written dialogue with texts
Mind wanderings and maps
Charts and graphs
Steps in problem solving
Process memos
Reader response

Demonstrating artifacts	Interacting artifacts
Illustrations	Photographs
Teacher assessments	Journal assessment
Lesson plans	Thinking exercises
Lesson critiques	In-class entries
Feedback from others	Group brainstorming charts
Video	Group consensus products
Checklists	Peer assessments
Teacher-made materials	Problems/solutions
Presentations	Projects

Writing artifacts
Formal papers
Publication piece
Philosophy of teaching and learning
Table of contents
Evaluation of artifacts
Descriptions of effective strategies
Self-evaluations of teaching
Goals

In my group one of the articles was on journals. A classroom teacher asked, "How do you really get students engaged?" One person suggested that the teacher share her journal with the students, saying that she actually puts journal pages on the overhead projector for students to discuss. This sounded like a great idea. Someone else suggested letting students respond to one another's journals. The first teacher responded, "I don't know if they want to share private writing." Another group member said, "If the students knew ahead that other students would be readers, they would be prepared for that audience." That is when I got the idea to have a different student each day share a journal re-

Figure 3
Peer evaluation of journals

Name_____ Date_____

1. List three examples of "evidence of learning and/or thinking" in this journal.
   a.
   b.
   c.
2. Can you describe a time when you actually observed this person writing in this journal?
3. Make a positive statement about this journal.
4. Do you think this person has kept a journal previously?
5. Read two entries and decide if they are thoughtful or done in haste. Comment.
6. How is this journal organized?
7. Can you hear the writer's voice in the entries?
8. Are notes from the texts complete?
9. How is this journal different from your own?
   _____This is an exceptional journal.
   _____This is a "good enough" journal.
   _____This journal needs some attention.

Figure 4
Smart portfolio lesson plan

   I. Objectives
      A. For student learning
      B. For teacher learning
  II. Introduction of lesson
 III. Procedures
      The teacher will...   The students will...

  IV. Closure
   V. Assignment with rationale
  VI. Materials
 VII. Ways to assess student learning
      A. Did I meet my objectives for student learning?
      B. What is the evidence? (Project, test, demonstration, essay, drawing, etc.)
VIII. Assessment of lesson delivery
      A. Were the teacher objectives met?
      B. Were the students engaged in learning? Why or why not?
      C. What did I learn? How do I know?

sponse on the overhead while the class critiqued the entry in small groups. It seemed to me that everyone would work harder for the public reading and be more engaged. Students would look for strengths and make suggestions for improvements.

Scaffolding has impact. Here is how it can work within a methods class. Students prepare a lesson plan with enough copies for the class. From the podium each one tells about the thoughtfully prepared lesson. In groups of four, students scrutinize the plan and the presentation. After this exercise one student wrote the following in her journal:

> Idea— Jury panels made up of students for music performance? I came up with this idea in class today as we were assessing each other's lesson plans. I felt that the activity was *very* helpful, as the groups were so honest and provided real feedback we were not getting from individuals. Perhaps I could do something similar with peer groups in music. Sometimes it's hard to assess instrumental or choral music, for example, because we don't generally give tests. My cooperating teacher gave "juries" but he was the only judge. Maybe a group of four kids could assess each performance. The assessment they did would also count as part of their [own] grade, so they would have to be fair and honest. They would learn even more about music by *evaluating* others for tone, musicality, rhythm, etc. This would give them a better idea of what makes a true musician. It also solves the assessment problem. I had never thought of a way to do cooperative learning in a performance-based music class before this.
>
> The same idea could apply to foreign language. Students could be given oral exams (dialogues, interviews, etc.) in front of the panel of peers....

Demonstrating

Teachers in training demonstrate their understandings of pedagogical theory by applying their reading to specific content as they present lessons to classmates. For example, they could set objectives for themselves as well as for their students. Then they could evaluate the teaching in terms of teacher objectives and learning in terms of student objectives. Such plans take time and require lots of thinking, but they exemplify "high road" transfer, as opposed to "low road" transfer that is automatic and mindless (Perkins, 1992, p. 124). These teachers learn to evaluate their success on a teaching level and determine the lesson's effectiveness on a learning level (see Figure 4). Traditionally, the lesson plan is concerned with objectives for students, but not for teachers, and assessment of teaching is rarely considered in a teacher's daily plan. It is, however, important to model a reflective thinking attitude, and the structured lesson plan makes it easy to do it systematically.

Each lesson includes "getting students ready" to learn, presenting the content (not always using direct instruction), and having the students apply or use the content to extend the learning experience. When teachers in training are asked to apply and demonstrate their learning, they question whether memorizing really leads to understanding. When teachers in training are asked to give a rationale for assignments, they consider their purposes more carefully. When asked to think of a variety of assessments, they wonder about the authenticity of one test. Connecting instruction and learning with student assessment and teacher effectiveness requires thoughtfulness in planning.

Making meaning

Hillocks shared his idea about the significance of writing:

> This is the self that must pull together, in meaningful ways, bits and pieces of one's experience in ways they have never been conjoined before. To the extent that one's self is a combination of one's total collection of memories *and* the manner in which one has placed them in relationship to each other, writing that shifts or adds to those relationships, such writing remakes the self to that extent. (1995, p. xi)

Hillocks went on to explain that as writers do research, meaning and relationships "formulate and reformulate." And, even though these changing formulations are not recorded, they are in the writer's mind. They become "part of the written texts—part of the writer's perspective and, therefore, personality" (p. 15).

However, if these changing formulations were recorded and revisited, might the connections and relationships be even stronger and more varied? Hillocks seemed to believe that each person is the integration of beliefs, memories, etc., and "our writing derives from the product of that integration." Therefore, he wrote, "Since those beliefs, memories, aspirations, and motives change from moment to moment, we find ourselves in a constant state of reintegration, of reinventing ourselves, as it were" (p. 23). This is how we make sense of our world.

As each semester brings new teachers in training to my class, they think that all the portfolios will be alike, but in the end each tells a different story,

Resources for reflective thinking strategies

Barton, J., & Collins, A. (1993). Portfolios in teacher education. *Journal of Teacher Education, 44,* 200–210.

Bauer, N. (1991). *Dewey and Schon: An analysis of reflective thinking.* Paper presented at the annual meeting of the American Educational Studies Association in Kansas City, MO. (ERIC Document Reproduction Service ED 344 299)

Black, L., Daiker, D., Sommers, J., & Stygall, G. (Eds.). (1994). *New directions in portfolio assessment.* Portsmouth, NH: Heinemann.

Brookfield, S. (1995). *Becoming a critically reflective teacher.* San Francisco: Jossey-Bass.

Brubacher, J., Case, C., & Reagan, T. (1994). *Becoming a reflective practitioner: How to build a culture of inquiry in the schools.* Thousand Oaks, CA: Corwin Press.

Bullough, R., Jr., & Gitlin, A. (1995). *Becoming a student of teaching.* New York: Garland.

Denus, J., & St. Hilaire, B. (1992). *Portfolios with real value: Teacher portfolios.* Winnipeg, MB: Seven Oaks School Division.

Fusco, E. (1994). *The portfolio assessment handbook: Teacher self-evaluation.* Roslyn, NY: Berrent.

Henderson, J. (1995). *Reflective teaching.* New York: Merrill.

Kochendorfer, L. (1994). *Becoming a reflective teacher.* Washington, DC: National Education Association.

Lasley, T., & Matezynske, T. (1995). Reflective teaching. In A. Ornstein (Ed.), *Teaching theory into practice* (pp. 307–321). Boston: Allyn & Bacon.

Loughran, J. (1996). *Developing reflective practice.* Washington, DC: Falmer Press.

Miller, J. (1990). *Creating spaces and finding voices: Teachers collaborating for empowerment.* Albany, NY: State University of New York Press.

Meyers, C., & Jones, T. (1993). *Promoting active learning.* San Francisco: Jossey-Bass.

Mezerow, J. (1990). *Fostering critical reflection in adulthood.* San Francisco: Jossey-Bass.

Newman, J. (Ed.). (1990). *Finding our own way: Teachers exploring their assumptions.* Portsmouth, NH: Heinemann.

(continued)

Resources for reflective thinking strategies (cont'd.)

Ormrod, J. (1995). *Human learning.* Englewood Cliffs, NJ: Prentice Hall.

Osterman, K., & Kottkamp, R. (1993). *Reflective practice for educators.* Newbury Park, CA: Corwin.

Pearson, J., & Santa, C. (1995). Students as researchers of their own learning. *Journal of Reading, 38,* 462–469.

Ross, D. (1989). First steps in developing a reflective approach. *Journal of Teacher Education, 40,* 22–30.

Schubert, W., & Ayers, W. (Eds.). (1992). *Teacher lore: Learning from our own experience.* White Plains, NY: Longman.

Shanahan, T. (Ed.). (1994). *Teachers thinking, teachers knowing.* Urbana, IL: National Council of Teachers of English and National Conference of Research on English.

Stahle, D., & Mitchell, J. (1993). Portfolio assessment in college methods courses: Practicing what we preach. *Journal of Reading, 36,* 538–542.

Valli, L. (Ed.). (1992). *Reflective teacher education.* Albany, NY: State University of New York Press .

Wildman, T., Magliaro, S., Niles, J., & McLaughlin, R. (1990). Promoting reflective practice among beginning and experienced teachers. In R. Clift, W. Houston, & M. Pugach (Eds.), *Encouraging reflective practice in education* (pp. 139–161). New York: Teachers College Press.

Wolf, K. (1991). *Teaching portfolios: Synthesis of research and annotated bibliography.* San Francisco: Far West Laboratory for Educational Research and Development.

Wolf, K., Whinery, B., & Hagerty, P. (1995, Spring). Teaching portfolios and portfolio conversations for teacher educators and teachers. *Action in Teacher Education,* pp. 30–39.

Zeichner, K., & Liston, D. (1987). Teaching student teachers to reflect. *Harvard Educational Review, 57,* 23–48.

Zubizarreta, J. (1994, December). Teaching portfolios and the beginning teacher. *Phi Delta Kappan,* pp. 323–326.

has a different personality, and holds artifacts very dear to each writer's heart. Writing to clarify, organize, and extend our thinking is necessary for making meaning, and making meaning is necessary for professional growth.

This is the key to the smart portfolio. Through constant connections in reading, writing, thinking, speaking, listening, and viewing, the portfolio takes on the personality of the writer. The artifacts show evidence of the ways we connect and pull things together, formulate new relationships, change our perspective, and "reinvent ourselves" as we integrate new knowledge. When teachers in training *see* and *feel* this kind of teaching and learning, they understand how the portfolio process facilitates learning.

Reflecting

Mitchell (1992) explained the importance of "thoughtfulness" at a secondary school in New York City (p. 79). Students asked and answered four questions: (a) Whose viewpoint are we seeing or reading or hearing? (b) How do we know what we know? What is the evidence? (c) How are things connected to each other? (d) So what? Who cares? Why does it matter? What does it mean? Could things be otherwise than they are? These are the questions reflective thinkers ask of and try to answer for themselves and others.

My students ask themselves questions as they view themselves on video. They ask themselves questions after they write or deliver a lesson. They ask for feedback from peers on their portfolio contents. They read others' journals and share their best learning strategies. We have no secrets. From studies on engagement, we have learned the importance of immediate feedback and using activities that hold interest through increasing complexity and skill level (Hillocks, 1995).

Connecting what we know with new information and new ways of knowing requires practice in reflective thinking. Following are some "writing to learn" exercises that facilitate thoughtfulness and a thinking attitude.

1. Have students reflect on their own teaching experiences for a moment or two and answer the following questions: Which of your own habits of

teaching might you consider altering? Where do you have the most opportunity or freedom to make changes? To become a thinker and learner in your own classroom, what do you need to do first? (Kirby & Kuykendall, 1991).

2. Ask students to consider these questions: How is language used in subjects other than in English class? In which classes did you learn to read and write? What is meant by the phrase "writing to learn?" Have you ever kept a journal or learning log? How did it affect you as a learner? (Strickland & Strickland, 1993).

3. Use this activity before students have read anything on the topic. Have students write everything they know about portfolios or portfolio assessment (or some other course topic). After 10 minutes make a list on the chalkboard. Ask students to write about one of the items on the board in as much detail as possible. After 10 minutes ask "What questions do you have about anything that came up today? What do you want to know? What are you wondering or thinking?" (Fulwiler, 1987).

4. I use the following exercise to show students how we actually integrate ideas. First, I ask them to list several ideas or innovations that interest them. Then, I ask them to choose one of the ideas or innovations and list some significant things they know about it. Next, we try to think of *where* or *how* we learned each of these significant things. Some students are perplexed at first and will seek more direction. I ask these kinds of questions to initiate their thinking: What did you read? What did you write? What did you see? What did others *tell* or explain to you? What did you share with others? Where did you do your thinking? Last, I ask students to draw a diagram of this learning.

There are many places to find ideas and strategies for teaching and learning reflective thinking (see Sidebar). Teachers in training often find that they can't immediately see how strategies can be easily changed to facilitate learning in different contexts. Just recently, for example, I demonstrated a lesson idea I read about in a journal article. The actual article explained several techniques for improving secondary students' reading skills (Caverly, Mandeville, & Nicholson, 1995). After sharing the

article with the class, I asked my students to do the following:

1. Draw a prediction map of a text they were going to read, *Creativity in the Classroom* (Starko, 1995).

2. Indicate with a check the things they thought they already knew something about.

3. Then, after reading, add information, questions, and ideas.

4. Look at their maps holistically and write a journal summary of their understandings.

5. Share their map with the class.

6. Share their thinking as to whether or not this exercise increased their learning and explain how they might change it to help students in their content area learn.

With this kind of a model, teachers in training quickly learn to transfer and adapt a variety of ideas and strategies from other content areas.

Evidence of thoughtful teaching and learning

Portfolios can facilitate professional growth as well as demonstrate it. Keeping track of reading, writing, thinking, speaking, listening, and viewing is necessary for teachers as learners; and collecting artifacts from observing, interpreting, applying, investigating, and assessing enhances learning and improves teaching. Artifacts that illustrate these kinds of thinking in classrooms offer others a way to see us and ensure that we see ourselves as we really are. This builds confidence and puts a classroom teacher in a better position to inquire, explore, and search for new and better ways of teaching and learning.

The smart portfolio becomes a place where thinking becomes visible, where it can be finely tuned, where the thinker is engaged, and where making meaning is personalized. A student wrote, "After all of this reading and thinking, writing and thinking, demonstrating and thinking, discussing and thinking, I ascertained the ultimate goal: the realization of the importance of metacognition on personal growth and how it can be cultivated in students and used to refine our own teaching."

The portfolio tells the story of the writer; not only the past but the present. And surely you will get an indication of what might come in the future. Smart schools, Perkins tells us, have to be "an informed and energetic setting for teachers' thoughtful learning, too" (1992, p. 221). Smart portfolios will hold the evidence of thoughtful teaching and learning. They will show that teachers who model a thinking attitude will be more thoughtful and have more thoughtful students.

Doing the kinds of thinking that a smart portfolio requires empowered me as a teacher and as a learner. Recording my ways of knowing, gathering new information, wondering whether these new ideas could be applied in my classroom, considering whether these new ideas would be helpful to my students, and deciding which to keep and which to throw away have made me a more thoughtful teacher. It isn't that one needs a smart portfolio to be a thoughtful teacher, but my portfolio contains the evidence that I am.

References

Anson, C., & Beach, R. (1995). *Journals in the classroom: Writing to learn.* Norwood, MA: Christopher-Gordon.

Barell, J. (1995). *Teaching for thoughtfulness.* White Plains, NY: Longman.

Caverly, D., Mandeville, T., & Nicholson, S. (1995). PLAN: A study-reading strategy for informational text. *Journal of Adolescent & Adult Literacy, 39,* 190–199.

Fisher, B. (1995). *Thinking and learning together.* Portsmouth, NH: Heinemann.

Fulwiler, T. (1987). *Teaching with writing.* Portsmouth, NH: Boynton/Cook.

Hillocks, G. (1995). *Teaching writing as reflective practice.* New York: Teachers College Press.

Kirby, D., & Kuykendall, C. (1991). *Mind matters: Teaching for thinking.* Portsmouth, NH: Boynton/Cook.

Mitchell, R. (1992). *Testing for learning.* New York: Macmillan.

Perkins, D. (1992). *Smart schools: From training memories to educating minds.* New York: The Free Press.

Perkins, D. (1995). *Outsmarting IQ: The emerging science of learnable intelligence.* New York: The Free Press.

Starko, A. (1995). *Creativity in the classroom.* White Plains, NY: Longman.

Strickland, K., & Strickland, J. (1993). *Uncovering the curriculum.* Portsmouth, NH: Boynton/Cook.

Tishman, S., Perkins, D., & Jay, E. (1995). *The thinking classroom.* Boston: Allyn & Bacon.

Taffy E. Raphael, Susan Florio-Ruane
Marcella J. Kehus, MariAnne George
Nina Levorn Hasty, Kathy Highfield

Thinking for ourselves: Literacy learning in a diverse teacher inquiry network

Collaboration and dialogue among diverse teachers led to knowledge and understanding.

At the annual convention of the International Reading Association (IRA), there is a long-standing tradition of presenting awards related to research (e.g., the Elva Knight Research Grants, Outstanding Dissertation Award). The presentation is followed by a research address, traditionally presented by a professor who studies literacy education. Last year's meeting in Indianapolis, May 2000, saw two significant changes to this tradition.

First, the topic suggested for the address was *teacher* research. This reflects a noteworthy acknowledgment of teacher research by IRA at a time when what "counts" as research is hotly contested. We value IRA's recognition, which underscores the importance of teacher research not only for the individual teacher, who learns more about his or her own practice by means of it, but for the field of literacy education as a whole (Richardson, 1990).

Second, our presentation in May 2000 reflected the first time the research awards address had been so visibly a collaborative venture. The authors of the research awards address, and this article, are members of the Teachers Learning Collaborative (TLC). Inviting a group of teachers and university-based teacher educators to present their work underscores IRA's recognition that to solve real problems in and out of schools, professionals with different expertise who work in different contexts must come together. It is precisely because we are not all the same that all our voices and perspectives are needed. In this article, based on our IRA Research Awards address, we describe collaborative teacher research on complex learning in the context of our practice as literacy educators.

The TLC is a network of three teacher study groups (Literary Circle, Book Club *Plus* Study Group, and the Literacy Circle Study Group) across southeastern Michigan, USA, supported in part by the Center for the Improvement of Early Reading Achievement and in part by the Walgreen Teachers in Residence Program at the University of Michigan. However, the network is supported primarily by individuals' voluntary commitment of time and energy to something in which we believe. Together, the six authors of this article represent a larger group of more than 30 Michigan teachers and teacher educators. Members of our group are actively engaged in teacher research in various stages, from defining questions to collecting data, to analyzing and publicizing what we have learned.

Common ground

We believe that inquiry is central to the work of teaching, that it requires community, and that communities of practice can take a myriad of forms. We live and work many miles from one another—along traffic-choked freeways throughout southeastern Michigan. We give up Saturdays and evenings to keep in touch about our work. We have had to become computer literate to communicate with one another by means of e-mail. What holds a group such as ours together? It is the common ground of a problem of practice with which we all struggle

Reprinted from *The Reading Teacher* (2001), 54, 596–607.

Figure 1
Influences on teaching and teacher learning

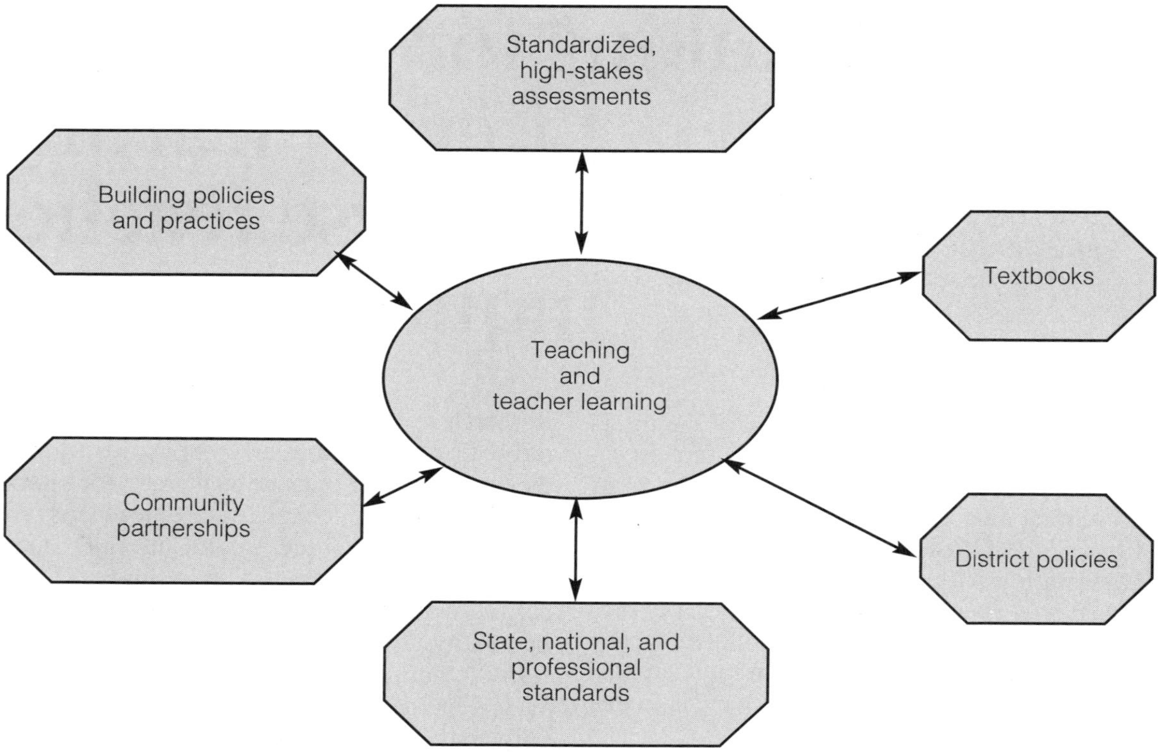

in our respective teaching contexts: How can we re-engage low-achieving readers?

We come to this question as experienced teachers who have often felt frustrated and isolated in our work. Too often, we have identified struggling readers and worried that our interventions to support their learning of skills and strategies have, in fact, derailed them from literacy. While these struggling readers spend most of their time in drill and practice, our more able readers seem to move quickly beyond grade-level expectations and engage in reading, writing, and talk about text in motivating and empowering ways. Thus, without intending to do so, we sometimes find that we have set up classrooms in which the rich get richer and the poor get poorer. How can we create classroom learning communities in which the skills and strategies we diligently teach are practiced by all of our students in powerful, engaging ways?

In TLC we have an opportunity to ask and answer this question in studies in our own classrooms and in conversation with one another. Some members of TLC teach in schools where there are many programs and pressures to raise literacy achievement. Some work in more affluent school districts and have greater autonomy to create individual programs, yet still are accountable for students' learning and their performance on high-stakes achievement tests. In each case, we find that it is easy to lose our way as we try to construct coherent, meaningful literacy experiences for all our students. Figure 1 illustrates an example of the forces that influence the teaching of literacy in one classroom.

Describing Figure 1 during our IRA Awards Address, Nina Hasty said the following:

> The circles in this diagram illustrate the various groups with a stake in literacy instruction in my district, and many people have had a voice in these—publishers, administrators, curriculum specialists, politicians, university professors. Notice

that the teacher is at the center of this diagram. I am in the center in terms of my direct work with children and my accountability, but it is hard for me to have a voice about my own practice outside the confines of my room. In a group such as TLC, I use my own voice to learn with other teachers so that I can improve literacy education for youngsters. In inquiring into the factors that shape my practice, I am discovering that the curriculum is not the reading series. It is not the [standardized] test or my district's exit skills for promotion to the next grade. The literacy curriculum is about spoken and written language. The curriculum is an ongoing conversation with and among my students.

This conversation, as Bruner (1986) has taught us, folds back on itself and gets more complex as we learn. It frames what we read, write, say, and hear in the process of learning literacy. In the learning conversation in Hasty's classroom, she and her students talk and wonder together about how language works, what written language is used for, how authors use different kinds of text to convey ideas, how to make sense of their lives through reading and writing, and how their lives are "storied."

Why we need one another

To understand how our community of practice worked to explore problems, it's useful, we believe, to understand the history of our network's development. All the members of the network were interested in re-engaging low achievers through authentic interactions with literature, and most of us were particularly intrigued by the idea of having our students participate in book clubs, using and adapting the Book Club program (McMahon, Raphael, Goatley, & Pardo, 1997; Raphael, Pardo, Highfield, & McMahon, 1997) for our classrooms. But we realized that two things stood in our way: (a) few of us had any experiences participating in book clubs with friends or colleagues, and (b) we wanted Book Club to be more than an enrichment activity for already-successful decoders.

In their roles as teacher educators, two authors of this article were particularly concerned with the problem of teachers being asked to teach in dialogic ways without having experienced this kind of teaching for themselves, and with a related problem of practice. Teacher education students and practicing teachers rarely have the opportunity to *experience sustained exploration of a complex idea*, let alone through dialogic practices. One such complex idea that we have found to be particularly challenging is that of culture—especially as it is manifest in classrooms throughout the United States, and as it affects literacy teaching and learning.

In the beginning of what became TLC, Florio-Ruane adapted the Book Club instructional framework developed by Raphael and her associates to teachers' learning about culture. Book Club had been developed to support youngsters' skill development in the areas of comprehension and interpretation of text. Florio-Ruane modified it to apply to adults and to develop the cultural theme in a master's-level course she then taught. In this initial book club course we read, wrote, and spoke about culture in response to autobiographical literature (Florio-Ruane & deTar, 1995, in press). In addition, we thought about our own development as literacy learners and as members of a culturally diverse society, as we developed vignettes revealing our autobiographies as literacy learners. Course members remained together, meeting monthly to form the Literary Circle (Florio-Ruane, 1994). Our ongoing teaching and research finds that because culture was so hard for us to talk about, sustained reading and repeated conversation on engaging multiple texts are needed repeatedly to explore the concept. Thus conversation can be a powerful way to learn about *complex concepts in indeterminate domains* (Spiro, Coulson, Feltovich, & Anderson, 1988; Spiro, Feltovich, Jacobson, & Coulson, 1992).

There is a family resemblance between teachers' leaning about a complex construct such as culture and the kind of curriculum conversations we want to see—and to support—through our students' reading, writing, and talking about text. Children's conceptions of culture, both in their own lives and as a key part of learning to contribute to a democratic society, are like our own—remarkably, but not surprisingly, impoverished (Dewey, 1944). Learning about democratic values—currently listed as one of the primary goals within U.S. and state social studies standards—requires not only the expository knowledge that typically is transmitted through textbooks, but also the important experiences that stem from engaging with that process. Thus, a second node in the TLC network formed through the creation of the Book Club *Plus* Study Group, focused on extending what we had

Figure 2
Book Club *Plus* curriculum framework

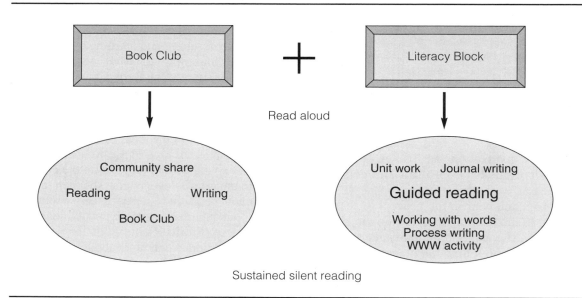

learned through the course and Literary Circle to develop meaningful literacy curriculum for diverse learners.

Our storied lives curriculum

Being a literate individual is more demanding today than ever before, and the challenge to educators is greater today than ever before. Not just the "college track" but "every school in America will ensure that all students learn to use their minds well" (National Education Goals Panel, 1995, p. 11). Political leaders in the U.S. have established as a national priority the goal that all students leave third grade able to read. However, in addition to decoding print, all children need to engage in the higher order thinking associated with literacy. To this end, the members of the TLC network recognize that as literacy teachers we have dual and what have sometimes been characterized as competing obligations.

On the one hand, we are obligated to make sure all students have decoding skills sufficient to read independently. Thus, it is vital for all students to have sufficient practice using reading materials that are at their instructional level. On the other hand, it is a crucial goal to make sure that students learn to *think* as readers and writers. Students must therefore also have access to age-appropriate material that challenges their thinking

and fosters thoughtful talk and writing about text. We cannot choose between these two obligations; nor must we view them as being in opposition. Good literacy education must involve both.

As things currently stand, low-achieving readers may conceivably go through school never engaging with challenging texts appropriate for their age level, texts that require higher order thinking and interpretation skills. Moreover, these struggling readers do not have the opportunity to talk with peers about such materials and the ideas they contain. Further, in such circumstances the classroom becomes stratified. It is difficult in that setting, if not impossible, for low-achieving readers to join or for the teacher to create a functioning community of learners. TLC identified this problem at the core of the reengagement of struggling readers. Over the past 3 years the teacher researchers in TLC have designed, taught, and evaluated a curricular framework aimed at solving this problem. We call the framework Book Club *Plus* (see Raphael, Florio-Ruane, & George, in preparation).

Book Club *Plus*

In Book Club *Plus*, we created thematic units that enable us to take advantage of two contexts for reading, writing, and talk about text as illustrated in Figure 2. These two contexts are

Family stories texts

Context	Patricia Polacco books used in Grade 3
Book Club book	*Chicken Sunday*
Guided reading	Above grade level: *Meteor!* At grade level: *Some Birthday!* Below grade level: *My Rotten Red-Headed Older Brother*
Read-alouds (also used as models for process writing activities)	*Babushka's Doll* *The Keeping Quilt* *Thank You, Mr. Falker* *The Bee Tree* *Boat Ride With Lillian Two Blossom* *Picnic at Mudsock Meadow* *Applemando's Dreams* *Pink and Say* *Thundercake* *Tikvah Means Hope* *Firetalking* (Polacco autobiography)
Viewing	*Dreamkeepers*

Book Club and Literacy Block. Each is an extended period of time in the school day within which important activities take place, each serving a different purpose in students' learning.

In one context, Literacy Block, activities related to the skills and strategies of reading and writing are taught and practiced. They may include writers' workshops, practice activities to foster word-level decoding skills, reading (or listening to) books individually or in peer groups, and so forth. However, one important feature of Literacy Block is guided reading, or teacher-led discussion around specific skills, strategies, and words to be taught. Students learn these within the guided reading groups using texts at their instructional level. These texts are all thematically linked to the unit in which the entire class participates and to the books that are discussed during Book Clubs.

In Book Club, heterogeneous student-led book clubs are the sites where students apply the strategies they have been taught by discussing compelling, age-appropriate literature. Access to the literature discussed in Book Club can involve a variety of routes: independent reading, buddy reading, listening or viewing centers, and teacher read-alouds. What is crucial is not that every child read every Book Club book independently, but that all children have access to the challenging, age-appropriate text and all students write and speak in response to it. As they respond to the texts and to one another, students learn to link texts to examine complex ideas.

Culture is one of the complex ideas we explored to anchor our yearlong curricular theme, "Our Storied Lives." Students address this theme in three 6- to 8-week units: Stories of Self, Family Stories, and Stories of Culture. This progression of units allows us to begin with a focus on the self, a concept that fits with curricular materials across grade levels, and it contextualizes the self within the broader areas of family, community, and society.

Each unit within the Storied Lives framework draws upon a set of books that allows the particular focus to be fully developed. Focus development occurs through the Book Club book, the guided reading books or stories, the teacher's read-aloud, shared reading books that are often the basis for minilessons during writers' workshop, and the classroom library that often serves students' sustained silent reading. Further, each unit includes a culminating project requiring students to apply and integrate language arts skills and strategies along with the overarching theme. Teachers alternated students' Book Club activities (2–3 days per week) with the guided reading and independent unit work of Literacy Block (2–3 days per week).

The Table lays out the books we used when teaching the Family Stories unit. We featured work of Patricia Polacco, a prolific Michigan author who bases her writings on her own life, highlighting relationships among family members, cultural heritage, and family stories. In describing this unit we make reference to students' work in the classroom of MariAnne George, one of the authors of this article.

The culminating project that students in George's third-grade classroom created involved oral retellings of family stories based upon artifacts that the students valued. For example, Nathan's (pseudonym) grandfather's father had come from Ireland. When it came time to share his family story, Nathan brought a pickle barrel he and his father had made and shared the story he had learned by interviewing his grandfather. As Nathan tells it, his great-grandfather had to leave Ireland rather suddenly and in secret, so he stowed away inside a pickle barrel and escaped on a boat. The interactions Nathan had with his father and grandfather brings home the importance of such assignments, while the family story content highlights one of the many histories of how the United States was built.

The variety of artifacts students brought to this task reflected what they had learned from reading picture books such as William Joyce's (1997) *The World of William Joyce Scrapbook* and hearing autobiographies of Roald Dahl (1984), Gary Paulsen (1998), Jean Craighead George (1996), and others. Moreover, they were informed by their continually developing reading, writing, and discussion skills as well as their knowledge of culture and of how lives are presented and re-presented. These family stories are so deeply rooted in the students' cultural heritage that it was a natural transition to the third unit in the theme, Stories of Culture.

The students learned what an artifact was and, in so doing, discovered culture in material aspects of everyday life. They saw how these everyday activities and artifacts matter—not just as festivals or tokens of ethnic identity, but as receptacles of collected and collective meaning, signals of the shared activities and understandings within social groups. Writing and oral language are artifacts of culture by this definition, as are such objects as pickle barrels.

In George's third-grade classroom, students learned about themselves and one another, and their relationship to other family members and their cultural heritage. In Marcella Kehus's eighth-grade class, students used different books but a similar thematic focus and instructional framework to explore more complex issues of identity, conformity, and social responsibility.

George's ongoing teacher research examines whether and how this curriculum supports students' learning to make intertextual connections—across texts, between the texts and their own lives, and across the contexts of writing, reading, and discussion—to understand a complex concept (Hartman, 1991). At least two decades of research document the importance of background knowledge for text understandings, and important sources for such knowledge include other texts students read, as well as the "texts" of their own lived experiences (Anderson, Hiebert, Scott, & Wilkinson, 1985; Sipe, 2000). George chose to study intertextual connections for many reasons, with one of the most important being how such connections affect students' response to literature, their text comprehension, and the interpretations they make.

Two examples illustrate the intertextual connections students make and why we teach so that students come to value such connections. In the first example, we highlight how George's students used text-to-text connections as they responded to books within the family stories unit. In the second, a connection from text to life helped one of her second-language learners find a way to talk about his own feelings of frustration in dealing with living in a new country.

The first example is taken from an entry George made in her teacher research log. Following a read-aloud, she was eavesdropping on her students as they talked during snack time. In her log, she wrote the following (all students' names are pseudonyms):

Today I was absolutely thrilled at the discussion that took place after my read aloud of Patricia Polacco's book *Thundercake*. As I finished, Megan said, "That story is a lot like 'Chicken Coop Monster' because Melissa's Grandpa helped her get over her fears like Patricia Polacco's grandmother did." Josh added, "Only it was her Babushka (grandmother) instead of her grandfather like in 'Chicken Coop Monster.'" Chelsea then chimed in, "It was kinda like that but the opposite in Tomie DePaola's book *Now One Foot Now the Other* because Tomie helped his grandpa get over his fears."

The children's intertextual connections began by noting that the role of the grandparents in each of two stories was quite similar, helping their grandchildren overcome a specific fear. They contrasted the two on the basis of gender. Chelsea's contribution was even more sophisticated, making a connection at the level of characters' agency in the story and highlighting that the two generations' roles were reversed in De Paola's story, where a child helps his grandfather overcome a fear. Their comments were spontaneous, rather than orchestrated by the teacher, the connections showed depth, and the fact that they occurred during snack time suggests that the students had internalized what they had been taught about both text interpretation and conversation.

When the unit drew to a close, the teacher led a whole-class discussion in which she asked the students to think about the big ideas or themes that reflected commonalities across their texts. Hands shot up, and one of the first themes to be identified was "facing your fears." We took this as evidence that conversations outside the formal context of Book Club and Literacy Block were as important to students' meaning making as those orchestrated within.

In the second example, the text of *Molly's Pilgrim* (1983) helps a second-language learner develop the language to talk about his often-frustrating school experiences. Johann, an ESL student from Germany, joined the classroom in February, speaking little English, though able to read at about a second-grade level. *Molly's Pilgrim* was the Book Club selection as part of the unit "Stories of Culture." Johann was "buddied" with a more proficient reader during the silent reading portion of Book Club. From George's teacher research log, we read the following:

> After reading the assigned chapters, the children moved into written response time in their literature logs. However, instead of writing, Johann put his head down on his desk. I walked over and sat with him trying to help him think of an idea to put down on paper. After a few probing questions, Johann responded "I didn't like the song 'Jolly Molly.'" "Why?" I asked. "The girls laugh at her." He then tried to explain to me that's how he felt at times because he was new and not from America. This exchange represented a breakthrough for us, since until this point I had not been able to engage Johann in writing or talking about text. The feelings he shared with Molly, the main character of the story, made the writing and talk meaningful. Johann wrote his two sentences (with my support) and was later able to share this with his Book Club group.

If, as Gavelek and Raphael (1996) have argued, learning is a complex, iterative process of social engagement, reflection, and transformation, then Book Club seems to foster learning about self, other, and text. The multiple texts students and teacher can reference include the published books they discuss, the writing they do in response, the oral stories they hear, and the stories they dare to tell one another. These intertextual connections make a fabric within which literature can be understood and the conventions of reading and writing practiced to powerful ends. Thus, in our network's research, we focus on them and hope to understand better the role of curricular frameworks in teaching and teacher thinking, and the effectiveness of a framework like Book Club *Plus* for re-engaging struggling readers.

Assessment research in Book Club *Plus*

It should be clear by now that our "problem of practice" of trying to re-engage struggling readers is an enormous one. Attempting to solve it opened the door to many associated and interesting problems, from literature selection to supporting materials to classroom organization to what was perhaps the most challenging—figuring out how to assess learning. With all the goals we were trying to accomplish, we engaged in *collaborative inquiry* to work out the details of the curriculum, teaching, and instruction. Even in one of our most hierarchically organized school districts, where teachers must use a particular textbook series for reading instruction, our members felt bold enough to work "outside the box," appropriating and transforming the units to make Book Club *Plus* come to life in classrooms, *putting our voices in the center of the conversation.*

The much harder task for us involved assessment in two major facets: (a) studying student learning in Book Club *Plus* to evaluate whether our framework was effective in supporting learning, and (b) finding ways to document student learning in terms that were useful within our classrooms' related communities, and responsive to the standards to which we are all accountable.

We looked around and learned from others, especially from Au (Au, Carroll, & Scheu, 1995) and Valencia (1999), and their teacher research colleagues in Hawaii and Washington,

Figure 3
Garland "I Can" statements

Reading
I can retell a story in my own words.
I can make meaning when I read a variety of texts.
I can make connections between my own life and what I am reading.
I can make connections within and between texts.
I can figure out a theme from my reading.

Writing
I can write to communicate my ideas.
I can use writing for different purposes and audiences.
I can show "me" in my writing.

Discussion
I can contribute to a good book club discussion.
    (a) I can stay on topic when I talk.
    (b) I can share my feelings and ideas.
    (c) I can respect others' ideas and opinions.
    (d) I can build on others' ideas.
    (e) I can bring others into the discussion.

Evaluation
I can show and/or tell what I learned and how I learned it.

Culture
I can use artifacts to describe
    (a) my own cultural heritage,
    (b) others' cultures, and
    (c) similarities and differences across cultures.

I can define culture and how cultures change.

stand in stark contrast to many of the assessments the teachers were required by their schools, districts, or state to undertake. They were devised in ways cognizant of other yardsticks against which teachers and pupils would be measured, but they were framed in terms that made sense within the TLC teachers' classrooms and Book Club *Plus* curriculum. To develop these statements, we moved from the formal statements of official documents from national, state, and district standards to language we could use with our students. For example, one standard in our Michigan English Language Arts Framework states the following:

> Students can engage in extended conversations with teachers and/or peers about subject matter in a way that builds an improved and shared understanding of ideas and topics.

Our own wording for that standard highlights specific ways our students could be expected to contribute to a good discussion. Thus, the "I can" for this discussion goal begins with the general statement, "I can contribute to a book club discussion," and then is broken down into much more specific indicators of what the student knows, can do, and, with the teacher, can accumulate evidence for having learned:

- I can stay on topic when I talk.
- I can share my feelings and ideas.
- I can respect others' ideas and opinions.
- I can build on others' ideas.
- I can bring others into the discussion.

These "I Can" statements provided the foundation from which grade-level benchmarks and subsequent rubrics could be developed. These rubrics and benchmarks became the basis of our assessment system, providing the framework for student self-evaluation, teacher evaluation, and portfolios that together provide evidence of learning. We aimed to make our language clear and simple for our students. Ironically, once we had made these "I Can" statements for each the standards, we found that we had also created language much preferred by our parents, administrators, and colleagues. Thus, the "I Can" statements gave us a common language to discuss our work both in going public with our colleagues and as we continue our research on student learning in Book Club *Plus*.

respectively. We began to think that we and our students might be able to put our own voices in the center of the assessment conversation. Thus, on one summer weekend a small group of us got together in a cabin in the lush countryside of Garland in northern Michigan to generate the "I Can" statements displayed in Figure 3.

We used these "I Can" statements to create an assessment system for Book Club *Plus* guided by our national, state, and district standards, but tailored to the goals and commitments of our curriculum framework. The Garland "I Can" statements pushed us to say in our own words, for the first time, what was important to teach, learn, and assess within Book Club *Plus*.

Perhaps tackling assessment is the strongest example of our efforts to "think for ourselves" as teachers of literacy. The "I Can" statements can be thought of as an artifact constructed within the TLC community of practice. As such, they

The "I Can" statements are divided into five related areas of learning: reading, writing, discussion, self-evaluation, and content knowledge. The first four areas cut across grade levels, differentiated only at the benchmark level, but the content goals often varied. In the unit George taught and researched, the focus was on culture. In Kehus's eighth-grade classroom, the focus was on social responsibility. Just as we worked collaboratively to define these "I Can" statements, so, too, did we want our students to feel a similar sense of ownership within our classrooms. To that end, we each turned to our students—from Hasty's second graders to George's third graders to Kehus's eighth graders—to identify the benchmarks that defined what we mean by "success" in a given area. Kehus's eighth-grade classroom is illustrative. After a series of student-led discussions, the eighth graders built from the "I Can" statements about discussion to create a set of criteria for a good discussion:

- Voice own opinions.
- Back up opinion with facts.
- Have good eye contact.
- Don't overuse "like."
- Ask good questions.
- Don't jump around topics.
- Make connections.
- Be polite.
- Speak clearly.
- Promote (and tolerate) some disagreements.
- Be open to everyone else talking.

These criteria, in turn, became the rubric for assessing students' progress, both as self-evaluation and from teacher observations. We did similar activities with students' writing, reading, and content learning. We feel confident that such a broad-sweeping assessment model meets the needs of all stakeholders in communicating about student achievement.

Our overall assessment system, reflected in Figure 4, flows from the "I Can" Statements. It is designed to track student learning in these five areas in a variety of ways—from the work samples collected in portfolios, to standardized tests of reading and language arts, to running records and teacher observations, to pre- and post-evaluations of student-led book club discussions.

We present one summative essay related to our reading theme to illustrate how we are able to assess at various levels and for different audiences or stakeholders. For this piece of writing, we began with a student's self-evaluation that informed both student and teacher as to how this student was performing in relation to his or her own learning goals. For our own teaching purposes, we also kept anecdotal notes to inform our teaching. This piece of writing would also be evaluated more formally using a rubric based on "I Can" statements and our negotiated benchmarks; such a rubric serves to inform multiple audiences, primarily the students and parents, as to how the work matches our criteria of success in the given area. This same rubric could also be translated into a number or letter grade for district report cards, communicating achievement for local school and district accountability. In the broadest sense, the work could be evaluated according to state or national standards, such as giving a holistic score to students' writing indicating their level of proficiency.

Building on the generative nature of the "I Can" statement for youngsters, we are also beginning to develop "I Can" statements for ourselves. Few studies in education have tried to link changes in teachers' knowledge with changes in pupils' knowledge. This means that we do not know well what makes for optimum teacher education in the service of literacy learning for all students. As we look at our roles as leaders in our profession and participants in the preparation of the next generation of teachers, we hope to devise "I Can" statements for teacher learning that are powerfully connected to the learning of youngsters. We believe this is important because we are coming to find that the teacher learning needed to teach literacy well is, like literacy learning itself, complex and multifaceted.

Thinking and speaking for ourselves

In this article, we have drawn on the Teachers Learning Collaborative to illustrate the potential of teacher research for informing our field, as well as to demonstrate a particular model within which such research can be accomplished. Teachers work with peers, as well as university-based researchers and teacher educators, to investigate complex problems of both theory and practice. Our focus stemmed from our concern about struggling readers. Specifically,

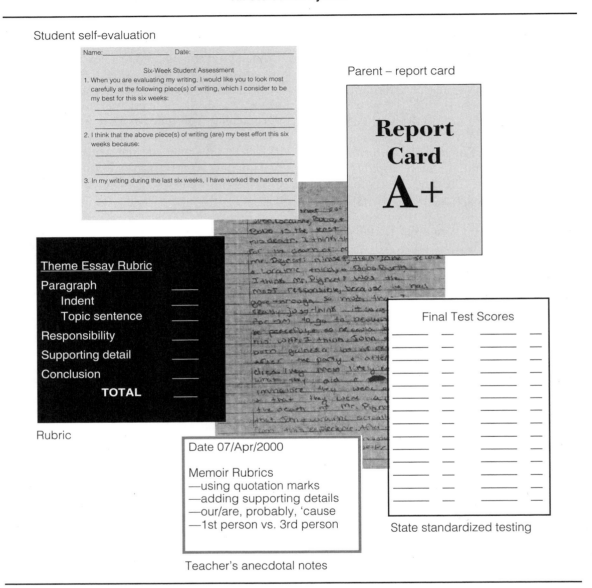

Figure 4
An evaluation system

Student self-evaluation

Name:_____ Date: _____

Six-Week Student Assessment

1. When you are evaluating my writing, I would like you to look most carefully at the following piece(s) of writing, which I consider to be my best for this six weeks:

_____
_____
_____

2. I think that the above piece(s) of writing (are) my best effort this six weeks because:

_____
_____
_____

3. In my writing during the last six weeks, I have worked the hardest on:

_____
_____
_____

Parent – report card

Report Card

A+

Theme Essay Rubric

Paragraph   _____
   Indent   _____
   Topic sentence   _____
Responsibility   _____
Supporting detail   _____
Conclusion   _____
         TOTAL   _____

Rubric

Final Test Scores

State standardized testing

Date 07/Apr/2000

Memoir Rubrics
—using quotation marks
—adding supporting details
—our/are, probably, 'cause
—1st person vs. 3rd person

Teacher's anecdotal notes

we wanted to create meaningful and rich literacy experiences for these students—experiences that stimulated their higher order and critical thinking, while still maintaining a place for instruction in basic skills in language conventions.

Through conversation in professional study groups, we became convinced that we needed a new, or at least a substantially modified, curriculum. In TLC, we met in book clubs and study groups for experience in conversation-based learning, emphasizing critical thinking, and work-

ing within a community of learners to solve a problem. We took from our experiences as readers, writers, and thinkers, insights for our own teaching. That led us to the design, teaching, and assessment of the Storied Lives curriculum and studying how our struggling readers both experienced and learned from that curriculum.

We have also begun to "go public" with our ideas through both informal and formal presentations. In doing this, we introduce our ideas to members of a broader professional community

Question for all
*How do we make time/skil
to improve our skil
+ practice?*

who, in turn, further our thinking by their response to our work. The contexts in which teachers work today tend to be isolated from other professionals. They are embedded within a hierarchical system in which the teachers' day-to-day activities are governed by external forces: administrative mandates, parental requests, and, somewhat unique to today's climate, legislative directives. Missing from the lives of teachers is the opportunity to articulate and investigate with others the means for improving our practice and the learning of those with whom we work. Study groups provide an activity setting in which these voices and views can be expressed as part of learning.

From psychological perspectives, teacher study groups are illustrative of the power of a learning community. For the past two decades, many literacy educators have drawn on the work of Ann Brown (Brown & Campione, 1990), Annemarie Palincsar (Palincsar & Brown, 1984), Barbara Rogoff (1990), Jean Lave (1990; Lave & Wenger, 1991) and others to detail the ways in which Vygotsky's (1978) theory of learning plays out in discourse practices. Vygotsky's basic tenet is that learning is a social phenomenon. Individuals learn, but that learning begins, and is based in, social activity or the social plane. This social plane is reflected in the public and shared discourse of the teacher study group as ideas are appropriated and transformed.

Sociolinguists such as Swales (1990) and Gee (1992) have helped us to understand the importance of this public discourse. Knowledge of the language practices within a discourse community provides access to that community and defines who the community members are. Language is a key factor in the development of our identities—as professionals, as educators, as literacy educators, and as teacher researchers. Understanding the importance of the discourse community helps us create opportunities for access and opportunities to harness the power of conversation to move beyond the immediate setting and effect important changes in practice.

In our collaborative research, we found that out of a dialogue among our diverse participants, we constructed knowledge that might otherwise have eluded us if we had conducted either traditional university-based research or innovative school-based practitioner research in isolation.

Rather than define practitioner research as alternative to or in opposition to university-based research on teaching, we hope to have argued persuasively for a model of "learning community" (Schwab, 1975), or negotiated knowledge and meaning within a diverse group with common concerns. Thus, while we are not naive about the historical privileging of academic research in which teachers serve as "subjects" or "informants," we are also not sanguine about such work. We underscore teacher research as another powerful, but—like university-driven research—also limited genre for the study of education.

In organizing our group explicitly to work against the traditional isolation of teacher from teacher, university from classroom, novice from experienced educator, we hope to craft a new professional community with a new discourse for the understanding and improvement of practice. From the content of our teaching, to our authorship of the curriculum, to our commitment to supporting diverse learners, to our reflections on the experience to date, TLC Network participants reflect the power of dialogic models of professional development.

References

Anderson, R.C., Hiebert, E.H., Scott, J.A., & Wilkinson, I.A.G. (1985). *Becoming a nation of readers: The report of the Commission on Reading.* Washington, DC: U.S. Department of Education.

Au, K.H., Carroll, J.H., & Scheu, J.R. (1995). *Balanced literacy instruction: A teacher's resource book.* Norwood, MA: Christopher-Gordon.

Brown, A.L., & Campione, J.C. (1990). Communities of learning and thinking, or a context by any other name. In D. Kuhn (Ed.), *Developmental perspectives on teaching and learning thinking skills* (pp. 108–126). Farmington, CT: Karger.

Bruner, J. (1986). *Actual minds, possible worlds.* Cambridge, MA: Harvard University Press.

Dewey, J. (1944). *Democracy and education.* New York: The Free Press.

Florio-Ruane, S. (1994) The future teachers' autobiography club: Preparing educators to support literacy learning in culturally diverse classrooms. *English Education, 26,* 52–66.

Florio-Ruane, S., & deTar, J. (1995). Conflict and consensus in teacher candidates' discussion of ethnic autobiography. *English Education, 27,* 11–39.

Florio-Ruane, S., & de Tar, J. (in press). *Teacher education and the cultural imagination: Autobiography, conversation, and narrative.* Mahwah, NJ: Erlbaum.

Gavelek, J.R., & Raphael, T.E. (1996). Changing talk about text: New roles for teachers and students. *Language Arts, 73,* 182–192.

Gee, J.P. (1992). *The social mind: Language, ideology, and social practice.* New York: Bergin & Garvey.

Hartman, D. (1991). The intertextual link of readers using multiple passages: A postmodern/semiotic/cognitive view of meaning making. In J. Zutell & S. McCormick (Eds.), *Learner factors/teacher factors: Issues in literacy research. 40th yearbook of the National Reading Conference* (pp. 616–636). Chicago: National Reading Conference.

Lave, J. (1990). The culture of acquisition and the practice of understanding. In J.W. Stigler, R.A. Shweder, & G. Herdt (Eds.), *Cultural psychology* (pp. 309–327). Cambridge, England: Cambridge University Press.

Lave, J., & Wenger, E. (1991). *Situated learning: Legitimate peripheral participation.* Cambridge, England: Cambridge University Press.

McMahon, S.I., Raphael, T.E., Goatley, V.J., & Pardo, L.S. (1990). *The book club connection: Literacy learning and classroom talk.* New York: Teachers College Press.

National Education Goals Panel. (1995). *The national education goals report: Building a nation of learners, 1995.* Washington, DC: U.S. Government Printing Office.

Palincsar, A.S., & Brown, A.L. (1984). Reciprocal teaching of comprehension-fostering and comprehension-monitoring activities. *Cognition and Instruction, 1,* 117–175.

Raphael, T.E., Florio-Ruane, S., & George, M.A. (in preparation). *Book Club* Plus: *A conceptual framework to organize literacy instruction.*

Raphael, T.E., Pardo, L., Highfield, K., & McMahon, S. (1997). *Book club: A literature-based curriculum.* Littleton, MA: Small Planet Communications.

Richardson, V. (1990). Significant and worthwhile change in teaching practice. *Educational Researcher, 19*(7), 10–18.

Rogoff, B. (1990). *Apprenticeship in thinking: Cognitive development in social context.* Oxford, England: Oxford University Press.

Schwab, J.J. (1975). On learning community: Education and the state. *The Center Magazine, 8*(3), 30–44.

Sipe, L.R. (2000). The construction of literacy understandings by first and second graders in oral response to picture storybook read-alouds. *Reading Research Quarterly, 35,* 252–275.

Spiro, R.J., Coulson, R.L., Feltovich, P.J., & Anderson, D.K. (1988). Cognitive flexible theory: advanced knowledge acquisition in ill-structures domains. In *10th Annual Conference of the Cognitive Science Society* (pp. 375–383). Hillsdale, NJ: Erlbaum.

Spiro, R.J., Feltovich, P.J., Jacobson, M.J., & Coulson, R.L. (1992). Knowledge representation, content specification, and the development of skill in situation-specific knowledge assembly: Some constructivist issues as they relate to Cognitive Flexibility Theory and hypertext. In T.M. Duffy & D.J. Jonassen (Eds.), *Constructivism and the technology of instruction: A conversation* (pp. 57–75). Hillsdale, NJ: Erlbaum.

Swales, J.M. (1990). *Genre analysis: English in academic and research settings.* Cambridge, England: Cambridge University Press.

Valencia, S. (1999). *Literacy portfolios in action.* Ft. Worth, TX: Harcourt College.

Vygotsky, L.S. (1978). *Mind in society: The development of higher psychological processes* (M. Cole, V. John-Steiner, S. Scribner, E. Souberman, Trans.). Cambridge, MA: Harvard University Press.

Children's books cited

Cohen, Barbara. (1983). *Molly's pilgrim.* New York: Morrow.

Dahl, Roald. (1984). *Boy: Tales of a childhood.* New York: Puffin.

DePaola, Tomie. (1998). *Now one foot now the other.* New York: Putnam.

George, Jean Craighead. (1996). *The tarantula in my purse and 172 other wild pets.* New York: HarperCollins.

Joyce, William. (1997). *The world of William Joyce scrapbook.* New York: HarperCollins.

McKissack, Patricia. (1992). Chicken coop monster. From *The dark thirty: Southern tales of the supernatural* (pp. 111–122). New York: Scholastic.

Paulsen, Gary. (1998). *My life in dog years.* New York: Delacorte Press.

Polacco, Patricia. (1989). *Boat ride with Lillian Two Blossom.* New York: Philomel.

Polacco, Patricia. (1990). *Thundercake.* New York: Putnam.

Polacco, Patricia. (1991). *Applemando's dreams.* New York: Philomel.

Polacco, Patricia. (1992). *Chicken Sunday.* New York: Philomel.

Polacco, Patricia. (1992). *Picnic at Mudsock Meadow.* New York: Putnam.

Polacco, Patricia. (1993). *The bee tree.* New York: Philomel.

Polacco, Patricia. (1994). *Babushka's doll.* New York: Simon & Schuster.

Polacco, Patricia. (1994). *Fire talking.* Katonah, NY: Richard C. Owen.

Polacco, Patricia. (1994). *The keeping quilt.* New York: Simon & Schuster.

Polacco, Patricia. (1994). *Pink and Say.* New York: Philomel.

Polacco, Patricia. (1994). *Some birthday!* New York: Simon & Schuster.

Polacco, Patricia. (1996). *Tikvah means hope.* New York: Yearling.

Polacco, Patricia. (1998). *My rotten red-headed older brother.* New York: Aladdin.

Polacco, Patricia. (1998). *Thank you, Mr. Falker.* New York: Philomel.

Polacco, Patricia. (1999). *Meteor!* New York: Philomel.

Teaching and Learning About Cultural Diversity

Becoming a multicultural teacher

Howard M. Miller

I am often asked to offer advice to nonminority teachers in the United States on how they might best work with minority students. Undoubtedly, the request is made out of a genuine desire to help these students be more successful in school, yet the inherent implications are many and disturbing:

- That minority students are, by their nature, less likely to be successful in school;
- That there is some formulaic methodology that can be employed to effectively teach particular groups of students on the basis of their cultural status;
- That all members of a particular minority group will respond in the same way to a given approach to teaching;
- That there is a need to teach minority students in ways that are different from how we teach nonminority students;
- That there is no need to teach in varied ways if we have no minority students in our classrooms; and
- That minority teachers will automatically be more successful than nonminority teachers in working with minority students.

Being multicultural teachers demands that we face a lengthy and com- plex set of issues, beginning with the understanding that good multicultural teaching has the bottom-line goal of helping every child be successful in our classrooms. Here are 10 recommendations for reaching that goal.

1. Let's start by being honest with ourselves. What are our own prejudices, beliefs, and values? To what extent do we make assumptions about our students on the basis of their background, socioeconomic status, language differences, physical appearance, health status, and cultural factors? No one is totally free of prejudice and xenophobia. These are emotional, not intellectual, responses that are shaped by our upbringing and experiences. We cannot help how we feel, but we do have the power to adjust how we act by improving the way we respond to and instruct our students.

2. We should work at being accepted and trusted by students and their parents, particularly if we are viewed as outsiders by the community. We ask parents to entrust us with their child, their most valued treasure, but unless we make a concerted effort to be worthy of that trust, negative feelings of suspicion and distrust can quickly take over and shut off communication. We need to reach out by being visible and active in the community, by being available to help, and by soliciting and accepting the advice and help of parents and community members.

3. When we do approach parents and community members for help, let's make sure that what we ask them to do has significance. It is not enough to invite them to bake cookies or photocopy papers for us; we need to use their skills and knowledge and let them know they are making a major contribution to our students'—their children's—learning. For example, we might call on persons who lived through the Holocaust or took part in the U.S. Civil Rights movement to share their experiences when we study these events in class. With real people telling personal stories, these issues and the lessons they teach will take on for our students an urgency far removed from abstract ideas of seemingly ancient and irrelevant history. We do not have to be experts in everything. How about bringing in a member of the Muslim community to talk about Ramadan, or the parent of a Deaf student to teach the class some signing? We need to think about what it will take to bring the curriculum to life and then look to our neighbors to help us.

4. We must always remember that textbooks and other teaching materials do not routinely portray minorities in nonstereotypical or "nontokenistic" ways. We need to make a genuine effort to seek out and incorporate materials that reflect the world's diversity, and to develop curriculum that consistently incorporates and respects minority perspectives in ways that are not merely for

show or that serve to single out cultural minorities as either heroes or victims of discrimination.

5. We should engage our students in culturally relevant activities and assignments. Turn lemons into lemonade, as the saying goes, by helping students to recognize stereotyping, tokenism, and bias in textbooks, magazines, newspapers, trade books, and popular culture. Get them involved in research or debates over issues such as slavery as it exists in the world today, the arguments for and against making English the official language of the United States, the fight over the role of religion in public education, the struggle for equal rights for women, the controversy over the "don't ask; don't tell" policy regarding gays in the military. Let's not avoid these issues in the name of protecting our students. School should be the place where ideas are studied along with facts, so that we can prepare students to be active and contributing members of society.

6. We must be on guard and prepared to take a stand against intolerance when it appears in the speech or actions of students, faculty, or staff at our schools. We must have a policy and a plan in place for dealing with issues of intolerance, including the often ignored bullying, name calling, and teasing that takes place in the hallways, bathrooms, and cafeteria. Sadly, U.S. schools are no longer viewed as totally safe environments, but we can support the efforts of our internal and external communities to envelop our own school in an atmosphere of respect and caring. When children form cliques or self-segregate in the cafeteria or shun other students, we need to make a big deal about it. When our students lack empathy for others, we need to encourage them to think, discuss, read, and write about how their actions affect the lives of others.

7. We need to provide direct instruction in cultural diversity for students, teachers, and staff and to be role models ourselves. We should make a deliberate and conscious effort to sit together in culturally mixed groups at meetings and at the faculty lunch table, and while there we need to have conversations about diversity issues. We should invite parents, community members, and staff to join us to provide programs for our students. In establishing learning groups in our classrooms, or organizing after-school activities, we should make an issue of diversity. Teach about it, talk about it, "do" it!

8. Let's get political. We do not necessarily have to embark on one-person crusades, but we do need to be involved as much we can in our school and at the district, state, and national levels. All the major education organizations, including the International Reading Association, have taken positions on the importance of cultural diversity and equity for all children. They offer relevant workshops, conferences, training, and support for teachers and schools. We can use the resources of these organizations to improve our own knowledge and teaching practices with respect to cultural diversity, and we can be instigators to broaden the understanding of our students and of other teachers, administrators, and school personnel.

9. If we see a wrong, we should try to find a way to right it. If children of minority status are being underserved or mis-served, then we need to speak up. If we witness acts of deliberate or unintentional discrimination, we must not give our silent consent to allowing these practices to continue. We need to ask ourselves the hard questions: What is the effect of high-stakes testing on these students? Does the way we enforce our discipline policies have an unfair impact on certain groups of children? Have our special education programs become "dumping grounds" for cultural minorities? Do we do enough community outreach to give a genuine ear to minority concerns? These are questions few of us care to face—particularly if the answers make us feel uncomfortable—but ask, answer, and act on them we must.

10. Finally, and always, let's be the best teachers we can be. Do we understand how to effectively incorporate learning styles and multiple-intelligences theory to help each child be successful? Do we have a real understanding of how to use cooperative learning to promote learning? Do we use authentic assessment practices? Do we actively engage our students in their own learning? Do we make a concerted effort to see to it that every child is recognized and celebrated as a genuine member of our classroom community? Instead of hunting for methods to teach particular groups of students on the basis of some cultural marker, let us make sure we understand how to effectively do the things we are doing. Therein lies the path to becoming multicultural teachers.

Rita M. Bean
Allison L. Swan
Rebecca Knaub

Reading specialists in schools with exemplary reading programs: Functional, versatile, and prepared

Principals and reading specialists in schools with exemplary reading programs were asked about the perceived role of the reading specialist. Results indicate that training programs for specialists should include more leadership skills.

There is increasing recognition of the importance of reading specialists in developing coherent, inclusive reading programs that meet the needs of all students (Snow, Burns, & Griffin, 1998). Indeed, the position statement, *Teaching All Children to Read: The Roles of the Reading Specialist* (International Reading Association, 2000), explicitly states, "schools must have reading specialists who can provide expert instruction, assessment, and leadership for the reading programs" (p. 1).

Reading specialists in schools are not a new phenomenon. In the 1960s, amid growing concern about students' lack of reading achievement, reading specialists were employed as "remedial reading teachers" to work directly with students experiencing difficulty. Although working with students has been the primary role of the reading specialist, there have been changes over the years. These changes have been influenced by federal guidelines, given that reading specialist positions often are funded by Title I monies. (Title I is a U.S. federally funded program for at-risk students.) For example, the criticism of pull-out programs (Kennedy, Birman, & Demaline, 1986) and a demand for congruence between classroom and specialized

instruction led reading specialists to work alongside teachers in the classroom.

Thus, although the instructional role was still an important one, more and more schools began to investigate different ways to deliver the instruction provided by the reading specialist. But researchers and reading specialists themselves have reported that reading specialists do much more than teach (Bean, McDonald, & Fotta, 1990; Jaeger, 1996; Quatroche, Bean, & Hamilton, 2001). Indeed, they provide resources to teachers, assess students with reading difficulties, develop and implement professional development experiences for teachers, and assume leadership of the school's reading program.

In response to a national survey (Bean, Cassidy, Grumet, Shelton, & Wallis, 2002), over 90% of U.S. reading specialists indicated that they were involved with instructing students on a daily basis; the same percentage indicated that they spent time daily or some of the time serving as a resource to teachers. Almost all were involved to some degree with curriculum development and in working with other professionals such as special educators and psychologists. Likewise, reading specialists, in a study conducted by Bean, Trovato, and Hamilton (1995),

Reprinted from *The Reading Teacher* (2003), 56, 446–455.

indicated that they performed many different tasks and, although they were very positive about their role, they expressed a great deal of frustration and confusion about these many tasks that they were asked to perform. In addition to their instructional role, they indicated that they had more and more responsibility as a resource or leader. Some felt that they were prepared to handle these responsibilities; others did not.

This leadership role is most often an informal one. Indeed, the notion of shared leadership (Lambert, 1998) best describes the role of reading specialists. Specifically, shared leadership is assumed by all educators in a school when they collaborate to improve instruction for all students. In other words, they assume responsibility for all students in the school, not just those with whom they work. Teachers and reading specialists cooperate with administrative personnel, school board members, parents, and other community members to improve the quality of instruction in the school. Jaeger (1996) described the reading specialist as a collaborative consultant, serving as a resource to teachers and parents, doing classroom demonstrations, and providing ideas about instructional strategies and ongoing staff development.

The importance of this leadership role was emphasized in Allington and Baker's (1999) description of the role of the reading specialist. They indicated that the reading specialist must provide specialized and intensive instruction needed by some children and that the specialist should also be responsible for improving the quality of classroom teaching. Such responsibility demands leadership of the reading specialist.

One way to investigate the leadership roles of reading specialists is to analyze how reading specialists in schools with exemplary reading programs function. This task was addressed by the Commission on the Role of the Reading Specialist, appointed by the International Reading Association to study the role of reading specialists. Commission members developed a questionnaire that could be sent to principals of such schools to obtain their views about the importance of reading specialists to the success of the reading program. In a second stage of the study, the authors developed an interview protocol that was used to talk with reading specialists themselves about their roles and responsibilities. These interviews enabled us to obtain an in-depth picture of how these reading specialists functioned.

Stage 1 methods

Three different sets of schools were identified: schools that had received recognition from the International Reading Association as having exemplary reading programs (1996–1999), schools that had been identified as having an exemplary Title I reading program (1994–1998), and schools that had achieved distinction because they had "beaten the odds" or performed at levels higher than expected, given student demographics. The data set consisted of 111 schools from across the United States.

The 19-item survey that was sent to the principals of the 111 schools included three sections: a request for demographic data, for information as to whether the school had a reading specialist and the "perceived" importance of that specialist, and for the principals' perceptions about the functions or tasks of the reading specialists in their schools. Principals responded to multiple-choice items and to a Likert scale item asking them to indicate the frequency with which reading specialists performed various tasks.

Stage 1 results

How important is the reading specialist? We received 58 responses (52% return) in which 39 schools indicated that they employed reading specialists. Over 97% of the principals in schools that had reading specialists stated that the reading specialists were important or very important to the success of the reading program.

What do reading specialists do? According to the principals, reading specialists performed many different tasks, from working with students to performing leadership roles in the schools (see Table). Indeed, results indicated that the most frequent tasks of reading specialists (performed on average more than several times a week) were instruction, diagnosis, and serving as a resource to teachers. In addition, specialists on average were involved more than several times a month in the following leadership roles: planning with teachers, selecting reading material, working with allied professionals, coordinating the reading program, developing curriculum, coteaching, and participating in school-based study teams. And more than once a month on average, specialists were involved in working with parents, guiding the work of paraprofessionals and volunteers, and conducting professional development activities.

Stage 2 methods

We wanted a more complete picture of how these specialists in schools with exemplary reading programs functioned. What did they do specifically that contributed to the success of these programs? We were hopeful that such information would be helpful to the field, providing data that would help other educators (e.g., administrators, reading specialists, and those who prepare reading specialists) to think about the qualifications, role demands, and expectations for reading specialists. Again, our assumption was that reading specialists who function in exemplary reading programs are performing in ways that contribute to the success of those programs and that they would have much to teach us about the role of the reading specialist. The next step was to talk with the reading specialists in these schools to get a more complete description of what they did to promote reading performance of students.

We contacted principals from the 30 schools with reading specialists who wished to participate in further research, asking that they forward our request for a telephone interview to the reading specialists. Because some principals had been transferred, taken a leave of absence, or were unreachable by telephone, our pool of principals was reduced to 23 who agreed to forward our request to specialists. Our interview sample consisted of 12 reading specialists from 12 states.

A 24-item structured interview protocol was designed to obtain detailed information about how reading specialists functioned. A large percentage of the questions focused on the following five leadership tasks identified through Stage 1: serving as a resource to teachers, developing curriculum, coordinating the reading program, selecting or identifying reading material, and providing professional development. The goal was to obtain a detailed description of the specific daily tasks performed by this sample of specialists. The remainder of the questions addressed other issues about the role of the reading specialist (e.g., instructional responsibilities, changes in the field of reading, specialist preparation, and typical day activities).

How reading specialists spend their time (according to principals)

Task	Mean
Instruction	4.50
Resource to teachers	4.21
Diagnosis	4.03
Plans with teachers	3.66
Selects reading material	3.53
Works with allied professionals	3.43
Coordinates reading program	3.21
Curriculum development	3.11
Coteaches with teachers	3.11
Study teams	3.02
Parents	2.95
Guides paraprofessionals	2.92
Conducts professional development	2.89
Works with volunteers	2.56
Not reading related	2.21

Note. 5 = daily; 4 = several times/week; 3 = several times/month; 2 = once/month.

Stage 2 results

Who they are. The majority of the 12 reading specialists interviewed were veteran teachers with total experience ranging from 10 to 39 years (M = 20.2). All participants were female. Eight of the 12 had 10–19 years of total experience; three fell within the 20–29 years range and one within the 30–39 years range. All had taught in the classroom for 5–16 years (M = 10.9). Although requirements from the various state education agencies are quite different as to the preparation, definition, and title for reading specialists, every respondent held some type of credential, certification, master's degree, endorsement, training, or equivalent in advanced reading education.

Nine of the 12 specialists interviewed worked in schools identified as exemplary by the International Reading Association, two worked in schools recognized by Title I, and one worked in a school identified as "beating the odds." The participants came from a variety of school settings, representing urban (42%), suburban (42%), and rural schools (16%). Size of school populations varied, ranging from 100 to 1,000

Figure 1
What do reading specialists do?

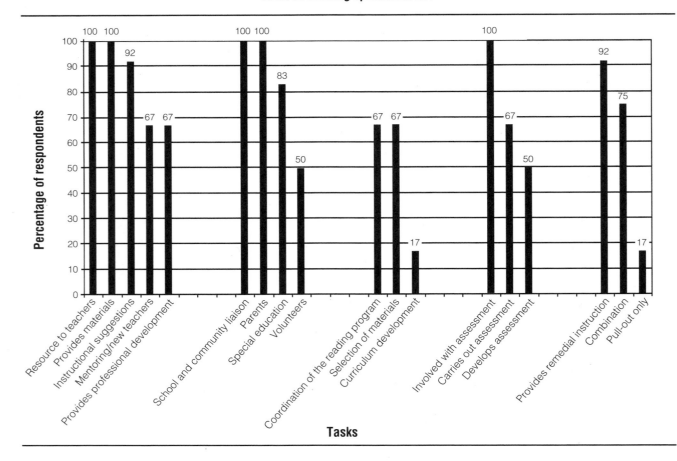

students. All reading specialists taught in buildings with an intermediate grade population. However, they worked almost exclusively with primary students, consistent with the current emphasis on early intervention.

What specialists do. As is evident from Figure 1, reading specialists were involved in five broad roles: resource to teachers, school and community liaison, coordinator of reading program, contributor to assessment, and instructor. All specialists served as a resource in some way, from providing materials, making instructional suggestions, and mentoring new teachers, to providing professional development. All were involved with serving as a liaison to other school personnel or parents. Fifty percent of the specialists worked with volunteers in the schools. A smaller percentage were involved in reading program coordination efforts and even fewer in

curriculum development. Assessment was a major responsibility, both conducting actual assessments and developing assessment tools. Finally, all but one of those interviewed worked with students—the majority using a combination of models, both pull-out and in-class. As is apparent, these reading specialists—in addition to their instructional and diagnostic responsibilities—were responsible for many tasks that, in our view, are leadership tasks. Yes, they worked with students (all but one), but in addition, they had responsibility for supporting the quality of the classroom teaching and for improving the school reading program as a whole.

In the sections below, we discuss each of the five broad roles, providing scenarios that describe how one or two of the reading specialists chose to fulfill these responsibilities. All specialists' names are pseudonyms. (Figure 2 provides a list of the many different ways in which the reading specialists implemented each of these responsibilities.)

> Marvine meets with a team of second-grade teachers on a regular basis to plan so that her instruction is congruent with what the teachers are providing for their students. The team then meets afterward to discuss what worked and what changes to make. The focus is on adjusting the instruction so that it meets the needs of each student. Marvine has responsibility for mentoring new teachers, helping them become more knowledgeable about the teaching of reading. She models various strategies for teaching reading (e.g., Making Words, reciprocal teaching) or for assessment (analyzing running records). She meets with teachers afterwards to discuss the lesson and to answer questions. She also observes teachers as they try these strategies, providing them with feedback about their instruction.

Resource to teachers. Reading specialists and teachers working together are better able to solve problems, whether they involve individual students or classroom instructional concerns. Every one of the reading specialists we talked with considered this resource role to be a major part of his or her responsibilities. The reading specialists in this study often provided professional materials for teachers, including journal articles and professional books, classroom materials such as book lists, children's books, poems, and computer software. Several specialists indicated that they worked closely with the school librarians to hold book talks and host book fairs.

The reading specialists indicated that they were often asked to provide information about various instructional strategies that were being promoted in the schools. Some of the specialists did demonstration lessons; others shared strategies through informal meetings and discussions. One specialist indicated that she and a group of fellow teachers observed each other and then held group discussions about best practice.

The specialists who were responsible for professional development identified the following among the many topics that they addressed: reading comprehension, use of technology (Internet and software) for teaching reading, state assessments, brain research, writing, guided reading, and balanced reading models. Some of the specialists actually conducted the professional development activities, while others indicated that they were responsible for coordinating literacy-related activities for teachers, parents,

mentors, and volunteers. All those interviewed indicated that they were very comfortable in this resource role and felt it was critical to improving the performance of students.

> When Hannah enters the small, urban K–5 school building where she is employed, she knows she is in for a morning that will test her knowledge of at-risk readers. Today Hannah will not be working with her Junior Great Books group or Title I students but instead will be attending a Building Consultation Team meeting. She will work collaboratively with a group that includes a guidance counselor, several resource teachers, and the school principal in a meeting designed to provide intervention solutions for students who are experiencing difficulties, both academically and socially.

School and community liaison. All reading specialists had some responsibility for working with allied professionals, parents and other community members, and with volunteers or tutors. All specialists indicated that they maintained ongoing communication with parents in the form of newsletters, communication sheets, report cards, or telephone calls. Further, the specialists were responsible for parent training on such topics as selecting books, homework suggestions, and reading strategies to use at home. One specialist reported a need to help parents understand specialized reading language (e.g., What is sight vocabulary?). At another school, the parent teacher organization members were given training by the specialists and then assisted in administering running records.

All reading specialists interviewed had some collaborative role with allied professionals, parents and other community members, and volunteers or tutors. Specialists who worked on coordinating volunteer efforts of parents, grandparents, community members, or college students indicated that they were involved in both training and scheduling. One specialist spoke of her visits to local colleges to recruit volunteers, highlighting the importance and value of having young adults in the schools as role models for children.

Reading specialists also indicated that they worked closely with special educators, even though they did not always share the same student population. As described previously, some specialists served on student assistance or instructional support teams. One specialist indicated that her relationship with special educators

Figure 2
Roles of reading specialists in schools with exemplary reading programs

Resource to classroom teachers

Discuss and share ideas with teachers about help for struggling readers, materials and ideas that enhance reading instruction, and assessment.

Hold collaborative planning sessions to develop lessons and strategies for working with students. These are held either on a systematic, regular basis (once a week during planning time), as needed, or "on the fly."

Serve as mentor to new teachers by modeling, providing feedback, and coaching.

Demonstrate strategies (especially those that are new) for teachers, observe, and provide feedback.

Participate in observations (teachers observing each other) for professional growth.

Lead study groups (read a professional book or article and then discuss).

Provide professional development for teachers as part of the school staff development program; also teach classes that teachers can take for credit. Work with teachers in planning and conducting professional development in the schools.

Provide a "friendly ear" for teachers who want to talk about issues, problems, or ideas that they have about reading instruction.

Resource to allied professionals, parents, other community members, volunteers, and tutors

Work closely with the principal in setting a schedule and making decisions about professional development.

Work with special educators and serve on instructional support or pupil personnel teams.

Work with librarians, speech therapists, counselors, and psychologists.

Serve as a resource for parents (communicate with parents, providing and accessing information); conduct workshops on how they can work with their children; provide workshops for parents of preschool students.

Work with volunteers (provide training sessions, coordinate schedules, recruit).

Coordinator of the reading program

Assist in the writing of curriculum.

Look for and assist in the selection of new materials (including development of criteria for determining quality of those materials); assist in the piloting of new materials.

Serve as a leader on curriculum committees.

Coordinate schedules for reading specialists and classroom teachers.

Maintain literacy center or location for various literacy materials.

Contributor to assessment

Assist in the development of assessment instruments (retelling protocols and running records) and selection of assessment instruments.

Conduct assessments for individuals or groups of students (e.g., assess all entering first graders).

Assist in interpretation of test results with teachers and parents.

Coordinate testing schedules.

Share results of assessments with public.

Instructor

Provide instruction for individuals or small groups of students, especially those identified as struggling readers. Such instruction tends to be supplemental to that provided by the classroom teachers.

Work on short-term basis with targeted students, then provide program for classroom teachers to follow.

Work in either pull-out or in-class settings, or both.

Provide instruction, using research supported programs (e.g., Reading Recovery, Junior Great Books).

---

was informal and that there was much sharing of materials and information.

Only a few specialists worked directly with paraprofessionals or educational aides. One specialist described the work of three paraprofes-sionals in her literacy resource lab; these individuals helped students by playing games, reinforcing skills, or listening to them read.

Last month, Jennifer attended a five-day curriculum alignment meeting with classroom teachers and other reading specialists. She was asked to participate in reviewing new materials and possibly piloting a new program that would meet the goals of the textbook advisory committee. After returning from a day of observing the Four Block Literacy Model (Cunningham, Hall, & Sigmon, 1999) in a neighboring school district, Jennifer wrote an analysis of the program to share with others.

Coordinator of reading program. Although few specialists had formal responsibility for coordination efforts, many were involved informally with such tasks as selecting materials for or disseminating information about the reading program. They were involved, to a lesser degree, with curriculum development. The majority of reading specialists in this study did not have a major role in the direct, formal coordination of the reading program, except for one respondent who was a Title I coordinator. However, a larger number of specialists assumed an informal leadership role in the development or selection of materials, including those for Title I, Reading Recovery, and schoolwide reading programs. Two specialists participated in curriculum development by serving voluntarily on districtwide advisory committees, which investigated or piloted programs before district adoption.

With the upcoming Title I assessments only five weeks away, Annette is organizing her assessment materials and coordinating a testing schedule that is least disruptive to the classroom teacher. As the school reading specialist, she is very familiar with student testing because she is in charge of individually testing all first-grade students, students referred by teachers, and new students who arrive throughout the school year. In addition, she meets with each teacher to discuss instructional implications of students' assessment scores. Annette also works with teachers to help them understand how reading standards and curriculum can be carried out in the classroom to prepare students for the state assessments.

Contributor to assessment. All specialists assumed some formal or informal responsibility for student assessment, by developing measures, conducting the assessments, or interpreting results. Many of these specialists formally assess all incoming students, both new students and those being referred to Title I. They also indicated that they conduct informal assessments by observing in classrooms and then conferring with classroom teachers about students. Specialists also assisted in the development and coordination of the school's assessment tests. Further, interviewees reported that even when the assessments

were the responsibility of the classroom teacher, the specialists assisted in preparation and administration.

After working 12 years as a classroom teacher, Josie took on a new role as a reading specialist. This position, which she has held for six years, is structured in a way that has enabled her to get back to the classroom by providing in-class instruction. Josie's vision of in-class instruction involves working as a coteacher and coach with students who have problems. She says she and the classroom teacher create "a very positive attitude" during the reading lessons they coteach. When she does, however, pull out any of the 45 students for individual or small-group tutoring, she makes a point of communicating with the classroom teacher regarding lesson planning, student accomplishment, and recommendations.

Instructor. One specialist in the study fulfilled a formal administrative role (Title I coordinator) and had no direct interaction with students. The other 11 specialists worked with students on a daily basis. These specialists had a caseload ranging from 20 to 80 students, with a mean caseload of 52. Each specialist described various research-based programs implemented in their schools (e.g., Reading Recovery, Four Block Model, and Junior Great Books). The majority of the reading specialists taught using both pull-out and in-class models. The in-class instruction involved team teaching and demonstrations and occurred most frequently in grades 1 and 2. The few specialists who provided instruction in pull-out settings indicated that these sessions were special tutorials (e.g., Reading Recovery or small-group Title I instruction). The reading specialists felt equally comfortable with both in-class and pull-out models of instruction. As they indicated, many factors need to be considered in making decisions about where instruction takes place (e.g., needs of students, purpose of the lesson, numbers of eligible students, grade level of students, and the working relationship with the individual teacher). All specialists realized the importance of communicating with teachers, regardless of where instruction occurred.

These reading specialists seemed to value the instructional role. When asked to describe what they liked best about their positions, the majority indicated their satisfaction with seeing children succeed, or as one specialist said, "seeing children get it." Moreover, even though specialists indicated that they needed more time to fulfill their many responsibilities, not one suggested eliminating the instructional role. As one specialist said, "I am a teacher at heart."

Leadership in exemplary schools

Principals of exemplary schools with reading specialists valued their presence and believed that these specialists contributed much to the success of their reading program. At the same time, principals saw specialists fulfilling a multitude of tasks that ranged from instruction to leadership, with instruction generally being seen as the predominant role of reading specialists. The reading specialists who were interviewed fulfilled an instructional and a leadership or resource role. This instructional responsibility seemed to give the reading specialists credibility and access to teachers to discuss both students and the school reading program in general. Indeed, it provided the pathway to a leadership role. The leadership role is a critical one, which was undertaken in diverse ways and included working not only with teachers but also with other professionals, administrators, and the community.

Reading specialists we interviewed in exemplary schools shared many traits and characteristics. All were experienced educators who had taught in the classroom, and all had participated in postgraduate work in the area of reading. All specialists were enthusiastic about their roles and passionate about the importance of effective literacy instruction for students. All who worked with students indicated that the instructional role was one that gave them much pleasure and satisfaction. At the same time, they acknowledged the importance of the leadership role, which had a significant influence on the reading programs within their schools. Given their prior experience, their enthusiasm and expertise, as well as the nature of their position, these specialists seemed to accept the leadership tasks that needed to be accomplished in each school.

These reading specialists in exemplary schools displayed behaviors and characteristics that promote shared leadership in schools (Lambert, 1998); that is, they are consummate learners, and they work with their fellow educators to make decisions that have far-reaching effects on each student individually and on the school as a whole. At the same time, they appeared to use the model suggested by Allington and Baker (1999): They had both an instruction-

al and a leadership role. All the reading specialists emphasized the importance of helping classroom teachers (and others in the school) to provide high-quality literacy instruction. They accomplished this by modeling, assisting, encouraging, and coaching. Thus, their resource or leadership role was carried out in many different ways. At the same time, they provided the intensive and specialized instruction needed by some children. Obviously, the extent to which these specialists accomplished both of these major focuses depended upon the way in which their positions were structured and the support they had from building administration as well as their own leadership capabilities.

The leadership requirements of these reading specialists call attention to the need for state certification offices and for universities preparing reading specialists to look more seriously at the standards or expectations related to leadership in their respective programs. Without support for the leadership role and without preparation, reading specialists may not be able to assume these responsibilities successfully. In summary, the position of reading specialist is one that requires an educator with multiple talents—one who can work with children and at the same time emerge as a leader, working collaboratively with colleagues to improve education for all students.

Implications

The results of this work have implications for many audiences—specifically, those who prepare reading specialists, school administrators who hire them, and reading specialists themselves. Those aspiring to be reading specialists must not only be knowledgeable about literacy teaching and learning; they also must have experiences that enable them to develop the leadership and communication skills necessary for their positions. The importance of such leadership roles is echoed in the position statement *Teaching All Children to Read: The Roles of the Reading Specialist* (International Reading Association, 2000). Thus, in any reading specialist certification program, there is a need for experiences that focus on leadership dimensions such as developing communication and interpersonal skills, working with groups, providing effective professional development, and serving as a coach in the school. These skills may require practica beyond that provided in a clinical setting and necessitate experiences in a classroom or school. Candidates may be required to work with school professionals, work with tutors such as those in America Read programs, or plan workshops for parents. In addition, standards at the state level for reading specialist certification may need to be more explicit in their call for leadership skills, thus requiring universities or colleges preparing reading specialists to modify their programs to include such experiences.

Those employing reading specialists need to think carefully about how the position is described and about what qualifications should be required of the individuals selected for that position. Even if the candidate is going to spend almost the entire day in an instructional role, the individual's ability to interact with classroom teachers, parents, and other adults is critical to his or her success. Therefore, school administrators must be confident that the candidate has the ability to work well with other adults and an interest in fulfilling the resource role of the reading specialist—in addition to providing specialized instruction to struggling readers.

The support of school administrators is critical to the success of reading specialists. Without the flexible scheduling that enables reading specialists to perform in the many aspects of their position, they and their classroom colleagues will have little opportunity to plan, interact, and affect the reading performance of students substantially. It is the principal who can encourage the reading specialist and classroom teacher to focus on improving quality classroom teaching. When principals and other administrators understand the role of reading specialists, they can establish a climate in which reading specialists work collaboratively with others in the school.

Finally, the results of this work speak directly to reading specialists themselves. The instructional role is an important one: Reading specialists can have a direct impact on the reading performance of individual students, they can serve as models for classroom teachers, and they can establish their credibility as caring, competent teachers. The instructional role, however, is essential, but not sufficient. Reading specialists must recognize the importance of the leadership

and resource roles they serve and be willing to move beyond the instructional role in order to make a difference in the reading performance of all students in the school.

Authors' note: This manuscript was developed in response to a charge to the Commission on the Role of the Reading Specialist, appointed by the Board of Directors, International Reading Association. Members of the Commission were instrumental in providing ideas and feedback about this work. Members included Melinda J. Beckwith, Lillian K. Boyd, Camille L. Blachowicz, Jack Cassidy, Judith Earle Grumet, Rebecca Hamilton, Nelda S. Hensley, Jane Matanzo, Alicia A. Moreyra, Diana J. Quatroche, Dorothy S. Shelton, MaryEllen Vogt, Dave Wallace, Sandra R. Wallis, and Rita Bean, chair.

References

Allington, R.L., & Baker, K. (1999). Best practices in literacy instruction for children with special needs. In L. Gambrell, L. Morrow, S. Neuman, & M. Pressley (Eds.), *Best practices in literacy instruction* (pp. 292–310). New York: Guilford.

Bean, R.M., Cassidy, J., Grumet, J.V., Shelton, D., & Wallis, S.R. (2002). What do reading specialists do? Results from a national survey. *The Reading Teacher, 55,* 736–744.

Bean, R.M., McDonald, L., & Fotta, B. (1990). *Survey of Chapter 1 programs in Pennsylvania.* Technical Report. Harrisburg, PA: Pennsylvania Department of Education.

Bean, R.M., Trovato, C.A., & Hamilton, R. (1995). Focus on Chapter 1 reading programs. Views of reading specialists, classroom teachers, and principals. *Reading Research and Instruction, 34*(3), 204–221.

Cunningham, P., Hall, D., & Sigmon, C. (1999). *The teacher's guide to Four Blocks: A multimethod, multilevel framework for grades 1–3.* Greensboro, NC: Carson Dellosa Publishing.

International Reading Association. (2000). *Teaching all children to read: The roles of the reading specialist.* Newark, DE: Author.

Jaeger, E.L. (1996). The reading specialist as collaborative consultant. *The Reading Teacher, 49,* 622–629.

Kennedy, M., Birman, B.F., & Demaline, R.E. (1986). *The effectiveness of Chapter 1 services.* Second Interim Report for the National Assessment of Chapter 1, Office of Educational Research and Improvement. Washington, DC: United States Department of Education.

Lambert, L. (1998). *Building leadership capacity in schools.* Alexandria, VA: Association for Supervision and Curriculum Development.

Quatroche, D.J., Bean, R.M., & Hamilton, R.L. (2001). The role of the reading specialist: A review of research. *The Reading Teacher, 55,* 282–294.

Snow, C., Burns, M.S., & Griffin, P. (Eds.). (1998). *Preventing reading difficulties in young children.* Washington, DC: National Academy Press.

Trends in Teacher Certification and Literacy

Teacher study groups: A strategic approach to promoting students' literacy development

Shirley Lefever-Davis, Cindy Wilson, Elizabeth Moore, Andrea Kent, Scott Hopkins

Changing classroom demographics and increasing demands for a more highly educated population have given rise to increased calls for education reform across the United States. In order to make meaningful, dynamic differences in the quality of education for students, educators and school districts must find professional development opportunities for teachers that are sustainable over a long period, are teacher-led in collaboration with peers, are based on meaningful inquiry, and are inexpensive. One such response to these demands is the creation of Professional Development and Inquiry Groups (Clark, 2001). In these groups, teachers meet to converse and to study teaching and learning. Such groups, also called teacher study groups (TSGs), are forming across the United States as teachers approach professional development as a way to learn about teaching and learning through conversation.

Key features of TSGs

A teacher study group is

a collaborative group organized and sustained by teachers to help them strengthen their professional development in areas of common interest. In these groups, teachers remain in charge of their own independent learning but seek to reach personal goals through interaction with others. (Cramer, Hurst, & Wilson, 1996)

Most TSGs are formed on a voluntary basis, with teachers selecting the topics for study and determining their own plan of action for implementation. The groups begin by exploring the purposes, processes, and goals of TSGs. Once a clear understanding of TSGs is established, the group identifies a topic or problem it wishes to investigate. In many cases, the topic or problem involves changing instructional practices to promote literacy achievement. Teachers then select a personal learning goal related to the broad topic chosen. For example, teachers might identify a particular strategy or approach designed to address an area of need in their own classrooms. Once a specific learning goal is identified, teachers tackle their topic by selecting learning opportunities most conducive to their own learning styles. In the past, methods chosen to learn about a topic have included reviewing related professional literature, attending a relevant workshop, or visiting a classroom where particular strategies are being used. While the methods for gaining information vary, what is important is that each teacher begin exploring the topic of interest through his or her best learning mode. When the study group meets, everyone has time to share what each has learned or accomplished before "discussion" of the topic occurs. Before the conclusion of the Teacher Study Group, new learning goals are set for the next session.

The effectiveness of TSGs as a means of professional development begins with a critical premise that teachers have control over their learning—they can define the topics or issues for exploration and approach learning through varied styles. Teacher study groups are often developed within schools and districts, reducing the isolation felt all too often by classroom teachers.

TSGs in action

Teacher study groups have been formed in a variety of ways for a variety of purposes, and all resulted in a change in teacher behavior. The following vignettes are examples of TSGs that were enacted to improve students' literacy development.

Elizabeth (coauthor), a veteran first-grade teacher with 19 years' experience, joined a teacher study group consisting of teachers going through the National Board for Professional Teaching Standards (NBPTS) certification process. Teachers seeking NBPTS certification develop a portfolio that engages them in self-reflection about their teaching and its impact on student learning. Each teacher must complete a required number of portfolio entries germane to their certification field. For example, teachers seeking certification in the early childhood generalist field must

Reprinted from *The Reading Teacher* (2003), 56, 782–784.

complete a portfolio entry requiring them to examine their students' literacy development. Teachers must describe the ways in which literacy is fostered in the classroom by analyzing work samples from two students, discussing the students' literacy development, and describing the approach taken to support the children's literacy learning. The teachers in Elizabeth's group met weekly to read and discuss the professional literature on teaching beginning readers and to plan how to implement needed changes in the classroom. During her participation in TSGs and while she worked through the NBPTS portfolio process, Elizabeth realized she needed to change the way she approached teaching reading, as the following comment illustrates.

> In order to fulfill requirements for the literacy entry in my portfolio, I had to look carefully at the literacy activities I was using in my classroom and explain why I was using those specific activities. In trying to describe my literacy instruction, I realized I was using a hodgepodge of reading strategies acquired during my teaching career of 19 years. I needed a streamlined, more focused approach to teaching literacy to make the instructional time as productive as possible. (personal communication, July 23, 2002)

The Teacher Study Group Elizabeth was in gave her the opportunity to read and explore new approaches to teaching reading. She read about literacy instruction specifically designed to help emergent readers use meaning and visual and syntax cues in their reading. This information provided the focus Elizabeth was seeking. She began to determine ways to align her literacy instruction with her new goal of having all her students use these cueing systems during reading. Moreover, Elizabeth learned how to evaluate her teaching practices to determine their impact on her students' literacy growth. Elizabeth credits the study groups for her success, as is indicated in the following quote.

> My study group was critical to my success. Nine of us met weekly to review best practice occurring in classrooms. The National Board certification process improved our knowledge of teaching by prompting us to review the education literature, collaborate, and reflect. Also valuable was the empathy we shared for what we were all going through. (personal communication, July 23, 2002)

Teacher study groups have also been used effectively on a larger scale, as in the example from the Alabama Reading Initiative (ARI). Teachers in Alabama formed a coalition with the express goal of improving students' literacy by enhancing teachers' professional development. The ARI began with a council of education, business, and industry leaders who met over a period of two years and developed a plan for a research-based, systematic approach to staff development for the state's teachers. The plan focused on engaging classroom teachers in extensive study of research-based practices and on improving students' literacy. Teacher study groups were formed, and they met over a period of two weeks in the summer to investigate three specific areas: strengthening reading instruction in the early grades, expanding all students' reading power and comprehension levels, and intervening effectively with struggling readers. Following the intensive summer study, teachers were expected to use a variety of assessment tools to monitor their students' literacy growth. A reading specialist met with the TSGs regularly during the school year to support their attempts to implement these strategies.

Another school in Missouri used TSGs to mentor new teachers. The school formed a study group that comprised several new teachers in the building, a few veteran teachers, and the principal. The participants chose different topics for each session and were responsible for finding some reading material related to the topic, implementing a related practice in their classroom, and sharing the results with the group. The study group was a success because it gave new teachers support during their first year of teaching and an opportunity to advance their learning through scheduled conversations and readings in areas relevant to their classrooms. One teacher, who chose to investigate the use of concept circles to support phonemic awareness, commented on the power of TSGs for her professional growth:

> I learned so much from our discussions [in the teacher study group] and examples the other teachers shared that I wasn't afraid to try concept circles in my classroom. Now we use them frequently, and more of my struggling students understand the sounds and letters connection.

The faculty at this school became so excited with the results of participating in TSGs that they decided to start study groups to solve other school-related problems and questions. However, perhaps the most exciting development for Missouri schools is that teachers can now be released from attending "one-shot" educational events that don't pertain to their classrooms and, instead, be allowed to schedule learning time when it is more conducive for their personal study.

Benefits of TSGs

Teacher study groups have the power to support change in today's classrooms. Outcomes described by Clark (2001) mirror those found in these vignettes of TSGs. The trusting, caring, and supportive environment that emerges in TSGs provides a safe place for teachers to articulate their understandings of teaching and learning and to challenge some of their long-held beliefs. Studies have shown that (a) the time teachers ultimately invest in these group opportunities is more productive than time spent in traditional inservice commitments and (b) teachers make greater gains and are more motivated to change when involved in TSGs (Birchak et al., 1998).

As a new vision of professional development spreads throughout the United States, repeated themes are being advanced, which often are addressed successfully through teacher study groups. Teacher learning thrives when professional development opportunities are focused on inquiry and problem solving; are based on the needs of teachers, learners, and schools; support lifelong learning for educators; acknowledge the professionalism of the educators; provide for safe practice, feedback, coaching, and reflection; are linked to student achievement; and are job related.

The benefits of teacher study groups are numerous because they allow integration of personal (individual) and school needs and because learning focuses on growth and change with support. For many groups, TSGs connect theory, application, and problem solving to real-life situations and provide a framework for educators to work together to accomplish shared goals (Cramer et al., 1996). TSGs also build a positive interdependence among teachers through face-to-face interactions. They strengthen leadership skills and provide new experiences for teachers in decision making, communicating, and conflict resolution.

Moving professional development opportunities away from top-down models of staff development will facilitate teacher learning and, ultimately, student achievement. Educators involved in TSGs explore literacy issues, instructional practices, curriculum, school safety, and other critical questions facing them as they take personal control of their continuing education.

References

Birchak, B., Connor, C., Crawford, K.M., Kahn, L.H., Kaser, S., Turner, S., et al. (1998). *Teacher study groups: Building community through dialogue and reflection.* Urbana, IL: National Council of Teachers of English.

Clark, C. (2001). Good conversations. In C. Clark (Ed.), *Talking shop: Authentic conversation and teacher learning* (pp. 172–182). New York: Teachers College Press.

Cramer, G., Hurst, B., & Wilson, C. (1996). *Teacher study groups for professional development.* Bloomington, IN: Phi Delta Kappa Educational Foundation.

JANICE A. DOLE

The changing role of the reading specialist in school reform

The role of the reading specialist in schools where many students struggle with reading is changing. This article discusses the evolution of the reading specialist's role to that of reading coach and research on how reading coaches meet an important need in teachers' professional development.

Recently, a new role for the reading specialist has been suggested for schools with large numbers of struggling readers. This role conceptualizes the reading specialist not as someone who works directly with students (Quatroche, Bean, & Hamilton, 2001) but as someone who works directly with teachers as a coach and mentor. In this new role the reading specialist supports teachers in their daily work—planning, modeling, team-teaching, and providing feedback on completed lessons in collaboration with classroom teachers in a school. In addition, the reading specialist assists teachers by helping them understand the assessment and instructional cycle and how that cycle can help them as they develop lessons and organize their classes for instruction. In the No Child Left Behind legislation, the Reading First Initiative views reading coaches as a viable and important professional development component for Reading First schools in the United States (U.S. Department of Education, 2002).

The purpose of this article is to discuss the changing role of reading specialists and their potential new role as reading coaches. The article begins with a discussion of the traditional role of the reading specialist as Title I teacher as it evolved under the Elementary and Secondary Education Act (ESEA) of 1965 and the new role of the reading specialist as coach under Title I of the new ESEA of 2000. I also discuss research on the benefits of coaches in the professional development of teachers. In the second half of the article I discuss what reading coaches can do in schools. I end with some rules of thumb for effectiveness based on the experiences of reading coaches.

Reading specialists under Title I of the ESEA of 1965 and 2000

In order to understand the changes that are taking place in federal funding for reading specialists in the United States today, it is helpful to begin with a look at the original Title I funding initiated through the ESEA of 1965. A comparison between this original funding and the new ESEA passed in 2000 sets up the context for understanding a new role for reading specialists today in schools with large numbers of struggling readers.

ESEA of 1965

Title I of the 1965 ESEA was the first federal initiative specifically designed to establish funding for compensatory reading education in U.S. schools. The goal of Title I funding was the improvement of reading achievement in schools with many students living in poverty. While Title I was established as a funding source for these schools rather than as a specific program, over time Title I became a special program for at-risk students. In this program a "Title I teacher," often a reading specialist, worked with struggling readers in what became known as a pullout program. Struggling readers would be pulled out of their regular classroom to receive compensatory small-group

Reprinted from *The Reading Teacher* (2004), 57, 462–471.

instruction implemented by the Title I teacher or the reading specialist.

Under Title I, the instructional focus was on supplementary intervention for students who struggled with reading. Classroom teachers continued to teach most of the students, and those students who were failing were sent to the Title I teacher for supplementary instruction. In this model little attention was paid to the instruction provided by the classroom teacher. Further, there was often not much interaction between the regular classroom teacher and the Title I teacher in terms of the kind of instruction students received and their progress.

Despite the large amount of time and effort as well as the literally billions of dollars funneled into pullout programs under Title I, researchers found very limited success in these programs. This finding has been replicated in study after study (for a review, see Allington & Walmsley, 1995). Of particular importance was the finding that help through these programs did not lead to students' continued success once they were mainstreamed back into regular classrooms (Puma et al., 1997). Thus, what gains students did make as a result of pullout programs were lost once they reentered regular classrooms.

Of course, this is not to say that all Title I programs have been ineffective or that reading specialists have made no differences in the lives of students. Certainly, lives have been positively changed and affected. These types of programs are still used in schools throughout the United States today (Bean, Cassidy, Grumet, Shelton, & Wallis, 2002). However, this model of intervention and the billions of dollars that went into it have not delivered the anticipated significant improvement in academic learning of at-risk students.

The new ESEA of 2000

In the year 2000, Congress authorized the revision of the ESEA of 1965 and the reissue of Title I as part of that act. Like the old Title I, the new Title I provides supplementary resources to districts and schools with large numbers of low-income students to ensure that all of them obtain a high-quality education. The goal of the new ESEA remains the same as that of the old—improved reading and academic achievement for all students.

However, under the new ESEA of 2000, the process of ensuring this achievement has changed quite substantially. There are three critical features of this new process.

- *All teachers need to be highly qualified to teach reading.* Under the new ESEA, a major focus is now on high-quality first instruction. In other words, what happens in regular classrooms is considered of foremost importance. High-quality reading instruction is needed in every primary-grade classroom in schools with many struggling readers. This high-quality first instruction is expected to minimize the number of students who will need intervention or supplementary instruction and also minimize the number of students recommended for special education services.

- *The reading instructional strategies and programs used to teach reading should be scientifically based.* Scientifically based reading instructional strategies and programs are those that have been shown to be effective through (a) the use of rigorous, systematic and empirical methods; (b) adequate data analyses; (c) reliance on measurements that provide valid data across evaluators and observers and across multiple measurements and observations; and (d) acceptance in peer-refereed journals (U.S. Department of Education, 2001). Many of these strategies and programs, but not all, are discussed in reports such as *Put Reading First: The Research Building Blocks for Teaching Students to Read* (Armbruster, Lehrer, & Osborn, 2001) and *Report of the National Reading Panel: Teaching Children to Read: An Evidence-Based Assessment of the Scientific Research Literature on Reading and Its Implications for Reading Instruction* (National Institute of Child Health and Human Development, 2000).

- *Effective and efficient informal assessment techniques should inform instruction and assist teachers in monitoring the progress of each child.* Beginning in kindergarten and continuing through the primary grades, teachers will need to frequently check the progress of each child, identify when a child needs extra help, specify what kind of extra help that child needs, and ensure that the child receives that help.

The changes in the new ESEA were made after careful consideration of a significant body of research pointing out what it takes to help all students achieve. For example, the need for high-quality reading instruction is supported by research indicating that the lowest performing students need the highest quality teachers. One of the most important findings in the research on teaching is that highly trained and qualified teachers make a significant difference in student achievement (Ferguson, 1991; Ferguson & Ladd, 1996). For example, in a recent study completed at Harvard, researchers found that four commonly used models of reading reform did not result in significant differences in first graders' reading achievement (Tivnan, Hemphill, & Ivins, 2002). Instead, there was a strong teacher effect. The best teachers produced students who progressed the most. In other words, the teacher was more important than the reading models or programs. Other documents, committees, and reports reiterate the importance of the teacher based on reviews of research on what matters most in classrooms (see, for example, Anderson, Hiebert, Scott, & Wilkinson, 1985; National Institute of Child Health and Human Development, 2000; Snow, Burns, & Griffin, 1998).

A second feature of the new ESEA legislation is that instructional strategies and programs used in federally funded schools in the United States must be scientifically based. Panel studies such as *Report of the National Reading Panel* (National Institute of Child Health and Human Development, 2000) and *Preventing Reading Difficulties in Young Children* (Snow et al., 1998) have looked at several areas where there was a significant body of research from which to draw instructional implications and recommendations. Their findings provide some (but not complete) guidelines for instructional strategies and programs. For example, phonemic awareness activities have not been a regular part of the K–1 curriculum up until quite recently. But these activities need to be taught. There is enough research to tell us that comprehension strategies should be taught to assist students in their understanding of texts. The National Reading Panel report recommended several comprehension strategies that should be taught because they improve comprehension. While primary-grade teach-

ers have always taught their students new vocabulary words, they have not typically taught their students the meanings of new words and concepts as a regular part of the curriculum. But, especially for at-risk students, learning the meanings of new words and concepts is critically important. Teachers should be teaching them.

Finally, a third feature for ensuring reading achievement, especially in the early grades, is the use of classroom-based assessment to inform instruction and to monitor reading progress. A body of research suggests that frequent monitoring of student progress increases student achievement and decreases the number of students reading below grade level (Good, Simmons, & Kame'enui, 2001). Torgeson (1998) summed up nicely this new way of looking at beginning readers with his title— "Catch Them Before They Fall." Students benefit when their teachers monitor their progress carefully beginning in kindergarten, catch students when they begin to fall behind in reading, and provide intervention to get them back on track as soon as possible. If teachers do catch students before they fall behind, fewer students will be identified and targeted for supplementary instructional intervention.

Regardless of the quality of any program or teacher, there will always be students who need supplementary instructional intervention. For these students, even high-quality first instruction is not enough. There are a variety of effective ways to provide that supplementary instruction, but they will look different from the traditional pullout program. Reading specialists certainly may play a role in this supplementary instruction.

How will this new instructional model for federally funded schools with low-performing students be realized? How can educators assist teachers in these and other schools in providing high-quality first instruction and monitoring carefully each student's progress in reading? Here reading specialists have an opportunity to play a unique role.

Coaches in the professional development of teachers

Many reading specialists working in schools today are in an excellent position to assume the role of reading coach and mentor in schools with many struggling readers. These specialists have the knowledge base to provide classroom teachers with the support they need to learn new content and research-based instruction and to assist teachers as they practice new strategies and programs in their classrooms until they become a part of teachers' daily work lives (Darling-Hammond & Sykes, 1999; Fullan, 1991; Fullan & Hargreaves, 1992).

Research on the role of coaches in professional development

Research on the role of coaches and mentors is small, although their value in the overall professional development of teachers is consistently advocated in the professional development literature (see, for example, Elmore & Burney, 1999; Fullan & Hargreaves, 1992; Guskey, 1995; Hawley & Valli, 1999). I have found the work of Joyce and Showers (1995) to be most helpful in understanding more precisely the role of coaches in the professional development of teachers.

Joyce and Showers (1995) have a model of professional development that lays out the different kinds of support and assistance that can be provided to teachers. This model clearly supports the importance of reading coaches in professional development (Bennett, 1987; Showers, Joyce, & Bennett, 1987). The Joyce and Showers model identifies five potential kinds of support for teachers.

- **Theory**—discussions, readings, and lectures where teachers learn the rationale or underlying reasoning behind particular teaching strategies or techniques. This knowledge provides teachers with an answer to the question "Why am I doing these activities?"

- **Demonstration**—opportunities for teachers to directly see the activities taught to students either through modeling of lessons or videotaping. This knowledge provides teachers with an answer to the question "What do these activities look like in a classroom?"

- **Practice**—opportunities in the session and in the workplace to practice the newly learned skills in front of other teachers or small groups of students. These opportunities provide teachers with an answer to the question "When I try these activities, what happens?"

- **Feedback**—assistance and support about teachers' practice from peers or more knowledgeable others. This assistance provides teachers with answers to questions like "What worked well in these activities?" "What could I have done differently?"

- **In-class coaching**—collaboration with more knowledgeable others and peers on newly learned activities and strategies taught and practiced in classrooms to solve problems and seek solutions to problems that arise during implementation. This collaboration provides teachers with answers to questions like "What do I do next?" and "Where do I go from here?"

What does research show about the role of coaching in this professional development model? The important part of the model is its increasing strength when more of the components of the model are included. For example, Joyce and Showers (1995) found that when feedback and in-class coaching were added to theory, demonstration, and practice, significant increases were found in teacher knowledge and skills. Further, the most significant increases occurred in the transfer of training to teachers' daily instructional practice. In other words, it was when feedback and in-class coaching were included that researchers saw actual transfer of the newly learned activities and skills directly into teachers' classrooms. Lest we become too complacent about the ease with which this can happen, Joyce and Showers (1995) pointed out that it took approximately 20 to 25 trials in the classroom before new activities became a part of a teacher's repertoire of instructional activities and strategies. Thus, it is no insignificant feat for teachers to learn about a new teaching skill or strategy and then have it become a routine in their teaching.

Joyce and Showers (1995) argued that teachers need to have opportunities to learn about new strategies and techniques, to observe demonstrations of the strategies, and to practice and receive feedback on the strategies in their own classrooms. It is apparent that theory or demonstration, do not provide teachers with sufficient support and guidance to apply new instructional strategies and programs in their own classrooms. Research suggests that teachers need consistent practice in their own work settings (Fullan, 1991; Hodges, 1996; Smylie, 1995).

Reading specialists as reading coaches

The importance of coaching and mentoring of teachers is becoming increasingly clear in the professional development literature (Darling-Hammond & Sykes, 1999; Guskey, 1995). In addition, professional development texts and programs now stress the need for the guidance of coaches in the classroom working side by side with teachers (see, e.g., Lyons & Pinnell, 2001).

However, other than the work of Joyce and Showers, there is little research on reading coaches to help administrators and specialists make important decisions about how to use reading coaches. For example, what makes an effective reading coach? How should reading coaches spend their time? Should they do any professional development with groups of teachers, or should they only work with individual teachers in classrooms? How much demonstration should they do, versus how much team teaching and direct observation and feedback? What education and experience should they have? All these questions await further research.

In Utah, we have worked with a coach and mentor model for reading specialists during the past seven years in over a dozen schools designated for Title I funds. The role of the reading specialist as coach has evolved over the period of the last several years in these schools. What follows is drawn from my colleagues' and my own experiences working with reading specialists as coaches and mentors to teachers. We believe our experiences may be useful to other professionals embarking on the use of reading coaches in their schools.

Coaching examples

Our experiences in Utah indicate that among the most important kinds of reading coaches' activities are teaching demonstrations and modeling of lessons. What follows is a compilation of the types of thinking and reasoning that our reading coaches go through as they plan for supporting teachers. Based on my work with reading coaches, here is a typical scenario that a reading coach might experience and a description of the coach's thinking through the issues involved in coaching and teaching.

During the summer professional development workshop in the district, my teachers learned about the importance of reading aloud as a way to develop the meanings of new vocabulary words. We had an outside consultant visit our district, and she told my teachers that reading aloud was an important way to help students acquire new vocabulary. My teachers were intrigued by this idea. Many of them had not thought of their reading aloud as a way to build vocabulary.

Some of the teachers became very excited about using read-aloud time to build vocabulary. But they didn't know how that time should be structured. They were unsure of which words to select for discussion, when and how to talk about the words, or what to do with them afterward. So I decided to do a demonstration lesson for several teachers.

I spoke with my principal, who helped me find substitutes and aides for teachers who would be observing me. I used a first-grade teacher's classroom. Before the lesson began, with several teachers at the back of the room taking notes, I explained what I had planned in the lesson. I told them what my purpose was and how I wanted it to proceed. That way, if I made changes, I could ask the teachers if they noticed those changes and discuss with them why I made them.

The book I had selected to read to the students was *Alexander and the Terrible, Horrible, No Good, Very Bad Day* (Viorst, 1972). I like this book because of the splendid vocabulary and relevant theme to which all students can relate. I began modeling the lesson with the first graders with a discussion in which I helped students activate their prior knowledge about bad days in their lives. Then I told students that we would be coming across some very interesting grown-up words in the story. I had written the four words on sentence strips, and as I showed students each word, we pronounced them together. I briefly explained what each word meant, using my own words rather than a difficult dictionary definition. I explained to students that I wanted them to raise their hands when they heard these words in the story.

My goal here was not to provide explicit instruction in vocabulary, but instead to make students aware of these unfamiliar words and to provide them with a beginning understanding of the words for later use. As we proceeded students became very engaged with the story and with listening for the words I had introduced. As each word was encountered, students' hands went up. I praised them for their good listening and repeated the sentence in which each word was used. At the end of the story, we discussed again what each word meant and how the word was used in the story. As a group, we generated other sentences using the same words. We decided that these were good words to listen for and to place on chart paper on the wall.

After the lesson, students were dismissed to recess while the principal supervised them. I had a vigorous discussion with the teachers about the lesson. We discussed the value of the activity, how to select specific stories for the activity, how to select the words for students to learn, and how to encourage students to be curious about words and to notice them.

After this demonstration lesson, second- and third-grade teachers created vocabulary lessons together with read-aloud books. Over the next several weeks, I observed four teachers during a read-aloud using the vocabulary lessons they had developed. So I saw the same lessons taught several times. But that was OK. Teachers were not yet ready to devise their own lessons without assistance and support. Their lessons went well, and I was able to support their instruction and their taking risks to try something quite new for many of them.

This example demonstrates a typical activity for reading coaches. They work with a group of teachers modeling a lesson that has been discussed in a recent workshop. In the workshop an outside consultant may have presented information about the importance of read-alouds in building vocabulary knowledge. But the information presented is often insufficient for teachers to take the ideas and implement them in their classrooms. Big questions remain for teachers including, "How do I go about teaching vocabulary while I read aloud to my students?" "What does this look like in a classroom?" "Where and when do I do the vocabulary part of the lesson?" "Which words do I select?" "Which stories do I read?" "What do I say?" "How do I incorporate the vocabulary into the other activities I already do?"

Here is where reading coaches can be most helpful. A coach may explain as follows:

By modeling how to conduct the lesson, I began to help teachers paint a mental picture of what the lesson might look like in their classrooms. By discussing the lesson with teachers and having them write lessons in their grade-level groups, I provided teachers with support as they tried to think through the how-to of the lesson. I wanted to help teachers become "reflective practitioners" (Schon, 1983) who think about their own learning, reflect and adjust their teaching based on that learning, and develop understandings about what they do and why they do it.

This reading coach also may have observed teachers in their classrooms and provided them with feedback about their lessons. Once this coach had built a positive rapport with teachers, the teachers would be comfortable inviting the coach into their classrooms for feedback and coaching. At this point in time, the teachers would see their coach as their support and view him or her as someone guiding them rather than evaluating them.

Another critical job for reading coaches is to provide feedback to teachers on their teaching. Here is a composite example of a teacher working with a reading coach after completing a lesson. The coach would have observed a read-aloud lesson and then "debriefed" the teacher as follows.

Coach: So, Margaret, tell me about the lesson.

Margaret: The other third-grade teachers and I developed this lesson together last week. I have to say that I was nervous about doing it, in part because you were here but also because this is not the way I do read-alouds with my students. My belief has always been that you should just read the story to the kids without all that teacher talk that takes away from the story. But I was encouraged when I saw that the kids listened to you when you demonstrated the lesson to us the other day.

Coach: So, how do you think your lesson went?

Margaret: Well, actually, I was surprised that the kids stayed as interested in the story as they did. I would have thought that they would become bored, but they didn't.

Coach: What did the kids do to show their interest?

Margaret: I couldn't believe how Mark, who hardly ever pays attention, was interested in the word *anxious*. The others, too, many of whom I would have thought would tune out with all the teacher talk—well, they really didn't.

Coach: (laughs) I agree with you.... I thought the kids were quite engaged. What was it that you did specifically to keep them engaged?

Margaret: Hmmm, I'm not sure I know. I did connect the words to the story and the characters. I think they liked that. I always read with expression, so I know they like that. I was surprised that they were actually interested in the words when we finished the story.

Coach: You may have tapped into something here that you can use in your teaching of reading in general, not just read-aloud time. What do you think you can do now with these words, Margaret?

Margaret: I don't really know. This is where I get stuck.

Coach: Well, OK, let me give you a couple of ideas. First, you could take the words the kids talked about today and put them on chart paper on the wall. An activity I like to give students is to have them look in magazines or newspapers and find sentences in which the words are used. They cut out the sentences and put them up on the chart paper. That way they see and hear the words used in different contexts. You also could ask kids to listen for the words as they watch TV and listen to adults speaking. Students can write down the words and the sentences in which they heard the words. Each morning for a week, you could spend a few minutes talking about the words, who heard them, and in what context.

The thing about these ideas, though, is this. If you want your students to really learn the words, you have to keep coming back to them and repeating them over and over. You have to ask each child to do more than just look at the words. You have to ensure that each student practices the words repeatedly.

In this debriefing example, the reading coach is just that, a coach to the teacher who is teaching reading. The coach provides feedback to the teacher about her teaching. In addition, the coach assists the teacher in becoming a reflective practitioner—thinking about the lesson, what went well and why, what to do next, and so forth. Here is what the coach might have been thinking:

I wanted to help Margaret to think about her lesson and what went well. I also realized that she needed to be able to pinpoint what she did that kept her kids engaged. Then, though, I realized that Margaret didn't know where to go with the lesson—what to do afterward with the vocabulary words. So, I gave her several suggestions from my own experiences. At this point, I felt I needed to be very explicit.

Reading coaches on reading coaches

As districts and schools with large numbers of struggling readers restructure and reorganize their reading programs, they should consider the use of reading coaches in their buildings. Research on professional development suggests that teachers need more than workshops to learn new instructional strategies and techniques (for a review, see Darling-Hammond & Sykes, 1999). Teachers benefit from support and assistance embedded within their

schools and their own classrooms. Reading specialists who are coaches can provide that support.

What makes an effective reading coach? A research-based answer to this question is at least five years away. Right now, little research exists on the use of reading coaches in schools. This will change as more educators and researchers begin to understand their potentially critical role in the professional development of teachers. Within a few years, I believe research on professional development will include and begin to study in depth how reading coaches can assist and support teachers in their learning.

However, those of us who are involved in school reform efforts need to make critical decisions now. We cannot wait five years for the research. To assist educators now, I asked a group of experienced and successful reading coaches what makes an effective reading coach. Here are their thoughts.

Effective reading coaches have to have a greater level of reading expertise than the teachers they are coaching. There is no substitute for a knowledgeable and skillful reading specialist in a school building. This knowledge is based on what students need to know and be able to do. Effective coaches can identify critically important skills and strategies that students need to learn, and they know different methods of instruction to teach those skills and strategies.

Current knowledge of research and practice is particularly critical when classroom teachers enter the middle stages of knowledge about the reading process and high-quality reading instruction. For example, effective reading coaches know how to help teachers determine whether students have mastered the concept of the lesson and whether they need to move on or not. We have seen several teachers in one school continue to teach one phonemic awareness skill long after students had mastered it. The reading coach in this school did not know enough about the content and curriculum of phonemic awareness to know what to do once students have mastered one stage. As a result, the students and teachers stagnated. We have also seen teachers build inappropriate prior knowledge before reading a story. The teachers followed the teacher's manual of their basal program, and the reading coach was not able to show teachers how to evaluate that instruction and choose a more appropriate prior knowledge activity. The reading coach in the school did not know enough about comprehension instruction to assist teachers at this intermediate stage of professional knowledge. Reading coaches whose reading knowledge is not deep enough are often not able to move teachers on to more advanced stages of reading instruction.

Reading coaches have to know how to teach reading extremely well and to have actually done it successfully. Reading coaches need to be able to "talk the talk" and, more important, "walk the walk." In order to be credible with teachers, reading coaches must have been successful with students themselves. They must have tried the strategies they are recommending and be able to pinpoint what problems might come up and how to resolve them. This knowledge gives coaches credibility with teachers.

Reading coaches must be reflective about their own instructional practice. Coaches will be asked to conduct model lessons and demonstrations for their teachers. However, not all of these lessons will proceed well. When they do not proceed as expected and when mistakes are made, coaches need to admit them and point out their own mistakes. This is what it means to be a reflective practitioner—someone who can think carefully and thoughtfully about their lessons and pinpoint what goes well and why, and what does not go well and why. In this way, reading coaches build trust with their teachers.

Reading coaches have to be able to articulate what they are seeing in a classroom. Reading coaches must be able to walk into a classroom and clearly articulate the teaching and learning that is going on in that classroom. For example, teachers may be thinking they are teaching one thing but really be teaching something else. They may invite a reading coach into a class and say, "I want you to watch how I teach this skill," only to have the reading coach realize that the teacher is really teaching a quite different skill. Or, teachers may not be aware of why they are teaching a particular skill that is required in their core curriculum or their basal reading program. Reading coaches must be able to quickly determine what teachers are

teaching—intentionally or not—and what students are learning—intentionally or not. Coaches must be able to articulate that knowledge in a way that teachers can understand.

Often times, this feedback is the first important kind of help a reading coach can give a teacher. Such feedback can help teachers see teaching and learning from a different lens, sometimes the first step toward becoming a reflective practitioner. One teacher remarked that it was the coach's pointing out to the teacher just what she was doing while she was teaching that helped the teacher begin to think about her teaching in a more reflective manner. The teacher remarked, "I was not even aware that I was doing those things."

Reading coaches need to support and nudge— balancing on a fine line between supporting the status quo and placing too much stress on teachers. Teachers need to know that their reading coach accepts them where they are and will assist them in moving forward from there. Coaches need to identify and articulate to teachers all the valuable knowledge and positive skills that teachers bring to their classrooms and their students. They need to articulate the positive aspects of each teacher's teaching. At the same time, coaches need to nudge teachers along, pushing them out of their comfort zone to more advanced stages of learning about teaching.

Coaches need to be able to plan and organize "on the run." Teachers may ask their reading coaches what they can do for their next writing or phonics lesson. They may ask for help with a particular student who is having difficulty. Coaches must have flexibility in their thinking and must be able to automatically assess a teaching and learning situation and make suggestions quickly to keep pace with teachers' fast-paced days.

Reading coaches need a sense of humor. Coaching, like teaching, can be stressful at times. A sense of humor is necessary for a reading coach in assisting teachers through the difficult task of learning new strategies, routines, and procedures. Coaches with a sense of humor can accept things that inevitably go wrong, appreciate and enjoy the teachers and students in their school, and marvel at the growth and progress made by everyone—including themselves.

A critical role

The bar has been raised on student achievement in the United States and on teaching quality as well. High-quality instruction is a first requirement for all schools with large numbers of at-risk students. This instruction only comes as a result of intensive professional development for teachers. But such intensive professional development does not come easily. Improving teaching quality requires great energy, time, commitment, and fiscal and personnel resources.

Reading specialists can play a critical role in the professional development of teachers. Most reading specialists have deep knowledge about the reading process and about high-quality reading instruction. Reading specialists can serve as coaches and mentors to teachers to help them apply in their classrooms the new strategies and practices they learn about. Research has shown that feedback and in-class coaching make it more likely that teachers will take ownership of the new strategies and teaching techniques they have learned (Joyce & Showers, 1995). Reading coaches are in a good position to provide that feedback and in-class coaching to teachers.

I am not suggesting that all reading specialists become reading coaches. It is clear that reading specialists have an important role to play in school leadership and instructional intervention in many schools. However, in schools where many students are far behind in reading, a reading specialist in the traditional role of support and intervention will not be enough. Such a school cannot have a reading specialist work with all the students who are behind in reading. There are simply too many students requiring intervention. It is in these schools that reading specialists can play the critical role of a coach to help teachers provide high-quality reading instruction for all students.

References

Allington, R.L., & Walmsley, S.A. (1995). *No quick fix: Rethinking literacy programs in America's elementary schools.* New York: Teachers College Press.

Anderson, R.C., Hiebert, E.F., Scott, J.A., & Wilkinson, I.A.G. (1985). *Becoming a nation of readers: The report of the commission on reading.* Washington, DC: The National Institute of Education.

Armbruster, B.B., Lehrer, F., & Osborn, J. (2001). *Put reading first: The research building blocks for teaching children to read.* Washington, DC: National Institute for Literacy.

Bean, R.M., Cassidy, J., Grumet, J.E., Shelton, D.S., & Wallis, S.R. (2002). What do reading specialists do? Results from a national survey. *The Reading Teacher, 55,* 736-744.

Bennett, B. (1987). *The effectiveness of staff development training practices: A meta-analysis.* Unpublished doctoral thesis, University of Oregon, Eugene.

Darling-Hammond, L., & Sykes, G. (1999). *Teaching as the learning profession: Handbook of policy and practice.* San Francisco: Jossey-Bass.

Elmore, R.F., & Burney, D. (1999). Investing in teacher learning: Staff development and instructional improvement. In L. Darling-Hammond & G. Sykes (Eds.), *Teaching as the learning profession: Handbook of policy and practice* (pp. 263-291). San Francisco: Jossey-Bass.

Ferguson, R.F. (1991). Paying for public education: New evidence on how and why money matters. *Harvard Journal on Legislation, 28,* 465-498.

Ferguson, R.F., & Ladd, H.F. (1996). How and why money matters: An analysis of Alabama schools. In H. Ladd (Ed.), *Holding schools accountable* (pp. 265-298). Washington, DC: Brookings Institution.

Fullan, M.G. (1991). *The new meaning of educational change.* New York: Teachers College Press.

Fullan, M.G., & Hargreaves, A. (1992). Teacher development and educational change. In M.G. Fullan & A. Hargreaves (Eds.), *Teacher development and educational change* (pp. 1-9). London: Falmer Press.

Good, R.H., Simmons, D.C., & Kame'enui, E.J. (2001). The importance of decision-making utility of a continuum of fluency-based indicators of foundational reading skills for third-grade high-stakes outcomes. *Scientific Studies of Reading, 5,* 257-288.

Guskey, T.R. (1995). Professional development in education: In search of an optimal mix. In T.R. Guskey & M. Huberman (Eds.), *Professional development in education: New paradigms and practices* (pp. 114-131). New York: Teachers College Press.

Hawley, W.D., & Valli, L. (1999). The essentials of effective professional development: A new consensus. In L. Darling-Hammond & G. Sykes (Eds.), *Teaching as a learning profession* (pp. 127-150). San Francisco: Jossey-Bass.

Hodges, H.L.B. (1996). Using research to inform practice in urban schools: Ten key strategies to success. *Educational Policy, 10,* 223-252.

Joyce, B., & Showers, B. (1995). *Student achievement through staff development.* White Plains, NY: Longman.

Lyons, C.A., & Pinnell, G.S. (2001). *Systems for change in literacy education: A guide to professional development.* Portsmouth, NH: Heinemann.

National Institute of Child Health and Human Development. (2000). *The report of the National Reading Panel:*

Teaching children to read: An evidence-based assessment of the scientific research literature on reading and its implications for reading instruction. Washington, DC: U.S. Government Printing Office.

Puma, M.J., Karweit, N., Price, C., Ricciuti, A., Thompson, W., & Vaden-Keirnan, M. (1997). *Prospects: Final report on student outcomes.* Cambridge, MA: Abt Associates.

Quatroche, D.J., Bean, R.M., & Hamilton, R.L. (2001). The role of the reading specialist: A review of research. *The Reading Teacher, 55,* 282–294.

Schon, D. (1983). *The reflective practitioner.* New York: Basic Books.

Showers, B., Joyce, B., & Bennett, B. (1987). Synthesis of research on staff development: A framework for future study and a state-of-the-art analysis. *Educational Leadership, 45,* 77–87.

Smylie, M.A. (1995). Teacher learning in the workplace: Implications for school reform. In T.R. Guskey & M. Huberman (Eds.), *Professional development in education:*

New paradigms and practices (pp. 92–113). New York: Teachers College Press.

Snow, C.E., Burns, M.S., & Griffin, P. (1998). *Preventing reading difficulties in young children.* Washington, DC: National Academy Press.

Tivnan, T., Hemphill, L., & Ivins, K. (April, 2002). *Evaluating comprehensive literacy models in the Boston Public Schools: Some results from first grade.* Paper presented at the annual meeting of the American Educational Research Association, New Orleans, LA.

Torgeson, J.K. (1998). Catch them before they fall. *American Educator, 22*(1 & 2), 32–39.

U.S. Department of Education. (2001). *No child left behind.* Washington, DC: Author.

U.S. Department of Education. (April, 2002). *Guidance for the Reading First program.* Washington, DC: U.S. Department of Education Office of Elementary and Secondary Education.

Viorst, J. (1972). *Alexander and the terrible, horrible, no good, very bad day.* New York: Atheneum.

Elizabeth L. Jaeger

The reading specialist as collaborative consultant

Special Ed Questions
Special vs inclus.

For a long time, reading specialists have been viewed as glorified mechanics, called in to fix problem readers. As site-based professionals responsible for helping students who struggle with reading, they have worked primarily with small groups of like-aged children in pull-out programs or, more recently, in-class models to teach the skills needed for them to catch up with classmates. Since many U.S. reading specialists work under the auspices of Title I funding, they often have been constrained to operate in this fashion by a fundamental misunderstanding of federal regulations (Allington & Johnston, 1989). It is clear, however, that this paradigm for reading assistance is no longer viable, if in fact it ever was. This is true for three essential reasons.

First, there continues to be disagreement about whether such "fix-it" programs are truly effective. Some research highlights the successes of Chapter 1 programs in raising standardized test scores (Jennings, 1991). Other research points out the many shortcomings of such remedial programs. There are statistical concerns such as an inability to raise test scores to the level of peers (LeTendre, 1991) and a tendency for the neediest children to make the least progress (Carter, 1984). Other problems not specifically related to statistical data include a lack of coordination between remedial and classroom services and negative effects on the self-esteem of students who are separated from their peers (Allington & Johnston, 1989; Bean & Wilson, 1981).

Second, we live in a society that demands more of our students than ever before. Basic literacy skills, emphasized by skill-oriented pull-out programs and measured by standard-

Reading specialists could function as collaborative consultants, spending the preponderance of their time working with other adults.

ized tests, are not sufficient to function adequately in today's world.

Third, in a time of great fiscal distress within school systems, we do not have the resources to offer programs of ongoing, small-group instruction to all who need assistance. More and more, reading assistance programs that have proved effective are using federal funds in more creative ways (Clayton, 1991).

In light of these concerns, I feel we need to rethink completely the role of the reading specialist at the school site level. The purpose of this article is to describe how reading specialists could function as collaborative consultants, spending the preponderance of their time working with other adults to meet the needs of students. I'll first examine some of the literature on educational consultation as it relates to reading specialists. Next I'll explain four dimensions that flesh out the reading specialist's collaborative role: curriculum development, instructional problem solving, assessment, and parent liaison. I'll conclude with some implications for the future.

Educational consultation

The concept of consultation within schools is clearly defined by Friend and Cook (1990)

Through regular, ongoing communication, reading specialists and teachers can reach the mutual understanding necessary to best provide for the students they serve. Photo by Cleo Freelance Photo

as "interaction between at least two co-equal parties voluntarily engaged in shared decision making as they work towards a common goal" (p. 72). To understand this concept, we need to take a look at the reasons why educational consultation has become popular (especially within special education), what attributes are characteristic of effective consultants, and what institutional changes would enhance the effectiveness of this model.

Since the 1970's there has been a significant trend toward such services for students with special educational needs (McKenzie et al., 1970). The movement toward adaptation of curriculum and instruction to meet the needs of these students within the regular classroom, rather than in full- or part-time pull-out programs, has its roots primarily in two areas. First, increases in special education staff are often quickly overtaken by the increase in referrals for placement in such programs. Second, there is movement, both philosophical and legal, away from segregation of special needs students (Friend, 1988). Studies have shown consultation to have positive effects for

both teaching and learning (Medway & Updike, 1985).

Teachers who operate effectively as consultants tend to share several basic characteristics and strategies. They attend to the internal motivation of colleagues and students, the environmental conditions present, and the process of consultation itself (Conoley & Conoley, 1988). They have a basic plan in mind prior to consultation but begin from the needs of teachers (Idol-Maestas & Ritter, 1985). Good interpersonal skills are evident in their interactions with others. They show a sincere interest in the needs of the classroom teacher, listen carefully, avoid the role of "expert," and focus on each situation as it exists (Heron & Kimball, 1988). Conoley and Conoley (1988) note that "the key task of the consultant is to use theory to inform practice, that is, to be sophisticated about what helps people change their skills, behaviors, attitudes, and expectations" (p. 19).

There is general agreement in the literature that several issues must be addressed before the power of the consulting process can be fully realized. First, consultation needs to take its place on a continuum of services that includes instruction of students and inservice to teachers and parents. Likewise, it must be adapted to fit the context of the particular situation and meet the needs of the people involved. Second, those professionals who will be involved in consultation, classroom teachers as well as consultants, need to be trained to operate effectively in these roles (Friend, 1988). Third, there must be a concerted effort to remove barriers to productive consultation, both pragmatic (e.g., lack of time) and conceptual (mistrust, conflict of mismatched knowledge bases, etc.) (Johnson, Pugach, & Hammitte, 1988).

Literacy learning and collaborative consultation

Johnson et al. (1988) suggest that, due to the frequent disparity between instructional methods chosen by classroom teachers versus those utilized by resource specialists, the special education teacher may not be "the most appropriate professional to be responsible for introducing changes into the general education classroom" (p. 45). However, the reading specialist is well suited to operating in this role, at least in part, because, as Vacca and Padak (1990) note, there are clear parallels between what we know about literacy learning and what we know about professional adult interaction; both are, at best, collaborative processes. Reading specialists can use their knowledge of literacy learning to inform their role as collaborative consultants.

Collaboration works best when the adults involved bring their own unique strengths to the process. Classroom teachers have the advantage of consistent, long-term experience with their students in all areas of the curriculum. Reading specialists bring a different perspective. They do not usually have the classroom teacher's breadth of knowledge about a given child. However, they are in a position to make in-depth observations of the student in tutorial, small-group, and large-group settings. They can focus substantial knowledge of the reading process, as well as significant amounts of time and energy, toward understanding a child's literacy development.

As a reading specialist works intensively with a child who is learning to read, this careful observation of the student's reading behav-

iors is crucial. The specialist notes which strategies the child uses effectively, which s/he struggles with, and which ones are new and unknown. Then the specialist develops a tentative plan that reinforces the child's strengths and expands her/his repertoire of strategies. As the specialist continues to teach, this initial plan is refined or even substantially revised to fit the student's needs.

Reading specialists need certain qualities in order to function effectively as collaborative consultants.

The same type of interaction is at the heart of the collaborative consultation process as well. As in the game of Mirrors, in which two people face each other and begin to move simultaneously with no real leader and no real follower, this collaboration occurs as a sometimes tentative exchange of ideas. It is a complex process.

Not all reading specialists are naturally comfortable in this role. Many years ago, Veatch (1968) lamented that "most reading specialists are genuinely frightened, insecure, and ignorant when it comes to working with teachers themselves. They are safe, secure, and satisfied when they work alone with children" (p. 23). Veatch insisted, even then, that such a model could not be allowed to continue indefinitely and that a different kind of person would have to emerge—a person with particular skills.

Reading specialists need certain qualities in order to function effectively as collaborative consultants. They must have a wealth of knowledge about all aspects of literacy and must be ever in search of new knowledge and experience that can be shared with students and teachers. They must have in mind an effective road map for the consultation process itself—where to begin, how to employ theory to inform practice, when and how to move from talk to action.

Of equal or greater importance is keeping the needs of teachers and students paramount. This includes beginning from and accepting the perspective of those with whom one consults, demonstrating a sensitivity to and genuine interest in the problem-solving process, using time well—in short, communicating effectively. Inevitably, the process of change will engender conflict. It is important that the reading specialist be able to work through such conflict in productive ways.

In the remainder of this article I explore examples of four significant dimensions of the reading specialist's role as collaborative consultant:

- curriculum development
- instructional problem solving
- assessment
- parent liaison

For each area, I will describe a conversation between a reading specialist (referred to as "me") and a classroom teacher, followed by a description of the actions taken by those professionals. I have made an effort to incorporate into these descriptions the qualities of effective collaborative consultation noted above.

Curriculum development

Carolyn, a second-grade teacher new to the district, makes an appointment to discuss with me her concerns about a lack of continuity within the literature curriculum. She is somewhat daunted by the number of literature selections at her grade level, none of which have lesson plans available. She worries that her teaching has become fragmented and that she is out of touch with what is really important for her students.

I tell Carolyn about an activity called "Gifts and Expectations" (H. Maniates, personal communication, February 11, 1993). Based on the work of Katz (1988), this activity asks teachers to focus very specifically on the knowledge, skills, and dispositions they wish children to have upon entering their classrooms and take with them when they move on at the end of the year. These standards then become the basis for any curriculum development in that area.

Carolyn takes this suggestion to her colleagues, and we all meet again after they have generated their lists of knowledge, skills, and dispositions. Most of the teachers are familiar with the minilesson format as it is used in Writing Workshop. The group agrees that we will work together to prepare a series of minilessons that address the reading-related knowledge, skills, and strategies teachers have designated and that can be taught in the context of the students' self-selected reading materials. These minilessons might include preparing to read, dealing with unknown words, and finding information. The classroom teachers also will focus on cultivating essential literacy dispositions such as curiosity, love of story, and interest in print.

The movement toward whole language instruction has placed our classroom teachers in an unparalleled state of flux. While exciting and stimulating, for many teachers it can be somewhat overwhelming. Gone are the basal reader teachers' manuals. Ideally, classroom teachers would have time to develop, in conjunction with colleagues, a literacy curriculum well suited to their children, chosen materials, and teaching style. Unfortunately, this rarely occurs. So, what frequently happens is an overreliance on teachers' guides for literature which are developed en masse by textbook companies or by firms set up specifically to fill this need. As might be expected, the plans developed by basal companies look much like basal plans, and even those developed by other groups tend to be formulaic. Curriculum codeveloped by teachers and reading specialists offers a good compromise. Because this curriculum begins from a foundation developed by school staff, it can be much better suited to the needs of the children of the district, without requiring each teacher to begin from scratch.

Instructional problem solving

Evan, a veteran intermediate teacher, has recently added Writing Workshop to his curriculum. He is excited about the progress of his students, but he still feels uncomfortable with the day-to-day management of process writing. He explains that he meets with a few kids each day, but seems to get caught up with those students and is then unsure about what the others are doing. I agree to observe in his classroom and, while his students seem to be more productive in their independent work time than he had thought, his perception that he touched base with only a few children is confirmed.

So much depends on the approach from...

As we talk further, it becomes clear that the real issue is grouping—if, how, and when to group, and what to do with the other students not meeting directly with him. I offer several selections from my professional library that focus primarily on establishing procedures for writing workshop—*Write On: A Conference Approach to Writing* by Parry and Hornsby (1985), and *Classroom Experiences: The Writing Process in Action* by Gordon (1984)—and we agree to meet again in a week or so. At this meeting, we talk at length about options—his own prior experiences with grouping, the pros and cons of forming groups, how kids can be grouped and for what purposes, how students might spend their time both in and out of groups.

Evan is interested in the idea of student-run writing response groups. He and I decide that, as a starting point, we need to prepare some lessons that will teach the students to work in independently functioning groups. We do so and observe each other teaching the lessons. Sharing responsibility for planning and instruction in this way increases the likelihood that these lessons will be incorporated into Evan's teaching repertoire. We meet regularly during the course of several weeks to refine what has occurred and plan for future work.

In the above example, I offered resources, personal suggestions, demonstration teaching, and team teaching as aids to problem solving. Often, however, depending on the nature of the situation, the teacher may be able to solve the problem almost independently; the specialist's role in such an interaction is to listen attentively, ask appropriate questions, and tease out possible solutions from the teacher's own mind. This relationship often results in the most effective, respectful, and long-lasting change (Idol, Paolucci-Whitcomb, & Nevin, 1986). An example of such an exchange is given below.

Barry is a third-grade teacher, well known on the staff as a person who can handle the needs of virtually any child. So I am a little surprised when he comes to me just before fall conference time. He's really puzzled by Belinda, a student in his class. Belinda seems to understand what she reads and once in a while contributes some wonderful ideas in discussion. But she has yet to read a single book cover to cover.

This discrepancy in Belinda's reading is puzzling to Barry. He has considered the possibility that the materials Belinda chooses are too difficult, but when he asks her to read a bit and talk about what she's read, Belinda can do both. Then Barry remembers Belinda's intense interest in science, an interest which may not be well served by Barry's classroom collection of predominantly fiction books.

Barry has generated a hypothesis about this student's reading: Belinda never finishes books because she does not enjoy the kind of reading material that is available to her (fiction). The next step in the process involves collecting some nonfiction science books, including Joanna Cole's (1987) *The Magic School Bus Inside the Earth* (and others in the series), a unique combination of fact and story. Then he'll test his hypothesis by offering the books to Belinda, and carefully observing her independent reading over the next few days. These procedures may confirm Barry's hypothesis, or he may need to reject or revise it.

How do classroom teachers make the transition to a stronger, more student-centered curriculum? For some, it is very much a personal odyssey, based on independent reading and attendance at workshops. But for many teachers, the support of knowledgeable colleagues is essential. While connections with other classroom teachers undergoing similar change are extremely useful, there are very real constraints on the amount of cooperative teaching and consultation that occur in the typical school setting. Ideally, the reading specialist can fill this role more effectively, allowing staff development to be an ongoing process, especially when regularly scheduled conference time is a part of the specialist's schedule.

Assessment

Point person

Because our staff has found the first few weeks to be crucial to a student's academic and social adjustment, we do all we can to make that transition a pleasant and productive one. I make it a point to check on the literacy progress of students new to our school—have they internalized the concept that reading is a meaning-based activity? Do they seem to enjoy reading? Do they have the skills needed to keep up with classroom work?

Frank has been a member of Maureen's fifth-grade class for about a week now.

Maureen notes that he can read fluently and that, when asked direct questions about what he's read, he can usually answer them. But when called upon to review a chapter read the previous day, Frank offers just one or two unrelated facts. He can't seem to sort out what's really important.

I suggest that, since we don't know much about Frank, it might be a good idea to assess his skills using an Informal Reading Inventory (IRI); this would give us a good idea of his strengths and weaknesses as a reader. Maureen reminds me that her instructional aide, Anna, has been trained to give an IRI. Frank seems to be somewhat uncomfortable with adults he doesn't know; so Anna, who works with him each day, will do the assessment. Maureen also agrees to keep anecdotal records on Frank's behavior in any situation that requires him to tell a story.

The results of the IRI serve to reinforce what Frank's teacher has noticed: He cannot structure a retelling of what he has read, but when asked direct questions about plot, he responds accurately most of the time. In contrast, Maureen observes that Frank seems to have little trouble offering summaries of events in which he has actually participated.

At this point, it seems profitable to talk with Frank about his reading. I ask Maureen which of us should conduct the interview and, expecting her to say that she should (due to Frank's discomfort with strangers), I plan to suggest that she and I might rehearse the interaction. But it turns out that Frank has noticed me helping out in the classroom and has asked who I am and what I do. Maureen mentions our idea to Frank, and he agrees to talk with me informally.

When asked to tell something about reading that is easy for him, Frank says that he cannot, that it is all hard. I remind him that he doesn't have much trouble figuring out words. Frank agrees, but adds that when his teacher asks him to tell what has happened in a story he doesn't know what to say. He also notes that his friend, Roberto, is good at summarizing.

This interview, though short, offers three salient bits of information. Frank has a reading strength, fluency, to which he reluctantly admits. He is aware of the trouble he has with retelling. And he has noticed someone in his class whose strength corresponds to his weakness.

Given this information, Maureen and I are able to do several things to help Frank. First, we give him the chance to do something in front of his peers that he does well—reading aloud. We encourage him to choose a selection he thinks other students will enjoy hearing. Second, Maureen and I develop a series of lessons, beginning with very simple stories, that will assist Frank in learning to recap what he has read. I train Frank's classmate Roberto to work through these lessons with Frank, gradually giving Frank more of the responsibility for the retelling. Roberto reads less fluently than Frank, so the potential exists for a balanced relationship between them as teacher and learner. Third, we alert Frank's parents to the focus of our work with him, and they agree to reinforce this work at home by listening to him retell chapters of a novel, preparing him to do the same in class the following day.

Obviously, if the reading specialist spends the majority of time engaged in activities other than direct instruction of needy students, it is even more important that the classroom teacher has substantial knowledge of students' literacy strengths and weaknesses. It is crucial for the reading specialist to find and/or develop assessment tools that provide accurate data about students' performance. These would include tests, such as an Informal Reading Inventory, and observational tools, like the keeping of anecdotal records. Both involve the ability to be acutely aware of clues exhibited by the child of his/her needs as a reader/writer.

Of equal importance is the ability to interpret the results of such assessments *with* the classroom teacher and together develop an instructional plan. If the specialist is no longer to be viewed as the fix-it person, then care must be taken to assist teachers in translating an awareness of the child's needs into effective classroom practice. A diagnostic scheme that connects data obtained by "kid watching/ listening" to a theoretical description and recommendations for instruction, like that developed by Phinney (1988), may be helpful. For example, a child who relies too heavily on print, rarely self-corrects, and has difficulty taking risks would be considered an underpredictive reader. Instruction that helped expand the child's repertoire of meaning-based, predictive strategies would be appropriate.

Parent liaison

Last year, several teachers from our school participated in a workshop that dealt with portfolio assessment. Jean, a first-grade teacher, was particularly taken with the process and began using portfolios with her students. After a parent education session, Jean tells me that parents from her classroom are enthusiastic about the portfolios. One father has asked how he and his child might keep a similar portfolio at home.

Jean likes this idea, but feels that having two separate portfolios for each child implies an artificial distinction between home and school literacy. She is considering the possibility that there could be one portfolio, including artifacts from both environments, but she is unsure how to guide this process. I suggest that, in much the same way that she and I have worked together informally, we might simply begin with a meeting for interested parents and see what evolves.

The meeting is well attended, and the families bring in all kinds of amazing things, from menus the children have read to notes written between family members to art projects. These artifacts relate quite clearly to the elements that are already present in the children's school portfolios—the usefulness of print, the connection between reading and writing, the importance of audience, the integration of curriculum. We talk a lot about similarities and differences exhibited by children in various settings, decide on an organizational scheme for the home/school portfolios, and set up a schedule for portfolios to "travel."

The reading specialist can serve as literacy liaison between home and school. Traditionally, this has meant little more than notifying parents that their child was enrolled in a special class and providing some suggestions for helping the child, but this limited role is not adequate.

Young readers benefit from quality literacy experiences at home as well as at school. In order for this to occur, parents need an understanding of the kind of instruction their children are receiving at school and how they can best complement that instruction at home. Home literacy experiences should be validated; parents should see the many interactions they have with their child each day as a potential literacy gold mine. Parents need the chance to work with their children at school, allowing children to expand the scope of their literacy activities. All these activities can be facilitated by the reading specialist.

Implications for the future

At the core of the reading specialist's role as collaborative consultant is a commitment to the process of instructional change. While the need for such change is not unique to school systems, the process suitable to schools differs from that in other environments. Because the nature of their day-to-day lives is so firmly rooted in the unique situation of their particular classrooms, teachers need to exercise ultimate control of the change to which they commit. Such a process of change can best succeed when classroom teachers work in close consort with another professional, such as a reading specialist.

It is not easy to expand the scope of the reading specialist's work to include the roles described above. The sooner site-based reading specialists confront the fact that they are no longer classroom teachers, yet have none of the administrative authority of a principal or district supervisor, the easier this transition will be.

But there needs to be a substantial change in the training offered to reading specialists, as well. Although the International Reading Association's *Guidelines for the Specialized Preparation of Reading Professionals* lists organizational tasks and staff/curriculum development responsibilities as falling within the scope of the reading resource teacher, it requires no course work in these areas (IRA's Professional Standards and Ethics Committee, 1986). As I informally surveyed reading specialist programs in California, there was little evidence that training programs currently emphasize the role of the specialist as resource person.

If we want reading specialists to become actively involved in the evolution of classroom teaching, we must carefully prepare them to take on this role. Such training would require coursework that emphasizes problem-solving and communication strategies as well as literacy education content. It would need to go further to include a practicum based in a school setting. The role of a collaborative consultant is a difficult one, primarily because of the complexities involved in maintaining a working relationship with dozens of adults as well as with children. To a certain extent only guided practice can allow the potential reading specialist to gain the experience needed to work with real teachers (both veterans and novices) dealing with real literacy issues. A reading specialist attempting to work in collaboration without such training and practice will face interpersonal issues that may be overwhelming.

Of equal importance is a concerted effort to diminish the pragmatic and conceptual barriers to collaboration that have plagued the reading specialist setting. This can best be accomplished by allowing significant flexibility in the specialist's schedule, thereby promoting communication with classroom staff. Without substantial blocks of time to plan together and a willingness on the part of all concerned to consider new ways of approaching problems, the collaborative consultation model is doomed to fail. It is only through such regular, ongoing communication that reading specialists and teachers can reach the mutual understanding necessary to best provide for the students they serve.

The move toward greater collaboration among educators will surely prove to be complex and challenging. Any number of factors addressed in this article have the potential to short-circuit this transition. Ultimately, however, children and adults alike will benefit from an educational process that makes the best possible use of teachers' time, energy, and expertise.

References

Allington, R.L., & Johnston, P. (1989). Coordination, collaboration, and consistency: The redesign of compensatory and special education interventions. In R.E. Slavin, N.L. Karweit, & N.A. Madden (Eds.), *Effective programs for students at risk* (pp. 320-354). Boston: Allyn & Bacon.

Bean, R.M., & Wilson, R.M. (1981). *Effecting change in school reading programs: The resource role.* Newark, DE: International Reading Association.

Carter, L. (1984). The sustaining effects study of compensatory and elementary education. *Educational Researcher, 13*(7), 4-13.

Clayton, C. (1991). Chapter I evaluation: Progress, problems and possibilities. *Educational Evaluation and Policy Analysis, 13*, 325-327.

Cole, J. (1987). *The magic school bus inside the earth.* New York: Scholastic.

Conoley, J., & Conoley, C. (1988). Useful theories in school-based consultation. *Remedial and Special Education, 9*(6), 14-20.

Friend, M. (1988). Putting consultation into context: Historical and contemporary perspectives. *Remedial and Special Education, 9*(6), 7-13.

Friend, M., & Cook, L. (1990). Collaboration as a predictor of success in school reform. *Journal of Educational and Psychological Consultation, 1*(1), 69-86.

Gordon, N. (Ed.). (1984). *Classroom experiences: The writing process in action.* Exeter, NH: Heinemann.

Heron, T.E., & Kimball, W.H. (1988). Gaining perspective with the educational consultation research base: Ecological considerations and further recommendations. *Remedial and Special Education, 9*(6), 21-28, 47.

Idol, L., Paolucci-Whitcomb, P., & Nevin, A. (1986). *Collaborative consultation.* Austin, TX: PRO-ED.

Idol-Maestas, L., & Ritter, S. (1985). A follow-up study of resource-consulting teachers: Factors that facilitate and inhibit teacher consultation. *Teacher Education and Special Education, 8*, 121-131.

International Reading Association's Professional Standards and Ethics Committee. (1986). *Guidelines for the specialized preparation of reading professionals.* Newark, DE: Author.

Jennings, J. (1991). Chapter I: A view from Congress. *Educational Evaluation and Policy Analysis, 13*, 335-338.

Johnson, L.J., Pugach, M.C., & Hammitte, D.J. (1988). Barriers to effective special education consultation. *Remedial and Special Education, 9*(6), 41-47.

Katz, L. (1988). What should young children be doing? *American Educator: The Professional Journal of the American Federation of Teachers, 12*(2), 28-33, 44-45.

LeTendre, M.J. (1991). The continuing evolution of a federal role in compensatory education. *Educational Evaluation and Policy Analysis, 13*, 328-334.

McKenzie, H.S., Egner, A.N., Knight, M.F., Perelman, P.F., Schneider, B.M., & Garvin, J.S. (1970). Training consulting teachers to assist elementary teachers in the management and education of handicapped children. *Exceptional Children, 37*, 137-143.

Medway, F.J., & Updike, J.F. (1985). Meta-analysis of consultation outcome studies. *American Journal of Community Psychology, 13*, 489-505.

Parry, J., & Hornsby, D. (1985) *Write on: A conference approach to writing.* Portsmouth, NH: Heinemann.

Phinney, M.Y. (1988). *Reading with the troubled reader.* Portsmouth, NH: Heinemann.

Vacca, J.L., & Padak, N.D. (1990). Reading consultants as classroom collaborators: An emerging role. *Journal of Educational and Psychological Consultation, 1*(1), 99-107.

Veatch, J. (1968). The clientele of the reading specialist. *Journal of the Reading Specialist, 8*, 22-25.

Having a LARC

Ann S. Parish

LARC has been a true stimulus for me. As a result of discussions and readings, I've tried and successfully implemented new techniques, strategies, and activities in my language arts curriculum. LARC was my support—I felt like I was working with a "net."

A teacher and LARC member

LARC stands for Language Arts Reading Club, a group of educators who meet monthly to discuss common professional reading and its impact on their thinking and classrooms. We started a LARC in the fall of 1992, and we've had at least one going in our school district ever since. Although the idea is not new, I'd like to answer some questions that educators wishing to begin LARCs frequently ask, such as how do I get started? What should I expect? And how do I keep it going?

1. Who should start the LARC? When?
   - Anyone can start a LARC—a teacher, a principal, a department chair, a team leader, a college professor. I happen to be a language arts supervisor for Grades K–12.
   - Don't worry about the time of year. You can start a LARC in March as easily as you can in September.

2. Why should I form such a group?
   - Perhaps you want someone to talk to about teaching, not about day-to-day trivia or the weekend or the latest diet. Some of us are fortunate enough to have teaching partners or teams with whom we do talk about strategies and learning theory as well as the triumphs and problems of everyday teaching.

     But many of us find teaching to be an isolated, lonely job. We walk into our classrooms and close the door and teach. If we are taking risks and trying new ideas, we hesitate to talk about them to our colleagues, especially if they never respond with stories of their own risks and new ideas. Some of us can share our ideas with spouses or friends, but those who aren't teachers often "just don't get it." So maybe you need people to talk with; people who share your enthu-

siasms and understand what you're trying to do and why.
   - Perhaps you need the structure of a deadline. Do you subscribe to journals and buy books but rarely find time to read them? If you have an "assignment" before the next meeting, you'll be far more likely to read it than to procrastinate—again.
   - Perhaps you realize you're stagnating. You've been using the same basic activities for months, even years. You remember the excitement of learning, the pure pleasure of playing with ideas. You're ready for new activities.

3. Whom should I invite?
   - You may decide to keep your group homogeneous in some way. Perhaps you will invite only teachers from your school, or perhaps you will invite only teachers from a certain grade level.
   - You may decide to mix everyone up. You may invite a mix of elementary, middle school, and high school teachers. You may invite teachers from several neighboring schools or districts, principals, aides, counselors—or not.
   - Keep the group to 10 or less. More than 10 people means too many people competing for talk time, and some people will get lost in the conversational crowd.
   - Be sure the potential members understand that a LARC is a discussion group, not a workshop. It is voluntary, so don't let anyone *require* membership in a LARC.

You may be disappointed at the response when you first send out invitations. I sent out vague invitations to all 250 elementary teachers (K–5) in my district via a language arts newsletter. The principals warned me I would be flooded with enthusiastic participants the first year—more teachers than I could handle. I had 4.

The next year I had 5, and then 7. (People kept bringing their friends.) This is our third year, and we have 11 (including 3 of the original members).

We decided, after some judicious experimentation, that we wanted to keep our group elementary because we had a hard time finding reading material

that interested everyone, yet was specific enough to be useful. The problems of a first-grade teacher coping with nonreaders were quite different from those of a ninth-grade teacher coping with nonreaders. We solved this particular problem by starting another group for secondary teachers.

4. What about logistics like place, time, frequency, food, and funding?
   - *Place.* I wanted the teachers to feel comfortable, without having a colleague or a principal drop in every 15 minutes to see what we were doing, so we meet at my house. We can put our feet up and even have a glass of wine—off campus and outside school hours. A LARC could also meet at a restaurant or rotate the meetings among the members' houses.
   - *Time.* We meet in the late afternoon from 4:30 to 6:30. By the time teachers do bus duty, gather their belongings, and drive across town from various schools, the earliest some of them can get to the meeting is 4:30. Other possibilities include early morning, evening, or Saturday meetings.

     We rarely have a meeting at which *everyone* shows up on time and stays the full 2 hours. But in spite of parent conferences, soccer games, and special choir practices, most people do show up for as long as schedules permit. And we usually have some people who stay late, talking about teaching.
   - *Frequency.* We meet once a month. This past year we even continued meeting once a month through the summer, juggling our dates around vacations just as we do during the school year. We try to bring our calendars to the first meeting and set the actual dates for the whole semester—or even the whole year—so people can avoid conflicts when possible.
   - *Food.* We assign someone to bring simple snacks (e.g., cookies or popcorn) to each meeting.
   - *Funding.* We received some district funding (under the heading of "Workshop Supplies") the first year, but after that we bought our own books. Everyone knows up front that personal purchase of the

books is part of the deal, so the cost of the books has not been an issue.

5. What should we read?

Journals. For the first meeting or two, you can read copies of articles from professional journals. In fact, everyone may want to subscribe to a journal or two and use articles for your reading all year. However, we found that different people selected different articles (and no one read the entire journal), so we didn't all have the same reading to discuss. We also found that once people joined the professional organization(s), they kept up their membership even if we didn't focus the LARC discussions on journal articles.

Books. What books you select will depend on your group. You may have teachers who are new to the world of professional literature, or you may have teachers who are already well read in their field. Perhaps the group wants to focus on one aspect of language arts, such as writing, portfolios, emergent literacy, or managing/organizing a workshop classroom. If possible, have the group members select the book(s) at the first meeting.

Helpful hints for book selection:

- Discuss how many books you want to read in a year. We usually select two a year, but sometimes we've picked two shorter books for one semester and a longer one for the other. You might pick one thick book for the whole year, or you could read one a month.
- Bring an assortment of books to the first meeting if possible. Everyone could look through them and then vote on the one(s) to buy.
- Use the catalogs from International Reading Association, National Council of Teachers of English, Heinemann, Richard Owen, Oryx, and/or Association for Supervision and Curriculum Development as an alternative, especially if you don't have an up-to-date professional library from which to pull samples. The catalogs not only provide descriptions of the contents but also tell you length and price.
- Try to select at least one book that the leader has not read so everyone explores together.

- Don't hesitate to switch topics. You may choose a book on elementary writing for one semester and a book on multiple intelligences the next. You may choose a how-to book one time and a theory book the next.
- Don't select a book that outlines neat ideas for lesson plans; select a substantive one that you can talk, think, and even argue about. A LARC is a discussion group, not a workshop.

6. Everyone has read the articles or the first 50 pages of the book. How do I start the talking?

- Remember to listen, not lecture. Don't let group members lecture either.
- Pay attention to who's talking. Be sure everyone gets at least one uninterrupted chance to talk at every meeting.
- Expect some "venting" about individual classrooms, students, parents, and maybe other staff. While letting off steam to trusted and understanding colleagues may be an important part of a LARC meeting, it is not the primary purpose. Confidentiality is essential; even if teachers don't name names, other members know what schools they come from or who their department chair is. Your job as leader is to let people voice their frustrations for a short while but then to get the discussion back on track even if you have to interrupt.
- Ask open-ended questions, preferably ones to which you do not know the answer. Some of my favorite questions are: What did you read that could or could not work in your classroom? Read a sentence or two that you underlined/highlighted or a place that you wrote notes in the margin. Why did you underline this passage? What comment did you make? What did the author say that you question or disagree with? What did the author say that confirmed or clarified your own beliefs?

If necessary, answer the question yourself. Your purpose is to start people talking about what they've read, and sometimes the easiest

way is to question or disagree with the author.

- Ask another open-ended question if the conversation drifts or dies. People come to LARCs to talk; all you have to do is open a topic and let them go.

7. Now that the first meeting is over, what do I do?

- Send out reminders about a week before the next meeting. Include not only the date and place, but also a reminder about the reading to be done and who is bringing the food.
- Check periodically with the group to see if LARC is meeting their needs and expectations. Are they having a good time? Do they want to come back? If not, why not? What can you change? You may even want to have a written survey at the end of the year.

8. Now that the first year is over, what do I do?

- Keep going. Select new books. Invite new members to join the group.
- If necessary, start a second group. Encourage members to start their own groups, perhaps on individual campuses. We now have several groups called WITs (Writing Institute Teachers), made up of K–12 teachers who have completed the New Jersey Writing Project in Texas. The math supervisor has started a similar group called SMART (Studying Math Articles Related to Teaching). Some teachers belong to two groups.
- At the end of the year, ask members to reflect on LARC and evaluate its impact and their reasons for coming—preferably in writing. When I asked, these were some of the responses:

I value the support from colleagues (e.g., suggestions that might work in my classroom), the affirmation of techniques and philosophies I employ in my room, and the encouragement to take risks.

I enjoy sharing, visiting, laughing, helping, and listening to each of our members; to me this is therapeutic support. I feel my teaching choices/learning opportunities for the students are validated when I am invited to share.

I found total acceptance, a focus on professional issues, top-notch teachers, exposure to new materials, and a break from routine.

I need as much support as I can get professionally. I enjoy the company [at LARC meetings] and bouncing ideas off compassionate knowledgeable colleagues. I'm used to being considered an "expert" on my campus. That is a scary position. I really want to help everyone, yet on my campus my ideas are often dismissed as too hard to follow. I often need lots of help emotionally. At LARC I'm not different.

LARC has been a steady, solid source of guidance and support. I can't imagine teaching without a LARC.

In 3 years we've gone from one LARC with 4 people to six groups with over 70 people. In my ideal world, every teacher would belong to a small group that reads books and meets once a month to talk about teaching. Every teacher would belong to at least one professional organization and read the journal. Every teacher would pause regularly to think about his or her philosophy of teaching. And every teacher would have a support group to provide encouragement for risk-taking. A LARC, if available, provides opportunities for such professional growth and risk-taking. So invite some people, order some books, and have a LARC!